Business Plans Handbook

Business Plans

A COMPILATION OF BUSINESS PLANS DEVELOPED BY INDIVIDUALS THROUGHOUT NORTH AMERICA

Handbook

VOLUME

23

Michelle Lee,
Project Editor

GALE
CENGAGE Learning

Detroit • New York • San Francisco • New Haven, Conn • Waterville, Maine • London

Business Plans Handbook, Volume 23

Project Editor: Michelle Lee

Product Manager: Jenai Drouillard

Product Design: Jennifer Wahi

Composition and Electronic Prepress: Evi Seoud

Manufacturing: Rita Wimberley

For product information and technology assistance, contact us at
Gale Customer Support, 1-800-877-4253.
For permission to use material from this text or product,
submit all requests online at **www.cengage.com/permissions.**
Further permissions questions can be emailed to
permissionrequest@cengage.com

Gale, a part of Cengage Learning
27500 Drake Rd.
Farmington Hills, MI 48331-3535

ISBN-13: 978-1-4144-6835-8
ISBN-10: 1-4144-6835-0
1084-4473

Printed in Mexico
1 2 3 4 5 6 7 13 12

Contents

BUSINESS PLANS

CONTENTS

Highlights

Business Plans Handbook, Volume 23 (BPH-23) is a collection of business plans compiled by entrepreneurs seeking funding for small businesses throughout North America. For those looking for examples of how to approach, structure, and compose their own business plans, *BPH-23* presents 20 sample plans, including plans for the following businesses:

- Automotive Detailing Business
- Biobased Metalworking Fluids Company
- Broker
- Business Consultant
- Cloud Computing Business
- Commercial Bank
- Debt Collection Agency
- Dispatched Trucking Service
- Energy Solutions Company
- Freelance Children's Librarian
- Nonprofit Pharmaceutical Research Center
- Online Dating/Matchmaking Service
- Online Job Service
- Process Serving Business
- Product Assembly Business
- Senior Relocation Service
- Specialty Food Manufacturer
- Student Art Gallery
- Tattoo Studio/Art Gallery
- Toy Rental Business

FEATURES AND BENEFITS

BPH-23 offers many features not provided by other business planning references including:

- Twenty business plans, each of which represent an attempt at clarifying (for themselves and others) the reasons that the business should exist or expand and why a lender should fund the enterprise.
- Two fictional plans that are used by business counselors at a prominent small business development organization as examples for their clients. (You will find these in the Business Plan Template Appendix.)
- A directory section that includes: listings for venture capital and finance companies, which specialize in funding start-up and second-stage small business ventures, and a comprehensive

listing of Service Corps of Retired Executives (SCORE) offices. In addition, the Appendix also contains updated listings of all Small Business Development Centers (SBDCs); associations of interest to entrepreneurs; Small Business Administration (SBA) Regional Offices; and consultants specializing in small business planning and advice. It is strongly advised that you consult supporting organizations while planning your business, as they can provide a wealth of useful information.

- A Small Business Term Glossary to help you decipher the sometimes confusing terminology used by lenders and others in the financial and small business communities.

- A cumulative index, outlining each plan profiled in the complete *Business Plans Handbook* series.

- A Business Plan Template which serves as a model to help you construct your own business plan. This generic outline lists all the essential elements of a complete business plan and their components, including the Summary, Business History and Industry Outlook, Market Examination, Competition, Marketing, Administration and Management, Financial Information, and other key sections. Use this guide as a starting point for compiling your plan.

- Extensive financial documentation required to solicit funding from small business lenders. You will find examples of: Cash Flows, Balance Sheets, Income Projections, and other financial information included with the textual portions of the plan.

Introduction

Perhaps the most important aspect of business planning is simply doing it. More and more business owners are beginning to compile business plans even if they don't need a bank loan. Others discover the value of planning when they must provide a business plan for the bank. The sheer act of putting thoughts on paper seems to clarify priorities and provide focus. Sometimes business owners completely change strategies when compiling their plan, deciding on a different product mix or advertising scheme after finding that their assumptions were incorrect. This kind of healthy thinking and re-thinking via business planning is becoming the norm. The editors of *Business Plans Handbook, Volume 23 (BPH-23)* sincerely hope that this latest addition to the series is a helpful tool in the successful completion of your business plan, no matter what the reason for creating it.

This twenty-third volume, like each volume in the series, offers business plans used and created by real people. *BPH-23* provides 20 business plans. The business and personal names and addresses and general locations have been changed to protect the privacy of the plan authors.

NEW BUSINESS OPPORTUNITIES

As in other volumes in the series, *BPH-23* finds entrepreneurs engaged in a wide variety of creative endeavors. Examples include a proposal for a Commercial Bank, a Dispatched Trucking Service, and a Toy Rental Business. In addition, several other plans are provided, including a Debt Collection Agency, a Specialty Foods Manufacturer, and a Student Art Gallery, among others.

Comprehensive financial documentation has become increasingly important as today's entrepreneurs compete for the finite resources of business lenders. Our plans illustrate the financial data generally required of loan applicants, including Income Statements, Financial Projections, Cash Flows, and Balance Sheets.

ENHANCED APPENDIXES

In an effort to provide the most relevant and valuable information for our readers, we have updated the coverage of small business resources. For instance, you will find: a directory section, which includes listings of all of the Service Corps of Retired Executives (SCORE) offices; an informative glossary, which includes small business terms; and a cumulative index, outlining each plan profiled in the complete *Business Plans Handbook* series. In addition we have updated the list of Small Business Development Centers (SBDCs); Small Business Administration Regional Offices; venture capital and finance companies, which specialize in funding start-up and second-stage small business enterprises; associations of interest to entrepreneurs; and consultants, specializing in small business advice and planning. For your reference, we have also reprinted the business plan template, which provides a comprehensive overview of the essential components of a business plan and two fictional plans used by small business counselors.

SERIES INFORMATION

If you already have the first twenty-two volumes of *BPH*, with this twenty-third volume, you will now have a collection of over 470 business plans (not including the updated plans); contact information for hundreds of organizations and agencies offering business expertise; a helpful business plan template; more than 1,500 citations to valuable small business development material; and a comprehensive glossary of terms to help the business planner navigate the sometimes confusing language of entrepreneurship.

ACKNOWLEDGEMENTS

The Editors wish to sincerely thank the contributors to *BPH-23*, including:

- AB Lane Communications
- BizPlanDB.com
- Charles J. Stankovic
- Don Brown
- Lisa Golden
- Eric Leander
- Heide Denler
- Kari Lucke
- Paul Greenland
- Susan Hartmann
- Vincent A. Marino

COMMENTS WELCOME

Your comments on *Business Plans Handbook* are appreciated. Please direct all correspondence, suggestions for future volumes of *BPH*, and other recommendations to the following:

Managing Editor, Business Product
Business Plans Handbook
Gale, a part of Cengage Learning
27500 Drake Rd.
Farmington Hills, MI 48331-3535
Phone: (248)699-4253
Fax: (248)699-8052
Toll-Free: 800-347-GALE
E-mail: BusinessProducts@gale.com

Automotive Detailing Business

Hands-On Car Wash & Detail Center Inc.

47 Green Bay Rd.
Winnetka, IL 60093

Paul Greenland

Hands-On Car Wash & Detail Center Inc. is a car wash and detailing business catering mainly to drivers of high-end automobiles.

EXECUTIVE SUMMARY

While managing the automotive detailing department at Stonecrest BMW in Chicago, Jeremy Rundle learned a great deal about customers who drive high-end automobiles. He also gained firsthand knowledge of the automotive detailing market in the Chicago area. In particular, Rundle discovered that a considerable number of luxury vehicle owners commute to the city from the suburbs via train, as opposed to driving their vehicles to work on a regular basis. In addition, many customers have second vehicles that are mainly used for suburban driving.

Convenience is important to drivers of high-end automobiles, many of whom are busy professionals. With this in mind, driving to the city for automotive detailing services, or having to make special pickup/drop-off arrangements, is often a hassle for them. Based on these observations, Rundle discovered that a strong market exists for a hand car wash and automotive detailing business serving the Chicago area's most affluent suburbs, and he has decided to establish Hands-On Car Wash & Detail Center in the community of Winnetka. In addition, a convenient drop-off service will be provided at the Hubbard Woods train station, which is utilized by residents of Winnetka and other nearby suburbs.

MARKET ANALYSIS

Primary Service Area

Hands-On Car Wash & Detail Center will consider Winnetka to be its primary service area. According to research from DemographicsNow, Winnetka was home to 4,112 households in the fall of 2010. This figure is expected to remain relatively unchanged through 2015. Average household income, which totaled $318,745, was expected to increase 3.9 percent by 2015, growing to $331,124. On average, each household had 2.1 vehicles in 2010, for a total of 8,694 vehicles. A total of 26.8 percent of homes had one vehicle, while 52.7 percent of homes had two vehicles, and 13.5 percent had three vehicles. Consumers in our primary service area spent an average of $2,440 annually on vehicle repair and maintenance.

Secondary Service Area

In addition to Winnetka, Hands-On Car Wash & Detail Center also will draw customers from the nearby towns of Kenilworth, Wilmette, Glenview, Northfield, Northbrook, and Glencoe. By expanding geographic boundaries to include these communities, our prospective customer base increases considerably. This larger region included 48,699 households in 2010, a figure that was not expected to change significantly within five years. The average household income in this larger region, although lower, is still substantial at $193,790. A near 5 percent increase is projected by 2015, when average household income will reach $203,246. On average, households had two vehicles each. A total of 29.2 percent of households had only one vehicle, while 48.9 percent had two, and 13.3 percent had three vehicles. Consumers in our secondary service area spent an average of $1,639 on vehicle repair and maintenance.

Competition

The majority of our competition will come from other businesses like ours that offer hand washing and automotive detailing services. Presently, there are no other businesses in Winnetka that offer the scope and level of services that we will offer. However, there are three businesses (in our primary and secondary service areas combined) that offer car washing services. These include the following:

- AutoProud, Winnetka, IL

- Bradfield's Car Wash LLC, Wilmette, IL

- Gleason's Car Wash, Skokie IL

Minimal competition will be attributed to these businesses because the majority of our customers would not utilize them for their premium vehicles. The majority of our true competition will come from high-end automotive detailing businesses located directly within the city of Chicago (including automotive dealerships). For residents who do not work in the city, we offer the very best option because we will provide the same level of expert service and care available within the city at the local level. For residents who do work in the city, we again offer convenience by enabling them to drop off their vehicles at the train station prior to their commute.

Future Markets

Although Hands-On Car Wash & Detail Center will concentrate primarily on residential customers, the business eventually will pursue commercial contracts from a number of businesses, including:

- Automotive Dealerships (sports cars and luxury vehicles)

- Body Shops

- Motorcycle Dealerships

- Marinas

A list of prospects will be developed during our first year of operations, and will serve as the basis of a commercial marketing effort that will commence during year two.

PERSONNEL

Jeremy Rundle (owner/manager)

Jeremy Rundle is a native of the Chicago suburb Evergreen Park. Growing up, he developed a knack for washing and waxing cars. During his high school years, fellow students began seeking him out for automotive detailing. Running with this natural ability, he began working for Smith Chevrolet after graduating from high school. Ultimately, his passion for cars landed him a job with Stonecrest BMW in Chicago.

After working at Stonecrest for three years, Jeremy was named manager of the automotive detailing department. He has held that position for five years, honing his human relations and business management skills. Along the way, Jeremy has learned a great deal about customers who drive high-end automobiles. He also gained first-hand knowledge of the automotive detailing market in the Chicago area. He plans to utilize this knowledge as the owner and manager of Hands-On Car Wash & Detail Center.

Detail Technicians

Hands-On Car Wash & Detail Center will require two additional employees for operations. Jeremy Rundle has had discussions with two prospective Chicago-area staff members (Jeff Stewart of Rexfield Lotus and Mike McCaskey of Euro Imports), who are both experienced and reliable. Detailed resumes for Jeff and Mike are available upon request.

Professional & Advisory Support

Hands-On Car Wash & Detail Center has established a business banking account with The Bank of Winnetka, as well as a merchant account for accepting credit card payments. Wakefield & Smith, a local accounting firm, will provide the business with accounting and tax advisory services. Jeremy Rundle has utilized a popular online legal document service to cost-effectively prepare the paperwork necessary for incorporating his new business.

GROWTH STRATEGY

Hands-On Car Wash & Detail Center has developed a formal strategy for growing the business during its first three years of operations.

- *Year One:* Focus on establishing Hands-On Car Wash & Detail Center's reputation in the local Winnetka community and surrounding suburbs. The prime emphasis will be on developing relationships with potential customers and ensuring efficient operations.

- *Year Two:* Maintain Hands-On Car Wash & Detail Center's excellent reputation for quality and customer service while continuing to grow the business. A strong focus will be placed on customer referrals and incentives for more frequent visits. By the year's end, achieve 75 percent capacity. Launch strategy for securing commercial accounts from body shops and upscale automotive dealers, and secure one to two commercial customers.

- *Year Three:* Continue growing the business and maintaining Hands-On Car Wash & Detail Center's excellent reputation for quality and customer service. By the year's end, achieve 85 percent capacity and have three to five commercial accounts in place.

SERVICES

The following services will be provided for cars, trucks, motorcycles, and boats:
- Hand Washing
- Detailing
- Engine Cleaning
- Upholstery & Carpet Shampooing
- Odor Removal
- Headlight Restoration
- Upholstery Repair

Packages

Hands-On Car Wash & Detail Center will offer a number of car wash and detailing packages for its clients:

Executive Deluxe $250

Our best package includes hand washing the entire vehicle and wheels. However, that is only the beginning. In addition, we will pressure wash and degrease the engine compartment, dry the engine with compressed air, and clean the area beneath the hood. A polish/wax will be applied, and vehicles will be buffed by hand. A dressing will be applied to the tires and exterior rubber trim. The entire interior of the car will be vacuumed, and all floor mats and carpets will be shampooed. Leather and vinyl interior surfaces will be cleaned, and the upholstery will be dressed. A brush and light air pressure will be utilized to clean interior surfaces, including vents.

Executive Special $200

This package includes hand washing the entire vehicle and wheels. In addition, a polish/wax will be applied, and vehicles will be buffed by hand. A dressing will be applied to the tires and exterior rubber trim. The entire interior of the car will be vacuumed, and all floor mats and carpets will be shampooed. Leather and vinyl interior surfaces will be cleaned, and the upholstery will be dressed. A brush and light air pressure will be utilized to clean interior surfaces, including vents.

The Outsider (vehicle exterior) $150

This package includes hand washing the entire vehicle and wheels. In addition, a polish/wax will be applied, and vehicles will be buffed by hand. A dressing will be applied to the tires and exterior rubber trim.

The Insider (vehicle interior) $150

The entire interior of the car will be vacuumed, and all floor mats and carpets will be shampooed. Leather and vinyl interior surfaces will be cleaned, and the upholstery will be dressed. A brush and light air pressure will be utilized to clean interior surfaces, including vents.

Running Clean (engine cleaning) $75

We will pressure wash and degrease the engine compartment, dry the engine with compressed air, and clean the area beneath the hood.

As a courtesy to our customers, we offer free pickup and delivery (cars only) at the Hubbard Woods train station, adding convenience for business commuters.

MARKETING & SALES

A marketing plan has been developed for Hands-On Car Wash & Detail Center that includes the following primary tactics:

Web Site: Hands-On Car Wash & Detail Center will develop a Web site that lists basic information about the services that we offer. In addition, the site will include an appointment request function that allows customers to view our schedule and book a tentative appointment (subject to staff approval). Following approval, a confirmation e-mail (or SMS text message) will be sent to the customer requesting the appointment.

Seasonal Consumer Direct Marketing: Hands-On Car Wash & Detail Center will develop a series of four (four-color, glossy) postcards that will be mailed in timing with the four seasons. Each will have a seasonal theme touting the advantages of our professional automotive detailing services. Mailing lists for our entire service area (primary and secondary) will be obtained from Chicago MailMaster, an area list broker and fulfillment house, which also will prepare and send the mailings. Quantities will be based on an average industry response rate of 2 percent and will be adjusted based on capacity/availability. We will incorporate the same graphic design from the postcards into seasonal-themed e-mails to existing customers, in order to encourage repeat business.

Business-to-Business Marketing: Beginning during our second year of operations, Hands-On Car Wash & Detail Center will begin marketing to prospective commercial accounts (see categories listed in the Market section of this business plan). Campaigns will consist of an introductory letter from owner Jeremy Rundle to top prospects. Following the mailing, Jeremy will personally follow up by telephone two weeks after the mailing. Based on the initial response, a second letter may be mailed to all non-respondents 90 days after the first mailing, and Jeremy will once again follow up by phone two weeks after the second letter mails.

Yellow Pages Advertising: We will run a small ad in the Yellow Pages.

Jeremy Rundle will evaluate Hands-On Car Wash & Detail Center's marketing plan on a semi-annual basis during the first three years of operations, and annually thereafter.

OPERATIONS

Liability

Hands-On Car Wash & Detail Center will secure a $2 million insurance policy from Rockwell Insurance Associates. In addition, we have secured a standard customer liability waiver form from a legal document service, which we will utilize for all jobs. Work will not be performed until the customer signs a damage waiver.

Location

Hands-On Car Wash & Detail Center is located on the corner of Tower and Green Bay Roads in Winnetka. This high-traffic area is a key location within the community. Our business is located in a former automotive repair shop. The facility has three indoor bays, each with two overhead doors. Vehicles enter from one side, and exit from the other. Each bay already is equipped with a floor drain. However, in order to equip the structure for use as a car wash and detailing shop, several modifications will need to be made (see Financial Analysis section).

Hours of Operation

Monday: 7:30 a.m.—7:00 p.m.

Tuesday: 7:30 a.m.—7:00 p.m.

Wednesday: 7:30 a.m.—7:00 p.m.

Thursday: 7:30 a.m.—7:00 p.m.

Friday: 7:30 a.m.—6:00 p.m.

Saturday: 8:00 a.m.—4:00 p.m.

Sunday: Closed

FINANCIAL ANALYSIS

Hands-On Car Wash & Detail Center has identified a suitable location for operations (a former automotive repair shop on the corner of Tower and Green Bay Roads in Winnetka) that will require several modifications for use as an automotive detailing center, including the following:

- Addition of two cinderblock walls (floor to ceiling) in order to completely separate each bay. ($10,000)

- Plumbing work (large-capacity water heaters, hot and cold water runs, water softeners) ($8,750)

- Vacuum system installation ($7,000)

- Commercial air compressors/accessories ($5,000)

- Moisture resistant fluorescent lighting ($2,000)

- Landmark and building signage ($4,500)

- Waiting room renovation & amenities ($3,500)

- Parking lot seal coating/striping ($2,000)

- Cash register ($750)

- PC & software ($1,500)

- Total investment required: $45,000

Three-Year Sales Forecast

Following are projections for growth sales during the first three years of operations, broken down by package type.

Package	Year one		Year two		Year three	
Executive deluxe	52	$ 13,000	104	$ 26,000	114	$ 28,500
Executive special	78	$ 15,600	156	$ 31,200	172	$ 34,400
The outsider	390	$ 58,500	780	$117,000	858	$128,700
The insider	260	$ 34,000	520	$ 78,000	572	$ 85,800
Running clean	51	$ 3,825	102	$ 7,650	112	$ 8,400
Gross revenue		$124,925		$259,850		$285,800
Packages sold	831		1,662		1,828	

Income Statement

In partnership with our accounting firm, a detailed pro forma income statement (available upon request) has been prepared, showing projected activity for our first three years of operations. This takes into account average operating costs (approximately 35 percent of gross revenues), as well as proposed mortgage terms for our facility.

Financing

Jeremy Rundle will contribute $30,000 of his own money to the business, from personal savings, and is seeking a business loan of $65,000 to cover the remaining start-up and operational costs.

Biobased Metalworking Fluids Company

EcoLubes

301 Galloway Oaks Drive
Ballwin, MO 63021

Eric Leander

The advantages of biobased lubricants far surpass the "feel good" incentives of buying green. Recent technological advances have afforded our biolubes benefits surpassing the productivity, safety, and cost of conventional lubricants. The complete product line will offer coolants, cutting oils, forming fluids, grinding oils, and rust preventatives. Based in Saint Louis, MO, EcoLubes is at the epicenter of American manufacturing. EcoLubes will be a new product line added to the existing Leander & Company, LLC brand of metalworking fluids.

EXECUTIVE SUMMARY

With the advent of the 21st century we are witnessing what some call the "Environmental Revolution." After decades of manufacturing overload, the global climate is showing adverse reaction to mankind's powerful industrialization. It is clear that if current manufacturing methods are sustained, our environment will continue to breakdown and eventually the world's resources will be fully depleted. With increased societal awareness and pressure from governments, businesses recognize they have responsibility to improve operations with the goal of environmental conservation. It is time to put the economical in economics. As a result, environmental impact has become a driving force in global business decisions.

While the importance of a greener economy is readily apparent, the necessary actions are still vague. No one company can save the environment. Widespread cooperation and collaboration toward climate change is necessary. Focusing locally on everyday actions and adjustments in daily operations can form the building blocks of a greener economy. In the metal manufacturing industry, there is rapidly growing demand toward alternative energy solutions and sustainable products. Prior to now, the transition from mineral or petroleum based lubricants toward eco-friendly products has been slow. The focus of EcoLubes is to provide biobased metalworking products and solutions that outperform conventional lubricants in productivity, cost, and most importantly, greater safety for workers and environment. Our goal is to create a company unlike all the other metalworking fluid companies. Instead of being a "me too," EcoLubes will stand out by offering complete green solutions to reform our customers local environmental impact while improving productivity and safety.

The advantages of biobased lubricants far surpass the "feel good" incentives of buying green. Recent technological advances have afforded our biolubes benefits surpassing the productivity, safety, and cost of conventional lubricants. The complete product line will offer coolants, cutting oils, forming fluids, grinding oils, and rust preventatives. Based in Saint Louis, MO, EcoLubes is at the epicenter of

American manufacturing. EcoLubes will be a new product line added to the existing Leander & Company, LLC brand of metalworking fluids. It is supported by the company's industry experience and superior technical support. Leander & Company currently generates over $600,000 annual revenues and has been growing steadily since its 2008 opening. The EcoLubes line is expecting to reach $50,000 in its first year at a targeted profit margin of 30% and we are projecting a 5-year growth rate of 25% annually. While a small portion of the worldwide 1.5 billion dollar metalworking fluids market, EcoLubes will be one of the industry's forerunning biobased lubricant suppliers. Our intentions are to pioneer a new market, by selling to the early adopters of biobased products and having a strong market segment by the time full integration of biobased products is an environmental necessity.

THE COMPANY

Focusing on the primary goal of reducing the carbon footprint of our customers, EcoLubes offers a complete line of industrial metalworking fluids formulated with biobased materials. Utilizing the mantra to "green it up and clean it up," these products will not only provide customers with an environmentally friendly product, but will increase their productivity and economic efficiency. Customers will "green it up" by purchasing products with positive environmental attributes which are less hazardous than traditional petroleum based metalworking fluids. Additionally customers will "clean it up" by using products which will reduce waste and reduce the company's environmental impact. Through cooperation with the U.S. Environmental Protection Agency's Environmentally Preferable Purchasing (EPP) program and the U.S. Department of Agriculture's BioPreferred Program, our aspiration is to reduce customers petroleum consumption, increase use of renewable resources, better manage the carbon cycle, and, ultimately reduce adverse environmental and health impacts.

Mission Statement

We supply customer-driven, environmentally friendly metalworking solutions. We partner with our customers to achieve goals of environmentally friendly, dependable, and safe metalworking solutions that deliver unsurpassed quality, innovation, productivity and cost effective results.

Company Description

The EcoLube line of products is a subsidiary venture of Leander & Company, LLC., which has been in the metalworking fluid industry since 2008. Leander's product line comes from its father company, Leander Lubricants Corporation, which manufactured metalworking fluids in Earth City, Missouri, from 1978 until its closing in early 2009. Operating under a lean business model, Leander & Company utilizes a consortium of industry partners to manufacture its line and now focuses solely on product development, sales, distribution, and customer support. Supplying customers primarily in the mid-western United States, Leander's distribution network reaches America, Mexico, Canada, South America, Europe and Southeast Asia.

Leander & Company has a strategic partnership with Hawkeye Industrial, a chemical service and technology provider. This partnership unites over 70 years experience in the metalworking fluids industry and ensures our ability to provide highly dependable and cost effective metalworking solutions. Through continuous research and development, the partners are constantly working to formulate high-technology products capable of outperforming corporate industry giants. Since it was formed in 2008, the Hawkeye-Leander partnership has netted over $1.2 million in revenues and forecasts continuous-stable growth as the world economy rebounds.

The current price comparison between biobased and conventional lubricants show biobased costing on average 25-50% more. With increasing petroleum prices, this figure is continuously shrinking. The Leander & Company current pricing model targets 25% profit margins. In order to maximize profit, EcoLubes will target 35% margins and increase that figure to 45% for online sales. Despite these high pricing levels our products will ultimately result in a cost-per-gallon equal to or less than our competitors due to our lean business model and lower operating costs.

The EcoLube competitive advantage is embracing multiple benefits and standing apart. We are not just another petroleum-based metalworking fluid supplier. Our products are structured to create value on a range of levels throughout the products life cycle. Each of our customers has unique manufacturing needs. Our goal is to provide improvements in troublesome production areas while equally or out-performing the competition. Our aim is to ultimately prove to our customers they will reap benefits of cost, productivity, safety, and environmental stability with our products.

Industry

Metalworking lubricants are an essential component in any type of industrial metal machining operation. They are used in a wide range of applications which involve abrading, cutting, bending, stamping, pressing, shaping and extruding metal into one form or another. These applications are diverse, and there is no one-size-fits-all metalworking lubricant. The lubricants are formulated for specific purposes based on performance, cost, and other factors. The three main types of metalworking lubricants are fluids, grease, and dry lubricants. Fluids are broadly categorized into coolants and liquid lubricants, and make up the largest part of the market. The main purpose of metalworking fluids is to reduce friction between machine tool and the item being manufactured. The reduced friction enhances performance and cuts costs, by preventing wear and tear on the machines and tools. Additional benefits include: increased machining speeds and feeds, rust and corrosion protection, improved metal surface finishing, lower energy consumption, narrower tolerances of the work piece size, cleaner cutting zones (carry away heat and debris), and longer tool life. Because of the wide range of requirements for metal forming operations, the metalworking lubricants can be engineered for use in any type of machine and for any type of application.

Metalworking fluids are made from three types of base stocks: petroleum or mineral-based, synthetic, and biobased. Complex mixtures of additives are combined to customize performance. These additives include emulsifiers, anti-weld agents, corrosion inhibitors, extreme pressure additives, buffers (alkaline reserve), and biocides. The generally accepted definition of biobased lubricants is that they are formulated with renewable and biodegradable base stock. This means they do not need to be composed entirely of an unaltered vegetable oil, but the base materials must be renewable. They can be products derived from renewable oils, such as fatty acids, and reacted with synthetic alcohols and polyols to produce esters. Natural vegetable oils can be treated to produce a modified product still considered biodegradable and renewable. The most widely used lubricant biobase stocks are soy and rapeseed oils. Other primary bio-oils come from sunflower, safflowers, palm oil trees and canola (a rapeseed hybrid) plants.

Until recent years, researchers trying to bring biobased lubricants to market encountered many hurdles, specifically related to performance and price. Improved technologies and environmental pressures for conservancy, have led to breakthroughs in performance, allowing effective cost competition with mineral-based and synthetic lubricants. Europe has been leading the biobased lubricant market for years. This is mostly because of regulations mandating use of biodegradables. Experts predict that by the end of 2010, 18% of all European lubricants will be biobased

The U.S. biobased market is changing rapidly through legislative initiatives. The Food, Conservation and Energy Act of 2008, the Farm Security and Rural Investment Act of 2002, the Presidential Executive Order #13423, and the Federal Acquisition Regulations (FAR) currently require government agencies the give preference to the purchase of biobased products over petroleum-based products. This is when such products are "readily available, reasonably priced and pass the required performance standards of their non-biobased counterparts." Formed from this legislation, the U.S. Department of Agriculture's BioPre-ferred Program not only instills a procurement preference for Federal agencies but campaigns a labeling program for consumer marketing of biobased products. Beginning February 21, 2011, this labeling program allows for certified biobased products to carry a distinctive label for consumer identification.

Additionally, the BioPreferred Program sets the U.S. standards and definitions of what can now be called BioPreferred products. For example, in some countries the biobased designation requires only 50% renewable content. The BioPreferred Program designation for metalworking fluids requires a minimum biobased content of 57% for general purpose lubricants, 40% for high performance lubricants, and 66% for straight oils, 68% for forming lubricants, and 53% for corrosion preventatives. The biodegradability requirements for metalworking biolubes requires the product to be "65% degraded in 28 days" when left outside or exposed.

The BioPreferred Program was adopted by the U.S. Environmental Protection Agency's Environmental Preferred Purchasing Program (EPP). This program focuses on stimulating market demand for green products and helps green businesses collaborate with one another. Industry analysts predict as these government programs become more fully integrated, they will provide a major driving force in the sales of biobased lubricants.

The market for lubricant oils and greases, SIC code 2992, demands about 13 billion gallons of fluid each year. Of these lubricants, only 2.8% are classified metalworking fluids. The U.S. market accounts for an estimated 28% of the demand, or between 2.5-3.5 billion gallons. Total sales of metalworking fluids are estimated at 1.5 billion dollars globally. While industry growth rates average approximately 2% annually, the fastest growing segment is synthetic and semi-synthetic products. The United States market for all metalworking fluids is estimated to be 246.6 million gallons, of which, 117.2 million gallons are metal removal fluids. The estimated 2010 market share of biobased products of all lubricant types in the U.S. was 4%; in the metalworking segment this figure would be lower. Industry analysts recognize the eco-friendly biobased market as underdeveloped and having high growth opportunities.

Product

The EcoLube line of biobased metalworking fluids will initially consist of 6 general types: general purpose cutting oil, heavy duty cutting oil, grinding oil, forming fluid, water-soluble machining coolant, and a corrosion inhibitor. Each of these products will be certified for labeling under the USDA's BioPreferred program. Developed by PhD chemists in our business consortium, these technologically advanced formulas provide biobased lubricants capable of out-performing synthetics. Usage of these formulas would be exclusive to Hawkeye and Leander, all toll blenders are restricted to use through existing legal contracts. In addition to the biobase stock, EcoLubes strives to use a minimum of chemical additives. Although necessary, our additive packages are less hazardous and have positive environmental attributes. Customization is key; we have the ability to tailor any of our products to improve critical aspects of our customer's application. Each of our products can be adjusted to meet the ISO viscosity range best suited for the operation. The majority of the EcoLubes line are soy based, however rapeseed and canola are also used frequently.

Product	Description	Applications
EcoCut 1000	General-purpose neat cutting oil	Safe on all types of ferrous and non-ferrous metals. Designed for cutting, grinding, milling, tapping, and reaming. Ideal in high pressure applications such as gear cutting, broaching, gun drilling, and screw machining.
EcoCut 1000 HD	High-performance neat cutting oil	Safe on all metals both ferrous and non-ferrous. Designed for cutting, grinding, milling, tapping, and reaming. Ideal in high pressure applications such as gear cutting, broaching, gun drilling, and screw machining.
EcoGrind 8000	Grinding oil	Safe on all metals both ferrous and non-ferrous. For grinding, milling, tapping, and reaming.
EcoForm 2000	Forming fluid	High viscosity forming fluid recommended for all types of metals. Highly effective on aluminum and stainless steal.
EcoCool 5000 WS	Water-Soluble metalworking concentrate	Ideal for ferrous metals, aluminum, cast iron, high-temp alloys. Used for milling, tapping, reaming, hobbing, gun drilling, broaching, and shaping.
EcoStop RP-200	Corrosion preventative	Solvent based rust preventative coating used on ferrous metals after they have been machined with water-soluble metalworking coolants.

The products will be manufactured by one of our business consortium partners (see Organization section for more details on business consortium). Depending on sales volume, we will stock finished products so they can ship immediately. Our distribution network is, for the most part, Midwestern U.S. (Missouri, Illinois, Indiana, Tennessee, Kentucky, Iowa, and Arkansas). Product will be sold in 5gal pails, 55gal drums, and 250 or 330 gallon totes; specialty arrangements can be made for larger orders requiring a tanker truck. The product will be shipped via LTL freight or UPS/Fed Ex ground.

Our pricing structure targets 35% profit margins. The online prices will reflect 45% margins, to allow for customer discounts as well as support our sales distributors pricing incentives. When later compared to our competitions pricing, this would fall into a moderate range.

EcoLubes	Manufacturing costs		Selling price		Website pricing	
Pricing	55 gal	5 gal	55 gal	5 gal	55 gal	5 gal
EcoCut 1000	$10.25	$11.75	$13.84	$15.86	$14.86	$17.04
EcoCut 1000 HD	$11.40	$12.90	$15.39	$17.42	$16.53	$18.71
EcoGrind 8000	$ 8.90	$10.40	$12.02	$14.04	$12.91	$15.08
EcoForm 2000	$11.89	$13.39	$16.06	$18.08	$17.24	$19.42
EcoCool 5000WS	$ 7.85	$ 9.35	$10.60	$12.62	$11.38	$13.56
EcoStop RP-200	$10.90	$12.40	$14.72	$16.74	$15.81	$17.98

All Leander & Company and EcoLube formulations are intellectual proprietary technology and are kept as trade secret. All parties to the business consortium operate under a Non-Disclosure Agreement and a Formulation Agreement.

The EcoLube Advantage

The EcoLube line will be successful because we offer a wide array of advantages, the most obvious being biodegradability. It is estimated that 50% of all used oil ends up in the environment. Mineral-based and synthetic lubricants do not degrade well, creating an environmental liability. Biobased lubricants are biodegradable, meaning microorganisms can break them down into innocuous carbon monoxide. Therefore, they are less toxic and cause less environmental damage. In the event of a spill, less remediation is needed and clean-up costs are significantly lower than non-biobased lubricants.

Higher Performance: All Biolubes have higher lubricity properties and a lower coefficient of friction compared to mineral-based lubricants. Superior lubricity reduces wear, which reduces the necessity of chemical additives for antiwear and extreme pressure. Most importantly, enhanced lubricity allows for faster machining (more parts per hour) and prolongs the tool life cycle. This gives customers an overall higher performance and cost savings for each tool.

Lower Volatility and Higher Shear Stability: Viscosity index (VI) is a critical measurement in lubrication. The lower an oil's VI, the more susceptible that oil is to change in temperatures. The VI range for basic mineral-based oil is 90 to 120 degrees F, while the VI range for equivalent viscosity biobased oil is 200 to 250 degrees F. This means biobased oil's optimum performance can be sustained in a wider range of thermal conditions than its mineral-based counterpart. The VI also indicates shear stability, a measurement of an oil's viscosity change while operating under stressful conditions. This means a greater load capacity is achieved with biobased over mineral-base lubricants.

Low Misting: Vegetable based oils have more density than their mineral-based counterparts. This means the airborne particles are heavier and gravity pulls them down faster. The result is less misting around the machines as the coolant will not "hang" as easily in the air. Coolant misting is a major occupational hazard for machine operators and can result in respiratory conditions such as hypersensitivity pneumotis (HP), chronic bronchitis, impaired lung function, and asthma. Work-related asthma (WRA) is one of today's most prevalent occupational disorders, imposing significant costs in healthcare and workers' compensation.

Less Carry Out: EcoLubes have less carry out on the parts and metal fines than mineral-based. This means less oil is removed during machining and oil needs to be replenished less often, thus saving the customer money.

Less Toxic: Natural ingredients make EcoLubes less hazardous. They contain low volatile organic compounds, and no sulfur or chlorine, a common cause of skin rash. According to NIOSH and OSHA, dermatologic exposures in the manufacturing industry are most commonly associated with allergic and irritant dermatitis or skin rash.

Safer: The flash point of EcoLubes is higher than mineral oils. This reduces smoking and fire hazards, as well as reducing freight costs associated with shipping more hazardous materials.

ISO 14000: Using less hazardous products will help companies comply with ISO: 14000 Environmental Management Standards.

Renewable and Agriculture Friendly: Dependence on foreign oil has been in the forefront of U.S. economic issues. EcoLubes support the growing interest in alternative energies and supports local farmers growing the biobased materials.

Reduced Packaging: EcoLubes uses only recyclable poly-urethane drums and totes.

Recyclable: All EcoLube products have the potential to be reclaimed, filtered, and reused through a coolant recycling system. This saves money on new coolant and reduces waste oil costs.

Waste Reduction: EcoLubes reduce waste. Used lubricants and fluid products containing a mixture of biobased oil and petroleum can be recycled under federal "used oil" management standards, which is much less costly than managing the used oil as hazardous waste. In some cases, used biobased oils can be treated as "solid waste," an even more flexible and low cost option.

While the added value from these advantages is impressive, Ecolubes are hindered by the same disadvantages of all biobased products. The most serious concern is the oxidative stability, which is the fluids resistance to decomposition from exposure to air and oxygen. This degradation can result in oxidative rancidification, whereby the product is broken down and chemical bonds are weakened, ultimately leaving the product susceptible to microbial attack from bacteria and fungus. The oxidation process is slow until the resistance is overcome, at which point the breakdown accelerates and rancidity becomes rapid. The second problem with biobased products are their higher pour points, requiring a higher temperature for the product to pour as a liquid. A result from their high viscosity, the high pour point can cause issues in winter months. Both these disadvantages are easily avoided through quality maintenance. Regular testing of the fluids can detect oxidation and bacteria before levels spiral out of control. And keeping the products stored at recommended temperatures, typically above 50F, can avoid pouring issues. Fluid maintenance is unfortunately often disregarded in our industry; operators usually do not catch issues until it's too late. EcoLubes will attempt to instill the importance of optimal fluid management, as well as provide regular free laboratory testing.

The biggest commercialization problem for EcoLubes is the lack of a performance track record. While biobased metalworking fluids are currently able to outperform conventional counterparts, the history of success is only a few years in the making. Some factors driving the success of biobased products are technology advancement, demand for petroleum, and federal/state incentives; however, it will take time for these products to fully penetrate the market and prove their value. Again, this hindrance is also an advantage as EcoLubes is targeting a small market segment to establish a strong presence amongst little competition and then growing with the market as biobased metalworking fluids are integrated.

The EcoLubes line will stand out in the field of biobased metalworking fluid suppliers by embracing existing Leander & Company attributes of efficiency, support and customization. Our strategic business consortium allows for supply chain efficiencies and faster availability than most companies—typically shipped in 3 business days. Our knowledgeable team is familiar with all types of metalworking operations and has experience with countless production challenges. This gives us the ability to provide outstanding customer support and rapidly fix problems. Unlike the competitors who recommend an "off-the-shelf" product that the customer must make work in their application, our products can be custom formulated to address critical aspects of customers' applications. We seek to understand the total process of a customer so we can offer products specifically formulated to achieve the best results.

In addition to fluids, we provide our customers complete green metalworking solutions by offering equipment, green cleaners, waste removal, and recycling systems. Through authorized distributor agreements with industry partners we offer full lines of equipment to accompany our products. These include application equipment delivering lubricant to the operation point and entire lubricant filtration systems which recycle contaminated (used) fluid and replenish it for continued use.

In conclusion, the EcoLubes line is able to provide our customers with companywide green solutions. Because EcoLubes offer a diverse array of benefits, our customers will receive value and advantages unobtainable with the mineral-based counterparts. Beyond the cost and productivity benefits, the best result of switching to EcoLubes will be significant reduction of each customer's local environmental impact. Every customer who switches to EcoLubes will make up the building blocks of our mission to improve the world environment. EcoLubes is not like every other metalworking fluid supplier. While our products do carry economic and productive advantages, switching to EcoLubes affirms each customer's social and environmental responsibility.

THE MARKET

Market Status and Target Customer

Metalworking fluids are found in almost every manufacturing industry and primarily from the SIC segments of 3200-Primairy Metal Industries, 3400-Fabricated Metal Products, 3500—Industrial and Commercial Machinery, and 3700-Transportation Equipment. Together these segments create the worldwide metalworking fluid industry which generates 1.5 billion dollars each year. Trade organizations of this industry include: Society of Tribologists and Lubrication Engineers (STLE), Precision Metalforming Association (PMA), North American Die Casting Association (NADCA), Independent Lubrication Manufactures Association (ILMA), Society of Manufacturing Engineers (SME), United Soybean Board, National Fluid Power Association, ASM International, StratSoy (National Soybean Research Laboratories), and the Biobased Manufacturers Association. Prominent industry publications are *Metalworking Fluids Magazine, Metalforming Magazine, Lubes 'n Greases Magazine, Production Machining Magazine, Modern Machineshop, Cutting Tool Engineering, Fabricating and Metalworking Trade Magazine, Metalworking Insiders' Report, Metalworking Production and Purchasing Magazine,* and dozens of similar international publications.

Our target customers are manufacturers of any type of products with metal components. The industries served are as diverse as the products sold. The target customer has a requirement for lubricity agents to assist with efficiently producing their end product. As an added benefit, because our products are used in the production of another product (and not an end usage product), they are most often classified sales tax free. Typically the customer will purchase metalworking fluids through a company PO system. Depending on their volume needs, orders are placed weekly, monthly, annually, or more often, right after they run out. We recommend a 1-year shelf life for our products. Because the wide range of applications and usage of metalworking fluids, each customer has different needs. The primary goals of these consumers is for a safe and cost-effective product which provides long sump life, high-productivity (longer tool life and faster production speeds), and a precision/quality metal finish.

EcoLubes will immediately target existing Leander & Company customers. Preliminary inquiries and research has indicated a good portion of them would be willing to test out the biobased products. While Leander & Company will continue supplying mineral-based and synthetic products, we will not cannibalize our own brand because EcoLubes has product offerings for which Leander could never compete. The neat or straight cutting oil market is dominated by corporate petroleum industry giants. These companies are able to utilize their logistical efficiencies and purchasing power to provide the product to customers with free delivery and very low margins. While these corporations may be unbeatable in their petroleum line, they currently do not offer biobased straight oils.

Competition

While the metalworking fluids industry has been around for over a century, the biobased metalworking fluid industry is still in its infancy. The largest company producing biobased lubricants is Autohydraulic Biolubes, Inc., based in Hartville, OH. Autohydraulic Biolubes is a leader in biobased greases, auto-motive, and hydraulics oils. They offer 12 biobased metalworking fluids which make up about 10% of their entire product line. While broadly focused, these metalworking fluids provide strong competition because of Autohydraulic Biolubes widespread distributor network. Primary distributors include T4 Bio Technologies of Tampa, Fl, and Freemont Wholesale Oil Co. of Sikeston, MO.

Other specific local competition comes from Eco-friendly Lubricants, Inc. EFL was created by Dr. Lorne Hoger, Director of the National Ag-Based Lubricant Center (NALB) at University of Northern Iowa. Through state and federal grants, NALB researchers have developed the world's most competitive and high-quality biobased lubricants. EFL began operations in 2006, initially offering biobased lubricants for any profitable application. Soon, they realized the scope of their products was far too widespread and concentrated mainly on greases, hydraulic, and general purpose lubricants. In turn, they sold the metalworking fluids division to a start-up company, BioPerformance, Inc., our strongest competitor. BioPerformance, Inc., has been selling only biobased metalworking lubricants since 2008. This is a private company based in Morton Grove, IL, with products toll blended by a manufacturer in Michigan. Sales manager, Glenn Schweiger, explained to me they have been doubling their revenues each year, and estimated revenues are about 1 million dollars.

In an industry investigation obtaining information from search engines, the Thomas Register, industry associations, and biobased industry contacts, researchers concluded there are 16 companies in the United States selling metalworking fluids considered as biobased that could be considered for inclusion in the Federal Biobased Products Preferred Procurement Program. The strongest of these competitors are detailed in the table below:

Company	Location	Product	Strength/weakness	Pricing*
Autohydraulic Biolubes, Inc.	Hartville, Ohio	Bio-Metal Cool GP Bio-Metal Cool HD	Wide range of products. Primarily sells hydraulic and automotive biolubes. Large networking of private labeling distributors.	Moderate to high
Envirolube Manufacturing, Inc.	Grundy Center, Iowa	SoyEasy Cool™ -XXL	Sold metalworking biolube division to Performance Biolubes. Only focus on grease, railroad lubes, and hydraulic fluids.	Average
Biosafe Products	Phoenix, Arizona	Safe Lube Grinding Fluid Safe Lube Cutting & Forming Fluid NF	Entirely biobased products. Sells cleaners, solvents, metalworking fluids, and anti-allergen soaps.	High
Johnson Industrial Oils & Lubricants	Minneapolis, Minnesota	Agri-Pure 420	Very large corporation. Small focus on biobased metalworking fluids.	Moderate
Specialty Chemical Corporation	Wickliffe, Ohio	LZ 7652	Company focus is as a specialty chemical supplier to manufactures of fluids. Not so much on end machining users.	Moderate
Fluidcare International, Inc.	Valley Forge, Pennsylvania	HOCUT V-400 HOCUT TR 2000C	Company focus is on fluidcare, an on-site fluid management service.	Moderate
USB Technology, Inc.	Lansdale, Pennsylvania	Desigreen Waterdilutable 100	Products sponsored by United Soybean Board. Small market share mostly in N.E. United States.	High
BioPerformance, Inc.	Morton Grove, Illinois	BioCool XXL BioSyn 100 NuCut Plus	Entirely biobased products. Only competitor who is solely focused on biobased metalworking fluids.	Average
T4 Bio Technologies	Tampa, Florida	Bio-Metal Cool GP Bio-Metal Cool HD	Distributor for many lubricant manufacturers. All biobased offerings come from partnership with Renewable Lubricants, Inc.	Moderate to High
BioRenew, LCC	Joliet, Illinois	BioCut 1500 BioCut FG	Entirely biobased products. Wide range of products including hydraulic, engine, greases, and metalworking.	Moderate to High
Freemont Wholesale Oil Co.	Sikeston, MO	Bio-Metal Cool GP Bio-Metal Cool HD	Distributor for an array of lubricants manufacturers, including Renewable Lubricants, Inc.	Moderate to High

*The pricing ranges in comparison to petroleum metalworking fluids—average=1.25 times, moderate=1.5 times, high=1.75 times cost of petro based.

While there is strong competition in the biobased field, our competitive advantage is our narrow focus, strategic partnerships, and ability to offer entire green solutions. Like many of these competitors, Leander & Company offers mineral-based and synthetic metalworking fluids. However, with the exception of BioPerformance, Inc., all these competitors are highly involved in other realms of lubricants. This hinders their ability to optimize their biobased metalworking fluid market segment. Additionally, because EcoLubes has dealership agreements we are a one-stop-shop for reforming a customer's environmental impact. This is a service none of these competitors currently offer and ensures EcoLubes ability to stand apart in the biobased metalworking industry.

Marketing Strategy

EcoLubes will use a range of marketing strategies to differentiate ourselves from the competition. While green business is our core focus, customers will benefit by switching to biolubes for any number of reasons. Key components of our overall sales strategy include custom solutions, companywide green results, and superior service. In addition to the Federal BioPreferred programs support, our products will be marketed through other avenues to enhance exposure and build our brand. Because "green" is an economic buzz-word, we intend to submit articles on our products to the industry publications. Editors of these publications have assured us that quality articles on green products written by an author with robust industry experience will likely be published, and at zero or little cost. Partnerships with machine manu-facturers will broaden our sales. For example, Green Emollients, Inc. is one of the area's largest producers of precision metalcutting machines, and they have a company directive toward eco-friendly operations. They currently supply or recommend products for use in every new machine they sell. Leveraging our existing contacts at Green Emollients could result in EcoLubes being an exclusive product endorsement.

EcoLubes uses third-party laboratories to test our products against the competitions. Key machining tests include torque and tap, pin and valve, and sheer stability. This allows our sales team to show certified results of EcoLubes durability against mineral-based or synthetic lubricants. While our sales pitch can be persuasive, the engineers in our industry demand evidence of performance, and extensive third-party testing will deliver that proof.

Our innovative product line will be supported by our contemporary website, providing 24/7 customer resources, support, and sales opportunities, located at www.LeanderAndCompany.com and www.EcoLu-bes.com (domain pending). Industry investigation has revealed significant opportunity in online marketing of metalworking fluids. While most of the corporate competitors have cutting-edge websites, the majority of our competition maintains very basic, rarely updated, and poorly indexed websites. We will capitalize on these inefficiencies and launch a continuous SEO campaign ensuring our company/products are easily found. It is certainly true that sales generated from metalworking fluid supplier's websites are not nearly as effective as other industries. This a result of industry purchasing practices, typically products are purchased through a company's purchasing order agent via fax, email, or direct call. Additionally, the industry and its representatives are typically behind in the digital age. However, we view this as an evolving opportunity. By establishing a strong web-based presence we will have a foothold ahead of our competition by the time the industry becomes more integrated with online technology.

Sales Plan: Existing Relationships

Initially, our sales team will focus on introducing EcoLubes to our existing customers. Because we have established relationships, these customers will be more easily persuaded to try biobased products. We have reached out to many of these customers and explained our new venture, this has been extremely well received and interest in eco-friendly products is very high. Since 2008, Leander & Company has sold to 160 customers currently, of these 134 have made repeat purchases. Of these, some customers purchase 2-3 times a month, where some buy once per year. Altogether, Leander & Company sells around 60,000 gallons of product annually. We believe the EcoLubes line can be successfully introduced to 40 existing customers, 30% of repeat buyers, within its first year. This expectation is supported by our research inquiries and knowledge that many of our customers' corporate culture is moving in a direction of sustainability and pro-green business operations.

Leander & Company currently has 5 sales distributors established. These companies represent our product line, in conjunction with their other product lines, in their respective sales territories. We sell them our products at a discounted rate and they in turn can distribute them at any rate they desire. We often give these reps sales leads when our office receives inquiries from prospects in their regions. And this has been a very successful inflow of sales and allowed us to establish a large presence without a fleet of company sales persons. EcoLubes will introduce and train these distributors on the new product line. The EcoLubes distributor pricing structure will target 15% profit margins, allowing for the distributors to set their pricing at levels able to handsomely compensate. For example, with EcoLubes priced at 45% margins on the website, the distributors will be able to significantly undercut this to demonstrate to their customers the value in purchasing through them, while still having lots of room from their own profit. Additionally, distributor prices will fluctuate based on sales volumes, payment terms, and other factors all designed to encourage their participation in pushing the EcoLubes line. We believe this distributor sales plan will not only succeed with current distributors, but EcoLubes hopes establish new distributors in other regions to help further grow the business.

Lastly, EcoLubes will leverage existing customer and distributor relationships to increase sales by networking and seeking introduction to new customers. We are confident that because EcoLubes is pursuing an eco-friendly solution to metalworking, our customers will be excited to announce their implementations toward more environmental conscious operations. Companies love to toot their own horn, and by publicizing their greener operations to vendors, suppliers, customers, shareholders, and so on, our own customers will be advertising the EcoLubes brand.

Sales Plan: New Customers

Securing new customers in the metalworking fluids business is a tough and time consuming endeavor. The most successful sales approach is a traditional in-person meeting with the prospective customers engineers/operators, purchasing agents, and/or plant managers. Once the potential customer agrees to a trial, it can take months to analyze machine performance before a companywide switch is made. We recognize the two toughest tasks of this sales procedure are establishing an introductory meeting which receives genuine consideration, and getting the product into the machine.

EcoLubes will clear these hurdles by differentiating our approach with the green aspect. We aren't just another metalworking fluid company promising lower cost and higher productivity. Our company presents complete green solutions, resulting in cleaner, more stable, safer products in addition to the cost and productivity benefits. Embracing the green revolution will get our foot in the door.

Next, our sales team will work with the customer to evaluate the current process and identity areas for improvement. Then we can begin the recommendation process and determine the best product for their application. Once a product is determined, a formulation review will take place where we look at adjusting the formula to better address critical aspects of the application. After this evaluation and formula review process, we recommend a specific product. That's why we say Leander & Company provides "Custom solutions, not stock answers."

The customer may be intrigued by our approach and our products, but allowing a test against the current fluid is a costly and time consuming process. Here is where we offer the array of benefits to comply with our prospective customers' company needs. For example, corporate management could be pushing green initiatives such as alternative energy, renewable products, or reduced dependency on foreign oil. Management may be interested in supporting a U.S. based supplier and the U.S. farming industry. There could be safety concerns from operator dermatitis, smoking issues, and fire potential, or the desire for less hazardous products. Management may be working toward achieving ISO 14000 Quality Management accreditation. There could be a push for a more valuable product with lower cost and higher productivity than conventional lubricants. The list goes on, and in most cases the customer will be seeking improvement in at least one of these criteria. Our selling point is that EcoLubes will provide its customers with additional benefits and value unobtainable with mineral-based lubricants.

Once the customer agrees to a trial, the last sales hurdle will be cleared through our "Proof of Performance" agreement. Simply put, we'll supply no-charge trial product and if they like it, they buy it. We work closely with the machine operators for input and feedback resulting in an analytical report which documents the performance, lab specs, and a price-per-piece breakdown. Additionally, we provide free laboratory testing to gauge pH, refractive index, bio-stability, and bacteria/fungus levels to continuously monitor the product's performance. This enhanced service will allow us to pinpoint areas for improvement and ensure the customers are using the products to their optimal performance. This analytical report is intended to affirm the value received from our products and make our customers believers in EcoLubes green solutions.

Milestones

Bringing EcoLubes to market will be a challenging venture. With the certain unforeseen obstacles and pitfalls, the company strategy will be open to pivoting objectives to ensure success. The following timetable identifies several milestones and the courses of action taken once reached:

Current: (May 2011—Introduction of EcoLubes to market)

- BioPreferrd label certifications—using American Society for Testing and Materials (ASTM.org) International

- Begin sales to existing customers

- Closely monitor performance of product in use, to gain as much knowledge of products before full introduction

- Logos and graphics for EcoLubes

- Build website to full functionality

- Fund third-party laboratory tests for EcoLubes vs competition

- Establish new relationships with other green businesses and find methods for cooperation or support

- Continue new product development

Introduction of EcoLubes to market (Anticipated January 1, 2012)

- Launch website—SEO, online advertising, email announcements

- Launch marketing plans—distributor training; submit articles to publications, and advertising campaign.

- Brian & Eric—on the road sales campaign

- Sales focus on establishing new customers

Reach $50,000 in sales to new customers (Expected between months 10-12)

- Hire additional company dedicate sales person(s)

- Develop more products—New licenses and certifications for these

- Being implementation of quality management certification, ISO:9001, using Det Norske Veritas.

Reach $250,000 in annual sales of EcoLubes (Expected in year 2-3)

- Being international sales development

- Additional sales persons, if needed

- Leverage EcoLubes performance history and success stories in marketing efforts.

- Begin feasibility study on eliminating toll blenders

- New locations? How can we make the supply chain more efficient?

Long Term

The EcoLube long-term strategy will guard its success by focusing on 5 key strategies: innovation, experience, partnerships, growth and international markets. The last decade has seen incredible developments in biobased lubricant technology. Our research and development team will continuously work to enhance our existing knowledge and embrace new techniques assuring an evolving, start-of-the-art product line. We will pioneer the biobased metalworking lubricants industry by keeping our products ahead of the competitions while establishing our company as the trusted industry leader. Through this recognition, we will build partnerships with distributors, non-competitor businesses in the industry, and most importantly, our own customers. Because we don't view our relationships as simply supplier-vendor, rather partners in facilitating our customers toward complete eco-friendly solutions.

Lastly, our long-term success will be fueled by the sheer market size and its untapped opportunities. The metalworking biolubes industry is in its earliest stages of development. Continued support from legislation and regulatory mandates, as well as societal desire to reduce petroleum usage, will provide the ammunition for the markets demand. Just as the U.S. is currently catching up to Europe's integration of metalworking biolubes, the rest of the world's industrialized nations will soon follow. Key economies include: Mexico, Brazil, China, and Southeast Asia. These international markets are the growing majority of metalworking fluid demand and essential to our business growth plan as more and more manufacturing leaves the United States. If EcoLubes are met with substantial demand, we will consider partnerships, private-labeling, licensing, or even organizational buy-out with our large corporate competitors. Our goal to provide green metalworking solutions and ultimately assist in changing the industrial world's environmental impact will best be achieved by widespread usage of biolubes. Cooperation with corporate competition would lower their restrictive barriers and drive a faster and more comprehensive integration of biolubes.

THE ORGANIZATION

Leander & Company currently operates as a LLC owned by a single proprietor and registered in the state of Missouri. The company has two full-time employees: Eric Leander, the owner and operations manager, and Brian Leander, the sales manager and technical advisor.

Eric received a Bachelor's of Science in Business Administration from Regis University in 2006 and is currently working toward an MBA in Entrepreneurship from Saint Louis University. As the Operations Manager, Eric handles all day-to-day business duties, including accounting, purchasing, order processing, logistics, inventory, and any business issues that may arise. His main purpose on a wider-scope is to make decisions regarding effective operating methods and efficient company direction. Since opening Leander & Company in 2008, Eric has effectively created a virtual company that allows for operations to be handled from any location with cell phone service and/or internet access. This lean business model means all employees can be out selling and visiting customers without interrupting business or service to other customers.

As the sales manager, Brian Leander's focus is customer driven. He is responsible for marketing, establishing new customers, and maintaining existing customers. His network of industry contacts is remarkably strong after working in the metalworking fluids business for over 35 years. He had significant success as president and CEO of the metalworking lubricants manufacturing company, Leander Lubricants Corporation, from 1977 until 2009. Located in Earth City, MO, Leander Lubricants was a regional leader in metalworking fluids, at its peak generating $4 million dollars in annual revenues and employing a staff of about 15. At the start of the economic recession in 2008, the customer-revenue base was about 85% automotive and as a result of multiple large customers filling Chapter 11 bankruptcy, Brian was forced to close Leander Lubricants. The entire product line at Leander Lubricants was developed by or under the direction of Brian. His formulation experience resulted in over 1000 unique products and is the line successfully sold by Leander & Company today. Brian's extensive knowledge of metalworking lubricant formulation makes him a perfect fit as the company's technical advisor. This positions duties include product development, customization of formulas, analyzing product performance, and is the technical contact for customer inquiries.

Related Service Providers

Leander & Company and the EcoLube line would not exist without the support of our business consortium. Our closest partners are Hawkeye Industrial Inc., a similar company supplying metalworking fluids and solutions through use of toll blenders. Together, Leander and Hawkeye share product information, develop new products, and facilitate all production through an order processing/invoicing system. All orders are processed by Hawkeye's operations secretaries who place the order with the optimal manufacturing company (toll blender) and once shipped Hawkeye handles all invoicing and collection duties. We have various toll blenders. Toll blending is a common practice in the industry and entails paying a small premium for custom product manufacturing. This allows Leander and Hawkeye to focus directly on sales, distribution, and customer support while bypassing the headaches and overhead costs of manufacturing. All our manufacturing partners are, at minimum, ISO:9001:2001 Quality Management registered. Each business in the consortium has extensive industry experience and incredibly knowledgeable personnel. By uniting our companies, we have compiled our industry know-how to develop products and reach markets unattainable alone.

Location

The EcoLubes product line will be broadcasted from its home-based at Leander & Company offices in greater Saint Louis, MO. We are currently in the processing of moving from a residential sales office in Ballwin, MO, to a new location at 403 Marshall Road in Valley Park, MO. This new office is adjoining our toll blender's 100,000 sqft building, and Leander & Company has a 2-year lease effective May 1st, 2011. A necessity for Leander & Company's growth, the new location will provide 4,600 sqft of space, 3,500 sqft of which is warehouse. The new warehouse will accommodate our plan to stock higher demand products, granting us the ability to ship in 1 business day, and reducing local customer freight costs. Our office has a high-tech laboratory with all the tools for testing, developing, and analyzing our products. The last added benefit of our consortium is the range of locations. Because our toll blenders are located in different regions throughout the Midwest, we can reduce customers' freight costs by supplying from the location closest to their facility.

FINANCIALS

The following financial documents are supported by actual 2009 and 2010 statements of Leander & Company. Critical assumptions are as follows:

- Leander & Company growth will increase 10% annually in 2011-2013.

- Profit margins will hit exactly the 25% target. Meaning COGS will be precisely 75% of revenues.

- EcoLubes will begin sales effective January 1, 2012.

- EcoLubes revenues will total $50,000 in its first year, growing 25% annually afterward.

- Pricing of EcoLubes are actual raw material costs from toll blenders, based on typical industry biolube pricing our 35% profit margin is very price competitive.

- Accounts receivable will be fully paid on a Net 30 day outlay.

- Annual expenses increase: office supplies +5%, travel/auto + 5%, accounting +5%, cell phones +5%, telephones +3%, insurance +3%, lab expenses +10%.

- $5000 would be allocated to advertising in 2012, growing 25% annually afterward.

- Auto Loan will be paid off in 1st quarter 2013.

- New blending equipment will be purchased in 2013: $25,000 total.

- Rental expenses will begin upon moving to new location effective May 1, 2011.

- Income taxes would total 13.3% of EBIT annually.

- Inflation rate is 3%.

Profit and loss projection (12 months)

Fiscal year begins   1/1/2012

					IND. %					
	Jan-12	% B/A	Feb-12	%	Mar-12	%	Apr-12	%	May-12	%
Revenue (sales)										
EcoCut 1000	761	1.5	761	1.5	1,552	3.0	1,552	2.4	1,552	2.4
EcoCut 1000 HD	846	1.7	846	1.7	846	1.6	1,693	2.6	1,693	2.6
EcoGrind 8000	140	0.3	140	0.3	281	0.5	281	0.4	576	0.9
EcoForm 2000	90	0.2	90	0.2	90	0.2	181	0.3	181	0.3
EcoCool 5000WS	63	0.1	63	0.1	63	0.1	63	0.1	63	0.1
EcoStop RP-200	84	0.2	167	0.3	167	0.3	167	0.3	345	0.5
Leander & Company	48,651	96.1	48,651	95.9	48,651	94.2	60,814	93.9	60,814	93.2
Total revenue (sales)	**50,636**	**100.0**	**50,720**	**100.0**	**51,652**	**100.0**	**64,752**	**100.0**	**65,224**	**100.0**
Cost of sales										
EcoCut 1000	564	74.1	564	74.1	1,128	72.7	1,128	72.7	1,128	72.7
EcoCut 1000 HD	627	74.1	627	74.1	627	74.1	1,254	74.1	1,254	74.1
EcoGrind 8000	104	74.1	104	74.1	208	74.0	208	74.0	416	72.2
EcoForm 2000	67	74.1	67	74.1	67	74.1	135	74.7	135	74.7
EcoCool 5000WS	47	74.5	47	74.5	47	74.5	47	74.5	47	74.5
EcoStop RP-200	62	74.1	124	74.1	124	74.1	124	74.1	248	71.9
Leander & Company	36,488	75.0	36,488	75.0	36,488	75.0	45,611	75.0	45,611	75.0
Total cost of sales	**37,959**	**75.0**	**38,021**	**75.0**	**38,689**	**74.9**	**48,507**	**74.9**	**48,839**	**74.9**
Gross profit	**12,677**	**25.0**	**12,699**	**25.0**	**12,963**	**25.1**	**16,245**	**25.1**	**16,386**	**25.1**
Expenses										
Labor expenses	4,167	8.2	4,167	8.2	4,167	8.1	4,167	6.4	4,167	6.4
Payroll expenses		0.0		0.0		0.0		0.0		0.0
Rent	1,674	3.3	1,674	3.3	1,674	3.2	1,674	2.6	1,674	2.6
Supplies (office and operating)	388	0.8	388	0.8	388	0.8	388	0.6	388	0.6
Repairs and maintenance		0.0		0.0		0.0		0.0		0.0
Advertising	492	1.0	492	1.0	492	1.0	492	0.8	492	0.8
Car, delivery and travel	707	1.4	707	1.4	707	1.4	707	1.1	707	1.1
Accounting and legal	223	0.4	223	0.4	223	0.4	223	0.3	223	0.3
Auto loan	272	0.5	272	0.5	272	0.5	272	0.4	272	0.4
Telephone	217	0.4	217	0.4	217	0.4	217	0.3	217	0.3
Cell phones	294	0.6	294	0.6	294	0.6	294	0.5	294	0.5
Lab expenses	229	0.5	229	0.5	229	0.4	229	0.4	229	0.4
Insurance	140	0.3	140	0.3	140	0.3	140	0.2	140	0.2
Interest		0.0		0.0		0.0		0.0		0.0
Depreciation		0.0		0.0		0.0		0.0		0.0
Mail (UPS, USPS, FedEX)	45	0.1	45	0.1	45	0.1	45	0.1	45	0.1
Product testing	600	1.2	600	1.2	600	1.2	800	1.2	800	1.2
Total expenses	**9,448**	**18.7**	**9,448**	**18.6**	**9,448**	**18.3**	**9,648**	**14.9**	**9,648**	**14.8**
Net profit	**3,229**	**6.4**	**3,251**	**6.4**	**3,514**	**6.8**	**6,597**	**10.2**	**6,738**	**10.3**

Profit and loss projection (12 months) cont.

Fiscal year begins   1/1/2012

	Jun-12	%	Jul-12	%	Aug-12	%	Sep-12	%	Oct-12	%
					IND. %					
Revenue (sales)										
EcoCut 1000	2,283	3.5	2,283	2.9	3,044	3.8	3,044	3.8	2,283	3.5
EcoCut 1000 HD	1,693	2.6	2,539	3.2	2,539	3.2	2,539	3.2	1,693	2.6
EcoGrind 8000	576	0.9	576	0.7	576	0.7	281	0.4	281	0.4
EcoForm 2000	181	0.3	362	0.5	362	0.5	362	0.5	181	0.3
EcoCool 5000WS	126	0.2	126	0.2	126	0.2	126	0.2	126	0.2
EcoStop RP-200	345	0.5	345	0.4	345	0.4	345	0.4	345	0.5
Leander & Company	60,814	92.1	71,977	92.0	72,977	91.3	72,977	91.6	60,814	92.5
Total revenue (sales)	**66,018**	**100.0**	**78,207**	**100.0**	**79,968**	**100.0**	**79,673**	**100.0**	**65,723**	**100.0**
Cost of sales										
EcoCut 1000	1,691	74.1	1,691	74.1	2,256	74.1	2,256	74.1	1,691	74.1
EcoCut 1000 HD	1,254	74.1	1,881	74.1	1,881	74.1	1,881	74.1	1,254	74.1
EcoGrind 8000	416	72.2	416	72.2	416	72.2	208	74.0	208	74.0
EcoForm 2000	135	74.7	270	74.7	270	74.7	270	74.7	135	74.6
EcoCool 5000WS	95	75.3	95	75.3	95	75.3	95	75.3	95	75.3
EcoStop RP-200	248	71.9	248	71.9	372	107.9	372	107.9	372	107.9
Leander & Company	45,611	75.0	53,983	75.0	53,983	74.0	54,733	75.0	45,611	75.0
Total cost of sales	**49,450**	**74.9**	**58,584**	**74.9**	**59,273**	**74.1**	**59,815**	**75.1**	**49,366**	**75.1**
Gross profit	**16,568**	**25.1**	**19,624**	**25.1**	**20,695**	**25.9**	**19,859**	**24.9**	**16,358**	**24.9**
Expenses										
Labor expenses	4,167	6.3	4,167	5.3	4,167	5.2	4,167	5.2	4,167	6.3
Payroll expenses		0.0		0.0		0.0		0.0		0.0
Rent	1,674	2.5	1,674	2.1	1,674	2.1	1,674	2.1	1,674	2.5
Supplies (office and operating)	388	0.6	388	0.5	388	0.5	388	0.5	388	0.6
Repairs and maintenance		0.0		0.0		0.0		0.0		0.0
Advertising	492	0.7	492	0.6	492	0.6	492	0.6	492	0.7
Car, delivery and travel	707	1.1	707	0.9	707	0.9	707	0.9	707	1.1
Accounting and legal	223	0.3	223	0.3	223	0.3	223	0.3	223	0.3
Auto loan	272	0.4	272	0.3	272	0.3	272	0.3	272	0.4
Telephone	217	0.3	217	0.3	217	0.3	217	0.3	217	0.3
Cell phones	294	0.4	294	0.4	294	0.4	294	0.4	294	0.4
Lab expenses	229	0.3	229	0.3	229	0.3	229	0.3	229	0.3
Insurance	140	0.2	140	0.2	140	0.2	140	0.2	140	0.2
Interest		0.0		0.0		0.0		0.0		0.0
Depreciation		0.0		0.0		0.0		0.0		0.0
Mail (UPS, USPS, FedEX)	45	0.1	45	0.1	45	0.1	45	0.1	45	0.1
Product testing	1,000	1.5	1,000	1.3	1,000	1.3	600	0.8	600	0.9
Total expenses	**9,848**	**14.9**	**9,848**	**12.6**	**9,848**	**12.3**	**9,448**	**11.9**	**9,448**	**14.4**
Net profit	**6,720**	**10.2**	**9,776**	**12.5**	**10,847**	**13.6**	**10,411**	**13.1**	**6,909**	**10.5**

BIOBASED METALWORKING FLUIDS COMPANY

Profit and loss projection (12 months) cont.

Fiscal year begins   1/1/2012

	Nov-12	%	Dec-12	%	Yearly	%
			IND. %			
Revenue (sales)						
EcoCut 1000	1,552	2.4	1,552	2.4	22,220	2.8
EcoCut 1000 HD	1,693	2.6	846	1.3	19,467	2.5
EcoGrind 8000	281	0.4	281	0.4	4,271	0.5
EcoForm 2000	181	0.3	181	0.3	2,441	0.3
EcoCool 5000WS	63	0.1	63	0.1	1,073	0.1
EcoStop RP-200	345	0.5	345	0.5	3,344	0.4
Leander & Company	60,814	93.7	60,814	94.9	728,767	
Total revenue (sales)	**64,929**	**100.0**	**64,082**	**100.0**	**781,584**	**6.8**
Cost of sales						
EcoCut 1000	1,691	109.0	1,128	72.7	16,916	76.1
EcoCut 1000 HD	1,254	74.1	627	74.1	14,421	74.1
EcoGrind 8000	208	74.0	208	74.0	3,120	73.1
EcoForm 2000	135	74.6	135	74.6	1,821	74.6
EcoCool 5000WS	47	74.5	47	74.5	804	75.0
EcoStop RP-200	248	71.9	248	71.9	2,790	83.4
Leander & Company	45,611	75.0	45,611	75.0	545,826	74.9
Total cost of sales	**49,194**	**75.8**	**48,004**	**74.9**	**585,697**	**74.9**
Gross profit	**15,735**	**24.2**	**16,078**	**25.1**	**195,887**	**25.1**
Expenses						
Labor expenses	4,167	6.4	4,167	6.5	50,004	6.4
Payroll expenses		0.0		0.0	0	0.0
Rent	1,674	2.6	1,674	2.6	20,084	2.6
Supplies (office and operating)	388	0.6	388	0.6	4,656	0.6
Repairs and maintenance		0.0		0.0	0	0.0
Advertising	492	0.8	492	0.8	5,905	0.8
Car, delivery and travel	707	1.1	707	1.1	8,484	1.1
Accounting and legal	223	0.3	223	0.3	2,681	0.3
Auto loan	272	0.4	272	0.4	3,259	0.4
Telephone	217	0.3	217	0.3	2,607	0.3
Cell phones	294	0.5	294	0.5	3,528	0.5
Lab expenses	229	0.4	229	0.4	2,750	0.4
Insurance	140	0.2	140	0.2	1,674	0.2
Interest		0.0		0.0	0	0.0
Depreciation		0.0		0.0	0	0.0
Mail (UPS, USPS, FedEX)	45	0.1	45	0.1	545	0.1
Product testing	600	0.9	600	0.9	8,800	1.1
Total expenses	**9,448**	**14.6**	**9,448**	**14.7**	**114,977**	**14.7**
Net profit	**6,287**	**9.7**	**6,630**	**10.3**	**80,910**	**10.4**

Profit and loss projection (2 years actual–3 projected)

	2009	%	2010	%	2011	%	2012	%	2013	%
Sales	$641,651	100.00%	$645,113	100.00%	$709,624	100.00%	$781,584	100.00%	$859,742	100.00%
Cost/Goods Sold (COGS)	491,159	76.55%	4,73,233	73.36%	532,218	75.00%	585,697	74.94%	644,807	75.00%
Gross profit	**$150,492**	**23.45%**	**$171,880**	**26.64%**	**$177,406**	**25.00%**	**$195,396**	**25.00%**	**$214,936**	**25.00%**
Operating expenses										
Salary (office & overhead)	$ 39,941	6.22%	$ 40,385	6.26%	$ 50,000	7.05%	$ 80,000	11.27%	$100,000	14.09%
Payroll (taxes etc.)	3,259	0.51%	—	0.00%	—	0.00%	—	0.00%	—	0.00%
Outside services	200	0.03%	—	0.00%	—	0.00%	—	0.00%	—	0.00%
Supplies (off and operation)	2,073	0.32%	4,221	0.65%	4,432	0.62%	4,654	0.66%	4,886	0.69%
Equipment	335	0.05%		0.00%	—	0.00%	—	0.00%	25,000	3.52%
Advertising	850	0.13%	580	0.09%	724	0.10%	905	0.13%	1,132	0.16%
Car, delivery and travel	3,155	0.49%	7,695	1.19%	8,080	1.14%	8,484	1.20%	8,908	1.26%
Accounting and legal	388	0.06%	2,260	0.35%	2,554	0.36%	2,681	0.38%	2,815	0.40%
Auto loan	2,886	0.45%	3,421	0.53%	3,259	0.46%	3,259	0.46%	824	0.12%
Telephone	3,759	0.59%	5,777	0.90%	2,531	0.36%	2,607	0.37%	2,685	0.38%
Cell phones	1,909	0.30%	3,806	0.59%	3,362	0.47%	3,530	0.50%	3,706	0.52%
Lab expenses	1,562	0.24%	446	0.07%	2,500	0.35%	2,750	0.39%	3,025	0.43%
Insurance	—	0.00%	1,578	0.24%	1,625	0.23%	1,674	0.24%	1,724	0.24%
Product testing	—	0.00%	—	0.00%	3,000	0.42%	8,800	1.24%	5,000	0.70%
Mail (UPS, FedEX, USPS)	419	0.07%	450	0.07%	495	0.07%	545	0.08%	599	0.08%
Misc. leander lube costs	4,837	0.75%	—	0.00%	—	0.00%	—	0.00%	—	0.00%
Total expenses	**$ 65,572**	**10.22%**	**$ 70,617**	**10.95%**	**$ 82,562**	**11.63%**	**$119,889**	**16.89%**	**$160,305**	**22.59%**
Net profit before tax	84,919		101,262		94,844		75,507		54,631	
Income taxes	9,021		15,379		12,614		10,042		7,266	
Net profit after tax	75,898		85,883		82,230		65,465		47,365	
Owner draw/dividends	32,158		35,841		40,000		41,200		42,436	
Adj. to retained earnings	**$ 43,740**		**$ 50,042**		**$ 42,230**		**$ 24,265**		**$4,929**	

Assumptions:
Revenues in 2011–2013 will grow by 10% annually.
Profit Margin for L&C and EcoLubes for 2011–2013 will be 25%, meaning COGS will be exactly 75% of revenues.
Office Suppliers Expense would grow by 5% each year.
Income Taxes would be consistent at 13.3% on EBIT.
Inflation rate is 3%.
Advertising Expenses would grow 25% each year.
Lab expenses and mail would grow 10% annually.
Travel/car, accounting, and cell phones would grow 5% annually $25,000 of new blending equipment in 2013.

BIOBASED METALWORKING FLUIDS COMPANY

Cash flow statement, 1 year

Starting date   Jan-12
Cash balance alert minimum   10,000

	Beginning	Jan-12	Feb-12	Mar-12	Apr-12	May-12	Jun-12
Cash on hand (beginning of month)	224,636	224,636	246,357	246,357	272,551	268,696	265,377
Cash receipts							
Cash sales		0	0	0	0	0	0
Returns and allowances		0	0	0	0	0	0
Collections on accounts receivable		65,472	63,924	50,563	50,644	51,512	64,577
Interest, other income		0	0	0	0	0	0
Owner contributions		0	0	0	0	0	0
Total cash receipts		65,472	63,924	50,563	50,664	51,512	64,577
Total cash available	224,636	290,108	310,281	317,031	323,195	320,208	329,954
Cash paid out							
Advertising		492	492	492	492	492	492
Rent		1,674	1,674	1,674	1,674	1,674	1,674
Contract labor		4,167	4,167	4,167	4,167	4,167	4,167
Insurance		140	140	140	140	140	140
Interest expense		0	0	0	0	0	0
Materials and supplies (in COGS)		37,959	38,021	38,689	48,507	48,839	49,450
Car, travel, and entertainment		707	707	707	707	707	707
Office expense		388	388	388	388	388	388
Lab expenses		229	229	229	229	229	229
Mail & shipping		45	45	45	45	45	45
Auto loan		272	272	272	272	272	272
Repairs and maintenance		0	0	0	0	0	0
Supplies (not in COGS)		0	0	0	0	0	0
Telephone		217	217	217	217	217	217
Cell phones		294	294	294	294	294	294
Product testing		600	600	600	800	800	1,000
Miscellaneous							
Subtotal		47,184	47,246	47,914	57,932	58,264	59,075
Loan principal payment							
Capital purchases							
Other startup costs							
To reserve and/or escrow							
Owners' withdrawal		3,433	3,433	3,433	3,433	3,433	3,433
Total cash paid out		43,751	43,813	44,481	54,499	54,831	55,642
Cash on hand (end of month)	224,636	246,357	266,468	272,551	268,696	265,377	274,313
Other operating data							
Sales volume (dollars)		50,563	50,644	51,512	64,577	65,010	65,803
Accounts receivable balance	129,396	114,487	101,207	102,156	116,089	129,587	130,813
Bad debt balance							
Inventory on hand	25,000	25,000	25,000	25,000	25,000	25,000	25,000
Accounts payable balance	8,431	8,431	8,431	8,431	8,431	8,431	8,431
Depreciation							

Cash flow statement, 1 year (cont.)

Starting date   Jan-12
Cash balance alert minimum   10,000

	Jul-12	Aug-12	Sep-12	Oct-12	Nov-12	Dec-12	Total
Cash on hand (beginning of month)	274,313	274,547	274,885	286,834	311,526	336,120	
Cash receipts							
Cash sales	0	0	0	0	0	0	0
Returns and allowances	0	0	0	0	0	0	0
Collections on accounts receivable	65,010	65,803	77,955	79,850	79,580	65,695	780,585
Interest, other income	0	0	0	0	0	0	0
Owner contributions	0	0	0	0	0	0	0
Total cash receipts	65,010	65,803	77,955	79,850	79,580	65,695	780,585
Total cash available	339,323	340,350	352,840	366,684	391,106	401,815	
Cash paid out							
Advertising	492	492	492	492	492	492	5,905
Rent	1,674	1,674	1,674	1,674	1,674	1,674	20,088
Contract labor	4,167	4,167	4,167	4,167	4,167	4,167	50,004
Insurance	140	140	140	140	140	140	1,675
Interest expense	0	0	0	0	0	0	0
Materials and supplies (in COGS)	58,584	59,273	59,815	49,366	49,194	48,004	585,701
Car, travel, and entertainment	707	707	707	707	707	707	8,484
Office expense	388	388	388	388	388	388	4,656
Lab expenses	229	229	229	229	229	229	2,750
Mail & shipping	45	45	45	45	45	45	545
Auto loan	272	272	272	272	272	272	3,259
Repairs and maintenance	0	0	0	0	0	0	0
Supplies (not in COGS)	0	0	0	0	0	0	0
Telephone	217	217	217	217	217	217	2,607
Cell phones	294	294	294	294	294	294	3,528
Product testing	1,000	1,000	1,000	600	600	600	9,200
Miscellaneous							0
Subtotal	68,209	68,898	69,440	58,591	58,419	57,229	698,401
Loan principal payment							0
Capital purchases							0
Other startup costs							0
To reserve and/or escrow							0
Owners' withdrawal	3,433	3,433	3,433	3,433	3,433	3,433	41,200
Total cash paid out	64,776	65,465	66,007	55,158	54,986	53,796	739,601
Cash on hand (end of month)	274,547	274,885	286,834	311,526	336,120	348,020	
Other operating data							
Sales volume (dollars)	77,955	79,850	79,580	65,695	65,472	63,924	
Accounts receivable balance	143,758	157,805	150,430	145,275	135,167	128,766	
Bad debt balance							
Inventory on hand	25,000	25,000	25,000	25,000	25,000	25,000	
Accounts payable balance	8,431	8,431	8,431	8,431	8,431	8,431	
Depreciation							

Cash flow projection

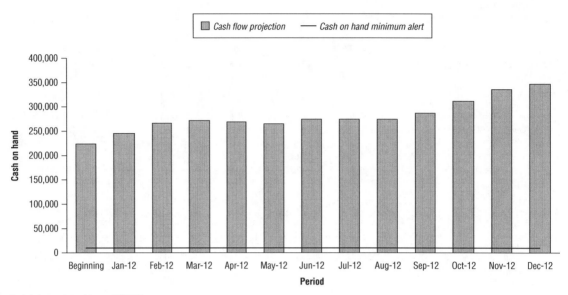

Cash balance alert minimum $10,000

Cash flow projection, 4 years

Starting date   Jan-10
Cash balance alert minimum   10,000

	Beginning	Q1 2010	Q2 2010	Q3 2010	Q4 2010	Q1 2011	Q2 2011	Q3 2011	Q4 2011
Cash on hand (beginning of month)		15,750	40,765	34,390	92,526	150,662	127,277	113,446	167,404
Cash receipts									
Cash sales		0	0	0	0	0	0	0	0
Returns and allowances									
Collections on accounts receivable		160,413	129,023	193,534	193,534	129,023	141,925	212,887	212,887
Interest, other income									
Owner contributions		0	0	0	0	0	0	0	0
Total cash receipts		160,413	129,023	193,534	193,534	129,023	141,925	212,887	212,887
Total cash available	0	176,163	169,788	227,924	286,060	279,685	269,202	326,333	380,292
Cash paid out									
Advertising		145	145	145	145	181	181	181	181
Rent		0	0	0	0	0	3,348	5,021	5,021
Contract labor		10,096	10,096	10,096	10,096	12,500	12,500	12,500	12,500
Insurance		395	395	395	395	406	406	406	406
Materials and supplies (in COGS)		118,308	118,308	118,308	118,308	133,055	133,055	133,055	133,055
Car, travel, and entertainment		1,924	1,924	1,924	1,924	2,020	2,020	2,020	2,020
Office expense		1,055	1,055	1,055	1,055	1,108	1,108	1,108	1,108
Lab expenses		112	112	112	112	625	625	625	625
Mail & shipping		113	113	113	113	124	124	124	124
Auto loan		855	855	855	855	816	816	816	816
Repairs and maintenance		0	0	0	0	0	0	0	0
Telephone		1,444	1,444	1,444	1,444	633	633	633	633
Cell phones		952	952	952	952	941	941	941	941
Product testing		n/a	n/a	n/a	n/a	n/a	n/a	1,500	1,500
Equipment									
Subtotal		135,398	135,398	135,398	135,398	152,408	155,756	158,929	158,929
Loan principal payment									
Capital purchases									
Other startup costs									
To reserve and/or escrow									
Owners' withdrawal									
Total cash paid out		135,398	135,398	135,398	135,398	152,408	155,756	158,929	158,929
Cash on hand (end of month)	0	40,765	34,390	92,526	150,662	127,277	113,446	167,404	221,363
Other operating data									
Sales volume (dollars)		129,023	193,534	193,534	129,023	141,925	212,887	212,887	141,925
Accounts receivable balance									
Bad debt balance									
Inventory on hand	25,000	25,000	25,000	25,000	25,000	25,000	25,000	25,000	25,000
Accounts payable balance									
Depreciation									

Cash Flow Projection, 4 yrs (cont.)

Starting date   Jan-10
Cash balance alert minimum   10,000

	Q1 2012	Q2 2012	Q3 2012	Q4 2012	Q1 2013	Q2 2013	Q3 2013	Q4 2013	Total
Cash on hand (beginning of month)	221,363	258,978	250,440	221,363	272,449	252,469	250,440	275,855	
Cash receipts									
Cash sales	0	0	0	0	0	0	0	0	0
Returns and allowances									0
Collections on accounts receivable	179,959	166,733	208,768	225,325	195,091	193,195	214,661	279,060	3,036,017
Interest, other income									0
Owner contributions	0	0	0	0	0	0	0	0	0
Total cash receipts	179,959	166,733	206,768	225,325	195,091	193,195	214,661	279,060	3,036,017
Total cash available	401,322	425,711	459,208	446,688	467,540	445,664	465,101	554,915	
Cash paid out									
Advertising	1,476	1,476	1,476	1,476	1,846	1,846	1,846	1,846	14,590
Rent	5,021	5,021	5,021	5,021	5,021	5,021	5,021	5,021	53,559
Contract labor	12,500	12,500	12,500	12,500	13,750	13,750	13,750	13,750	195,385
Insurance	420	420	420	420	431	431	431	431	6,607
Materials and supplies (in COGS)	114,669	146,796	177,672	146,564	160,996	160,996	160,996	160,996	2,235,135
Car, travel, and entertainment	2,121	2,121	2,121	2,121	2,227	2,227	2,227	2,227	33,167
Office expense	1,164	1,164	1,164	1,164	1,222	1,222	1,222	1,222	18,195
Lab expenses	687	687	687	687	756	756	756	756	8,718
Mail & shipping	136	136	136	136	150	150	150	150	2,089
Auto loan	816	816	816	816	824	0	0	0	10,773
Repairs and maintenance	0	0	0	0	0	0	0	0	0
Telephone	652	652	652	652	671	671	671	671	13,601
Cell phones	882	882	882	882	927	927	927	927	14,804
Product testing	1,800	2,600	3,000	1,800	1,250	1,250	1,250	1,250	17,200
Equipment					25,000				25,000
Subtotal	142,344	175,271	206,547	174,239	215,070	189,246	189,246	189,246	2,648,823
Loan principal payment									0
Capital purchases									0
Other startup costs									0
To reserve and/or escrow									0
Owners' withdrawal									0
Total cash paid out	142,344	175,271	206,547	174,239	215,070	189,246	189,246	189,246	2,648,823
Cash on hand (end of month)	258,978	250,440	252,661	272,449	252,469	256,418	275,855	365,668	
Other operating data									
Sales volume (dollars)	152,719	195,390	237,385	195,091	193,195	214,661	279,060	171,729	
Accounts receivable balance									
Bad debt balance									
Inventory on hand	25,000	25,000	25,000	25,000	25,000	25,000	25,000	25,000	
Accounts payable balance	25,293	25,293	25,293	25,293	25,293	25,293	25,293	25,293	
Depreciation									

Cash flow projection

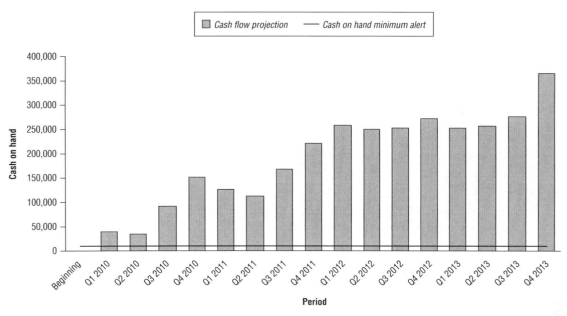

Cash balance alert minimum $10,000

Balance sheet (projected)

	Beginning as of 04/1/2011	Projected as of 1/1/2012	Projected as of 1/1/2013
Assets			
Current assets			
Cash in bank	$ 35,645	$224,636	$357,220
Accounts receivable	59,135	129,396	128,766
Inventory	25,000	25,000	25,000
Prepaid expenses	—	—	—
Other current assets	—	—	—
Total current assets	**$119,780**	**$379,032**	**$510,986**
Fixed assets			
Machinery & equipment	$ —	$ —	$ 25,000
Furniture & fixtures	—	—	—
Leasehold improvements	—	—	—
Land & buildings	—	—	—
Other fixed assets	—	—	—
(LESS accumulated depreciation on all fixed assets)	—	—	—
Total fixed assets (net of depreciation)	**$ —**	**$ —**	**$ 25,000**
Other assets			
Intangibles	$ —	$ —	$ —
Deposits	—	—	—
Goodwill	—	—	—
Other	—	—	—
Total other assets	**$ —**	**$ —**	**$ —**
Total assets	**$119,780**	**$379,032**	**$535,986**
Liabilities and equity			
Current liabilities			
Accounts payable	$ 15,492	$ 16,862	$ 17,565
Interest payable	—	—	—
Taxes payable	—	—	—
Notes, short-term (due within 12 months)	—	—	—
Current part, long-term debt	—	—	—
Other current liabilities	—	—	—
Total current liabilities	**$ 15,492**	**$ 16,862**	**$ 17,565**
Long-term debt			
Bank loans payable	$ —	$ —	$ —
Notes payable to stockholders	—	—	—
LESS: Short-term portion	—	—	—
Other long term debt	—	—	—
Total long-term debt	**$ —**	**$ —**	**$ —**
Total liabilities	**$ 15,492**	**$ 16,862**	**$ 17,565**
Owners' equity			
Invested capital	$ —	$ —	$ —
Retained earnings-beginning	50,042	104,288	387,170
Retained earnings-current	54,246	257,882	131,251
Total owners' equity	**$104,288**	**$362,170**	**$518,421**
Total liabilities & equity	**$119,780**	**$379,032**	**$535,986**

Broker

Marshall Financial Services

98989 E. Washington St.
New York, NY 10012

BizPlanDB.com

Marshall Financial Services is a New York-based corporation that will provide brokering of stocks and other financial instruments as well as financial advice within the Company's targeted market of New York. The Company was founded by Jeff Marshall.

1.0 EXECUTIVE SUMMARY

The purpose of this business plan is to raise $100,000 for the development of a broker dealer while showcasing the expected financials and operations over the next three years. Marshall Financial Services is a New York-based corporation that will provide brokering of stocks and other financial instruments as well as financial advice within the Company's targeted market of New York. The Company was founded by Jeff Marshall.

1.1 The Services

Marshall Financial Services' primary revenue center will come from the ongoing trades and orders placed for stocks, options, and other investment instruments on behalf of its client base. The business will earn approximately $7 to $9 per trade placed by a client.

The business will also earn ongoing revenues from advisory fees based on the size of accounts maintained by clients. On a per annum basis, the business will charge an amount equal to 1% of assets under management.

The third section of the business plan will further describe the services offered by the Private Placement Broker, Inc.

1.2 Financing

Mr. Marshall is seeking to raise $100,000 from a private investment. The business is seeking to sell a 45% interest in the business in exchange for the requisite capital sought in this business plan. The investor will also receive a seat on the board of directors and a regular stream of dividends. The financing will be used for the following:

- Development of the Company's location.

- Financing for the first six months of operation.

- Capital to purchase a company vehicle.

1.3 Mission Statement

The mission of Marshall Financial Services is to develop a business that provides outstanding execution for trades while concurrently providing insightful financial advice to its clients throughout the New York metropolitan area.

1.4 Management Team

The Company was founded by Jeff Marshall. Mr. Marshall has more than 10 years of experience in the stock brokering and investment advisory industry. Through his expertise, he will be able to bring the operations of the business to profitability within its first year of operations.

1.5 Sales Forecasts

Mr. Marshall expects a strong rate of growth at the start of operations. Below are the expected financials over the next three years.

Proforma profit and loss (yearly)

Year	1	2	3
Sales	$833,250	$899,910	$971,903
Operating costs	$504,842	$536,725	$570,151
EBITDA	$245,083	$273,194	$304,561
Taxes, interest, and depreciation	$ 97,239	$107,921	$119,840
Net profit	$147,844	$165,273	$184,721

Sales, operating costs, and profit forecast

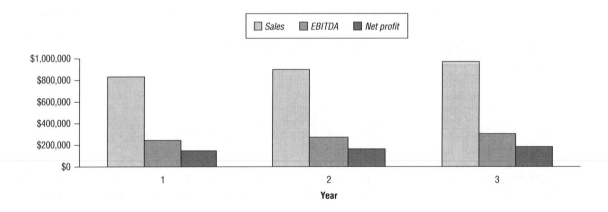

1.6 Expansion Plan

The Founder expects that the business will aggressively expand during the first three years of operation. Mr. Marshall intends to implement marketing campaigns that will effectively target individuals that are in need of specialized trading accounts, IRAs, and general investment advice in addition to providing broker dealer services.

2.0 COMPANY AND FINANCING SUMMARY

2.1 Registered Name and Corporate Structure

Marshall Financial Services is registered as a corporation in the State of New York.

2.2 Required Funds

At this time, Marshall Financial Services requires $100,000 of equity funds. Below is a breakdown of how these funds will be used:

Projected startup costs

Broker dealer licensing	$ 10,000
Working capital	$ 35,000
FF&E	$ 23,000
Leasehold improvements	$ 5,000
Security deposits	$ 5,000
Insurance	$ 2,500
Vehicle	$ 17,000
Marketing budget	$ 7,500
Miscellaneous and unforeseen costs	$ 5,000
Total startup costs	**$110,000**

Use of funds

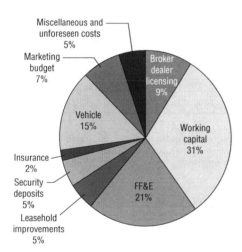

2.3 Investor Equity

Mr. Marshall is seeking to sell a 45% equity interest in the business in exchange for the capital required in order to launch the operations of Marshall Financial Services.

2.4 Management Equity

Jeff Marshall owns 100% of Marshall Financial Services. This capital structure will change once the requisite capital has been raised.

2.5 Exit Strategy

If the business is very successful, Mr. Marshall may seek to sell the business to a third party for a significant earnings multiple. Most likely, the Company will hire a qualified investment bank to sell the business on behalf of Marshall Financial Services. Based on historical numbers, the business could fetch a sales premium of up to 4 times earnings.

3.0 PRODUCTS AND SERVICES

Below is a description of the investment and stock brokering services offered by Marshall Financial Services.

3.1 Stock Brokering Services

As discussed in the executive summary, the primary revenue center for the business will come from the ongoing placing of orders for stocks and options purchases on behalf of clients that hold accounts with Marshall Financial Services. On each trade, the business will generate approximately $7 to $9 of revenue. However, these fees may be higher if the trade is specific for options or a large order of securities.

Mr. Marshall is currently acquiring all of the appropriate licensure so that the business can act in a multifaceted capacity when it comes to placing stock trades, mutual fund purchases, and options trades on behalf of its clients.

3.2 Investment Advisory Services

Marshall Financial Services' secondary revenue center will come from the ongoing advisory services provided to clients that are seeking to effectively have a well balanced portfolio that mitigates risk and provides above market average returns for its investors. The business will charge a yearly fee equal to 1% of the total assets under management for each client enrolled in the Company's investment advisory and broker dealer programs.

4.0 STRATEGIC AND MARKET ANALYSIS

4.1 Economic Outlook

This section of the analysis will detail the economic climate, the broker industry, the customer profile, and the competition that the business will face as it progresses through its business operations.

At this time, the economy is coming out of its recession. The job market has improved, and businesses are beginning to make investments into expansion. As such, the demand among companies that are seeking capital to expand is immense. Marshall Financial Services will be able to remain profitable and cash flow positive at all times given the highly recurring streams of revenue generated from the Company's investment advisory services.

4.2 Industry Analysis

Within the United States, there are approximately 30,000 businesses that are registered as broker dealer with the Securities and Exchange Commission. The industry employs approximately 350,000 people. In each of the last five years, annual revenues among broker dealers have exceeded $107 billion while annual payrolls have reached an all time high of $50 billion.

This is a mature industry, and the expected future growth rate is expected to remain in line with the United States economy in general. However, there are a number of pieces of legislation, SEC rulings, and FINRA requirements that the Company will need to remain aware of as time progresses. As such, one of the most common trends within the industry is to hire an in-house or outsourced compliance officer or compliance company to ensure that these businesses remain within the letter of the law at all times.

4.3 Customer Profile

Marshall Financial Services' average client will be a company that is seeking to invest in stocks, bonds, or other financial instruments. Below is an overview of the demographics anticipated by the Company:

• Is based in the New York metropolitan area.

• Has $100,000 to $1,000,000 if investment capital.

• Will spend $1,000 to $10,000 on services from Marshall Financial Services on a yearly basis including fees related to asset management.

Based on statistics relating to the New York metropolitan area, there are approximately one million individuals that fall into the Company's demographic profile. Management intends to develop a large scale marketing campaign that will showcase the brokering and asset management services offered by Marshall Financial Services.

4.4 Competition

As discussed above, there are 30,000 businesses within the United States that act in a broker-dealer capacity. As such, it is extremely important that the business retain a competitive advantage by providing regular traders with substantial discounts as it relates to their trading. Additionally, as it relates to financial advice, Management must hire qualified and seasoned professionals that can provide guidance for clients so that their asset portfolios remain stable in any economic climate.

5.0 MARKETING PLAN

Marshall Financial Services intends to maintain an extensive marketing campaign that will ensure maximum visibility for the business in its targeted market. Below is an overview of the marketing strategies and objectives of Marshall Financial Services.

5.1 Marketing Objectives

• Establish relationships with area investment banks, other stock brokerages, and private investors.

• Develop a broad range website that showcases the licensure and stock brokering, options brokering, and mutual fund sales available through Marshall Financial Services.

• Maintain a strong database of registered representatives that can assist the business with exponential growth over the next three years of operation.

5.2 Marketing Strategies

Mr. Marshall intends on using a number of strategies that will aggressively showcase broker services and investment advisory services available through Marshall Financial Services. These advertisements will focus on the local New York metropolitan market. The marketing messages to be used by the business will focus on the experience of the Company's principals and Founders while concurrently showcasing the low cost associated with using Marshall Financial Services for investment purposes.

The business will also develop a highly informative website that shows the operations of the business, its past track record, and how an individual or business can become a client of Marshall Financial Services. This website will also feature specialized login features so that individuals can see their account balances on a real time basis. This website will also allow individuals to place trades with Marshall Financial Services in an online basis.

Finally, the Company intends to develop a broad network of Series 7 and Series 65 licensed stock brokers and investment advisors that can actively market their services and that of the Broker-Dealer. As these individuals operate as independent contracts, they will spend a significant amount of their time acquiring new clients for the firm. Management will need to approve all marketing materials produced by these third party agents.

5.3 Pricing

As discussed earlier, Management anticipates that each trade will generate $7 to $9 for the business. In regards to asset management services, the business will receive a fee equal to 1% of the aggregate assets managed by the business on behalf of a client.

6.0 ORGANIZATIONAL PLAN AND PERSONNEL SUMMARY

6.1 Corporate Organization

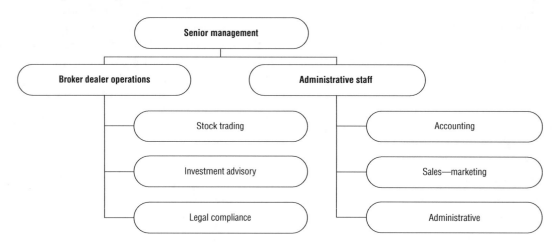

6.2 Organizational Budget

Personnel plan—yearly

Year	1	2	3
Senior management	$ 80,000	$ 82,400	$ 84,872
Principals	$105,000	$108,150	$111,395
Analysts	$130,000	$133,900	$137,917
Accountant	$ 37,500	$ 51,500	$ 66,306
Administrative	$ 22,000	$ 22,660	$ 23,340
Total	**$374,500**	**$398,610**	**$423,830**

Numbers of personnel

Senior management	2	2	2
Principals	3	3	3
Analysts	4	4	4
Accountant	3	4	5
Administrative	1	1	1
Totals	**13**	**14**	**15**

Personnel expense breakdown

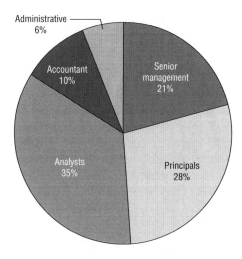

7.0 FINANCIAL PLAN

7.1 Underlying Assumptions

The Company has based its proforma financial statements on the following:

- Marshall Financial Services will have an annual revenue growth rate of 15% per year.

- Management will acquire $100,000 of investor funds to launch the operations of Marshall Financial Services.

- Management will settle most short term payables on a monthly basis.

7.2 Sensitivity Analysis

In the event of an economic downturn, the business may have a decline in its revenues. However, the business will generate highly recurring streams of revenue from the ongoing sales of securities coupled with investment advisory services on an ongoing basis. This will ensure that Marshall Financial Services remains profitable and cash flow positive at all times.

7.3 Source of Funds

Financing

Equity contributions	
Investor(s)	$100,000.00
Management	$ 10,000.00
Total equity financing	**$110,000.00**
Banks and lenders	
Total debt financing	**$ 0.00**
Total financing	**$110,000.00**

7.4 General Assumptions

General assumptions

Year	1	2	3
Short term interest rate	9.5%	9.5%	9.5%
Long term interest rate	10.0%	10.0%	10.0%
Federal tax rate	33.0%	33.0%	33.0%
State tax rate	5.0%	5.0%	5.0%
Personnel taxes	15.0%	15.0%	15.0%

7.5 Profit and Loss Statements

Proforma profit and loss (yearly)

Year	1	2	3
Sales	**$833,250**	**$899,910**	**$971,903**
Cost of goods sold	$ 83,325	$ 89,991	$ 97,190
Gross margin	90.00%	90.00%	90.00%
Operating income	**$749,925**	**$809,919**	**$874,713**
Expenses			
Payroll	$374,500	$398,610	$423,830
General and administrative	$ 25,200	$ 26,208	$ 27,256
Marketing expenses	$ 4,166	$ 4,500	$ 4,860
Professional fees and licensure	$ 5,219	$ 5,376	$ 5,537
Insurance costs	$ 1,987	$ 2,086	$ 2,191
Travel and vehicle costs	$ 7,596	$ 8,356	$ 9,191
Rent and utilities	$ 20,000	$ 21,000	$ 22,050
Miscellaneous costs	$ 9,999	$ 10,799	$ 11,663
Payroll taxes	$ 56,175	$ 59,792	$ 63,574
Total operating costs	**$504,842**	**$536,725**	**$570,151**
EBITDA	**$245,083**	**$273,194**	**$304,561**
Federal income tax	$ 80,877	$ 90,154	$100,505
State income tax	$ 12,254	$ 13,660	$ 15,228
Interest expense	$ 0	$ 0	$ 0
Depreciation expenses	$ 4,107	$ 4,107	$ 4,107
Net profit	**$147,844**	**$165,273**	**$184,721**
Profit margin	**17.74%**	**18.37%**	**19.01%**

Sales, operating costs, and profit forecast

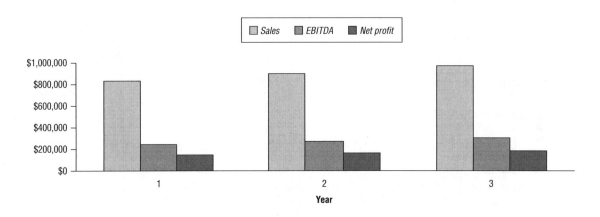

7.6 Cash Flow Analysis

Proforma cash flow analysis—yearly

Year	1	2	3
Cash from operations	$151,951	$169,380	$188,828
Cash from receivables	$ 0	$ 0	$ 0
Operating cash inflow	**$151,951**	**$169,380**	**$188,828**
Other cash inflows			
Equity investment	$110,000	$ 0	$ 0
Increased borrowings	$ 0	$ 0	$ 0
Sales of business assets	$ 0	$ 0	$ 0
A/P increases	$ 37,902	$ 43,587	$ 50,125
Total other cash inflows	**$147,902**	**$ 43,587**	**$ 50,125**
Total cash inflow	**$299,853**	**$212,967**	**$238,953**
Cash outflows			
Repayment of principal	$ 0	$ 0	$ 0
A/P decreases	$ 24,897	$ 29,876	$ 35,852
A/R increases	$ 0	$ 0	$ 0
Asset purchases	$ 57,500	$ 25,407	$ 28,324
Dividends	$121,561	$135,504	$151,062
Total cash outflows	**$203,958**	**$190,787**	**$215,238**
Net cash flow	**$ 95,895**	**$ 22,180**	**$ 23,715**
Cash balance	**$ 95,895**	**$118,075**	**$141,790**

Proforma cash flow (yearly)

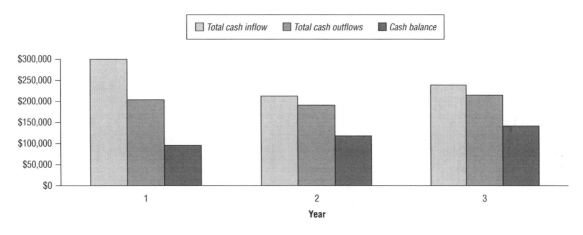

7.7 Balance Sheet

Proforma balance sheet—yearly

Year	1	2	3
Assets			
Cash	$ 95,895	$118,075	$141,790
Amortized development/expansion costs	$ 17,500	$ 39,096	$ 63,172
Company vehicle	$ 17,000	$ 17,000	$ 17,000
FF&E	$ 23,000	$ 26,811	$ 31,060
Accumulated depreciation	($ 4,107)	($ 8,214)	($ 12,321)
Total assets	**$149,288**	**$192,768**	**$240,700**
Liabilities and equity			
Accounts payable	$ 13,005	$ 26,716	$ 40,990
Long term liabilities	$ 0	$ 0	$ 0
Other liabilities	$ 0	$ 0	$ 0
Total liabilities	**$ 13,005**	**$ 26,716**	**$ 40,990**
Net worth	**$136,283**	**$166,052**	**$199,710**
Total liabilities and equity	**$149,288**	**$192,768**	**$240,700**

Proforma balance sheet

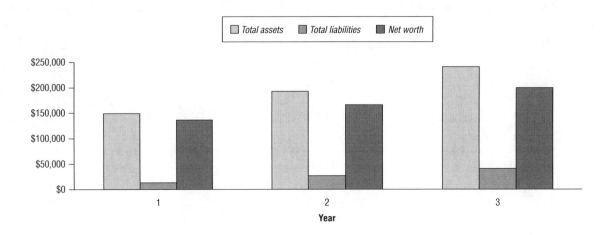

7.8 Breakeven Analysis

Monthly break even analysis

Year	1	2	3
Monthly revenue	$ 46,745	$ 49,697	$ 52,792
Yearly revenue	$560,936	$596,362	$633,501

Break even analysis

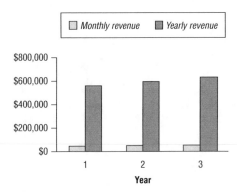

7.9 Business Ratios

Business ratios—yearly

Year	1	2	3
Sales			
Sales growth	0.00%	8.00%	8.00%
Gross margin	90.00%	90.00%	90.00%
Financials			
Profit margin	17.74%	18.37%	19.01%
Assets to liabilities	11.48	7.22	5.87
Equity to liabilities	10.48	6.22	4.87
Assets to equity	1.10	1.16	1.21
Liquidity			
Acid test	7.37	4.42	3.46
Cash to assets	0.64	0.61	0.59

7.10 Three Year Profit and Loss Statement

Profit and loss statement (first year)

Months	1	2	3	4	5	6	7
Sales	$68,750	$68,875	$69,000	$69,125	$69,250	$69,375	$69,500
Cost of goods sold	$ 6,875	$ 6,888	$ 6,900	$ 6,913	$ 6,925	$ 6,938	$ 6,950
Gross margin	90.00%	90.00%	90.00%	90.00%	90.00%	90.00%	90.00%
Operating income	$61,875	$61,988	$62,100	$62,213	$62,325	$62,438	$62,550
Expenses							
Payroll	$ 31,208	$ 31,208	$ 31,208	$ 31,208	$ 31,208	$ 31,208	$ 31,208
General and administrative	$ 2,100	$ 2,100	$ 2,100	$ 2,100	$ 2,100	$ 2,100	$ 2,100
Marketing expenses	$ 347	$ 347	$ 347	$ 347	$ 347	$ 347	$ 347
Professional fees and licensure	$ 435	$ 435	$ 435	$ 435	$ 435	$ 435	$ 435
Insurance costs	$ 166	$ 166	$ 166	$ 166	$ 166	$ 166	$ 166
Travel and vehicle costs	$ 633	$ 633	$ 633	$ 633	$ 633	$ 633	$ 633
Rent and utilities	$ 1,667	$ 1,667	$ 1,667	$ 1,667	$ 1,667	$ 1,667	$ 1,667
Miscellaneous costs	$ 833	$ 833	$ 833	$ 833	$ 833	$ 833	$ 833
Payroll taxes	$ 4,681	$ 4,681	$ 4,681	$ 4,681	$ 4,681	$ 4,681	$ 4,681
Total operating costs	$42,070	$42,070	$42,070	$42,070	$42,070	$42,070	$42,070
EBITDA	$19,805	$19,917	$20,030	$20,142	$20,255	$20,367	$20,480
Federal income tax	$ 6,673	$ 6,685	$ 6,697	$ 6,709	$ 6,772	$ 6,734	$ 6,746
State income tax	$ 1,011	$ 1,013	$ 1,015	$ 1,017	$ 1,018	$ 1,020	$ 1,022
Interest expense	$ 0	$ 0	$ 0	$ 0	$ 0	$ 0	$ 0
Depreciation expense	$ 342	$ 342	$ 342	$ 342	$ 342	$ 342	$ 342
Net profit	$11,778	$11,877	$11,975	$12,074	$12,173	$12,271	$12,370

Profit and loss statement (first year cont.)

Month	8	9	10	11	12	1
Sales	$69,625	$69,750	$69,875	$70,000	$70,125	$833,250
Cost of goods sold	$ 6,963	$ 6,975	$ 6,988	$ 7,000	$ 7,013	$ 83,325
Gross margin	90.00%	90.00%	90.00%	90.00%	90.00%	90.00%
Operating income	$62,663	$62,775	$62,888	$63,000	$63,113	$749,925
Expenses						
Payroll	$ 31,208	$ 31,208	$ 31,208	$ 31,208	$ 31,208	$374,500
General and administrative	$ 2,100	$ 2,100	$ 2,100	$ 2,100	$ 2,100	$ 25,200
Marketing expenses	$ 347	$ 347	$ 347	$ 347	$ 347	$ 4,166
Professional fees and licensure	$ 435	$ 435	$ 435	$ 435	$ 435	$ 5,219
Insurance costs	$ 166	$ 166	$ 166	$ 166	$ 166	$ 1,987
Travel and vehicle costs	$ 633	$ 633	$ 633	$ 633	$ 633	$ 7,596
Rent and utilities	$ 1,667	$ 1,667	$ 1,667	$ 1,667	$ 1,667	$ 20,000
Miscellaneous costs	$ 833	$ 833	$ 833	$ 833	$ 833	$ 9,999
Payroll taxes	$ 4,681	$ 4,681	$ 4,681	$ 4,681	$ 4,681	$ 56,175
Total operating costs	$42,070	$42,070	$42,070	$42,070	$42,070	$504,842
EBITDA	$20,592	$20,705	$20,817	$20,930	$21,042	$245,083
Federal income tax	$ 6,758	$ 6,770	$ 6,782	$ 6,794	$ 6,807	$ 80,877
State income tax	$ 1,024	$ 1,026	$ 1,028	$ 1,029	$ 1,031	$ 12,254
Interest expense	$ 0	$ 0	$ 0	$ 0	$ 0	$ 0
Depreciation expense	$ 342	$ 342	$ 342	$ 342	$ 342	$ 4,107
Net profit	$12,468	$12,567	$12,665	$12,764	$12,862	$147,844

Profit and loss statement (second year)

Quarter	Q1	2 Q2	Q3	Q4	2
Sales	$179,982	$224,978	$242,976	$251,975	$899,910
Cost of goods sold	$ 17,998	$ 22,498	$ 24,298	$ 25,197	$ 89,991
Gross margin	90.00%	90.00%	90.00%	90.00%	90.00%
Operating income	$161,984	$202,480	$218,678	$226,777	$809,919
Expenses					
Payroll	$ 79,722	$ 99,653	$107,625	$111,611	$398,610
General and administrative	$ 5,242	$ 6,552	$ 7,076	$ 7,338	$ 26,208
Marketing expenses	$ 900	$ 1,125	$ 1,215	$ 1,260	$ 4,500
Professional fees and licensure	$ 1,075	$ 1,344	$ 1,451	$ 1,505	$ 5,376
Insurance costs	$ 417	$ 522	$ 563	$ 584	$ 2,086
Travel and vehicle costs	$ 1,671	$ 2,089	$ 2,256	$ 2,340	$ 8,356
Rent and utilities	$ 4,200	$ 5,250	$ 5,670	$ 5,880	$ 21,000
Miscellaneous costs	$ 2,160	$ 2,700	$ 2,916	$ 3,024	$ 10,799
Payroll taxes	$ 11,958	$ 14,948	$ 16,144	$ 16,742	$ 59,792
Total operating costs	$107,345	$134,181	$144,916	$150,283	$536,725
EBITDA	$ 54,639	$ 68,298	$ 73,762	$ 76,494	$273,194
Federal income tax	$ 18,031	$ 22,538	$ 24,342	$ 25,243	$ 90,154
State income tax	$ 2,732	$ 3,415	$ 3,688	$ 3,825	$ 13,660
Interest expense	$ 0	$ 0	$ 0	$ 0	$ 0
Depreciation expense	$ 1,027	$ 1,027	$ 1,027	$ 1,027	$ 4,107
Net profit	$ 32,849	$ 41,318	$ 44,706	$ 46,400	$165,273

Profit and loss statement (third year)

Quarter	Q1	3 Q2	Q3	Q4	3
Sales	$194,381	$242,976	$262,414	$272,133	$971,903
Cost of goods sold	$ 19,438	$ 24,298	$ 26,241	$ 27,213	$ 97,190
Gross margin	90.00%	90.00%	90.00%	90.00%	90.00%
Operating income	$174,943	$218,678	$236,172	$244,920	$874,713
Expenses					
Payroll	$ 84,766	$105,957	$114,434	$118,672	$423,830
General and administrative	$ 5,451	$ 6,814	$ 7,359	$ 7,632	$ 27,256
Marketing expenses	$ 972	$ 1,215	$ 1,312	$ 1,361	$ 4,860
Professional fees and licensure	$ 1,107	$ 1,384	$ 1,495	$ 1,550	$ 5,537
Insurance costs	$ 438	$ 548	$ 591	$ 613	$ 2,191
Travel and vehicle costs	$ 1,838	$ 2,298	$ 2,482	$ 2,574	$ 9,191
Rent and utilities	$ 4,410	$ 5,513	$ 5,954	$ 6,174	$ 22,050
Miscellaneous costs	$ 2,333	$ 2,916	$ 3,149	$ 3,266	$ 11,663
Payroll taxes	$ 12,715	$ 15,894	$ 17,165	$ 17,801	$ 63,574
Total operating costs	$114,030	$142,538	$153,941	$159,642	$570,151
EBITDA	$ 60,912	$ 76,140	$ 82,232	$ 85,277	$304,561
Federal income tax	$ 20,101	$ 25,126	$ 27,136	$ 28,141	$100,505
State income tax	$ 3,046	$ 3,807	$ 4,112	$ 4,264	$ 15,228
Interest expense	$ 0	$ 0	$ 0	$ 0	$ 0
Depreciation expense	$ 1,027	$ 1,027	$ 1,027	$ 1,027	$ 4,107
Net profit	$ 36,739	$ 46,180	$ 49,957	$ 51,845	$184,721

7.11 Three Year Cash Flow Analysis

Cash flow analysis (first year)

Month	1	2	3	4	5	6	7
Cash from operations	$ 12,121	$12,219	$12,318	$ 12,416	$ 12,515	$ 12,613	$ 12,712
Cash from receivables	$ 0	$ 0	$ 0	$ 0	$ 0	$ 0	$ 0
Operating cash inflow	**$ 12,121**	**$12,219**	**$12,318**	**$ 12,416**	**$ 12,515**	**$ 12,613**	**$ 12,712**
Other cash inflows							
Equity investment	$110,000	$ 0	$ 0	$ 0	$ 0	$ 0	$ 0
Increased borrowings	$ 0	$ 0	$ 0	$ 0	$ 0	$ 0	$ 0
Sales of business assets	$ 0	$ 0	$ 0	$ 0	$ 0	$ 0	$ 0
A/P increases	$ 3,159	$ 3,159	$ 3,159	$ 3,159	$ 3,159	$ 3,159	$ 3,159
Total other cash inflows	**$113,159**	**$ 3,159**	**$ 3,159**	**$ 3,159**	**$ 3,159**	**$ 3,159**	**$ 3,159**
Total cash inflow	**$125,279**	**$15,378**	**$15,476**	**$ 15,575**	**$ 15,673**	**$ 15,772**	**$ 15,870**
Cash outflows							
Repayment of principal	$ 0	$ 0	$ 0	$ 0	$ 0	$ 0	$ 0
A/P decreases	$ 2,075	$ 2,075	$ 2,075	$ 2,075	$ 2,075	$ 2,075	$ 2,075
A/R increases	$ 0	$ 0	$ 0	$ 0	$ 0	$ 0	$ 0
Asset purchases	$ 57,500	$ 0	$ 0	$ 0	$ 0	$ 0	$ 0
Dividends	$ 0	$ 0	$ 0	$ 0	$ 0	$ 0	$ 0
Total cash outflows	**$ 59,575**	**$ 2,075**	**$ 2,075**	**$ 2,075**	**$ 2,075**	**$ 2,075**	**$ 2,075**
Net cash flow	**$ 65,704**	**$13,303**	**$13,402**	**$ 13,500**	**$ 13,599**	**$ 13,697**	**$ 13,796**
Cash balance	**$ 65,704**	**$79,007**	**$92,409**	**$105,909**	**$119,508**	**$133,205**	**$147,000**

Cash flow analysis (first year cont.)

Month	8	9	10	11	12	1
Cash from operations	$ 12,810	$ 12,909	$ 13,007	$ 13,106	$ 13,205	$151,951
Cash from receivables	$ 0	$ 0	$ 0	$ 0	$ 0	$ 0
Operating cash inflow	**$ 12,810**	**$ 12,909**	**$ 13,007**	**$ 13,106**	**$ 13,205**	**$151,951**
Other cash inflows						
Equity investment	$ 0	$ 0	$ 0	$ 0	$ 0	$110,000
Increased borrowings	$ 0	$ 0	$ 0	$ 0	$ 0	$ 0
Sales of business assets	$ 0	$ 0	$ 0	$ 0	$ 0	$ 0
A/P increases	$ 3,159	$ 3,159	$ 3,159	$ 3,159	$ 3,159	$ 37,902
Total other cash inflows	**$ 3,159**	**$ 3,159**	**$ 3,159**	**$ 3,159**	**$ 3,159**	**$147,902**
Total cash inflow	**$ 15,969**	**$ 16,067**	**$ 16,166**	**$ 16,264**	**$ 16,363**	**$299,853**
Cash outflows						
Repayment of principal	$ 0	$ 0	$ 0	$ 0	$ 0	$ 0
A/P decreases	$ 2,075	$ 2,075	$ 2,075	$ 2,075	$ 2,075	$ 24,897
A/R increases	$ 0	$ 0	$ 0	$ 0	$ 0	$ 0
Asset purchases	$ 0	$ 0	$ 0	$ 0	$ 0	$ 57,500
Dividends	$ 0	$ 0	$ 0	$ 0	$121,561	$121,561
Total cash outflows	**$ 2,075**	**$ 2,075**	**$ 2,075**	**$ 2,075**	**$123,636**	**$203,958**
Net cash flow	**$ 13,894**	**$ 13,993**	**$ 14,091**	**$ 14,190**	**−$107,273**	**$ 95,895**
Cash balance	**$160,894**	**$174,887**	**$188,978**	**$203,168**	**$ 95,895**	**$ 95,895**

Cash flow analysis (second year)

Quarter	Q1	2 Q2	Q3	Q4	2
Cash from operations	$ 33,876	$ 42,345	$ 45,733	$ 47,426	$169,380
Cash from receivables	$ 0	$ 0	$ 0	$ 0	$ 0
Operating cash inflow	**$ 33,876**	**$ 42,345**	**$ 45,733**	**$ 47,426**	**$169,380**
Other cash inflows					
Equity investment	$ 0	$ 0	$ 0	$ 0	$ 0
Increased borrowings	$ 0	$ 0	$ 0	$ 0	$ 0
Sales of business assets	$ 0	$ 0	$ 0	$ 0	$ 0
A/P increases	$ 8,717	$ 10,897	$ 11,769	$ 12,204	$ 43,587
Total other cash inflows	**$ 8,717**	**$ 10,897**	**$ 11,769**	**$ 12,204**	**$ 43,587**
Total cash inflow	**$ 42,593**	**$ 53,242**	**$ 57,501**	**$ 59,631**	**$212,967**
Cash outflows					
Repayment of principal	$ 0	$ 0	$ 0	$ 0	$ 0
A/P decreases	$ 5,975	$ 7,469	$ 8,067	$ 8,365	$ 29,876
A/R increases	$ 0	$ 0	$ 0	$ 0	$ 0
Asset purchases	$ 5,081	$ 6,352	$ 6,860	$ 7,114	$ 25,407
Dividends	$ 27,101	$ 33,876	$ 36,586	$ 37,941	$135,504
Total cash outflows	**$ 38,157**	**$ 47,697**	**$ 51,513**	**$ 53,420**	**$190,787**
Net cash flow	**$ 4,436**	**$ 5,545**	**$ 5,989**	**$ 6,210**	**$ 22,180**
Cash balance	**$100,331**	**$105,876**	**$111,865**	**$118,075**	**$118,075**

Cash flow analysis (third year)

Quarter	Q1	3 Q2	Q3	Q4	3
Cash from operations	$ 37,766	$ 47,207	$ 50,984	$ 52,872	$188,828
Cash from receivables	$ 0	$ 0	$ 0	$ 0	$ 0
Operating cash inflow	**$ 37,766**	**$ 47,207**	**$ 50,984**	**$ 52,872**	**$188,828**
Other cash inflows					
Equity investment	$ 0	$ 0	$ 0	$ 0	$ 0
Increased borrowings	$ 0	$ 0	$ 0	$ 0	$ 0
Sales of business assets	$ 0	$ 0	$ 0	$ 0	$ 0
A/P increases	$ 10,025	$ 12,531	$ 13,534	$ 14,035	$ 50,125
Total other cash inflows	**$ 10,025**	**$ 12,531**	**$ 13,534**	**$ 14,035**	**$ 50,125**
Total cash inflow	**$ 47,791**	**$ 59,738**	**$ 64,517**	**$ 66,907**	**$238,953**
Cash outflows					
Repayment of principal	$ 0	$ 0	$ 0	$ 0	$ 0
A/P decreases	$ 7,170	$ 8,963	$ 9,680	$ 10,038	$ 35,852
A/R increases	$ 0	$ 0	$ 0	$ 0	$ 0
Asset purchases	$ 5,665	$ 7,081	$ 7,648	$ 7,931	$ 28,324
Dividends	$ 30,212	$ 37,766	$ 40,787	$ 42,297	$151,062
Total cash outflows	**$ 43,048**	**$ 53,810**	**$ 58,114**	**$ 60,267**	**$215,238**
Net cash flow	**$ 4,743**	**$ 5,929**	**$ 6,403**	**$ 6,640**	**$ 23,715**
Cash balance	**$122,818**	**$128,747**	**$135,150**	**$141,790**	**$141,790**

Business Consultant

Cartwright Business Consultants, LLC

78989 W. 59th St.
New York, New York 10012

BizPlanDB.com

Cartwright Business Consultants, LLC is a New York-based corporation that will provide business and general consulting to small and medium-sized businesses in its targeted market. The Company was founded in 2009 by Kent Cartwright.

1.0 EXECUTIVE SUMMARY

The purpose of this business plan is to raise $50,000 for the development of a general business consulting firm while showcasing the expected financials and operations over the next three years. Cartwright Business Consultants, LLC is a New York-based corporation that will provide business and general consulting to small and medium-sized businesses in its targeted market. The Company was founded in 2009 by Kent Cartwright.

1.1 The Services

The Company will specialize in providing multifaceted advice related to the operation of small- and medium-sized businesses. At the onset of operations, Mr. Cartwright intends to hire four consultants of varying educational and experience backgrounds so that Cartwright Business Consultants can market its services to a broad spectrum of clients within the target market.

The business will generate revenues from per hour fees and as well as per project fees rendered to clients.

The third section of the business plan will further describe the services offered by Cartwright Business Consultants.

1.2 Financing

Mr. Cartwright is seeking to raise $50,000 from a bank loan. The interest rate and loan agreement are to be further discussed during negotiation. This business plan assumes that the business will receive a 10-year loan with a 9% fixed interest rate. The financing will be used for the following:

- Development of the Company's office location.
- Financing for the first six months of operation.
- Capital to purchase computer and technology equipment.

Mr. Cartwright will contribute $10,000 to the venture.

1.3 Mission Statement

Cartwright Business Consultants' mission is to become the recognized leader in its targeted market for small- and medium-sized business consulting services.

1.4 Management Team

The Company was founded by Kent Cartwright. Mr. Cartwright has more than 10 years of experience in the consulting industry. Through his expertise, he will be able to bring the operations of the business to profitability within its first year of operations.

1.5 Sales Forecasts

Mr. Cartwright expects a strong rate of growth at the start of operations. Below are the expected financials over the next three years.

Proforma profit and loss (yearly)

Year	1	2	3
Sales	$549,000	$658,800	$770,796
Operating costs	$496,639	$548,981	$573,655
EBITDA	$ 24,911	$ 76,879	$158,601
Taxes, interest, and depreciation	$ 16,692	$ 34,592	$ 65,441
Net profit	$ 8,219	$ 42,287	$ 93,160

Sales, operating costs, and profit forecast

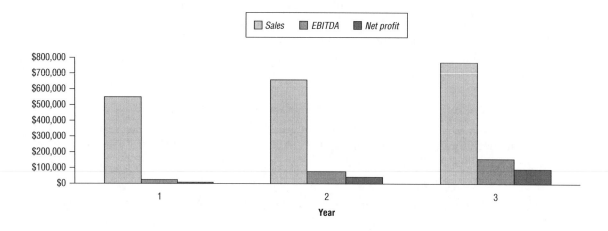

1.6 Expansion Plan

The Founder expects that the business will aggressively expand during the first three years of operation. Mr. Cartwright intends to implement marketing campaigns that will effectively target small- and medium-sized businesses within the target market.

2.0 COMPANY AND FINANCING SUMMARY

2.1 Registered Name and Corporate Structure

Cartwright Business Consultants, LLC is registered as a corporation in the State of New York.

2.2 Required Funds

At this time, Cartwright Business Consultants requires $50,000 of debt funds. Below is a breakdown of how these funds will be used:

Projected startup costs

Initial lease payments and deposits	$ 5,000
Working capital	$10,000
FF&E	$15,000
Leasehold improvements	$ 2,500
Security deposits	$ 2,500
Insurance	$ 2,500
Computer and technology equipment	$15,000
Marketing budget	$ 5,000
Miscellaneous and unforeseen costs	$ 2,500
Total startup costs	**$60,000**

Use of funds

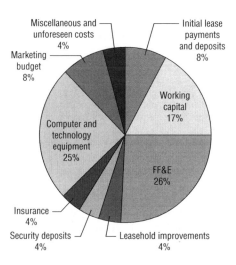

2.3 Investor Equity

Mr. Cartwright is not seeking an investment from a third party at this time.

2.4 Management Equity

Kent Cartwright owns 100% of Cartwright Business Consultants, LLC.

2.5 Exit Strategy

If the business is very successful, Mr. Cartwright may seek to sell the business to a third party for a significant earnings multiple. Most likely, the Company will hire a qualified business broker to sell the business on behalf of Cartwright Business Consultants. Based on historical numbers, the business could fetch a sales premium of up to 3 times earnings.

It should be noted that Mr. Cartwright may sell Cartwright Business Consultants, LLC to a current consultant employed by the business that is familiar with the firm's clients and business operations.

3.0 PRODUCTS AND SERVICES

Below is a description of the consulting services offered by Cartwright Business Consultants.

3.1 Per Hour Consulting Services

The primary source of income for the business will come from per hour consulting services rendered to small- and medium-sized businesses that have a specific issue that needs to be addressed. For instance, if a small business is developing a new product, the Company, through its consultants, will be able to assist the business with determining pricing, marketing, and the economic viability of the new venture. The business will charge a per hour rate of $150 to $300 depending on the complexity of the business or financial consulting rendered to the client.

3.2 Special Project Management and Consulting Services

In addition to per hour consulting, the business will also generate secondary streams of revenue by undertaking special projects such as business efficiency, business valuation, and economic viability analyses that are performed on site. Cartwright Business Consultants, at the onset of operations, will hire two specialized consultants that can provide these services onsite to clients. These services differ from the per hour consulting services in that these projects will typically be larger in scope, and as such, the client will want a fixed-price project based pricing for these services.

4.0 STRATEGIC AND MARKET ANALYSIS

4.1 Economic Outlook

This section of the analysis will detail the economic climate, the consulting industry, the customer profile, and the competition that the business will face as it progresses through its business operations.

Currently, the economic market condition in the United States is sluggish. This slowdown in the economy has also greatly impacted real estate sales, which has halted to historical lows. Many economists expect that this sluggish will continue for a significant period of time, at which point the economy will begin a prolonged recovery period. However, Consulting Firms tend to do well in any economic climate as during times of deleterious economic conditions business owners and business managers will require specialized advice on how to keep their organizations profitable.

4.2 Industry Analysis

The consulting industry is a highly fragmented group of individual practitioners, small firms, and large auditing institutions. There are over 621,000 consulting in the United States. The industry generates over $38 billion dollars a year, and employs over 390,000 Americans.

The demand for consulting services is expected to increase as companies seek to outsource non-core functions advisory and project analysis to private firms. Additionally, as the economy continues to have specialized labor needs, the Company can continually hire new employees with specialty expertise that will provide clients with informative research regarding their specific business issue. As stated earlier, the Company intends to provide a multitude of business development and related consulting services, which will allow business to balance its economic risk by operating among many industries.

4.3 Customer Profile

By acting in a multifaceted business capacity, the Company will be able to instruct and guide small businesses and corporate clients based on their specific research, project, or development needs. Below is a demographic profile of the businesses that Management will continue to target as potential clientele:

- Is a privately owned business

- Has less than $1,000,000 per year of revenue

- Has EBITDA of $50,000 to $250,000 per year

4.4 Competition

As discussed above, there are many consultants that operate a nationwide, regional, and local basis. As such, it is imperative that Cartwright Business Consultants differentiate itself from other consulting firms in operating in a multifaceted capacity as it relates to specialized business projects. The business will be able to appropriately source additional consultants, at anytime, should a specific company need consulting advice pertaining to an esoteric or complex subject.

5.0 MARKETING PLAN

Cartwright Business Consultants intends to maintain an extensive marketing campaign that will ensure maximum visibility for the business in its targeted market. Below is an overview of the marketing strategies and objectives of Cartwright Business Consultants.

5.1 Marketing Objectives

- Implement a local campaign with the Company's targeted market via the use of local newspaper advertisements, and word of mouth.

- Establish relationships with other business consultants within the targeted market.

5.2 Marketing Strategies

Mr. Cartwright intends on using a number of marketing strategies that will allow Cartwright Business Consultants to easily target small- and medium-sized businesses within the market. Management's first marketing strategy is to develop referral relationships with local accountants and attorneys that will continually provide the business with clients that have specialized consulting needs. Additionally, Management may act in a third party capacity on behalf of accountants.

The Company will maintain a sizable amount of print and traditional advertising methods among business journals within local markets to promote the business consulting services that the Company is selling.

Cartwright Business Consultants will maintain a broad website that showcases the individual profiles of consultants, costs relating to business consulting, and how to contact the firm. Management may use pay per click advertising and search engine optimization strategies so that the website can become prominently found when people search for New York metropolitan area consultants.

5.3 Pricing

Management anticipates that the business will generate $150 to $300 per hour based on the complexity of the project or depending on the skill of the individual consultant. Per project fees will typically range from $2,500 to $10,000.

6.0 ORGANIZATIONAL PLAN AND PERSONNEL SUMMARY

6.1 Corporate Organization

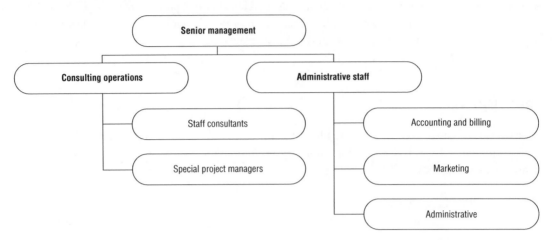

6.2 Organizational Budget

Personnel plan—yearly

Year	1	2	3
Senior management	$ 75,000	$ 77,250	$ 79,568
Business advisors and consultants	$110,000	$113,300	$116,699
Project managers	$ 90,000	$ 92,700	$ 95,481
Accountant	$ 32,500	$ 33,475	$ 34,479
Administrative	$ 25,000	$ 51,500	$ 53,045
Total	**$332,500**	**$368,225**	**$379,272**

Numbers of personnel

Senior management	1	1	1
Business advisors and consultants	2	2	2
Project managers	2	2	2
Accountant	1	1	1
Administrative	1	2	2
Totals	**7**	**8**	**8**

Personnel expense breakdown

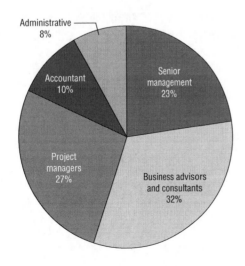

7.0 FINANCIAL PLAN

7.1 Underlying Assumptions

The Company has based its proforma financial statements on the following:

- Cartwright Business Consultants will have an annual revenue growth rate of 13% per year.

- The Owner will acquire $50,000 of debt funds to develop the business.

- The loan will have a 10-year term with a 9% interest rate.

7.2 Sensitivity Analysis

In the event of an economic downturn, the business may have a decline in its revenues. However, specialized consulting services are typically in demand despite difficult economic climates as small- and medium-sized businesses seek advice in order to keep their companies profitable and cash flow positive. Additionally, the very high margin revenues generated from per hour consulting fees and special project fees will ensure that the business can continually satisfy its debt obligations despite declines in top line income.

7.3 Source of Funds

Financing

Equity contributions	
Investor(s)	$10,000.00
Total equity financing	**$10,000.00**
Banks and lenders	
Banks and lenders	$50,000.00
Total debt financing	**$50,000.00**
Total financing	**$60,000.00**

7.4 General Assumptions

General assumptions

Year	1	2	3
Short term interest rate	9.5%	9.5%	9.5%
Long term interest rate	10.0%	10.0%	10.0%
Federal tax rate	33.0%	33.0%	33.0%
State tax rate	5.0%	5.0%	5.0%
Personnel taxes	15.0%	15.0%	15.0%

7.5 Profit and Loss Statements

Proforma profit and loss (yearly)

Year	1	2	3
Sales	**$549,000**	**$658,800**	**$770,796**
Cost of goods sold	$ 27,450	$ 32,940	$ 38,540
Gross margin	95.00%	95.00%	95.00%
Operating income	**$521,550**	**$625,860**	**$732,256**
Expenses			
Payroll	$332,500	$368,225	$379,272
General and administrative	$ 12,000	$ 12,480	$ 12,979
Marketing expenses	$ 13,176	$ 15,811	$ 18,499
Professional fees and licensure	$ 2,500	$ 2,575	$ 2,652
Insurance costs	$ 10,000	$ 10,500	$ 11,025
Travel and vehicle costs	$ 55,000	$ 60,500	$ 66,550
Rent and utilities	$ 15,000	$ 15,750	$ 16,538
Miscellaneous costs	$ 6,588	$ 7,906	$ 9,250
Payroll taxes	$ 49,875	$ 55,234	$ 56,891
Total operating costs	**$496,639**	**$548,981**	**$573,655**
EBITDA	**$ 24,911**	**$ 76,879**	**$158,601**
Federal income tax	$ 8,221	$ 24,029	$ 51,106
State income tax	$ 1,246	$ 3,641	$ 7,743
Interest expense	$ 4,369	$ 4,066	$ 3,734
Depreciation expenses	$ 2,857	$ 2,857	$ 2,857
Net profit	**$ 8,219**	**$ 42,287**	**$ 93,160**
Profit margin	**1.50%**	**6.42%**	**12.09%**

Sales, operating costs, and profit forecast

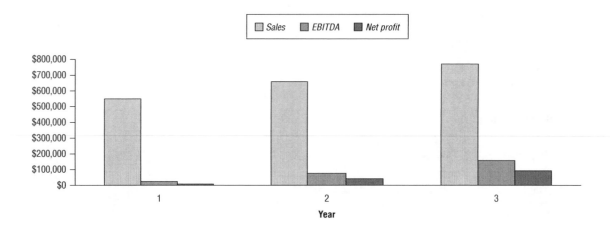

7.6 Cash Flow Analysis

Proforma cash flow analysis—yearly

Year	1	2	3
Cash from operations	$11,076	$45,145	$ 96,018
Cash from receivables	$ 0	$ 0	$ 0
Operating cash inflow	**$11,076**	**$45,145**	**$ 96,018**
Other cash inflows			
Equity investment	$10,000	$ 0	$ 0
Increased borrowings	$50,000	$ 0	$ 0
Sales of business assets	$ 0	$ 0	$ 0
A/P increases	$ 7,500	$ 8,625	$ 9,919
Total other cash inflows	**$67,500**	**$ 8,625**	**$ 9,919**
Total cash inflow	**$78,576**	**$53,770**	**$105,936**
Cash outflows			
Repayment of principal	$ 3,232	$ 3,535	$ 3,866
A/P decreases	$ 6,000	$ 7,200	$ 8,640
A/R increases	$ 0	$ 0	$ 0
Asset purchases	$40,000	$11,286	$ 24,004
Dividends	$ 7,753	$31,601	$ 67,212
Total cash outflows	**$56,985**	**$53,622**	**$103,723**
Net cash flow	**$21,591**	**$ 147**	**$ 2,213**
Cash balance	**$21,591**	**$21,738**	**$ 23,952**

Proforma cash flow (yearly)

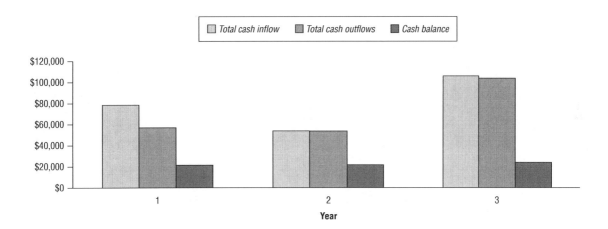

7.7 Balance Sheet

Proforma balance sheet—yearly

Year	1	2	3
Assets			
Cash	$21,591	$21,738	$23,952
Amortized expansion costs	$10,000	$11,129	$13,529
Computer and technology assets	$15,000	$23,465	$41,468
FF&E	$15,000	$16,693	$20,294
Accumulated depreciation	($ 2,857)	($ 5,714)	($ 8,571)
Total assets	**$58,734**	**$67,310**	**$90,671**
Liabilities and equity			
Accounts payable	$ 1,500	$ 2,925	$ 4,204
Long term liabilities	$46,768	$43,233	$39,699
Other liabilities	$ 0	$ 0	$ 0
Total liabilities	**$48,268**	**$46,158**	**$43,902**
Net worth	**$10,466**	**$21,152**	**$46,768**
Total liabilities and equity	**$58,734**	**$67,310**	**$90,671**

Proforma balance sheet

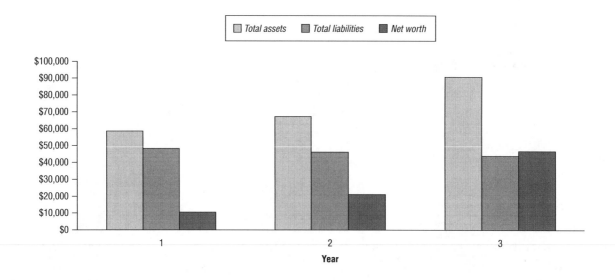

7.8 Breakeven Analysis

Monthly break even analysis

Year	1	2	3
Monthly revenue	$ 43,565	$ 48,156	$ 50,321
Yearly revenue	$522,778	$577,874	$603,847

Break even analysis

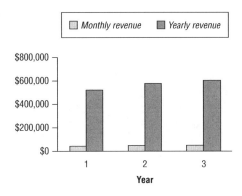

7.9 Business Ratios

Business ratios—yearly

Year	1	2	3
Sales			
Sales growth	0.00%	20.00%	17.00%
Gross margin	95.00%	95.00%	95.00%
Financials			
Profit margin	1.50%	6.42%	12.09%
Assets to liabilities	1.22	1.46	2.07
Equity to liabilities	0.22	0.46	1.07
Assets to equity	5.61	3.18	1.94
Liquidity			
Acid test	0.45	0.47	0.55
Cash to assets	0.37	0.32	0.26

7.10 Three Year Profit and Loss Statement

Profit and loss statement (first year)

Months	1	2	3	4	5	6	7
Sales	$37,500	$39,000	$40,500	$42,000	$43,500	$45,000	$46,500
Cost of goods sold	$ 1,875	$ 1,950	$ 2,025	$ 2,100	$ 2,175	$ 2,250	$ 2,325
Gross margin	95.00%	95.00%	95.00%	95.00%	95.00%	95.00%	95.00%
Operating income	$35,625	$37,050	$38,475	$39,900	$41,325	$42,750	$44,175
Expenses							
Payroll	$27,708	$27,708	$27,708	$27,708	$27,708	$27,708	$27,708
General and administrative	$ 1,000	$ 1,000	$ 1,000	$ 1,000	$ 1,000	$ 1,000	$ 1,000
Marketing expenses	$ 1,098	$ 1,098	$ 1,098	$ 1,098	$ 1,098	$ 1,098	$ 1,098
Professional fees and licensure	$ 208	$ 208	$ 208	$ 208	$ 208	$ 208	$ 208
Insurance costs	$ 833	$ 833	$ 833	$ 833	$ 833	$ 833	$ 833
Travel and vehicle costs	$ 4,583	$ 4,583	$ 4,583	$ 4,583	$ 4,583	$ 4,583	$ 4,583
Rent and utilities	$ 1,250	$ 1,250	$ 1,250	$ 1,250	$ 1,250	$ 1,250	$ 1,250
Miscellaneous costs	$ 549	$ 549	$ 549	$ 549	$ 549	$ 549	$ 549
Payroll taxes	$ 4,156	$ 4,156	$ 4,156	$ 4,156	$ 4,156	$ 4,156	$ 4,156
Total operating costs	$41,387	$41,387	$41,387	$41,387	$41,387	$41,387	$41,387
EBITDA	−$ 5,762	−$ 4,337	−$ 2,912	−$ 1,487	−$ 62	$ 1,363	$ 2,788
Federal income tax	$ 562	$ 584	$ 606	$ 629	$ 651	$ 674	$ 696
State income tax	$ 85	$ 88	$ 92	$ 95	$ 99	$ 102	$ 105
Interest expense	$ 375	$ 373	$ 371	$ 369	$ 367	$ 365	$ 363
Depreciation expense	$ 238	$ 238	$ 238	$ 238	$ 238	$ 238	$ 238
Net profit	−$ 7,021	−$ 5,620	−$ 4,219	−$ 2,818	−$ 1,417	−$ 16	$ 1,385

Profit and loss statement (first year cont.)

Month	8	9	10	11	12	1
Sales	$48,000	$49,500	$51,000	$52,500	$54,000	$549,000
Cost of goods sold	$ 2,400	$ 2,475	$ 2,550	$ 2,625	$ 2,700	$ 27,450
Gross margin	95.00%	95.00%	95.00%	95.00%	95.00%	95.00%
Operating income	$45,600	$47,025	$48,450	$49,875	$51,300	$521,550
Expenses						
Payroll	$27,708	$27,708	$27,708	$27,708	$27,708	$332,500
General and administrative	$ 1,000	$ 1,000	$ 1,000	$ 1,000	$ 1,000	$ 12,000
Marketing expenses	$ 1,098	$ 1,098	$ 1,098	$ 1,098	$ 1,098	$ 13,176
Professional fees and licensure	$ 208	$ 208	$ 208	$ 208	$ 208	$ 2,500
Insurance costs	$ 833	$ 833	$ 833	$ 833	$ 833	$ 10,000
Travel and vehicle costs	$ 4,583	$ 4,583	$ 4,583	$ 4,583	$ 4,583	$ 55,000
Rent and utilities	$ 1,250	$ 1,250	$ 1,250	$ 1,250	$ 1,250	$ 15,000
Miscellaneous costs	$ 549	$ 549	$ 549	$ 549	$ 549	$ 6,588
Payroll taxes	$ 4,156	$ 4,156	$ 4,156	$ 4,156	$ 4,156	$ 49,875
Total operating costs	$41,387	$41,387	$41,387	$41,387	$41,387	$496,639
EBITDA	$ 4,213	$ 5,638	$ 7,063	$ 8,488	$ 9,913	$ 24,911
Federal income tax	$ 719	$ 741	$ 764	$ 786	$ 809	$ 8,221
State income tax	$ 109	$ 112	$ 116	$ 119	$ 123	$ 1,246
Interest expense	$ 361	$ 359	$ 357	$ 355	$ 353	$ 4,369
Depreciation expense	$ 238	$ 238	$ 238	$ 238	$ 238	$ 2,857
Net profit	$ 2,787	$ 4,188	$ 5,589	$ 6,990	$ 8,391	$ 8,219

Profit and loss statement (second year)

Quarter	Q1	2 Q2	Q3	Q4	2
Sales	**$131,760**	**$164,700**	**$177,876**	**$184,464**	**$658,800**
Cost of goods sold	$ 6,588	$ 8,235	$ 8,894	$ 9,223	$ 32,940
Gross margin	95.00%	95.00%	95.00%	95.00%	95.00%
Operating income	**$125,172**	**$156,465**	**$168,982**	**$175,241**	**$625,860**
Expenses					
Payroll	$ 73,645	$ 92,056	$ 99,421	$103,103	$368,225
General and administrative	$ 2,496	$ 3,120	$ 3,370	$ 3,494	$ 12,480
Marketing expenses	$ 3,162	$ 3,953	$ 4,269	$ 4,427	$ 15,811
Professional fees and licensure	$ 515	$ 644	$ 695	$ 721	$ 2,575
Insurance costs	$ 2,100	$ 2,625	$ 2,835	$ 2,940	$ 10,500
Travel and vehicle costs	$ 12,100	$ 15,125	$ 16,335	$ 16,940	$ 60,500
Rent and utilities	$ 3,150	$ 3,938	$ 4,253	$ 4,410	$ 15,750
Miscellaneous costs	$ 1,581	$ 1,976	$ 2,135	$ 2,214	$ 7,906
Payroll taxes	$ 11,047	$ 13,808	$ 14,913	$ 15,465	$ 55,234
Total operating costs	**$109,796**	**$137,245**	**$148,225**	**$153,715**	**$548,981**
EBITDA	**$ 15,376**	**$ 19,220**	**$ 20,757**	**$ 21,526**	**$ 76,879**
Federal income tax	$ 4,806	$ 6,007	$ 6,488	$ 6,728	$ 24,029
State income tax	$ 728	$ 910	$ 983	$ 1,019	$ 3,641
Interest expense	$ 1,046	$ 1,027	$ 1,007	$ 986	$ 4,066
Depreciation expense	$ 714	$ 714	$ 714	$ 714	$ 2,857
Net profit	**$ 8,082**	**$ 10,562**	**$ 11,566**	**$ 12,078**	**$ 42,287**

Profit and loss statement (third year)

Quarter	Q1	3 Q2	Q3	Q4	3
Sales	**$154,159**	**$192,699**	**$208,115**	**$215,823**	**$770,796**
Cost of goods sold	$ 7,708	$ 9,635	$ 10,406	$ 10,791	$ 38,540
Gross margin	95.00%	95.00%	95.00%	95.00%	95.00%
Operating income	**$146,451**	**$183,064**	**$197,709**	**$205,032**	**$732,256**
Expenses					
Payroll	$ 75,854	$ 94,818	$102,403	$106,196	$379,272
General and administrative	$ 2,596	$ 3,245	$ 3,504	$ 3,634	$ 12,979
Marketing expenses	$ 3,700	$ 4,625	$ 4,995	$ 5,180	$ 18,499
Professional fees and licensure	$ 530	$ 663	$ 716	$ 743	$ 2,652
Insurance costs	$ 2,205	$ 2,756	$ 2,977	$ 3,087	$ 11,025
Travel and vehicle costs	$ 13,310	$ 16,638	$ 17,969	$ 18,634	$ 66,550
Rent and utilities	$ 3,308	$ 4,134	$ 4,465	$ 4,631	$ 16,538
Miscellaneous costs	$ 1,850	$ 2,312	$ 2,497	$ 2,590	$ 9,250
Payroll taxes	$ 11,378	$ 14,223	$ 15,361	$ 15,929	$ 56,891
Total operating costs	**$114,731**	**$143,414**	**$154,887**	**$160,623**	**$573,655**
EBITDA	**$ 31,720**	**$ 39,650**	**$ 42,822**	**$ 44,408**	**$158,601**
Federal income tax	$ 10,221	$ 12,777	$ 13,799	$ 14,310	$ 51,106
State income tax	$ 1,549	$ 1,936	$ 2,091	$ 2,168	$ 7,743
Interest expense	$ 966	$ 945	$ 923	$ 901	$ 3,734
Depreciation expense	$ 714	$ 714	$ 714	$ 714	$ 2,857
Net profit	**$ 18,270**	**$ 23,279**	**$ 25,296**	**$ 26,315**	**$ 93,160**

7.11 Three Year Cash Flow Analysis

Cash flow analysis (first year)

Month	1	2	3	4	5	6	7
Cash from operations	−$ 6,783	−$ 5,382	−$ 3,981	−$ 2,580	−$1,179	$ 222	$ 1,623
Cash from receivables	$ 0	$ 0	$ 0	$ 0	$ 0	$ 0	$ 0
Operating cash inflow	**−$ 6,783**	**−$ 5,382**	**−$ 3,981**	**−$ 2,580**	**−$1,179**	**$ 222**	**$ 1,623**
Other cash inflows							
Equity investment	$10,000	$ 0	$ 0	$ 0	$ 0	$ 0	$ 0
Increased borrowings	$50,000	$ 0	$ 0	$ 0	$ 0	$ 0	$ 0
Sales of business assets	$ 0	$ 0	$ 0	$ 0	$ 0	$ 0	$ 0
A/P increases	$ 625	$ 625	$ 625	$ 625	$ 625	$ 625	$ 625
Total other cash inflows	**$60,625**	**$ 625**	**$ 625**	**$ 625**	**$ 625**	**$ 625**	**$ 625**
Total cash inflow	**$53,842**	**−$ 4,757**	**−$ 3,356**	**−$ 1,955**	**−$ 554**	**$ 847**	**$ 2,248**
Cash outflows							
Repayment of principal	$ 258	$ 260	$ 262	$ 264	$ 266	$ 268	$ 270
A/P decreases	$ 500	$ 500	$ 500	$ 500	$ 500	$ 500	$ 500
A/R increases	$ 0	$ 0	$ 0	$ 0	$ 0	$ 0	$ 0
Asset purchases	$30,000	$ 0	$ 0	$ 0	$ 0	$ 0	$ 0
Dividends	$ 0	$ 0	$ 0	$ 0	$ 0	$ 0	$ 0
Total cash outflows	**$30,758**	**$ 760**	**$ 762**	**$ 764**	**$ 766**	**$ 768**	**$ 770**
Net cash flow	**$23,083**	**−$ 5,517**	**−$ 4,118**	**−$ 2,719**	**−$1,320**	**$ 79**	**$ 1,478**
Cash balance	**$23,083**	**$17,566**	**$13,448**	**$10,729**	**$9,409**	**$9,488**	**$10,966**

Cash flow analysis (first year cont.)

Month	8	9	10	11	12	1
Cash from operations	$ 3,025	$ 4,426	$ 5,827	$ 7,228	$ 8,629	$11,076
Cash from receivables	$ 0	$ 0	$ 0	$ 0	$ 0	$ 0
Operating cash inflow	**$ 3,025**	**$ 4,426**	**$ 5,827**	**$ 7,228**	**$ 8,629**	**$11,076**
Other cash inflows						
Equity investment	$ 0	$ 0	$ 0	$ 0	$ 0	$10,000
Increased borrowings	$ 0	$ 0	$ 0	$ 0	$ 0	$50,000
Sales of business assets	$ 0	$ 0	$ 0	$ 0	$ 0	$ 0
A/P increases	$ 625	$ 625	$ 625	$ 625	$ 625	$ 7,500
Total other cash inflows	**$ 625**	**$ 625**	**$ 625**	**$ 625**	**$ 625**	**$67,500**
Total cash inflow	**$ 3,650**	**$ 5,051**	**$ 6,452**	**$ 7,853**	**$ 9,254**	**$78,576**
Cash outflows						
Repayment of principal	$ 272	$ 274	$ 276	$ 278	$ 281	$ 3,232
A/P decreases	$ 500	$ 500	$ 500	$ 500	$ 500	$ 6,000
A/R increases	$ 0	$ 0	$ 0	$ 0	$ 0	$ 0
Asset purchases	$ 0	$ 0	$ 5,000	$ 0	$ 5,000	$40,000
Dividends	$ 0	$ 0	$ 0	$ 0	$ 7,753	$ 7,753
Total cash outflows	**$ 772**	**$ 774**	**$ 5,776**	**$ 778**	**$13,534**	**$56,985**
Net cash flow	**$ 2,877**	**$ 4,277**	**$ 676**	**$ 7,075**	**−$ 4,279**	**$21,591**
Cash balance	**$13,843**	**$18,120**	**$18,796**	**$25,870**	**$21,591**	**$21,591**

Cash flow analysis (second year)

Quarter	Q1	2 Q2	Q3	Q4	2
Cash from operations	$ 9,029	$11,286	$12,189	$12,640	$45,145
Cash from receivables	$ 0	$ 0	$ 0	$ 0	$ 0
Operating cash inflow	**$ 9,029**	**$11,286**	**$12,189**	**$12,640**	**$45,145**
Other cash inflows					
Equity investment	$ 0	$ 0	$ 0	$ 0	$ 0
Increased borrowings	$ 0	$ 0	$ 0	$ 0	$ 0
Sales of business assets	$ 0	$ 0	$ 0	$ 0	$ 0
A/P increases	$ 1,725	$ 2,156	$ 2,329	$ 2,415	$ 8,625
Total other cash inflows	**$ 1,725**	**$ 2,156**	**$ 2,329**	**$ 2,415**	**$ 8,625**
Total cash inflow	**$10,754**	**$13,442**	**$14,518**	**$15,055**	**$53,770**
Cash outflows					
Repayment of principal	$ 854	$ 874	$ 893	$ 914	$ 3,535
A/P decreases	$ 1,440	$ 1,800	$ 1,944	$ 2,016	$ 7,200
A/R increases	$ 0	$ 0	$ 0	$ 0	$ 0
Asset purchases	$ 2,257	$ 2,822	$ 3,047	$ 3,160	$11,286
Dividends	$ 6,320	$ 7,900	$ 8,532	$ 8,848	$31,601
Total cash outflows	**$10,872**	**$13,395**	**$14,417**	**$14,938**	**$53,622**
Net cash flow	**−$ 118**	**$ 47**	**$ 101**	**$ 117**	**$ 147**
Cash balance	**$21,473**	**$21,520**	**$21,621**	**$21,738**	**$21,738**

Cash flow analysis (third year)

Quarter	Q1	3 Q2	Q3	Q4	3
Cash from operations	$19,204	$24,004	$25,925	$26,885	$ 96,018
Cash from receivables	$ 0	$ 0	$ 0	$ 0	$ 0
Operating cash inflow	**$19,204**	**$24,004**	**$25,925**	**$26,885**	**$ 96,018**
Other cash inflows					
Equity investment	$ 0	$ 0	$ 0	$ 0	$ 0
Increased borrowings	$ 0	$ 0	$ 0	$ 0	$ 0
Sales of business assets	$ 0	$ 0	$ 0	$ 0	$ 0
A/P increases	$ 1,984	$ 2,480	$ 2,678	$ 2,777	$ 9,919
Total other cash inflows	**$ 1,984**	**$ 2,480**	**$ 2,678**	**$ 2,777**	**$ 9,919**
Total cash inflow	**$21,187**	**$26,484**	**$28,603**	**$29,662**	**$105,936**
Cash outflows					
Repayment of principal	$ 934	$ 956	$ 977	$ 999	$ 3,866
A/P decreases	$ 1,728	$ 2,160	$ 2,333	$ 2,419	$ 8,640
A/R increases	$ 0	$ 0	$ 0	$ 0	$ 0
Asset purchases	$ 4,801	$ 6,001	$ 6,481	$ 6,721	$ 24,004
Dividends	$13,442	$16,803	$18,147	$18,819	$ 67,212
Total cash outflows	**$20,906**	**$25,920**	**$27,938**	**$28,959**	**$103,723**
Net cash flow	**$ 282**	**$ 564**	**$ 664**	**$ 703**	**$ 2,213**
Cash balance	**$22,020**	**$22,584**	**$23,249**	**$23,952**	**$ 23,952**

Cloud Computing Business

Premier Cloud Infrastructure, Inc.

12345 First Ave.
New York, NY 10013

BizPlanDB.com

The purpose of this business plan is to raise $100,000 for the development of a cloud computing and virtual machine company while showcasing the expected financials and operations over the next three years.

1.0 EXECUTIVE SUMMARY

The purpose of this business plan is to raise $100,000 for the development of a cloud computing and virtual machine company while showcasing the expected financials and operations over the next three years. Premier Cloud Infrastructure, Inc. is a New York-based corporation that will provide offsite management of customer's domain names, cloud computing machines, and security certificates to customers on a nationwide basis. The Company was founded by Peter Halestrom.

1.1 The Services

The primary source of revenue for the business will come from the direct hosting and management of virtual machines and cloud computing software on behalf of customers on the Company's server network. At the onset of operations, the Company will have the capacity to host up to 2,000 separate cloud computing systems. The Company will also have specialized servers for customers that have extensive dedicated server needs (this is especially true of businesses that have a high volume of bandwidth needs). From this segment of the business, the Company will generate monthly recurring revenues for providing these services.

Premier Cloud Infrastructure, Inc. will also generate secondary streams of revenue from the sale of domain names (as a third party vendor) as well as security certificates. The Company's final revenue stream will come from affiliate revenues among vendors that can provide customers with virtual machine development solutions.

The third section of the business plan will further describe the services offered by Premier Cloud Infrastructure, Inc.

1.2 Financing

Mr. Halestrom is seeking to raise $100,000 from a bank loan. The interest rate and loan agreement are to be further discussed during negotiation. This business plan assumes that the business will receive a 10-year loan with a 9% fixed interest rate. The financing will be used for the following:

- Development of the Company's physical location.

- Financing for the first six months of operation.

- Capital to purchase servers.

Mr. Halestrom will contribute $10,000 to the venture.

1.3 Mission Statement

Premier Cloud Infrastructure's mission is to become the recognized leader in its targeted market for outstanding cloud computing and virtual machine services.

1.4 Management Team

The Company was founded by Peter Halestrom. Mr. Halestrom has more than 10 years of experience in the information technology industry. Through his expertise, he will be able to bring the operations of the business to profitability within its first year of operations.

1.5 Sales Forecasts

Mr. Halestrom expects a strong rate of growth at the start of operations. Below are the expected financials over the next three years.

Proforma profit and loss (yearly)

Year	1	2	3
Sales	$570,840	$627,924	$690,716
Operating costs	$361,246	$376,488	$392,585
EBITDA	$180,839	$219,806	$263,338
Taxes, interest, and depreciation	$ 81,921	$ 93,032	$109,163
Net profit	$ 98,918	$126,774	$154,175

Sales, operating costs, and profit forecast

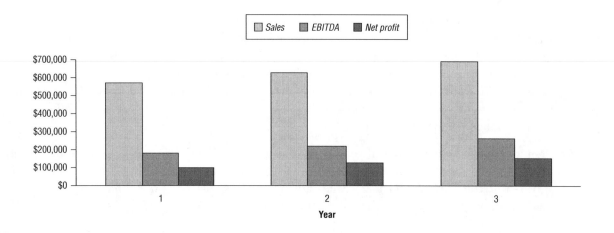

1.6 Expansion Plan

The Founder expects that the business will aggressively expand during the first three years of operation. Mr. Halestrom intends to implement marketing campaigns that will effectively target mid-sized to large businesses within the target market.

2.0 COMPANY AND FINANCING SUMMARY

2.1 Registered Name and Corporate Structure

Premier Cloud Infrastructure, Inc. is registered as a corporation in the State of New York.

2.2 Required Funds

At this time, Premier Cloud Infrastructure, Inc. requires $100,000 of debt funds. Below is a breakdown of how these funds will be used:

Projected startup costs

Initial lease payments and deposits	$ 10,000
Working capital	$ 15,000
FF&E	$ 20,000
Leasehold improvements	$ 15,500
Security deposits	$ 5,000
Insurance	$ 2,500
Servers	$ 30,000
Marketing budget	$ 7,500
Miscellaneous and unforeseen costs	$ 5,000
Total startup costs	**$110,000**

Use of funds

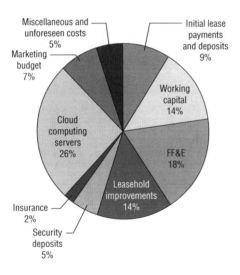

2.3 Investor Equity

Mr. Halestrom is not seeking an investment from a third party at this time.

2.4 Management Equity

Peter Halestrom owns 100% of Premier Cloud Infrastructure, Inc.

2.5 Exit Strategy

If the business is very successful, Mr. Halestrom may seek to sell the business to a third party for a significant earnings multiple. Most likely, the Company will hire a qualified business broker to sell the business on behalf of Premier Cloud Infrastructure, Inc. Based on historical numbers, the business could fetch a sales premium of up to 6 times earnings based on the recurring revenues generated from cloud computing and virtual machine services.

3.0 PRODUCTS AND SERVICES

Below is a description of the services offered by Premier Cloud Infrastructure, Inc.

3.1 Cloud Computing Services

The primary revenue center for the business will come from the ongoing dedicated virtual machine and cloud computing services that will be offered to medium- and large-sized businesses within the Company's targeted market. These virtual machines and cloud computing services will allow businesses to more effectively communicate by allowing individuals to connect to a broad spectrum of programs from one centrally located server.

3.2 Ancillary Products

In addition to cloud computing and dedicated server services, the business will also provide customers with the ability to register domain names, obtain security certificates (issued by certified authorities), dedicated customer support, and other ancillary services that complement the Company's primary revenue center. Mr. Halestrom expects that these ancillary services will generate 25% of the business's revenues.

3.3 Affiliate Revenues

The final revenue stream for the business will come from affiliate marketing revenues generated from third party companies that provide cloud computing and IT management services. The Company will receive a commission based stream of income when a Premier Cloud Infrastructure, Inc. client uses one of the Company's preferred vendors. Management anticipates that this revenue center will generate 3% to 5% of the Company's top line income.

4.0 STRATEGIC AND MARKET ANALYSIS

4.1 Economic Outlook

This section of the analysis will detail the economic climate, the technology services industry, the customer profile, and the competition that the business will face as it progresses through its business operations.

Currently, the economic market condition in the United States is sluggish. This slowdown in the economy has also greatly impacted real estate sales, which has halted to historical lows. Many economists expect that this sluggish will continue for a significant period of time, at which point the economy will begin a prolonged recovery period. However, cloud computing businesses operate with great economic stability as the recurring streams of revenue ensure that these businesses remain profitable despite deleterious economic climates.

4.2 Industry Analysis

The dedicated web hosting industry, server collocation industry, and general technology industries are extremely important to both businesses and individual users. This industry aggregately generates in excess of $160 billion dollars a year. The market is comprised of approximately 12,000 businesses that operate throughout the continental United States. Additionally, the industry employs more than 300,000 people and generates gross annual payrolls of $50 billion dollars.

The industry has had tremendous growth over the last twenty years. As more businesses and individuals demand more sophisticated technology systems, the industry has seen its growth increase to an average five year compounded growth rate of 70.1%.

This trend is expected to continue as the need for Internet, intranet, and communications continues to grow beyond the standard economic rate of growth. Additionally, the technology landscape is an ever-changing arena of business where new technologies and businesses are being developed on a regular basis and with this growth is the need for continually upgrading and improving existing information technology platforms.

Approximately 40% of the industry revenues are generated from information technology expenditures. As businesses continually need greater levels of internet connectivity (including the introduction of cloud computing), the market share of IT is expected to increase as a function of the technology industry as a whole.

4.3 Customer Profile

Premier Cloud Infrastructure, Inc. will have two primary client groups: small businesses and corporations. Common traits among small business clients will include:

- Annual revenues of $100,000 to $1,000,000

- Will spend $500 on cloud computing services and virtual machine services

Among business clients, Mr. Halestrom has outlined the following demographics that will be used to target this customer segment:

- Annual revenues of $1,000,000+

- Maintains a large scale information infrastructure

- 50% of clients will want their server to have secure cloud computing functionality

4.4 Competition

As stated above, the recurring streams of revenue and economic stability of virtual machine hosting businesses have driven several thousand market agents into the industry. As such, one of the ways that cloud computing and dedicated server companies remain competitive is by providing superior customer service to its client base. Major competitors in this field, include, but are not limited to the following:

- GoDaddy.com (largest by volume competitor)

- UplinkEarth.com (well regarded, but has recently had severe technical issues)

5.0 MARKETING PLAN

Premier Cloud Infrastructure, Inc. intends to maintain an extensive marketing campaign that will ensure maximum visibility for the business in its targeted market. Below is an overview of the marketing strategies and objectives of the Company.

5.1 Marketing Objectives
- Develop an online presence by developing a website and placing the Company's name and contact information with online directories.

- Establish relationships with web development firms that operate on a national basis.

- Implement a large scale search engine optimization and pay per click campaign at the onset of operations.

5.2 Marketing Strategies

Mr. Halestrom intends to use a high-impact marketing campaign that will generate a substantial amount of traffic to Premier Cloud Infrastructure, Inc.'s online platform. These strategies primarily include the use of search engine optimization and pay per click marketing.

Foremost, Management intends to develop a number of relationships with website development firms that work with small businesses, medium-sized businesses, and large corporations. As these companies' clients have extensive needs for cloud computing services, Management feels that the most economically viable way of executing this marketing plan is to engage website development companies as well as IT consulting firms that will refer or outsource their clients cloud computing needs to that of the Company. In time, this will become an invaluable source of revenue for the business.

Additionally, Premier Cloud Infrastructure, Inc. will use several pay methods for increasing the Company's visibility. This strategy is expensive, but the results can be phenomenal if this marketing strategy is properly executed. These advertisements appear along the border and side of a website, and each time a person clicks on the website, a small fee ranging from fifty cents to one dollar is charged to the Company's account. This will be the primary method for generating visitors at the onset of operations.

5.3 Pricing

Management anticipates that the average business user will spend $150 to $200 per month on having a dedicated server or virtual server that can host their applications directly or on a co-location basis.

6.0 ORGANIZATIONAL PLAN AND PERSONNEL SUMMARY

6.1 Corporate Organization

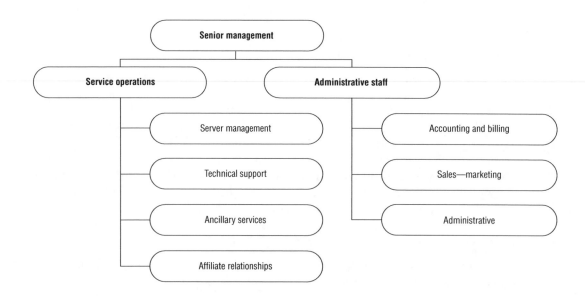

6.2 Organizational Budget

Personnel plan—yearly

Year	1	2	3
Owner	$ 50,000	$ 51,500	$ 53,045
Technical manager	$ 45,000	$ 46,350	$ 47,741
Technical support staff	$ 66,000	$ 67,980	$ 70,019
Bookkeeper (P/T)	$ 12,500	$ 12,875	$ 13,261
Administrative	$ 44,000	$ 45,320	$ 46,680
Total	**$217,500**	**$224,025**	**$230,746**

Numbers of personnel

Owner	1	1	1
Technical manager	1	1	1
Technical support staff	3	3	3
Bookkeeper (P/T)	1	1	1
Administrative	2	2	2
Totals	**8**	**8**	**8**

Personnel expense breakdown

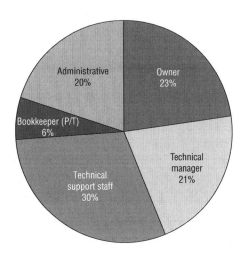

7.0 FINANCIAL PLAN

7.1 Underlying Assumptions

The Company has based its proforma financial statements on the following:

- Premier Cloud Infrastructure will have an annual revenue growth rate of 10% per year.

- The Owner will acquire $100,000 of debt funds to develop the business.

- The loan will have a 10-year term with a 9% interest rate.

7.2 Sensitivity Analysis

In the event of an economic downturn, the business may have a decline in its revenue growth. However, Premier Cloud Infrastructure will generate recurring streams of revenue from its developed client base that will ensure the Company's profitability on a monthly basis. Additionally, the margins generated by the business are extremely high while operating costs are moderately low.

7.3 Source of Funds

Financing

Equity contributions

Management investment	$ 10,000.00
Total equity financing	**$ 10,000.00**

Banks and lenders

Banks and lenders	$100,000.00
Total debt financing	**$100,000.00**
Total financing	**$110,000.00**

7.4 General Assumptions

General assumptions

Year	1	2	3
Short term interest rate	9.5%	9.5%	9.5%
Long term interest rate	10.0%	10.0%	10.0%
Federal tax rate	33.0%	33.0%	33.0%
State tax rate	5.0%	5.0%	5.0%
Personnel taxes	15.0%	15.0%	15.0%

7.5 Profit and Loss Statements

Proforma profit and loss (yearly)

Year	1	2	3
Sales	**$570,840**	**$627,924**	**$690,716**
Cost of goods sold	$ 28,755	$ 31,631	$ 34,794
Gross margin	94.96%	94.96%	94.96%
Operating income	**$542,085**	**$596,294**	**$655,923**
Expenses			
Payroll	$217,500	$224,025	$230,746
General and administrative	$ 25,200	$ 26,208	$ 27,256
Marketing expenses	$ 39,959	$ 43,955	$ 48,350
Professional fees and licensure	$ 7,500	$ 7,725	$ 7,957
Insurance costs	$ 2,500	$ 2,625	$ 2,756
Equipment maintenance costs	$ 10,000	$ 11,000	$ 12,100
Rent and utilities	$ 24,250	$ 25,463	$ 26,736
Miscellaneous costs	$ 1,713	$ 1,884	$ 2,072
Payroll taxes	$ 32,625	$ 33,604	$ 34,612
Total operating costs	**$361,246**	**$376,488**	**$392,585**
EBITDA	**$180,839**	**$219,806**	**$263,338**
Federal income tax	$ 59,677	$ 69,853	$ 84,437
State income tax	$ 9,042	$ 10,584	$ 12,793
Interest expense	$ 8,738	$ 8,131	$ 7,468
Depreciation expenses	$ 4,464	$ 4,464	$ 4,464
Net profit	**$ 98,918**	**$126,774**	**$154,175**
Profit margin	**17.33%**	**20.19%**	**22.32%**

Sales, operating costs, and profit forecast

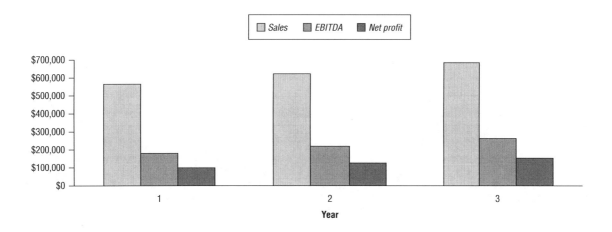

7.6 Cash Flow Analysis

Proforma cash flow analysis—yearly

Year	1	2	3
Cash from operations	$103,382	$131,238	$158,639
Cash from receivables	$ 0	$ 0	$ 0
Operating cash inflow	**$103,382**	**$131,238**	**$158,639**
Other cash inflows			
Equity investment	$ 10,000	$ 0	$ 0
Increased borrowings	$100,000	$ 0	$ 0
Sales of business assets	$ 0	$ 0	$ 0
A/P increases	$ 37,902	$ 43,587	$ 50,125
Total other cash inflows	**$147,902**	**$ 43,587**	**$ 50,125**
Total cash inflow	**$251,284**	**$174,825**	**$208,765**
Cash outflows			
Repayment of principal	$ 6,463	$ 7,070	$ 7,733
A/P decreases	$ 24,897	$ 29,876	$ 35,852
A/R increases	$ 0	$ 0	$ 0
Asset purchases	$ 57,500	$ 32,810	$ 39,660
Dividends	$ 72,368	$ 91,867	$111,047
Total cash outflows	**$161,228**	**$161,622**	**$194,292**
Net cash flow	**$ 90,056**	**$ 13,203**	**$ 14,473**
Cash balance	**$ 90,056**	**$103,259**	**$117,732**

Proforma cash flow (yearly)

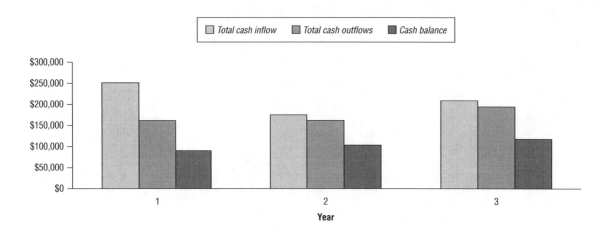

7.7 Balance Sheet

Proforma balance sheet—yearly

Year	1	2	3
Assets			
Cash	$ 90,056	$103,259	$117,732
Amortized development/expansion costs	$ 17,500	$ 20,781	$ 24,747
Servers	$ 30,000	$ 46,405	$ 66,235
FF&E	$ 15,000	$ 28,124	$ 43,988
Accumulated depreciation	($ 4,464)	($ 8,929)	($ 13,393)
Total assets	**$148,092**	**$189,640**	**$239,309**
Liabilities and equity			
Accounts payable	$ 13,005	$ 26,716	$ 40,990
Long term liabilities	$ 93,537	$ 86,467	$ 79,397
Other liabilities	$ 0	$ 0	$ 0
Total liabilities	**$106,542**	**$113,183**	**$120,387**
Net worth	**$ 41,550**	**$ 76,458**	**$118,922**
Total liabilities and equity	**$148,092**	**$189,640**	**$239,309**

Proforma balance sheet

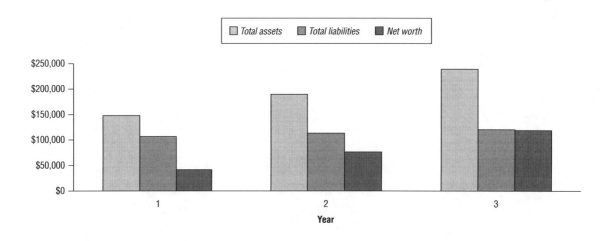

7.8 Breakeven Analysis

Monthly break even analysis

Year	1	2	3
Monthly revenue	$ 31,701	$ 33,038	$ 34,451
Yearly revenue	$380,409	$396,459	$413,410

Break even analysis

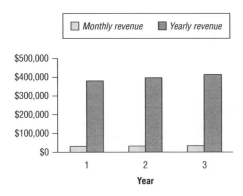

7.9 Business Ratios

Business ratios—yearly

Year	1	2	3
Sales			
Sales growth	0.00%	10.00%	10.00%
Gross margin	95.00%	95.00%	95.00%
Financials			
Profit margin	17.33%	20.19%	22.32%
Assets to liabilities	1.39	1.68	1.99
Equity to liabilities	0.39	0.68	0.99
Assets to equity	3.56	2.48	2.01
Liquidity			
Acid test	0.85	0.91	0.98
Cash to assets	0.61	0.54	0.49

7.10 Three Year Profit and Loss Statement

Profit and loss statement (first year)

Months	1	2	3	4	5	6	7
Sales	$40,200	$41,540	$42,880	$44,220	$45,560	$46,900	$48,240
Cost of goods sold	$ 2,025	$ 2,093	$ 2,160	$ 2,228	$ 2,295	$ 2,363	$ 2,430
Gross margin	95.00%	95.00%	95.00%	95.00%	95.00%	95.00%	95.00%
Operating income	$38,175	$39,448	$40,720	$41,993	$43,265	$44,538	$45,810
Expenses							
Payroll	$18,125	$18,125	$18,125	$18,125	$18,125	$18,125	$18,125
General and administrative	$ 2,100	$ 2,100	$ 2,100	$ 2,100	$ 2,100	$ 2,100	$ 2,100
Marketing expenses	$ 3,330	$ 3,330	$ 3,330	$ 3,330	$ 3,330	$ 3,330	$ 3,330
Professional fees and licensure	$ 625	$ 625	$ 625	$ 625	$ 625	$ 625	$ 625
Insurance costs	$ 208	$ 208	$ 208	$ 208	$ 208	$ 208	$ 208
Equipment maintenance costs	$ 833	$ 833	$ 833	$ 833	$ 833	$ 833	$ 833
Rent and utilities	$ 2,021	$ 2,021	$ 2,021	$ 2,021	$ 2,021	$ 2,021	$ 2,021
Miscellaneous costs	$ 143	$ 143	$ 143	$ 143	$ 143	$ 143	$ 143
Payroll taxes	$ 2,719	$ 2,719	$ 2,719	$ 2,719	$ 2,719	$ 2,719	$ 2,719
Total operating costs	$30,104	$30,104	$30,104	$30,104	$30,104	$30,104	$30,104
EBITDA	$ 8,071	$ 9,344	$10,616	$11,889	$13,161	$14,434	$15,706
Federal income tax	$ 4,203	$ 4,343	$ 4,483	$ 4,623	$ 4,763	$ 4,903	$ 5,043
State income tax	$ 637	$ 658	$ 679	$ 700	$ 722	$ 743	$ 764
Interest expense	$ 750	$ 746	$ 742	$ 738	$ 734	$ 730	$ 726
Depreciation expense	$ 372	$ 372	$ 372	$ 372	$ 372	$ 372	$ 372
Net profit	$ 2,110	$ 3,225	$ 4,340	$ 5,455	$ 6,570	$ 7,685	$ 8,801

Profit and loss statement (first year cont.)

Month	8	9	10	11	12	1
Sales	$49,580	$50,920	$52,260	$53,600	$54,940	$570,840
Cost of goods sold	$ 2,498	$ 2,565	$ 2,633	$ 2,700	$ 2,768	$ 28,755
Gross margin	95.00%	95.00%	95.00%	95.00%	95.00%	95.00%
Operating income	$47,083	$48,355	$49,628	$50,900	$52,173	$542,085
Expenses						
Payroll	$18,125	$18,125	$18,125	$18,125	$18,125	$217,500
General and administrative	$ 2,100	$ 2,100	$ 2,100	$ 2,100	$ 2,100	$ 25,200
Marketing expenses	$ 3,330	$ 3,330	$ 3,330	$ 3,330	$ 3,330	$ 39,959
Professional fees and licensure	$ 625	$ 625	$ 625	$ 625	$ 625	$ 7,500
Insurance costs	$ 208	$ 208	$ 208	$ 208	$ 208	$ 2,500
Equipment maintenance costs	$ 833	$ 833	$ 833	$ 833	$ 833	$ 10,000
Rent and utilities	$ 2,021	$ 2,021	$ 2,021	$ 2,021	$ 2,021	$ 24,250
Miscellaneous costs	$ 143	$ 143	$ 143	$ 143	$ 143	$ 1,713
Payroll taxes	$ 2,719	$ 2,719	$ 2,719	$ 2,719	$ 2,719	$ 32,625
Total operating costs	$30,104	$30,104	$30,104	$30,104	$30,104	$361,246
EBITDA	$16,979	$18,251	$19,524	$20,796	$22,069	$180,839
Federal income tax	$ 5,183	$ 5,323	$ 5,463	$ 5,603	$ 5,744	$ 59,677
State income tax	$ 785	$ 807	$ 828	$ 849	$ 870	$ 9,042
Interest expense	$ 722	$ 718	$ 714	$ 710	$ 706	$ 8,738
Depreciation expense	$ 372	$ 372	$ 372	$ 372	$ 372	$ 4,464
Net profit	$ 9,916	$11,031	$12,146	$13,262	$14,377	$ 98,918

Profit and loss statement (second year)

Quarter	Q1	2 Q2	Q3	Q4	2
Sales	$125,585	$156,981	$169,539	$175,819	$627,924
Cost of goods sold	$ 6,326	$ 7,908	$ 8,540	$ 8,857	$ 31,631
Gross margin	95.00%	95.00%	95.00%	95.00%	95.00%
Operating income	$119,259	$149,073	$160,999	$166,962	$596,294
Expenses					
Payroll	$ 44,805	$ 56,006	$ 60,487	$ 62,727	$224,025
General and administrative	$ 5,242	$ 6,552	$ 7,076	$ 7,338	$ 26,208
Marketing expenses	$ 8,791	$ 10,989	$ 11,868	$ 12,307	$ 43,955
Professional fees and licensure	$ 1,545	$ 1,931	$ 2,086	$ 2,163	$ 7,725
Insurance costs	$ 525	$ 656	$ 709	$ 735	$ 2,625
Equipment maintenance costs	$ 2,200	$ 2,750	$ 2,970	$ 3,080	$ 11,000
Rent and utilities	$ 5,093	$ 6,366	$ 6,875	$ 7,130	$ 25,463
Miscellaneous costs	$ 377	$ 471	$ 509	$ 527	$ 1,884
Payroll taxes	$ 6,721	$ 8,401	$ 9,073	$ 9,409	$ 33,604
Total operating costs	$ 75,298	$ 94,122	$101,652	$105,417	$376,488
EBITDA	$ 43,961	$ 54,951	$ 59,348	$ 61,546	$219,806
Federal income tax	$ 13,971	$ 17,463	$ 18,860	$ 19,559	$ 69,853
State income tax	$ 2,117	$ 2,646	$ 2,858	$ 2,963	$ 10,584
Interest expense	$ 2,092	$ 2,053	$ 2,013	$ 1,973	$ 8,131
Depreciation expense	$ 1,116	$ 1,116	$ 1,116	$ 1,116	$ 4,464
Net profit	$ 24,666	$ 31,673	$ 34,500	$ 35,934	$126,774

Profit and loss statement (third year)

Quarter	Q1	3 Q2	Q3	Q4	3
Sales	$138,143	$172,679	$186,493	$193,401	$690,716
Cost of goods sold	$ 6,959	$ 8,698	$ 9,394	$ 9,742	$ 34,794
Gross margin	95.00%	95.00%	95.00%	95.00%	95.00%
Operating income	$131,185	$163,981	$177,099	$183,658	$655,923
Expenses					
Payroll	$ 46,149	$ 57,686	$ 62,301	$ 64,609	$230,746
General and administrative	$ 5,451	$ 6,814	$ 7,359	$ 7,632	$ 27,256
Marketing expenses	$ 9,670	$ 12,088	$ 13,055	$ 13,538	$ 48,350
Professional fees and licensure	$ 1,591	$ 1,989	$ 2,148	$ 2,228	$ 7,957
Insurance costs	$ 551	$ 689	$ 744	$ 772	$ 2,756
Equipment maintenance costs	$ 2,420	$ 3,025	$ 3,267	$ 3,388	$ 12,100
Rent and utilities	$ 5,347	$ 6,684	$ 7,219	$ 7,486	$ 26,736
Miscellaneous costs	$ 414	$ 518	$ 559	$ 580	$ 2,072
Payroll taxes	$ 6,922	$ 8,653	$ 9,345	$ 9,691	$ 34,612
Total operating costs	$ 78,517	$ 98,146	$105,998	$109,924	$392,585
EBITDA	$ 52,668	$ 65,834	$ 71,101	$ 73,735	$263,338
Federal income tax	$ 16,887	$ 21,109	$ 22,798	$ 23,642	$ 84,437
State income tax	$ 2,559	$ 3,198	$ 3,454	$ 3,582	$ 12,793
Interest expense	$ 1,932	$ 1,889	$ 1,846	$ 1,802	$ 7,468
Depreciation expense	$ 1,116	$ 1,116	$ 1,116	$ 1,116	$ 4,464
Net profit	$ 30,174	$ 38,522	$ 41,887	$ 43,592	$154,175

7.11 Three Year Cash Flow Analysis

Cash flow analysis (first year)

Month	1	2	3	4	5	6	7
Cash from operations	$ 2,482	$ 3,597	$ 4,712	$ 5,827	$ 6,942	$ 8,057	$ 9,173
Cash from receivables	$ 0	$ 0	$ 0	$ 0	$ 0	$ 0	$ 0
Operating cash inflow	**$ 2,482**	**$ 3,597**	**$ 4,712**	**$ 5,827**	**$ 6,942**	**$ 8,057**	**$ 9,173**
Other cash inflows							
Equity investment	$ 10,000	$ 0	$ 0	$ 0	$ 0	$ 0	$ 0
Increased borrowings	$100,000	$ 0	$ 0	$ 0	$ 0	$ 0	$ 0
Sales of business assets	$ 0	$ 0	$ 0	$ 0	$ 0	$ 0	$ 0
A/P increases	$ 3,159	$ 3,159	$ 3,159	$ 3,159	$ 3,159	$ 3,159	$ 3,159
Total other cash inflows	**$113,159**	**$ 3,159**	**$ 3,159**	**$ 3,159**	**$ 3,159**	**$ 3,159**	**$ 3,159**
Total cash inflow	**$115,640**	**$ 6,755**	**$ 7,870**	**$ 8,986**	**$10,101**	**$11,216**	**$12,331**
Cash outflows							
Repayment of principal	$ 517	$ 521	$ 525	$ 528	$ 532	$ 536	$ 540
A/P decreases	$ 2,075	$ 2,075	$ 2,075	$ 2,075	$ 2,075	$ 2,075	$ 2,075
A/R increases	$ 0	$ 0	$ 0	$ 0	$ 0	$ 0	$ 0
Asset purchases	$ 57,500	$ 0	$ 0	$ 0	$ 0	$ 0	$ 0
Dividends	$ 0	$ 0	$ 0	$ 0	$ 0	$ 0	$ 0
Total cash outflows	**$ 60,092**	**$ 2,595**	**$ 2,599**	**$ 2,603**	**$ 2,607**	**$ 2,611**	**$ 2,615**
Net cash flow	**$ 55,549**	**$ 4,160**	**$ 5,271**	**$ 6,382**	**$ 7,494**	**$ 8,605**	**$ 9,716**
Cash balance	**$ 55,549**	**$59,709**	**$64,980**	**$71,362**	**$78,856**	**$87,461**	**$97,176**

Cash flow analysis (first year cont.)

Month	8	9	10	11	12	1
Cash from operations	$ 10,288	$ 11,403	$ 12,518	$ 13,634	$14,749	$103,382
Cash from receivables	$ 0	$ 0	$ 0	$ 0	$ 0	$ 0
Operating cash inflow	**$ 10,288**	**$ 11,403**	**$ 12,518**	**$ 13,634**	**$14,749**	**$103,382**
Other cash inflows						
Equity investment	$ 0	$ 0	$ 0	$ 0	$ 0	$ 10,000
Increased borrowings	$ 0	$ 0	$ 0	$ 0	$ 0	$100,000
Sales of business assets	$ 0	$ 0	$ 0	$ 0	$ 0	$ 0
A/P increases	$ 3,159	$ 3,159	$ 3,159	$ 3,159	$ 3,159	$ 37,902
Total other cash inflows	**$ 3,159**	**$ 3,159**	**$ 3,159**	**$ 3,159**	**$ 3,159**	**$147,902**
Total cash inflow	**$ 13,446**	**$ 14,562**	**$ 15,677**	**$ 16,792**	**$17,908**	**$251,284**
Cash outflows						
Repayment of principal	$ 545	$ 549	$ 553	$ 557	$ 561	$ 6,463
A/P decreases	$ 2,075	$ 2,075	$ 2,075	$ 2,075	$ 2,075	$ 24,897
A/R increases	$ 0	$ 0	$ 0	$ 0	$ 0	$ 0
Asset purchases	$ 0	$ 0	$ 0	$ 0	$ 0	$ 57,500
Dividends	$ 0	$ 0	$ 0	$ 0	$72,368	$ 72,368
Total cash outflows	**$ 2,619**	**$ 2,623**	**$ 2,627**	**$ 2,632**	**$75,004**	**$161,228**
Net cash flow	**$ 10,827**	**$ 11,938**	**$ 13,049**	**$ 14,161**	**−$57,096**	**$ 90,056**
Cash balance	**$108,004**	**$119,942**	**$132,991**	**$147,152**	**$90,056**	**$ 90,056**

Cash flow analysis (second year)

Quarter	Q1	2 Q2	Q3	Q4	2
Cash from operations	$26,248	$32,810	$35,434	$ 36,747	$131,238
Cash from receivables	$ 0	$ 0	$ 0	$ 0	$ 0
Operating cash inflow	**$26,248**	**$32,810**	**$35,434**	**$ 36,747**	**$131,238**
Other cash inflows					
Equity investment	$ 0	$ 0	$ 0	$ 0	$ 0
Increased borrowings	$ 0	$ 0	$ 0	$ 0	$ 0
Sales of business assets	$ 0	$ 0	$ 0	$ 0	$ 0
A/P increases	$ 8,717	$10,897	$11,769	$ 12,204	$ 43,587
Total other cash inflows	**$ 8,717**	**$10,897**	**$11,769**	**$ 12,204**	**$ 43,587**
Total cash inflow	**$34,965**	**$43,706**	**$47,203**	**$ 48,951**	**$174,825**
Cash outflows					
Repayment of principal	$ 1,708	$ 1,747	$ 1,787	$ 1,827	$ 7,070
A/P decreases	$ 5,975	$ 7,469	$ 8,067	$ 8,365	$ 29,876
A/R increases	$ 0	$ 0	$ 0	$ 0	$ 0
Asset purchases	$ 6,562	$ 8,202	$ 8,859	$ 9,187	$ 32,810
Dividends	$18,373	$22,967	$24,804	$ 25,723	$ 91,867
Total cash outflows	**$32,619**	**$40,385**	**$43,516**	**$ 45,102**	**$161,622**
Net cash flow	**$ 2,346**	**$ 3,321**	**$ 3,687**	**$ 3,849**	**$ 13,203**
Cash balance	**$92,402**	**$95,723**	**$99,410**	**$103,259**	**$103,259**

Cash flow analysis (third year)

Quarter	Q1	3 Q2	Q3	Q4	3
Cash from operations	$ 31,728	$ 39,660	$ 42,833	$ 44,419	$158,639
Cash from receivables	$ 0	$ 0	$ 0	$ 0	$ 0
Operating cash inflow	**$ 31,728**	**$ 39,660**	**$ 42,833**	**$ 44,419**	**$158,639**
Other cash inflows					
Equity investment	$ 0	$ 0	$ 0	$ 0	$ 0
Increased borrowings	$ 0	$ 0	$ 0	$ 0	$ 0
Sales of business assets	$ 0	$ 0	$ 0	$ 0	$ 0
A/P increases	$ 10,025	$ 12,531	$ 13,534	$ 14,035	$ 50,125
Total other cash inflows	**$ 10,025**	**$ 12,531**	**$ 13,534**	**$ 14,035**	**$ 50,125**
Total cash inflow	**$ 41,753**	**$ 52,191**	**$ 56,366**	**$ 58,454**	**$208,765**
Cash outflows					
Repayment of principal	$ 1,869	$ 1,911	$ 1,954	$ 1,999	$ 7,733
A/P decreases	$ 7,170	$ 8,963	$ 9,680	$ 10,038	$ 35,852
A/R increases	$ 0	$ 0	$ 0	$ 0	$ 0
Asset purchases	$ 7,932	$ 9,915	$ 10,708	$ 11,105	$ 39,660
Dividends	$ 22,209	$ 27,762	$ 29,983	$ 31,093	$111,047
Total cash outflows	**$ 39,181**	**$ 48,551**	**$ 52,325**	**$ 54,235**	**$194,292**
Net cash flow	**$ 2,572**	**$ 3,640**	**$ 4,041**	**$ 4,219**	**$ 14,473**
Cash balance	**$105,832**	**$109,472**	**$113,513**	**$117,732**	**$117,732**

Commercial Bank

Bronx Community Bank

66697 East 187th St.
Bronx, NY 10451

BizPlanDb.com

The purpose of this business plan is to raise $10,000,000 for the development of the Bronx Community Bank, founded by Charles Doherty.

1.0 EXECUTIVE SUMMARY

The purpose of this business plan is to raise $10,000,000 for the development of a commercial bank while showcasing the expected financials and operations over the next three years. Bronx Community Bank is a New York-based corporation that will provide traditional commercial banking services for its investors in its targeted market. The Company was founded by Charles Doherty.

1.1 The Services

As stated above, the Company will act in a traditional banking capacity by offering loans, checking accounts, savings accounts, and other financial products normally associated with banks. At this time, Mr. Doherty is securing the capital that is required in order to receive a banking license from the U.S. Federal Reserve. The Founder is also undergoing the process of acquiring the needed licensure to operate this business.

The third section of the business plan will further describe the underwriting services and investment management services offered by Bronx Community Bank.

1.2 Financing

At this time, the Company is seeking to raise $10,000,000 for the development of Bronx Community Bank's operations. Mr. Doherty is seeking to sell an 80% ownership interest in the business in exchange for this capital. 85% of the invested capital will be used for direct investments into the firm's investments. Briefly, the capital will be used as follows:

- Financing for lending activities.

- Development of the Company's initial branch.

- General working capital.

1.3 Mission Statement

Management's mission is to provide the greater New York metropolitan area with an extensive line of banking and financial services that are affordable and convenient.

1.4 Management Team

The Company was founded by Charles Doherty. Mr. Doherty has more than 10 years of experience in the commercial banking industry. Through his expertise, he will be able to bring the operations of the business to profitability within its first year of operations.

1.5 Income Forecasts

Mr. Doherty expects a strong rate of growth at the start of operations. Below are the expected financials over the next three years.

Proforma profit and loss (yearly)

Year	1	2	3
Sales	$3,748,770	$4,498,524	$5,263,273
Operating costs	$1,596,763	$1,924,691	$2,005,350
EBITDA	$1,964,569	$2,348,906	$2,994,759
Taxes, interest, and depreciation	$ 781,786	$ 927,834	$1,173,259
Net profit	$1,182,783	$1,421,072	$1,821,501

Sales, operating costs, and profit forecast

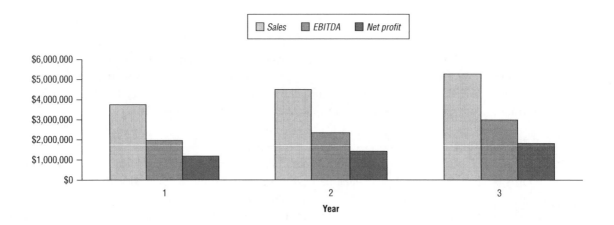

1.6 Expansion Plan

The Company plans on positioning itself toward becoming a leading financial services provider among middle-income people. Over time, Bronx Community Bank intends to not only expand its geographic reach by establishing relationships and offices in other major metropolitan areas but also by acquiring banks.

2.0 COMPANY AND FINANCING SUMMARY

2.1 Registered Name and Corporate Structure

Bronx Community Bank is registered as a corporation in the State of New York.

2.2 Required Funds

At this time, Bronx Community Bank requires $10,000,000 of equity funds. Below is a breakdown of how these funds will be used:

Projected startup costs

Initial lease payments and deposits	$ 50,000
Working capital	$ 1,000,000
FF&E	$ 125,000
Leasehold improvements	$ 100,000
Security deposits	$ 100,000
Insurance	$ 25,000
Initial bank capital	$ 8,500,000
Marketing budget	$ 75,000
Miscellaneous and unforeseen costs	$ 25,000
Total startup costs	**$10,000,000**

2.3 Investor Equity

At this time, Mr. Doherty is seeking to sell an 80% interest in Bronx Community Bank in exchange for the capital sought in this business plan. Please reference the Company's private placement memorandum regarding more information regarding the Company's fee and ownership structure.

2.4 Management Equity

Charles Doherty currently owns 100% of Bronx Community Bank, Inc.

2.5 Exit Strategies

The Management has planned for three possible exit strategies. The first strategy would be to sell the Company to a larger entity at a significant premium. Since the financial management and commercial banking industry maintains a very low-risk profile once the business is established, the Management feels that the Company could be sold for ten to fifteen times earnings.

The second exit scenario would entail selling a portion of the Company via an initial public offering (or "IPO"). After a detailed analysis, it was found that the Company could sell for twenty to thirty times earnings on the open market depending on the business's annual growth rate and strength of earnings. However, taking a company public involves significant legal red tape. Bronx Community Bank would be bound by the significant legal framework of the Sarbanes-Oxley Act in addition to the legal requirements set forth in form S1 of the Securities and Exchange Commission. The Company would also have to comply with the Securities Act of 1933 and the Exchange Act of 1934.

The last exit scenario would involve the use of a private placement memorandum to raise capital from private sources. This is also a significantly expensive process that requires the assistance of both an experienced securities law firm and an investment bank. Funds would be raised from private equity and merchant banking sources in exchange for a percentage of the Company's stock.

2.6 Investor Divesture

This will be discussed during negotiations.

3.0 BANKING OPERATIONS

Below is a description of the commercial banking services offered by the company.

3.1 Customer Accounts

The primary service offered by Bronx Community Bank is the management of checking accounts, savings accounts, and money market accounts. The bank, in turn, will use these deposits for financing customer loans and for making acquisitions of debt instruments in the secondary markets. The Company will provide Visa/MasterCard branded debit cards that can be used in any ATM or at stores that accept EBT payments.

At all times, the Company will comply with the myriad of federal, state, and central bank regulations (specifically Regulation U) that guide the operations of thrifts, trusts, and financial companies.

3.2 Loans

Through its branches, the business will be able to provide its customers with a variety of lending products, including the following:

- First-time homebuyer mortgages

- Second mortgages

- Home equity lines of credit/loans

- Commercial Mortgages

- Mortgage refinancing

- Automotive Loans

- Marine Loans

- Business Loans (SBA and traditional commercial loans)

- Student Loans

- Debt Consolidation

- Credit Cards (Secured, Unsecured, and Prepaid Cards)

4.0 STRATEGIC AND MARKET ANALYSIS

4.1 Economic Outlook

This section of the analysis will detail the economic climate, the banking industry, the customer profile, and the competition that the business will face as it progresses through its business operations.

Currently, the economic market condition in the United States is sluggish. This slowdown in the economy has also greatly impacted real estate sales, which has halted to historical lows. Many economists expect that this recession will continue for a significant period of time, at which point the economy will begin a prolonged recovery and sluggish growth period. However, Bronx Community Bank intends to only work with qualified borrowers as it pertains to their lending needs. As such, this, along with the protections provided by the Federal Reserve, will ensure that the business is able to remain profitable and cash flow positive at all times.

4.2 Industry Analysis

In the United States there are over 8,000 businesses that operate as depository credit institutions. Among these business, aggregates receipts from closed loan fees, interest, and other banking fees over each of the last five years has been in excess of $400 billion dollars of interest revenue. These businesses employ over 2.2 million people and provide gross annual payrolls in excess of $167 billion dollars.

The Internet has revolutionized the way that many lenders do business. It is not uncommon for small lenders (and thrifts), like Bronx Community Bank to lend among a broad geographical base and to a wide variety of clients that have varying incomes and credit qualities. Additionally, since the Internet has created a method of receiving information at a much faster rate, information relating to the credit quality of borrowers is readily available. The Company will pride itself on its ability to make fast credit decisions for clients.

4.3 Customer Profile

The Company has established several lending procedures that will ensure that the Company's default rate is less than 1.5% of the Company's total loan portfolio. Among people that will use the Company's services for borrowing money, Management has developed the following demographic profile:

- Male or Female

- Between the ages of 28 and 65

- Household income of $35,000+

- Will borrow for an automotive or home purchase

4.4 Competition

There is a tremendous amount of competition among lending companies to acquire and finance loans. Not only will the business face competition from other loan financiers but from traditional banks and finance companies as well.

Bronx Community Bank understands the complicated borrowing needs of low-, middle- and high-income borrowers. As such, the Company will differentiate itself by providing loans to these customers while concurrently using other factors (outside of the credit report) to determine whether or not to lend to a customer.

5.0 MARKETING PLAN

Bronx Community Bank intends to maintain an extensive marketing campaign that will ensure maximum visibility for the business in its targeted market. Below is an overview of the marketing strategies and objectives of Bronx Community Bank.

5.1 Marketing Objectives

- Establish relationships with industrial registered banks within the United States.

- Work closely with mortgage banking companies and mortgage brokerage firms that will work on the Company's behalf as it relates to closing appropriate loans.

5.2 Marketing Strategies

Management intends to use a number of marketing strategies to generate depositors and borrowers for Bronx Community Bank. The Company intends to use traditional print and media advertising as well as online sales tactics which will further increase visibility of the bank.

The business will regularly distribute a number of flyers while concurrently engaging in a massive grand opening in order to inform potential depositors and borrowers of the Company's banking operations. The grand opening period will last three to six months depending on the success of the marketing campaign. Additionally, higher interest rates and lower loan rates will be used in order to convince people to switch their checking accounts and loan needs to Bronx Community Bank, Inc.

As discussed above, the business intends to develop ongoing affinity relationships with mortgage banks and mortgage brokers that will solicit business on behalf of their clients. This is of an immense importance to the Company's marketing strategy as the bank will be able to source loans from anywhere within the United States once mortgage bankers/brokers see that Bronx Community Bank is able to make quick lending decisions to qualified borrowers.

5.3 Pricing

Below is the preliminary pricing schedule that Management intends to use from the onset of operations.

- Closed loans will yield approximately 5% of the borrowed amount.

- The Company will also receive 4% to 8% of the interest rate generated from each loan currently managed by Bronx Community Bank, Inc.

6.0 ORGANIZATIONAL PLAN AND PERSONNEL SUMMARY

6.1 Corporate Organization

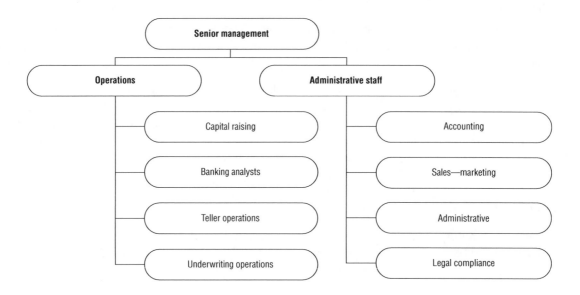

6.2 Organizational Budget

Personnel plan—yearly

Year	1	2	3
Senior management	$ 250,000	$ 257,500	$ 265,225
Vice presidents	$ 500,000	$ 618,000	$ 636,540
Accountants	$ 85,000	$ 175,100	$ 180,353
Customer service	$ 130,000	$ 167,375	$ 172,396
Administrative	$ 90,000	$ 92,700	$ 95,481
Total	**$1,055,000**	**$1,310,675**	**$1,349,995**

Numbers of personnel

Senior management	2	2	2
Vice presidents	5	6	6
Accountants	1	2	2
Customer service	4	5	5
Administrative	2	2	2
Totals	**14**	**17**	**17**

Personnel expense breakdown

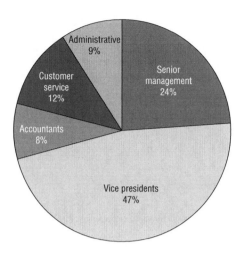

7.0 FINANCIAL PLAN

7.1 Underlying Assumptions

The Company has based its proforma financial statements on the following:

- Commercial Bank will have an annual revenue growth rate of 20% per year.

- The Owner will acquire $10,000,000 of equity funds to develop the business.

- The Company will earn a compounded annual return of 30% on its proprietary loan based investment trading portfolio.

7.2 Sensitivity Analysis

The Company's revenues are sensitive to the overall condition of the financial markets. Revenues derived from the lending portfolio are directly tied to the prevailing prime credit interest rate. As such, the Company must strive to invest in high credit quality investments that have "staying power" during times of economic recession or pullback. Management will enact stringent credit control and screening policies to ensure that losses resulting from defaulted loans are kept below 1.5% of the Company's closed loan portfolio.

7.3 Source of Funds

Financing

Equity contributions

Investor(s)	$ 10,000,000.00
Total equity financing	**$10,000,000.00**
Banks and lenders	
Total debt financing	**$ 0.00**
Total financing	**$10,000,000.00**

7.4 General Assumptions

General assumptions

Year	1	2	3
Short term interest rate	9.5%	9.5%	9.5%
Long term interest rate	10.0%	10.0%	10.0%
Federal tax rate	33.0%	33.0%	33.0%
State tax rate	5.0%	5.0%	5.0%
Personnel taxes	15.0%	15.0%	15.0%

7.5 Profit and Loss Statements

Proforma profit and loss (yearly)

Year	1	2	3
Sales	**$3,748,770**	**$4,498,524**	**$5,263,273**
Cost of goods sold	$ 187,439	$ 224,926	$ 263,164
Gross margin	95.00%	95.00%	95.00%
Operating income	**$3,561,332**	**$4,273,598**	**$5,000,109**
Expenses			
Payroll	$1,055,000	$1,310,675	$1,349,995
General and administrative	$ 41,988	$ 43,668	$ 45,414
Marketing expenses	$ 37,488	$ 44,985	$ 52,633
Professional fees and licensure	$ 55,219	$ 56,876	$ 58,582
Insurance costs	$ 61,987	$ 65,086	$ 68,341
Travel and vehicle costs	$ 77,596	$ 85,356	$ 93,891
Rent and utilities	$ 64,250	$ 67,463	$ 70,836
Miscellaneous costs	$ 44,985	$ 53,982	$ 63,159
Payroll taxes	$ 158,250	$ 196,601	$ 202,499
Total operating costs	**$1,596,763**	**$1,924,691**	**$2,005,350**
EBITDA	**$1,964,569**	**$2,348,906**	**$2,994,759**
Federal income tax	$ 648,308	$ 775,139	$ 988,271
State income tax	$ 98,228	$ 117,445	$ 149,738
Interest expense	$ 0	$ 0	$ 0
Depreciation expenses	$ 35,250	$ 35,250	$ 35,250
Net profit	**$1,182,783**	**$1,421,072**	**$1,821,501**
Profit margin	**31.55%**	**31.59%**	**34.61%**

Sales, operating costs, and profit forecast

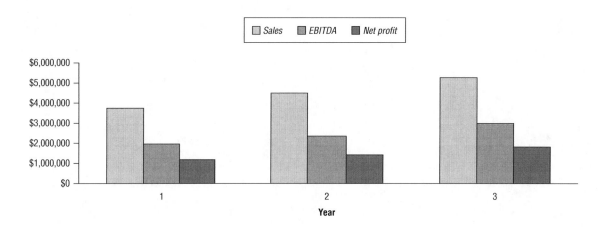

7.6 Cash Flow Analysis

Proforma cash flow analysis—yearly

Year	1	2	3
Cash from operations	$ 1,218,033	$ 1,456,322	$ 1,856,751
Cash from receivables	$ 0	$ 0	$ 0
Operating cash inflow	**$ 1,218,033**	**$ 1,456,322**	**$ 1,856,751**
Other cash inflows			
Equity investment	$10,000,000	$ 0	$ 0
Increased borrowings	$ 0	$ 0	$ 0
Sales of business assets	$ 0	$ 0	$ 0
A/P increases	$ 37,902	$ 43,587	$ 50,125
Total other cash inflows	**$10,037,902**	**$ 43,587**	**$ 50,125**
Total cash inflow	**$11,255,935**	**$ 1,499,909**	**$ 1,906,876**
Cash outflows			
Repayment of principal	$ 0	$ 0	$ 0
A/P decreases	$ 24,897	$ 29,876	$ 35,852
A/R increases	$ 0	$ 0	$ 0
Asset purchases	$ 8,875,500	$ 873,793	$ 1,114,050
Dividends	$ 0	$ 509,713	$ 649,863
Total cash outflows	**$ 8,899,897**	**$ 1,413,382**	**$ 1,799,765**
Net cash flow	**$ 2,356,038**	**$ 86,527**	**$ 107,111**
Cash balance	**$ 2,356,038**	**$ 2,442,565**	**$ 2,549,676**

Proforma cash flow (yearly)

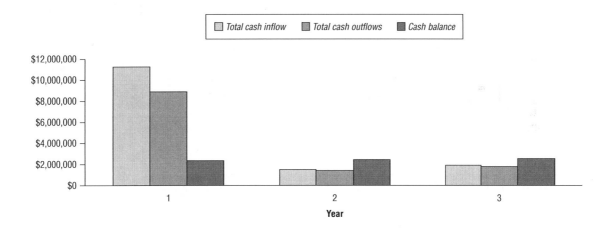

7.7 Balance Sheet

Proforma balance sheet—yearly

Year	1	2	3
Assets			
Cash	$ 2,356,038	$ 2,442,565	$ 2,549,676
Amortized development/expansion costs	$ 250,000	$ 337,379	$ 448,784
Loan portfolio	$10,200,000	$14,831,659	$21,376,311
FF&E	$ 125,000	$ 212,379	$ 323,784
Accumulated depreciation	($ 35,250)	($ 70,500)	($ 105,750)
Total assets	**$12,895,788**	**$17,753,482**	**$24,592,805**
Liabilities and equity			
Accounts payable	$ 13,005	$ 26,716	$ 40,990
Long term liabilities	$ 0	$ 0	$ 0
Other liabilities	$ 0	$ 0	$ 0
Total liabilities	**$ 13,005**	**$ 26,716**	**$ 40,990**
Net worth	**$12,882,783**	**$17,726,766**	**$24,551,816**
Total liabilities and equity	**$12,895,788**	**$17,753,482**	**$24,592,805**

Proforma balance sheet

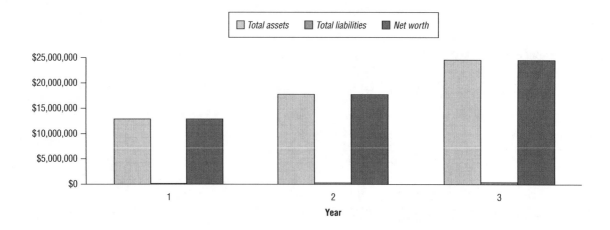

7.8 Breakeven Analysis

Monthly break even analysis

Year	1	2	3
Monthly revenue	$ 140,067	$ 168,833	$ 175,908
Yearly revenue	$1,680,803	$2,025,991	$2,110,895

Break even analysis

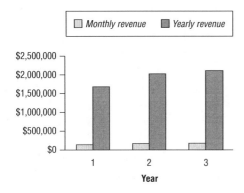

7.9 Business Ratios

Business ratios—yearly

Year	1	2	3
Sales			
Sales growth	0.00%	20.00%	17.00%
Gross margin	95.00%	95.00%	95.00%
Financials			
Profit margin	31.55%	31.59%	34.61%
Assets to liabilities	991.60	664.53	599.98
Equity to liabilities	990.60	663.53	598.98
Assets to equity	1.00	1.00	1.00
Liquidity			
Acid test	181.16	91.43	62.20
Cash to assets	0.18	0.14	0.10

7.10 Three Year Profit and Loss Statement

Profit and loss statement (first year)

Months	1	2	3	4	5	6	7
Sales	$310,500	$310,845	$311,190	$311,535	$311,880	$312,225	$312,570
Cost of goods sold	$ 15,525	$ 15,542	$ 15,560	$ 15,577	$ 15,594	$ 15,611	$ 15,629
Gross margin	95.00%	95.00%	95.00%	95.00%	95.00%	95.00%	95.00%
Operating income	$294,975	$295,303	$295,631	$295,958	$296,286	$296,614	$296,942
Expenses							
Payroll	$ 87,917	$ 87,917	$ 87,917	$ 87,917	$ 87,917	$ 87,917	$ 87,917
General and administrative	$ 3,499	$ 3,499	$ 3,499	$ 3,499	$ 3,499	$ 3,499	$ 3,499
Marketing expenses	$ 3,124	$ 3,124	$ 3,124	$ 3,124	$ 3,124	$ 3,124	$ 3,124
Professional fees and licensure	$ 4,602	$ 4,602	$ 4,602	$ 4,602	$ 4,602	$ 4,602	$ 4,602
Insurance costs	$ 5,166	$ 5,166	$ 5,166	$ 5,166	$ 5,166	$ 5,166	$ 5,166
Travel and vehicle costs	$ 6,466	$ 6,466	$ 6,466	$ 6,466	$ 6,466	$ 6,466	$ 6,466
Rent and utilities	$ 5,354	$ 5,354	$ 5,354	$ 5,354	$ 5,354	$ 5,354	$ 5,354
Miscellaneous costs	$ 3,749	$ 3,749	$ 3,749	$ 3,749	$ 3,749	$ 3,749	$ 3,749
Payroll taxes	$ 13,188	$ 13,188	$ 13,188	$ 13,188	$ 13,188	$ 13,188	$ 13,188
Total operating costs	$133,064	$133,064	$133,064	$133,064	$133,064	$133,064	$133,064
EBITDA	$161,911	$162,239	$162,567	$162,895	$163,222	$163,550	$163,878
Federal income tax	$ 53,697	$ 53,757	$ 53,817	$ 53,876	$ 53,936	$ 53,996	$ 54,055
State income tax	$ 8,136	$ 8,145	$ 8,154	$ 8,163	$ 8,172	$ 8,181	$ 8,190
Interest expense	$ 0	$ 0	$ 0	$ 0	$ 0	$ 0	$ 0
Depreciation expense	$ 2,938	$ 2,938	$ 2,938	$ 2,938	$ 2,938	$ 2,938	$ 2,938
Net profit	$ 97,140	$ 97,400	$ 97,659	$ 97,918	$ 98,177	$ 98,436	$ 98,695

Profit and loss statement (first year cont.)

Month	8	9	10	11	12	1
Sales	$312,915	$313,260	$313,605	$313,950	$314,295	$3,748,770
Cost of goods sold	$ 15,646	$ 15,663	$ 15,680	$ 15,698	$ 15,715	$ 187,439
Gross margin	95.00%	95.00%	95.00%	95.00%	95.00%	95.0%
Operating income	$297,269	$297,597	$297,925	$298,253	$298,580	$3,561,332
Expenses						
Payroll	$ 87,917	$ 87,917	$ 87,917	$ 87,917	$ 87,917	$1,055,000
General and administrative	$ 3,499	$ 3,499	$ 3,499	$ 3,499	$ 3,499	$ 41,988
Marketing expenses	$ 3,124	$ 3,124	$ 3,124	$ 3,124	$ 3,124	$ 37,488
Professional fees and licensure	$ 4,602	$ 4,602	$ 4,602	$ 4,602	$ 4,602	$ 55,219
Insurance costs	$ 5,166	$ 5,166	$ 5,166	$ 5,166	$ 5,166	$ 61,987
Travel and vehicle costs	$ 6,466	$ 6,466	$ 6,466	$ 6,466	$ 6,466	$ 77,596
Rent and utilities	$ 5,354	$ 5,354	$ 5,354	$ 5,354	$ 5,354	$ 64,250
Miscellaneous costs	$ 3,749	$ 3,749	$ 3,749	$ 3,749	$ 3,749	$ 44,985
Payroll taxes	$ 13,188	$ 13,188	$ 13,188	$ 13,188	$ 13,188	$ 158,250
Total operating costs	$133,064	$133,064	$133,064	$133,064	$133,064	$1,596,763
EBITDA	$164,206	$164,533	$164,861	$165,189	$165,517	$1,964,569
Federal income tax	$ 54,115	$ 54,175	$ 54,234	$ 54,294	$ 54,354	$ 648,308
State income tax	$ 8,199	$ 8,208	$ 8,217	$ 8,226	$ 8,235	$ 98,228
Interest expense	$ 0	$ 0	$ 0	$ 0	$ 0	$ 0
Depreciation expense	$ 2,938	$ 2,938	$ 2,938	$ 2,938	$ 2,938	$ 35,250
Net profit	$ 98,954	$ 99,213	$ 99,472	$ 99,731	$ 99,990	$1,182,783

Profit and loss statement (second year)

Quarter	Q1	2 Q2	Q3	Q4	2
Sales	$899,705	$1,124,631	$1,214,601	$1,259,587	$4,498,524
Cost of goods sold	$ 44,985	$ 56,232	$ 60,730	$ 62,979	$ 224,926
Gross margin	95.0%	95.0%	95.0%	95.0%	95.0%
Operating income	$854,720	$1,068,399	$1,153,871	$1,196,607	$4,273,598
Expenses					
Payroll	$262,135	$ 327,669	$ 353,882	$ 366,989	$1,310,675
General and administrative	$ 8,734	$ 10,917	$ 11,790	$ 12,227	$ 43,668
Marketing expenses	$ 8,997	$ 11,246	$ 12,146	$ 12,596	$ 44,985
Professional fees and licensure	$ 11,375	$ 14,219	$ 15,356	$ 15,925	$ 56,876
Insurance costs	$ 13,017	$ 16,272	$ 17,573	$ 18,224	$ 65,086
Travel and vehicle costs	$ 17,071	$ 21,339	$ 23,046	$ 23,900	$ 85,356
Rent and utilities	$ 13,493	$ 16,866	$ 18,215	$ 18,890	$ 67,463
Miscellaneous costs	$ 10,796	$ 13,496	$ 14,575	$ 15,115	$ 53,982
Payroll taxes	$ 39,320	$ 49,150	$ 53,082	$ 55,048	$ 196,601
Total operating costs	$384,938	$ 481,173	$ 519,667	$ 538,914	$1,924,691
EBITDA	$469,781	$ 587,227	$ 634,205	$ 657,694	$2,348,906
Federal income tax	$155,028	$ 193,785	$ 209,288	$ 217,039	$ 775,139
State income tax	$ 23,489	$ 29,361	$ 31,710	$ 32,885	$ 117,445
Interest expense	$ 0	$ 0	$ 0	$ 0	$ 0
Depreciation expense	$ 8,813	$ 8,813	$ 8,813	$ 8,813	$ 35,250
Net profit	$282,452	$ 355,268	$ 384,394	$ 398,958	$1,421,072

Profit and loss statement (third year)

Quarter	Q1	3 Q2	Q3	Q4	3
Sales	$1,052,655	$1,315,818	$1,421,084	$1,473,716	$5,263,273
Cost of goods sold	$ 52,633	$ 65,791	$ 71,054	$ 73,686	$ 263,164
Gross margin	95.0%	95.0%	95.0%	95.0%	95.0%
Operating income	$1,000,022	$1,250,027	$1,350,030	$1,400,031	$5,000,109
Expenses					
Payroll	$ 269,999	$ 337,499	$ 364,499	$ 377,999	$1,349,995
General and administrative	$ 9,083	$ 11,354	$ 12,262	$ 12,716	$ 45,414
Marketing expenses	$ 10,527	$ 13,158	$ 14,211	$ 14,737	$ 52,633
Professional fees and licensure	$ 11,716	$ 14,645	$ 15,817	$ 16,403	$ 58,582
Insurance costs	$ 13,668	$ 17,085	$ 18,452	$ 19,834	$ 68,341
Travel and vehicle costs	$ 18,778	$ 23,473	$ 25,351	$ 26,290	$ 93,891
Rent and utilities	$ 14,167	$ 17,709	$ 19,126	$ 19,834	$ 70,836
Miscellaneous costs	$ 12,632	$ 15,790	$ 17,053	$ 17,685	$ 63,159
Payroll taxes	$ 40,500	$ 50,625	$ 54,675	$ 56,700	$ 202,499
Total operating costs	$ 401,070	$ 501,338	$ 541,445	$ 561,498	$2,005,350
EBITDA	$ 598,952	$ 748,690	$ 808,585	$ 838,533	$2,994,759
Federal income tax	$ 197,654	$ 247,068	$ 266,833	$ 276,716	$ 988,271
State income tax	$ 29,948	$ 37,434	$ 40,429	$ 41,927	$ 149,738
Interest expense	$ 0	$ 0	$ 0	$ 0	$ 0
Depreciation expense	$ 8,813	$ 8,813	$ 8,813	$ 8,813	$ 35,250
Net profit	$ 362,538	$ 455,375	$ 492,510	$ 511,078	$1,821,501

7.11 Three Year Cash Flow Analysis

Cash flow analysis (first year)

Month	1	2	3	4	5	6	7
Cash from operations	$ 100,078	$ 100,337	$ 100,596	$ 100,855	$ 101,114	$ 101,373	$ 101,632
Cash from receivables	$ 0	$ 0	$ 0	$ 0	$ 0	$ 0	$ 0
Operating cash inflow	**$ 100,078**	**$ 100,337**	**$ 100,596**	**$ 100,855**	**$ 101,114**	**$ 101,373**	**$ 101,632**
Other cash inflows							
Equity investment	$10,000,000	$ 0	$ 0	$ 0	$ 0	$ 0	$ 0
Increased borrowings	$ 0	$ 0	$ 0	$ 0	$ 0	$ 0	$ 0
Sales of business assets	$ 0	$ 0	$ 0	$ 0	$ 0	$ 0	$ 0
A/P increases	$ 3,159	$ 3,159	$ 3,159	$ 3,159	$ 3,159	$ 3,159	$ 3,159
Total other cash inflows	**$10,003,159**	**$ 3,159**	**$ 3,159**	**$ 3,159**	**$ 3,159**	**$ 3,159**	**$ 3,159**
Total cash inflow	**$10,103,236**	**$ 103,496**	**$ 103,755**	**$ 104,014**	**$ 104,273**	**$ 104,532**	**$ 104,791**
Cash outflows							
Repayment of principal	$ 0	$ 0	$ 0	$ 0	$ 0	$ 0	$ 0
A/P decreases	$ 2,075	$ 2,075	$ 2,075	$ 2,075	$ 2,075	$ 2,075	$ 2,075
A/R increases	$ 0	$ 0	$ 0	$ 0	$ 0	$ 0	$ 0
Asset purchases	$ 8,875,000	$ 0	$ 0	$ 0	$ 0	$ 0	$ 0
Dividends	$ 0	$ 0	$ 0	$ 0	$ 0	$ 0	$ 0
Total cash outflows	**$ 8,877,075**	**$ 2,075**	**$ 2,075**	**$ 2,075**	**$ 2,075**	**$ 2,075**	**$ 2,075**
Net cash flow	**$ 1,226,162**	**$ 101,421**	**$ 101,680**	**$ 101,939**	**$ 102,198**	**$ 102,457**	**$ 102,716**
Cash balance	**$ 1,226,162**	**$1,327,582**	**$1,429,262**	**$1,531,201**	**$1,633,399**	**$1,735,856**	**$1,838,572**

Cash flow analysis (first year cont.)

Month	8	9	10	11	12	1
Cash from operations	$ 101,891	$ 102,150	$ 102,409	$ 102,668	$ 102,927	$ 1,218,033
Cash from receivables	$ 0	$ 0	$ 0	$ 0	$ 0	$ 0
Operating cash inflow	**$ 101,891**	**$ 102,150**	**$ 102,409**	**$ 102,668**	**$ 102,927**	**$ 1,218,033**
Other cash inflows						
Equity investment	$ 0	$ 0	$ 0	$ 0	$ 0	$10,000,000
Increased borrowings	$ 0	$ 0	$ 0	$ 0	$ 0	$ 0
Sales of business assets	$ 0	$ 0	$ 0	$ 0	$ 0	$ 0
A/P increases	$ 3,159	$ 3,159	$ 3,159	$ 3,159	$ 3,159	$ 37,902
Total other cash inflows	**$ 3,159**	**$ 3,159**	**$ 3,159**	**$ 3,159**	**$ 3,159**	**$10,037,902**
Total cash inflow	**$ 105,050**	**$ 105,309**	**$ 105,568**	**$ 105,827**	**$ 106,086**	**$11,255,935**
Cash outflows						
Repayment of principal	$ 0	$ 0	$ 0	$ 0	$ 0	$ 0
A/P decreases	$ 2,075	$ 2,075	$ 2,075	$ 2,075	$ 2,075	$ 24,897
A/R increases	$ 0	$ 0	$ 0	$ 0	$ 0	$ 0
Asset purchases	$ 0	$ 0	$ 0	$ 0	$ 0	$ 8,875,000
Dividends	$ 0	$ 0	$ 0	$ 0	$ 0	$ 0
Total cash outflows	**$ 2,075**	**$ 2,075**	**$ 2,075**	**$ 2,075**	**$ 2,075**	**$ 8,899,897**
Net cash flow	**$ 102,975**	**$ 103,234**	**$ 103,493**	**$ 103,752**	**$ 104,011**	**$ 2,356,038**
Cash balance	**$1,941,547**	**$2,044,781**	**$2,148,274**	**$2,252,026**	**$2,356,038**	**$ 2,356,038**

Cash flow analysis (second year)

Quarter	Q1	2 Q2	Q3	Q4	2
Cash from operations	$ 291,264	$ 364,081	$ 393,207	$ 407,770	$ 1,456,322
Cash from receivables	$ 0	$ 0	$ 0	$ 0	$ 0
Operating cash inflow	**$ 291,264**	**$ 364,081**	**$ 393,207**	**$ 407,770**	**$1,456,322**
Other cash inflows					
Equity investment	$ 0	$ 0	$ 0	$ 0	$ 0
Increased borrowings	$ 0	$ 0	$ 0	$ 0	$ 0
Sales of business assets	$ 0	$ 0	$ 0	$ 0	$ 0
A/P increases	$ 8,717	$ 10,897	$ 11,769	$ 12,204	$ 43,587
Total other cash inflows	**$ 8,717**	**$ 10,897**	**$ 11,769**	**$ 12,204**	**$ 43,587**
Total cash inflow	**$ 299,982**	**$ 374,977**	**$ 404,976**	**$ 419,975**	**$1,499,909**
Cash outflows					
Repayment of principal	$ 0	$ 0	$ 0	$ 0	$ 0
A/P decreases	$ 5,975	$ 7,469	$ 8,067	$ 8,365	$ 29,876
A/R increases	$ 0	$ 0	$ 0	$ 0	$ 0
Asset purchases	$ 174,759	$ 218,448	$ 235,924	$ 244,662	$ 873,793
Dividends	$ 101,943	$ 127,428	$ 137,622	$ 142,720	$ 509,713
Total cash outflows	**$ 282,676**	**$ 353,346**	**$ 381,613**	**$ 395,747**	**$1,413,382**
Net cash flow	**$ 17,305**	**$ 21,632**	**$ 23,362**	**$ 24,228**	**$ 86,527**
Cash balance	**$2,373,343**	**$2,394,975**	**$2,418,337**	**$2,442,565**	**$2,442,565**

Cash flow analysis (third year)

Quarter	Q1	3 Q2	Q3	Q4	3
Cash from operations	$ 371,350	$ 464,188	$ 501,323	$ 519,890	$ 1,856,751
Cash from receivables	$ 0	$ 0	$ 0	$ 0	$ 0
Operating cash inflow	**$ 371,350**	**$ 464,188**	**$ 501,323**	**$ 519,890**	**$1,856,751**
Other cash inflows					
Equity investment	$ 0	$ 0	$ 0	$ 0	$ 0
Increased borrowings	$ 0	$ 0	$ 0	$ 0	$ 0
Sales of business assets	$ 0	$ 0	$ 0	$ 0	$ 0
A/P increases	$ 10,025	$ 12,531	$ 13,534	$ 14,035	$ 50,125
Total other cash inflows	**$ 10,025**	**$ 12,531**	**$ 13,534**	**$ 14,035**	**$ 50,125**
Total cash inflow	**$ 381,375**	**$ 476,719**	**$ 514,857**	**$ 533,925**	**$1,906,876**
Cash outflows					
Repayment of principal	$ 0	$ 0	$ 0	$ 0	$ 0
A/P decreases	$ 7,170	$ 8,963	$ 9,680	$ 10,038	$ 35,852
A/R increases	$ 0	$ 0	$ 0	$ 0	$ 0
Asset purchases	$ 222,810	$ 278,513	$ 300,794	$ 311,934	$1,114,050
Dividends	$ 129,973	$ 162,466	$ 175,463	$ 181,962	$ 649,863
Total cash outflows	**$ 359,953**	**$ 449,941**	**$ 485,937**	**$ 503,934**	**$1,799,765**
Net cash flow	**$ 21,422**	**$ 26,778**	**$ 28,920**	**$ 29,991**	**$ 107,111**
Cash balance	**$2,463,987**	**$2,490,765**	**$2,519,685**	**$2,549,676**	**$2,549,676**

Debt Collection Agency

Zerri Collection Agency

9963 Washington Ave.
New York, NY 10023

BizPlanDB.com

Zerri Collection Agency ("the Company") is a New York-based corporation that will arrange for the collection of debts on behalf of clients within the target market. The business will also provide credit advisory services as an ancillary service. The Company was founded by Tony Zerri.

1.0 EXECUTIVE SUMMARY

The purpose of this business plan is to raise $100,000 for the development of a debt collection and credit advisory firm while showcasing the expected financials and operations over the next three years. Zerri Collection Agency is a New York-based corporation that will arrange for the collection of debts on behalf of clients within the target market. The business will also provide credit advisory services as an ancillary service. The Company was founded by Tony Zerri.

1.1 The Services

Debt Collection Agency is the in the business of purchasing debt obligations from creditors that are "writing off" specific debts as a result of the debtors failure to remit payment. The Company will purchase these debt obligations at ten to twelve percent of their face value with the intent to settle the obligation with the debtor for a substantially reduced payment amount. The business will also act in a third party capacity for securing bad debts on behalf of clients for a fee equal to 30% of the amount collected.

The Company will also directly assist clients with credit advisory issues as most people that require debt collection also have issues with their credit profiles. Approximately 40% of the U.S. population has issues with their credit profiles and as such, the market for credit advisory services is extremely strong, especially in today's economic climate. The business will receive per hour fees from the client for these services.

The third section of the business plan will further describe the services offered by Zerri Collection Agency.

1.2 Financing

Mr. Zerri is seeking to raise $100,000 from a bank loan. The interest rate and loan agreement are to be further discussed during negotiation. This business plan assumes that the business will receive a 10-year loan with a 9% fixed interest rate. The financing will be used for the following:

- Development of the Company's office location.

- Financing for the first six months of operation.

- Capital to purchase FF&E and obtain the Company's licensure.

Mr. Zerri will contribute $10,000 to the venture.

1.3 Mission Statement

Zerri Collection Agency's mission is to become a recognized leader within its target market for assisting people with collecting bad debts.

1.4 Management Team

The Company was founded by Tony Zerri. Mr. Zerri has more than 10 years of experience in the lending industry. Through his expertise, he will be able to bring the operations of the business to profitability within its first year of operations.

1.5 Sales Forecasts

Mr. Zerri expects a strong rate of growth at the start of operations. Below are the expected financials over the next three years.

Proforma profit and loss (yearly)

Year	1	2	3
Sales	$727,920	$873,504	$1,022,000
Operating costs	$451,552	$471,057	$ 536,961
EBITDA	$209,642	$322,376	$ 391,355
Taxes, interest, and depreciation	$ 92,509	$131,651	$ 157,453
Net profit	$117,133	$190,724	$ 233,903

Sales, operating costs, and profit forecast

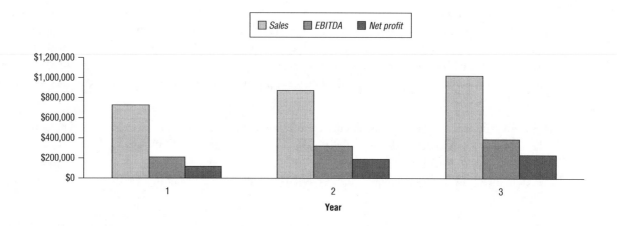

1.6 Expansion Plan

The Founder expects that the business will aggressively expand during the first three years of operation. Mr. Zerri intends to implement marketing campaigns that will effectively target companies that have outstanding receivables within the target market.

2.0 COMPANY AND FINANCING SUMMARY

2.1 Registered Name and Corporate Structure
Zerri Collection Agency is registered as a corporation in the State of New York.

2.2 Required Funds
At this time, the Debt Collection Agency requires $100,000 of debt funds. Below is a breakdown of how these funds will be used:

Projected startup costs

Initial lease payments and deposits	$ 10,000
Working capital	$ 35,000
FF&E	$ 30,000
Leasehold improvements	$ 5,000
Security deposits	$ 5,000
Insurance	$ 2,500
Professional fees and licensure	$ 10,000
Marketing budget	$ 7,500
Miscellaneous and unforeseen costs	$ 5,000
Total startup costs	**$110,000**

Use of funds

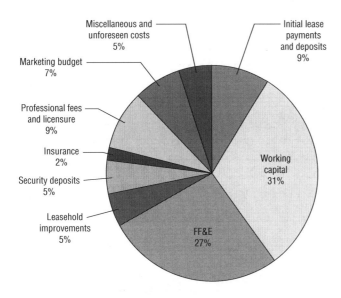

2.3 Investor Equity
Mr. Zerri is not seeking an investment from a third party at this time.

2.4 Management Equity
Tony Zerri owns 100% of the Zerri Collection Agency.

2.5 Exit Strategy
If the business is very successful, Mr. Zerri may seek to sell the business to a third party for a significant earnings multiple. Most likely, the Company will hire a qualified business broker to sell the business on

behalf of the Debt Collection Agency. Based on historical numbers, the business could fetch a sales premium of up to 4 to 6 times the previous year's operations by the fifth year of operation.

3.0 PRODUCTS AND SERVICES

Below is a description of the debt collection and credit advisory services offered by the Company.

3.1 Debt Collection Services

The primary function of the Debt Collection Agency is to purchase defaulted loan and receivables portfolios that have not been properly serviced by the debt for more than 180 days. The business intends to purchase these portfolios for three to four percent of their face value. The secondary market for defaulted debts is immensely large, and debts are regularly sold and divested among debt collection agencies.

The business will maintain a call center that will house 2 to 3 debt collection staff members that will be responsible for managing the phone calling and correspondence with each debtor of the Debt Collection Agency. Management estimates that on any given day, a staff member will make 100 to 150 phone calls, and will service approximately 100 accounts. The Company will provide incentives for these agents by providing them with 20% commissions on each dollar of debt collected after their monthly quota. The Company is currently developing its procedures for employee incentives.

The business will also act in a third party capacity among companies that contract with the Company for collecting debts on their behalf. The business will charge a fee equal to 30% of the amount collected.

3.2 Credit Advisory Services

The Company's secondary source of revenue for the business will come from the direct consultation to clients who have minor or substantial credit issues. The Company will also offer per hour advice to clients regarding how to properly maintain their credit scores. Finally, the business will develop an internal program that monitors clients' credit profiles on a monthly basis for an ongoing yearly fee.

In regards to fees, the client will pay directly for these counseling services, which will be offered at a fixed rate. The Company will maintain extensive policies on fee disclosures to ensure that client's clearly understand the costs associated with the Company's services as well as all other applicable disclaimers and warranties.

4.0 STRATEGIC AND MARKET ANALYSIS

4.1 Economic Outlook

This section of the analysis will detail the economic climate, the debt collection and credit counseling/advisory industry, the customer profile, and the competition that the business will face as it progresses through its business operations.

Currently, the economic market condition in the United States is moderate. The meltdown of the subprime mortgage market coupled with increasing gas prices has led many people to believe that the U.S. is on the cusp of a double dip economic recession. This slowdown in the economy has also greatly impacted real estate sales, which has halted to historical lows. However, debt collection businesses typically operate with a great degree of economic immunity as people will continue to require these services on an ongoing basis, especially during deleterious economic climates. As such, Management feels that the current economic climate is actually an excellent time to launch this type of business as millions of people are currently having substantial issues with their debts.

4.2 Industry Analysis

Below is an overview of the industries in which Zerri Collection Agency will operate.

4.2.1 Debt Collection Credit Intermediation Industry

In the United States there are over 7,000 businesses that operate as credit intermediaries (which includes debt collection businesses). Among debt collection agencies, annual revenues are approximately $10 billion per year. Aggregately, the industry employs approximately 100,000 people and provides more than $2 billion of annual payrolls.

There has been a substantial increase in the demand among debt collection agencies over the past ten years for their services among both companies that collect debts on a third party basis as well as for businesses that purchase bad debt portfolios. This is primarily due to the fact that the technology associated with these businesses have allowed them to very quickly contact default borrowers while very quickly processing bad debt repayments.

4.2.2 Credit Advisory Industry

The credit counseling and credit management industry represents over 3,000 established businesses that employ more than 15,000. Each year, these businesses aggregately generate more than $2 billion dollars a year of revenue and provide gross annual payrolls of $600 million dollars. The growth rate for this industry has been tremendous over the last five years as the growth of financial transaction over the Internet has increased significantly. Over the last five years, the number of agents operating within this market more than doubled, with income received by these firms increasing more than 300%.

As lending has become much more scientific over the last fifteen years with the implementation of electronic credit reporting, FICO scores, and electronic employment records, the need for consumers to maintain strong credit profiles is tremendous. This is especially true in today's economy where millions of people have over extended themselves with debt, and require professional assistance with loan renegotiations, credit repair services, and credit advisory services.

4.3 Customer Profile

Management expects that a diverse group of companies will use the Company's services. The target market sought by the Company will consist of businesses that have substantial owed debts or receivables. The business, after obtaining licensure to operate in multiple states will be able to effectively assist thousands of businesses with their debt collection needs. Approximately 40% of adult Americans currently have past due payments or debts that require collection or renegotiation. As such, the potential market for this type of service exceeds 70 million people. Mr. Zerri expects that the average income of a collection customer will be $28,000 to $45,000 per year.

4.4 Competition

As stated above, there are a number of debt collection agencies and credit improvement services that provide identical or substantially similar services to that of the Company. Management intends to maintain a substantial competitive advantage over other debt collection agencies and credit improvement services that cater to both businesses and individuals by providing services at a lower cost than is typically associated within the industry. As this is a commoditized business, it is imperative that the Company is able to effectively compete on cost as well as providing comprehensive debt collection and credit repair services.

5.0 MARKETING PLAN

Zerri Collection Agency intends to maintain an extensive marketing campaign that will ensure maximum visibility for the business in its targeted market. Below is an overview of the marketing strategies and objectives of the Company.

5.1 Marketing Objectives

- Establish relationships with accountants within the targeted market.

- Develop relationships with companies that maintain a large amount of unpaid receivables.

5.2 Marketing Strategies

Mr. Zerri intends on using a number of marketing strategies that will allow Zerri Collection Agency to easily target businesses and individuals with credit issues within the target market. These strategies include traditional print advertisements and ads placed on search engines on the Internet.

The Company will maintain a sizable amount of print and traditional advertising methods within local markets to promote the debt collection services and credit advisory that the Company is offering. Mr. Zerri will also develop ongoing referral relationships with accountants and small business associations within the Company's local market who will refer clients with significant debt issues. In time, this will become an invaluable source of new business for the Company.

Zerri Collection Agency will also maintain an expansive website that showcases its services to both individuals and businesses that have credit issues. As it relates to individuals, the Company will showcase how the business is able to settle debts for substantially less than the outstanding amount of the debt while also showcasing how the business is able to provide licensed third party debt collection services to the business public.

5.3 Pricing

Management anticipates that the business will receive $500 to $2,000 for providing credit repair services. In regards to debt collection operations, Management anticipates that the Company will receive $300 to $1,000 on each successfully collected debt for third party companies and for its own portfolio of bad debts.

6.0 ORGANIZATIONAL PLAN AND PERSONNEL SUMMARY

6.1 Corporate Organization

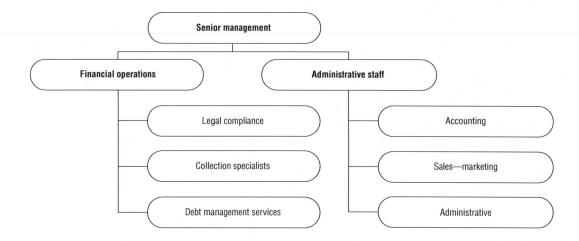

6.2 Organizational Budget

Personnel plan—yearly

Year	1	2	3
Owner	$ 60,000	$ 61,800	$ 63,654
General manager	$ 55,000	$ 56,650	$ 58,350
Debt collection specialists	$112,000	$115,875	$159,135
Bookkeeper (P/T)	$ 20,000	$ 20,600	$ 21,218
Administrative	$ 50,000	$ 51,500	$ 53,045
Total	**$297,500**	**$306,425**	**$355,402**

Numbers of personnel

Owner	1	1	1
General manager	1	1	1
Debt collection specialists	3	3	4
Bookkeeper (P/T)	1	1	1
Administrative	2	2	2
Totals	**8**	**8**	**9**

Personnel expense breakdown

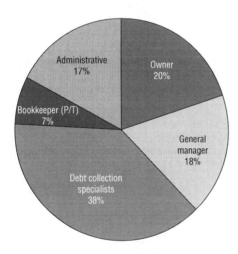

7.0 FINANCIAL PLAN

7.1 Underlying Assumptions

The Company has based its proforma financial statements on the following:

- Zerri Collection Agency will have an annual revenue growth rate of 14% per year.

- The Owner will acquire $100,000 of debt funds to develop the business.

- The loan will have a 10 year term with a 9% interest rate.

7.2 Sensitivity Analysis

The Company's revenues are not sensitive to changes in the general economy. In fact, during deleterious economic conditions (like the current economy), Mr. Zerri expects an increase in revenue as more businesses turn to debt collection companies to assist with the collection of existing debts. Additionally, the Company generates high margin income from its services, which will allow the business to thrive in any economic climate.

7.3 Source of Funds

Financing

Equity contributions

Management investment	$ 10,000.00
Total equity financing	**$ 10,000.00**

Banks and lenders

Banks and lenders	$ 100,000.00
Total debt financing	**$100,000.00**
Total financing	**$110,000.00**

7.4 General Assumptions

General assumptions

Year	1	2	3
Short term interest rate	9.5%	9.5%	9.5%
Long term interest rate	10.0%	10.0%	10.0%
Federal tax rate	33.0%	33.0%	33.0%
State tax rate	5.0%	5.0%	5.0%
Personnel taxes	15.0%	15.0%	15.0%

7.5 Profit and Loss Statements

Proforma profit and loss (yearly)

Year	1	2	3
Sales	**$727,920**	**$873,504**	**$1,022,000**
Cost of goods sold	$ 66,726	$ 80,071	$ 93,683
Gross margin	90.83%	90.83%	90.83%
Operating income	**$661,194**	**$793,433**	**$ 928,316**
Expenses			
Payroll	$297,500	$306,425	$ 355,402
General and administrative	$ 25,200	$ 26,208	$ 27,256
Marketing expenses	$ 21,838	$ 26,205	$ 30,660
Professional fees and licensure	$ 15,000	$ 15,450	$ 15,914
Insurance costs	$ 12,500	$ 13,125	$ 13,781
Travel and vehicle costs	$ 10,000	$ 11,000	$ 12,100
Rent and utilities	$ 21,250	$ 22,313	$ 23,428
Miscellaneous costs	$ 3,640	$ 4,368	$ 5,110
Payroll taxes	$ 44,625	$ 45,964	$ 53,310
Total operating costs	**$451,552**	**$471,057**	**$ 536,961**
EBITDA	**$209,642**	**$322,376**	**$ 391,355**
Federal income tax	$ 69,182	$103,701	$ 126,683
State income tax	$ 10,482	$ 15,712	$ 19,194
Interest expense	$ 8,738	$ 8,131	$ 7,468
Depreciation expenses	$ 4,107	$ 4,107	$ 4,107
Net profit	**$117,133**	**$190,724**	**$ 233,903**
Profit margin	**16.09%**	**21.83%**	**22.89%**

Sales, operating costs, and profit forecast

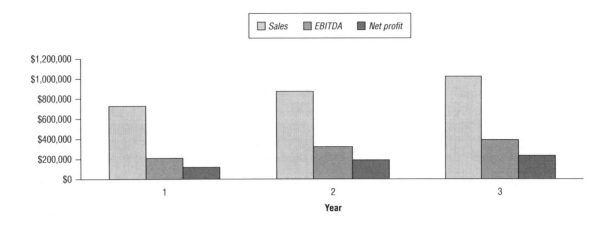

7.6 Cash Flow Analysis

Proforma cash flow analysis—yearly

Year	1	2	3
Cash from operations	$121,240	$194,832	$238,010
Cash from receivables	$ 0	$ 0	$ 0
Operating cash inflow	**$121,240**	**$194,832**	**$238,010**
Other cash inflows			
Equity investment	$ 10,000	$ 0	$ 0
Increased borrowings	$100,000	$ 0	$ 0
Sales of business assets	$ 0	$ 0	$ 0
A/P increases	$ 37,902	$ 43,587	$ 50,125
Total other cash inflows	**$147,902**	**$ 43,587**	**$ 50,125**
Total cash inflow	**$269,142**	**$238,419**	**$288,135**
Cash outflows			
Repayment of principal	$ 6,463	$ 7,070	$ 7,733
A/P decreases	$ 24,897	$ 29,876	$ 35,852
A/R increases	$ 0	$ 0	$ 0
Asset purchases	$ 57,500	$ 19,483	$ 23,801
Dividends	$ 96,992	$155,865	$190,408
Total cash outflows	**$185,853**	**$212,295**	**$257,794**
Net cash flow	**$ 83,290**	**$ 26,124**	**$ 30,342**
Cash balance	**$ 83,290**	**$109,414**	**$139,756**

Proforma cash flow (yearly)

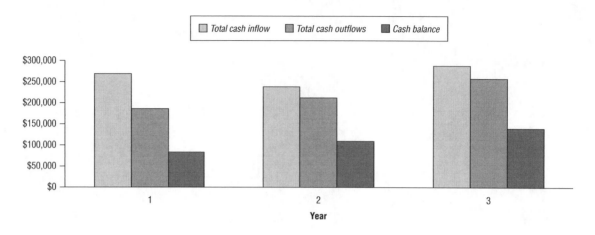

7.7 Balance Sheet

Proforma balance sheet—yearly

Year	1	2	3
Assets			
Cash	$ 83,290	$109,414	$139,756
Amortized development/expansion costs	$ 37,500	$ 39,448	$ 41,828
FF&E	$ 20,000	$ 37,535	$ 58,956
Accumulated depreciation	($ 4,107)	($ 8,214)	($ 12,321)
Total assets	**$136,683**	**$178,183**	**$228,219**
Liabilities and equity			
Accounts payable	$ 13,005	$ 26,716	$ 40,990
Long term liabilities	$ 93,537	$ 86,467	$ 79,397
Other liabilities	$ 0	$ 0	$ 0
Total liabilities	**$106,542**	**$113,183**	**$120,387**
Net worth	**$ 30,141**	**$ 65,000**	**$107,832**
Total liabilities and equity	**$136,683**	**$178,183**	**$228,219**

Proforma balance sheet

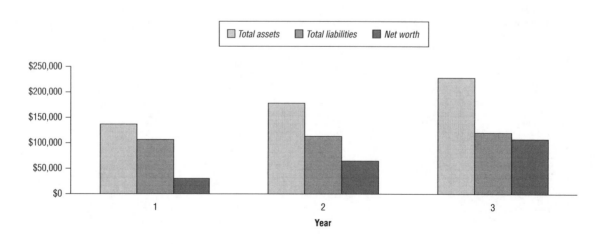

7.8 Breakeven Analysis

Monthly break even analysis

Year	1	2	3
Monthly revenue	$ 41,427	$ 43,216	$ 49,262
Yearly revenue	$497,122	$518,595	$591,150

Break even analysis

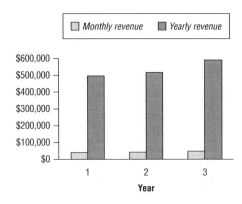

7.9 Business Ratios

Business ratios—yearly

Year	1	2	3
Sales			
Sales growth	0.00%	20.00%	17.00%
Gross margin	90.80%	90.80%	90.80%
Financials			
Profit margin	16.09%	21.83%	22.89%
Assets to liabilities	1.28	1.57	1.90
Equity to liabilities	0.28	0.57	0.90
Assets to equity	4.53	2.74	2.12
Liquidity			
Acid test	0.78	0.97	1.16
Cash to assets	0.61	0.61	0.61

7.10 Three Year Profit and Loss Statement

Profit and loss statement (first year)

Months	1	2	3	4	5	6	7
Sales	**$60,000**	**$60,120**	**$60,240**	**$60,360**	**$60,480**	**$60,600**	**$60,720**
Cost of goods sold	$ 5,500	$ 5,511	$ 5,522	$ 5,533	$ 5,544	$ 5,555	$ 5,566
Gross margin	90.80%	90.80%	90.80%	90.80%	90.80%	90.80%	90.80%
Operating income	**$54,500**	**$54,609**	**$54,718**	**$54,827**	**$54,936**	**$54,045**	**$55,154**
Expenses							
Payroll	$24,792	$24,792	$24,792	$24,792	$24,792	$24,792	$24,792
General and administrative	$ 2,100	$ 2,100	$ 2,100	$ 2,100	$ 2,100	$ 2,100	$ 2,100
Marketing expenses	$ 1,820	$ 1,820	$ 1,820	$ 1,820	$ 1,820	$ 1,820	$ 1,820
Professional fees and licensure	$ 1,250	$ 1,250	$ 1,250	$ 1,250	$ 1,250	$ 1,250	$ 1,250
Insurance costs	$ 1,042	$ 1,042	$ 1,042	$ 1,042	$ 1,042	$ 1,042	$ 1,042
Travel and vehicle costs	$ 833	$ 833	$ 833	$ 833	$ 833	$ 833	$ 833
Rent and utilities	$ 1,771	$ 1,771	$ 1,771	$ 1,771	$ 1,771	$ 1,771	$ 1,771
Miscellaneous costs	$ 303	$ 303	$ 303	$ 303	$ 303	$ 303	$ 303
Payroll taxes	$ 3,719	$ 3,719	$ 3,719	$ 3,719	$ 3,719	$ 3,719	$ 3,719
Total operating costs	**$37,629**	**$37,629**	**$37,629**	**$37,629**	**$37,629**	**$37,629**	**$37,629**
EBITDA	**$16,871**	**$16,980**	**$17,089**	**$17,198**	**$17,307**	**$17,416**	**$17,525**
Federal income tax	$ 5,702	$ 5,714	$ 5,725	$ 5,737	$ 5,748	$ 5,759	$ 5,771
State income tax	$ 864	$ 866	$ 867	$ 869	$ 871	$ 873	$ 874
Interest expense	$ 750	$ 746	$ 742	$ 738	$ 734	$ 730	$ 726
Depreciation expense	$ 342	$ 342	$ 342	$ 342	$ 342	$ 342	$ 342
Net profit	**$ 9,212**	**$ 9,312**	**$ 9,411**	**$ 9,511**	**$ 9,611**	**$ 9,711**	**$ 9,811**

Profit and loss statement (first year cont.)

Month	8	9	10	11	12	1
Sales	**$60,840**	**$60,960**	**$61,080**	**$61,200**	**$61,320**	**$727,920**
Cost of goods sold	$ 5,577	$ 5,588	$ 5,599	$ 5,610	$ 5,621	$ 66,726
Gross margin	90.80%	90.80%	90.80%	90.80%	90.80%	90.80%
Operating income	**$55,263**	**$55,372**	**$55,481**	**$55,590**	**$55,699**	**$661,194**
Expenses						
Payroll	$24,792	$24,792	$24,792	$24,792	$24,792	$297,500
General and administrative	$ 2,100	$ 2,100	$ 2,100	$ 2,100	$ 2,100	$ 25,200
Marketing expenses	$ 1,820	$ 1,820	$ 1,820	$ 1,820	$ 1,820	$ 21,838
Professional fees and licensure	$ 1,250	$ 1,250	$ 1,250	$ 1,250	$ 1,250	$ 15,000
Insurance costs	$ 1,042	$ 1,042	$ 1,042	$ 1,042	$ 1,042	$ 12,500
Equipment maintenance costs	$ 833	$ 833	$ 833	$ 833	$ 833	$ 10,000
Rent and utilities	$ 1,771	$ 1,771	$ 1,771	$ 1,771	$ 1,771	$ 21,250
Miscellaneous costs	$ 303	$ 303	$ 303	$ 303	$ 303	$ 3,640
Payroll taxes	$ 3,719	$ 3,719	$ 3,719	$ 3,719	$ 3,719	$ 44,625
Total operating costs	**$37,629**	**$37,629**	**$37,629**	**$37,629**	**$37,629**	**$351,552**
EBITDA	**$17,634**	**$17,743**	**$17,852**	**$17,961**	**$18,070**	**$209,642**
Federal income tax	$ 5,782	$ 5,794	$ 5,805	$ 5,816	$ 5,828	$ 69,182
State income tax	$ 876	$ 878	$ 880	$ 881	$ 883	$ 10,482
Interest expense	$ 722	$ 718	$ 714	$ 710	$ 706	$ 8,738
Depreciation expense	$ 342	$ 342	$ 342	$ 342	$ 342	$ 4,107
Net profit	**$ 9,911**	**$10,011**	**$10,111**	**$10,211**	**$10,311**	**$117,133**

Profit and loss statement (second year)

Quarter	Q1	2 Q2	Q3	Q4	2
Sales	$174,701	$218,376	$235,846	$244,581	$873,504
Cost of goods sold	$ 16,014	$ 20,018	$ 21,619	$ 22,420	$ 80,071
Gross margin	90.8%	90.8%	90.8%	90.8%	90.8%
Operating income	$158,687	$198,358	$214,227	$222,161	$793,433
Expenses					
Payroll	$ 61,285	$ 76,606	$ 82,735	$ 85,799	$306,425
General and administrative	$ 5,242	$ 6,552	$ 7,076	$ 7,338	$ 26,208
Marketing expenses	$ 5,241	$ 6,551	$ 7,075	$ 7,337	$ 26,205
Professional fees and licensure	$ 3,090	$ 3,863	$ 4,172	$ 4,326	$ 15,450
Insurance costs	$ 2,625	$ 3,281	$ 3,544	$ 3,675	$ 13,125
Travel and vehicle costs	$ 2,200	$ 2,750	$ 2,970	$ 3,080	$ 11,000
Rent and utilities	$ 4,463	$ 5,578	$ 6,024	$ 6,248	$ 22,313
Miscellaneous costs	$ 874	$ 1,092	$ 1,179	$ 1,223	$ 4,368
Payroll taxes	$ 9,193	$ 11,491	$ 12,410	$ 12,870	$ 45,964
Total operating costs	$ 94,211	$117,764	$127,185	$131,896	$471,057
EBITDA	$ 64,475	$ 80,594	$ 87,041	$ 90,265	$322,376
Federal income tax	$ 20,740	$ 25,925	$ 27,999	$ 29,036	$103,701
State income tax	$ 3,142	$ 3,928	$ 4,242	$ 4,399	$ 15,712
Interest expense	$ 2,092	$ 2,053	$ 2,013	$ 1,973	$ 8,131
Depreciation expense	$ 1,027	$ 1,027	$ 1,027	$ 1,027	$ 4,107
Net profit	$ 37,474	$ 47,661	$ 51,760	$ 53,830	$190,724

Profit and loss statement (third year)

Quarter	Q1	3 Q2	Q3	Q4	3
Sales	$204,400	$255,500	$275,940	$286,160	$1,022,000
Cost of goods sold	$ 18,737	$ 23,421	$ 25,294	$ 26,231	$ 93,683
Gross margin	90.8%	90.8%	90.8%	90.8%	90.8%
Operating income	$185,663	$232,079	$250,645	$259,929	$ 928,316
Expenses					
Payroll	$ 71,080	$ 88,850	$ 95,958	$ 99,512	$ 355,402
General and administrative	$ 5,451	$ 6,814	$ 7,359	$ 7,632	$ 27,256
Marketing expenses	$ 6,132	$ 7,665	$ 8,278	$ 8,585	$ 30,660
Professional fees and licensure	$ 3,183	$ 3,978	$ 4,297	$ 4,456	$ 15,914
Insurance costs	$ 2,756	$ 3,445	$ 3,721	$ 3,859	$ 13,781
Travel and vehicle costs	$ 2,420	$ 3,025	$ 3,267	$ 3,388	$ 12,100
Rent and utilities	$ 4,686	$ 5,857	$ 6,326	$ 6,560	$ 23,428
Miscellaneous costs	$ 1,022	$ 1,277	$ 1,380	$ 1,431	$ 5,110
Payroll taxes	$ 10,662	$ 13,328	$ 14,394	$ 14,927	$ 53,310
Total operating costs	$107,392	$134,240	$144,979	$150,349	$ 536,961
EBITDA	$ 78,271	$ 97,839	$105,666	$109,580	$ 391,355
Federal income tax	$ 25,337	$ 31,671	$ 34,204	$ 35,471	$ 126,683
State income tax	$ 3,839	$ 4,799	$ 5,182	$ 5,374	$ 19,194
Interest expense	$ 1,932	$ 1,889	$ 1,846	$ 1,802	$ 7,468
Depreciation expense	$ 1,027	$ 1,027	$ 1,027	$ 1,027	$ 4,107
Net profit	$ 46,137	$ 58,454	$ 63,406	$ 65,906	$ 233,903

7.11 Three Year Cash Flow Analysis

Cash flow analysis (first year)

Month	1	2	3	4	5	6	7
Cash from operations	$ 9,554	$ 9,654	$ 9,754	$ 9,854	$ 9,953	$ 10,053	$ 10,153
Cash from receivables	$ 0	$ 0	$ 0	$ 0	$ 0	$ 0	$ 0
Operating cash inflow	**$ 9,554**	**$ 9,654**	**$ 9,754**	**$ 9,854**	**$ 9,953**	**$ 10,053**	**$ 10,153**
Other cash inflows							
Equity investment	$ 10,000	$ 0	$ 0	$ 0	$ 0	$ 0	$ 0
Increased borrowings	$100,000	$ 0	$ 0	$ 0	$ 0	$ 0	$ 0
Sales of business assets	$ 0	$ 0	$ 0	$ 0	$ 0	$ 0	$ 0
A/P increases	$ 3,159	$ 3,159	$ 3,159	$ 3,159	$ 3,159	$ 3,159	$ 3,159
Total other cash inflows	**$113,159**	**$ 3,159**	**$ 3,159**	**$ 3,159**	**$ 3,159**	**$ 3,159**	**$ 3,159**
Total cash inflow	**$122,713**	**$12,812**	**$12,912**	**$13,012**	**$ 13,112**	**$ 13,212**	**$ 13,312**
Cash outflows							
Repayment of principal	$ 517	$ 521	$ 525	$ 528	$ 532	$ 536	$ 540
A/P decreases	$ 2,075	$ 2,075	$ 2,075	$ 2,075	$ 2,075	$ 2,075	$ 2,075
A/R increases	$ 0	$ 0	$ 0	$ 0	$ 0	$ 0	$ 0
Asset purchases	$ 57,500	$ 0	$ 0	$ 0	$ 0	$ 0	$ 0
Dividends	$ 0	$ 0	$ 0	$ 0	$ 0	$ 0	$ 0
Total cash outflows	**$ 60,092**	**$ 2,595**	**$ 2,599**	**$ 2,603**	**$ 2,607**	**$ 2,611**	**$ 2,615**
Net cash flow	**$ 62,621**	**$10,217**	**$10,313**	**$10,409**	**$ 10,505**	**$ 10,601**	**$ 10,696**
Cash balance	**$ 62,621**	**$72,838**	**$83,151**	**$93,560**	**$104,065**	**$114,665**	**$125,362**

Cash flow analysis (first year cont.)

Month	8	9	10	11	12	1
Cash from operations	$ 10,253	$ 10,353	$ 10,453	$ 10,553	$10,653	$121,240
Cash from receivables	$ 0	$ 0	$ 0	$ 0	$ 0	$ 0
Operating cash inflow	**$ 10,253**	**$ 10,353**	**$ 10,453**	**$ 10,553**	**$10,653**	**$121,240**
Other cash inflows						
Equity investment	$ 0	$ 0	$ 0	$ 0	$ 0	$ 10,000
Increased borrowings	$ 0	$ 0	$ 0	$ 0	$ 0	$100,000
Sales of business assets	$ 0	$ 0	$ 0	$ 0	$ 0	$ 0
A/P increases	$ 3,159	$ 3,159	$ 3,159	$ 3,159	$ 3,159	$ 37,902
Total other cash inflows	**$ 3,159**	**$ 3,159**	**$ 3,159**	**$ 3,159**	**$ 3,159**	**$147,902**
Total cash inflow	**$ 13,412**	**$ 13,511**	**$ 13,611**	**$ 13,711**	**$13,812**	**$269,142**
Cash outflows						
Repayment of principal	$ 545	$ 549	$ 553	$ 557	$ 561	$ 6,463
A/P decreases	$ 2,075	$ 2,075	$ 2,075	$ 2,075	$ 2,075	$ 24,897
A/R increases	$ 0	$ 0	$ 0	$ 0	$ 0	$ 0
Asset purchases	$ 0	$ 0	$ 0	$ 0	$ 0	$ 57,500
Dividends	$ 0	$ 0	$ 0	$ 0	$96,992	$ 96,992
Total cash outflows	**$ 2,619**	**$ 2,623**	**$ 2,627**	**$ 2,632**	**$99,628**	**$185,853**
Net cash flow	**$ 10,792**	**$ 10,888**	**$ 10,984**	**$ 11,080**	**−$85,816**	**$ 83,290**
Cash balance	**$136,154**	**$147,042**	**$158,026**	**$169,106**	**$83,290**	**$ 83,290**

Cash flow analysis (second year)

Quarter	Q1	2 Q2	Q3	Q4	2
Cash from operations	$38,966	$48,708	$ 52,605	$ 54,553	$194,832
Cash from receivables	$ 0	$ 0	$ 0	$ 0	$ 0
Operating cash inflow	**$38,996**	**$48,708**	**$ 52,605**	**$ 54,553**	**$194,832**
Other cash inflows					
Equity investment	$ 0	$ 0	$ 0	$ 0	$ 0
Increased borrowings	$ 0	$ 0	$ 0	$ 0	$ 0
Sales of business assets	$ 0	$ 0	$ 0	$ 0	$ 0
A/P increases	$ 8,717	$10,897	$ 11,769	$ 12,204	$ 43,587
Total other cash inflows	**$ 8,717**	**$10,897**	**$ 11,769**	**$ 12,204**	**$ 43,587**
Total cash inflow	**$47,684**	**$59,605**	**$ 64,373**	**$ 66,757**	**$238,419**
Cash outflows					
Repayment of principal	$ 1,708	$ 1,747	$ 1,787	$ 1,827	$ 7,070
A/P decreases	$ 5,975	$ 7,469	$ 8,067	$ 8,365	$ 29,876
A/R increases	$ 0	$ 0	$ 0	$ 0	$ 0
Asset purchases	$ 3,897	$ 4,871	$ 5,260	$ 5,455	$ 19,483
Dividends	$31,173	$38,966	$ 42,084	$ 43,642	$155,865
Total cash outflows	**$42,753**	**$53,053**	**$ 57,197**	**$ 59,290**	**$212,295**
Net cash flow	**$ 4,930**	**$ 6,551**	**$ 7,176**	**$ 7,467**	**$ 26,124**
Cash balance	**$88,220**	**$94,771**	**$101,947**	**$109,414**	**$109,414**

Cash flow analysis (third year)

Quarter	Q1	3 Q2	Q3	Q4	3
Cash from operations	$ 47,602	$ 59,503	$ 64,263	$ 66,643	$238,010
Cash from receivables	$ 0	$ 0	$ 0	$ 0	$ 0
Operating cash inflow	**$ 47,602**	**$ 59,503**	**$ 64,263**	**$ 66,643**	**$238,010**
Other cash inflows					
Equity investment	$ 0	$ 0	$ 0	$ 0	$ 0
Increased borrowings	$ 0	$ 0	$ 0	$ 0	$ 0
Sales of business assets	$ 0	$ 0	$ 0	$ 0	$ 0
A/P increases	$ 10,025	$ 12,531	$ 13,534	$ 14,035	$ 50,125
Total other cash inflows	**$ 10,025**	**$ 12,531**	**$ 13,534**	**$ 14,035**	**$ 50,125**
Total cash inflow	**$ 57,627**	**$ 72,034**	**$ 77,797**	**$ 80,678**	**$288,135**
Cash outflows					
Repayment of principal	$ 1,869	$ 1,911	$ 1,954	$ 1,999	$ 7,733
A/P decreases	$ 7,170	$ 8,963	$ 9,680	$ 10,038	$ 35,852
A/R increases	$ 0	$ 0	$ 0	$ 0	$ 0
Asset purchases	$ 4,760	$ 5,950	$ 6,426	$ 6,664	$ 23,801
Dividends	$ 38,082	$ 47,602	$ 51,410	$ 53,314	$190,408
Total cash outflows	**$ 51,881**	**$ 64,426**	**$ 69,471**	**$ 72,016**	**$257,794**
Net cash flow	**$ 5,746**	**$ 7,608**	**$ 8,326**	**$ 8,662**	**$ 30,342**
Cash balance	**$115,160**	**$122,768**	**$131,094**	**$139,756**	**$139,756**

Dispatched Trucking Service

Preferred Trucking

12354 55th St.
New York, NY 10063

BizPlanDB.com

The purpose of this business plan is to raise $150,000 for the development of a dispatched trucking and transportation company while showcasing the expected financials and operations over the next three years. Preferred Trucking is a New York-based corporation that will provide dispatched focused long and short haul transportation services to customers in its targeted market.

1.0 EXECUTIVE SUMMARY

The purpose of this business plan is to raise $150,000 for the development of a dispatched trucking and transportation company while showcasing the expected financials and operations over the next three years. Preferred Trucking is a New York-based corporation that will provide dispatched focused long and short haul transportation services to customers in its targeted market. The Company was founded by Bill Masinick.

1.1 The Services

Preferred Trucking has been developed to provide an extremely comprehensive management service of long and short distance trucking for companies and people in the Company's target market area. The Company will offer its clients the ability to manage all of their localized or long distance hauling needs through one business that will provide its clients the ability to manage their shipments in a cost and time effective manner.

At this time, Management is sourcing the trucks that it will lease in order to provide services to its customer base. The business will also develop third party relationships with other trucking companies within the target market.

The third section of the business plan will further describe the services offered by Preferred Trucking.

1.2 Financing

Mr. Masinick is seeking to raise $150,000 from a bank loan. The interest rate and loan agreement are to be further discussed during negotiation. This business plan assumes that the business will receive a 10-year loan with a 9% fixed interest rate. The financing will be used for the following:

- Development of the Company's office location.

- Financing for the first six months of operation.

- Capital to finance deposits for leasing of trucks.

Mr. Masinick will contribute $25,000 to the venture.

1.3 Mission Statement

Preferred Trucking's mission is to become the recognized leader in its targeted market for long and short haul trucking and transportation services.

1.4 Management Team

The Company was founded by Bill Masinick. Mr. Masinick has more than 10 years of experience in the transportation industry. Through his expertise, he will be able to bring the operations of the business to profitability within its first year of operations.

1.5 Sales Forecasts

Mr. Masinick expects a strong rate of growth at the start of operations. Below are the expected financials over the next three years.

Proforma profit and loss (yearly)

Year	1	2	3
Sales	$973,590	$1,168,308	$1,366,920
Operating costs	$297,003	$ 310,535	$ 324,590
EBITDA	$ 79,734	$ 141,549	$ 204,349
Taxes, interest, and depreciation	$ 52,155	$ 70,101	$ 93,348
Net profit	$ 27,579	$ 71,448	$ 111,001

Sales, operating costs, and profit forecast

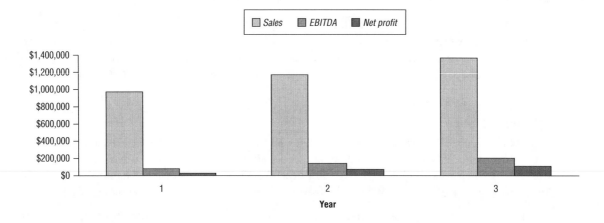

1.6 Expansion Plan

The Founder expects that the business will aggressively expand during the first three years of operation. Mr. Masinick intends to implement marketing campaigns that will effectively target individuals and businesses within the target market.

2.0 COMPANY AND FINANCING SUMMARY

2.1 Registered Name and Corporate Structure

Preferred Trucking is registered as a corporation in the State of New York.

2.2 Required Funds

At this time, Preferred Trucking requires $150,000 of debt funds. Below is a breakdown of how these funds will be used:

Projected startup costs

Initial lease payments and deposits	$ 15,000
Working capital	$ 35,000
FF&E	$ 25,000
Leasehold improvements	$ 7,500
Security deposits	$ 12,500
Insurance	$ 5,000
Vehicle deposits	$ 50,000
Marketing budget	$ 17,500
Miscellaneous and unforeseen costs	$ 7,500
Total startup costs	**$175,000**

Use of funds

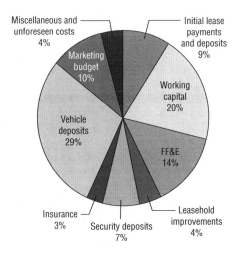

2.3 Investor Equity

Mr. Masinick is not seeking an investment from a third party at this time.

2.4 Management Equity

Bill Masinick owns 100% of Preferred Trucking.

2.5 Exit Strategy

If the business is very successful, Mr. Masinick may seek to sell the business to a third party for a significant earnings multiple. Most likely, the Company will hire a qualified business broker to sell the business on behalf of Preferred Trucking.

Based on historical numbers, the business could fetch a sales premium of up to 6 times earnings. However, with recent fuel costs rising, the premiums for trucking businesses have declined due to the volatility of the oil markets. It should be noted that Mr. Masinick intends to operate this business for a significant period of time, and a potential exit strategy would not be executed for at least five to seven years.

3.0 PRODUCTS AND SERVICES

Below is a description of the trucking and transportation services offered by the Company.

3.1 Freight Transportation

Mr. Masinick believes that the key to maintaining a successful business operation will be to ensure that our clients can easily and quickly place orders for shipping their large merchandise trucking needs for short or long distances throughout the local or regional target market.

At the onset of the operations, Preferred Trucking will operate three trucks and will provide dry freight hauling services to retailers and product distributors. Once the business expands, Mr. Masinick may include specialty hauling services for perishable materials. The Company will also provide moving services to individual customers.

The business will also maintain connections with third-party trucking companies that can be dispatched to locations when the Company's trucking fleet is fully in use.

3.2 Logistics and Supply Chain Management

In addition to the service provided above, the Company will make sure that each transportation order is handled in a safe and professional manner. The most important key to maintaining and developing successful business operations is to be able to consistently deliver high-quality trucking services at reasonable prices. With the recent increase in the price of diesel fuels, it is especially important, more now than ever, that Management develops and implements strategies to minimize the possibility of mistakes.

4.0 STRATEGIC AND MARKET ANALYSIS

4.1 Economic Outlook

This section of the analysis will detail the economic climate, the transportation industry, the customer profile, and the competition that the business will face as it progresses through its business operations.

Currently, the economic market condition in the United States is moderate. The meltdown of the subprime mortgage market coupled with increasing gas prices has led many people to believe that the U.S. is on the cusp of a double dip economic recession. This slowdown in the economy has also greatly impacted real estate sales, which has halted to historical lows.

A primary concern for the Company is its ability to price its services affordably during times of economic recession or spikes of oil prices. Within this year, the price of oil and its associated refined energy products have reached multi-year highs. This increase in oil prices has caused the freight and trucking industries costs to rise significantly during last six months. While this is a concern for the business, it is a risk and an issue faced by all other businesses as well. Mr. Masinick will continue to increase prices (at a standardized rate of markup) to ensure the profitability of the business.

4.2 Industry Analysis

Freight transportation is one of the United States biggest industries. Within the continental U.S., trucking is the most cost efficient method for managing shipments. The freight transportation industry generates $100 billion dollars per year and provides jobs for more than 800,000 people. Each year the industry provides average annual payrolls in excess of $12.6 billion dollars per year. Over the last five years the number of established trucking businesses has increased from 40,821 businesses to 47,000. Gross receipts increased by 38.2%, primarily because of the increases in fuel costs over the last three years.

Logistics Management services generate more than $3 billion dollars per year of revenue among 3,000 businesses in the United States. The industry employs more than 25,000 people and has grown at a rate that is much faster than the economy in general. As technology related to transportation has increased significantly over the last ten years, it has become imperative for companies to integrate new technologies into their supply chain management systems. The industry has experienced growth rates in excess of 20% for each of the last five years. This trend is expected to continue as the increase in technological advancements has allowed smaller firms to compete with larger competitors.

4.3 Customer Profile

Preferred Trucking intends to operate as a general carrier of merchandise, household goods, and other items for companies and individuals across the state. As such, it is difficult to determine the average customer of the Company as the business will have the licensure and the ability to effectively move any type of merchandise. Management anticipates that the business will receive orders for service from both companies seeking to move merchandise as well as people relocating to different areas of the target and regional market area.

4.4 Competition

As with any commoditized industry, the competition within the trucking services, freight management services, and logistics management services is substantial. The primary competitive advantage that the business will maintain is the Company's continued ability to price its services at a standardized markup despite continuing increases in oil prices. Additionally, Management intends to maintain an expansive marketing infrastructure to ensure that businesses will continue to call on Preferred Trucking for their merchandise/personal goods transportation needs.

5.0 MARKETING PLAN

Preferred Trucking intends to maintain an extensive marketing campaign that will ensure maximum visibility for the business in its targeted market. Below is an overview of the marketing strategies and objectives of Preferred Trucking.

5.1 Marketing Objectives

- Establish relationships with freight brokerages within the targeted market.

- Implement a localized marketing campaign that targets individuals that are moving to a different residence.

5.2 Marketing Strategies

The Company intends to use a multitude of marketing strategies to promote and expand the business operations. The Company will maintain its listing in the Yellow pages, create marketing campaigns within local newspapers, and promote the business through word of mouth advertising. The business actively advertises its affordable trucking and freight logistics contracting services.

Mr. Masinick intends to maintain a website that allows customers to contact Management directly over email for more information regarding Preferred Trucking and pricing quotes. As the Company expands, the business will upgrade the website to include higher levels of functionality and support.

Additionally, Management intends to continually develop a number of referral and contractual relationships within among other trucking companies, retailers, distribution companies, and moving businesses. Since these businesses regularly require trucking/tracking services, Management sees a significant opportunity to partner with these firms.

5.3 Pricing

Management anticipates that the business will receive $800 to $3,000 for each transaction. For each dollar of revenue generated, Management anticipates gross margins of approximately 39%.

6.0 ORGANIZATIONAL PLAN AND PERSONNEL SUMMARY

6.1 Corporate Organization

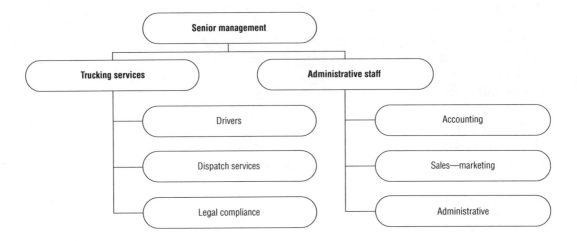

6.2 Organizational Budget

Personnel plan—yearly

Year	1	2	3
Owner	$ 40,000	$ 41,200	$ 42,436
Assistant Manager	$ 29,000	$ 29,870	$ 30,766
Drivers	$ 93,000	$ 95,790	$ 98,664
Bookkeeper (P/T)	$ 9,000	$ 9,270	$ 9,548
Administrative (P/T)	$ 17,000	$ 17,510	$ 18,035
Total	**$188,000**	**$193,640**	**$199,449**

Numbers of personnel

Owner	1	1	1
Assistant Manager	1	1	1
Drivers	3	3	3
Bookkeeper (P/T)	1	1	1
Administrative (P/T)	1	1	1
Totals	**7**	**7**	**7**

Personnel expense breakdown

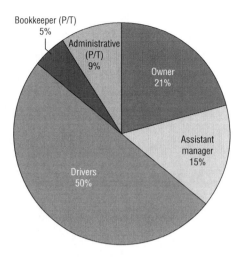

7.0 FINANCIAL PLAN

7.1 Underlying Assumptions

The Company has based its proforma financial statements on the following:

- Preferred Trucking will have an annual revenue growth rate of 14% per year.

- The Owner will acquire $150,000 of debt funds to develop the business.

- The loan will have a 10 year term with a 9% interest rate.

7.2 Sensitivity Analysis

The Company's revenues are sensitive to many external factors. Should the cost of oil increase significantly, Management fully expects that its bottom line income will decrease. However, the Company has priced its services so that increases in the price of oil will not severely impact the Company's ability to operate both profitably and cash flow positive. In the event of a dramatic increase in price, Management will seek to increase the price of its freight trucking services to reflect the higher transportation costs.

7.3 Source of Funds

Financing

Equity contributions	
Management investment	$ 25,000.00
Total equity financing	**$ 25,000.00**
Banks and lenders	
Banks and lenders	$ 150,000.00
Total debt financing	**$150,000.00**
Total financing	**$175,000.00**

7.4 General Assumptions

General assumptions

Year	1	2	3
Short term interest rate	9.5%	9.5%	9.5%
Long term interest rate	10.0%	10.0%	10.0%
Federal tax rate	33.0%	33.0%	33.0%
State tax rate	5.0%	5.0%	5.0%
Personnel taxes	15.0%	15.0%	15.0%

7.5 Profit and Loss Statements

Proforma profit and loss (yearly)

Year	1	2	3
Sales	**$973,590**	**$1,168,308**	**$1,366,920**
Cost of goods sold	$596,853	$ 716,224	$ 837,982
Gross margin	38.70%	38.70%	38.70%
Operating income	**$376,737**	**$ 452,084**	**$ 528,939**
Expenses			
Payroll	$188,000	$ 193,640	$ 199,449
General and administrative	$ 25,200	$ 26,208	$ 27,256
Marketing expenses	$ 4,868	$ 5,842	$ 6,835
Professional fees and licensure	$ 5,219	$ 5,376	$ 5,537
Insurance costs	$ 1,987	$ 2,086	$ 2,191
Truck maintenance costs	$ 17,596	$ 19,356	$ 21,291
Rent and utilities	$ 14,250	$ 14,963	$ 15,711
Miscellaneous costs	$ 11,683	$ 14,020	$ 16,403
Payroll taxes	$ 28,200	$ 29,046	$ 29,917
Total operating costs	**$297,003**	**$ 310,535**	**$ 324,590**
EBITDA	**$ 79,734**	**$ 141,549**	**$ 204,349**
Federal income tax	$ 26,312	$ 42,686	$ 63,738
State income tax	$ 3,987	$ 6,468	$ 9,657
Interest expense	$ 13,107	$ 12,197	$ 11,202
Depreciation expenses	$ 8,750	$ 8,750	$ 8,750
Net profit	**$ 27,579**	**$ 71,448**	**$ 111,001**
Profit margin	**2.83%**	**6.12%**	**8.12%**

Sales, operating costs, and profit forecast

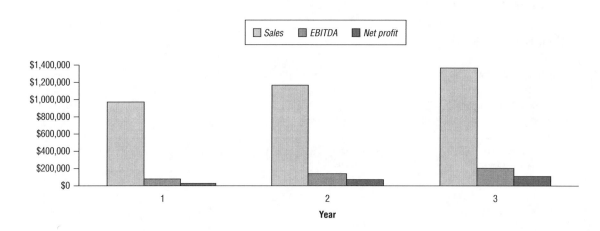

7.6 Cash Flow Analysis

Proforma cash flow analysis—yearly

Year	1	2	3
Cash from operations	$ 36,329	$ 80,198	$119,751
Cash from receivables	$ 0	$ 0	$ 0
Operating cash inflow	**$ 36,329**	**$ 80,198**	**$119,751**
Other cash inflows			
Equity investment	$ 25,000	$ 0	$ 0
Increased borrowings	$150,000	$ 0	$ 0
Sales of business assets	$ 0	$ 0	$ 0
A/P increases	$ 37,902	$ 43,587	$ 50,125
Total other cash inflows	**$212,902**	**$ 43,587**	**$ 50,125**
Total cash inflow	**$249,231**	**$123,786**	**$169,876**
Cash outflows			
Repayment of principal	$ 9,695	$ 10,605	$ 11,599
A/P decreases	$ 24,897	$ 29,876	$ 35,852
A/R increases	$ 0	$ 0	$ 0
Asset purchases	$122,500	$ 20,050	$ 29,938
Dividends	$ 25,430	$ 56,139	$ 83,826
Total cash outflows	**$182,522**	**$116,669**	**$161,214**
Net cash flow	**$ 66,708**	**$ 7,116**	**$ 8,662**
Cash balance	**$ 66,708**	**$ 73,825**	**$ 82,487**

Proforma cash flow (yearly)

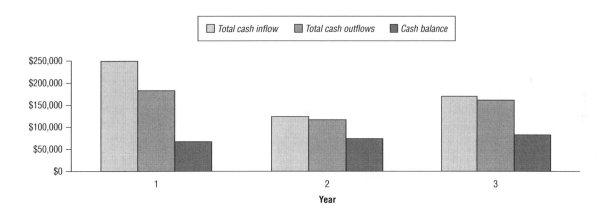

7.7 Balance Sheet

Proforma balance sheet—yearly

Year	1	2	3
Assets			
Cash	$ 66,708	$ 73,825	$ 82,487
Amortized expansion costs	$ 47,500	$ 49,505	$ 52,499
Vehicle deposits	$ 50,000	$ 65,037	$ 87,490
FF&E	$ 25,000	$ 28,007	$ 32,498
Accumulated depreciation	($ 8,750)	($ 17,500)	($ 26,250)
Total assets	**$180,458**	**$198,874**	**$228,724**
Liabilities and equity			
Accounts payable	$ 13,005	$ 26,716	$ 40,990
Long term liabilities	$140,305	$129,700	$119,096
Other liabilities	$ 0	$ 0	$ 0
Total liabilities	**$153,310**	**$156,416**	**$160,085**
Net worth	**$ 27,149**	**$ 42,458**	**$ 68,639**
Total liabilities and equity	**$180,458**	**$198,874**	**$228,724**

Proforma balance sheet

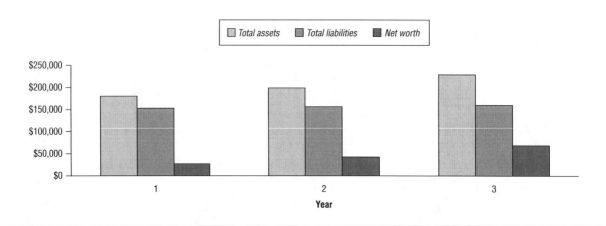

7.8 Breakeven Analysis

Monthly break even analysis

Year	1	2	3
Monthly revenue	$ 63,961	$ 66,876	$ 69,902
Yearly revenue	$767,536	$802,507	$838,828

Break even analysis

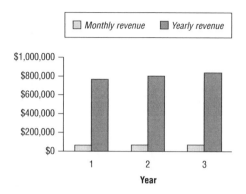

7.9 Business Ratios

Business ratios—yearly

Year	1	2	3
Sales			
Sales growth	0.00%	20.00%	17.00%
Gross margin	38.70%	38.70%	38.70%
Financials			
Profit margin	2.83%	6.12%	8.12%
Assets to liabilities	1.18	1.27	1.43
Equity to liabilities	0.18	0.27	0.43
Assets to equity	6.65	4.68	3.33
Liquidity			
Acid test	0.44	0.47	0.52
Cash to assets	0.37	0.37	0.36

7.10 Three Year Profit and Loss Statement

Profit and loss statement (first year)

Months	1	2	3	4	5	6	7
Sales	**$80,500**	**$80,615**	**$80,730**	**$80,845**	**$80,960**	**$81,075**	**$81,190**
Cost of goods sold	$49,350	$49,421	$49,491	$49,562	$49,632	$49,703	$49,773
Gross margin	38.70%	38.70%	38.70%	38.70%	38.70%	38.70%	38.70%
Operating income	**$31,150**	**$31,195**	**$31,239**	**$31,284**	**$31,328**	**$31,373**	**$31,417**
Expenses							
Payroll	$15,667	$15,667	$15,667	$15,667	$15,667	$15,667	$15,667
General and administrative	$ 2,100	$ 2,100	$ 2,100	$ 2,100	$ 2,100	$ 2,100	$ 2,100
Marketing expenses	$ 406	$ 406	$ 406	$ 406	$ 406	$ 406	$ 406
Professional fees and licensure	$ 435	$ 435	$ 435	$ 435	$ 435	$ 435	$ 435
Insurance costs	$ 166	$ 166	$ 166	$ 166	$ 166	$ 166	$ 166
Truck maintenance costs	$ 1,466	$ 1,466	$ 1,466	$ 1,466	$ 1,466	$ 1,466	$ 1,466
Rent and utilities	$ 1,188	$ 1,188	$ 1,188	$ 1,188	$ 1,188	$ 1,188	$ 1,188
Miscellaneous costs	$ 974	$ 974	$ 974	$ 974	$ 974	$ 974	$ 974
Payroll taxes	$ 2,350	$ 2,350	$ 2,350	$ 2,350	$ 2,350	$ 2,350	$ 2,350
Total operating costs	**$24,750**	**$24,750**	**$24,750**	**$24,750**	**$24,750**	**$24,750**	**$24,750**
EBITDA	**$ 6,400**	**$ 6,444**	**$ 6,489**	**$ 6,533**	**$ 6,578**	**$ 6,622**	**$ 6,667**
Federal income tax	$ 2,176	$ 2,179	$ 2,182	$ 2,185	$ 2,188	$ 2,191	$ 2,194
State income tax	$ 330	$ 330	$ 331	$ 331	$ 332	$ 332	$ 332
Interest expense	$ 1,125	$ 1,119	$ 1,113	$ 1,107	$ 1,101	$ 1,095	$ 1,089
Depreciation expense	$ 729	$ 729	$ 729	$ 729	$ 729	$ 729	$ 729
Net profit	**$ 2,040**	**$ 2,087**	**$ 2,134**	**$ 2,181**	**$ 2,181**	**$ 2,274**	**$ 2,321**

Profit and loss statement (first year cont.)

Month	8	9	10	11	12	1
Sales	**$81,305**	**$81,420**	**$81,535**	**$81,650**	**$81,765**	**$973,590**
Cost of goods sold	$49,844	$49,914	$49,985	$50,055	$50,126	$596,853
Gross margin	38.70%	38.70%	38.70%	38.70%	38.70%	38.70%
Operating income	**$31,462**	**$31,506**	**$31,551**	**$31,595**	**$31,640**	**$376,737**
Expenses						
Payroll	$ 15,667	$ 15,667	$ 15,667	$ 15,667	$ 15,667	$ 188,000
General and administrative	$ 2,100	$ 2,100	$ 2,100	$ 2,100	$ 2,100	$ 25,200
Marketing expenses	$ 406	$ 406	$ 406	$ 406	$ 406	$ 4,868
Professional fees and licensure	$ 435	$ 435	$ 435	$ 435	$ 435	$ 5,219
Insurance costs	$ 166	$ 166	$ 166	$ 166	$ 166	$ 1,987
Truck maintenance costs	$ 1,466	$ 1,466	$ 1,466	$ 1,466	$ 1,466	$ 17,596
Rent and utilities	$ 1,188	$ 1,188	$ 1,188	$ 1,188	$ 1,188	$ 14,250
Miscellaneous costs	$ 974	$ 974	$ 974	$ 974	$ 974	$ 11,683
Payroll taxes	$ 2,350	$ 2,350	$ 2,350	$ 2,350	$ 2,350	$ 28,200
Total operating costs	**$24,750**	**$24,750**	**$24,750**	**$24,750**	**$24,750**	**$297,003**
EBITDA	**$ 6,711**	**$ 6,756**	**$ 6,800**	**$ 6,845**	**$ 6,889**	**$ 79,734**
Federal income tax	$ 2,197	$ 2,200	$ 2,204	$ 2,207	$ 2,210	$ 26,312
State income tax	$ 333	$ 333	$ 334	$ 334	$ 335	$ 3,987
Interest expense	$ 1,083	$ 1,077	$ 1,071	$ 1,065	$ 1,059	$ 13,107
Depreciation expense	$ 729	$ 729	$ 729	$ 729	$ 729	$ 8,750
Net profit	**$ 2,368**	**$ 2,415**	**$ 2,463**	**$ 2,510**	**$ 2,557**	**$ 27,579**

Profit and loss statement (second year)

Quarter	Q1	2 Q2	Q3	Q4	2
Sales	**$233,662**	**$292,077**	**$315,443**	**$327,126**	**$1,168,308**
Cost of goods sold	$143,245	$179,056	$193,380	$200,543	$ 716,224
Gross margin	38.70%	38.70%	38.70%	38.70%	38.70%
Operating income	**$ 90,417**	**$113,021**	**$122,063**	**$126,584**	**$ 452,084**
Expenses					
Payroll	$ 38,728	$ 48,410	$ 52,283	$ 54,219	$ 193,640
General and administrative	$ 5,242	$ 6,552	$ 7,076	$ 7,338	$ 26,208
Marketing expenses	$ 1,168	$ 1,460	$ 1,577	$ 1,636	$ 5,842
Professional fees and licensure	$ 1,075	$ 1,344	$ 1,451	$ 1,505	$ 5,376
Insurance costs	$ 417	$ 522	$ 563	$ 584	$ 2,086
Truck maintenance costs	$ 3,871	$ 4,383	$ 5,226	$ 5,420	$ 19,356
Rent and utilities	$ 2,993	$ 3,741	$ 4,040	$ 4,190	$ 14,963
Miscellaneous costs	$ 2,804	$ 3,505	$ 3,785	$ 3,926	$ 14,020
Payroll taxes	$ 5,809	$ 7,262	$ 7,842	$ 8,133	$ 29,046
Total operating costs	**$ 62,107**	**$ 77,634**	**$ 83,845**	**$ 86,950**	**$ 310,535**
EBITDA	**$ 28,310**	**$ 35,387**	**$ 38,218**	**$ 39,634**	**$ 141,549**
Federal income tax	$ 8,537	$ 10,672	$ 11,525	$ 11,952	$ 42,686
State income tax	$ 1,294	$ 1,617	$ 1,746	$ 1,811	$ 6,468
Interest expense	$ 3,138	$ 3,080	$ 3,020	$ 2,959	$ 12,197
Depreciation expense	$ 2,188	$ 2,188	$ 2,188	$ 2,188	$ 8,750
Net profit	**$ 13,154**	**$ 17,832**	**$ 19,739**	**$ 20,724**	**$ 71,448**

Profit and loss statement (third year)

Quarter	Q1	3 Q2	Q3	Q4	3
Sales	$273,384	$341,730	$369,068	$382,738	$1,366,920
Cost of goods sold	$167,596	$209,495	$226,255	$234,635	$ 837,982
Gross margin	38.70%	38.70%	38.70%	38.70%	38.70%
Operating income	$105,788	$132,235	$142,813	$148,103	$ 528,939
Expenses					
Payroll	$ 39,890	$ 49,862	$ 53,851	$ 55,846	$ 199,449
General and administrative	$ 5,451	$ 6,814	$ 7,359	$ 7,632	$ 27,256
Marketing expenses	$ 1,367	$ 1,709	$ 1,845	$ 1,914	$ 6,835
Professional fees and licensure	$ 1,107	$ 1,384	$ 1,495	$ 1,550	$ 5,537
Insurance costs	$ 438	$ 548	$ 591	$ 613	$ 2,191
Truck maintenance costs	$ 4,258	$ 5,323	$ 5,749	$ 5,962	$ 21,291
Rent and utilities	$ 3,142	$ 3,928	$ 4,242	$ 4,399	$ 15,711
Miscellaneous costs	$ 3,281	$ 4,101	$ 4,429	$ 4,593	$ 16,403
Payroll taxes	$ 5,983	$ 7,479	$ 8,078	$ 8,377	$ 29,917
Total operating costs	$ 64,918	$ 81,147	$ 87,639	$ 90,885	$ 324,590
EBITDA	$ 40,870	$ 51,087	$ 55,174	$ 57,218	$ 204,349
Federal income tax	$ 12,748	$ 15,935	$ 17,209	$ 17,847	$ 63,738
State income tax	$ 1,931	$ 2,414	$ 2,607	$ 2,704	$ 9,657
Interest expense	$ 2,897	$ 2,834	$ 2,769	$ 2,702	$ 11,202
Depreciation expense	$ 2,188	$ 2,188	$ 2,188	$ 2,188	$ 8,750
Net profit	$ 21,106	$ 27,717	$ 30,401	$ 31,777	$ 111,001

7.11 Three Year Cash Flow Analysis

Cash flow analysis (first year)

Month	1	2	3	4	5	6	7
Cash from operations	$ 2,770	$ 2,816	$ 2,863	$ 2,910	$ 2,957	$ 3,004	$ 3,051
Cash from receivables	$ 0	$ 0	$ 0	$ 0	$ 0	$ 0	$ 0
Operating cash inflow	$ 2,770	$ 2,816	$ 2,863	$ 2,910	$ 2,957	$ 3,004	$ 3,051
Other cash inflows							
Equity investment	$ 25,000	$ 0	$ 0	$ 0	$ 0	$ 0	$ 0
Increased borrowings	$150,000	$ 0	$ 0	$ 0	$ 0	$ 0	$ 0
Sales of business assets	$ 0	$ 0	$ 0	$ 0	$ 0	$ 0	$ 0
A/P increases	$ 3,159	$ 3,159	$ 3,159	$ 3,159	$ 3,159	$ 3,159	$ 3,159
Total other cash inflows	$178,159	$ 3,159	$ 3,159	$ 3,159	$ 3,159	$ 3,159	$ 3,159
Total cash inflow	$180,928	$ 5,975	$ 6,022	$ 6,068	$ 6,115	$ 6,162	$ 6,209
Cash outflows							
Repayment of principal	$ 775	$ 781	$ 787	$ 793	$ 799	$ 805	$ 811
A/P decreases	$ 2,075	$ 2,075	$ 2,075	$ 2,075	$ 2,075	$ 2,075	$ 2,075
A/R increases	$ 0	$ 0	$ 0	$ 0	$ 0	$ 0	$ 0
Asset purchases	$122,500	$ 0	$ 0	$ 0	$ 0	$ 0	$ 0
Dividends	$ 0	$ 0	$ 0	$ 0	$ 0	$ 0	$ 0
Total cash outflows	$125,350	$ 2,856	$ 2,862	$ 2,867	$ 2,873	$ 2,879	$ 2,885
Net cash flow	$ 55,578	$ 3,119	$ 3,160	$ 3,201	$ 3,242	$ 3,283	$ 3,324
Cash balance	$ 55,578	$58,697	$61,857	$65,058	$68,300	$71,583	$74,906

DISPATCHED TRUCKING SERVICE

Cash flow analysis (first year cont.)

Month	8	9	10	11	12	1
Cash from operations	$ 3,098	$ 3,145	$ 3,192	$ 3,239	$ 3,286	$ 36,329
Cash from receivables	$ 0	$ 0	$ 0	$ 0	$ 0	$ 0
Operating cash inflow	**$ 3,098**	**$ 3,145**	**$ 3,192**	**$ 3,239**	**$ 3,286**	**$ 36,329**
Other cash inflows						
Equity investment	$ 0	$ 0	$ 0	$ 0	$ 0	$ 25,000
Increased borrowings	$ 0	$ 0	$ 0	$ 0	$ 0	$150,000
Sales of business assets	$ 0	$ 0	$ 0	$ 0	$ 0	$ 0
A/P increases	$ 3,159	$ 3,159	$ 3,159	$ 3,159	$ 3,159	$ 37,902
Total other cash inflows	**$ 3,159**	**$ 3,159**	**$ 3,159**	**$ 3,159**	**$ 3,159**	**$212,902**
Total cash inflow	**$ 6,256**	**$ 6,303**	**$ 6,350**	**$ 6,397**	**$ 6,445**	**$249,231**
Cash outflows						
Repayment of principal	$ 817	$ 823	$ 829	$ 835	$ 842	$ 9,695
A/P decreases	$ 2,075	$ 2,075	$ 2,075	$ 2,075	$ 2,075	$ 24,897
A/R increases	$ 0	$ 0	$ 0	$ 0	$ 0	$ 0
Asset purchases	$ 0	$ 0	$ 0	$ 0	$ 0	$122,500
Dividends	$ 0	$ 0	$ 0	$ 0	$25,430	$ 25,430
Total cash outflows	**$ 2,892**	**$ 2,898**	**$ 2,904**	**$ 2,910**	**$28,346**	**$182,522**
Net cash flow	**$ 3,365**	**$ 3,406**	**$ 3,446**	**$ 3,487**	**−$21,902**	**$ 66,708**
Cash balance	**$78,271**	**$81,676**	**$85,123**	**$88,610**	**$66,708**	**$ 66,708**

Cash flow analysis (second year)

Quarter	Q1	2 Q2	Q3	Q4	2
Cash from operations	$16,040	$20,050	$21,654	$22,456	$ 80,198
Cash from receivables	$ 0	$ 0	$ 0	$ 0	$ 0
Operating cash inflow	**$16,040**	**$20,050**	**$21,654**	**$22,456**	**$ 80,198**
Other cash inflows					
Equity investment	$ 0	$ 0	$ 0	$ 0	$ 0
Increased borrowings	$ 0	$ 0	$ 0	$ 0	$ 0
Sales of business assets	$ 0	$ 0	$ 0	$ 0	$ 0
A/P increases	$ 8,717	$10,897	$11,769	$12,204	$ 43,587
Total other cash inflows	**$ 8,717**	**$10,897**	**$11,769**	**$12,204**	**$ 43,587**
Total cash inflow	**$24,757**	**$30,946**	**$33,422**	**$34,660**	**$123,786**
Cash outflows					
Repayment of principal	$ 2,563	$ 2,621	$ 2,680	$ 2,741	$ 10,605
A/P decreases	$ 5,975	$ 7,469	$ 8,067	$ 8,365	$ 29,876
A/R increases	$ 0	$ 0	$ 0	$ 0	$ 0
Asset purchases	$ 4,010	$ 5,021	$ 5,413	$ 5,614	$ 20,050
Dividends	$11,228	$14,035	$15,157	$15,719	$ 56,139
Total cash outflows	**$23,776**	**$29,137**	**$31,318**	**$32,439**	**$116,669**
Net cash flow	**$ 981**	**$ 1,809**	**$ 2,104**	**$ 2,221**	**$ 7,116**
Cash balance	**$67,690**	**$69,499**	**$71,604**	**$73,825**	**$ 73,825**

Cash flow analysis (third year)

Quarter	Q1	Q2	Q3	Q4	3
		3			
Cash from operations	$23,950	$29,938	$32,333	$33,530	$119,751
Cash from receivables	$ 0	$ 0	$ 0	$ 0	$ 0
Operating cash inflow	**$23,950**	**$29,938**	**$32,333**	**$33,530**	**$119,751**
Other cash inflows					
Equity investment	$ 0	$ 0	$ 0	$ 0	$ 0
Increased borrowings	$ 0	$ 0	$ 0	$ 0	$ 0
Sales of business assets	$ 0	$ 0	$ 0	$ 0	$ 0
A/P increases	$10,025	$12,531	$13,534	$14,035	$ 50,125
Total other cash inflows	**$10,025**	**$12,531**	**$13,534**	**$14,035**	**$ 50,125**
Total cash inflow	**$33,975**	**$42,469**	**$45,867**	**$47,565**	**$169,876**
Cash outflows					
Repayment of principal	$ 2,803	$ 2,867	$ 2,932	$ 2,998	$ 11,599
A/P decreases	$ 7,170	$ 8,963	$ 9,680	$10,038	$ 35,852
A/R increases	$ 0	$ 0	$ 0	$ 0	$ 0
Asset purchases	$ 5,988	$ 7,484	$ 8,083	$ 8,383	$ 29,938
Dividends	$16,765	$20,956	$22,633	$23,471	$ 83,826
Total cash outflows	**$32,726**	**$40,270**	**$43,328**	**$44,890**	**$161,214**
Net cash flow	**$ 1,249**	**$ 2,199**	**$ 2,539**	**$ 2,675**	**$ 8,662**
Cash balance	**$75,074**	**$77,273**	**$79,812**	**$82,487**	**$ 82,487**

Energy Solutions Company

Abaka Energy Solutions

1200 Manistee Way
Portland, OR 97209

Abaka Energy Solutions will empower the world's underdeveloped communities through the application of solar and wind energy technologies. The company will become the world's leading provider of renewable energy (RE) products and services, with projects potentially spanning all seven continents by 2026.

This plan appeared in Business Plans Handbook, Volume 8. It has been updated for this volume.

EXECUTIVE SUMMARY

Company Overview

Abaka Energy Solutions will empower the world's underdeveloped communities through the application of solar and wind energy technologies. The company will become the world's leading provider of renewable energy (RE) products and services, with projects potentially spanning all seven continents by 2026.

Industry & Marketplace Analysis

A significant portion of the world's population has no electricity. The majority of these people live in rural, remote areas of the world's poorest nations. Global development is a multi-billion dollar industry, with the World Bank providing huge sums of money to fund large-scale projects.

Globally, energy demand is expected to increase. According to data from the U.S. Energy Information Administration, world marketed energy consumption is projected to rise 49 percent between 2007 and 2035. Specifically, global net electricity generation is projected to climb 87 percent during this time frame, growing from 18.8 trillion kWh to 35.2 trillion kWh. Growth is expected to be strongest in developing countries with unmet demand.

Electricity generation through the use of RE is expected to grow at an annual rate of 3 percent between 2007 and 2035. Accounting for 18 percent of world electricity generation in 2007, RE is expected to account for 23 percent of total generation by 2035. Even though wind and hydropower account for the majority of electricity generated by renewable means, solar power is expected to make meaningful gains as an energy source over the next few decades. From almost nonexistent levels in 2007, solar is expected to account for roughly 180 billion kWh by 2035, according to the Energy Information Administration.

Industrialization of developing countries will largely fuel the demand for energy in the coming decades. As a specialty provider and integrator of RE systems designed for developing communities, Abaka will position itself to capitalize on this explosive trend. Abaka will establish its first project in Kiseru, Tanzania, which lies near the western shore of Lake Victoria, deep in sub-Saharan Africa.

Products & Services

Abaka will introduce affordable electricity to Kiseru by offering attractive financing options for solar electric systems. This will enable families to make purchases in small monthly installments, in the same way that a consumer would buy an automobile in the United States. In addition, Abaka will construct a 15,000-watt solar/wind power station and community center, where services such as electric coffee processing, water pumping, refrigeration, computing, telecommunications access, and Internet browsing will be sold. This community center will also serve as a nucleus of education, where Kiseru residents will be exposed to a contagious spirit of entrepreneurship. The services provided here will enable, motivate, and educate people to start new businesses. In this way, Abaka's presence in Kiseru will substantially boost the region's economic prosperity.

Marketing Strategy

Kiseru is a dispersed farming community of 350,000 people. The area is so remote that power lines may never be extended there, and only 2 percent of the population has electricity. Abaka's target customer is a Kiseru family that earns about $900 per year. A basic solar electric system will be priced at $378, or $31.50 per month. Market research conducted in Kiseru strongly suggests that this price is feasible, despite the fact that it represents 45 percent of a typical family's annual income. Currently, Kiseru families use crude and dangerous kerosene lamps to light their homes, and expensive dry-cell batteries to power their radios. A solar electric system is safer, more reliable, provides better lighting, and promises better value than the alternatives mentioned above. Construction of the power station and community center will advertise Abaka's dedication to a sustainable, long-term presence within the community. Abaka has partnered with a local company called the Seattle Solar Electronics Workshop (SSEW). Working with SSEW, Abaka will sponsor informational forums to educate customers about the economic benefits of financing, the technology behind solar electricity, and the use of electricity in cultivating a prosperous economy.

Operations and Development

In October 2012, Abaka will begin building the power station and community center.

An expert in the RE field has been recruited to design this station, and to oversee its construction. SSEW will run all operations of the business in Kiseru, including inventory handling, payment collection, product distribution, and maintenance repair. All power systems will be sold to customers as pre-packaged kits, assembled by SSEW employees.

Management Team

Liam Stiller, Abaka's founder, is completing his M.B.A. in Entrepreneurship at the University of Oregon. He has traveled extensively in East Africa, and has forged a business partnership with Ghin Patel, owner of SSEW. As permanent employees, the founders will seek, identify, and finance lucrative new project opportunities all over the world. Mr. Patel will also oversee Abaka's operations in Kiseru.

Summary of Financials and Offering to Investors

In Kiseru, solar kit financing will generate almost $1 million of net income, and $3.5 million in accumulated cash, by 2018. Abaka will seek $1.3 million in a single round of seed financing to fund the construction of the power station and community center. Abaka will seek this capital from private accredited investors, nonprofit relief agencies, or possibly as a partnership with a global technology company interested in penetrating emerging markets. Abaka's presence in Kiseru will drastically improve the community's prosperity, thereby building real demand for electronics and telecommunications products and services. In exchange for capital and strategic support, Abaka will offer an investor equity, and will additionally offer a partner company direct, unlimited access to these markets at the grass-roots level. Abaka is dedicated to improving the lives of the world's underprivileged people by promoting the use of clean renewable energy. Therefore, Abaka also offers investors association with this noble initiative.

COMPANY OVERVIEW

The commitment of Abaka Energy Solutions will be to spread technologies for harnessing renewable energy (RE). The term "renewable" refers to sources of energy that can never be diminished or exhausted, such as wind and sun. The most common commercial RE technologies are photovoltaic (PV) modules, wind turbines, and, increasingly, fuel cells, which produce electricity from solar radiation, wind, and hydrogen, respectively.

Vision Statement

To become the world leader in the creation, development, and deployment of technologies that converge the advancement of human civilization with that of the environmental condition.

Three-Year Mission Statement

To profitably and sustainably introduce renewable energy into the world's underdeveloped communities.

Current Status

Abaka Energy Solutions will be organized as a Delaware C-corporation, with an executive office in Portland, Oregon, USA, during the first quarter of 2012. The company will serve as a for-profit holding, investing, and consulting agency, and will work in partnership with developing communities to establish sustainable RE projects all over the world.

Market & Services

Abaka will immediately specialize in providing electricity and electric services for rural communities, and will utilize two different business strategies to distribute power. First, Abaka will sell solar electric systems for home and commercial applications by allowing customers to finance the cost of these systems over time. Second, the company will offer end-user services direct to customers by establishing electrified community centers in the heart of their villages. At these centers, people will be able to purchase services ranging from crop processing to refrigeration to telecommunications access to internet browsing.

Objectives

Abaka's first RE project will be in Kiseru, Tanzania, a remote agricultural community in East Africa. The company will aggressively expand into a global provider of RE products and services by seeking new opportunities in other parts of Africa, as well as in Asia and Latin America. By 2026, Abaka will be the world's undisputed leading provider of RE products and services, and will operate Research & Development divisions for creating innovative novel technologies that address the environmental crises of the twenty-first century. This business plan will present Abaka's strategy for getting started, by establishing a profitable and sustainable RE business in Kiseru, Tanzania.

PRODUCTS & SERVICES

Description of Services

Abaka will offer financing packages for home and commercial-scale solar electric systems. The retail price of a small solar electric system in rural Africa is around $1,000. Abaka will enable Kiseru customers to purchase systems in affordable monthly installments, similar to the way most people in the United States purchase automobiles. These financing options will be especially popular in poor communities such as Kiseru, where affordability drives a preventative wedge in a customer's ability to buy. This business plan will mainly describe the financing aspect of Abaka's operation in Kiseru.

To solidify people's confidence in these financing options, and to demonstrate the company's dedication to the community, a 15,000-watt solar/wind power station and community center will be constructed in Kiseru. A number of end-user services will eventually be provided at this community center, such as coffee bean processing, food storage and refrigeration, battery charging, water distilling, computing, telecommunications access, and Internet browsing. In addition, an educational center will be instituted, where customers will learn how to use electricity and technology to start new businesses, or to expand existing ones. Most of these services will be provided within a year after Abaka's initial establishment in Kiseru, but eventually they will generate as much as 75 percent of the company's revenue. All of these services will be designed to help Kiseru residents augment their incomes. In this way, Abaka hopes to foster economic activity, and thus prosperity, within the community. This business plan will not describe the community center aspect of Abaka's operation in detail, but the offering of these services is part of the company's long-range plan for development in Kiseru.

Proprietary Rights

In Kiseru, and in all other project sites, Abaka will seek partnership with a local organization to help with operations, marketing, legal negotiations, and other important aspects of conducting business. Abaka's partner in Kiseru is a natively owned company called the Seattle Solar Electronics Workshop (SSEW). SSEW was founded in April 2011 by Mr. Ghin Patel, a Tanzanian electrical engineer and entrepreneur. Mr. Patel and Mr. Stiller, Abaka's founder, are close friends, and have been in business together for close to two years. It is virtually impossible for any foreign company to conduct effective or sustainable business in a poor, developing community without trustworthy local contacts. Besides SSEW, there is no company in Kiseru that has the technical capability, or the entrepreneurial innovation, to establish a joint venture of this kind. As such, Abaka is confident that no other foreign company will be able to enter this market.

Stage of Development

Although fifty years of market exposure have proven RE technologies to be unequivocally reliable and durable, the commercial RE industry is still in its infancy, and the electricity markets in developing parts of the world remain almost completely untapped. A business solution is needed to meet the challenge of profitably selling this expensive, high technology equipment to people with meager incomes. In recent years, a number of strategies have been implemented in rural, developing markets with astounding success. Almost all of these models have extended a micro-credit or financing option to their customers. These successful companies, which will be further discussed in the Industry Analysis section, have proven the efficacy of the business model that Abaka will apply in Kiseru.

INDUSTRY & MARKETPLACE ANALYSIS

Industry Analysis

As an RE service provider targeting emerging markets, Abaka will compete in the industry known as Renewables for Sustainable Village Power (RSVP). RSVP is a small, but fast-growing subset of the gigantic global energy industry, which is currently experiencing an economic revolution. One significant characteristic of this revolution has been astonishing growth.

According to data from the U.S. Energy Information Administration, world marketed energy consumption is projected to rise 49 percent between 2007 and 2035. Specifically, global net electricity generation is projected to climb 87 percent during this time frame, growing from 18.8 trillion kWh to 35.2 trillion kWh. Growth is expected to be strongest in developing countries with unmet demand. Experts predict that, as industrialization sweeps developing countries, current demand will increase significantly. Because so many new electricity users live in remote areas, most of this increased demand has been, and will continue to be, serviced by RE. As a result, renewables are a fast growing segment of world energy use.

The second trend of importance is privatization and deregulation—especially in developing countries, where governments continue to implement aggressive policies designed to attract foreign investment. Tanzania, for instance, adopted the National Investment Promotion and Protection Act in 1990, which guaranteed the privatization of several key industries, including energy. The opening of these economies has sparked the proliferation of scores of small, entrepreneurial energy companies striving to profitably satisfy the need for rural energy development. Some, such as the Grameen Bank of Bangladesh, the Solar Electric Light Fund of Thailand, and Soluz of the Dominican Republic, have developed profitable business models based on selling solar electric systems through micro-credit arrangements. Meanwhile, large companies such as Enron, Shell Oil, and BP have established dedicated RE divisions, and are aggressively executing multi-million-dollar RE projects in places such as Indonesia and South Africa.

But despite this recent surge of activity, the RSVP industry still faces some imposing challenges. For example, the vast majority of people who most need RE technologies still cannot afford them. Substantial increases in end-user purchasing power have remained elusive, and, as a result, sales are not close to what they could be. Consequently, RE manufacturers have been unable to drive economies of scale enough to cost-compete with fossil fuels. Another problem is the lack of skilled RE technicians in developing countries. There are only a handful of training centers in the world teaching RE system installation. Finally, international turmoil remains an imposing obstacle. In many countries, political and economic instability has prevented the long-term investment and presence needed to sustain RE projects.

These challenges are typical of any global industry that is only just beginning to mature, and real progress is being made to address them. As prosperity builds demand for electricity, RE training centers are being established in the developing world, such as the highly respected Institute for Solar Training in Kiseru. Furthermore, despite civil wars and social unrest, there are scores of developing countries, like Tanzania, where political stability harbors fantastic economic opportunity. Many experts predict that this global "Energy Revolution" contains the seed that will become the world's premier growth industry of the twenty-first century.

Marketplace Analysis

Tanzania. Tanzania is among the largest and most peaceful nations in East Africa. The country has demonstrated many years of political stability. According to data from the Tanzania National Web site, obtained in mid-2011, approximately 25 percent of the country (mostly non-urban areas) is not connected to the national power grid. However, one important objective is to supply some 8,200 villages with electricity, in an effort to hinder deforestation efforts. This is because some 93 percent of energy consumption is attributed to biomass energy resources, namely fuel-wood and charcoal obtained from plantations and natural forests.

According to the Tanzanian government, "very little attempt" has been made to utilize wind and solar energy in the country. However, the government recognizes, and indeed promotes, these sources of RE as viable alternatives to wood and other energy sources. In addition to concerns over deforestation, Tanzania has contended with an erratic supply of electricity. The majority of Tanzania's commercial electricity consumers are served by hydroelectric power, and the country experiences generation shortfalls during drought conditions. This situation has been exacerbated by economic growth and the increasing demand for electricity.

Tanzania has enjoyed relative political stability for many years. The country has held two elections since 1995. According to information from the Central Intelligence Agency's *World Factbook*, these elections have been contentious, with allegations of voting irregularities raised among members of the international community. Most recently, Jakaya Kikwete was elected president (for a second five-year term) on October 31, 2010. That year, electoral tensions were minimized thanks to the establishment of a government of national unity comprised of the two leading parties in Zanzibar. The next election is scheduled for 2015.

Kiseru. Kiseru is a remote farming community in the northwestern corner of Tanzania, roughly 100 kilometers from the western shore of Lake Victoria. The region experiences two dependable rainy seasons per year, and receives an annual average of about five peak sun hours per day, roughly 10 percent more than Denver, Colorado. About 350,000 people, or 60,000 households, live in this region, which is situated on a wide, sloping ridge at an elevation of 1,650 meters (5,400 feet) above sea level. The prominence of this ridge above the surrounding plain leaves it exposed to the tropical trade winds, which consistently blow from the west. There are few regions in the world that boast such abundant RE natural resources. Almost every household in Kiseru is surrounded by a plantation of several hectares, and coffee is the community's chief cash crop. The average yearly income is about $900 per family, and although this is strikingly poor by Western standards, Kiseru is one of Tanzania's most prosperous rural communities.

Customer Analysis

Kiseru is an extremely dispersed village, with 350,000 people living in an area of 3,200 square kilometers. As a result, only 1.4 percent of Kiseru's most centralized homes and businesses are electrified by the regional utility grid, while 0.6 percent are electrified with solar power. The remaining 98 percent have no hope of seeing the grid extended to their homes during the next ten years. Residents of Kiseru realize that modernization cannot take place without electricity, and that access to electricity will significantly enhance their economic prosperity and quality of life. As a result, it is no surprise that 100 percent of the fifty or so Kiseru residents surveyed during the summer of 2011 indicated a strong desire to participate in a financing program that would allow them to afford a solar electric system.

Kiseru families live in large houses, typically constructed of brick and concrete. Each house has three to five bedrooms, a kitchen, a living room, a washroom, and an animal pen. Families submit no property taxes or mortgage payments. Furthermore, because Kiseru is a farming community, residents spend very little on food, except for the few items, such as rice and fish that must be imported from surrounding districts. Very few people in this village possess an automobile, and those who do earn three to ten times more than the average yearly income. Aside from a handful of bars, restaurants, grocery stores, and weekly farmers' markets, Kiseru offers very little for the consumer. Because there is not much in this community to spend money on, Kiseru families tend to retain a purchasing power that is greater than half of their annual income. Nevertheless, due in large part to the inflationary pressures and banking crises that have plagued Tanzania ever since the 1960s, people are generally unfamiliar with the concept of saving money. Only in the past few years have stabilized banks begun to earn the trust of Tanzanian consumers, and in the rural parts of the country, this trend is proceeding quite slowly.

Despite these simplistic financial tendencies, the typical Kiseru resident is quite sophisticated, and understands the benefits of solar electricity. Kiseru is home to Africa's most distinguished solar training facility, where Abaka's Africa Operations Officer, Mr. Ghin Patel, is chief of faculty. Because of the international recognition of this school, Kiseru residents know that solar electricity represents a clean, safe, and reliable way to power their homes. Unfortunately, however, even a small solar electric system costs about $1,000 retail in Africa, and only the richest families can afford this price. As a result, most families continue to light their homes with crude kerosene lamps, and to power their radios with inefficient dry-cell batteries. Nevertheless, the demand for solar electric systems latently exists in Kiseru, and it is up to Abaka to tap this market potential by making these systems affordable for the average Kiseru family.

Competitor Analysis

Competing Technologies. Because solar electric systems are so expensive in Kiseru, they are viewed as luxury items. Almost every family would love to have one, but affordability is a preventative issue. As such, people must use more conventional methods of lighting their homes. Kerosene and dry-cell batteries are readily available in Kiseru, but neither item is particularly cheap. Kerosene sells for about fifty cents per liter, and a typical family uses four to six liters per month; many organizations, such as schools and health clinics, use twenty to fifty liters per month. Dry-cell batteries retail for nearly $4.00, and may last two or three weeks at the rate most families use their radios. Some families also own gasoline gensets, while still others own automobile batteries, which they charge with gensets, or at a grid station in the central part of the village. Abaka's chief competition in Kiseru is certainly kerosene and disposable batteries, and solar has several advantages over them. First, kerosene lamps are crude and dangerous; it is easy to find an adult in Kiseru who has been burned, at some point in his or her life, by a kerosene lamp leaking, spilling, or completely exploding. Furthermore, kerosene lamps provide lighting that is only somewhat better than a large candle, and they tend to be noisy and smelly during operation. Dry-cell batteries are expensive because they must be replaced so frequently, and their disposal poses a serious environmental threat. Also, many appliances cannot be powered with batteries. A solar electric system, on the other hand, is clean and safe, and provides the familiar fluorescent, white light that can illuminate an entire room. Furthermore, a solar electric system can be used to power any electric appliance. It offers modularity, flexibility, and expandability, so that one single power source can be used for the house's every electrical need. Additionally, these systems are extremely reliable, and require only minimal maintenance on, and periodic replacement of, the battery. If well maintained, a solar electric system will last for thirty years. Solar electric systems are more expensive than conventional alternatives in the short-term, but in the long run provide a far superior value for the money.

Competing Service Providers

Aside from Abaka's partner, SSEW, there are no businesses or organizations providing solar electricity in Kiseru. Furthermore, there is not a single organization in all of northwestern Tanzania that offers financing for solar electric systems. The national utility, the Tanzania Electric Supply Company (TANESCO), has no intention of expanding the utility grid into the periphery of Kiseru for at least ten years. Furthermore, this company has no understanding of solar electricity, and maintains only a minimal presence in Kiseru. TANESCO is not equipped to effectively compete in this marketplace.

MARKETING STRATEGY

Target Market Strategy

In order to make solar electricity affordable, Abaka will offer families and businesses the option of paying for their system in twelve monthly installments. The smallest kit offered will be priced at $31.50 per month. This translates into a year-end price of $378, which is a tremendous saving over retail. Because people in this region maintain a purchasing power equivalent to about 50 percent of their annual income, Abaka's principal target market is families that earn at least $800 per year. It is estimated that roughly one-third of Kiseru's households earn this amount or more, meaning that Abaka's primary target market in Kiseru consists of about 19,000 families.

Service Strategy

Financing Terms. Many micro-credit programs have failed in developing communities because customers have been allowed to default on their loans. It can be extremely difficult both logistically and financially to repossess equipment in remote villages of foreign countries. To circumvent this problem, Abaka will offer "pre-financing" plans to its customers. Under the terms of these pre-financing options, customers will have to pay their entire balance before Abaka will give them a system. There are two reasons why this is necessary in Kiseru. First, people in developing countries often do not understand the concept of credit, and, especially when an American company is the lender, regularly assume that "credit" means "free." Second, industrialized nations have repeatedly allowed governments and businesses in the developing world to default on their debt. People in these communities, Kiseru included, are accustomed to receiving free handouts from the World Bank and industrialized governments. It is unlikely that Abaka can establish a high-growth, sustainable business in Kiseru if expensive electrical systems are provided, but money is not collected. As such, customers will pay for their systems first, in entirety, before they receive them; no exceptions will be allowed.

Because the financing plans will have one-year terms, Abaka must offer customers something while they pay for their electric systems. This is where the community center will be useful. During the terms of their financing contracts, Abaka's customers will be allowed to utilize all services at this community center free of charge. These privileges will end upon fulfillment of the financing agreement, or if a customer defaults on several payments. This strategy will allow Abaka to collect money before distributing systems, and will encourage customers to fulfill their financing agreements. Abaka will gladly accept down payments for customers desiring shorter financing terms.

Solar Electric Kits. Abaka's solar electric systems will be sized to meet the needs of a typical Kiseru household.

Very few Kiseru homes have the need to power anything more extravagant than a few fluorescent lights and a radio, and therefore these systems will be small by Western standards. Each system will come with a solar panel, a deep-cycle battery, a charge controller, lights, a radio, wiring, connectors, and mounting materials. In order to serve the expected high demand for affordable solar electric systems in Kiseru, all systems will be sold as pre-assembled kits. These kits will be designed to be so simple that end-users will be able to perform the installations themselves. In this way, Abaka will minimize the size of its technical staff. Initially, there will be three kit sizes offered. The following table presents a spec and price comparison of Abaka's introductory product line. For homes or businesses requiring more power, customized systems will also be available. Furthermore, as the community becomes more prosperous, people will develop more extravagant tastes for electric appliances and equipment, such as television sets, satellite dish receivers, refrigerators, and computers. Abaka will continuously readjust this product line according to customers' power needs. In addition, attractive trade-in and scale-up plans will be offered to customers in subsequent years, so that smaller systems can be traded in and upgraded to larger ones.

Abaka's Initial Product Line

Kit	Size	Components	Price/month	Price/year
1	13 watts	1 light, 1 radio	$31.50	$ 378
2	30 watts	2 lights, 1 radio	$63.00	$ 756
3	48 watts	3 lights, 1 radio	$94.50	$1,134

Pricing Strategy

Abaka will price these kits as low as possible while still yielding an attractive profit. Based on Prouffer's experience in Indonesia between 2006 and 2010, it is expected that a family living in an impoverished, rural agricultural community will surrender about half of its yearly income for a necessary item such as reliable electricity. With the pricing strategy that Abaka has adopted, Kiseru consumers will pay less than half of what a comparable solar electric system would cost from a typical African retailer.

Distribution Strategy

The community center will be used as Abaka's administrative office and distribution hub. Most of the components of the solar electric kits will be shipped by sea from suppliers in the U.S. or Europe to the Indian Ocean port of Dar es Salaam, then trucked overland to Kiseru. Abaka will also attempt to identify reliable suppliers in South Africa to reduce its dependence on overseas shipping. Upon arrival in Kiseru, SSEW will be responsible for assembling all components into complete solar electric kits, ready for installation. When customers have satisfied their payment schedules, they will be cordially thanked for their business, and invited to pick up their kits from the community center. At this time, customers will be given written instructions on how to install and maintain their new systems. During their payment period, and throughout their duration of ownership, all Abaka customers will be invited to attend free educational workshops on using, maintaining, optimizing, and expanding their solar electric systems.

Advertising & Promotion Strategy

Abaka will rely greatly on publicity and word-of-mouth advertising to promote these financing plans. The construction of a 15,000-watt solar/wind power station and community center will be tremendous news in Kiseru, and will therefore serve as a very useful promotional tool. Residents will be unable to avoid noticing the sheer scale of this project. Over 100 people will be employed in this undertaking, and every newspaper and radio station in the region will publicly monitor its progress. Like many rural agricultural villages, Kiseru is a tight-knit community, and people tend to be extremely social. Abaka will have to do little to instigate excitement and conversation about this project. Once built, the generating facility, featuring a 10,000-watt wind turbine perched on an eighty-foot tower, and a 5,000-watt array of sleek solar panels mounted on a 10,000-square-foot scaffold, will serve as a constant advertisement of the electricity that Abaka offers.

Due to the visibility of this project, Abaka will ensure that high standards of professionalism are maintained at all times. Embroidered uniforms will be distributed to the SSEW technicians that maintain and operate the community center. New, high-quality equipment will be purchased, and the community center itself will have a clean, modern design. Service will be prompt and courteous, and technicians will be well trained and well paid. To complement the publicity aspect, Abaka will also post billboards in the heavily trafficked "downtown" area of the Kiseru district. The main purpose of these billboard advertisements will be to inform and remind customers of scheduled educational training sessions and technical demonstrations being held at the community center. In addition, posters will be used to announce new service offerings or price adjustments, as needed. Finally, professionally printed brochures, featuring concise descriptions of the financing plans offered, as well as general information about solar energy, will be widely distributed.

Sales Strategy

Ghin Patel, the founder and executive officer of SSEW, is a native of Kiseru, and has been installing solar energy systems there for eight years. Mr. Patel's expert reputation is common knowledge in the community. All sales and operational responsibilities will be contracted to SSEW, taking advantage of Mr. Patel's contacts and stature in Kiseru as a solar energy professional. Because SSEW's name is already well known to the community, customers will be dealing directly with a local company that they trust. A customer service office and reception desk will be established at the community center, and SSEW will collect payments at this location. In exchange for these services, and for using the SSEW name to generate trust and loyalty, Abaka will pay SSEW a contracting fee based on sales volume. Therefore, SSEW will have an incentive to aggressively generate sales by subscribing new customers, in whatever fashion they deem appropriate or effective.

Marketing & Sales Forecasts

Abaka's projected target market in Kiseru is about 19,000 families. There are 58,000 families in the region without electricity. However, these pre-financing plans will be expensive. Furthermore, customers will have to pay all of their monthly installments before receiving any equipment. Abaka recognizes that this will initially dissuade many potential customers. However, the construction of the power station and community center, as well as the partnership with SSEW, will help to reinforce Abaka's trustworthiness, and should neutralize some of these concerns. In addition, Abaka will allow subscribed customers to use the community center for free during their contract term. This means that customers will be able to enjoy free access to computers, refrigeration, water distilling, coffee bean processing, telecommunications access, and other services, for up to a year. Abaka anticipates subscribing about 250 families in 2013, the first year of operation. After one year, Kiseru residents will witness the delivery of solar electric systems purchased the previous year by their friends, neighbors, and relatives. The demand for these financing contracts will therefore increase exquisitely over the next five years, as Abaka's trustworthiness becomes confirmed, and its presence accepted, by the community. Furthermore, similar projects in other parts of the world have demonstrated that the availability of energy systems motivates people to increase their income by working harder, and then to save more of that income, in anticipation of having something valuable to buy. As a result, more Kiseru families will be able and willing to afford Abaka's financing plans over time, and the growth rates built into Abaka's revenue forecasts reflect this expectation. The following table shows sales and revenue forecasts for the years 2013-2018.

	2013	2014	2015	2016	2017	2018
Units sold	250	750	1,875	3,750	5,625	8,438
Revenues	$110,541	$331,033	$829,060	$1,658,119	$2,487,178	$3,730,768

OPERATIONS STRATEGY

Bim Stiletto, a primary schoolteacher in Kiseru, arrives home after a long day of work. It is nighttime in Africa, and pitch black envelops the quiet community. There are no street lights, no glows in the neighbors' windows; only the brilliant stars of the Southern Cross provide illumination. But on this night, Mr. Stiletto arrives to find his house teeming with activity. The solar electric system he spent a year buying has finally arrived, and his family is already putting it to good use. His wife is busily cooking in the kitchen, his eldest son studiously doing homework, and his two youngest children playing Monopoly, all possible due to the streaming radiance provided by the fluorescent lamp in the living room. Had this been a typical night in a typical Kiseru house, Mr. Stiletto would have to wait his turn to use one of the household's two kerosene lamps, for he has about thirty exams to grade. In other words, he would be up late, long after his family had retired for the night. But as he greets his family working and playing under this new artificial sun, Mr. Stiletto realizes that the "typical" Kiseru evening has now changed forever.

Customers will start their lifetime relationship with Abaka upon receipt of their first solar electric kit. In time, they will learn to effectively apply the full potential of solar energy, and they will completely replace archaic kerosene lamps and dry cell batteries with the solar electricity that will become the routine hallmark of the future for communities like Kiseru.

All of Abaka's operations in Kiseru will be contracted out to SSEW. Mr. Ghin Patel, founder and CEO of SSEW, will serve as Abaka's Chief Operating Officer for this project. Mr. Patel will facilitate dealings with the Tanzanian government, as well as with Karadea, an influential UN-funded nongovernment organization that will be heavily utilized, both in the construction of the power station and in ongoing operations.

Scope of Operations

SSEW will be responsible for conducting the following activities in Kiseru:

- Operating and maintaining the power station and community center

- Placing supply orders and maintaining inventory

- Overseeing and orchestrating solar kit assembly and distribution

- Collecting customer payments

- Servicing customer repair calls and manufacturer's warranties

- Printing and distributing advertisements, such as billboards, posterboards, and brochures

- Subscribing new customers and upgrading current and past customers

- Organizing informational forums and instructional demonstrations

Abaka will negotiate the most attractive supply agreements possible, and all purchases will be made directly from manufacturers at wholesale prices. Additionally, all shipping will occur via ocean, to the Tanzanian port of Dar es Salaam. Supplies will be trucked overland to Kiseru from the Indian Ocean coast. To avoid import duties, all batteries will be purchased in bulk directly from the Acme Exide Company, a Tanzania manufacturer. Lights, charge controllers, wiring, connectors, and radios will be purchased in bulk from wholesale suppliers in the United States, Europe, or South Africa. Solar modules will be purchased directly from WorldSolar, Inc., a Eugene, Oregon-based company with production facilities in India. Wind turbines and towers will be purchased from and installed by Rossimond Light & Power, of Forrestville, Wisconsin. Building and security materials will be purchased in the United States, South Africa, or Kenya. Abaka will be able to legally avoid all import duties through Mr. Patel's association with Karadea, which enjoys complete exemption from most Tanzanian tariff laws. A temporary workforce of about 100 will be hired in Kiseru to build the power station and community center. Rossimond Light & Power will design, oversee, and orchestrate the construction project, with all Abaka officers present to oversee progress and to direct funding.

Ongoing Operations

After the power station and community center are completed, a full-time workforce of three to five maintenance technicians and two to four security agents will be hired and paid directly by SSEW for salaries in excess of $1,000 per year. Rossimond Light & Power will thoroughly train SSEW technicians on proper maintenance and operation of the power station. Insurance on hard assets will be purchased from a trustworthy agency in Tanzania.

SSEW will be charged with the responsibility of maintaining customer relations and satisfaction. This will include subscribing new customers and taking care of existing ones. SSEW will provide free maintenance or repair visits to customers' homes for one year after the equipment's initial installation. Additionally, SSEW will help and encourage customers to upgrade to larger power systems. Used components in good working condition will be accepted as trade-in for credit on a larger system. Furthermore, customers will be encouraged to return their used batteries to SSEW, which will send them out for proper recycling. Price credits towards the purchase of new batteries will be given to all customers who dispose of their old batteries in this manner.

SSEW will be in charge of hiring and maintaining a trained local workforce. Because Mr. Patel has taught at the Institute for Solar Training for six years, he knows who the most competent technicians are, and how to find them in East Africa. Abaka will provide the financial resources to help Mr. Patel attract these technicians to Kiseru.

Operating Expenses

The following table shows Abaka's anticipated operating expenses from 2013-2018.

Operating expenses	2013	2014	2015	2016	2017	2018
SSEW contracting fees	$ 6,500	$13,000	$26,000	$52,000	$104,000	$208,000
Maintenance expenses	$ 4,000	$ 4,135	$ 4,341	$ 4,557	$ 4,786	$ 5,024
Marketing expenses	$ 4,000	$ 4,725	$ 5,669	$ 6,802	$ 8,163	$ 9,796
Insurance and security	$10,500	$10,500	$10,500	$10,500	$ 10,500	$ 10,500
Total	$25,000	$32,360	$46,510	$73,859	$127,449	$233,320

DEVELOPMENT STRATEGY

Abaka will assemble a legal team and incorporate during the first quarter of 2012. After completing and revising the business plan, the company will begin to seek grants and investments from accredited private investors, multi-national relief agencies, and, possibly, from large corporations.

There will be some need for product development and prototyping in Kiseru. Solar electric systems consist of four main components. The solar panel harnesses photon energy from the sun, converting radiation into electricity. This electricity is then conditioned by a charge controller before it is sent to a battery for storage. The charge controller regulates the battery's state of charge, preventing it from being damaged. The appliance, then, receives its power directly from the battery. This system has been used and perfected for well over fifty years, and Abaka's kits will not deviate from this simple design. Nevertheless, Abaka's solar electric systems will be sold as pre-assembled kits. Because customers will be expected to perform their own installations, Abaka will need to test customer reaction to these kits. Specifically, Abaka will assemble several versions in order to develop a packaging method that optimizes simplicity for the customer. Prototype testing will be conducted simultaneously with the construction of the power station and will take less than one month to complete.

Once in Kiseru, Abaka and SSEW will focus on developing market demand for the financing services. Because these financing plans will be expensive, and because no equipment will be distributed until all payments have been received, it will take time for Abaka to earn the trust of Kiseru's consumers. However, Abaka is convinced that this can be done within one year. First, utilization of SSEW, a Kiseru company that people already know and trust, will help to lend credibility to Abaka's promises. Second, the power station and community center will represent a symbol of Abaka's long-term commitment to the community. Finally, Abaka will lead by example; when working solar kits are delivered to the first wave of customers, Abaka's trustworthiness will be ultimately confirmed. By this time, Kiseru's demand for these systems will be growing fantastically.

Development Timeline

Project Kiseru will be launched in five major phases, during the following estimated dates:

- Phase 1—Incorporation: Finalize business plan, incorporate, file with the U.S. SEC, build project website: January-March 2012

- Phase 2—Venture Financing: $1.3 million for construction of power station and community center, and to jump-start operations: February-September 2012

- Phase 3—Construction of power station and community center: October-December 2012

- Phase 4—Optimize solar kit packaging and assembly: November 2012

- Phase 5—Subscribe customers to solar kit financing plans: December 2012

Development Expenses

Abaka estimates that the company will need $2,500 to $6,500 for incorporation and legal fees, which will be paid by Mr. Stiller during the first quarter of 2012.

MANAGEMENT TEAM

Company Organization

Abaka's principal founders, Liam Stiller and Ghin Patel, will control the majority of the company's equity. Abaka will employ both Mr. Stiller and Mr. Patel on a full-time basis. A Board of Directors will be assembled if and when investors demand one. A Board of Advisers has been compiled in the meanwhile. This Board is composed of experts with extensive experience relevant to the area of international rural development. All of these advisers have agreed to lend their assistance free of charge. Please see the Appendix for a detailed description of Abaka's Board of Advisers, and Appendix F for the resume of one of Abaka's founders.

Liam Stiller, Executive Officer. Mr. Stiller is Abaka's primary visionary. He will earn his M.B.A. degree in entrepreneurship from the University of Oregon in May 2012. He has taken formal coursework in both PV and wind system design and installation at International Natural Energy (INE), arguably the most respected and well-known RE training facilities in the world. Mr. Stiller has many contacts in the industry, and knows key people at the Renewable Energy Sources Laboratory (RESL), the Public Service Company of Oregon, WorldSolar, Inc., Energy Choices Africa, and the Tanzania Investment Center. He has traveled extensively in East Africa, and conducted market research on solar financing in Kiseru while doing an internship for SSEW during the summer of 2011.

Ghin Patel, Africa Operations Officer. Mr. Patel, Abaka's principal co-founder, will serve as the company's Officer for Africa Operations. Mr. Patel is a native of Kiseru, Tanzania, and is a master electrician. In 2011, he founded the Seattle Solar Electronics Workshop (SSEW) with financial backing from Mr. Stiller. SSEW offers a wide range of electrical services in the Kiseru area and beyond. Mr. Patel has installed over 500 solar electric systems in his career, and he has taught the PV systems design and installation course at the Institute for Solar Training for six years. For the last three of those years, Mr. Patel has served as the school's resident chief of staff. The school itself is located in Kiseru, and is operated and funded by one of Tanzania's most important non-government organizations, the Kiseru Development Association (KARADEA), with which Mr. Patel has very close ties. In a period of only eight years, the Institute for Solar Training has arguably become the most respected solar energy technical school in the southern Hemisphere. Mr. Patel has earned the distinction "Fundi," which, in Kiswahili means "Master Technician." He is unquestionably Tanzania's premier installer of PV systems, and one of the most admired men in Kiseru.

Administrative Expenses

The following table shows Abaka's expected administrative expenses for 2013-2018.

Administrative expenses	2013	2014	2015	2016	2017	2018
Salary, Mr. Stiller	$39,000	$47,000	$56,688	$ 68,825	$ 81,630	$ 97,957
Benefits, Mr. Stiller	$ 3,900	$ 4,700	$ 5,668	$ 6,882	$ 8,163	$ 9,795
Salary, Mr. Patel	$ 3,500	$ 4,000	$ 4,725	$ 5,669	$ 6,803	$ 8,163
Travel expenses	$ 5,250	$ 6,300	$ 7,560	$ 9,070	$ 10,884	$ 13,060
Legal & accounting services	$ 5,250	$ 6,300	$ 7,560	$ 9,070	$ 10,884	$ 13,060
Office expenses	$ 650	$ 787	$ 945	$ 1,134	$ 1,361	$ 1,632
Total	$57,550	$69,087	$83,146	$100,650	$119,725	$143,667

FINANCIAL SUMMARY

Assumptions

The financial statements presented in the Appendix reflect only Abaka's forecasted sales of pre-financing contracts in Kiseru. Revenues generated from community center services are not included in these forecasts, nor are potential revenues generated from projects in locations other than Kiseru. In addition, the financial statements assume that Abaka makes no capital expenditures during the explicit period of 2013-2018. Due to the nature of the pre-financing plans, the bulk of customer payments will be collected before kit components will be ordered. This will have a positive effect on net income and cash flow. The following table presents Abaka's expected operational calendar and shows why reported net income and cash flow will be increased by the nature of the pre-financing plans.

Operational Calendar

Year 0 - Nov. to Dec.—Sign-Up New Customers

Year 1 - Jan. to Dec.—Collect Monthly Payments

Year 1 - Sep. to Oct.—Order Kit Components

Year 1 - Oct. to Dec.—Assemble Kits

Year 2 - Jan. to Feb.—Distribute Kits

Year 2 - Jan. to Feb.—Charge off Cost of Kits Sold

Capital Requirements

Abaka requires $1 million in start-up capital for the construction of the power station and community center. An additional infusion of $300,000 in cash at the end of 2012 will be needed to jump-start operations; this includes a significant safety cushion in case of financial emergency.

Financial Risks

Currency Translation. All of Abaka's revenues will be collected in Tanzanian shillings, and almost every shilling collected will have to be converted into U.S. dollars in order to meet the company's major expense accounts. As far as the founders know, there are no market-based instruments available for hedging currency risks, such as the deflation of the Tanzanian shilling against the dollar. As such, all financial forecasts assume that Abaka will lose 5 percent of its revenue to currency exchange fluctuations and expenses. In order to minimize exposure, almost all collected Tanzanian money will be immediately converted into U.S. dollars by establishing a corporate forex account at the Tanzania National Bank. This account will allow for currency exchange at a competitive market rate, and will also enable Abaka to automatically wire transfer all funds directly into a corporate account at either Citibank or the Chase Manhattan Bank in Eugene. This will be Abaka's short-term answer to contending with currency risk. For the long-term, Abaka will neutralize currency risk by diversifying its operations and holdings into other areas of the world.

Political and Economic Stability. The countries surrounding Tanzania's western border have experienced a great deal of strife over the years, characterized by anarchy, exodus, bloody violence, and massive inflation. In Tanzania, these regional pressures have contributed to high unemployment and double-digit inflation. Nevertheless, Tanzania has enjoyed relative political stability for many years. The country has held two elections since 1995. According to information from the Central Intelligence Agency's *World Factbook*, these elections have been contentious, with allegations of voting irregularities raised among members of the international community. Most recently, Jakaya Kikwete was elected president (for a second five-year term) on October 31, 2010. That year, electoral tensions were minimized thanks to the establishment of a government of national unity comprised of the two leading parties in Zanzibar. The next election is scheduled for 2015. There is a substantial World Bank presence in Tanzania, as well as in Kenya and Uganda. The Tanzanian government has set up an Investment Center to aid foreigners in identifying lucrative opportunities in Tanzania. Consistent with this measure, the government has also adopted extremely liberal tax and import laws in an effort to attract foreign investment. Abaka is confident that the political and economic climate in Tanzania is becoming more and more favorable for business every day, and that real progress is being made to protect Tanzania's economy and infrastructure from the instability occurring in neighboring regions.

Coffee. Kiseru residents depend heavily on coffee for their revenue. Economically, coffee harvests can be affected by climate or market prices, and this cannot be ignored as a potential threat to Abaka's success in Kiseru. However, Abaka's presence in Kiseru will drastically improve the region's prosperity, and the community center will help to spark an entrepreneurial spirit by providing new opportunities for small businesses in Kiseru. In short, Abaka's commitment for a long-term, value-enhancing presence in Kiseru will itself significantly neutralize this risk by helping the community to diversify and expand its economy. Furthermore, Abaka will explore the possibility of accepting coffee as payment for solar kits, which might prove to be another effective strategy for neutralizing currency translation risk.

Cross-Cultural. There is an operational risk inherent whenever a company in one country attempts to do business in another. This "distance" risk will be mitigated in Kiseru through the partnership with SSEW, which will handle all day-to-day operations of the business. Additionally, Abaka will maintain a full-time Oregon-based staff, as well as an expanding travel budget, so that Kiseru, and future sites in other countries, will be visited on a regular basis.

Exit Strategy

This proposed project in Kiseru will require a long-term commitment. In Kiseru, Abaka will generate cash flows that will be used to finance project expansions into other areas of the world, such as West Africa, Asia, and Latin America. Once Abaka's concept has been proven, and the potential for further growth demonstrated, Abaka will most likely exit via a management buyout. Another real possibility will be to take the company public. Demonstration of substantial and sustainable growth, combined with the establishment of global brand name recognition, should make this a viable exit option. Over the past few decades, several mutual funds have been established that explicitly invest with environmental companies, and this demonstrates that there is a public capital market willing to purchase equity in a company like Abaka. In any case, Abaka does not foresee an exit occurring until at least 2018.

For a comprehensive background on the challenges of conducting business in Tanzania, please see the author's paper entitled "Tanzania: Developing Strategies for Effective Business Practices," available in Adobe Acrobat format from the Abaka website, www.Abaka.com.

OFFERING

Investment Requirements

Mr. Stiller has already invested $10,500 in administrative, travel, and research expenses to write this business plan. In the near future, Abaka will require an additional $2,500 to $6,500 for incorporation and legal expenses, plus $1.3 million in seed venture financing to launch the project in Kiseru. The following table presents an itemized breakdown of the venture financing needed.

Itemization of investment needed

Power station

5,000-watt solar array	$ 60,000
10,000-watt wind generator	$ 60,000
Power conditioning equipment	$ 60,000
Power storage equipment	$ 60,000
Security equipment	$ 13,000
Wiring and connectors	$ 13,000
Labor	$ 34,000
Total cost of power station	**$ 300,000**

Community center

Coffee and fruit processors	$ 212,500
Refrigeration & freezing equipment	$ 104,000
Computing and telecommunications center	$ 130,000
Water pumping facility	$ 78,000
Convention center and theatre	$ 32,500
Battery charging station	$ 26,000
2 work vans	$ 26,000
Workshops	$ 19,500
Office space	$ 6,500
Furniture	$ 6,500
Security equipment	$ 6,500
Labor	$ 52,000
Total cost of community center	**$ 700,000**

Totals

Power station	$ 300,000
Community center	$ 700,000
Cash for operations	$ 300,000
Total venture round B investment	**$1,300,000**

In addition, the company will seek assistance in further developing legal, distribution, marketing, and financial strategies for conducting business internationally. Therefore, Abaka will require significant strategic support, as well as capital, in launching this venture.

Offering

Abaka's required $1.3 million capital investment will be obtained through a venture round financing period conducted during the first half of 2012. Abaka will attempt to obtain the majority of this capital either from an environmental project investment agency or in the form of a partnership with a large, multinational corporation interested in penetrating emerging market. Ideally, this will be an electronics or telecommunications company that has substantial financial, marketing, and legal resources. Potential corporate partners include companies such as General Electric, Philips, Sharp, Magnavox, Toshiba, and a host of streamlined, globally-aggressive telecommunications companies. Abaka will also seek and accept financing from private, accredited investors, in accordance with all U.S. and Tanzanian securities laws.

Abaka will prefer to structure this investment agreement as an exchange of services partnership agreement, but, if necessary, equity can and will be granted in return for capital. Because the founders want to maintain cash flows for use in future project expansions, and not to buy back common stock, Abaka will attempt to retain 67 percent of its equity in the control of management throughout both rounds of financing. Additionally, the company will explore the possibility of leveraging a partnership or equity investment with a loan from a government or nonprofit relief agency such as USAID or the Africa Project Development Fund.

The markets in which Abaka will operate have a tremendous long-term potential for economic development. Abaka has the knowledge and the local contacts to bring electricity and prosperity to these regions. Eventually, these markets will develop a substantial demand for electronics, telecommunication, and information technologies. Abaka's ideal investor and/or corporate partner will have the vision and the desire to penetrate these markets early and aggressively. They will have the resources to provide significant financial, logistical, operational, marketing, and legal support. In exchange, a partner company will be granted exclusive supply and branding rights for all products and services that Abaka offers. In addition, Abaka will actively help a partner company to market its product(s) at the grassroots level by employing locals to build a loyal, long-term customer base within their communities. By providing underdeveloped communities with affordable and dependable electricity, Abaka will help pave the way for prosperity and economic development to permeate emerging markets all over the world.

APPENDICES

Organization	Type	Location
CAT Consultancy	Profit	Wales
Cinergy Global Power	Profit	United Kingdom
E & Company	Profit	New Jersey, USA
Econergy International	Profit	Oregon, USA
EnergyEnviro Ventures LLC	Profit	New England, USA
Energy Alternatives Africa	Profit	Kenya
Energy Power Resources, Ltd.	Profit	England
Enersol	Nonprofit	New England, USA
Global Impressions, Ltd.	Profit	United Kingdom
Hyder	Profit	Wales
Intermediate Technology	Profit	United Kingdom
Nykomb Synergetics AB	Profit	Sweden
Plenum Energy	Profit	Germany
PowerGen	Profit	United States
Ramboll	Profit	Denmark
Solar Bank International	Profit	United States
Soluz	Profit	New England, USA
SunTree	Profit	Israel
The Grameen Bank	Nonprofit	Bangladesh
TradeWind Insurance	Profit	United States

Survey

During the Summer of 2011, Mr. Stiller conducted an informal survey of Kiseru citizens. As an American, it is very difficult to obtain reliable information from people there, because they will always try to make themselves sound poorer than they really are, in the hope of receiving a handout or "sponsorship." Therefore, questions concentrated on qualitative measures rather than quantitative. In other words, discussion of actual dollar figures was avoided. Nevertheless, a good measure of Kiseru's demand for solar electricity, and why it is not being met, was obtained from these conversations. In some cases, a translator was used. The following questions were posed, generally in this order:

1. What other electrical appliances do you own?

2. How do you feel about the currently available energy sources in Kiseru?

3. What do you know about solar energy?

4. Do you know Ghin Patel?

5. Why is solar energy not used more readily in Kiseru?

6. In which village do you live?

7. How big is your house?

8. How do you light your house and power your radios?

9. What would you use solar energy for, if you could get it?

It is important to note that these questions were not posed in a formal interview environment, but during casual conversation with almost every local that Mr. Stiller met. Most of these conversations took place on the streets, in bars and restaurants, or on shuttle rides between villages. Overwhelmingly, the results of these conversations demonstrated that, in Kiseru, solar power is viewed as an expensive luxury item that only the richest families possess.

Furthermore, it was clear that almost every individual had a basic understanding of what solar energy is, and what it can do. The most important message of these conversations is that a tremendous latent demand for solar energy exists in Kiseru, and that the major obstacle impeding its widespread use is affordability.

Board of Advisors

Mary Flinger. Ms. Flinger has developed RE policy in Bangladesh, in Egypt, and in many parts of Latin America. She worked at RESL's International Programs Division for three years, and graduated from International Natural Energy's RE education program. Most significantly, Ms. Flinger was instrumental in aiding the Grameen Bank of Bangladesh to develop a working micro-finance plan for solar electric systems. The Grameen model is now regarded to be the most successful solar leasing program in the history of the industry, and the bank has become one of the most fortuitous lending institutions in the world with a 95 percent pay-back rate. Ms. Flinger is currently earning her M.B.A. degree at New York University in New York. Her experience developing a successful business plan to bring affordable solar energy systems to families in Bangladesh will be extremely valuable to this project.

Jane Winger. Ms. Winger has over six years of experience in the energy industry, as well as several years' experience in the global development field. Currently, she is employed by Energy Resources International (ERI), where she develops training curriculum for electric utility managers in developing countries. This curriculum, which has been implemented in Ghana, Brazil, and Mexico, teaches utility managers strategies for maximizing energy efficiency. Ms. Winger is currently earning her M.B.A. degree in entrepreneurship and marketing from the University of Oregon. She played an instrumental role in the preparation of this business plan, and, as one of Abaka's most accessible advisers, will maintain close involvement with Abaka in years to come. At some point in the future, Ms. Winger may join the company's full-time staff.

Rudolph Heisemann. Mr. Bartholf is a director at Energy Resources International (ERI), and has over twenty years of experience in the RE industry. During his impressive career, Mr. Bartholf has provided strategic planning, project development, and technical assistance as a consultant to numerous organizations all over the world. Prior to joining ERI, Mr. Bartholf served as a Senior Program Officer at Prouffer International, a nonprofit development assistance organization. While at Prouffer, Mr. Bartholf spearheaded the development of RE projects in several Asian countries. His advice on technical and economic matters, as well as his contacts within the industry, will prove highly valuable to Abaka.

Miller Fried. Mr. Byrne is a British ex-patriot who has been installing solar electric systems off and on in eastern and southern Africa for twelve years. Currently, he is working with the Maasai people in Arusha, Tanzania, on a large-scale solar project to electrify several remote community centers and schools on tribal lands. Mr. Byrne is literally in the trenches, both as a system installer and integrator, and as a fundraiser. He has important contacts with non-government organizations throughout Europe and Africa, and knows key RE producers and distributors. His assistance with the Tanzanian government, with suppliers and distributors, and with private fundraisers, will prove vital to Abaka's success in Kiseru. He will also serve as an ideal sounding board for idea testing.

Justin Sangria, Ph.D. Dr. Sangria is a Professor of Finance at the University of Oregon. He specializes in the area of risk management, particularly as it relates to international finance and currency exchange. A native of Peru, Professor Sangria has consulted for numerous banks in Latin America on currency hedging, and has developed financial strategies to help these banks effectively conduct business across international borders. Professor Sangria's expertise in this realm will help Abaka to manage the serious financial risks associated with doing business in Tanzania.

Felicia Strong, M.B.A. Ms. Strong has worked in the U.S. RE industry for over seven years in both the public and private sectors. Most recently, she worked for Kyocera Solar International, one of the world's largest producers of PV technology, as well as for the U.S. Export Council for RE. She is now working for Prouffer International. Ms. Strong has lived and worked in Brazil, and knows the global RE industry as well as anybody. She will aid in developing strategies for executing this business plan, and in locating potential investors.

Joseph Rosenthal, Ph.D. Dr. Rosenthal is a Senior Economist at the National Energy Sources Laboratory (NESL) in Eugene, Oregon. He has been the Senior Analyst of NESL's International and Village Power Program for nine years, and has worked in the RE field since 1990. He specializes in conducting feasibility and optimization analyses for RE projects in developing nations. Dr. Rosenthal will continue to assist Abaka by reviewing and editing the business plan, by providing fresh ideas and approaches, and by connecting Abaka's management team with other key people in the industry.

Samuel Obago. Mr. Obago is a native of Kenya, and is the Chief Operations Officer at Energy Choices Africa (ECA), probably Kenya's pre-eminent large-scale RE consulting firm. He has seven years of hands-on experience installing solar electric systems. For ECA, Mr. Obago evaluates project financing and feasibility, and negotiates contracts with the World Bank and other international lenders. He is fluent in Kiswahili, and knows key people in East African government, financial, and nonprofit organizations.

Jake Rossimond. Mr. Rossimond, owner of Rossimond Power and Light, has been designing, installing, repairing, and building wind generators for twenty years. He is perhaps the nation's best-known specialist in the commercial wind energy industry, and has worked on RE development projects in 23 foreign countries. He has consulted for NESL, as well as numerous other energy organizations all over the world, and has taught the wind energy class at INE for the past six years. In addition to serving as a consultant for the business plan, he has agreed to oversee the design and construction of Abaka's power station and community center in Kiseru.

Mitchell Bumholtz. Mr. Bumholtz served two years in Paraguay with the Peace Corps, and has since graduated from INE's RE education program. He has consulted for the World Conservation Project, and for the past two years has been instrumental in the establishment of a large-scale commercial wind power project in New England. Mr. Bumholtz has been a dedicated proponent of this project since its inception, and may join the Abaka management team as a full-time employee within a year.

Jimmy Wise. Mr. Wise has been an Executive Director of International Natural Energy (INE), arguably the world's most respected RE training center, since 2003. He has been training people in RE installation since 1993, and has nearly thirty years of experience as a licensed general contractor in solar home building and design. During his career, Mr. Wise has taught solar installation in developing countries all over the world. He has agreed to assist with the on-site design and construction of Abaka's power station and community center.

Jacob Black, Ph.D. Dr. Black is a Senior Analyst at NESL's International Programs Division. He has over twenty years of experience advising and consulting on RE projects in sub-Saharan Africa, and has traveled extensively in the region. As one of Abaka's most accessible and supporting advisers, Dr. Black will continue to provide constructive criticism, new ideas, and liaison with potential consultants and investors.

RESUME OF LIAM STILLER

OBJECTIVE

To build Abaka Energy Solutions into a global provider of renewable energy products and services

EDUCATION & EXPERIENCE

University of Oregon

Master's Degree in Business Administration

Expected Graduation, May 2012

- Major in Entrepreneurship; 3.7 cumulative GPA

- Awarded $5,000 in merit-based fellowships for study in Entrepreneurship

- Helped WorldSolar, Inc. of Eugene, OR develop a marketing strategy for introducing their solar module into East Africa as an independent project for M.B.A. credit

- Teaching Assistant, M.B.A. Business Statistics course

Seattle Solar Electronics Workshop, Kiseru, Kagera, Tanzania

Summer Internship, June-August 2011

- Conducted the feasibility analysis for the Abaka business concept

- Forged a business partnership with Ghin Patel, Tanzania's leading installer of solar electric systems

- Made contacts with key industry people including Samuel Obago and Miller Fried, as well as officials at the Kiseru Development Association (KARADEA), the Tanzania Foreign Investment Center, the Tanzania Revenue Authority, the Tanzania Electric Supply Company, and the Africa Projects Development Fund

International Natural Energy, Eugene, OR

Renewable Energy Education Program, June-August 2010

- Completed coursework in PV system design and installation

- Helped to install a 1.5 kW grid-tied PV system on a home in Edwards, CO

- Completed coursework in the fundamentals of wind generator operation and installation

- Helped to install a 1.5 kW wind generator on a remote home near Fairplay, CO

Amgen, Inc., Portland OR

Department of Inflammation November 2005-May 2010

Research Associate in Cell Biology & Immunology

- Worked on over 20 project teams to develop novel therapeutics for treating inflammatory diseases

- Responsible for researching the effects of drugs on cells and organ systems, reporting data at team meetings, contributing to strategies for drug development, and coordinating cell biology research efforts with those of other departments

- Supervised 3 student interns to help with research and project implementation

- Wrote 2 and co-authored 7 scientific papers

- Promoted twice for ability to work in teams, handle multiple responsibilities, conduct sound science, function without supervision, and take primary initiative

- Presented data in front of 200 cell biologists at the international Keystone Symposium

University of Chicago, Chicago, IL

Bachelor's Degree in History & Immunology, Graduated June 2005

- Chairman of fraternity committee; led the most successful recruitment program on campus

- Chairman of Philanthropy committee; led an effort which raised $85,000 for cancer research, and honored by the Saturn Corporation for dedication to community service

ADDITIONAL INFORMATION

- Skilled in Microsoft Office, including Excel spreadsheets for financial analyses and optimization modeling (maximizing profits or minimizing costs)

- Written and conversational literacy in Spanish

- Able to travel extensively, and to remote locations (have been to 17 countries on 4 continents); self-sufficient and culturally adaptive

---

FINANCIAL STATEMENTS

Sales & Revenue Forecasts

Anticipated sales breakdown	Plan 1	Plan 2	Plan 3
Percent of total sales	85%	13%	2%

Sales forecasts	2013	2014	2015	2016	2017	2018
Sales growth rate	200%	150%	100%	50%	50%	
Kits sales, plan 1	212	637	1,593	3,187	4,781	7,172
Kits sales, plan 2	33	98	244	488	731	1097
Kits sales, plan 3	5	15	38	75	113	169
Total kits sold	**250**	**750**	**1,875**	**3,750**	**5,625**	**8,438**

Total Customers Served, 2013-2018: 20,688

Revenue forecasts	2013	2014	2015	2016	2017	2018
Units sold	250	750	1,875	3,750	5,625	8,438
Revenues	$110,541	$331,033	$829,060	$1,658,119	$2,487,178	$3,730,768

Additional Financial Data

The financial data incorporated throughout the narrative portion of this business plan was obtained from detailed financial statements, which have been prepared with assistance from our certified public accountant. Available upon request, these include:

- Pro-Forma Cost of Kits Sold and Inventory Holding Schedule

- Consolidated Pro-Forma Financial Statements, 2013-2018

- Consolidated Monthly Pro-Forma Financial Statements, Year 2013

- Consolidated Monthly Pro-Forma Financial Statements, Year 2014

Freelance Children's Librarian

Storytime Alternatives

PO Box 123456
Armada, Michigan 48005

AB Lane Communications

Storytime Alternatives is a freelance company offering programming and services by a certified and degreed children's librarian to libraries, city recreation centers, and preschools.

EXECUTIVE SUMMARY

Storytime Alternatives is a freelance company offering programming and services by a certified and degreed children's librarian to libraries, city recreation centers, and preschools. These institutions can offer programming to their patrons with much less cost than hiring a librarian on a more permanent basis.

RATIONALE

Libraries and city recreation centers are suffering from the same financial concerns as the rest of the country. Funding comes at least partially from the collection of property taxes; as the housing market has plummeted and foreclosures abound, the monies collected from property taxes has dwindled. Additional funding comes from federal, state, and local governments, all of which have cut funding to some extent, further exaggerating the funding problem and forcing these institutions to carefully review their expenditures and try to maximize their spending potential.

Preschools are also money-conscious, as they try to cap costs for families to maintain affordability, while at the same time trying to instruct children in a fun environment that utilizes the latest educational resources. The costs of running preschools are going up as the price of things like electricity and personnel increase, but the price they are able to charge families to remain competitive remains stagnant.

As a consequence, libraries, city recreation departments, and preschools are looking for ways to save money so that they can avoid having to cut available services. One way of doing this is by "outsourcing" their programs to qualified individuals on a freelance basis to avoid the costs of healthcare, retirement, taxes, vacation time, and other costs associated with regular employees.

MARKET

The primary market for Storytime Alternatives is the small-to-medium sized public library. These libraries typically have limited budgets and rely on non-certified staff to act in the role of a librarian in order to save costs. These libraries may be better served by hiring freelance staff to run storytimes, plan or perform summer reading programs, and cover other staff roles during emergency situations.

City recreation departments also offer children's programming that a certified librarian would be qualified to run, including things like "Music and Movement," "Mommy and Me," and "Baby Lapsit" classes.

Preschools are another potential area for Storytime Alternatives, especially in terms of special programming such as storytelling or events related to "March is Reading Month."

PROGRAMS AND SERVICES

There are various programs and services offered, including the following:

- Baby Storytime (Lapsit): For children ages 9 to 24 months old. Parents or caregivers must remain with the child. Class sizes are limited to 15 children.

- Toddler Storytime: For children ages 2 to 4 years of age. Parents or caregivers must remain with the child. Class sizes are limited to 20 children.

- Preschool Storytime: For 3.5 to 6 years of age. Parents or caregivers may remain with the child if they prefer, or they may leave their independent child at storytime while they remain in the facility. Class sizes are limited to 25 children.

- Music & Movement: Concentrates on songs, rhymes, movement with streamers and scarves, and use of rhythm instruments while helping to promote a positive adult-child interaction and emergent literacy skills for children ages 2-4.

- After-school Storytime: For elementary school-age students. Class sizes are limited to 15 children.

- Family Storytime: Generally held during evening or weekend hours so that entire families can attend. Class sizes may vary.

Summer Reading-Themed Programs

Summer Reading Programs are an essential service offered by libraries for kids of all ages. Kids read books and record their progress, either in time spent reading or books read, and submit their results to the library for prizes and other rewards. This system encourages kids to read during a time that they normally do not, and studies have shown that reading during the summer helps ease "summer slide." It also gets kids into the library and exposes them to all of the programs and services the library has to offer.

One organization, the Collaborative Summer Library Program (CSLP), provides a yearly summer reading program theme. They include the overall theme, program ideas, lists of appropriate resources, book lists, prizes, and advertising and promo materials. Most libraries subscribe to the service and use the theme and related materials as the basis for their program, using the pieces from the kit that fit their budget and interests, and adding ones of their own. While the service is only available to libraries and Storytime Alternatives is not permitted to use the materials, we can be aware of the upcoming themes are prepare and market related programs.

For instance, the 2011 Summer Reading theme is "One World, Many Stories." There are many programs that would be a perfect fit for this theme, including:

- Multicultural crafts

- Multicultural games

- Storytelling stories from around the world

- Geography-related program

- Food from around the world

The 2012 theme for children is "Dream Big - Read." Possible program ideas include:

- Pajama party

- Nocturnal animals

- Stars and planets

- Shadow puppets

Other, special programs include:

- Parachute games

- Lego club

- Movies

- Holiday storytimes

- Arts and crafts

- Science programs

- Dance party

- Summer reading-themed programs

STATISTICS

One way of measuring success is to record and track statistics from all delivered programs. A database will be kept noting the event, place, payment amount, and number of attendees. This information will be invaluable in proving the cost-effectiveness of the programs and tracking any increase in program attendance due to name recognition and reputation.

SCHEDULING AND PAYMENT

There are three ways clients may utilize the services of Storytime Alternatives.

- Regularly scheduled programs: Some institutions may opt to hire Storytime Alternatives on a regular basis to do weekly or monthly programs. Examples of this type of program include weekly storytimes for various ages.

- One-time programs: This option is usually reserved for institutions who need help with bigger, theme-specific programs such as movie nights, holiday parties, and the like. These "extra" programs may not fit into the schedule of current staff but are very popular with patrons.

- Emergency substitute programs: These last-minute programs are available to cover staff sickness, vacations, maternity leave, and other emergencies.

Regularly scheduled programs including storytimes and lapsits are generally charged at a rate of $25 per hour.

One time, specialty programs are quoted based on the specific parameters desired. The basic rate is still $25 per hour, but more time or money may be quoted based on special materials or additional prep time that is necessary.

Emergency substitutes are paid at the basic substitute rate of the institution, which varies from $15 to $25 an hour.

ADVERTISING

- Glossy program flyers

- Business cards

- Website

- Social media (Facebook, LinkedIn)

PERSONNEL

The company was founded by Linda Pierce. Linda graduated with an MLIS from Wayne State University two years ago and has been working as a librarian intern and substitute librarian since that time. In addition to this, Linda worked part-time in the publishing industry and recently left this job to pursue her dream of working exclusively with children. For the past six years, Linda has also volunteered her time working with children through the schools as a classroom parent organizing parties and helping on special projects; as a PTA officer at school book fairs, ice cream socials, poetry slams, author day, and the like; and planning activities for girls as a Girl Scout leader. All of this experience has helped her prepare for a career as a freelance children's librarian.

SAMPLE PRESCHOOL STORYTIME

Theme: Dogs

Age Range: 3.5 to 6 years old

Time: Approximately 45 minutes

- Greeting

- Book: Move Over, Rover!

- Action Rhyme: "Rags the Dog"

- Song: "Puppy Dog" from Welcome to Ralph's World

- Book: Dog's Colorful Day

- Poem: From the Doghouse: Poems to Chew On

- Action Rhyme: "Puppy Dog, Puppy Dog"

- Book: The Pigeon Wants a Puppy

- Felt board: "Five Little Puppies"

- Farewell

- Puppy print hand stamp

- "D is for Dog" coloring sheet to take home

START-UP COSTS

Item	Cost
Laptop	$1,000
Scanning/copying printer	$ 250
Software, including Microsoft Word, Microsoft Publisher, Quicken, and Readerware	$ 500
Book cases	$ 300
File cabinet	$ 75
Desk	$ 150
Books—children's	$1,000
Books/periodicals—professional	$ 500
Craft supplies, including scissors, glue, paint and brushes, paper, and totes	$ 100
Felt sets/felt board	$ 250
CD player	$ 45
Children's music	$ 150
Scarves—24	$ 20
Puppets—10	$ 250
20' Parachute & accessories	$ 250
Wrist Bells—25	$ 75
Music shakers—30	$ 50
Ukulele	$ 50
Rolling travel case	$ 50
ALA & ALSC memberships	$ 110
Conference attendance	$ 525
Marketing and Advertising materials (flyers, website, business cards, etc.)	$ 300
Portfolio	$ 100
Legos	$ 250
Various science apparatus	$ 250
Cricut machine & cartridges	$ 400
Total	**$7,000**

Nonprofit Pharmaceutical Research Center

The Center

8652 W. Market St.
Greensboro, North Carolina 27410

Susan Hartmann
Charles J. Stankovic

Business Plan for Growth, 2011-2016

1. EXECUTIVE SUMMARY

The Center is a nonprofit drug discovery group dedicated to the discovery and development of medicines to treat diseases that afflict the underprivileged and underserved. Consisting of a team of former pharmaceutical industry professionals, The Center looks to apply its robust expertise in translational research in order to accomplish its mission.

When a major pharmaceutical company announced the closure of a local research site, hundreds of local jobs were lost. As part of a region-wide effort to create jobs and keep scientists in the area, a local university decided to form a research institute dedicated to treating diseases of the under-privileged and underserved. In addition, the research site closure meant that the university could hire the entire research complement of this institute at once. The Center contains most of the components of a drug discovery group. Not only does The Center provide the university with a group of scientists possessing unparalleled research expertise, these researchers are also applying their years of drug discovery experience towards serving those in need. The goal is for The Center to partner with academic researchers at the university and worldwide, in order to translate basic science discoveries into clinically relevant therapies. The university operates The Center through the Office of Research in order to provide it with the autonomy needed to form collaborations efficiently. Funding is provided though a 2-year grant from the University Opportunity Fund. In addition, the donation of equipment allowed The Center to quickly begin conducting research. Since its creation in July of 2010, The Center has demonstrated a remarkable ability to quickly form collaborations and deliver results. Besides the initial funding from the university, other funding has been realized from intramural grants, external collaborators, and fee for service operations. It is from these initial results that The Center seeks to build a plan towards sustainability, in order to continue serving those in need.

The demand for safe and effective treatments for diseases of the developing world is ever-present, and involvement from high profile philanthropists, such as Warren Buffet and Bill Gates, has only heightened public awareness. While pharmaceutical companies allocate some resources to these efforts, much of the research in this disease space falls to the nonprofit sector. It is the intent of the scientists of The Center to apply the expertise they gained in the for profit world to a nonprofit mission.

2. NEED AND OPPORTUNITY

Despite major advances in drug development over recent decades there is an unmet need for medicines to treat diseases that predominantly affect the world's poor and underserved patient populations. Existing treatments are either too expensive, ineffective, or possess undesirable side effects. One major reason for this is the lack of significant research and development efforts dedicated to discovering new medicines for these diseases. While pharmaceutical companies spend large amounts on drug research and development, commercial viability and profit potential drive their research efforts. As a result, they largely focus on diseases of the developed world where patient populations have the means to pay. To put this in perspective, in 2007 the U.S. spent $2.9 billion on research on neglected diseases, with over 60% of that money coming from the public (governmental) funding. This seems like a lot until it is compared to the over $58 billion spent on drug discovery and development research by the pharmaceutical and biotech industry during the same period (see Endnotes 1 and 2).

Figure 1: U.S. R&D Spending on Neglected Diseases

Funders of neglected disease R&D in 2007

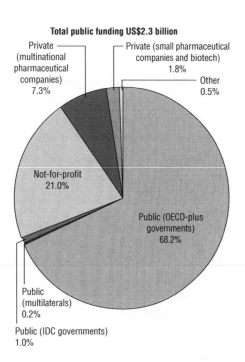

In the absence of significant pharmaceutical research in this area, the bulk of the research into neglected diseases occurs in academic, governmental, and nonprofit organizations where the focus is placed on basic research and in-depth understanding of a specific disease. While these institutions are able to produce high quality leads, they lack the skills and expertise necessary to convert or "translate" these leads into compounds suitable for clinical development. Thus there currently exists a gap in the ability to translate basic scientific discoveries into clinically relevant therapies. The Center for World Health and Medicine seeks to fill this gap by partnering with researchers around the world. By providing translational expertise (via medicinal chemistry optimization and disease pharmacology) basic initial discoveries can be translated into quality lead compounds and ultimately clinically viable compounds.

2.1 Causes and Barriers

Ultimately, the root cause of the lack of treatments for neglected diseases is the general apathy towards the problems of the world's poorest nations. It is an extension of the problem that most people focus on the needs of their families and immediate communities first, and spend less attention on problems beyond that scope. This coupled with the seemingly overwhelming problems of the developing world such as poverty and political unrest; make most people wonder if there is anything they can really do. As a result, they do nothing. Despite the apathy displayed by the general public, there are multiple governmental and nongovernmental organizations, which are devoted to alleviating the suffering of people in developing countries. Organizations such as the World Health Organization (WHO) have over a 30-year history of involvement in funding the discovery and development of treatments for diseases of the developing world. In 1975, the WHO established Tropical Disease Research (TDR) program, a global program of scientific collaboration to coordinate efforts and develop medicines for major diseases of the poor and disadvantaged. Administered by the World Health Organization, TDR is also sponsored by the United Nations Children's Fund (UNICEF), the United Nations Development Program (UNDP), the World Bank and WHO. The US government also provides some funding for research into treatments for neglected diseases through the National Institutes for Health (NIH), but this funding is primarily directed towards basic early stage research.

In the late 1990s, Product Development Partnerships (PDPs) were established as a response to the lack of commercial incentive to research treatments for diseases of the developing world. These organizations do not have any internal research and development efforts. Instead, they act as "matchmakers" pairing financing, mostly from philanthropic foundations, such as the Gates Foundation, with researchers. In contrast to the NIH, PDPs focus primarily on late stage projects that can deliver clinically relevant results.

Another major problem in treating diseases of the developing world is that pharmaceutical and biotech companies, who discover and develop most new drugs, have little financial incentive to develop treatments for populations who lack the means to provide a monetary reward. The cost to discover and develop a new medication can exceed $800 million, which means these companies mainly focus their efforts on diseases of the developed world, where there is a sufficiently large and wealthy patient population to recover these costs and realize a profit. In fairness, pharmaceutical and biotech companies do devote some efforts toward neglected diseases, but in most cases there is some opportunistic benefit, either through the ability to treat a related disease of the developed world, or through government incentives, or more generally as part of their efforts to maintain their good corporate citizenship status.

The most notable story of pharmaceutical company involvement for a developing world disease is the story of Ivermectin. In the 1970s, Merck scientists discovered that Ivermectin, which was originally developed for veterinary use to kill parasitic worms, was also potent against the parasite that causes River Blindness. Merck spent millions on the development of a human formulation hoping that governments, charitable foundations, or international health agencies would purchase Ivermectin, and fund its distribution. When none came forward, the company pledged to provide the drug free of charge in perpetuity to anyone, anywhere who needed it. Success stories such as this are not common in this disease space.

Although a lack of treatment for many diseases is still the main problem, many other factors contribute to the overall poor quality of healthcare in the developing world. Poverty contributes in that most of the populations in these countries cannot afford treatment. The patient populations live in famine stricken areas, where malnutrition contributes to poor health. Similarly, a lack of resources does not allow access to adequate sanitation and clean water. Poor sanitation only compounds this problem by enabling the spread of disease. The inadequate healthcare and general infrastructure in these countries also are obstacles to medicine distribution efforts, even when treatments are available. Finally, the existing poor health of many people in these countries contributes to susceptibility to new infections. This is especially true in areas with large HIV infected populations, where their severely compromised immune systems make them prone to other infections, such as tuberculosis, which is a growing problem in the developing and developed world. In fact, the World Health Organization (WHO) has declared tuberculosis a Global Public Health Emergency (see Endnote 3).

2.1.1 Diseases of Poverty

Diseases of poverty are conditions, which are most commonly found in low-income populations, usually in the developing world. They can also include neglected tropical diseases (NTD's), a group of diseases officially categorized as such by the World Health Organization [Buruli Ulcer, Chagas disease (American trypanosomiasis), Cysticercosis, Dengue/dengue haemorrhagic fever, Dracunculiasis (guinea-worm disease), Echinococcosis, Fascioliasis, Human African trypanosomiasis, Leishmaniasis, Leprosy, Lymphatic filariasis, Onchocerciasis, Rabies, Schistosomiasis, Soil transmitted helminthiasis, Trachoma, Yaws]. Below are more detailed explanations of the diseases of poverty that Center is currently researching.

Childhood Diarrhea

Surprisingly, childhood diarrhea is one of the leading causes of mortality in the developing world, responsible for annual deaths of approximately 1.5 million infants and children, and 2 million people of all ages. In addition, diarrhea-associated morbidity has long-term consequences for growth and cognitive development. While there are multiple infectious agents responsible for the onset of diarrhea, lack of adequate sanitation and limited access to clean water contribute to its ongoing proliferation. Current treatments for diarrhea have made significant strides in reducing deaths, but suffer from impractical dosing regimens and undesirable side effects. Loperamide (Imodium) must be taken multiple times per day and can cause life-threatening complications in children. Other commonly administered therapies, such as oral rehydration therapy (ORT) and zinc supplementation simply rehydrate after fluid loss, and do not target the underlying cause of fluid loss.

Malaria

Each year, there are approximately 300-500 million cases of malaria, resulting in the deaths of 1-3 million people worldwide. The majority of these deaths are young children in sub-Saharan Africa, where ninety percent of malaria-related deaths occur. Malaria is a mosquito-borne infectious disease caused by a parasite of the genus Plasmodium. While malaria is commonly associated with poverty, it is also a cause of poverty, and presents a major obstacle to economic growth in the developing world. Current therapies include the new class of Artemisinin-like compounds (a traditional Chinese herbal medicine), often in combination with the standard treatments of quinine or chloroquine. Unfortunately, drug resistance has developed for all of these treatments and new therapies are still needed.

Tuberculosis

Tuberculosis (TB) continues to be the most prevalent causes of infectious disease related morbidity and death worldwide. It disproportionally impacts impoverished and immunocompromised populations. Nearly one-third of the global population is infected with Mycobacterium Tuberculosis, the major causative bacteria of TB, and 2 million people die from TB annually. It is estimated that if present trends continue, TB incidence will increase by 41% in the next 20 years. Current therapies require lengthy dosing regimens, over several months, to clear bacterial infection. These types of therapies are difficult to complete, and when not completed lead to the formation of drug resistance due to significant under-dosing of patients. Multidrug-resistant (MDR) TB is increasing in incidence, and is not isolated to the developing world.

2.1.2 Orphan Diseases

Orphan or rare diseases are conditions with patient populations too small to realize substantial resources from pharmaceutical companies. In the United States, a disease is categorized as an orphan disease if it afflicts fewer than 2000 people. The Center also has a small portfolio of orphan disease projects, and looks to pursue these opportunistically where there is overlap with its expertise, and collaborators within the university.

Sickle Cell Disease

Sickle-cell disease (SCD) is a blood disorder caused by a genetic mutation in hemoglobin. SCD causes refolding of human hemoglobin or "sickling" when oxygen levels are low in the blood. These irregularly shaped sickle cells obstruct blood flow in the vessels that lead to limbs and organs. This results in pain, and can lead to infection and organ damage. The gene mutation that causes SCD is most commonly found in people of African ancestry. In the United States, it is estimated that SCD affects 70,000−100,000 people. It is also prevalent in parts of the developing world, especially in West and Central Africa. There is no cure for sickle cell disease and improvements in treatment are greatly needed.

Ophthalmology Related Diseases

Retinitis Pigmentosa (RP), Familial Exudative Vitreoretinopathy (FEVR) and Retinopathy of Prematurity (ROP) are orphan diseases with distinct etiology, but are all characterized by abnormalities in the retina which lead to vision loss that often initiates at an early age. There are currently no effective drug treatments for these rare and debilitating conditions, although recent advances in basic research have significantly advanced knowledge of the underlying molecular causes of blindness.

2.2 External Landscape

Although The Center occupies a fairly unique position within the underserved disease research community, there are several other types organizations dedicated to the same mission, from both the for profit and nonprofit worlds, including, nonprofit biotechs, academic institutions, for profit pharmaceutical and biotech companies.

Several major pharmaceutical and biotech companies conduct at least some nominal and relatively minimal research into diseases of the underserved; the most notable examples are Novartis and GlaxoSmithKline who have recently created entire research institutes dedicated to this cause. There are also several nonprofit biotechs such as Seattle Biomed and the Infectious Diseases Research Institute (also based in Seattle) which conduct research in many different neglected disease areas, and have large research groups (over 300 and 100 researchers respectively), with multimillion-dollar budgets (over $40mm for Seattle Biomed in 2010). Within academia, similar research groups have recently been created at UC-Berkeley, UCSF, Notre Dame, and George Washington University. *Table 1* lists many of these organizations, their locations, and the disease targets they currently pursue. (For more information on each center, see *Appendix 1*)

Table 1: Organizations Researching Underserved Diseases

Organization	Location	Type	Disease targets
Infectious Disease Research Institute	Seattle, WA	Not for profit biotech	Leishmaniasis, TB, Malaria, Leprosy, Chagas disease
Seattle BioMed	Seattle, WA	Not for profit biotech	African Sleeping Sickness, Candidiasis, Chagas disease, HIV/AIDS, Leishmaniasis, Malaria, Toxoplasmosis, Tuberculosis
Center for Emerging and Neglected Diseases	Berkeley, CA	Academic center	Tuberculosis, HIV/AIDS, Malaria, Diarrheal diseases, Bacterial infections, Viral infections, Parasitic infections
The Center for Rare and Neglected Diseases at the University of Notre Dame	South Bend, IN	Academic center	Malaria, Niemann-Pick C, Anemia, Lymphatic Filariasis, Salmonella, Thalassemia, Tuberculosis, Leishmaniasis
The Sandler Center for Basic Research in Parasitic Diseases	San Francisco, CA	Academic center	Malaria, Pneumonia, HIV/AIDS, Diarrheal diseases, Tuberculosis
George Washington University	Washington, DC	Academic institution	Neglected Infections of Poverty (US), Neglected Tropical Diseases (developing world)
Barcelona Centre for International Health Research	Barcelona, Spain	Academic and biomedical research institution	Malaria, Pneumonia, HIV/AIDS, Diarrheal diseases, Tuberculosis
GlaxoSmithKline	Tres Cantos, Spain	Pharmaceutical company	Malaria, Tuberculosis
Novartis Institute for Tropical Diseases	Singapore	Pharmaceutical company	Dengue, Tuberculosis, Malaria

2.3: Opportunity

Taking an initial lead compound and optimizing it to be a good drug candidate is challenging, and is somewhat of an art that requires years of experience to master. Issues such as absorption, solubility, and stability amongst others must be optimized and balanced to find a compound with the right combination of properties. Additional efforts are necessary to formulate this compound for proper dosing and delivery. Finally, appropriate and often complex animal testing is required to ensure efficacy and to increase the likelihood of success in human clinical trials. The scientists at The Center have mastered this art and are committed to using their skills to help find new treatments for neglected and orphaned diseases.

As indicated above The Center fills a gap not being fully addressed by the other academic centers, which is the need for translational research. Translational research is defined as the process needed to span the gap between basic lab discoveries and compounds that are suitable and ready for clinical development. This gap is often referred to, especially in the venture capital world, as the "Valley of Death," since so many projects tend to die here, either due to technical failures or lack of funding (see *Figure 2*). This process is beset with difficult and unpredictable scientific challenges, and can consume unpredictable amounts of time and money. It also occupies a gap in funding sources, between early stage discovery and basic research, which is traditionally funded by the NIH, and clinical development, which is primarily funded by pharmaceutical and biotech companies.

Funding in this space has traditionally been scarce, with the NIH and other governmental agencies reluctant to support such directed and applied research. Conversely, most projects at this stage are too premature to garner support from the pharmaceutical industry, which is generally interested in acquiring projects closer to clinical development. Venture capital firms provide some funding for companies in this space but not to academic laboratories. Finally, this funding gap was one of the primary drivers for the formation of the PDP's mentioned above.

Figure 2: Translational Research and Center Expertise

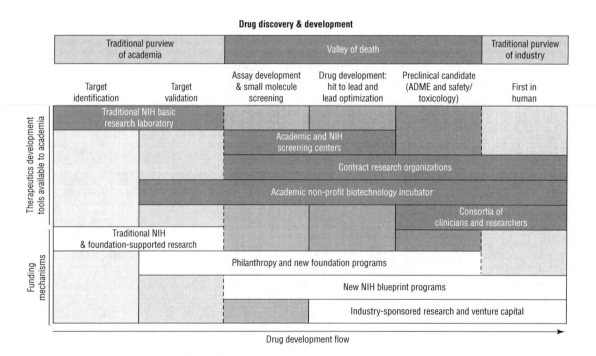

The Center is focused on addressing the need for safe and affordable treatments for diseases of poverty by providing the translational component to the drug development pipeline. It is uniquely positioned to help bridge the existing scientific gap, and plans to use a variety of funding sources to span the funding gap (vide infra). By virtue of their drug discovery and development experience in the pharmaceutical industry, The Center scientists are experts in the area of translational research. This ability is The Center's key strength, and what differentiates it from all the other academic centers focused on research into neglected diseases. This expertise makes them ideal partners for academic groups worldwide that might have identified a promising drug lead, but need the help that Center can provide to bring that initial discovery to the point that it is ready for human clinical trials.

The Center will initiate and coordinate targeted research and development projects in collaboration with the internal university research departments, the international research community at large, government organizations, the pharmaceutical industry, private foundations, and other relevant partners. The primary objective is to establish a strong project portfolio by focusing on translating early stage exploratory projects, emerging from the basic research partners, into promising drug candidates for human clinical trials. The Center will look to form strong global alliances and partnerships with entities already possessing the needed expertise and infrastructure for clinical trials, registration, and distribution, as well as for sources of funding.

3. SOCIAL IMPACT MODEL

3.1 Overview of Organization

The Center consists of a multidisciplinary team of former pharmaceutical company scientists with extensive translational research experience and skills. These accomplished scientists represent nearly all the necessary skill sets required to discover and develop small molecule drug therapeutics. They are most experienced in advancing drugs into human clinical trials.

The Center is actively engaged in almost all aspects of the drug discovery and development process, as outlined below. The only major discipline not covered is drug safety, where The Center plans to partner with existing Contract Research Organizations to provide this service as needed.

Medicinal Chemistry—the design, synthesis and development of drug candidates, which contain the desired efficacy, safety, pharmaceutical, pharmacokinetic and pharmacodynamic properties. The Center medicinal chemists utilize structure-based drug design, and intuitive medicinal chemistry analogue synthesis to transform lead molecules into promising clinical compounds. They are also knowledgeable of the intellectual property landscape, with experience in writing and evaluating patents.

Indications Discovery—the evaluation of existing drugs, drug combinations and discontinued drug candidates for utility in diseases and disease mechanisms that differ from the original intended or existing indication.

Molecular and Cellular Biology—the design and execution of in vitro and ex vivo biological assays against a targeted mechanism of action that are predictive of in vivo efficacy in models of the target disease. These scientists work closely with our medicinal chemists and in vivo pharmacologists to advance promising molecules for specific disease targets.

In vivoPharmacology—the design, execution and analysis of pre-clinical in vivo models of human disease and the evaluation of drug candidates in models for the prediction of efficacy and safety in human clinical trials.

Molecular Pharmacology—the analysis of the pharmacokinetic and pharmacodynamic properties of potential drug candidates in in vivo models of disease This data is used in combination with in vitro analysis, to predict bioavailability, exposure, safety, and efficacy in human clinical trials.

Biomarker Pharmacology—the design and development of in vivo biomarker assays to establish proof of mechanism analysis in pre-clinical and human clinical trials.

In a broader context, the scientists representing the various disciplines are experienced in working together as a results oriented team that demands stringent scientific rigor and a strong desire to deliver therapies to those in need of them.

3.2 Social Impact Model

Social Problem Definition

The lack of adequate healthcare and sanitation provide for the proliferation of many diseases with in the developing world. These diseases remain primarily untreated due to their poor profit potential for pharmaceutical companies. Although significant governmental and nonprofit resources are being spent to understand the underlying basic biology of these diseases, there currently exists a gap in the translation of basic scientific discoveries into clinically relevant therapies.

Mission

The Center is a multidisciplinary team that discovers and develops new medicines to support the improvement of human health with a special emphasis on unmet medical needs of the underprivileged and underserved. We collaborate with international institutions and researchers that best complement our robust translational research expertise.

Vision

We envisage a future in which preventable diseases no longer claim millions of lives each year.

3.3 Description of Operating Model

The primary operational goal of The Center is to secure a self-sustaining stream of funding. Although several funding streams are envisaged, including fee-for-service work, endowment building, and collaborations with the pharmaceutical industry, the primary sources of funding will be through grants from governmental agencies, foundations, and PDP's in support of various projects and collaborations. The first step in this process is the identification of key partners who share a common interest in treating diseases of the developing world, and who are in need of the translational research expertise of The Center. Once collaboration is agreed to, the difficult work of securing funding begins.

The Center will need to focus on developing its current grant writing abilities. Although each of the directors is an established researcher with many publications to his name, grant writing is a practiced art and needs to develop with time, as does name recognition in the disease space The Center is pursuing. The directors are currently working with a professor in the School of Medicine, and one of The Center's faculty advisors, to enhance grant-writing skills. They also rely heavily on the academic collaborators to assist in the grant building process. An external grant writer has also been identified with whom The Center can work with on a per project basis to augment their grant writing efforts. The Center also receives grant support from the Office of Research. Given the relatively large budget of The Center, and the large number of projects being pursued, additional help will ultimately be required to administer and manage the grants they receive.

With funding secured, The Center can turn its attention to executing its research plans. Research is by definition unpredictable, but scientists at The Center will leverage their years of experience managing projects within the pharmaceutical industry to keep projects focused on the most important experiments and milestones, giving them the best chance of success.

The final step necessary in this process is to advance refined compounds into human clinical trials. At this point expenses can escalate quickly, and The Center will use its expertise to identify the appropriate funding sources for this step. This could be through additional funding from PDP's, or by forming an alliance or licensing arrangement with a neglected disease center within the pharmaceutical industry, such as the Novartis Institute for Tropical Diseases or the GlaxoSmithKline's diseases of the developing world initiative, amongst others.

3.4 Description of Program Strategies

The main goal of The Center is to translate promising early stage basic research discoveries into compounds suitable for human clinical trial development and ultimately into human therapies. Although The Center is staffed with world-class scientists, it is not and could not ever be large enough to do all of the necessary discovery research on the numerous targets and diseases possible in the neglected and orphan diseases space. The Center will need to collaborate with academic researchers within the university and worldwide to identify promising drug candidates and disease targets, and to assist them in advancing their initial leads into clinically viable candidates.

As a relative newcomer to the academic research community, The Center needs to initially establish itself as a valuable research partner. Initial efforts are and have been focused on reaching out to the university research community. Initial successes have led to establishing the following collaborations:

- Department of Biology (Ophthalmology Related Diseases)

- School of Medicine (Tuberculosis)

- University Hospital (Sickle Cell)

The effort to obtain external collaborators must also continue to be developed, and The Center must reach out to experts in the disease areas it researches. It is imperative The Center uses its current collaborations to demonstrate expertise, which will make it more marketable to the leading scientists in the fields of neglected and orphan diseases.

The Center has also established a multi-center collaboration with a Chinese research institute, and professors at local universities to focus on the treatment of malaria. Although no funding is being provided by this collaboration, each group is providing in-kind services. This collaboration offers good exposure for The Center at the international level.

The Center recently received funding from research to treat childhood diarrhea. This research proposal provides significant funding for The Center and is a beachhead for additional PDP collaboration.

4. IMPLEMENTATION STRATEGY

As implied above, the success of The Center hinges on its ability to form multiple, effective collaborations with internal and external researchers, and funding and development partners such as PDP's. The key strength of The Center is its robust experience in translational research, but they lack expertise in neglected, tropical and orphan diseases. To bolster this gap, The Center will need to establish collaborations with relevant disease experts both within the university and worldwide. Forming and executing effective collaborations will be the main driver of The Center strategy for success.

The timeline below outlines the steps initially needed to establish the necessary collaborations, and how to maintain them going forward, establishing a steady stream of projects and resources.

4.1 Business Plan Timeline

The business plan is structured into three phases over five plus years and is outlined in *Table 2*. Details in this business plan will focus on Phase 1 and 2 cover the first 3 years for The Center, from July 2010 to July 2013. The main goals in each phase are listed in the table below.

Table 2: Goals by Phase

Phases	Goals
Phase 1: Establish initial reputation of center and key collaborations July 2010–July 2011 (1 year)	• Establish at least 2–3 local collaborations • Establish 1 national or international collaboration • Bring labs to full operating capacity and deliver results for collaborators • Explore fee-for-service options • Secure one major grant or contract • Establish research goals • Develop research prioritization scheme and goals
Phase 2: Grow national and international reputation of center July 2011–July 2013 (2 years)	• Identify and connect with potential local collaborators • Establish 2–4 new national or international collaborations • Demonstrate feasibility and demand for fee-for-service component • Submit sufficient grant proposals to provide funding of at least 40% of their costs (including fee-for-service) • Grow training program (students, post-docs, and visiting scholars) • Begin public policy efforts and collaborations with School of Public Health • Explore ways to collaborate with other research centers focused on neglected and orphan diseases
Phase 3: Establish CENTER as a world leader and sought out partner in research for diseases of the underprivileged and underserved July 2013–July 2015 (2 years)	• Establish and expand ongoing collaborations with internationally recognized researchers • Establish and grow fee-for-service component (always <20% of efforts) • Provide funding of at least 50% of their costs (including fee-for-service) • Expand training and visiting scholar program

4.2 Strategy

The main goals for The Center for its first year are to achieve full operation, and to establish initial baseline operations and procedures. In addition, The Center will focus on establishing itself as a new contributor in the area of diseases of poverty. Beyond the goals list in *Table 2*, The Center should also focus on achieving the following goals to help clarify its operational strategy and plans.

•   Identification of groups within the University instrumental to execution of strategy, including Office of Research, IP and Technology Transfer, Grant Writing; School of Medicine; Governmental Relations; Communications and Marketing; Development Office

•   Develop familiarity with funding agencies

•   Assignment of Center staff to research disease targets

4.2.1 Internal and Local Strategy

Ongoing efforts include reaching out and meeting as many faculty members as possible, to explain the mission of The Center, and seek out potential collaborations. The key targets are researchers within the University who seek a means to convert their basic discoveries into clinical therapies. Secondary targets would be researchers with research interests or expertise in ancillary or supportive areas, such as diagnostics, clinical trial design, or even health policy. This group could also assist in the identification of other possible collaborators, though their network of contacts, which might also be interested in collaborating with or supporting The Center.

Additional future efforts could include hosting/co-hosting a local seminar series on neglected and orphan diseases, which would help raise awareness and visibility of The Center both internally to the University and externally, especially within the local external community (local universities and local biotechs) to which these seminars would be open. In addition, this would provide The Center an opportunity to network with researchers in the local life science community. Participation in local charity events, nonprofit advisory boards, and task forces would also provide ample opportunity to network with policy makers and others involved in social enterprise.

Each of these events or approaches strikes at a different aspect of their message and target audience, from potential research partners and collaborators to potential supporters or donors. Each event or effort helps build the visibility of The Center within the local community.

4.2.2 National and International Strategy

Beyond internal and local collaborations The Center needs to establish its reputation for providing translational research excellence within the external environment both nationally and internationally. This effort is initially focused on attending and presenting at external conferences, and reaching out to key personal and scientific contacts of the directors.

Beyond the initial goal outline above The Center also needs to establish its reputation within the funding community. Granting Agencies, such as the NIH, philanthropic foundations, and PDP's, which fund research for treatments of rare, neglected, and orphan diseases (Gates Foundation, Institute for One World Health) are all generally favorably impressed by results, and the existence of other collaborations and contracts. With each collaboration established and grant awarded The Center status increases as a reputable recipient of funding and heightens the odds of securing additional funds and contracts.

A long-range goal for The Center is to partner with the School of Public Health to address issues, in areas where there is sufficient overlap in scope and interests. This work could include partnerships with the above-mentioned PDP's, and other centers to combine resources and efforts, and develop a unified effort that influences public policy both domestically and internationally.

4.2.3 Fee-for-Service Strategy

A unique strength of the researchers in The Center is an expertise in the design and execution of sophisticated in vivo pharmacology studies. In addition, they have access to and expertise in the use of radio-telemetry monitoring and automated blood sampling instrumentation. This instrumentation is highly specialized, and not readily available to small companies and academic laboratories.

The combination of expertise and specialized equipment uniquely positions The Center to provide these services to academic and small biotechs. In doing so, The Center also has chance to be part of the entrepreneurial community, and to establish this fee-for-service model within the university community.

Beyond the obvious addition to the revenue stream, this opportunity allows The Center to contribute to the local life science community, and establish itself as a regional leader in biomedical research, which in turn provides a further opportunity to market the strengths of The Center.

A final possible offering would be fee-for-service consulting to biotechs and pharmaceutical companies. This service would provide another source of revenue, but again would enhance the reputation of the directors and The Center and is thus part of the overall strategy.

4.3 Organizational Capacity Building

The Center is currently comprised entirely of experienced scientific staff, but its size and mission create a large number of administrative, operational and strategic resource demands. While these activities are currently distributed amongst the directors, it would be a better use of their time to focus on value added activities and allow new people with expertise in these areas to perform them in a more cost efficient manner.

To address these issues The Center plans to or needs to hire the following key personnel list in order of their most critical need and ease of hiring. Presently, there is one opening for scientific staff to fill an open headcount.

- Current headcount of 11, plus one opening.

- Administrative support—the Office of Research will use money from its budget to hire a part-time administrative assistant.

- Grant writer—Center is currently not highly experienced in this area. In order to achieve the funding necessary, they must continuously search for collaborators, and grant opportunities. Once funding is obtained, grant accounting will be necessary. Grant writing can be contracted out on a per project basis.

- Business Manager—allow directors to focus more time on scientific duties and building collaborations with disease experts. The Business manager would manage budgets, develop financing strategy, manage fee for service operations, research market landscape, develop partnerships and new programs, etc.

Further headcount additions to the staff will be made as budgets allow, although the irregularities of grants monies will likely mean a shift towards a more flexible work staff, including contractors, students, and post-docs. The latter also allows The Center to begin to offer a training component to the mission and operation. Expansion of the fee for service operations could also mean that future headcount is added to work exclusively on these activities.

In the absence of any additional headcount, the directors should assign certain responsibilities to the remaining staff. For example, one team member could assist in grant writing. Also, continuing research into the other players in the area of neglected and orphan diseases could be distributed throughout the team. Beyond simply filling these critical operational gaps, these activities also provide a means of career development for the scientists at The Center.

4.4 Technology

Beyond their strengths and expertise in translational research, The Center is also endowed with over $2 million worth of the most cutting edge technology and equipment in the industry. These tools allow them to quickly and efficiently address the technical aspects of many of the problems they tackle and also make them a sought after partner for academic and small biotech collaborators. This combination of experience and intellectual expertise combined with access to a wide range of cutting edge technologies allows the center to rapidly and efficiently advance their research collaborations. A list of notable facilities and technologies available to The Center is included in *Appendix 2.*

4.5 Public Policy

Although The Center is not primarily focused on shaping public policy, its broader mission is highly dependent on and interwoven with public policy surrounding research funding, pharmaceutical industry regulations, orphan drug legislation, and foreign aid, especially aid directed at providing health care in the developing world.

The Center is working closely with the Director of Governmental Relations to address these issues and others, which might impact The Center. He has over 10 years experience working for both houses of Congress, and within the administration working, giving him an extensive network of contacts on Capitol Hill.

The primary goal of these interactions is to build awareness of The Center within the state and federal Congressional delegations, and to keep abreast of any opportunities or threats posed by the ever-shifting sea of regulations and public policies. Initial efforts were successful in securing earmark funds for The Center; unfortunately, these were lost when all earmarks were dropped by the current congress.

As part of its effort in this area The Center needs to develop a one-page overview of itself and its mission, which is directed at a congressional audience. It should explain The Center and its mission, and highlight the current and long-term plans to address the following issues:

- Job creation

- Training opportunities (post-doc, visiting researchers)

- Spin out opportunities and IP generation

- Fee-for-service opportunities

- Philanthropic outreach

- Educational outreach—high school co-ops

- Partnerships on the School of Public Health initiatives

To maximize their efforts in this area The Center needs to add the Director of Governmental Relations to the key stakeholders who receive regular updates on current and upcoming activities and developments of the center, so that he is able to proactively support the packaging and distribution of this information to his key constituencies.

4.6 Performance and Impact Measurement

4.6.1 Indicators and Targets

The Center will establish a set of key indicators and performance targets or goals, which can be used by The Center and its key stakeholders to judge ongoing performance and success against these goals. Some initial key indicators and performance targets include:

- Number of collaborations created and on-going

- Funding levels

- Grants applied for and received

- Number of publications and presentations

4.6.2 Feedback Loop

Create dashboards and report cards to monitor progress against key goals and indicators or performance, and use these forms and data to create reports to key stakeholders. This data can then be used to adjust efforts as necessary to get back on track or to adjust the goals if needed to reflect changes in the current dynamic.

5. TEAM AND GOVERNANCE

The Center has a unique placement within the University. It is an independent entity that reports through the Office of Research, not tied to any academic department. This provides The Center a high degree of autonomy. Center scientists are thus not affiliated with a specific academic department, although they do have specific academic training and experience. The Center staff is comprised of 11 highly experienced pharmaceutical scientists, an expertise not typically found within academia.

The goal of all these scientists is to apply their drug discovery and translational research knowledge to diseases of the developing world, orphan, and neglected diseases, through collaboration with researchers worldwide, to hopefully eliminate the suffering caused by many of these diseases.

5.1 Key Personnel

- Executive Director of Research

- Director of Pharmacology

- Director of Biology

- Director of Chemistry

The Center's Leadership Team consists of former pharmaceutical company research leaders and represents a lifetime of experience. Their breadth and depth of drug discovery and development accomplishments are key differentiators, and key contributors to future research success in the discovery and development of safe and effective treatments for the neglected, rare, and orphan diseases that disproportionately affect those in the developing world. Experienced in being integral members of multidisciplinary project teams, they are well versed in forming environments of open collaboration. This will enable the advancement of research both within the university and research community at-large.

Executive Director

As the visionary architect of The Center, he is the liaison to stakeholders who share The Center's mission. He fosters an environment of open collaboration, creativity and innovation. He combines a strong medicinal chemistry and molecular biology background with an exceptional ability to organize and lead cross-disciplinary teams.

Director of Pharmacology

The director of pharmacology is responsible for management of the preclinical pharmacology that provides confidence in viability of targets, disease relevance, and compound pharmacology. The goal of preclinical pharmacology is to achieve appropriate selection and characterization of compounds, which allows for a seamless transition into clinical evaluation. Prior to joining The Center, he achieved an impressive track record of success in the pharmaceutical industry. As a project and group leader over a ten-year career, he successfully led drug discovery and development teams that advanced five compounds from Lead Development through Phase I/II clinical studies. He also served as Discovery representative on the Global Cardiovascular and Metabolic Disease Development Team. This team was responsible for the early development portfolio of treatments for cardiovascular and metabolic diseases such as hypertension, heart failure, and diabetes.

Director of Cellular and Molecular Biology

The Director of Cell and Molecular Biology manages the development and implementation of in vitro and ex vivo assays that generate results critical to project decision-making. The expertise provided by his group includes high throughput screening of compounds, assessment of target potency and selectivity for lead optimization, and development of biomarker assays for translational pharmacology studies. During his successful seventeen-year career in drug discovery he specialized in target validation, where his skills and efforts significantly impacted research programs in multiple therapeutic areas including inflammation, oncology, bone disease, and ophthalmology.

Director of Chemistry

The Director of Chemistry oversees the synthesis and design of tool compounds and clinical leads. These compounds are to be used to assess target viability, disease relevance, and compound pharmacology. The selection and design of compounds are based on the optimal physiochemical and pharmacokinetic properties, as well as overall safety to ensure the best possible candidates for clinical evaluation. He was an accomplished group leader, chemistry team leader, project leader, and medicinal chemistry director in drug discovery and development over a twenty-five year career. During his notable tenure in the pharmaceutical industry, he led teams that advanced eight compounds from Lead Development through Phase I/II clinical studies. His research efforts have spanned a number of therapeutic areas including CNS, cardiovascular, oncology, and inflammation.

5.2 Roles and Responsibilities

Advisory Board

The Advisory Board serves to provide scientific and operational advice to The Center. The current core advisory board consists of faculty from the university. External members will be engaged as the projects develop. *Table 3* lists the members of the Advisory Board, their department affiliations, and research interests.

Table 3: The Center for World Health and Medicine Advisory Board

School of Medicine		
Board member	**Department**	**Research area**
John Hutchins	Professor of internal medicine, and director of the division of infectious diseases, allergy, and immunology	Expertise is in immunology and mechanisms of pathogenesis and inflammation.
Maria Bixel	Associate professor of molecular microbiology and immunology	Expert in systems biology, with published contributions in immunology, inflammation, cell signaling, and virology.
Lisa Schoenberg	Professor of pharmacological and physiological sciences	Expertise is in the physiology and pharmacology of neural signaling, particularly as it pertains to cardiovascular function.
Michael Navarro	Professor of biochemistry and molecular biology	Described the first case of Mucopolysaccharidosis type VII ("Sly Syndrome") and the first case of Carbonic Anhydrase II deficiency. His expertise is in lysosomal storage diseases, carbonic anydrase deficiencies, and hemachromatosis.
Jacob Smith	Professor and associate chair for research in the department of pediatrics	Research focuses on neutrophil function in newborn infants.
Jennifer Lee	Professor and vice chair of the department of pharmacological and physiological sciences	Research centers on the molecular and genetic basis for sensory signaling by the peripheral nervous system.
	Associate professor of biochemistry and molecular biology	Expertise in the enzymology of methionineaminopeptidases, as well as development of molecular tools for detection of substances in serum samples.
Thomas Reynolds	Professor of biochemistry and molecular biology and associate dean for research	Expertise in mechanisms of transcriptional regulation of gene expression.

Local university professor		
Board member	**Department**	**Research area**
Sarah Jankowitz	Distinguished professor of chemistry, biochemistry, and biology, and associate director of the center for nanoscience	Research interests include syntheticion channels and molecular capsules and nanotubes.

Directors

Although each of the directors shares responsibility for the ultimate success of The Center, leadership roles have been distributed to leverage each director's strengths. The Executive Director's role is to focus on marketing, fundraising, business development, and to serve as the primary voice for The Center. The other directors assume research leadership for their respective scientific disciplines while focusing on building a stable and efficient operation. Each also provides a key strategic role such as grant writing, sourcing new collaborations, or business planning and finance. Further responsibilities are outlined in *Table 4.*

Table 4: Directors' Roles and Responsibilities

Roles	Responsibilities
Founder and Executive Director	• Co-leads the implementation of the business plan, reporting to the Vice president of research • Leads the development of all national partnerships • Leads all fundraising activities • Primary spokesperson for CENTER to the public, attending industry, public policy, corporate, nonprofit, and fundraising meetings
Director of Pharmacology	• Manages all preclinical pharmacology studies and design • Manages financials for CENTER • Leads and manages development and implementation of fee for service operations • Project leadership
Director of Cellular and Molecular Biology	• Lead development and implementation of *in vitro and ex vivo* assays including high throughput screening and potency and selectivity assays • Lead development of biomarker assays for translational pharmacology studies • Leads all grant writing for CENTER • Project leadership
Director of Chemistry	• Lead compound design and synthesis efforts • Oversees design and selection of compounds with optimal physiochemical, pharmacokinetic, and safety properties • Interpretation of pharmacokinetic/toxicology data • Project leadership

6. MARKETING

The primary marketing goal of The Center is to establish the necessary marketing tools, programs, and partnerships needed to improve the regional, national and international reputation of The Center. These activities will establish The Center as a leader and key partner in the development of treatments for diseases of poverty.

6.1 Brand

The Center is currently trying to define and refine its brand image; in doing so it is imperative to focus on the fact that a strong brand is simple, unique, relevant and consistent. Building a successful brand in general requires three attributes:

- Differentiation, or how is your product or service unique?

- Segmentation, or what is unique about your target consumers?

- Positioning—Combining the two previous points allows you to create your unique message.

For The Center, the unique product and service is expertise in translational research; taking early stage research discoveries and translating them into compounds suitable and ready for clinical development. This is an expertise not generally found in academic research centers, and is normally reserved to biotech and big pharmaceutical companies. Their customers are in general academic groups and some small biotechs who cannot support this type of expertise internally. All of the groups, along with The Center belong to the small niche of researchers interested in neglected diseases. Combining their strengths with the existing gap in translational research, gives The Center a differentiator within the market and research community.

Tagline

The Center is currently considering a variety of tag lines, with the goal of identifying one with the best market appeal that resonates with donors, and captures the mission of the center. Some current examples are shown below, although the final choice may yet come from beyond this list.

- Developing medicines for the developing world

- Discovering medicines, discovering hope

- Prescriptions for hope

- Discovering medicines for the developing world

Elevator Pitch

As with any marketing strategy, The Center needs to be able to tell a compelling story. The following is a good example of a typical elevator pitch for The Center.

Do you realize that 1.5 million infants and children die from childhood diarrhea each year? Did you know that the World Health Organization has declared tuberculosis a Global Public Health Emergency? These are two of the many diseases that cause suffering to the poorest of the world's population. Who is there to help them? Not drug companies, because the poor can't pay for new medicines. The Center looks to fill that need and serve those who have been underserved. We combine lifetimes of experience in the pharmaceutical industry, with the basic research discoveries of university researchers and collaborators worldwide, to discover and develop new medicines for diseases of poverty. Your support is needed so we can bring new medicines to those who need them desperately. Please help us develop medicines for the developing world.

6.2 Target Market

The target market for The Center is primarily split into two somewhat overlapping groups, potential funding sources such as:

Funding Agencies/Sources

- Granting Agencies, such as the NIH

- Philanthropic foundations

- Product Development Partnerships—PDP's

Potential Partnerships:

- Product Development Partnerships—PDP's

- Academic collaborators/experts in specific disease targets

- Small biotechs

Each of these potential clients or partners has its own unique set of interests and criteria for collaborating with the center, but each shares in its desire to partner with The Center to access its expertise in translational research. Each partner also offers The Center unique benefits ranging from funding to access to renowned experts to visibility and recognition within this research community.

6.3 Partnerships

Since its creation in July of 2010, The Center has demonstrated a remarkable ability to quickly form collaborations and deliver results. Some of these initial collaborators are listed in *Table 5*. In addition, *Appendix 3* contains a more detailed list of current and potential collaborators and funding partners.

Table 5: Initial Research Collaborations and Partners

Research area	Partner
Childhood diarrhea	PDP
Malaria	Chinese government-funded institute
	Local university researchers
Malaria	National university researchers
Tuberculosis	Internal university collaboration
Retinal degeneration	Internal university collaboration

Each of these collaborations brings a different benefit to the CHWM. Some bring significant funding for The Center. Others, like the collaborations with internal university researchers, help build the reputation within the university, and some, like the multi-center collaboration, bring national and international visibility to the center.

7. FINANCIAL SUSTAINABILITY

The Center is currently funded through the Opportunity Fund. This is a grant distributed for fiscal years 2011 and 2012. It is the intent of the Office of Research that for 2013, The Center be placed into the operational budget of the university. The expectation is that by FY2013 The Center will be able to cover close to half of their expenses through external funding sources.

The Center is looking at grants as the primary source of external funding for the immediate and near term: Grants can be awarded from governmental agencies, foundations, and Product Development Partnerships (PDP's). Fee-for-service research operations are also being pursued as a means to generate revenue for The Center. Longer-range sources of funding are establishing an endowment for The Center (through the university development office), individual donors, and partnerships with the pharmaceutical industry.

Governmental Granting Agencies, Foundations, and Product Development Partnerships

Since The Center acts as a translational research group, it is able to partner with investigators at the university and worldwide, and provide resources that these investigators do not have in their individual groups. This will enable investigators to be more competitive for federal grant dollars. It is critical that The Center conduct due diligence in identifying the best potential collaborators in the disease space in which they operate.

Granting foundations and PDP's are closely related as many PDP's receive funding from large philanthropic organizations. This is the customer category for which the center is best aligned. As a translational research group, The Center is not in the business of conducting basic research. Philanthropic foundations and PDP's mostly seek late stage projects that can deliver clinically relevant results. The Center received almost immediate notice from a PDP and was awarded a grant for a childhood diarrhea project. Other PDP's that fund research into diseases of poverty include Medicines for Malaria, TB Initiative, and Drugs for Neglected Diseases Initiative, among others.

Fee for Service Operations

The Center has an opportunity to leverage their robust translational research experience into a revenue stream. When the University created The Center it not only received intellectual capital in the form of experienced scientists, it also received a large donation of highly specialized, expensive equipment. Much of this equipment is not readily available to small companies and academic laboratories. The combination of a need for a near-term revenue stream, and the abundance of resources not widely available elsewhere provide The Center the unique chance to be part of the entrepreneurial community. Delivery of research results to biotechs and academics can be provided with in vivo pharmacology services. In addition to the revenue stream, this opportunity allows The Center to contribute something valuable to the local life science community, and establish itself as a regional leader in biomedical research.

It is not uncommon for nonprofits to offer a service as a means to generate revenue, and there are examples of academic groups offering similar services. A local company has already subcontracted to The Center, to conduct an animal model study.

8. RISK MITIGATION

The following is a list of the key risks facing The Center. Adequate planning to both try to prevent these scenarios from happening in the first place can mitigate each, and to have plans to correct or compensate for them if they do occur anyway.

* Lack of Focus—too many projects
* Inability to secure adequate funding
* Inability to build collaborations with tropical disease experts
* Loss of key personnel
* Use SWOT analysis in developing strategies to mitigate risks (*Appendix 5*)

9. APPENDICES

Appendix 1: Competitor table

Appendix 2: Notable Facilities and Technologies Possessed by The Center

Appendix 3: SWOT Analysis

Appendix 1: Competitor Table

Organization	Location	Category	Website	Disease areas
Seattle BioMed	Seattle, WA	Not for Profit Biotech	http://www.seattlebiomed.org/	African sleeping sickness, Candidiasis, Chagas' disease,
Infectious Disease Research Institute	Seattle, WA	Not for Profit Biotech	idri.org	Leishmaniasis, TB, Malaria, Leprosy, Chagas disease
Center for Emerging and Neglected Diseases	Berkeley, CA	Academic Center	globalhealth.berkeley.edu/cend/	Tuberculosis, HIV/AIDS, Malaria, Diarrheal diseases,
The Center for Rare and Neglected Diseases at the University of Notre	South Bend, IN	Academic Center	nd.edu/~crnd/	Malaria, Niemann-Pick C Anemia, Lymphatic filariasis
The Sandler Center for Basic Research in Parasitic Diseases	San Francisco, CA	Academic Center	sandler.ucsf.edu/sandler.html	African sleeping sickness, Chagas disease, Leishmaniasis
Center for Global Health and Diseases at Case Western Reserve University	Cleveland, OH	Academic Center	http://www.case.edu/orgs/cghd/index.html	
Neglected Global Disease Initiative at UBC	Vancouver BC	Academic Center	http://ngdi.wordpress.com/about/	
Barcelona Centre for International Health Research	Barcelona, Spain	Academic and Biomedical Research Institution	cresib.cat/en/	Malaria, Pneumonia, HIV/AIDS, Diarrheal diseases,
George Washington University	Washington, DC	Academic Institution	GWU Newstory	Neglected infections of poverty (US), neglected tropical
European Solutions Enterprise for Neglected Diseases (euSend)				
Scynexis	Research Triangle Park, NC	For Profit CRO		
GlaxoSmithKline	Tres Cantos, Spain	Pharmaceutical Company	http://www.gsk.com/research/about/about_diseases.html	
Novartis Institute for Tropical Diseases	Singapore	Pharmaceutical Company	http://www.nibr.com/research/developing_world/NITD/index.shtml	Malaria, Tuberculosis Dengue, Tuberculosis, Malaria

Appendix 2: Tables of Facilities and Technologies

Research cores and equipment–university core facilities	
Small animal imaging facility	IVIS Spectrum system captures both fluorescent and luminescent light sources, which is viewable in both planar and 3D reconstructions.
Research microscopy core	Provide histology services, confocal microscopy, epifluorescencemicroscopy, laser capture technique, electron microscopy, and cell motility imaging resources.
Microarray core	AffymetrixGeneChip® System-provides a systems biology perspective for both expression profiling and DNA analysis.
Multimode plate readers	
Tecan Safire 2	Flexible monochromator-based detection system for 96 & 384 microplates with capabilities for top and bottom fluorescence intensity measurements, fluorescence polarization studies, multi-channel absorbance, TRF & FRET measurements.
Molecular devices flex station	Scanning fluorometer with integrated pipeting for endpoint or kinetic experiments. Excellent for calcium release or aequorin assays.
Specialized plate detection	
Perkin Elmer Topcount HTS	Sensitive scintillation and luminescence detector for 96 & 384 microplates.
Luminex 100	Liquid array multiplexing using bead based xMAP technology. Useful for immunoassays, receptor–ligand and nucleic acid assays.
Micro volume liquid handling	
Digilab hummingbird pipettor	Nanoliter transfer using glass capillaries in 384 format.
Thermo LabsystemsMicroMultidrop	Non-contact dispenser in 1uL increments for 96 or 384 formats with low dead volume.
Matrix platemate plus	Automated pipetting system with 4-position deck, allowing 96 & 384 plates, tip washing and reagent reservoirs to be configured into a walk away application.
Genomic tools	
Agilent 2100 Bioanalyzer	Microfluidics for sizing, quantification & quality control of DNA, RNA proteins and cells.
ABI Prism 6100 Nucleic Acid PrepStation	Automated isolation and purification of total RNA and genomic DNA from biological samples.
BioRad gene pulser II	An electroporation system for transforming eukaryotic and prokaryotic cells.
ABI 7500 RT-PCR system	Access through the University Department of Molecular Microbiology and Immunology.
Mass spectometry	
Sciex ABI 4000 - LC/MS/MS	Excellent sensitivity for low detection limits, industry standard, auto-injector holds up to six 96-well plates in chilled environment until sample run.
Thermo finnigan LCQ Deca XP	Ion trap LC/MS/MS, large dynamic range for small and large molecules, performs multiple MS stages within same run
Hematology analyzer, Cell-Dyn 3700	Fully automated hematology analysis, white blood cell counts and red blood cell and platelet analysis for medium to high volume laboratories.
Chemistry	
Biotage SP1	Automated preparative normal and reverse phase liquid chromatography for purification of organic compounds on milligram to multigram scale.
Agilent 1100 analytical HPLC	Auto sampler and diode array detector.
Genevac EZ2+	Centrifugal evaporation of low to high boiling point organic and aqueous solvents in round-bottom flasks, vials, test tube or plate formats.
Cambridge soft	Compound database and electronic notebook software.
Schrödinger maestro	A powerful, all-purpose molecular modeling environment for structure based drug design.
***In vivo* pharmacology**	
Implantable telemetry system	Monitors and collects data from conscious, freely moving laboratory animals: blood pressure, temperature, heart rate, ECG, EEG, etc.
Radnoti tissue bath systems	Monitors drug metabolism and kinetics, radio labels, muscle force, and stress measurements in passive and stimulated muscle preparations for cardiac muscle, skeletal muscle, smooth muscle such as aortic rings, bladder or intestine as well as many other experiments.
Culex automated *in vivo* sampling system	Collects samples for pharmacokinetic and pharmacodynamic analysis.

Appendix 3: Center—SWOT Analysis

Strengths

- Financial backing the university

- Experience in translational research

- Physical infrastructure (labs, vivarium, overhead)

- Intellectual infrastructure (university researchers)

- Center team has familiarity, worked with each other on teams in industry

- Knowledgeable of drug discovery process

- Proven track record of innovation—over 90 issued patents

- Great cause

- Network of contacts

- Enhance resources available to University researchers—improve funding opportunities

- Leverage School of Public Health

Weaknesses

- New venture, not experienced as "social entrepreneurs"

- New therapeutic areas, developing diseases expertise

- Too many projects will spread resources too thin

- Resource constraints will limit which projects can be on-boarded (early stage projects likely to be too resource intensive)

- Insufficient internal medicinal chemistry

- Not yet established reputation in academia

- Grant writing and administration

- Lab space limitations within the university campus

- Lack of internal GLP/GMP capability

Opportunities

- Early notice by strong external partners

- Entrepreneurial avenues (gaps in regional research resources create FFS opportunities for in vivo pharmacology and biological assays)

- Partnerships with similar groups which lack translational research

- Diseases of poverty and orphan diseases mostly ignored by Big Pharma

- Continued consolidation of Pharmaceutical industry may be a catalyst for collaboration in neglected and orphan disease research

- Center as pharma portal/library creation and distribution

Threats

- No formal ties to developing world translational partners

- Access to compounds from the pharmaceutical industry

ENDNOTES

1. "R&D Spending by US Pharma and Biotech Firms Reaches Record High—Pharmaceutical Technology." Pharmaceutical Technology—Pharmaceutical Manufacturing & Development News & Research for Scientists. Web. 26 Apr. 2011. http://pharmtech.findpharma.com/pharmtech/News/RampD-Spending-by-US-Pharma-and-Biotech-Firms-Reac/ArticleStandard/Article/detail/507255.

2. Nordling, Linda. "Lack of Support Keeps African Discoveries Languishing in Labs: Nature News." Nature Publishing Group: Science Journals, Jobs, and Information. Web. 26 Apr. 2011. http://www.nature.com/news/2010/101212/full/news.2010.666.html?WT.ec_id=NEWS-20101214.

3. http://www.who.int/dg/speeches/2009/mxdr_tb_prevention_20090401/en/index.html

Online Dating/Matchmaking Service

MatchMate Inc.

200 Elm St.
Boston, MA 02290

The authors of this plan are attempting to diversify their business by offering matchmaking franchises to others.

This business plan appeared in **Business Plans Handbook, Volume 3.** *It has been updated for this volume.*

DESCRIPTION OF COMPANY

MatchMate is an online dating/matchmaking service created by a marriage counselor and Fortune 100 software designer. The company focuses on the 50-plus market and provides local matchmaking services to Boston-area singles; national and international matchmaking services to singles worldwide via the Internet; and exclusive licenses to other entrepreneurs to own and operate MatchMate software using the MatchMate name and system within geographic boundaries around the world. To date, 110 local MatchMates operate in the United States and a dozen more operate internationally.

In addition to offering matchmaking services, the MatchMate Web site hosts a singles' mall with photo gallery listings in a variety of geographic locations, and markets other singles-related services and products. Our online speed dating service, which utilizes video chat technology, differentiates us from our competitors. This has proven to be extremely popular with our customers because it adds yet another dimension to the matchmaking experience. Individuals can go beyond e-mails and static photographs (which may not be entirely representative) before committing to a deeper level of involvement. Another differential is that, when desired, our specially trained franchisees offer personal assistance to customers at the local level.

The company employs three full-time staff, three outside sales representatives, and several contract programmers who maintain and develop the Web site and other interactive technologies.

LEGAL STATUS

MatchMate, Inc., headquartered in Boston, Massachusetts, is a limited Massachusetts company incorporated in June of 2008. From its inception in December of 2003 until incorporation, MatchMate operated as a D.B.A./Proprietorship.

MISSION STATEMENT/PURPOSE

MatchMate's explicit purpose is to help singles over the age of 50 to find compatible long-term or life partners by offering psycho-social screening through the sale of memberships to the service. The unique matchmaking system matches and cross-matches each client for 350 items of compatibility that are deemed by university researchers to be the most compelling elements in long-lasting relationships. The internal scoring system, based on surveys of how singles rank various categories, declares only those who score at 60% percent or higher.

The implicit purpose of the system is to educate and raise awareness about one's individual dating patterns and needs in terms of romantic partnership. In completing the application form, singles evaluate themselves and potential partners in terms of race, religion, education, personality traits, physical description, health, interests, lifestyle, sexual orientation, children, personal habits, and relationship goals. In the course of both completing the application and experiencing the results, singles gain valuable self-awareness and self-esteem.

The MatchMate system was designed by a marriage counselor and former social worker who believes that too much emphasis has been placed on online dating services for the younger market. A number of trends are driving market opportunities for the 50-plus market. One major trend is that people are living longer than ever before. This has led to a redefinition of what is considered to be "middle age." In fact, the U.S. Census Bureau now considers this time of life to be the period from age 45 to age 75. By 2010 the average life expectancy was 78, compared to 47 back in 1900. In addition to living longer, medical advances are improving the quality of life for those over 50. For example, the importance of intimacy has been supported by new pharmaceuticals for those with problems such as impotence.

Over a seven-year period, singles who met and married using the MatchMate system report only a 1% divorce rate, implying that matching for compatibility first is a more accurate method for predicting long-term relationship success.

STAGE OF DEVELOPMENT

MatchMate began as a small, local matchmaking service in Marlborough, Massachusetts. In addition to matching compatible individuals, the company's founder originally offered personal service to clients for an additional fee. The original client base grew to 200 clients during the first year.

The owners moved to Springfield, Massachusetts, and began pursuing a growth and expansion strategy. Western Massachusetts was added as a second base of operations. Within three years the service grew to offering database matching in all of Massachusetts and Rhode Island. The total client base in 2009 comprised 1,800 singles.

In March of 2008, MatchMate began offering franchise opportunities. The United States was divided into 150 geographic zones based on population demographics. By April of 2011, 110 units were sold in the United States. The international territory was divided into 220 zones, and 13 have been sold since March of 2008. Since December of 2009, visibility on the Internet has increased sales to potential buyers in foreign countries by 40%. Franchisees receive specific training that qualifies them to offer the optional personalized services that set us apart from other online dating services.

In December of 2009, MatchMate launched a Web site with several pages of information and an online application for local and national bases. International bases were added in the summer of 2009. By the first anniversary, the MatchMate home page was recording 140,000 hits a month. By early 2011, that figure had doubled.

In the spring of 2010 MatchMate sold its interest in Western Massachusetts as an existing base and moved its headquarters to Boston, Massachusetts. A new Boston-area base serving the metropolitan area was developed. To date, it is the only local database that the corporation owns. The corporation also exclusively owns and operates the national and international databases.

It also was in 2010 that MatchMate added singles' mall features to its home page. This included a photo gallery and biographical data about singles who posted in a special section called American Ads (listed by state). That section grew in the second month to include Canadian and Asian photo personals and will be further expanded to include Russian and Brazilian personals. As more international sites are sold, personals pages will be added as a service to singles who do not wish to undergo matchmaking. While this portion of the service does not match-make, it accommodates those singles who wish only to view photos and contact other singles.

In February of 2011, the advice feature was added to the home page. This page allows singles over 50 to ask founder Susan Hamilton, M.S.W., questions on relationships, marriage, and dating. Initially, it is a free service. Eventually, there will be a nominal charge and the pages will become interactive. Ms. Hamilton intends this section to have an educational format in which guided discussion occur. She will monitor the discussion group at specific times, answering and posing questions. Singles' mall pages also include other products and services for singles to purchase. To date, vendors include those who provide books, DVDs, newsletters, downloadable audio files, gifts, and other singles-related services.

We currently are developing a mobile app for the Apple iPhone, as well as the Android operating system. This will enable our customers to conveniently access services wherever they are, and potentially take advantage of location-based services. Finally, we are exploring the integration of our online dating services with popular social media sites, including Facebook.

PRODUCT/SERVICES

- Matchmaking: National and international online databases.

- Online Speed Dating: Customers can take advantage of video chat technology to get a better feel for prospective mates. This option allows them to go beyond e-mails and static photographs (which may not be entirely representative) before committing to a deeper level of involvement.

- Enhanced Services: One-on-one, personalized services for singles who have more complicated needs. Involves personal interviews and more detailed screening of matches. Fees vary. Availability of enhanced services is at owner's discretion. Not available in all markets.

- Worldwide Photo Ads: Browse a photo gallery and leave messages for other singles.

- Licensed business opportunities in the United States and internationally.

- Advice Forum, a question-and-answer page offering free; professional advice on life's pressing romantic/relationship issues.

- "Myths about Love over 50," a video seminar (available on DVD and online) presentation in three chapters, based on common myths about love, romance, and finding a soul mate over age 50. The video features Susan Hamilton, marriage counselor and founder of the MatchMate system.

INDUSTRY/MARKET ANALYSIS

Industry Overview

The dating services industry is big business. According to a fifth edition Marketdata study released in early 2011, the U.S. dating services market is valued at $1.8 billion. Online dating services account for more than 50% of that total. According to the January 1, 2011, issue of *The Economist,* the research firm

ComScore reported that, in November 2010, two leading online dating sites (Match.com and Zoosk) had roughly 4.5 million visitors each. The online dating industry has received widespread media attention, both nationally and internationally. In addition to leading newspapers and magazines, there are a number of blogs devoted exclusively to the subject. One example is Online Dating Insider.

Target Market

The target market for our business is adults over the age of 50. However, we have segmented our offerings into two distinct categories. One is targeted toward individuals ages 50-64, while another is targeted toward individuals over age 65. Whenever possible, our online products are interoperable, so that customers with broader interests are not limited in any way.

By 2010 the first members of the baby boom generation (76 million people) began retiring. In time, this phenomenon will lead to the largest over-65 population in the U.S. history. According to U.S. Census Bureau data, those aged 65 or older totaled a mere 3.1 million in 1900. However, this figure had increased to 12.3 million by 1950, 25.5 million by 1980, 35 million by 2000, and is projected to reach 88.5 million by 2050.

A number of trends are driving the popularity of online dating sites for those over age 50. One major trend is that people are living longer than ever before. This has led to a redefinition of what is considered to be "middle age." In fact, the U.S. Census Bureau now considers this time of life to be the period from age 45 to age 75. By 2010 the average life expectancy was 78, compared to 47 back in 1900. In addition to living longer, medical advances are improving the quality of life for those over 50. For example, the importance of intimacy has been supported by new pharmaceuticals for those with problems such as impotence.

Finally, older adults are adopting technology in growing numbers. The Pew Internet Foundation reported that the use of social media among the 55-to-64-year-old age category increased substantially from 2008 to 2010, growing from 9 percent to 43 percent, outclassing growth in all other categories.

Competition

By the 21st century's second decade, market saturation had led to cutthroat competition within our industry. According to some research reports, we compete against more than 1,500 providers of online dating/matchmaking services. This competition has been heightened by the rising popularity of social media.

In order to be successful, industry players need a strong differential. Beyond popular sites such as Match.com, Yahoo Personals, True.com, Plenty of Fish, and eHarmony, a wide range of niche sites have emerged. For example, People Media, which was established in 2002, operates sites focused on African Americans (BlackPeopleMeet.com), as well as sites for Christians and individuals with very specific or unconventional interests. Vampire Passions is yet another example of online dating sites that cater to those with interests that fall outside of the mainstream.

Given the need for specialization, it's no surprise that the 50-plus market has a number of options for online dating. For example, WhiteLabelDating began operating Fun at 50 in October of 2008. The site is based in the United Kingdom, but allows users to search by several different countries. In mid-2011 publicly-traded IAC (People Media) brought members of several of its sites together on OurTime.com, an online dating site for people over 50 that is one of the largest of its kind worldwide.

Differentials

We stand out among the crowded sea of competitors by excelling in three areas: security, science, and speed.

In terms of security, we pride ourselves on offering the most secure online matchmaking/dating environment for the 50-plus market in the world. Unlike many services, we require that all members undergo criminal background checks. Although this is a "turnoff" to a small segment of prospective customers, it creates such tremendous peace of mind for members of online communities.

Our "secret sauce" is the science behind the compatibility matrix that we use to match prospective mates. This is gleaned from both published research, and years of clinical experience counseling individuals over age 50. In addition to offering the matrix online, our franchisees are able to utilize even more in-depth/robust analysis for customers with specialized needs.

Finally, our employment of optional online speed dating techniques really set us apart from others. We regularly give clusters of compatible prospects the option to engage in online speed dating services via video chat. This has proven to be extremely popular with our customers, because it adds yet another dimension to the matchmaking experience. Individuals can get a much better feel for one another, going beyond e-mails and static photographs (which may not be entirely representative) before committing to a deeper level of involvement.

Online speed dating sessions are hosted several times per day, seven days a week. Participants "date" approximately 15 to 20 people per session. Each encounter lasts four minutes. Following the encounter, participants have 10 seconds to give the experience a "thumbs up" or a "thumbs down" rating. In the case of a thumbs-up rating, participants then complete a secondary rating of 1 to 5 stars. When the overall session ends, thumbs-up ratings are added to a participant's queue, where they are sorted according to the aforementioned star ranking. A queue may contain prospective partners from multiple speed dating sessions.

MARKETING/ADVERTISING/SALES STRATEGIES

Direct mail is a prime form of marketing the MatchMate name and service. Inexpensive post cards outlining the advantages of this unique form of matchmaking are sent to singles over the age of 50 in a targeted community (including individuals recently divorced or widowed). Mailing lists can be obtained from list brokers or lists can be cross-referenced from business or client lists the owner has accumulated.

For prospective customers over the age of 65, lists also can be obtained for retirement communities and apartment complexes. Some indicators suggest, in most communities, that condominiums, townhomes, and apartments are home to the majority of singles in this category.

Distribution of door-hanger direct marketing materials provides inexpensive exposure in upscale senior apartment/town home communities. The marketing pieces go directly to the occupant and can be passed along to family and friends. Discount coupons are incorporated so occupants feel they are getting a better price and are more apt to join. Each piece is marked with a two-week coupon mandating an immediate response.

Pundits of advertising report that the wise advertiser "hits" the prospect with material three times. The MatchMate business plan includes second and third mailers to prospects who did not join the service after requesting information. The second mailer, sent three to four weeks after the initial inquiry, offers the service at a moderate 10% discount. The third mailer, sent annually in June or July, offers a significant 30% discount. (The "Summer Special" compensates for the slower registration rate that traditionally occurs during summer months, when singles are either on vacation or more socially active).

The name and address of every single who inquired about the service is entered into a master mailing list for future use. No lead is considered "dead" until that person has received at least three "hits."

Owners are encouraged to contact activity/interest groups and churches to make presentations about the service. Informal presentations provide valuable information and encourage singles to participate without sales pressure.

Informational form letters are sent to local counselors/therapists/psychologists outlining the benefits of the MatchMate system to professionals who traditionally endorse compatibility matching. The letter explains how the service operates—by matching key, holistic elements of compatibility—and that it was designed by a certified professional. Many referrals come from therapists who have urged their clients to pursue relationships in a more realistic and logical manner than random dating offers.

Free or nominally-priced educational seminars offered to the public using the video "Myths about Love over 50," by founder Susan Hamilton, also are effective. Corporate research indicates that singles over the age of 50 are hungry for specific information on how to meet and how to select the appropriate partner. This 90-minute video answers the most frequently asked questions and, although generic, is a subtle promotion of the MatchMate system. Ms. Hamilton is available via online video for a question-and-answer period following the presentation. If the owner is using a hotel meeting room for the seminar, a broadband Internet connection, along with a Web cam and microphone/speakers, are required.

A 45-minute audio presentation is provided to all owners. This CD master can be duplicated at the owner's expense and mailed to prospective clients along with the brochure and application form. The CD answers the most frequently asked questions about the service and provides background information on how and why it functions so accurately. The advantage to the CD is that if the prospect isn't interested, perhaps they will give the CD to another single friend, making it an automatic distribution tool.

A marketing packet of successful ads, direct-mail post cards, DVDs/CDs, and door hangers is provided to all owners as part of the purchase price.

MANAGEMENT

MatchMate, Inc., the parent company, is owned and operated by Susan Hamilton, M.S.W., and Lawrence Hamilton, M.ED.

Ms. Hamilton is a relationship counselor, freelance writer, and lecturer. She received her Master's in Social Work from Central University. She held numerous administrative social work positions with charitable agencies in Massachusetts and California before establishing her own counseling practice concentrating on the needs of adults over age 50.

Ms. Hamilton is a recipient of a Commissioner's award for Excellence in Community Service. She is the author of feature articles in numerous national magazines, a frequent radio and TV talk show guest, and is recognized as a leading computer matchmaking/online dating expert. Thousands of people follow her on Twitter and are regular readers of her blog.

As the president of MatchMate, Inc., Ms. Hamilton functions as the marketing and sales director for services and licensees. She also provides enhanced services to members who desire the personalized, one-to-one matchmaking service.

Mr. Hamilton is a computer and Internet consultant and a freelance technical writer. He holds a Master's in Education from Dalhousie University. He taught mathematics for several years before being recruited by a major computer firm to teach computer programming. Mr. Hamilton has held positions in Fortune 500 and 1000 companies. His software design of the MatchMate system is technically unparalleled.

He is the vice president of MatchMate, Inc., and functions as technical support director and chief financial officer. He is also responsible for Internet marketing and development.

Cheryl Smith is executive administrative assistant. She is in charge of database management, employees, outside sales representatives, and client support.

LONG-TERM GOALS

MatchMate's primary goals are two-fold. First, to continue the growth of local, national, and international memberships and to experience no less than the current annual 30%-40% growth rate. Second, to continue to sell licensed business opportunities to entrepreneurs throughout the world. We fully expect to continue our growth and become the world's largest online dating/matchmaking service for those over age 50. As the availability of zones in the United States and Canada diminishes, the corporate goals will focus on the sale of international zones and the addition of personals for individual countries.

On the technical front, our goals include the continued evolution of new interactive offerings. We currently are developing a mobile app for the Apple iPhone, as well as the Android operating system. This will enable our customers to conveniently access services wherever they are, and potentially take advantage of location-based services. Finally, we are exploring the integration of our online dating services with popular social media sites, including Facebook.

MatchMate's future plans also include making the Advice Forum pages interactive and presenting seminars on topics of interest to singles. These topics will include issues on single health, investments, travel, and romantic relations, and will be delivered by other esteemed professionals. This service will be available by the middle of 2012.

For licensees, MatchMate plans to coordinate singles' fairs in major cities in the United States. A singles' exhibition organizer has been hired to deliver these one-day events, which draw thousands of singles to a full day of exhibits, seminars, games, and a dance. The prototype was developed in the Boston market in November of 2010. The event, the first ever held in the Boston area, drew 800 singles and was considered a huge success. Similar events are planned for major cities as licensees develop their local singles lists and gain knowledge of other singles-related organizations in their communities. Not only does this marketing format produce on-the-spot registrations, the end result is a community-wide mailing list garnered from competitors who also attract attendees.

MatchMate expects to produce two additional videos, each containing three more chapters of "Myths about Love over 50." As promotion for the videos and the matchmaking service, Susan Hamilton will appear on various national talk shows.

MILESTONES

- 2008 MatchMate was voted the number 1 matchmaking service by the New England Singles Association.

- 2009/2010 MatchMate was rated by *Entrepreneur* magazine as one of the top 500 business opportunities in America and listed in their July "Business 500" edition. MatchMate will also be included in the July 2011 edition.

- 2010 Susan Hamilton was selected as a member of the U.S. Society of Ethical Dating Services and appointed the nation's expert on computer matchmaking for older adults. Membership to this organization is not purchased, but given for outstanding merit.

- 2011 MatchMate joined the Worldwide Association of Matchmaking and was appointed the northeastern USA expert on computer matchmaking. Membership is purchased, but expert status is voted.

- 2011 MatchMate's Internet home page was selected for a Magellan Three Star award for home page content and design.

FINANCIAL STATEMENTS

Balance Sheet—December 31, 2010

Assets

Current assets

Cash clearing	$32,079
Total current assets	$32,079

Fixed assets

Computer/equipment	$ 8,182
Depr/computer/equipment	($ 5,157)
Total fixed assets	$ 3,025

Other assets

Organization expense	$ 324
Amortization/organization	($ 166)
Security deposit	$ 860
Total other assets	**$ 1,018**
Total assets	**$36,122**

Liabilities and equity

Current liabilities

Visa payable	$ 2,279
Total current liabilities	$ 2,279

Long term liabilities

L/P—Lawrence Hamilton	$27,929
Total long-term liabilities	$27,929

Equity

Capital	($ 7,590)
Current income (loss)	$13,504
Total equity	**$ 5,914**
Total liabilities & equity	**$36,122**

Income Statement for the Year Ended December 31, 2010

Revenue

Sales/licensed software	$121,059
Sales/profiles	$ 6,538
Sales/programming	$ 7
Sales/registration	$ 27,198
Total revenue	$154,802

Cost of sales

Returns & allowance	$ 5,279
Total cost of sales	$ 5,279
Gross profit	$149,523

Operating expenses

Contract labor	$ 10,511
Advertising	$ 32,996
Accounting	$ 724
Amortization expense	$ 65
Auto expense	$ 17,926
Bank charges	$ 377
Commission expense	$ 4,683
Contributions	$ 2,001
Depreciation expense	$ 4,646
Dues & subscriptions	$ 1,045
Entertainment	$ 330
Insurance expense	$ 1,667
Legal expense	$ 1,154
Licenses	$ 49
Office expense	$ 3,870
Office supplies	$ 2,193
Office/computer expense	$ 923
Office/computer supplies	$ 387
Operation expenses	$ 5,976
Postage	$ 10,169
Rent	$ 19,565
Tax/other	$ 625
Telephone	$ 17,251
Travel expense	$ 70
Utilities/other	$ 2,549
Total expenses	**$141,752**
Operating income	**$ 7,771**
Net income (loss)	**$ 7,771**

Online Job Service

The Job Authority, Inc.

9996 W. 53rd St., Ste. 909
New York, NY 10012

BizPlanDB.com

The purpose of this business plan is to raise $150,000 for the development of an online jobs website that will provide a platform for businesses to promote positions that are available within their organization. The Company was founded by Larry Downs.

1.0 EXECUTIVE SUMMARY

The purpose of this business plan is to raise $150,000 for the development of an online jobs website that will provide a platform for businesses to promote positions that are available within their organization. This business plan will also showcase the expected financials and operations over the next three years. The Job Authority is a New York-based corporation that will sell advertising space while generating revenues through advertising sales via its online platform to users. The Company was founded by Larry Downs.

1.1 The Site

As stated above, the primary revenue center for the business will come from the ongoing posting of available positions among employers that are seeking to fill positions within their organization. Management anticipates that the business will charge $100 for each position posted.

The business will generate revenues from static and dynamic advertisements that generate revenues on a per 1000 impressions basis while concurrently earning other income from affiliate partner revenues. The third section of the business plan will further describe the services offered by The Job Authority.

1.2 Financing

Mr. Downs is seeking to raise $150,000 from a bank loan. The interest rate and loan agreement are to be further discussed during negotiation. This business plan assumes that the business will receive a 10-year loan with a 9% fixed interest rate. The financing will be used for the following:

- Development of the Company's online website platform

- Financing for the first six months of operation

- Capital to purchase servers, computers, and related technology

Mr. Downs will contribute $25,000 to the venture

1.3 Mission Statement

The Job Authority's mission is to become the recognized leader in its targeted market as a platform where people can find jobs.

1.4 Management Team

The Company was founded by Larry Downs. Mr. Downs has more than 10 years of experience in the online and Internet industry. Through his expertise, he will be able to bring the operations of the business to profitability within its first year of operations.

1.5 Sales Forecasts

Mr. Downs expects a strong rate of growth at the start of operations. Below are the expected financials over the next three years.

Proforma profit and loss (yearly)

Year	1	2	3
Sales	$990,450	$1,436,153	$1,938,806
Operating costs	$429,373	$ 480,774	$ 536,571
EBITDA	$462,033	$ 811,763	$1,208,354
Taxes, interest, and depreciation	$197,607	$ 324,961	$ 475,048
Net profit	$264,425	$ 486,802	$ 733,305

Sales, operating costs, and profit forecast

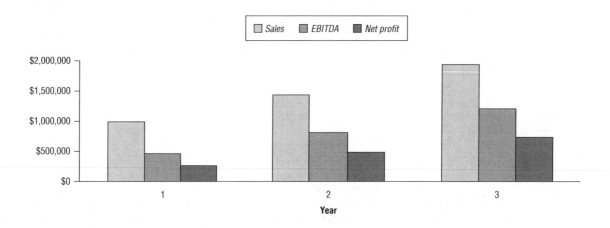

1.6 Expansion Plan

The Founder expects that the business will aggressively expand during the first three years of operation. Mr. Downs intends to implement marketing campaigns that will effectively target individuals and businesses that are seeking to hire within the Company's demographic.

2.0 COMPANY AND FINANCING SUMMARY

2.1 Registered Name and Corporate Structure

The Job Authority is registered as a corporation in the State of New York.

2.2 Required Funds

At this time, The Job Authority requires $150,000 of debt funds. Below is a breakdown of how these funds will be used:

Projected startup costs

Initial lease payments and deposits	$ 15,000
Working capital	$ 25,000
FF&E	$ 30,000
Website development	$ 42,500
Security deposits	$ 5,000
Insurance	$ 5,500
Servers and technology equipment	$ 25,000
Marketing budget	$ 25,000
Miscellaneous and unforeseen costs	$ 5,000
Total startup costs	**$175,000**

Use of funds

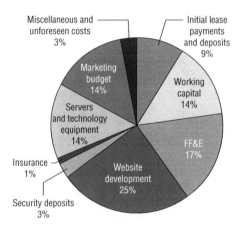

2.3 Investor Equity

Mr. Downs is not seeking an investment from a third party at this time.

2.4 Management Equity

Larry Downs owns 100% of The Job Authority, Inc.

2.5 Exit Strategy

If the business is very successful, Mr. Downs may seek to sell the business to a third party for a significant earnings multiple. Most likely, the Company will hire a qualified business broker to sell the business on behalf of The Job Authority. Based on historical numbers, the business could fetch a sales premium of up to 6 times earnings.

3.0 PRODUCTS AND SERVICES

Below is a description of the benefits (to both users and businesses) offered by The Job Authority.

3.1 Benefits of The Job Authority

As discussed earlier, the business will specialize in allowing employers to place advertisements for available positions on The Job Authority. The business will charge a flat rate of approximately $100 for each position posted on the website.

In the future, the business may offer services to job seekers such as interview coaching, resume development, and online job fairs. This could be a substantial additional revenue stream for the business once the Company commences operations.

3.2 Advertising Revenues

The revenues will come from the sale of advertising space to businesses. At the onset of operations the business will develop a relationship with Google AdSense so that the business can immediately generate revenue. Each time a visiting user clicks on one of the advertisements for the business, the Company receives a payment from Google. These ads will be tastefully placed throughout the Online Job Website's platform.

The Company also intends to develop its own internal advertising programs that will feature static advertisements within the website. These advertisements will be sold directly to advertisers rather than through a third party system, like Google AdSense. In the future, the Online Job Website will also seek to develop product affiliation and corporate sponsorship relationships which would further the Company's visibility and revenue streams.

4.0 STRATEGIC AND MARKET ANALYSIS

4.1 Economic Outlook

This section of the analysis will detail the economic climate, the online advertising and e-commerce industry, the customer profile, and the competition that the business will face as it progresses through its business operations.

Currently, the economic market condition in the United States is moderate. The meltdown of the subprime mortgage market coupled with increasing gas prices has led many people to believe that the U.S. is on the cusp of a double dip economic recession. This slowdown in the economy has also greatly impacted real estate sales, which has halted to historical lows. However, this should not have an impact on the Company's ability to generate revenues given the strong demand among companies to hire qualified candidates coupled with the demand among job seekers to post their resumes to websites that can potentially provide them with employment.

4.2 Industry Analysis

In the United States there are 13,000 companies that specialize in the placement of job candidates and providing temporary labor (this industry includes online businesses that are seeking to place candidates for available job positions). Each year, these businesses generate more than $4.7 billion dollars per year, and employ more than 113,000 people. These businesses provide over $2.6 billion dollars of payrolls.

The annualized growth rate over the last five years for firms entering this market has been 2.4% per year. However, over the same time period, the revenues collectively generated by these businesses have exceeded 13% per year.

4.3 Customer Profile

The Job Authority's average client will be a young middle- to upper-middle class male or female that has a broadband internet connection. Common traits among end users will include:

- Is currently seeking a position that pays $25,000 to $100,000 per year

- Between the ages of 18 and 59

- Has high speed internet access

- Is familiar with the concept and operations of online job websites

- May need assistance with interview coaching, resume development, and related services

At this time, the estimated market of individuals that are seeking jobs is enormous given the recent severe recession within the United States. Although unemployment figures have dropped moderately over the past twelve months (starting in 2010), it is still estimated that 9 million people are either unemployed or underemployed. As such, the demand for companies and individuals that are providing jobs and seeking jobs is substantial.

4.4 Competition

As many individuals now seek to find a job online, a number of major competitors have entered the market with platforms that are substantially similar to The Job Authority, Inc. These competitors include, but are not limited to the following:

- Monster.com, Inc.

- HotJobs

- CareerBuilder.com

As such, Management will need to make a strong differentiation regarding its online jobs Internet-based portal in order to remain competitive within this market. Management intends to focus heavily on locally available jobs in order to provide employers with a number of targeted resumes and cover letters from individuals that are seeking jobs within localized markets.

5.0 MARKETING PLAN

The Job Authority intends to maintain an extensive marketing campaign that will ensure maximum visibility for the business in its targeted market. Below is an overview of the marketing strategies and objectives of The Job Authority.

5.1 Marketing Objectives

- Establish relationships with advertisers that are targeting a computer savvy younger demographic.

- Develop ongoing relationships with medium-sized and large corporations that will continue to need the services of The Job Authority as time progresses.

5.2 Marketing Strategies

Mr. Downs intends to use a high impact marketing campaign that will generate a substantial amount of traffic to the website. These strategies include the use of search engine optimization and pay per click marketing.

The Company intends to focus a substantial amount of its marketing budget on booths at major job fairs that will not only assist in placing qualified candidates with jobs, but it will also increase the brand name of The Job Authority. As time progresses, Management anticipates that this will become an invaluable source of traffic and brand recognition as it pertains to increasing awareness of the Company's online job offering website while concurrently generating substantial revenues for the business.

Additionally, the business will continue to develop ongoing relationships with major corporations, medium-sized companies, and small businesses that are regularly seeking to hire individuals for specific positions. This is extremely important as this will assist in normalizing revenues for the business as time progresses.

At the onset of operations, Management will use pay per click marketing in order to drive immediate traffic to the website.

5.3 Pricing

The Company intends to charge employers a fixed flat rate fee of approximately $100 each time they intend to offer a position to qualified candidates within their localized market.

The Job Authority, Inc. will also generate incomes through its advertising operations. For each 1,000 visitors that come to the website, Management anticipates approximately $20 of revenue.

6.0 ORGANIZATIONAL PLAN AND PERSONNEL SUMMARY

6.1 Corporate Organization

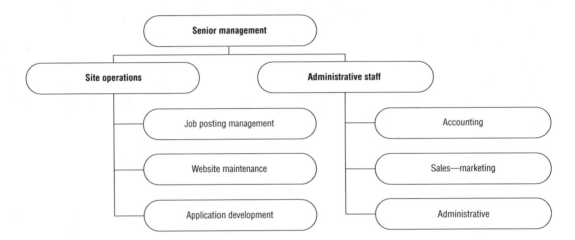

6.2 Organizational Budget

Personnel plan—yearly

Year	1	2	3
Owners	$ 80,000	$ 82,400	$ 84,872
Website manager	$ 35,000	$ 36,050	$ 37,132
Assistant	$ 32,500	$ 33,475	$ 34,479
Website marketing staff	$ 37,500	$ 51,500	$ 66,306
Administrative	$ 44,000	$ 45,320	$ 46,680
Total	**$229,000**	**$248,745**	**$269,469**

Numbers of personnel

Owners	2	2	2
Website manager	1	1	1
Assistant	1	1	1
Website marketing staff	3	4	5
Administrative	2	2	2
Totals	**9**	**10**	**11**

Personnel expense breakdown

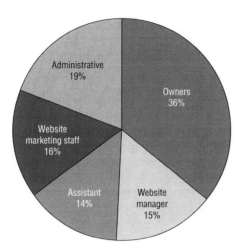

7.0 FINANCIAL PLAN

7.1 Underlying Assumptions

The Company has based its proforma financial statements on the following:

- The Job Authority will have an annual revenue growth rate of 31% per year.

- The Owner will acquire $150,000 of debt funds to develop the business.

- The loan will have a 10-year term with a 9% interest rate.

7.2 Sensitivity Analysis

The demand for online jobs websites has increased significantly as the economy has improved. As such, Management fees that the low operating cost infrastructure of the business coupled with the high margin revenues generated by the Company will ensure that the business is able to remain profitable and cash flow positive at all times.

7.3 Source of Funds

Financing

Equity contributions	
Management investment	$ 25,000.00
Total equity financing	**$ 25,000.00**
Banks and lenders	
Banks and lenders	$ 150,000.00
Total debt financing	**$150,000.00**
Total financing	**$175,000.00**

7.4 General Assumptions

General assumptions

Year	1	2	3
Short term interest rate	9.5%	9.5%	9.5%
Long term interest rate	10.0%	10.0%	10.0%
Federal tax rate	33.0%	33.0%	33.0%
State tax rate	5.0%	5.0%	5.0%
Personnel taxes	15.0%	15.0%	15.0%

7.5 Profit and Loss Statements

Proforma profit and loss (yearly)

Year	1	2	3
Sales	**$990,450**	**$1,436,153**	**$1,938,806**
Cost of goods sold	$ 99,045	$ 143,615	$ 193,881
Gross margin	90.00%	90.00%	90.00%
Operating income	**$891,405**	**$1,292,537**	**$1,744,925**
Expenses			
Payroll	$229,000	$ 248,745	$ 269,469
General and administrative	$ 32,500	$ 33,800	$ 35,152
Marketing expenses	$ 39,618	$ 57,446	$ 77,552
Professional fees and licensure	$ 17,000	$ 17,510	$ 18,035
Insurance costs	$ 12,000	$ 12,600	$ 13,230
Server and technology costs	$ 25,000	$ 27,500	$ 30,250
Rent and utilities	$ 30,000	$ 31,500	$ 33,075
Miscellaneous costs	$ 9,905	$ 14,362	$ 19,388
Payroll taxes	$ 34,350	$ 37,312	$ 40,420
Total operating costs	**$429,373**	**$ 480,774**	**$ 536,571**
EBITDA	**$462,033**	**$ 811,763**	**$1,208,354**
Federal income tax	$152,471	$ 263,857	$ 395,060
State income tax	$ 23,102	$ 39,978	$ 59,858
Interest expense	$ 13,107	$ 12,197	$ 11,202
Depreciation expenses	$ 8,929	$ 8,929	$ 8,929
Net profit	**$264,425**	**$ 486,802**	**$ 733,305**
Profit margin	**26.70%**	**33.90%**	**37.82%**

Sales, operating costs, and profit forecast

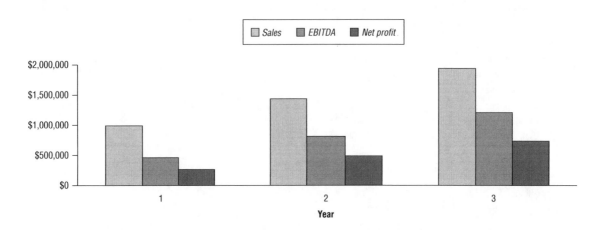

7.6 Cash Flow Analysis

Proforma cash flow analysis—yearly

Year	1	2	3
Cash from operations	$273,354	$495,731	$742,234
Cash from receivables	$ 0	$ 0	$ 0
Operating cash inflow	**$273,354**	**$495,731**	**$742,234**
Other cash inflows			
Equity investment	$ 25,000	$ 0	$ 0
Increased borrowings	$150,000	$ 0	$ 0
Sales of business assets	$ 0	$ 0	$ 0
A/P increases	$ 37,902	$ 43,587	$ 50,125
Total other cash inflows	**$212,902**	**$ 43,587**	**$ 50,125**
Total cash inflow	**$486,256**	**$539,318**	**$792,359**
Cash outflows			
Repayment of principal	$ 9,695	$ 10,605	$ 11,599
A/P decreases	$ 24,897	$ 29,876	$ 35,852
A/R increases	$ 0	$ 0	$ 0
Asset purchases	$125,000	$123,933	$185,558
Dividends	$191,348	$347,012	$519,564
Total cash outflows	**$350,940**	**$511,425**	**$752,573**
Net cash flow	**$135,316**	**$ 27,893**	**$ 39,786**
Cash balance	**$135,316**	**$163,209**	**$202,995**

Proforma cash flow (yearly)

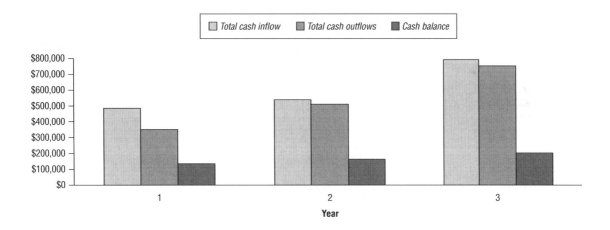

7.7 Balance Sheet

Proforma balance sheet—yearly

Year	1	2	3
Assets			
Cash	$135,316	$163,209	$202,995
Amortized development costs	$ 70,000	$ 82,393	$100,949
Servers and technology equipment	$ 25,000	$117,950	$257,118
FF&E	$ 30,000	$ 48,590	$ 76,424
Accumulated depreciation	($ 8,929)	($ 17,857)	($ 26,786)
Total assets	**$251,387**	**$394,284**	**$610,700**
Liabilities and equity			
Accounts payable	$ 13,005	$ 26,716	$ 40,990
Long term liabilities	$140,305	$129,700	$119,096
Other liabilities	$ 0	$ 0	$ 0
Total liabilities	**$153,310**	**$156,416**	**$160,085**
Net worth	**$ 98,078**	**$237,868**	**$450,615**
Total liabilities and equity	**$251,387**	**$394,284**	**$610,700**

Proforma balance sheet

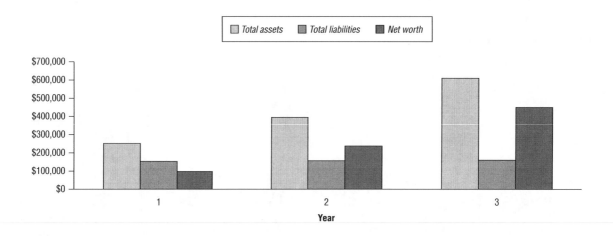

7.8 Breakeven Analysis

Monthly break even analysis

Year	1	2	3
Monthly revenue	$ 39,757	$ 44,516	$ 49,683
Yearly revenue	$477,081	$534,194	$596,191

Break even analysis

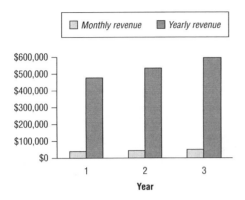

7.9 Business Ratios

Business ratios—yearly

Year	1	2	3
Sales			
Sales growth	0.00%	45.00%	35.00%
Gross margin	90.00%	90.00%	90.00%
Financials			
Profit margin	26.70%	33.90%	37.82%
Assets to liabilities	1.64	2.52	3.81
Equity to liabilities	0.64	1.52	2.81
Assets to equity	2.56	1.66	1.36
Liquidity			
Acid test	0.88	1.04	1.27
Cash to assets	0.54	0.41	0.33

7.10 Three Year Profit and Loss Statement

Profit and loss statement (first year)

Months	1	2	3	4	5	6	7
Sales	**$69,750**	**$72,075**	**$74,400**	**$76,725**	**$79,050**	**$81,375**	**$83,700**
Cost of goods sold	$ 6,975	$ 7,208	$ 7,440	$ 7,673	$ 7,905	$ 8,138	$ 8,370
Gross margin	90.00%	90.00%	90.00%	90.00%	90.00%	90.00%	90.00%
Operating income	**$62,775**	**$64,868**	**$66,960**	**$69,053**	**$71,145**	**$73,238**	**$75,330**
Expenses							
Payroll	$ 19,083	$ 19,083	$ 19,083	$ 19,083	$ 19,083	$ 19,083	$ 19,083
General and administrative	$ 2,708	$ 2,708	$ 2,708	$ 2,708	$ 2,708	$ 2,708	$ 2,708
Marketing expenses	$ 3,302	$ 3,302	$ 3,302	$ 3,302	$ 3,302	$ 3,302	$ 3,302
Professional fees and licensure	$ 1,417	$ 1,417	$ 1,417	$ 1,417	$ 1,417	$ 1,417	$ 1,417
Insurance costs	$ 1,000	$ 1,000	$ 1,000	$ 1,000	$ 1,000	$ 1,000	$ 1,000
Server and technology costs	$ 2,083	$ 2,083	$ 2,083	$ 2,083	$ 2,083	$ 2,083	$ 2,083
Rent and utilities	$ 2,500	$ 2,500	$ 2,500	$ 2,500	$ 2,500	$ 2,500	$ 2,500
Miscellaneous costs	$ 825	$ 825	$ 825	$ 825	$ 825	$ 825	$ 825
Payroll taxes	$ 2,863	$ 2,863	$ 2,863	$ 2,863	$ 2,863	$ 2,863	$ 2,863
Total operating costs	**$35,781**	**$35,781**	**$35,781**	**$35,781**	**$35,781**	**$35,781**	**$35,781**
EBITDA	**$26,994**	**$29,086**	**$31,179**	**$33,271**	**$35,364**	**$37,456**	**$39,549**
Federal income tax	$ 10,737	$ 11,095	$ 11,453	$ 11,811	$ 12,169	$ 12,527	$ 12,885
State income tax	$ 1,627	$ 1,681	$ 1,735	$ 1,790	$ 1,844	$ 1,898	$ 1,952
Interest expense	$ 1,125	$ 1,119	$ 1,113	$ 1,107	$ 1,101	$ 1,095	$ 1,089
Depreciation expense	$ 744	$ 744	$ 744	$ 744	$ 744	$ 744	$ 744
Net profit	**$12,761**	**$14,447**	**$16,133**	**$17,819**	**$19,506**	**$21,192**	**$22,878**

Profit and loss statement (first year cont.)

Month	8	9	10	11	12	1
Sales	$86,025	$88,350	$90,675	$93,000	$95,325	$990,450
Cost of goods sold	$ 8,603	$ 8,835	$ 9,068	$ 9,300	$ 9,533	$ 99,045
Gross margin	90.00%	90.00%	90.00%	90.00%	90.00%	90.00%
Operating income	**$77,423**	**$79,515**	**$81,608**	**$83,700**	**$85,793**	**$891,405**
Expenses						
Payroll	$19,083	$19,083	$19,083	$19,083	$19,083	$229,000
General and administrative	$ 2,708	$ 2,708	$ 2,708	$ 2,708	$ 2,708	$ 32,500
Marketing expenses	$ 3,302	$ 3,302	$ 3,302	$ 3,302	$ 3,302	$ 39,618
Professional fees and licensure	$ 1,417	$ 1,417	$ 1,417	$ 1,417	$ 1,417	$ 17,000
Insurance costs	$ 1,000	$ 1,000	$ 1,000	$ 1,000	$ 1,000	$ 12,000
Server and technology costs	$ 2,083	$ 2,083	$ 2,083	$ 2,083	$ 2,083	$ 25,000
Rent and utilities	$ 2,500	$ 2,500	$ 2,500	$ 2,500	$ 2,500	$ 30,000
Miscellaneous costs	$ 825	$ 825	$ 825	$ 825	$ 825	$ 9,905
Payroll taxes	$ 2,863	$ 2,863	$ 2,863	$ 2,863	$ 2,863	$ 34,350
Total operating costs	**$35,781**	**$35,781**	**$35,781**	**$35,781**	**$35,781**	**$429,373**
EBITDA	**$41,641**	**$43,734**	**$45,826**	**$47,919**	**$50,011**	**$462,033**
Federal income tax	$13,243	$13,601	$13,959	$14,317	$14,674	$152,471
State income tax	$ 2,006	$ 2,061	$ 2,115	$ 2,169	$ 2,223	$ 23,102
Interest expense	$ 1,083	$ 1,077	$ 1,071	$ 1,065	$ 1,059	$ 13,107
Depreciation expense	$ 744	$ 744	$ 744	$ 744	$ 744	$ 8,929
Net profit	**$24,565**	**$26,251**	**$27,938**	**$29,624**	**$31,311**	**$264,425**

Profit and loss statement (second year)

Quarter	Q1	2 Q2	Q3	Q4	2
Sales	$287,231	$359,038	$387,761	$402,123	$1,436,153
Cost of goods sold	$ 28,723	$ 35,904	$ 38,776	$ 40,212	$ 143,615
Gross margin	90.00%	90.00%	90.00%	90.00%	90.00%
Operating income	**$258,507**	**$323,134**	**$348,985**	**$361,910**	**$1,292,537**
Expenses					
Payroll	$ 49,749	$ 62,186	$ 67,161	$ 69,649	$ 248,745
General and administrative	$ 6,760	$ 8,450	$ 9,126	$ 9,464	$ 33,800
Marketing expenses	$ 11,489	$ 14,362	$ 15,510	$ 16,085	$ 57,446
Professional fees and licensure	$ 3,502	$ 4,378	$ 4,728	$ 4,903	$ 17,510
Insurance costs	$ 2,520	$ 3,150	$ 3,402	$ 3,528	$ 12,600
Server and technology costs	$ 5,500	$ 6,875	$ 7,425	$ 7,700	$ 27,500
Rent and utilities	$ 6,300	$ 7,875	$ 8,505	$ 8,820	$ 31,500
Miscellaneous costs	$ 2,872	$ 3,590	$ 3,878	$ 4,021	$ 14,362
Payroll taxes	$ 7,462	$ 9,328	$ 10,074	$ 10,447	$ 37,312
Total operating costs	**$ 96,155**	**$120,194**	**$129,809**	**$134,617**	**$ 480,774**
EBITDA	**$162,353**	**$202,941**	**$219,176**	**$227,294**	**$ 811,763**
Federal income tax	$ 52,771	$ 65,964	$ 71,241	$ 73,880	$ 263,857
State income tax	$ 7,996	$ 9,995	$ 10,794	$ 11,194	$ 39,978
Interest expense	$ 3,138	$ 3,080	$ 3,020	$ 2,959	$ 12,197
Depreciation expense	$ 2,232	$ 2,232	$ 2,232	$ 2,232	$ 8,929
Net profit	**$ 96,216**	**$121,670**	**$131,888**	**$137,028**	**$ 486,802**

Profit and loss statement (third year)

Quarter	Q1	3 Q2	Q3	Q4	3
Sales	**$387,761**	**$484,701**	**$523,478**	**$542,866**	**$1,938,806**
Cost of goods sold	$ 38,776	$ 48,470	$ 52,348	$ 54,287	$ 193,881
Gross margin	90.00%	90.00%	90.00%	90.00%	90.00%
Operating income	**$348,985**	**$436,231**	**$471,130**	**$488,579**	**$1,744,925**
Expenses					
Payroll	$ 53,894	$ 67,367	$ 72,757	$ 75,451	$ 269,469
General and administrative	$ 7,030	$ 8,788	$ 9,491	$ 9,843	$ 35,152
Marketing expenses	$ 15,510	$ 19,388	$ 20,939	$ 21,715	$ 77,552
Professional fees and licensure	$ 3,607	$ 4,509	$ 4,870	$ 5,050	$ 18,035
Insurance costs	$ 2,646	$ 3,308	$ 3,572	$ 3,704	$ 13,230
Server and technology costs	$ 6,050	$ 7,563	$ 8,168	$ 8,470	$ 30,250
Rent and utilities	$ 6,615	$ 8,269	$ 8,930	$ 9,261	$ 33,075
Miscellaneous costs	$ 3,878	$ 4,847	$ 5,235	$ 5,429	$ 19,388
Payroll taxes	$ 8,084	$ 10,105	$ 10,913	$ 11,318	$ 40,420
Total operating costs	**$107,314**	**$134,143**	**$144,874**	**$150,240**	**$ 536,571**
EBITDA	**$241,671**	**$302,088**	**$326,256**	**$338,339**	**$1,208,354**
Federal income tax	$ 79,012	$ 98,765	$106,666	$110,617	$ 395,060
State income tax	$ 11,972	$ 14,964	$ 16,162	$ 16,760	$ 59,858
Interest expense	$ 2,897	$ 2,834	$ 2,769	$ 2,702	$ 11,202
Depreciation expense	$ 2,232	$ 2,232	$ 2,232	$ 2,232	$ 8,929
Net profit	**$145,558**	**$183,293**	**$198,427**	**$206,028**	**$ 733,305**

7.11 Three Year Cash Flow Analysis

Cash flow analysis (first year)

Month	1	2	3	4	5	6	7
Cash from operations	$ 13,505	$15,191	$16,877	$ 18,563	$ 20,250	$ 21,936	$ 23,622
Cash from receivables	$ 0	$ 0	$ 0	$ 0	$ 0	$ 0	$ 0
Operating cash inflow	**$ 13,505**	**$15,191**	**$16,877**	**$ 18,563**	**$ 20,250**	**$ 21,936**	**$ 23,622**
Other cash inflows							
Equity investment	$ 25,000	$ 0	$ 0	$ 0	$ 0	$ 0	$ 0
Increased borrowings	$150,000	$ 0	$ 0	$ 0	$ 0	$ 0	$ 0
Sales of business assets	$ 0	$ 0	$ 0	$ 0	$ 0	$ 0	$ 0
A/P increases	$ 3,159	$ 3,159	$ 3,159	$ 3,159	$ 3,159	$ 3,159	$ 3,159
Total other cash inflows	**$178,159**	**$ 3,159**	**$ 3,159**	**$ 3,159**	**$ 3,159**	**$ 3,159**	**$ 3,159**
Total cash inflow	**$191,663**	**$18,349**	**$20,036**	**$ 21,722**	**$ 23,408**	**$ 25,095**	**$ 26,781**
Cash outflows							
Repayment of principal	$ 775	$ 781	$ 787	$ 793	$ 799	$ 805	$ 811
A/P decreases	$ 2,075	$ 2,075	$ 2,075	$ 2,075	$ 2,075	$ 2,075	$ 2,075
A/R increases	$ 0	$ 0	$ 0	$ 0	$ 0	$ 0	$ 0
Asset purchases	$125,000	$ 0	$ 0	$ 0	$ 0	$ 0	$ 0
Dividends	$ 0	$ 0	$ 0	$ 0	$ 0	$ 0	$ 0
Total cash outflows	**$127,850**	**$ 2,856**	**$ 2,862**	**$ 2,867**	**$ 2,873**	**$ 2,879**	**$ 2,885**
Net cash flow	**$ 63,813**	**$15,494**	**$17,174**	**$ 18,854**	**$ 20,535**	**$ 22,215**	**$ 23,895**
Cash balance	**$ 63,813**	**$79,307**	**$96,481**	**$115,335**	**$135,870**	**$158,085**	**$181,981**

Cash flow analysis (first year cont.)

Month	8	9	10	11	12	1
Cash from operations	$ 25,309	$ 26,995	$ 28,682	$ 30,368	$ 32,055	$273,354
Cash from receivables	$ 0	$ 0	$ 0	$ 0	$ 0	$ 0
Operating cash inflow	**$ 25,309**	**$ 26,995**	**$ 28,682**	**$ 30,368**	**$ 32,055**	**$273,354**
Other cash inflows						
Equity investment	$ 0	$ 0	$ 0	$ 0	$ 0	$ 25,000
Increased borrowings	$ 0	$ 0	$ 0	$ 0	$ 0	$150,000
Sales of business assets	$ 0	$ 0	$ 0	$ 0	$ 0	$ 0
A/P increases	$ 3,159	$ 3,159	$ 3,159	$ 3,159	$ 3,159	$ 37,902
Total other cash inflows	**$ 3,159**	**$ 3,159**	**$ 3,159**	**$ 3,159**	**$ 3,159**	**$212,902**
Total cash inflow	**$ 28,467**	**$ 30,154**	**$ 31,840**	**$ 33,527**	**$ 35,214**	**$486,256**
Cash outflows						
Repayment of principal	$ 817	$ 823	$ 829	$ 835	$ 842	$ 9,695
A/P decreases	$ 2,075	$ 2,075	$ 2,075	$ 2,075	$ 2,075	$ 24,897
A/R increases	$ 0	$ 0	$ 0	$ 0	$ 0	$ 0
Asset purchases	$ 0	$ 0	$ 0	$ 0	$ 0	$125,000
Dividends	$ 0	$ 0	$ 0	$ 0	$191,348	$191,348
Total cash outflows	**$ 2,892**	**$ 2,898**	**$ 2,904**	**$ 2,910**	**$194,264**	**$350,940**
Net cash flow	**$ 25,576**	**$ 27,256**	**$ 28,937**	**$ 30,617**	**−$159,051**	**$135,316**
Cash balance	**$207,557**	**$234,813**	**$263,749**	**$294,366**	**$135,316**	**$135,316**

Cash flow analysis (second year)

Quarter	Q1	2 Q2	Q3	Q4	2
Cash from operations	$ 99,146	$123,933	$133,847	$138,805	$495,731
Cash from receivables	$ 0	$ 0	$ 0	$ 0	$ 0
Operating cash inflow	**$ 99,146**	**$123,933**	**$133,847**	**$138,805**	**$495,731**
Other cash inflows					
Equity investment	$ 0	$ 0	$ 0	$ 0	$ 0
Increased borrowings	$ 0	$ 0	$ 0	$ 0	$ 0
Sales of business assets	$ 0	$ 0	$ 0	$ 0	$ 0
A/P increases	$ 8,717	$ 10,897	$ 11,769	$ 12,204	$ 43,587
Total other cash inflows	**$ 8,717**	**$ 10,897**	**$ 11,769**	**$ 12,204**	**$ 43,587**
Total cash inflow	**$107,864**	**$134,830**	**$145,616**	**$151,009**	**$539,318**
Cash outflows					
Repayment of principal	$ 2,563	$ 2,621	$ 2,680	$ 2,741	$ 10,605
A/P decreases	$ 5,975	$ 7,469	$ 8,067	$ 8,365	$ 29,876
A/R increases	$ 0	$ 0	$ 0	$ 0	$ 0
Asset purchases	$ 24,787	$ 30,983	$ 33,462	$ 34,701	$123,933
Dividends	$ 69,402	$ 86,753	$ 93,693	$ 97,163	$347,012
Total cash outflows	**$102,727**	**$127,826**	**$137,902**	**$142,971**	**$511,425**
Net cash flow	**$ 5,137**	**$ 7,004**	**$ 7,714**	**$ 8,038**	**$ 27,893**
Cash balance	**$140,453**	**$147,456**	**$155,171**	**$163,209**	**$163,209**

Cash flow analysis (third year)

Quarter	Q1	3 Q2	Q3	Q4	3
Cash from operations	$148,447	$185,558	$200,403	$207,826	$742,234
Cash from receivables	$ 0	$ 0	$ 0	$ 0	$ 0
Operating cash inflow	**$148,447**	**$185,558**	**$200,403**	**$207,826**	**$742,234**
Other cash inflows					
Equity investment	$ 0	$ 0	$ 0	$ 0	$ 0
Increased borrowings	$ 0	$ 0	$ 0	$ 0	$ 0
Sales of business assets	$ 0	$ 0	$ 0	$ 0	$ 0
A/P increases	$ 10,025	$ 12,531	$ 13,534	$ 14,035	$ 50,125
Total other cash inflows	**$ 10,025**	**$ 12,531**	**$ 13,534**	**$ 14,035**	**$ 50,125**
Total cash inflow	**$158,472**	**$198,090**	**$213,937**	**$221,861**	**$792,359**
Cash outflows					
Repayment of principal	$ 2,803	$ 2,867	$ 2,932	$ 2,998	$ 11,599
A/P decreases	$ 7,170	$ 8,963	$ 9,680	$ 10,038	$ 35,852
A/R increases	$ 0	$ 0	$ 0	$ 0	$ 0
Asset purchases	$ 37,112	$ 46,390	$ 50,101	$ 51,956	$185,558
Dividends	$103,913	$129,891	$140,282	$145,478	$519,564
Total cash outflows	**$150,998**	**$188,110**	**$202,995**	**$210,471**	**$752,573**
Net cash flow	**$ 7,474**	**$ 9,980**	**$ 10,942**	**$ 11,390**	**$ 39,786**
Cash balance	**$170,683**	**$180,663**	**$191,605**	**$202,995**	**$202,995**

Process Serving Business

Morgan Legal Services

789 E. 33rd St.
New York, New York 10153

BizPlanDB.com

Morgan Legal Services will provide serving of legal documents to individuals on behalf of attorneys and the courts in its targeted market. The Company was founded by Robert Morgan.

1.0 EXECUTIVE SUMMARY

The purpose of this business plan is to raise $100,000 for the development of a process serving business while showcasing the expected financials and operations over the next three years. Morgan Legal Services ("the Company") is a New York-based corporation that will provide serving of legal documents to individuals on behalf of attorneys and the courts in its targeted market. The Company was founded by Robert Morgan.

1.1 The Services

The primary revenue center will come from serving official court documents to individuals on behalf of courts and attorneys throughout the New York metropolitan area. The business will be appropriately licensed to go onto people's premises to hand official court documents to persons and businesses. At all times, the business will comply with all state and federal laws regarding the serving of official legal documents. At no time will an employee violate these laws especially as they relate to trespassing.

The third section of the business plan will further describe the services offered by the Morgan Legal Services.

1.2 Financing

Mr. Morgan is seeking to raise $100,000 from a bank loan. The interest rate and loan agreement are to be further discussed during negotiation. This business plan assumes that the business will receive a 10-year loan with a 9% fixed interest rate. The financing will be used for the following:

- Development of the office.

- Financing for the first six months of operation.

- Capital to purchase a company vehicle.

Mr. Morgan will contribute $10,000 to the venture.

1.3 Mission Statement

The Process Serving mission is to become the recognized leader in its targeted market for processing serving services.

1.4 Management Team

The Company was founded by Robert Morgan. Mr. Morgan has more than 10 years of experience in the paralegal and legal support industry. Through his expertise, he will be able to bring the operations of the business to profitability within its first year of operations.

1.5 Sales Forecasts

Mr. Morgan expects a strong rate of growth at the start of operations. Below are the expected financials over the next three years.

Proforma profit and loss (yearly)

Year	1	2	3
Sales	$407,778	$440,400	$475,632
Operating costs	$295,209	$331,695	$370,169
EBITDA	$ 71,791	$ 64,666	$ 57,900
Taxes, interest, and depreciation	$ 40,125	$ 33,722	$ 30,739
Net profit	$ 31,666	$ 30,944	$ 27,160

Sales, operating costs, and profit forecast

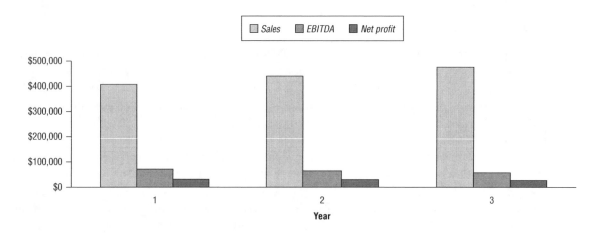

1.6 Expansion Plan

The Founder expects that the business will aggressively expand during the first three years of operation. Mr. Morgan intends to implement marketing campaigns that will effectively target law firms that have process serving needs within the target market.

2.0 COMPANY AND FINANCING SUMMARY

2.1 Registered Name and Corporate Structure

Morgan Legal Services is registered as a corporation in the State of New York.

2.2 Required Funds

At this time, Morgan Legal Services requires $100,000 of debt funds. Below is a breakdown of how these funds will be used:

Projected startup costs

Initial lease payments and deposits	$ 10,000
Working capital	$ 35,000
FF&E	$ 23,000
Leasehold improvements	$ 5,000
Security deposits	$ 5,000
Insurance	$ 2,500
Vehicle(s)	$ 17,000
Marketing budget	$ 7,500
Miscellaneous and unforeseen costs	$ 5,000
Total startup costs	**$110,000**

Use of funds

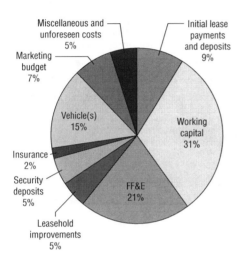

2.3 Investor Equity

Mr. Morgan is not seeking an investment from a third party at this time.

2.4 Management Equity

Robert Morgan owns 100% of the Morgan Legal Services.

2.5 Exit Strategy

If the business is very successful, Mr. Morgan may seek to sell the business to a third party for a significant earnings multiple. Most likely, the Company will hire a qualified business broker to sell the business on behalf of Morgan Legal Services. Based on historical numbers, the business could fetch a sales premium of up to 2 to 4 times the previous year's earnings.

3.0 PRODUCTS AND SERVICES

Below is a description of the services offered by Morgan Legal Services.

3.1 Process Serving

As discussed in the executive summary, Morgan Legal Services (through its employees) will provide legal support services as it relates serving individuals with court papers, official documents, and subpoenas to individuals and businesses throughout the New York metropolitan area. The business is currently in the process of receiving its appropriate licensure to act as a process serving business within the State of New York.

Mr. Morgan is also developing a number of protocols and procedures that ensure that process servers comply with all laws regarding the serving of government issued and court issued documents.

4.0 STRATEGIC AND MARKET ANALYSIS

4.1 Economic Outlook

This section of the analysis will detail the economic climate, the process serving industry, the customer profile, and the competition that the business will face as it progresses through its business operations.

Currently, the economic market condition in the United States is moderate. The meltdown of the subprime mortgage market coupled with increasing gas prices has led many people to believe that the U.S. is on the cusp of a double dip economic recession. This slowdown in the economy has also greatly impacted real estate sales, which has halted to historical lows. However, Morgan Legal Services is relatively immune from deleterious changes from the economy as the serving of court issued documents is required in any economic climate.

4.2 Industry Analysis

Within the United States, there are approximately 2,500 companies that are involved with serving official and legal documents to individuals and businesses. Each year, these businesses generate approximately $1.9 billion of revenue while providing jobs to more than 15,000 people. Annual payrolls in each of the last five years have exceeded $500 million.

This is a mature industry, and the future expected growth rate is anticipated to remain on par with that of the general economy. Again, this industry is relatively immune from negative changes in the economy. There is no pending legislation related to the ongoing operation of process serving businesses.

4.3 Customer Profile

Morgan Legal Services's average client will be a law firm or individual attorney practicing in the Company's target market. Common traits among clients will include:

- Annual billings exceeding $300,000 per year.

- Operates within 15 miles from the Company's location.

- Will spend $200 per serving of documents to an individual or business.

Within the Company's targeted market, there are more than 50,000 practicing attorneys within approximately 1/3 of these practitioners operating in a group practice capacity. As such, the business will be able to call on a number of potential clients for their process serving needs.

4.4 Competition

Within the New York metropolitan market, there are approximately 400 companies that are able to provide process serving services on behalf of attorneys, paralegals, and courts. In order to successfully launch business operations, it will be imperative for Morgan Legal Services to provide discounts to new clients. Management will also need to clearly showcase the firm's ability to quickly and properly serve individuals with paperwork.

5.0 MARKETING PLAN

Morgan Legal Services intends to maintain an extensive marketing campaign that will ensure maximum visibility for the business in its targeted market. Below is an overview of the marketing strategies and objectives of Morgan Legal Services.

5.1 Marketing Objectives

- Establish relationships with individually practicing attorneys, law firms, and government agencies within the Company's targeted New York market.

- Develop ongoing relationships with other organizations that frequently need process serving and delivery of legal documents.

5.2 Marketing Strategies

Mr. Morgan intends on using a number of marketing strategies that will allow Morgan Legal Services to easily market to the demographics discussed in the fifth section of the business plan within the target market.

The first prong of the Company's marketing strategy consists of Mr. Morgan directly contact attorneys, law firms, law enforcement agencies, and courts in regards to developing ongoing relationships for their process serving needs.

Morgan Legal Services will also use an internet based strategy. This is very important as many attorneys, paralegals, and law firms frequently begin their searches for finding process servers by searching the internet. The business will have a web development company establish a highly interactive website that showcases the services of the company, costs associated with process serving, the Company's licensure to act as a process serving company in the State of New York, and how to contact the business.

Finally, the Company will regularly take out print advertisements within prominent New York based legal periodicals and within publications that are produced and distributed by the American Bar Association and the New York Bar Association.

5.3 Pricing

For each serving of legal documents, the business will generate $100 to $300 per transaction. Fees will range depending on how difficult it was to serve the party with legal documents.

6.0 ORGANIZATIONAL PLAN AND PERSONNEL SUMMARY

6.1 Corporate Organization

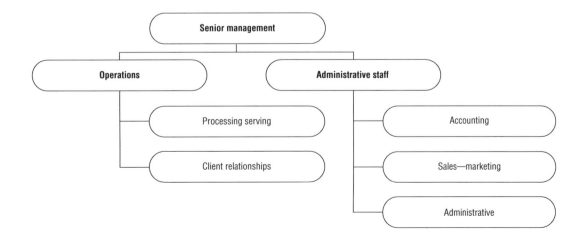

6.2 Organizational Budget

Personnel plan—yearly

Year	1	2	3
Owner	$ 40,000	$ 41,200	$ 42,436
General manager	$ 35,000	$ 36,050	$ 37,132
Owner's assistant	$ 32,500	$ 33,475	$ 34,479
Process servers	$ 66,000	$ 90,640	$116,699
Administrative	$ 25,000	$ 25,750	$ 26,523
Total	**$198,500**	**$227,115**	**$257,268**

Numbers of personnel

Owner	1	1	1
General manager	1	1	1
Owner's assistant	1	1	1
Process servers	3	4	5
Administrative	2	2	2
Totals	**8**	**9**	**10**

Personnel expense breakdown

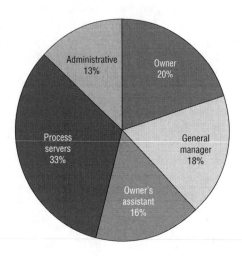

7.0 FINANCIAL PLAN

7.1 Underlying Assumptions

The Company has based its proforma financial statements on the following:

- Morgan Legal Services will have an annual revenue growth rate of 13.3% per year.

- The Owner will acquire $100,000 of debt funds to develop the business.

- The loan will have a 10-year term with a 9% interest rate.

- Management will settle most short term payables on a monthly basis.

7.2 Sensitivity Analysis

Management does not anticipate that any further negative issues with the economy will hinder the Company's ability to generate revenues as courts and law firms will continue to require process serving in any economic climate.

7.3 Source of Funds

Financing

Equity contributions

Management investment	$ 10,000.00
Total equity financing	**$ 10,000.00**

Banks and lenders

Banks and lenders	$ 100,000.00
Total debt financing	**$100,000.00**
Total financing	**$110,000.00**

7.4 General Assumptions

General assumptions

Year	1	2	3
Short term interest rate	9.5%	9.5%	9.5%
Long term interest rate	10.0%	10.0%	10.0%
Federal tax rate	33.0%	33.0%	33.0%
State tax rate	5.0%	5.0%	5.0%
Personnel taxes	15.0%	15.0%	15.0%

7.5 Profit and Loss Statements

Proforma profit and loss (yearly)

Year	1	2	3
Sales	**$407,778**	**$440,400**	**$475,632**
Cost of goods sold	$ 40,778	$ 44,040	$ 47,563
Gross margin	90.00%	90.00%	90.00%
Operating income	**$367,000**	**$396,360**	**$428,069**
Expenses			
Payroll	$198,500	$227,115	$257,268
General and administrative	$ 25,200	$ 26,208	$ 27,256
Marketing expenses	$ 2,039	$ 2,202	$ 2,378
Professional fees and licensure	$ 5,219	$ 5,376	$ 5,537
Insurance costs	$ 1,987	$ 2,086	$ 2,191
Travel and vehicle costs	$ 7,596	$ 8,356	$ 9,191
Rent and utilities	$ 20,000	$ 21,000	$ 22,050
Miscellaneous costs	$ 4,893	$ 5,285	$ 5,708
Payroll taxes	$ 29,775	$ 34,067	$ 38,590
Total operating costs	**$295,209**	**$331,695**	**$370,169**
EBITDA	**$ 71,791**	**$ 64,666**	**$ 57,900**
Federal income tax	$ 23,691	$ 18,656	$ 16,642
State income tax	$ 3,590	$ 2,827	$ 2,522
Interest expense	$ 8,738	$ 8,131	$ 7,468
Depreciation expenses	$ 4,107	$ 4,107	$ 4,107
Net profit	**$ 31,666**	**$ 30,944**	**$ 27,160**
Profit margin	**7.77%**	**7.03%**	**5.71%**

Sales, operating costs, and profit forecast

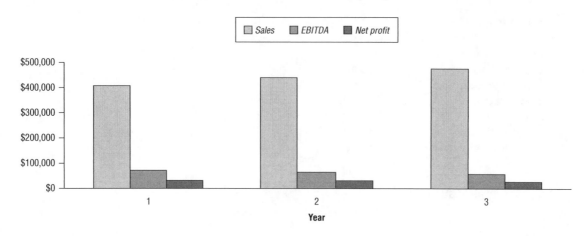

7.6 Cash Flow Analysis

Proforma cash flow analysis—yearly

Year	1	2	3
Cash from operations	$ 35,773	$ 35,051	$ 31,268
Cash from receivables	$ 0	$ 0	$ 0
Operating cash inflow	**$ 35,773**	**$ 35,051**	**$ 31,268**
Other cash inflows			
Equity investment	$ 10,000	$ 0	$ 0
Increased borrowings	$100,000	$ 0	$ 0
Sales of business assets	$ 0	$ 0	$ 0
A/P increases	$ 37,902	$ 43,587	$ 50,125
Total other cash inflows	**$147,902**	**$ 43,587**	**$ 50,125**
Total cash inflow	**$183,675**	**$ 78,639**	**$ 81,393**
Cash outflows			
Repayment of principal	$ 6,463	$ 7,070	$ 7,733
A/P decreases	$ 24,897	$ 29,876	$ 35,852
A/R increases	$ 0	$ 0	$ 0
Asset purchases	$ 57,500	$ 5,258	$ 4,690
Dividends	$ 28,618	$ 28,041	$ 25,014
Total cash outflows	**$117,479**	**$ 70,245**	**$ 73,289**
Net cash flow	**$ 66,196**	**$ 8,394**	**$ 8,104**
Cash balance	**$ 66,196**	**$ 74,590**	**$ 82,694**

Proforma cash flow (yearly)

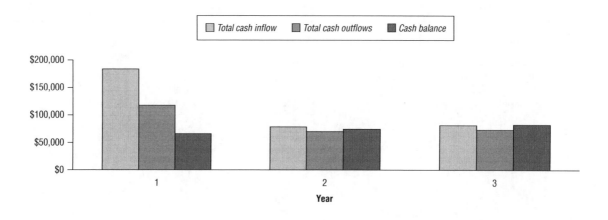

7.7 Balance Sheet

Proforma balance sheet—yearly

Year	1	2	3
Assets			
Cash	$ 66,196	$ 74,590	$ 82,694
Amortized development/expansion costs	$ 17,500	$ 18,026	$ 18,495
Vehicles	$ 17,000	$ 20,943	$ 24,461
FF&E	$ 23,000	$ 23,789	$ 24,492
Accumulated depreciation	($ 1,107)	($ 8,214)	($ 12,321)
Total assets	**$119,589**	**$129,133**	**$137,821**
Liabilities and equity			
Accounts payable	$ 13,005	$ 26,716	$ 40,990
Long term liabilities	$ 93,537	$ 86,467	$ 79,397
Other liabilities	$ 0	$ 0	$ 0
Total liabilities	**$106,542**	**$113,183**	**$120,387**
Net worth	**$ 13,047**	**$ 15,951**	**$ 17,434**
Total liabilities and equity	**$119,589**	**$129,133**	**$137,821**

Proforma balance sheet

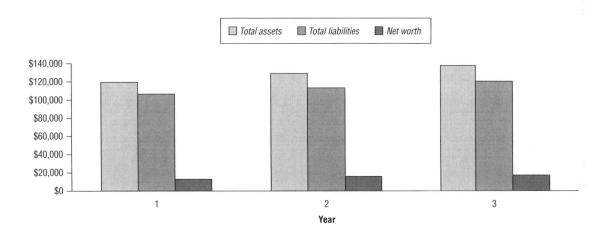

7.8 Breakeven Analysis

Monthly break even analysis

Year	1	2	3
Monthly revenue	$ 27,334	$ 30,712	$ 34,275
Yearly revenue	$328,010	$368,550	$411,299

Break even analysis

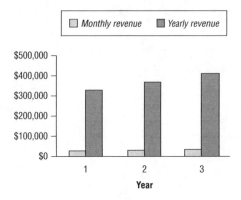

7.9 Business Ratios

Business ratios—yearly

Year	1	2	3
Sales			
Sales growth	0.00%	8.00%	8.00%
Gross margin	90.00%	90.00%	90.00%
Financials			
Profit margin	7.77%	7.03%	5.71%
Assets to liabilities	1.12	1.14	1.14
Equity to liabilities	0.12	0.14	0.14
Assets to equity	9.17	8.10	7.91
Liquidity			
Acid test	0.62	0.66	0.69
Cash to assets	0.55	0.58	0.60

7.10 Three Year Profit and Loss Statement

Profit and loss statement (first year)

Months	1	2	3	4	5	6	7
Sales	$33,250	$33,383	$33,516	$33,649	$33,782	$33,915	$34,048
Cost of goods sold	$ 3,325	$ 3,338	$ 3,352	$ 3,365	$ 3,378	$ 3,392	$ 3,405
Gross margin	90.00%	90.00%	90.00%	90.00%	90.00%	90.00%	90.00%
Operating income	$29,925	$30,045	$30,164	$30,284	$30,404	$30,524	$30,643
Expenses							
Payroll	$16,542	$16,542	$16,542	$16,542	$16,542	$16,542	$16,542
General and administrative	$ 2,100	$ 2,100	$ 2,100	$ 2,100	$ 2,100	$ 2,100	$ 2,100
Marketing expenses	$ 170	$ 170	$ 170	$ 170	$ 170	$ 170	$ 170
Professional fees and licensure	$ 435	$ 435	$ 435	$ 435	$ 435	$ 435	$ 435
Insurance costs	$ 166	$ 166	$ 166	$ 166	$ 166	$ 166	$ 166
Travel and vehicle costs	$ 633	$ 633	$ 633	$ 633	$ 633	$ 633	$ 633
Rent and utilities	$ 1,667	$ 1,667	$ 1,667	$ 1,667	$ 1,667	$ 1,667	$ 1,667
Miscellaneous costs	$ 408	$ 408	$ 408	$ 408	$ 408	$ 408	$ 408
Payroll taxes	$ 2,481	$ 2,481	$ 2,481	$ 2,481	$ 2,481	$ 2,481	$ 2,481
Total operating costs	$24,601	$24,601	$24,601	$24,601	$24,601	$24,601	$24,601
EBITDA	$ 5,324	$ 5,324	$ 5,564	$ 5,683	$ 5,803	$ 5,923	$ 6,042
Federal income tax	$ 1,932	$ 1,939	$ 1,947	$ 1,955	$ 1,963	$ 1,970	$ 1,978
State income tax	$ 293	$ 294	$ 295	$ 296	$ 297	$ 299	$ 300
Interest expense	$ 750	$ 746	$ 742	$ 738	$ 734	$ 730	$ 726
Depreciation expense	$ 342	$ 342	$ 342	$ 342	$ 342	$ 342	$ 342
Net profit	$ 2,008	$ 2,122	$ 2,237	$ 2,352	$ 2,466	$ 2,581	$ 2,696

Profit and loss statement (first year cont.)

Month	8	9	10	11	12	1
Sales	$34,181	$34,314	$34,447	$34,580	$34,713	$407,778
Cost of goods sold	$ 3,418	$ 3,431	$ 3,445	$ 3,458	$ 3,471	$ 40,778
Gross margin	90.00%	90.00%	90.00%	90.00%	90.00%	90.00%
Operating income	$30,763	$30,883	$31,002	$31,122	$31,242	$367,000
Expenses						
Payroll	$16,542	$16,542	$16,542	$16,542	$16,542	$198,500
General and administrative	$ 2,100	$ 2,100	$ 2,100	$ 2,100	$ 2,100	$ 25,200
Marketing expenses	$ 170	$ 170	$ 170	$ 170	$ 170	$ 2,039
Professional fees and licensure	$ 435	$ 435	$ 435	$ 435	$ 435	$ 5,219
Insurance costs	$ 166	$ 166	$ 166	$ 166	$ 166	$ 1,987
Travel and vehicle costs	$ 633	$ 633	$ 633	$ 633	$ 633	$ 7,596
Rent and utilities	$ 1,667	$ 1,667	$ 1,667	$ 1,667	$ 1,667	$ 20,000
Miscellaneous costs	$ 408	$ 408	$ 408	$ 408	$ 408	$ 4,893
Payroll taxes	$ 2,481	$ 2,481	$ 2,481	$ 2,481	$ 2,481	$ 29,775
Total operating costs	$24,601	$24,601	$24,601	$24,601	$24,601	$295,209
EBITDA	$ 6,162	$ 6,282	$ 6,402	$ 6,521	$ 6,641	$ 71,791
Federal income tax	$ 1,986	$ 1,994	$ 2,001	$ 2,009	$ 2,017	$ 23,691
State income tax	$ 301	$ 302	$ 303	$ 304	$ 306	$ 3,590
Interest expense	$ 722	$ 718	$ 714	$ 710	$ 706	$ 8,738
Depreciation expense	$ 342	$ 342	$ 342	$ 342	$ 342	$ 4,107
Net profit	$ 2,811	$ 2,926	$ 3,041	$ 3,156	$ 3,271	$ 31,666

Profit and loss statement (second year)

Quarter	Q1	Q2	Q3	Q4	2
Sales	$88,080	$110,100	$118,908	$123,312	$440,400
Cost of goods sold	$ 8,808	$ 11,010	$ 11,891	$ 12,331	$ 44,040
Gross margin	90.00%	90.00%	90.00%	90.00%	90.00%
Operating income	$79,272	$ 99,090	$107,017	$110,981	$396,360
Expenses					
Payroll	$45,243	$ 56,779	$ 61,321	$ 63,592	$227,115
General and administrative	$ 5,242	$ 6,552	$ 7,076	$ 7,338	$ 26,208
Marketing expenses	$ 440	$ 551	$ 595	$ 617	$ 2,202
Professional fees and licensure	$ 1,075	$ 1,344	$ 1,451	$ 1,505	$ 5,376
Insurance costs	$ 417	$ 552	$ 563	$ 584	$ 2,086
Travel and vehicle costs	$ 1,671	$ 2,089	$ 2,256	$ 2,340	$ 8,356
Rent and utilities	$ 4,200	$ 5,250	$ 5,670	$ 5,880	$ 21,000
Miscellaneous costs	$ 1,057	$ 1,321	$ 1,427	$ 1,480	$ 5,285
Payroll taxes	$ 6,813	$ 8,517	$ 9,198	$ 9,539	$ 34,067
Total operating costs	$66,339	$ 82,924	$ 89,558	$ 92,874	$331,695
EBITDA	$12,933	$ 16,166	$ 17,460	$ 18,106	$ 64,666
Federal income tax	$ 3,731	$ 4,664	$ 5,037	$ 5,224	$ 18,656
State income tax	$ 565	$ 707	$ 763	$ 791	$ 2,827
Interest expense	$ 2,092	$ 2,053	$ 2,013	$ 1,973	$ 8,131
Depreciation expense	$ 1,027	$ 1,027	$ 1,027	$ 1,027	$ 4,107
Net profit	$ 5,518	$ 7,716	$ 8,619	$ 9,091	$ 30,944

Profit and loss statement (third year)

Quarter	Q1	3 Q2	Q3	Q4	3
Sales	$95,126	$118,908	$128,421	$133,177	$475,632
Cost of goods sold	$ 9,513	$ 11,891	$ 12,842	$ 13,318	$ 47,563
Gross margin	90.00%	90.00%	90.00%	90.00%	90.00%
Operating income	$85,614	$107,017	$115,579	$119,859	$428,069
Expenses					
Payroll	$51,454	$ 64,317	$ 69,462	$ 72,035	$257,268
General and administrative	$ 5,451	$ 6,814	$ 7,359	$ 7,632	$ 27,256
Marketing expenses	$ 476	$ 595	$ 642	$ 666	$ 2,378
Professional fees and licensure	$ 1,107	$ 1,384	$ 1,495	$ 1,550	$ 5,537
Insurance costs	$ 438	$ 548	$ 591	$ 613	$ 2,191
Travel and vehicle costs	$ 1,838	$ 2,298	$ 2,482	$ 2,574	$ 9,191
Rent and utilities	$ 4,410	$ 5,513	$ 5,954	$ 6,174	$ 22,050
Miscellaneous costs	$ 1,142	$ 1,427	$ 1,541	$ 1,598	$ 5,708
Payroll taxes	$ 7,718	$ 9,648	$ 10,419	$ 10,805	$ 38,590
Total operating costs	$74,034	$ 92,542	$ 99,946	$103,647	$370,169
EBITDA	$11,580	$ 14,475	$ 15,633	$ 16,212	$ 57,900
Federal income tax	$ 3,328	$ 4,161	$ 4,493	$ 4,660	$ 16,642
State income tax	$ 504	$ 630	$ 681	$ 706	$ 2,522
Interest expense	$ 1,932	$ 1,889	$ 1,846	$ 1,802	$ 7,468
Depreciation expense	$ 1,027	$ 1,027	$ 1,027	$ 1,027	$ 4,107
Net profit	$ 4,789	$ 6,768	$ 7,586	$ 8,018	$ 27,160

7.11 Three Year Cash Flow Analysis

Cash flow analysis (first year)

Month	1	2	3	4	5	6	7
Cash from operations	$ 2,350	$ 2,464	$ 2,579	$ 2,694	$ 2,809	$ 2,923	$ 3,038
Cash from receivables	$ 0	$ 0	$ 0	$ 0	$ 0	$ 0	$ 0
Operating cash inflow	$ 2,350	$ 2,464	$ 2,579	$ 2,694	$ 2,809	$ 2,923	$ 3,038
Other cash inflows							
Equity investment	$ 10,000	$ 0	$ 0	$ 0	$ 0	$ 0	$ 0
Increased borrowings	$100,000	$ 0	$ 0	$ 0	$ 0	$ 0	$ 0
Sales of business assets	$ 0	$ 0	$ 0	$ 0	$ 0	$ 0	$ 0
A/P increases	$ 3,159	$ 3,159	$ 3,159	$ 3,159	$ 3,159	$ 3,159	$ 3,159
Total other cash inflows	$113,159	$ 3,159	$ 3,159	$ 3,159	$ 3,159	$ 3,159	$ 3,159
Total cash inflow	$115,508	$ 5,623	$ 5,738	$ 5,852	$ 5,967	$ 6,082	$ 6,197
Cash outflows							
Repayment of principal	$ 517	$ 521	$ 525	$ 528	$ 532	$ 536	$ 540
A/P decreases	$ 2,075	$ 2,075	$ 2,075	$ 2,075	$ 2,075	$ 2,075	$ 2,075
A/R increases	$ 0	$ 0	$ 0	$ 0	$ 0	$ 0	$ 0
Asset purchases	$ 57,500	$ 0	$ 0	$ 0	$ 0	$ 0	$ 0
Dividends	$ 0	$ 0	$ 0	$ 0	$ 0	$ 0	$ 0
Total cash outflows	$ 60,092	$ 2,595	$ 2,599	$ 2,603	$ 2,607	$ 2,611	$ 2,615
Net cash flow	$ 55,417	$ 3,028	$ 3,138	$ 3,249	$ 3,360	$ 3,471	$ 3,582
Cash balance	$ 55,417	$58,444	$61,583	$64,832	$68,192	$71,663	$75,244

Cash flow analysis (first year cont.)

Month	8	9	10	11	12	1
Cash from operations	$ 3,153	$ 3,268	$ 3,383	$ 3,498	$ 3,613	$ 35,773
Cash from receivables	$ 0	$ 0	$ 0	$ 0	$ 0	$ 0
Operating cash inflow	**$ 3,153**	**$ 3,268**	**$ 3,383**	**$ 3,498**	**$ 3,613**	**$ 35,773**
Other cash inflows						
Equity investment	$ 0	$ 0	$ 0	$ 0	$ 0	$ 10,000
Increased borrowings	$ 0	$ 0	$ 0	$ 0	$ 0	$100,000
Sales of business assets	$ 0	$ 0	$ 0	$ 0	$ 0	$ 0
A/P increases	$ 3,159	$ 3,159	$ 3,159	$ 3,159	$ 3,159	$ 37,902
Total other cash inflows	**$ 3,159**	**$ 3,159**	**$ 3,159**	**$ 3,159**	**$ 3,159**	**$147,902**
Total cash inflow	**$ 6,312**	**$ 6,427**	**$ 6,541**	**$ 6,656**	**$ 6,771**	**$183,675**
Cash outflows						
Repayment of principal	$ 545	$ 549	$ 553	$ 557	$ 561	$ 6,463
A/P decreases	$ 2,075	$ 2,075	$ 2,075	$ 2,075	$ 2,075	$ 24,897
A/R increases	$ 0	$ 0	$ 0	$ 0	$ 0	$ 0
Asset purchases	$ 0	$ 0	$ 0	$ 0	$ 0	$ 57,500
Dividends	$ 0	$ 0	$ 0	$ 0	$28,618	$ 28,618
Total cash outflows	**$ 2,619**	**$ 2,623**	**$ 2,627**	**$ 2,632**	**$31,254**	**$117,479**
Net cash flow	**$ 3,692**	**$ 3,803**	**$ 3,914**	**$ 4,025**	**−$24,482**	**$ 66,196**
Cash balance	**$78,937**	**$82,740**	**$86,654**	**$90,679**	**$66,196**	**$ 66,196**

Cash flow analysis (second year)

Quarter	Q1	2 Q2	Q3	Q4	2
Cash from operations	$ 7,010	$ 8,763	$ 9,464	$ 9,814	$35,051
Cash from receivables	$ 0	$ 0	$ 0	$ 0	$ 0
Operating cash inflow	**$ 7,010**	**$ 8,763**	**$ 9,464**	**$ 9,814**	**$35,051**
Other cash inflows					
Equity investment	$ 0	$ 0	$ 0	$ 0	$ 0
Increased borrowings	$ 0	$ 0	$ 0	$ 0	$ 0
Sales of business assets	$ 0	$ 0	$ 0	$ 0	$ 0
A/P increases	$ 8,717	$10,897	$11,769	$12,204	$43,587
Total other cash inflows	**$ 8,717**	**$10,897**	**$11,769**	**$12,204**	**$43,587**
Total cash inflow	**$15,728**	**$19,660**	**$21,232**	**$22,019**	**$78,639**
Cash outflows					
Repayment of principal	$ 1,708	$ 1,747	$ 1,787	$ 1,827	$ 7,070
A/P decreases	$ 5,975	$ 7,469	$ 8,067	$ 8,365	$29,876
A/R increases	$ 0	$ 0	$ 0	$ 0	$ 0
Asset purchases	$ 1,052	$ 1,314	$ 1,420	$ 1,472	$ 5,258
Dividends	$ 5,608	$ 7,010	$ 7,571	$ 7,851	$28,041
Total cash outflows	**$14,343**	**$17,541**	**$18,844**	**$19,516**	**$70,245**
Net cash flow	**$ 1,384**	**$ 2,119**	**$ 2,388**	**$ 2,502**	**$ 8,394**
Cash balance	**$67,580**	**$69,699**	**$72,087**	**$74,590**	**$74,590**

Cash flow analysis (third year)

Quarter	Q1	3 Q2	Q3	Q4	3
Cash from operations	$ 6,254	$ 7,817	$ 8,442	$ 8,755	$31,268
Cash from receivables	$ 0	$ 0	$ 0	$ 0	$ 0
Operating cash inflow	**$ 6,254**	**$ 7,817**	**$ 8,442**	**$ 8,755**	**$31,268**
Other cash inflows					
Equity investment	$ 0	$ 0	$ 0	$ 0	$ 0
Increased borrowings	$ 0	$ 0	$ 0	$ 0	$ 0
Sales of business assets	$ 0	$ 0	$ 0	$ 0	$ 0
A/P increases	$10,025	$12,531	$13,534	$14,035	$50,125
Total other cash inflows	**$10,025**	**$12,531**	**$13,534**	**$14,035**	**$50,125**
Total cash inflow	**$16,279**	**$20,348**	**$21,976**	**$22,790**	**$81,393**
Cash outflows					
Repayment of principal	$ 1,869	$ 1,911	$ 1,954	$ 1,999	$ 7,733
A/P decreases	$ 7,170	$ 8,963	$ 9,680	$10,038	$35,852
A/R increases	$ 0	$ 0	$ 0	$ 0	$ 0
Asset purchases	$ 938	$ 1,173	$ 1,266	$ 1,313	$ 4,690
Dividends	$ 5,003	$ 6,254	$ 6,754	$ 7,004	$25,014
Total cash outflows	**$14,980**	**$18,300**	**$19,654**	**$20,354**	**$73,289**
Net cash flow	**$ 1,299**	**$ 2,048**	**$ 2,322**	**$ 2,436**	**$ 8,104**
Cash balance	**$75,889**	**$77,937**	**$80,258**	**$82,694**	**$82,694**

Product Assembly Business

AssemblyPro LLC

2130 Times St.
Willows Bay, FL 00887

Paul Greenland

AssemblyPro offers professional assembly and installation services to consumers for a wide range of products, including furniture, outdoor/patio items, sporting goods/recreation, and lawn/garden equipment.

EXECUTIVE SUMMARY

When it comes to consumer products, there's no denying that we live in a world where, more often than not, some assembly is required. This especially is the case with larger products. AssemblyPro provides an assembly solution to individuals who are unable to, or not interested in, assembling products themselves.

Located in Willows Bay, Florida, AssemblyPro is the brainchild of John Davis, who has devoted most of his career to the retail sector. Davis' first employer was the Fortune 500 retailer, BuyMart. Because of his natural mechanical aptitude, Davis was given the task of assembling and disassembling a wide range of display merchandise in the Sporting Goods, Home Furnishings, Office Furniture, and Baby Needs departments. Five years later, he went to work for Milton Assemblers, a national company providing assembly services directly to leading retailers.

An entrepreneurial spirit, along with the desire for independence and flexibility, has led Davis to establish his own assembly business that focuses on the consumer market. By combining his experience providing similar services to retailers, and combining it with knowledge gained while pursuing his Associates degree in business management from Smith Community College, Davis has excellent prospects for success. Importantly, he has located his business in a geographic area where there is significant demand for an assembly services business.

MARKET ANALYSIS

Although AssemblyPro will provide services to anyone, the company will concentrate its initial marketing efforts on the following target audiences in the community of Willows Bay:

- Disabled individuals
- Elderly individuals
- Busy professionals

Willows Bay is a coastal city in southwest Florida, with a population of approximately 65,000 people. According to market data from Arrowhead Research, the community's population was projected to grow nearly 5 percent by 2015.

The community is well-suited for an assembly services business because it is home to an especially high concentration of elderly individuals. Arrowhead Research's analysis revealed that more than 58 percent of the Willows Bay population was over the age of 55. Specifically, those aged 55 to 64 accounted for 14.4 percent of the population in 2010. Individuals aged 65 to 74 represented 17.8 percent of the population. Finally, 26 percent of the population was over the age of 75.

Willows Bay is sub-divided into seven different geographic areas. Of these, four hold the greatest potential for AssemblyPro. Considering this, our business will concentrate its marketing efforts on the communities of Ocean Bank, Seaview, and Stoneridge, which have the highest concentrations of elderly individuals. In addition, Rogers Park is a small, but upscale, area that is home to busy working professionals.

An analysis of household income data in Willows Bay, obtained in 2011 from Arrowhead Research, revealed that the city's residents have high levels of disposable income. Specifically, 12.3 percent of residents had household incomes between $75,000 and $99,999. Those earning between $100,000 and $149,999 accounted for 18.7 percent of the population, while 24.9 percent of the population had household income levels of more than $150,000.

PERSONNEL

John Davis (owner)

John Davis has devoted most of his career to the retail sector. Davis' first employer was the Fortune 500 retailer, BuyMart. Because of his natural mechanical aptitude, Davis was given the task of assembling and disassembling a wide range of display merchandise in the Sporting Goods, Home Furnishings, Office Furniture, and Baby Needs departments. Five years later, he went to work for Milton Assemblers, a national company providing assembly services directly to leading retailers.

An entrepreneurial spirit, along with the desire for independence and flexibility, has led Davis to establish his own assembly business that focuses on the consumer market. By combining his experience providing similar services to retailers, and combining it with knowledge gained while pursuing his Associates degree in business management from Smith Community College, Davis has excellent prospects for success. Importantly, he has located his business in a geographic area where there is significant demand for an assembly services business.

Bill Davis (independent contractor)

John's father, Bill Davis, who is a resident of Willows Bay, will provide occasional assistance when two people are needed for an assembly job. A former machine shop owner, Bill will provide John with guidance gained from many years of business ownership. As a resident of Willows Bay, he will serve as the perfect goodwill ambassador for AssemblyPro, helping to give the business credibility during its formative stages and beyond.

John and Bill Davis also have identified several able-bodied individuals who can be utilized on occasion when very large or heavy objects need to be lifted or moved.

BUSINESS STRATEGY

The overall objective of AssemblyPro is to provide independence and flexibility for the owner. However, John Davis will adhere to the following strategy during the first three years of operations:

Year One: Establish AssemblyPro in the Willows Bay community. Focus on developing a reputation for excellent customer service and quality workmanship, realizing that word-of-mouth referrals will be essential to growing the business. Develop and execute a consistent direct marketing campaign focusing on the communities named in the Market Analysis section of this plan. Perform 1,225 hours of billable work.

Year Two: Continue to build AssemblyPro's reputation in Willows Bay. Perform 1,715 hours of billable work.

Year Three: Focus on maintaining AssemblyPro's reputation in the community. Consider the addition of one regular part-time employee, while maintaining one independent contractor when occasional assistance is needed. Perform 2,205 hours of billable work.

SERVICES

AssemblyPro will offer professional assembly and installation services for virtually every type of consumer product. Examples of the items we will assemble and install include, but are not limited to, the following:

Furniture

- Barstool
- Bed Frame
- Bedside Table
- Bench
- Bookcase
- Bottle Rack
- Bunk Bed
- Cabinet Lighting
- CD Tower
- Chair
- Changing Table
- Chest of Drawers
- Coffee Table
- Computer Unit/Drawers
- Corner Shelf
- Crib
- Daybed
- Desk
- Dining Table
- Dressing Table with Mirror
- Entertainment Center
- File Cabinet

- Footstool
- Head/Footboard
- Hutch
- Kitchen Cart
- Kitchen Island
- Laptop Table
- Linen Cabinet
- Media Storage
- Pedestal Table
- Secretary
- Shelf Unit
- Side Table
- Spice Rack
- Step-Stool
- Storage Unit
- Swivel Chair
- Table
- Wall Lamp
- Wardrobe
- Wash-Stand
- Work Lamp

Exercise Equipment/Recreation
- Treadmill
- Elliptical Machine
- Free Weight Rack
- Recombinant Exercise Bike
- Standard Exercise Bike
- Home Gym
- Pool Table
- Foosball Table
- Ping-Pong Table
- Shuffleboard Table
- Air Hockey Table

Lawn & Garden
- String Trimmer
- Lawnmower

- Wheelbarrow
- Spreader
- Garden Cart
- Edger

Outdoor & Patio

- Awning
- Basketball Hoop
- Box Garden
- Charcoal Grill
- Gas Grill
- Gazebo
- Tiki Hut
- Patio Furniture
- Planter
- Play Set
- Storage Shed
- Umbrella
- Swing Set
- Trampoline

In addition to assembly, we also will offer customers store pickup/delivery services (50-mile radius of Willows Bay; same flat rate that we charge for assembly applies). We require that customers pre-pay for the given item, or accompany us to the store.

MARKETING & SALES

We have identified a number of key marketing tactics to drive the growth of our business. These mainly focus on the target market of older adults, as well as the children of older adults who purchase services for their parents. The key tactics we have identified include the following:

- An attractive, four-color panel card will be developed to promote our business. In addition to serving as a leave-behind item following live sales presentations, the brochure also can be utilized in direct marketing efforts or given to people requesting information about our services.

- We will run regular newspaper ads in *The Senior Gazette,* a local free newspaper serving the senior market in Willows Bay. This publication has a solid readership base, and the advertising rates are very affordable.

- A direct marketing program focusing on the aforementioned communities in Willows Bay.

- A customer loyalty program that provides a 10 percent discount to those referring a friend or family member to our business.

- Magnetic signage that can be affixed to our vehicle in order to promote the business.

- Magnetic business cards that will double as advertising specialties.

- Active membership in the local Chamber of Commerce.

- Trade show marketing at the semi-annual Willows Bay Senior Expo.

- AssemblyPro will develop a Web site that provides basic information about our services, along with a presence on popular social networking sites, such as Facebook.

OPERATIONS

Fees

AssemblyPro will charge a flat rate of $40 per hour for its assembly services (one-hour minimum). Although every job is different, a ballpark estimate will be provided to the customer before beginning any work.

A flyer showing typical assembly times for common/popular items will be provided. For example:

- Bikes (1.5-2 hours)

- Charcoal Grills (1-2 hours)

- Gas Grills (2-3 hours)

- Wall Cabinet (20 minutes)

- Base Cabinet with Drawer (40 minutes)

Location

John Davis will operate AssemblyPro as a home-based business. He has dedicated a small room in his house that will be used as a home office for administrative tasks. Consultations with prospective customers, as well as the actual assembly work, will always occur in a customer's home. Customers can communicate with John by dialing his mobile telephone number.

Equipment

Davis will use his existing 2008 Ford pickup truck for business purposes and will keep track of mileage used for all work related to AssemblyPro. Although he already owns all of the basic hand tools needed to begin work (e.g., screwdrivers, wrenches, socket set, pliers, hammer, etc.), there are a few items that he will need to purchase:

- Commercial quality cordless drill

- Laser level

- Stud finder

- Small adjustable clamps (4)

- Medium adjustable clamps (4)

The total investment for these items will be less than $500.

Liability

Estimates for a business liability policy were obtained from three different insurance companies. John Davis has selected a policy from Mountain Insurance Co., because it offered comprehensive coverage at the most competitive price. More details about specific terms and coverage levels are available upon request. In addition to liability insurance, AssemblyPro has obtained a basic damage waiver, which customers will be required to sign prior to any project.

FINANCIAL ANALYSIS

AssemblyPro will require virtually no overhead or start-up costs, aside from the minimal investment required for the items listed in the Operations section of this plan. The business essentially will break even during its first three years. The addition of another employee would provide an opportunity for expansion if desired. John Davis will contribute $15,000 of his own money from personal savings to start the business, and will draw a modest salary during the first year.

	2012	2013	2014
Revenue	**$49,000**	**$68,600**	**$88,200**
Expenses			
Advertising & marketing	$ 7,500	$ 5,000	$ 5,000
Miscellaneous items	$ 500	$ 500	$ 500
Accounting & legal	$ 1,500	$ 1,000	$ 1,000
Office supplies	$ 500	$ 300	$ 300
Computers/peripherals	$ 1,500	$ 250	$ 250
Business insurance	$ 750	$ 750	$ 750
Health insurance	$ 1,400	$ 1,500	$ 1,600
Independent contractors	$ 3,500	$ 7,500	$10,000
Salary	$25,000	$45,000	$60,000
Taxes	$ 3,250	$ 4,800	$ 6,000
Postage	$ 125	$ 125	$ 125
Telecommunications	$ 1,200	$ 1,200	$ 1,200
Total expenses	**$48,725**	**$67,925**	**$86,725**
Net income	**$ 2,275**	**$ 675**	**$ 1,475**

Senior Relocation Service

A New Day

3305 Deer Tail Way
Columbia, Missouri 65202

Kari Lucke

A New Day (AND) is a moving company that specializes in the specific needs of older people who are downsizing and moving to a different residence or some type of retirement community. The company was started by Maureen and John Welch.

1.0 INTRODUCTION

1.1. Mission Statement

Our purpose is to provide senior (55 and older) clients with affordable, efficient, stress-free relocation services in Columbia, Missouri, and surrounding areas.

1.2. Executive Summary

A New Day (AND) is a moving company that specializes in the specific needs of older people who are downsizing and moving to a different residence or some type of retirement community. These situations typically involve moving into a smaller home. John and Marsha Welch work with seniors as well as their grown children, caregivers, and other involved parties to help with the sometimes overwhelming task of downsizing and relocating. Many times downsizing for seniors means sorting through and reducing the number of belongings, sometimes including years' or decades' worth of personal memorabilia, as well as a myriad of other tasks that can seem insurmountable, especially if the older person is in ill health, has recently lost a spouse, or is in some other emotionally or physically disadvantaged position.

According to the National Association of Senior Move Managers (NASMM), more than 70 percent of people who use senior move managers are relocating to an independent living community or an assisted living community. The downsizing required means reducing the number of items the person owns in order to "fit" into the smaller home. This can be an emotionally taxing task for many older people, on top of the complexities of moving itself. AND helps these people get organized; sort and pack their belongings; reduce the amount of belongings through recycling, selling, or donating; coordinate with other businesses to provide loading, transporting, and unloading services; and take care of necessary paperwork involved in a move such as turning utilities on/off, negotiating leases with landlords and/or working with a realtor to sell the senior's current home, and much more. An important aspect of working with relocating seniors is being especially sensitive to the emotional trauma that can accompany such a move, most noticeable when people are moving from a house in which they have raised children, established neighborhood relationships and routines, and/or collected dozens or even hundreds of sentimentally valuable items.

There are basically two types of senior move managers (SMM): One type helps people "age in place," or make changes in their current environment in order to accompany changing physical capabilities and health needs; the other specializes in assisting older adults with the emotional and physical aspects of relocation. The owners and operators of AND, John and Marsha Welch, are SMMs of the latter type.

1.3. Business Philosophy

The philosophy of AND Senior Relocation Service is summed up in three words: "Well worth it." Some people (sometimes grown children who live at a distance) have the impression that helping a parent move is a task that can be handled easily with (a) a couple of weekend visits to pack and (b) hiring a moving company. However, these people do not realize the complications, emotional and physical trauma, and intricacies that can be involved in this type of moving. Senior relocation services may receive calls from overwhelmed and frustrated people halfway (or less) through the process, with reports such as "She won't get rid of anything!" or "We spent all weekend and only got three boxes packed!" or "I have to get back to work!" Family tensions can also run high, as siblings may disagree about the best way to go about moving their parents, or who is responsible for what, or even who gets what. These types of problems are just a few of the numerous reasons people use senior move managers. AND has a firm belief in the idea that using a SMM makes the process easier, more organized, less traumatic, and even less damaging to family relationships. In addition, the physical, emotional, and mental demands required of older people are greatly reduced, making the move a smooth transition to a new life rather than a devastating uprooting amid chaos and confusion.

1.4. Goals and Objectives

*   Provide affordable and reliable relocation services to area seniors

*   Help seniors have a positive moving experience

*   Establish AND as the premier senior move management service in the Columbia area

2.0. INDUSTRY AND MARKET

2.1. Industry Analysis

By 2030, the elderly (over age 65) will account for one-fifth of the total U.S. population, according to *Direction: The Magazine of the American Moving & Storage Association*, as members of the baby boom generation retire (2010-2030), and Americans age 85 and above represent the fastest growing segment of the U.S. population. In addition, the NASMM reported that by 2040, more middle-aged parents will care for parents than for children. According to the NASMM, the resulting increase in retirement housing together with the twenty-first century trend toward adult children leaving their hometowns and settling in various places across the country has created a niche for the senior move management industry. In 2010, more than 50,000 families used senior move management services, as compared to 30,000 in 2008. Part of the reason for this growth is that adult children are often the go-to families that seniors count on for assistance (Smooth Mooove in Tucker, Georgia, reported in 2011 that one in every three adults between the ages of 35 and 54 has provided hands-on help for older family members); however, often adult children live far away from their parents' home and are not able to be there to help. These adult children may take time off from work to travel to their parents' home and help them pack and move. The problem is that, because downsizing and moving seniors is a complicated process, especially if the person has lived in the home for a long time, all that needs to be done cannot happen in one weekend or even one week. Thus the adult children may leave the parents' home after several days with a few boxes packed but a long list of other things to be done left unchecked and family tensions high. According to Patrick Egan, "Hundreds of necessary decisions and actions can swallow time the family may not have; the inevitable negotiations and concessions can trouble even the best parent-child relationships." This is where the importance of a senior move manager comes in.

With the growth of the senior population in the United States, the opportunities for senior move managers will expand, and the demand for services may well exceed the number of people certified to help seniors move in an organized, efficient, and positive way.

2.2. Market Analysis

The market for AND Senior Relocation Service consists of residents of Columbia, Missouri, and surrounding areas. Columbia is a town of approximately 94,000. The population of Boone County, which includes the towns of Ashland, Centralia, and Hallsville, is around 146,000. The median household income of Columbia residents is $42,163, with a race distribution of 83 percent white, 9 percent black, and 8 percent other. In 2009, 13.7 percent of the population of the state of Missouri was age 65 and older, higher than the national average of 12.9 percent.

Potential clients for AND include the elderly as well as their adult children. Most often the services are used for older people who (a) have grown kids and/or are unable to keep up their current home and need to move into a smaller house, senior community, or assisted living for physical or financial reasons; (b) have lost a spouse or contracted an illness; (c) do not have grown children or whose children cannot help them due to time or geographic limitations; (d) any combination of the above or other circumstances.

Other than the elderly person planning to move, those who are most likely to contact a senior relocation specialist include family members, bank and trust officers, attorneys, senior living community managers, realtors, geriatric care personnel, and others. In a 2009 survey, the NASMM found that in 2009 the elderly person contacted the relocation specialist 44 percent of the time; 31 percent of the contacts were made by the person's adult children or other family members, whereas 19 percent of contacts came from senior living communities managers.

The fact that Columbia has scores of retirement, assisted living, and other elderly communities—many of which have waiting lists—demonstrates the high senior relocation rate and the need for a senior relocation service in Columbia. In addition, Columbia is home to three hospitals (University of Missouri, Boone Hospital, and the VA Hospital) and therefore offers a prime location for seniors with or without health concerns who want to be close to medical care facilities. Due to these factors and others, Columbia offers significant potential for a senior relocation service.

2.3. Competition

There is only one other company specifically targeted to helping seniors more and downsize in Columbia: Smooth Transitions of Mid-Missouri, which is part of the Smooth Transitions franchise. The Fry Wagner franchise includes a senior moving services division in its services, but that sector of the business is not emphasized. Therefore, AND has the potential to become the largest and most used senior relocation firm in the area.

3.0. PERSONNEL

3.1. Management

John and Marsha Welch, married since 2002, are the owners and managers of AND Senior Relocation Service. John brings valuable financial and business planning skills from his education at the University of Missouri, where he earned a bachelor of science degree in business. With a Master of Arts degree in psychology, Marsha balances the team with a focus on the emotional aspects of relocating, as well as an ability to help seniors deal well with issues such as family dynamics, communication among all the related parties involved in the move, and other aspects of relocating, many of which can be overwhelming to the person(s) moving. Together the Welches constitute a highly reliable and skilled team that can assist seniors with every aspect of their move while treating them with respect and compassion.

Both John and Marsha are certified as Senior Move Managers by the National Association of Senior Move Managers and keep up-to-date on the industry with active participation in conferences, webinars, publications, and other activities of the association. Together they exemplify what the NASMM requires of a Senior Move Manager: "a profound commitment to connecting with older adults and a desire to perform meaningful work."

The NASMM has a Code of Ethics and Standards of Practice that all members are expected to follow, and continued certification as a SMM requires ongoing training in the form of classes (in person or online) that keep the managers up-to-date with current trends, laws, and other important issues related to senior moving.

3.2. Staffing

Contract staff, such as packers and movers, will be hired as needed. There will no full-time or part-time on-staff employees, although John and Marsha will develop relationships with the best and most cost-efficient independent contractors in the area in order to offer the highest quality service possible at the lowest cost to the customer.

This hiring structure is typical of many senior relocation specialists; the NASMM found that at least half of member businesses use independent contractors and only 20 percent had employees, most of which were part-time. Illustrating the growth in the industry, 45 percent of those surveyed planned to add staff in the upcoming year (2011).

3.3. Professional and Advisory Support

Owners John and Marsha Welch have been members of the NASMM (National Association of Senior Move Managers) since 2005. According to its website, the NASMM is a "not-for-profit, professional association of organizations dedicated to assisting older adults and families with the physical and emotional demands of later life living including downsizing, relocating, or modifying their homes." NASMM is also "the only professional association in North America devoted to helping the rapidly increasing 55+ population with middle and later life transition issues." Founded in 2002 and head-quartered in Hinsdale, Illinois, the association had about 600 members in 2011. Professionals that have been trained and certified by the NASMM can legally advertise themselves as Senior Move Managers. Benefits of membership in the NASMM include an annual national conference, publications, networking opportunities, and other advantages of participation in an organization that upholds certain standards and ethics in the senior relocation industry.

4.0. GROWTH STRATEGY

The most logical area for growth for AND Senior Relocation Services is in the number of moves that can be accomplished in a certain amount of time. Whereas AND estimates it will complete an average of one move per month in the first year of business, by Year 3 that figure will hopefully have grown to three moves per month on average, thus tripling the businesses income and raising its position in the community as a vital service to Columbia seniors.

In an article addressed to families of seniors who are relocating, the American Association of Retired Persons (AARP) noted that "the downsizing process can be especially difficult since it will involve long walks down memory lane and having to part with much-loved possessions. But done correctly—and in enough time—the process can be less painful and more productive." Many grown children of seniors who are trying to help do not have this kind of time, or the knowledge or skills that lead to a smooth and successful relocation. The AARP recommends: "When in doubt, hire out" and affirms the positive contribution and benefits for the whole family that SMMs can have on senior relocations. More positive press and overall public education of the benefits of these services will help increase AND's sales in the upcoming years.

5.0. PRODUCTS AND SERVICES

5.1. Description

AND helps seniors prepare and manage all aspects of the moving process, regardless of their situation. It can provide as many or as few services needed by each individual. The first step is a free initial appointment and cost estimate, after which AND will provide all or any combination of the following services:

- Developing an overall moving plan

- Organizing and sorting household items and possessions

- Arranging for the disposal of unwanted items through auction, estate sale, buy-out, consignment, donation, or a combination of these

- Supervising professional packing and unpacking services

- Arranging for shipment and storage of items if necessary

- Scheduling and overseeing movers

- Designing furniture lay-out plans and strategies for use in the new home

- Contracting and coordinating related services, such as cleaning and preparing a home for sale; listing a home for sale through a realtor and following through with the paperwork involved in the sale; transferring utilities, telephone, and other services to the new location; initiating address changes where needed; making arrangements for transportation, deliveries, and other such services that may be necessary after the move; and various other services depending on each individual situation.

By taking care of all the details of moving, SMMs relieve much of the stress and pressure that seniors may feel when facing a relocation. In addition, through compassionate and appropriate counsel, AND helps seniors deal with the emotional aspects of moving, which might include leaving a home they have lived in for years, letting go of a variety of possessions, and coming to grips with the common but sometimes depressing idea that "things will never be the same." John and Marsha work hard to present a positive and encouraging attitude through every stage of the moving process. Because a senior's relocation and dispersal of possessions can cause tension and conflict within the larger family unit, Marsha can also provide real-time family counseling sessions if needed.

5.2. Unique Features/Niche

AND fills a particular niche in the moving services business by focusing on seniors and the special considerations involved when they choose or are forced to relocate. AND not only ensures that items are packed and moved but also that this happens after careful and guided consideration of what to keep, donate, sell, or give to other family members.

Compared to other senior relocation specialists, AND is especially attentive to all of the senior populations' special needs, including emotional, financial, and physical. In addition, even though some stages of the moving process are contracted out, either John or Marsha is on site at all times; there is never a time when the senior is left alone when things are being packed or moved. Finally, a specialized moving plan is made for each individual client. Rather than following a generic formula, as many moving and relocation companies might do, AND personalizes each plan based on individual needs and circumstances.

5.3. Pricing

The cost of AND's services is $50 an hour, which is comparable to other similar businesses in the area. Clients are also charged for any outside contracting work, such as movers, packing supplies, moving truck charges, and so on. An estimate is provided to the client at the initial interview, after John and/or Marsha has determined (roughly) how much time may be involved. Factors that can affect this figure range from how many possessions seniors have to how willing and/or able they are to make the move. Every client or responsible family member will sign a contract that specifies that the figure given is an estimate only and that the true price will depend on the time involved in conducting a successful move.

6.0. MARKETING AND SALES

6.1. Advertising and Promotion

John and Marsha Welch will advertise their new senior relocation service via three main avenues: an interactive website, a regular ad in the *Columbia Senior Times* (monthly circulation of 5,000), and pamphlets/brochures. This has been determined to be the most cost-efficient way to promote the service; the only cost will be for printing brochures and running the ad in the *Senior Times*. The latter is directed toward seniors who are considering a move soon or in the future and will emphasize the idea of planning ahead. The website, on the other hand, will be directed more toward grown children and other family members, as older people have less of a tendency to utilize the Internet for research. John will design the website to emphasize the benefits of using a senior relocation service as well as the affordability and the care with which AND treats all senior members of society. The pamphlet or brochure will combine an approach for both families and seniors and will be placed in permitted locations such as hair salons, libraries, grocery stores, doctor's offices, and so on. In addition, free word-of-mouth advertising will be stimulated after AND has served several clients successfully; testimonials from these clients will also be posted on the website and possibly used in the brochures.

6.2. Cost

The main cost for advertising will come from the ad in the *Senior Times*, which will average $1,200 a year. Because John can create the brochure, the only cost involved there will be for printing on high-quality paper, estimated at roughly $400 per year.

7.0. OPERATIONS

7.1. Customers

The customers of AND include seniors who are facing an upcoming relocation. In some cases, the elderly are not able to contract services due to physical or mental limitations, so adult children or other family members may contact AND. Other people who may look for such services are those who act on behalf of the senior or in the place of the family, and these can include a variety of professionals such as bankers, realtors, attorneys, elderly care managers, and so on. Ultimately, however, it is the seniors themselves who are considered the most important customer of AND.

7.2. Suppliers

Material suppliers will include the local U-HAUL retailer for boxes, packing materials, and other moving supplies. Service suppliers will include moving companies, house cleaners, lawn care providers, and so on, all of which will be researched and contracted in the best interest of the client in terms of cost and service.

7.3. Hours

As a special service provider, AND does not keep standard business hours. The business line will be answered 24 hours a day, 7 days a week, and consultations may be scheduled at any time based on the clients' needs.

7.4. Facility and Location

John and Marsha Welch will operate out of their home at 3305 Deer Tail Way in Columbia, Missouri. Although most business will be conducted outside of their own house, the Welches' home does include an office that will be used for paperwork/office tasks and is available for consultations when necessary.

7.5. Legal Environment

Due to the nature of the business, AND has contracted an attorney to provide all necessary legal paperwork and contracts in order to protect their investment. John and Marsha Welch will be licensed and bonded, and all other considerations such as liability insurance and disclaimers will be covered in the contract signed by the client and the business owners.

8.0. FINANCIAL ANALYSIS

Some recent statistics about the senior relocation business are helpful in estimating the expected income for AND. For example, according to a survey of member organizations by NASMM, approximately 50 percent have gross annual revenues of more than $50,000, and 25 percent earn more than $100,000 per year. Just under half of the surveyed members charge between $41 and $60 an hour.

Although senior relocation services can seem expensive at first, especially to adult children who are contributing to the endeavor, they can end up saving a significant amount of money. According to a report by the Metropolitan Life Insurance Company, cost due to lost employee productivity related to senior care needs is more than $11 billion a year. The Smooth Mooove Senior Relocation franchise provided the following breakdown that shows the savings that using a senior relocation service can create as compared to lost employee time when family members do it themselves.

In 2010 the NASSM estimated that the average cost of moving a senior from a two-bedroom home to another location was between $1,500 and $4,000. The following projected figures are based on an average of one move per month the first year, two per month the second year, and three per month the third year. Because the customer pays for any subcontracted services, the only significant ongoing costs are insurance and advertising, which here are estimated to increase 10 percent annually.

Senior downsizing time comparison move from house to one bedroom retirement community

	Employee time loss	SMSRS service benefit	Total time savings
Packing old home for move	40 hours	5 hours	35 hours
Truck loading, unloading	12 hours	6 hours	6 hours
New home setup	24 hours	3 hours	21 hours
Prepare old home for yard sale	120 hours (Less $ return)	40 hours estate sale (higher $ for items)	80 hours
Charity delivery	3 hours	1 hour liquidation buyer	2 hours
Sort and clear old home	40 hours	6 hours	34 hours
Clean old home	8 hours	3 hours	5 hours
Total	**207 hours (26 days)**	**64 hours (8 days)**	**143 hours (18 days) Savings**

	2012	2013	2014
Projected sales	$30,000	$60,000	$90,000
Projected advertising costs	$ 1,600	$ 1,760	$ 1,940
Projected insurance costs	$ 1,200	$ 1,320	$ 1,450
Estimated profit	$27,200	$56,920	$86,610

Specialty Food Manufacturer

TOFU Beanery, LLC

123 Main St.
St. Louis, MO 63101

Don Brown
Lisa Golden

"We let the bean shine through!"—Don Brown, founder of TOFU Beanery

---

EXECUTIVE SUMMARY

TOFU Beanery is excited to bring premium soy foods to the Saint Louis market. The time is right for TOFU Beanery to enter the market as we have identified a niche untapped by other soy foods companies in the Midwest. TOFU Beanery specializes in soy foods handcrafted with Organic Missouri-grown soybeans. Specifically, TOFU Beanery crafts firm tofu, value added tofu, soymilk and soy jerky. Each product is full of nuances and subtleties normally left out by large, mass-production companies.

When the 2008 recession forced consumers to cut back their spending, a movement developed where consumers seek out local versions of products they used to buy from large national and multinational conglomerates. The locavore movement has also taken hold in restaurants and markets where freshness and knowing your food producer are stressed. TOFU Beanery is a St. Louis based company owned by a native St. Louisan. TOFU Beanery will capitalize on the locavore movement by selling at farmer's markets and by targeting restaurants that use soy foods and that advertise their use of local foods. This strategy will also provide free advertising as many of these restaurants make a substantial effort to share where they got their food from with their customers on menus and chalkboards. Branding and guerilla marketing are key components to TOFU Beanery's success by creating "buzz" and boosting demand for the product. TOFU Beanery's goal is to create a solid customer base and sound business so as to acquire funding to increase production and distribution with a long-term goal of penetrating local independent groceries and regional branches of high-end groceries like Whole Foods.

TOFU Beanery was founded and is currently owned by Don Brown. Food and nutrition have been Don's passions since a young age. In pursuit of doing what he loves, Don underwent professional culinary training and is currently finishing a Master's Degree in Nutrition Culinary Entrepreneurship. While working on a project studying food and culture Don did an experiment where he tried to make his own tofu. After much trial and error, he crafted the best tofu he had ever had. At that point the idea of starting a soy beanery sprouted and he has been pursuing the dream ever since.

Currently Don has two accounts open with Lothers in Maplewood, Missouri, and Fresh Food Cafe. He landed the Lothers account after giving the head chef a sample of the product and asking him to try it and give him feedback. Two days later the chef called him and asked him if he could buy 20 packages of TOFU Beanery Firm Tofu. Using similar sales techniques Don plans to penetrate the local restaurant, café, and coffee house market growing net sales to $17,500 in the first year of production with nearly $10,000 dollars net profit.

18-MONTH PLAN

April/May/June/July

- Meet with various industry experts and potential clients to establish relationship and expose product offerings.

- Finish research and development on first line of value added products (expected finish May 20th).

- Create rigid quality control standards and implement total manufacturing process control system (expected finish May 24th).

- Secure Organic soybean purveyor with a back up purveyor.

- Move from individual tofu package orders to case orders of 10 packages/case.

- Solidify logo by middle to end of May and create initial labeling to begin selling at farmers market by first market in June.

- Solidify packaging with new bags that fit product better and reduce "crinkling."

- Start selling at farmers market by first week in June with firm tofu, medium tofu, and 4 value-added products. While doing this I will work hard to connect with people converting them into TOFU Beanery evangelicals.

- Develop additional restaurant accounts: 1 in May, 2 in June, and 2 in July for a total of 7.

- Continue to create buzz via grass roots efforts: Blogs, local magazines, and social media. Create QR code with link to website and 20-30 second video describing how TOFU Beanery does tofu. Print these codes on stickers and guerilla stamp the city in key areas.

- Identify additional winter farmers markets for additional sales opportunities.

- Approach local grocery stores with product for sale.

- Find professional photographer to shot images of product and me producing for PR purposes. Create standard PR package.

August/September/October

- I am presenting at conference in San Diego towards the end of September. During this trip I will visit another tofu manufacturer to tour their plant to learn the equipment they use and where they got it.

- Continue selling at farmers markets through end of October.

- Continue to develop and strengthening the relationship with existing accounts providing support for product usage expansion.

- Apply for two additional farmers markets to sell at in 2012. Conduct research on demographic of each potential market to better inform the decision making process.

- Continue research and development on value added products adding an additional line using different methods.

- Purchase bottles for soy milk sales.

- Soft launch plain and vanilla soymilk to local coffee shops.

November/December/January

- Continue selling at farmers market on Saturdays.

- Continue to develop and strengthen the relationships with existing accounts providing support for product usage expansion. Replace flaccid accounts with new ones or supplement to maintain desired number of sales.

- Solidify Market selection for 2012 season.

- Work with local chocolate maker/producer to develop chocolate soymilk. Co-branding power.

February/March/April

- Create job descriptions for farmers market booth workers. Hire one to two for each market depending on the size of market by the end of March.

- Find PR consultant willing to work pro-bono based on business potential and interest in company.

- Obtain source for funding of $5,000.

May/June/July

- Master the art of selling at the farmers market. Create a loyal customer following.

- Maintain relationships with restaurants and possible expand to other restaurants depending on sales mix and production capacity.

- Push hard for PR.

- Serve Tofu to President Obama or The First Lady and her "Lets Move" campaign.

- Continually monitor and rate the "this works, that doesn't" at the farmers markets and create a system of how to operate the best way.

August/September/October

- Further develop business looking for best growth opportunities: Groceries, Web sales.

- Start reaching out to the Whole Foods Market, et al.

- Start networking with other companies using refrigerated trucks or create network of local producers whom would like to co-op and effort to buy a truck and hire a driver.

GENERAL COMPANY DESCRIPTION

TOFU Beanery brings the traditional goodness of tofu made in Missouri by supplanting conventional soy stereotypes with eye-opening soy food experiences.

Using only the finest Missouri-grown, non-genetically modified (non-gmo) soybeans, TOFU Beanery creates handmade artisan tofu and soymilk. We will craft each batch as if it were a small batch coffee roasting. You can even find the minute and subtle nuances in TOFU Beanery products just as you do a fine coffee or wine. Our competitors have left behind these subtleties in large-scale plants in exchange for a bottom line driven by quantity, not quality. We celebrate the endless possibilities in small batch soy products and deliver a second-to-none experience for our customers.

Business Philosophy: Owning and operating a business is a privilege. Every day is another opportunity to be better, to improve the business financially and in the eyes of the community. It's important to remember that a business is an integral part of the community and vice versa. TOFU Beanery is not a subsidiary of another company or a conglomerate or several companies. It is a company run by an individual with a passion for the best tasting soy foods around, period.

TOFU Beanery was born from a desire to share the benefits of soy with the St. Louis community. As such, our guiding principles are simple:

- Integrity of ingredients and final product

- Nourishment of customers, both nutritionally and communally

- Responsible business growth and success

MARKET OPPORTUNITY

To say that the marketplace has changed since the 2008 recession would be an understatement. As Americans tightened their belts, they started to drive less, spent more time looking for bargains, and learned how to cook! Since then, urban gardening has mainstreamed and the demand for locally grown food has skyrocketed. In fact, growth of the farmer's market channel actually *accelerated* with the onset of the 2008 recession, growing 30.9% from 2008 to 2010, compared to only 6.8% growth from 2006 to 2008 (see Endnote 1). In 2010 there were approximately 6,132 farmers' markets in the U.S., and there are currently 22 farmers' markets within a 25-mile radius of St. Louis (see Endnote 2).

The consumer has also changed. More than half of Americans have purchased food at farmers' markets (see Endnote 3). Many just like the market experience: the free samples and the chance to interact with vendors who can really tell them where their produce originated or how their tofu was made. In an economy where people are looking for cheaper entertainment, farmers' markets are often the sites of free live music and annual festivals. As consumers looked to save money on food, lose weight and improve their nutrition, they started cooking at home, and this, more than any other factor, has increased the demand for the freshest locally produced food.

The time is right for TOFU Beanery to start selling at farmers' markets. Tofu is not sold at any farmers' markets in St. Louis, and we think that the heightened demand for local produce and meats applies to tofu as well. Tofu is a great alternative for many consumers who are concerned about their cholesterol or who are sensitive to dairy, though the number one reason people who buy tofu do so is because they like the taste (see Endnote 4). And the fresher tofu is, the better it tastes. Since TOFU Beanery's tofu is handcrafted in small batches using organic soybeans and then sold within 3 days of manufacture, it has flavor and texture superior to that of national brands that have been sitting in grocery stores for weeks.

TOFU Beanery is a small company that focuses on handcrafted artisan soy foods. Using small batch recipes and techniques every product is cared for from start to consumer. The ability to "know" your food is lost when dealing with major corporations and that's just one reason TOFU Beanery is special. Customers will be able to know who made their food, how it was made, and exactly where it came from. The desire for local foods not only at farmer's markets and groceries but also in restaurants is only on the increase.

COMPETITION

Competitive analysis

Factor	TOFU retail	TOFU restaurants	US tofu	565 firm tofu	East SOY firm tofu	Tasoya	Soy Gourmet	Importance to customer
Products	14 oz	14 oz	14 oz	14 oz	14 oz	14 oz	12 oz	
Price	$4.00	$3.00	$1.33	$1.69	$2.49	$2.69	$3.09	
Quality 1–10	10	10		5	7	7.5	7	
Taste	Beaney, natural sweetness, nutty, crisp, clean	Beaney, natural sweetness, nutty, crisp, clean		Mineral	Clean, crisp, edamame	Clean, crisp	nutty	Think it doesn't have taste until had TOFU
Texture	Dense, firm, body, has bite	Dense, firm, body, has bite		Silky smooth, no body, no bite	Body and very firm, some grit	Dense, some air wholes, rubbery	Very firm	Customers want a "Meatier" product
Aroma	Beany, green	Beany, green		Mineral	Bitter	Sweet	Mineral	Pleasant
Packaging	Vacuum pack	Vacuum pack	MAP plastic	MAP plastic	Vacuum pack	MAP plastic	Vaccum	
Advertising			Wholesale	Private label	Bold and Blue	Soft and Airy	Asian pasture	

TOFU Beanery is entering a niche untapped in St. Louis and the surrounding area. However, there is direct competition from major distributors and companies. Due to the economies of scale inherent in large operations, their cost of production is much lower and this allows them to sell tofu for about half the price of TOFU Beanery tofu. However, we believe that the superior quality of TOFU Beanery tofu along with the social mission of TOFU Beanery will persuade our customers to choose us over these national brands.

Inconvenience is another competitive disadvantage. It is much more convenient for restaurant managers to order all or most of their ingredients from one supplier. TOFU Beanery sells few items and requires lead-time on orders. However, as the locavore movement ramps up in St. Louis, more and more restaurants are proud to source their ingredients from many small, local operations. And they make sure to inform their own customers of the origins of their ingredients: from using prominent chalkboard displays to noting directly on the menu, restaurants want their customers to know that they are serving local ingredients.

Meat and dairy milk are indirect competitors among the omnivore consumer base. Both tofu and soymilk can be substituted for the equivalent animal products, and are great alternatives for omnivores trying to decrease the meat in their diets. In Mintel's March 2011 *Soy Food and Beverages* report, over half of survey respondents use soy simply because they like the taste. In fact, taste is the key market driver—even more so than the health benefits. Since TOFU Beanery products taste even better than the mass-market versions our customers are used to, we think that our local, artisan offering will be very well received.

TOFU Beanery does not have direct competition against the value added TOFU Beanery. However, it does face stiff competition from other flavored protein alternatives. There is an extensive amount of these analogs at groceries, most of which are takes on common meat products like chicken nuggets or sausage. TOFU Beanery has an advantage in that its products are made of tofu and are meant to be tofu. They are simply flavored and made ready to go for a customer to enjoy on a sandwich, wrap, or salad. This is unique to TOFU Beanery as is the freshness of each value added product.

NICHE

TOFU Beanery is the only artisan soy foods producer in the greater St. Louis area. Freshness and locality are not new to the restaurant and food business, but there has yet to be a soy food offering. TOFU Beanery will capitalize on this opportunity by producing the freshest and highest quality soy foods unrivaled by any current offering in St. Louis. TOFU Beanery value added tofu products will also be new to the market. Currently there are no offerings like those that TOFU Beanery will bring to market. The community will know where their soy foods come from and who produced it!

CUSTOMERS

TOFU Beanery is planning a two-tiered customer approach. While one of the goals of TOFU Beanery is to sell directly to and educate the end-consumer, in order to establish good cash flow we will start by selling to restaurants. The benefits of starting with restaurants are many:

- Can sell in bulk vacuum packs to restaurants, don't need end-user packaging

- Starts creating a predictable revenue stream by landing standing order contracts with restaurants with specific payment terms

- Builds the company's reputation and begins to inform the end-user customers about the product

TOFU Beanery's second tier customer are people who patronize St. Louis farmer's markets. Industry data show that people who report shopping at farmer's markets are likely to be the following:

- 25+ years old—reflects a greater interest in cooking and nutrition among older adults

- From wealthier households with incomes of $100K—these consumers tend to be more health-conscious than those of lesser means, and are generally more likely to purchase organic foods

- Interested in where their food comes from (see Endnote 5)

While there is a high correlation between income and shopping at farmer's markets, it is certainly not a limiting factor. It is important to remember that while organic produce at the market may not be cheaper than that available at the grocery store, as more people cook at home *instead of eating out* they are more likely to spend extra money on high-quality, locally grown ingredients (see Endnote 6).

Within this customer base, TOFU Beanery's target customers are the subset of farmer's market shoppers who are interested in tofu and other soy foods. Just as some shoppers may not be interested in meat vendors at the market, there may be some who are not interested in soy. TOFU Beanery plans to aggressively sample product at the markets as we believe that soy can play a role in almost anyone's diet, and we want to capture all farmers' market patrons in our customer base. We believe that we can depend upon regular sales from patrons who are already familiar with tofu and who use it regularly; as TOFU Beanery will provide the only locally produced, extremely fresh, handcrafted tofu available in the St. Louis area, we foresee becoming a favorite among these customers. But one of TOFU Beanery's goals is getting our tofu into the mouths of non-tofu eaters, and blowing their minds in the process.

PRODUCT, PACKAGING, PRICING, PROMOTION

Tofu

TOFU Beanery Firm and Medium Tofu are artisan small batch tofus made with Missouri grown soybeans that are identity preserved and not genetically modified. By small batch, we mean that in one production run we produce thirty 14-ounce blocks or cakes of tofu. The process is carefully watched and every step involves human involvement. This is a longer, more laborious process, but it leads to a much richer, higher quality, better tasting tofu.

TOFU Beanery's competitive advantage lies in the artisan production method which yields a better texture and taste, and the freshness of the product upon delivery to the consumer. Another advantage is the ability to get direct feedback and alter products upon request from local chefs. The direct connection to the producer allows continual feedback and support from consumers.

Value Added TOFU Beanery

TOFU Beanery will offer three flavored products when we go to market. This is tofu that has been deep fried and simmered in a flavoring sauce. TOFU Beanery believes that 60% of farmer's market sales will come from this category. The flavors will be outside the box from what consumers are used to with traditional companies (the most common is Five-Spiced). TOFU Beanery will offer an initial line that targets the most commonly eaten cuisines in the United States: American, Mexican, and Italian. I will craft each recipe to perfection from my chef background and research. This product mix will be adapted after taking to market to best optimize sales. Three additional flavored products will be launched as the product life cycle starts to level off on the initial offering.

TOFU Beanery Milk

TOFU Beanery Milk is very thick, comparable to whole milk from a cow. The essence of soybeans comes through very strong on the palate and has a subtle sweetness due to the carbohydrates of the soybean.

TOFU Beanery Milk is unlike soymilk you would find in the grocery store. It is not overly sweet and bland. It also does not contain any preservatives or protein isolates for fortification. One of the weaknesses of TOFU Beanery Milk is that it is not fortified with vitamin D or calcium. Many consumers look to fortified milk products as a source of these minerals and vitamins, but TOFU Beanery believes that this product is superior in taste and experience. TOFU Beanery plans to launch a line of soymilk in October 2011. It will include plain, vanilla, and chocolate soymilk. TOFU Beanery will approach a chocolate manufacturer in Missouri to work on proprietary chocolate blend for TOFU Beanery Milk.

Jerky

TOFU Beanery jerky is made with the trimmings from shaping the firm and medium tofu into perfect blocks. It is the perfect use for the scraps because as they are cut just as meat would be for jerky. It does not have fibrous texture that meat jerky does but has a similar bite and the tofu allows for an intense and pure flavor. This line is being developed. Currently the only flavor is applewood smoked BBQ.

Packaging

TOFU Beanery is vacuum packaged in food grade bags. This maintains the freshness of the product. Interviews with chefs have revealed that they like being able to open the bag and use the product without washing it or pressing it as you have to do with tofu packaged in water. A customer testimonial has also proved the same thing. TOFU Beanery will be looking at purchasing bags that better fit the product shape to decrease the amount of crinkling and for better label adherence.

TOFU Beanery Milk will be packaged in glass bottles with the TOFU Beanery logo on them. These bottles will require a deposit from the customers to cover the liability of them not being returned. The customers will return the bottles and purchase more without an additional deposit or receive cash back if they do not want to make another purchase. Glass bottles are the most logical choice for this stage of TOFU Beanery. They will be a key marketing feature because they represent small artisan production.

Features and Benefits

Every TOFU Beanery product is made from whole soybeans grown locally and raised in a sustainable way. Our artisan traditional methods highlight the soybeans flavor and create a texture not available on the market. Customers want almost all food products they purchase to be fresh. Why would they not want tofu that is fresh? They do not know that it matters, but TOFU Beanery will educate to people that it applies to tofu as well. Aside from being a superior product, customers can enjoy TOFU Beanery knowing that they are supporting the community and contributing to the sustainability of our world.

People are also becoming more and more health conscious. This includes heart health, keeping a healthy weight, and eating healthier to have more energy among a list of other health concerns. The popularity of health related TV reality shows and the growing "health food" sections in grocery stores evidence this. TOFU Beanery offers healthy foods for consumers to enjoy. Our take on classic flavors used in our value added products taste great but are also healthy. For instance, the "buffalo" tofu uses a hot sauce made by me and contains very little sodium compared to the tradition buffalo sauce found in restaurants. The "mole" flavored tofu is also healthy in that it does not contain an overwhelming amount of fat and the fat it does contain come from nuts and healthy oils. We believe our customers will appreciate that TOFU Beanery is a healthy alternative to what is currently available.

Customer service is a key component of the success and growth of TOFU Beanery. Chefs from restaurants can call me and speak to the maker of the product they are ordering. This is an aspect of business that is leaving some industries but in the restaurant business it is a key part to the local movement. The same goes for the customers at the farmer's market who are looking to know who, when, where, and how of their food. They will not find this from other companies.

Just to be safe, because we do not anticipate this problem often, we will offer a refund policy ensuring our customers always leave satisfied. Product not up to par will be replaced with fresh, proper product at no cost. If the customer doesn't want an immediate replacement, we will give them a credit for their next order. However, we will try to limit the occurrences of subpar product. The production section below details how we go about that.

Pricing

TOFU Beanery sells a product that is of greater value than its competitors and that is reflected in the price. Tofu is priced at $3.00 for restaurants and $4.00 at the farmer's market with 10.3% and 7.7% margin respectively. Value added TOFU Beanery will cost the consumer $6.00 which provides about a 15% margin. TOFU Beanery Milk will also be a higher price. It will be offered to restaurants at $4.00 a liter and $5.00 to the public at farmer's markets. TOFU Beanery Milk at the market will provide a 2.9% margin. This premium pricing strategy sets the bar for best product available. It also reflects the quality, amount of time, effort and care that went into creating the product. Jerky will cost the consumer $3.00 a package.

Promotion

Once initial product testing is complete and TOFU Beanery starts participating in local farmers' markets, we will start building buzz by way of local press. We sell a unique, high-end product, and people are more likely to try such a product if they've heard something good about it. Our customers educate themselves before making buying decisions, using a variety of media to learn about products they are interested in.

For these reasons, we are currently developing a press package. Through the Saint Louis University network we will receive a brief list of local press contacts. Then, using a simple email distribution list, we'll start sending them TOFU Beanery news. Press are very receptive to new, small, startup businesses, but they prefer writing on businesses that are actually selling product. The first press package is going out two weeks before TOFU Beanery starts selling at the Farmers' Market on June 2.

At this point we will also ramp up TOFU Beanery's social media presence. TOFU Beanery already has a Facebook page and a twitter account, and plans for a blog and YouTube videos are in process. We are also going to make QR code stickers and guerilla stamp the city in key areas. When scanned by a smart phone equipped with a QR code reader, the code will link to a 20-30 second video showing how TOFU Beanery does tofu. Our target customers are those with a higher level of income and education, who care about buying local produce at the peak of flavor and nutrition. That demographic profile also describes the smartphone user who has used a QR code before (see Endnote 7).

In addition to the PR plan, TOFU Beanery samples aggressively. Missouri is called the "Show-Me State" for a reason! St. Louisans want to try before they buy. We believe we've got a great product and we're building a name, but it is vital that our customers be able to taste the tofu so they can experience the disintegration of the widely held belief that all tofu is bland and rubbery.

TOFU Beanery is targeting restaurants, cafes and coffee shops that identify themselves as users of local ingredients and also those who currently have tofu and soymilk offerings on their menus. These restaurants try very hard to let their clientele know they use local ingredients and furthermore like to tell them exactly where they came from. People will see this and drive traffic to the booth during farmers markets.

After a logo is acquired it will be used to create T-shirts to be worn at the farmers market, stickers, business cards and letterhead. When able, TOFU Beanery will support local programs and clubs that promote health and wellness, events that promote sustainability and health, and provide product for the independent restaurant scene in St. Louis.

Promotional Budget

TOFU Beanery is seeking the help of students from Washington University Sam Fox School of Art and Design to work on designing a TOFU Beanery logo. Going this route will be free or very low cost. The downside is that the process is slow and there is little ability to push the process along. It's ready when it's ready. The tofu and soymilk samples given to potential customers are very low cost. The most expensive part of the sample is the time that went into making it. One block of tofu cost about $0.34 cents. The left over product from research and development is also used as samples if it meets the criteria used for market sales.

Sales Strategy

TOFU Beanery will target restaurants, cafes, and coffee shops that already have tofu and soymilk offerings. We will give our customers free samples of the products and explain the TOFU Beanery brand and why it is unique. Don will leave them contact information and tell them to call after they experiment with the products. If they do not call after 5 days Don will revisit and check in to see how they liked the product.

TOFU Beanery will also sell at the farmer's market on Wednesdays from 4-7pm. Farmer's markets are an opportunity to deliver excellent customer service and employ sales strategies to sell TOFU Beanery, both product and brand. Chef Don will have product samples to taste at each farmer's market. I will sample the value added products. I assume that people know nothing about tofu: how it's made, the different types, and the different ways to work with it. By having them taste the value added product it is more likely to generate a sale when we can say, "I have it ready right here for you to enjoy at home!" Also at the table will be a poster of the process to make TOFU Beanery and TOFU Beanery Milk to use as an educational tofu. If customers want a recipe they can visit the TOFU Beanery website where they can find recipes and sign up for the newsletter and interact with additional features of the site.

OPERATIONS

Management

TOFU Beanery is owned and operated by Don Brown, a professionally trained chef and registered dietitian. Currently Don is one semester away from attaining a Master's degree in Nutrition Culinary Entrepreneurship. Since early high school Don has worked about every position in the restaurant business. He is now interested in supplying some of those same restaurants with the best tofu and soymilk available.

Don is young, fit and energetic, ready to take on the long days and tremendous effort involved in this venture. His passion is to work with food and share it with as many people as possible and he believes this is the way to do it. TOFU Beanery represents a fresh take on soy foods and Don is passionate about making it a success.

Credit

TOFU Beanery will sell on credit Net30. It is customary for restaurants to run on Net30 credit with their suppliers. It will always be policy to pursue check/cash on delivery (COD) whenever possible. If needed, invoices can be sent to customers prior to delivery.

Collection of receivables will be dealt with in the following manner. Five days after a payment is due and missed, a phone call will be made to the customer. If payment is still not received, during the next delivery, their balance will have to be paid in full and then the delivery will be left. The company will continue to be able to pay on credit at Net30. If it happens again, then the account will move to COD.

Production

All of TOFU Beanery's products are produced at a FDA approved processing center. The facility is equipped with a 15'x30' walk in refrigerator, 10'x30' deep freezer, 40'x30' deep freezer, multiple storage closets, an industrial three-compartment sink system, full gas range and convection oven system, two 40-gallon steam jacketed kettles, a small commercial food dehydrator, and a small commercial vacuum packaging system. The kitchen is also fully equipped with standard commercial kitchen small wares.

Quality control is done with each batch of soymilk and tofu. Products are tasted after each production run to ensure the desired attributes are present. If the product is subpar and missing attributes it will be further analyzed to uncover the shortcomings in the production process. All HACCP procedures are followed.

Part of TOFU Beanery's company philosophy is to deliver the freshest product possible. Because our products are made weekly and to order, we require a lead-time of 5 business days. This allows our customers to get the freshest product available. By doing this we keep our quality standards high and have low product inventory on hand. As the company grows and takes on more orders this strategy will be modified to reflect the increase in scale.

INVENTORY

Inventory will be controlled tightly with detailed in/out logs and production logs. TOFU Beanery's key inventory item is soybeans. Orders will be about 1600 pounds or 26.7 bushels. Inventory will depletion happens at 200 different times of the year. Lead time on soybean orders is about two weeks so when inventory hits three weeks capacity new inventory will be ordered for pickup 5 days from the order date. The commodity rate of soybeans fluctuates but soybeans seem to average at around $0.30 per pound which equals $480 per order. At any given time inventory could range from $70-$500.

Finished product inventory will be kept at a minimum. Orders are taken weekly with five day lead-time. Any product left in inventory will be kept for the following week or rolled into product development. Tofu will last 3 weeks when vacuum packaged. Soymilk can last 3 weeks but quality starts to deteriorate after 2 weeks because of the high water content. Soymilk will separate at 27-30 days after production.

FINANCIALS

Assumptions—Sales Forecast

- Assumes 3 restaurant accounts in May, 5 in June, then 7 in July. There is not an increase in restaurants until year 2012.

- Restaurant sales are based off speculation of restaurant size and data collected from sales.

- Assumes farmer's market sales to start May 25th.

- Assumes TOFU Beanery Milk launch in October 2011 with full year sales in 2012-2014. TOFU Beanery Milk does not include sales at farmer's markets.

- Assumes that prices do not change and cost stay the same.

- Total man-hours was collected by breaking up total sales into batches. This method may not represent the true hours in jerky production or for the actual amount of batches of TOFU Beanery Milk. 2011=586 hours, 2012=1364 hours, 2013=1913 hours, 2014=2875 hours. These hours include production time, farmer's market time, and sales time/delivery time.

- Hours include hiring someone to work farmer's market booths on weekends when I cannot be at each.

- Year 2012 assumes sales at 3 farmer's markets. Years 2013 and 2014 do not assume an increase in farmer's markets, just an increase in sales. Most likely additional farmers markets will be needed to reach stated sales levels.

Assumptions—Cash Flow and P&L

- Assumes all accounts receivable are current and all outstanding balances have been collected on time.

- Assumes sales are consistent except for off season during winter.

- Assumes using facility at $250 rental fee/ month starting December 2011-2013. In 2014, a new facility will be rented at $1800/ month. Rent figures also include the booth rental fees for farmer's markets.

- Assumes labor cost of $4,800 in 2011, $27,285 in 2012, $38,269 in 2013, and $25,994 in 2014. I will hire a part time worker in 2014 at $13/hour to help with production. That number is represented in the 2014 gross wages. I will pull a $50,000 salary at that point.

- Assumes $1,650 research and development in first year. $1,500 for nutrition analysis of products.

- Assumes $1,300 capital expenditure for glass bottle purchase in first year. Assumes additional bottles and small wares will be needed in 2012 and 2013.

- Does not include the cost of refitting a new facility in 2014 per needs of business.

12 month sales forecast

	Apr-11	May-11	Jun-11	Jul-11	Aug-11	Sep-11	Oct-11
Firm Tofu restaurants	46	76	150	190	190	200	200
Bottleworks	40	40	40	40	40	40	40
Fresh gatherings	6	16	20	20	20	30	30
Restaurant 3		20	30	30	30	30	30
Restaurant 4			40	40	40	40	40
Restaurant 5			20	20	20	20	20
Restaurant 6				20	20	20	20
Restaurant 7				20	20	20	20
Sale price @ unit	$ 3.00	$ 3.00	$ 3.00	$ 3.00	$ 3.00	$ 3.00	$ 3.00
Total	**$138.00**	**$228.00**	**$ 450.00**	**$ 570.00**	**$ 570.00**	**$ 600.00**	**$ 600.00**
Firm and medium Tofu retail	0	15	60	80	80	80	70
Maplewood (wed.)		15	60	80	80	80	70
Sale price @ unit	$ 4.00	$ 4.00	$ 4.00	$ 4.00	$ 4.00	$ 4.00	$ 4.00
Total	**$ —**	**$ 60.00**	**$ 240.00**	**$ 320.00**	**$ 320.00**	**$ 320.00**	**$ 280.00**
% of plain Tofu sales at market			38%	50%	50%	50%	44%
Value added products retail	0	30	160	160	160	160	160
Maplewood (wed.)		30	160	160	160	160	160
Sale price @ unit		$ 6.00	$ 6.00	$ 6.00	$ 6.00	$ 6.00	$ 6.00
Total	**$ —**	**$180.00**	**$ 960.00**	**$ 960.00**	**$ 960.00**	**$ 960.00**	**$ 960.00**
Craft soy milk coffee shop							20
Coffee shop 1							20
Coffee shop 2							
Coffee shop 3							
Sale price @ unit							$ 4.00
Total	**$ —**	**$ —**	**$ —**	**$ —**	**$ —**	**$ —**	**$ 80.00**
Vanilla soy milk coffee shop							0
Coffee shop 1							
Coffee shop 2							
Coffee shop 3							
Sale price @ unit							$ 4.00
Total	**$ —**	**$ —**	**$ —**	**$ —**	**$ —**	**$ —**	**$ —**
Tofu jerky retail		10	40	40	40	40	40
Maplewood (wed.)		10	40	40	40	40	40
Sale price @ unit		$ 3.00	$ 3.00	$ 3.00	$ 3.00	$ 3.00	$ 3.00
Total	**$ —**	**$ 30.00**	**$ 120.00**	**$ 120.00**	**$ 120.00**	**$ 120.00**	**$ 120.00**
Monthly totals: all categories	**$138.00**	**$498.00**	**$1,770.00**	**$1,970.00**	**$1,970.00**	**$2,000.00**	**$ 2,040.00**
Running total	**$138.00**	**$636.00**	**$2,406.00**	**$4,376.00**	**$6,346.00** (Breakeven sales)	**$8,346.00**	**$10,386.00**

Inventory required for sales	Apr-11	May-11	Jun-11	Jul-11	Aug-11	Sep-11	Oct-11
Soy bean in pounds	38	101	308	358	358	367	359
CaCl in grams	307	807	2,467	2,867	2,867	2,933	2,867
Vacuum baas	46	91	210	270	270	280	270
Bottle lids				160	160	160	180

12 month sales forecast (cont.)

	Nov-11	Dec-11	Jan-12	Feb-12	Mar-12	Annual totals
Firm Tofu restaurants	200	200	200	200	200	2,052
Bottleworks	40	40	40	40	40	
Fresh gatherings	30	30	30	30	30	
Restaurant 3	30	30	30	30	30	
Restaurant 4	40	40	40	40	40	
Restaurant 5	20	20	20	20	20	
Restaurant 6	20	20	20	20	20	
Restaurant 7	20	20	20	20	20	
Sale price @ unit	$ 3.00	$ 3.00	$ 3.00	$ 3.00	$ 3.00	
Total	**$ 600.00**	**$ 600.00**	**$ 600.00**	**$ 600.00**	**$ 600.00**	**$ 6,156.00**
Firm and medium Tofu retail	20	20	20	20	20	485
Maplewood (wed.)	20	20	20	20	20	
Sale price @ unit	$ 4.00	$ 4.00	$ 4.00	$ 4.00	$ 4.00	
Total	**$ 80.00**	**$ 80.00**	**$ 80.00**	**$ 80.00**	**$ 80.00**	**$ 1,940.00**
% of plain Tofu sales at market	33%	33%	33%	33%	33%	
Value added products retail	60	60	60	60	60	1,130
Maplewood (wed.)	60	60	60	60	60	
Sale price @ unit	$ 6.00	$ 6.00	$ 6.00	$ 6.00	$ 6.00	
Total	**$ 360.00**	**$ 360.00**	**$ 360.00**	**$ 360.00**	**$ 360.00**	**$ 6,780.00**
Craft soy milk coffee shop	60	60	60	60	60	320
Coffee shop 1	20	20	20	20	20	
Coffee shop 2						
Coffee shop 3	40	40	40	40	40	
Sale price @ unit	$ 4.00	$ 4.00	$ 4.00	$ 4.00	$ 4.00	
Total	**$ 240.00**	**$ 240.00**	**$ 240.00**	**$ 240.00**	**$ 240.00**	**$ 1,280.00**
Vanilla soy milk coffee shop	20	20	30	30	30	130
Coffee shop 1						
Coffee shop 2	20	20	30	30	30	
Coffee shop 3						
Sale price @ unit	$ 4.00	$ 4.00	$ 4.00	$ 4.00	$ 4.00	
Total	**$ 80.00**	**$ 80.00**	**$ 120.00**	**$ 120.00**	**$ 120.00**	**$ 520.00**
Tofu jerky retail	40	40	40	40	40	410
Maplewood (wed.)	40	40	40	40	40	
Sale price @ unit	$ 3.00	$ 3.00	$ 3.00	$ 3.00	$ 3.00	
Total	**$ 120.00**	**$ 120.00**	**$ 120.00**	**$ 120.00**	**$ 120.00**	**$ 1,230.00**
Monthly totals: all categories	**$ 1,480.00**	**$ 1,480.00**	**$ 1,520.00**	**$ 1,520.00**	**$ 1,520.00**	**$17,906.00**
Running total	**$11,866.00**	**$13,346.00**	**$14,866.00**	**$16,386.00**	**$17,906.00**	

Inventory required for sales	Nov-11	Dec-11	Jan-12	Feb-12	Mar-12	Annual totals
Soy bean in pounds	235	235	235	235	235	
CaCl in grams	1,867	1,867	1,867	1,867	1,867	
Vacuum baas	220	220	220	220	220	
Bottle lids	120	120	120	120	120	Total lids 1,260

12 month sales forecast (cont.)

	2011 totals	225% 2012	175% 2013	175% retail growth due to new facility/restaurant stays same as 2013 2014	
Firm Tofu restaurants	68	4,617	8,080	14,140	
Bottleworks	137	154	269	471	
Fresh gatherings					
Restaurant 3					
Restaurant 4					
Restaurant 5					
Restaurant 6					
Restaurant 7					
Sale price @ unit		0	0	0	
Total		**$13,851.00**	**$24,239.25**	**$42,418.69**	
Firm and medium Tofu retail	16	1,091	1,637	2,865	
Maplewood (wed.)	32	36	55	95	
Sale price @ unit		300% farmers market growth from additional markets			
Total		**$ 4,365.00**	**$ 6,547.50**	**$11,458.13**	
% of plain Tofu sales at market		0	0	0	
Value added products retail	38	2,543	4,449	7,786	
Maplewood (wed.)	113	85	148	260	
Sale price @ unit		300% farmers market growth from additional markets			
Total		**$15,255.00**	**$26,696.25**	**$46,718.44**	
Craft soy milk coffee shop	5	1,440	2,520	4,410	Full year + 200% growth
Coffee shop 1	20	24	41	72	
Coffee shop 2					
Coffee shop 3					
Sale price @ unit		0	0	0	
Total		**$ 5,760.00**	**$10,080.00**	**$17,640.00**	
Vanilla soy milk coffee shop	2	585	1,024	1,792	Full year + 200% growth
Coffee shop 1	20	10	17	29	
Coffee shop 2					
Coffee shop 3					
Sale price @ unit					
Total		**$ 2,340.00**	**$ 4,095.00**	**$ 7,166.25**	
Tofu jerky retail	44	923	1,614	2,825	
Maplewood (wed.)		23	40	71	
Sale price @ unit					
Total		**$ 2,767.50**	**$ 4,843.13**	**$ 8,475.47**	
Monthly totals: All categories		**$44,338.50**	**$76,501.13**	**$133,876.97**	
Running total					
Total man hours	366	732	1,281	2,243	
Total market hours	120	432	432	432	
Total sales hours	100	200	200	200	4 × 50
Total hours/year guestimate	586	1,364	1,913	2,875	
Full time with 2 week holiday		2,000	Hire for 875		

SPECIALTY FOOD MANUFACTURER

12 month cash flow projections

	Pre-startup	Apr-11	May-11	Jun-11	Jul-11	Aug-11	Sep-11
Cash on hand beginning of month	$1,300.00	$1,300.00	$1,355.00	$1,299.75	$2,688.50	$2,781.25	$3,391.00
Cash receipts							
Cash sales			$270.00	$1,320.00	$1,400.00	$1,400.00	$1,400.00
Collections from CR accounts		$55.00	$—	$399.00	$570.00	$570.00	$585.00
Loan/other cash inj.							
Total cash receipts	$—	$55.00	$270.00	$1,659.00	$1,910.00	$1,970.00	$1,985.00
Total cash available before OUT	$1,300.00	$1,355.00	$1,625.00	$2,958.75	$4,598.50	$4,751.25	$5,376.00
Cash paid OUT							
Inventory purchases							
CaCl2	$35.00			$35.00			$70.00
Soy beans	$257.00	$—			$257.00		$257.00
Value added inventory needs			$15.00	$50.00	$50.00	$50.00	$50.00
Packaging purchases							
6" × 8" vacuum bags, 1000ct/bx (2)	$75.00			$75.00			$125.00
Labels, 4500ct	$—		$100.00				$100.00
Total COGs	$367.00	$—	$115.00	$160.00	$307.00	$50.00	$602.00
Salary							
Gross wages		$—	$—		$1,200.00	$1,200.00	$1,200.00
Payroll expenses	$—						
Repairs and maintenance	$—						
Car, Delivery, pick-up (gas)			$50.00	$50.00	$50.00	$50.00	$50.00
Accounting and legal							
Rent	$—	$—	$—	$—	$—	$—	$—
Telephone (cell phone)	$—	$25.00	$25.00	$25.00	$25.00	$25.00	$25.00
Utilities (include in rent)							
Insurance		$35.25	$35.25	$35.25	$35.25	$35.25	$35.25
Taxes							
Interest							
License	$410.00						
Bottle purchase							
Bottle lids							
Subtotal	$777.00	$60.25	$225.25	$270.25	$1,617.25	$1,360.25	$1,912.25
Loan principle payment							
Capital purchase					$200.00		
Research and development			$100.00				$50.00
Owners withdrawl							
Total cash paid OUT	$777.00	$60.25	$325.25	$270.25	$1,817.25	$1,360.25	$1,962.25
Cash position (EOM)	$523.00	$1,294.75	$1,299.75	$2,688.50	$2,781.25	$3,391.00	$3,413.75
Essential operating data							
Sales volume ($)		$138.00	$498.00	$1,770.00	$1,970.00	$1,970.00	$2,000.00
Accounts receivable		$69.00	$183.00	$339.00	$510.00	$570.00	$585.00
Bad debit (EOM)							
Needed inventory	$257.00	$11.50	$30.25	$92.50	$107.50	$107.50	$110.00
Packaging supplies on hand (EOM)			$(86.40)	$(97.80)	$(184.20)	$(270.60)	$(132.00)
Accounts payable (EOM)							
Depreciation							

12 month cash flow projections (cont.)

	Oct-11	Nov-11	Dec-11	Jan-12	Feb-12	Mar-16
Cash on hand beginning of month	$3,413.75	$1,200.50	$2,400.25	$3,345.00	$4,107.75	$4,717.50
Cash receipts						
Cash sales	$1,360.00	$ 560.00	$ 560.00	$ 560.00	$ 560.00	$ 560.00
Collections from CR accounts	$ 640.00	$ 800.00	$ 920.00	$ 940.00	$ 960.00	$ 960.00
Loan/other cash inj.						
Total cash receipts	**$2,000.00**	**$1,360.00**	**$1,480.00**	**$1,500.00**	**$1,520.00**	**$1,520.00**
Total cash available before OUT	**$5,413.75**	**$2,560.50**	**$3,880.25**	**$4,845.00**	**$5,627.75**	**$6,237.50**
Cash paid OUT						
Inventory purchases						
CaCl2				$ 70.00		
Soy beans	$ —		$ —	$ 257.00	$ —	
Value added inventory needs	$ 50.00	$ 50.00	$ 50.00	$ 50.00	$ 50.00	$ 50.00
Packaging purchases						
6" × 8" vacuum bags, 1000ct/bx (2)			$ 125.00			$ 125.00
Labels, 4500ct					$ 500.00	
Total COGs	**$ 50.00**	**$ 50.00**	**$ 175.00**	**$ 377.00**	**$ 550.00**	**$ 175.00**
Salary						
Gross wages	$1,200.00					
Payroll expenses						
Repairs and maintenance						
Car, Delivery, pick-up (gas)	$ 50.00	$ 50.00	$ 50.00	$ 50.00	$ 50.00	$ 50.00
Accounting and legal						
Rent	$ —	$ —	$ 250.00	$ 250.00	$ 250.00	$ 250.00
Telephone (cell phone)	$ 25.00	$ 25.00	$ 25.00	$ 25.00	$ 25.00	$ 25.00
Utilities (include in rent)						
Insurance	$ 35.25	$ 35.25	$ 35.25	$ 35.25	$ 35.25	$ 35.25
Taxes						
Interest						
License						
Bottle purchase						
Bottle lids	$ 253.00					
Subtotal	**$1,613.25**	**$ 160.25**	**$ 535.25**	**$ 737.25**	**$ 910.25**	**$ 535.25**
Loan principle payment						
Capital purchase	$1,100.00					
Research and development	$1,500.00					
Owners withdrawl						
Total cash paid OUT	**$4,213.25**	**$ 160.25**	**$ 535.25**	**$ 737.25**	**$ 910.25**	**$ 535.25**
Cash position (EOM)	$1,200.50	$2,400.25	$3,345.00	$4,107.75	$4,717.50	$5,702.25
Essential operating data						
Sales volume ($)	$2,040.00	$1,480.00	$1,480.00	$1,520.00	$1,520.00	$1,520.00
Accounts receivable	$ 600.00	$ 600.00	$ 600.00	$ 600.00	$ 600.00	$ 600.00
Bad debit (EOM)						
Needed inventory	$ 107.60	$ 70.39	$ 70.39	$ 70.44	$ 70.44	$ 70.44
Packaging supplies on hand (EOM)	$ (218.40)	$ (304.80)	$ (266.20)	$ (395.80)	$ (25.40)	$ (115.00)
Accounts payable (EOM)						
Depreciation						

12 month cash flow projections (cont.)

	Total item EST year	Year 2 150%	Year 3 175%	Year 4 175%
Cash on hand beginning of month	$ 5,702.25	$ 7,258.35	$ 1,852.72	$ 8,122.61
Cash receipts				
Cash sales	$ 9,950.00	$22,387.50	$38,086.88	$ 66,652.03
Collections from CR accounts	$ 7,279.00	$21,951.00	$38,414.25	$ 67,224.94
Loan/other cash inj.				
Total cash receipts	**$17,906.00**	**$44,338.50**	**$76,501.13**	**$133,876.97**
Total cash available before OUT	**$23,608.25**	**$51,596.85**	**$78,353.84**	**$141,999.58**
Cash paid OUT		$ —	$ —	$ —
Inventory purchases		$ —	$ —	$ —
CaCl2	$ 210.00	$ 420.00	$ 840.00	$ 1,680.00
Soy beans	$ 1,028.00	$ 2,056.00	$ 3,598.00	$ 6,296.50
Value added inventory needs	$ 515.50	$ 1,030.00	$ 1,802.50	$ 2,703.75
Packaging purchases	$ —	$ —	$ —	$ —
6" × 8" vacuum bags, 1000ct/bx (2)	$ 525.00	$ 1,050.00	$ 1,500.00	$ 2,000.00
Labels, 4500ct	$ 700.00	$ 1,400.00	$ 2,450.00	$ 4,287.50
Total COGs	**$ 2,978.00**	**$ 5,956.00**	**$10,190.50**	**$ 16,967.75**
Salary	$ —			$ 50,000.00
Gross wages	$ 4,800.00	$27,285.33	$38,269.33	$ 25,994.37
Payroll expenses	$ —	$ 200.00	$ 200.00	$ 200.00
Repairs and maintenance	$ —	$ 1,000.00	$ 1,000.00	$ 1,000.00
Car, Delivery, pick-up (gas)	$ 550.00	$ 1,500.00	$ 1,500.00	$ 2,000.00
Accounting and legal	$ —	$ 500.00	$ 1,000.00	$ 1,000.00
Rent	$ 1,000.00	$ 4,584.00	$ 4,584.00	$ 23,184.00
Telephone (cell phone)	$ 300.00	$ 300.00	$ 300.00	$ 300.00
Utilities (include in rent)	$ —	$ —	$ —	$ —
Insurance	$ 423.00	$ 1,000.00	$ 2,000.00	$ 3,000.00
Taxes	$ 2,685.90	$ 4,092.80	$ 5,740.40	$ 3,899.16
Interest	$ —			
License	$ 410.00	$ 820.00	$ 1,435.00	$ 2,511.25
Bottle purchase	$ —			
Bottle lids	$ 253.00	$ 506.00	$ 1,012.00	
Subtotal	**$10,421.90**	**$41,788.13**	**$57,040.73**	**$113,088.77**
Loan principle payment		$ —		
Capital purchase	$ 1,300.00	$ 2,000.00	$ 1,000.00	
Research and development	$ 1,650.00		$ 2,000.00	$ 2,000.00
Owners withdrawl		$ —	$ —	$ —
Total cash paid OUT	**$16,349.90**	**$49,744.13**	**$70,231.23**	**$132,056.52**
Cash position (EOM)	$ 7,259.35	$ 1,852.72	$ 8,122.61	$ 9,943.06
Essential operating data		$ —	$ —	$ —
Sales volume ($)	$17,906.00	$44,338.50	$76,501.13	$133,876.97
Accounts receivable		$ —	$ —	$ —
Bad debit (EOM)		$ —	$ —	$ —
Needed inventory		$ —	$ —	$ —
Packaging supplies on hand (EOM)		$ —	$ —	$ —
Accounts payable (EOM)				
Depreciation				

Projected balance sheet

	Beginning as of 4/7/2011	Projected as of 3/31/2012
Assets		
Current assets		
Cash in bank	$1,300	$4,718
Accounts receivable	—	960
Inventory	300	300
Prepaid expenses	—	—
Other current assets	—	—
Total current assets	**$1,600**	**$5,978**
Fixed assets		
Machinery & equipment	$ 250	$ 250
Total fixed assets (net of depreciation)	**$ 250**	**$ 250**
Other assets		
Other	—	—
Total other assets	**$ —**	**$ —**
Total assets	**$1,850**	**$6,228**
Liabilities and equity		
Current liabilities		
Accounts payable	$ 300	$ 300
Interest payable	—	—
Taxes payable	—	1,000
Notes, short-term (due within 12 months)	—	—
Current part, long-term debt	—	—
Other current liabilities	—	—
Total current liabilities	**$ 300**	**$1,300**
Long-term debt		
Bank loans payable	$ —	
Notes payable to stockholders	—	—
LESS: Short-term portion	—	—
Other long term debt	—	—
Total long-term debt	**$ —**	
Total liabilities	**$ 300**	**$1,300**
Owners' equity		
Invested capital	$1,550	$ 550
Retained earnings—beginning	—	—
Retained earnings—current	—	4,378
Total owners' equity	**$1,550**	**$4,928**
Total liabilities & equity	**$1,850**	**$6,228**

Breakeven analysis

Cost description	Fixed costs ($)	Variable costs (%)
Variable costs		
Cost of goods sold		12.6%
Direct labor (includes payroll taxes)		31.7%
Fixed costs		
Supplies	$ 253	
Car, delivery and travel	$ 550	
Accounting and legal	$ —	
Rent	$ 1,000	
Telephone	$ 300	
Insurance	$ 423	
Miscellaneous expenses	$ —	
Owner's draw	$ —	
Total fixed costs	**$ 2,526**	
Total variable costs		**44%**
Breakeven sales level	**$4,536.89**	

Sources of capital

Owners' investment (some and percent ownership)	%	
Don Brown, owner	**100**	$1,550
Total investment		**$1,550**
Goodwill		
Nutrition and diabetics-HELP		$ 257
Total Goodwill		**$ 257**
Startup expenses		
Leasehold improvements		$ —
Total Leasehold improvements		**$ —**
Capital equipment unit		
Muslin cheesecloth		$ 50
Total capital equipment		**$ 50**
Location and admin expenses		
Rental		$ —
Legal and accounting fees		—
Quickbooks		200
Total location and admin expenses		**$ 200**
Opening inventory		
Soy beans		$ 257
CaCl2		35
Packaging		50
Total inventory		**$ 342**
Advertising and promotional expenses		
Advertising		$ —
Printing		—
Total advertising/promotional expenses		**$ —**
Other expenses		$ —
Total other expenses		**$ —**
Reserve for contingencies		$ —
Working capital		$ —
Summary statement		
Source of capital		
Owners' and other investments		$1,500
Other loans		
Total source of funds		**$1,500**
Startup expenses		
Capital equipment		50
Location/administration expenses		200
Opening inventory		342
Total startup expenses		**$ 592**

ENDNOTES

1. Mintel. (2011, January). *American Lifestyles - US.* Retrieved from http://academic.mintel.com/.

2. "Farmers' Market Map." http://mda.mo.gov. Missouri Department of Agriculture. Web. 5 May 2011.

3. Mintel. (2011, January). *American Lifestyles - US.* Retrieved from http://academic.mintel.com/.

4. Mintel. (2011, March). *Soy Foods and Beverages - US.* Retrieved from http://academic.mintel. com/.

5. Mintel. (2011, January). *American Lifestyles - US.* Retrieved from http://academic.mintel.com/.

6. Ibid.

7. (2011, April 4). Surprising Familiarity with QR Codes. Retrieved from http://www.emarketer.com/ Article.aspx?R=1008318.

Student Art Gallery

Pozzo Gallery

127 Gallman Hall
St. Louis, MO 63109

Vincent A. Marino

St. Louis University needs a student art gallery to display and sell student-created works of art as well as provide practical experience for those seeking employment in the art industry.

EXECUTIVE SUMMARY

Currently, Saint Louis University is the only local university or college that does not have an art gallery dedicated to student work.

As a result, students have limited options when it comes to displaying and selling their works of art. Twice a year, the Boileau Hall Art Gallery, on SLU's campus, hosts two juried student exhibitions where students can show and make their pieces available for purchase. Although these shows are beneficial for art students, they need a more consistent opportunity to establish themselves as artists. A permanent student art gallery would give these students that needed forum.

Furthermore, many students in the program will embark on art related careers after graduation; some of these students will create works for galleries, will manage a gallery or will even start their own gallery. To enhance their chances of success, Saint Louis University is investigating the potential for a student run art gallery with the primary goal to give students exposure to the business of art. The gallery will enhance the curricula that students are studying by providing the opportunity for real-world, practical experience in the business of art. It will also provide students who wish to sell pieces the experience of working with a gallery to sell their works.

As an extension of the University, the gallery will be able to utilize many of the resources that the University has available, especially those related to promotion. Additionally, the gallery will also take advantage of the community relationships that the University has developed with businesses in the area.

The gallery will act as an educational tool for students. In the context of an actual course, students will manage and operate the gallery on their own, which will give them experience in running an art related business. A faculty advisor will supervise the students, but he or she will allow them to run all aspects of the business, thus, maximizing the educational value.

The gallery will need financial support from the University to initiate the endeavor and, most likely, to support it in the long-term. Ideally, the gallery will strive to be self-sustaining but that may be unlikely. The primary goal of the gallery is to enhance the education that students receive, not profit, but an aspect of the educational experience is making the gallery as self-reliant as possible.

This business plan outlines the different aspects of establishing a student art gallery either on or off campus. It provides a framework for how the business would be structured and operated. The plan also lays out the possible costs and potential benefits that the University could expect if this venture is undertaken.

COMPANY DESCRIPTION

The Name

Andrea Pozzo was an Italian Jesuit brother who lived from 1642 to 1709. Pozzo was a gifted artist, designer and art theoretician. His skill as an artist quickly earned him virtuosic reputation; and he was commissioned by the highest ranking officers of the Jesuit Order to paint frescoes in Jesuit churches that lacked ornamentation.

In 1685, he was tasked to paint the ceiling of the Sant' Ignazio (St. Ignatius) church in Rome. The church had been consecrated in 1642 but was never completed because a dispute with the primary donors. As a result, the dome of the church was never completed. Brother Pozzo proposed that he paint an illusionistic dome on a flat canvas that would be suspended from the ceiling. Many were skeptical of his idea, not only because of the sheer magnitude of the undertaking, but also because it was a groundbreaking concept. His work depicts, among other things, the elevation of St. Ignatius to divine status. It still exists today and is considered to be his masterpiece:

On the flat ceiling he painted an allegory of the Apotheosis of S. Ignatius, in breathtaking perspective. The painting, 17 m in diameter, is devised to make an observer, looking from a spot marked by a brass disc set into the floor of the nave, seem to see a lofty vaulted roof decorated by statues, while in fact the ceiling is flat. (wikipedia.org)

His illusionary work became the model of church decoration for many years and influenced countless other artists. In addition to his ingenious creations, Pozzo published two volumes that contained his artistic theory and instructions in architectural painting. Titled the *Perspectiva Pictorum et Architectorum,* it is one of the first manuals on the concept of perspective for artists. These writings were translated into a multitude of languages and retained a presence in other art instruction publications for centuries.

Considering Brother Pozzo's artistic and educational contributions to the art world, Saint Louis University's tradition of naming buildings of academia after celebrated Jesuits, and the gallery's close proximity to the Hotel Ignacio; it is apropos that the gallery takes his name and be known as the Pozzo Gallery.

The Need

The genesis for this enterprise emerged from a need. Fr. Nowak recognized that Saint Louis University needed a permanent student art gallery where members of the SLU community, especially students, could share their artistic expressions with SLU and the surrounding community.

Saint Louis University is the only college institution in the St. Louis area that does not have a permanent student art gallery. Most colleges and universities in the country have some form of a student art gallery. A student gallery is intended to enhance the educational aspects of a school's fine arts department by providing students exposure to the art world and a taste of what it is like to be an artist.

Recognizing that a need existed, Fr. Nowak reached out to members of the University for assistance in finding a way to address that need. This plan is a response to the need and this recommendation is a general design for a student art gallery.

The Pozzo Gallery

The Pozzo Gallery will be a nonprofit art gallery run by Saint Louis University students and will feature works of art, in several media, created by SLU students that are available for purchase. The gallery will also act as an extension of the Fine and Performing Arts Department and serve as a real world educational tool for students.

Vision Statement

Student arts' gateway to the world.

Mission Statement

The Pozzo Gallery provides all Saint Louis University students a forum to display and sell their artwork while providing students who aspire to achieve a career in the arts with an invaluable educational experience of running and managing a business.

Goals

The goals of the Pozzo Gallery center around two aspects: education and community involvement. More specifically, the intended goals are to do the following:

- Educate art students in the entrepreneurial and commercial aspects of the business of art, by presenting them with the opportunity to manage and operate all aspects of the gallery as if it were their own business.

- Provide the opportunity and a forum for Saint Louis University students, especially those in fine arts, the satisfaction of displaying and selling their own works.

- Instill the importance of the role community involvement can play in the livelihood of a business.

- Strengthen the University's bond with the surrounding art community.

- Further the reputation of Saint Louis University as a leader in the community.

Objectives

The Pozzo Gallery will use the following objectives to accomplish the stated goals:

- Establish the Pozzo Gallery Management Board (PGMB) that will consist of a faculty advisor and a team of dedicated fine art students who will create the articles by which the board, as well as the business, will operate.

- Act as an ambassador of the University by engaging with local organizations, such as Grand Center and Midtown Alley, through events and membership to further establish it as a leader in the area.

Company Background

In late February 2011, the President of Saint Louis University, Fr. Lawrence Nowak, S.J., requested that a business plan be created for a student art gallery located in the space at 3331 Locust Street, just north of the school's Frost campus. With the approaching grand opening of the Hotel Ignacio, another University venture, Fr. Nowak saw both a short and long term need for this 460 square-foot street level property. In the short term, he wanted something to occupy the space by April 1st that would be both aesthetically pleasing and visible from the main entrance of the Hotel Ignacio. In the long term, he wanted to see a permanent retail location that would benefit the both the school and the neighborhood. As a passionate supporter of the arts, Fr. Nowak wanted a plan that would realize his vision of an art gallery that exhibited art by students. He requested Dr. Gary Kile to instruct someone who could develop the long term business plan for the concept.

The first phase of the gallery was completed in late March when SLU Facilities' crews laid new tile and installed track lighting in the room. Faculty members of the fine arts department hung student art on the walls and glass works from the University's inventory were brought in for display. Since that time work has continued on developing the concept with that location in mind; however, on April 28th, parties involved with the project were informed that the location was no longer available because another lessee had been found. This information was disappointing as many aspects of the proposal revolved around the physical location, which had changed. Despite the setback, work on the plan has continued with the same focus as before, that pertaining to the educational and social benefits of the proposition, but with a more general framework as to its locale. Real estate location plays a considerable role in operations and strategy development for almost any business. Fortunately, the general location for a future gallery can be logically assumed—either residing on the Frost campus or just outside its perimeter. Consequently, some assumptions related to location can still be included in the business plan.

The original business plan determined the financial requirements for the space at 3331 Locust. A new location is unknown, but the financial statements from the original plan can serve as an example for a future gallery. Of course, some of the costs will vary, but the types of expenses have been identified, so this plan can be used to provide the financial framework in the future. Depending on the location, whether on campus or off, and if off campus whether or not SLU owns the property, differences in cost structure may exist. In essence, three scenarios for the art gallery location exist: on campus; off campus in a SLU owned property; or off campus in a third-party owned property. Many of the costs will be incurred in every scenario, such as, hardware supplies, transaction fees and phone services; however, rental, insurance and security expenses are incredibly dependent on the situation. This plan attempts to identify the possible costs for two of the scenarios, on campus and off campus in a SLU property. The third scenario is not economically feasible for the gallery because of the hard dollar costs associated with it.

As stated before, this plan is intended to outline the general requirements of a student gallery so that it can be used as the basis for a new plan when a location becomes available.

PRODUCTS & SERVICES AND INDUSTRY

Product & Service Features

The Pozzo Gallery will showcase student works of art and sell them at a reasonable price. Initially, works will consist of two dimensional art, i.e. paintings, graphic designs, drawings, photographs and sketches, and will eventually include three dimensional pieces such as ceramics, small sculptures, handmade jewelry and metal working.

Pricing for works of art will be determined by the artist and approved by the student management board. The artist and gallery will split the revenues from the sale equally. It is anticipated that the majority of the two dimensional art will range in price from $50 to $250, depending on several factors such as medium and size. For most three dimensional works, the prices will likely range from $20 to $125.

In the surrounding area, including the Grand Center Arts and Mid Town Alley districts, no gallery sells works at a lower-end price. The galleries that sell works in the area feature works by known artists and are typically priced significantly higher than those at the Pozzo Gallery. In the art world, price is often determined by how well-established an artist is. College students have not built a reputation in the art community; thus, command a lower price for their works. In this situation, a lower price level is not necessarily reflective of inferior work quality; rather, it is reflective of their level of exposure in the art world.

Customers will have the opportunity to view and purchase pieces during the gallery's published business hours, but will also have the ability to preview the works in the virtual gallery on the company website, which will be designed and maintained by the students.

Customers who purchase works will utilize them for decorations in their homes and businesses or give them as gifts. More importantly, the gallery will help customers act on their altruistic desires to help students, the local community and Saint Louis University. Many patrons may make a purchase, not only for the art itself, but also for what that purchase means to them. Some customers may simply feel good about aiding students in their educational pursuits. Local residents may believe that by supporting the gallery they are doing their part in ensuring the health of the neighborhood in which they live. Likewise, alumni may see a purchase at the gallery as another opportunity to give back to the University.

The focus of the gallery is on students, but an opportunity exists to involve other members of the SLU community, such as faculty, staff and, especially, alumni. Including these SLU related parties in the gallery would provide additional support channels and increase the awareness of the gallery itself. At least a few alumni who indulge in artistic hobbies would probably like to show someone, other than their spouses, what they have created in their spare time. Even though painting, drawing, photographing or sculpting may be a pastime activity for these artists, they may feel the urge to share their artistic expression with others who appreciate their efforts. Limited options, outside the one or two day community art fair, exist for them to do so. By reaching out to these alumni, students can offer them the vehicle to do this in a more meaningful way. These alumni would invite their friends, family and coworkers to visit the SLU campus to see their official exhibition. This could be a tremendous experience for the artist which, in turn, would translate into increased goodwill towards the University. A couple options exist for how the gallery can offer this service to alumni. The gallery could offer to host the exhibition for a possible donation to support gallery operations. Or, the service could be offered for free to interested alumni with the purpose to generate alumni engagement with the gallery.

An additional service investigated for the 3331 Locust St. location involved renting the space out to groups before events at the Fox Theatre. A group of ten to thirty people could rent the room for a pre-event two hours before the Fox show time. The idea would be that people could gather and mingle and then walk over to the theatre to see the show. A group would have the option to have the event catered with food and drink. The gallery would book the events and hire an outside service to do the catering.

While creating the plan for the Locust location, preliminary discussions with the Hotel Ignacio indicated that working with them was a possibility. The hotel's close proximity to the gallery made it a logical partner for this service. Other restaurants in the area may also be interested in offering catering services too. In fact, the person booking the gallery could choose from a list of preferred caterers. Food offerings would be constrained to appetizers that could be kept warm in chafing dishes. The catering service could also serve beverages, beer and wine. In addition, the gallery would need to purchase three or four bar tables, the taller circular tables around three feet in diameter, and nine to twelve stools. Theses tables do not take up a lot of space, and would offer guests a choice of sitting or standing. Most guests would probably stand as they circulated and socialized. The Locust gallery is small but would provide a delightful setting for an event. The possibility for offering this service at other gallery sites would depend on the size and layout of the space, and its geographical location. 3331 Locust St. is ideal for Fox events, but another place may not be as well suited. Needless to say, the gallery can be rented for any occasion and not just restricted to Fox events.

The gallery would charge an hourly rate to rent the room which would include making arrangements with the caterer. This potential service could bring in additional income for the gallery; it might even become the main source of revenue. It is not unusual for an art gallery to derive its main source of income from services other than art sales. Event rental is a common way that galleries supplement their income and this service will give students experience selling that service, working with caterers and planning events.

Product & Service Benefits

The Pozzo Gallery will provide numerous benefits to several groups; the most recognizable ones are students, Saint Louis University, and the surrounding community. Of course, when students benefit, the University also benefits as the students are part of the University. The benefits are usually not mutually exclusive and can be shared by multiple parties. These benefits will be a determining factor in the decision to go forward with the endeavor, as they will act as the counter balance to offset the tangible financial costs. The benefits can be viewed as the social profits that the gallery will generate for students, Saint Louis University and the community.

Student Benefits

The increase in the value of students' education is obviously the greatest benefit of the gallery. At the gallery, learning will be an active experience and students will learn by doing, which is a much more effective educational approach than the passive one associated with the traditional classroom setting. Students involved in managing the gallery will gain experience in the following areas:

- Creating a strategic direction for a business
- Establishing a business model
- Working with artists
- Keeping business records
- Managing a budget
- Dealing with limited financial resources
- Writing grants
- Brainstorming and experimenting with new approaches to the business model
- Establishing, retaining and growing a client base
- Working with staff
- Networking within the art community
- Prepping and displaying artwork to increase appeal
- Promoting artists and the gallery itself
- Designing and maintaining a website for business purposes
- Hanging and displaying pieces
- Establishing best practices for dealing with customers
- Handling the highs and lows that come from running a business
- Understanding that the unexpected is expected
- Sourcing donations, sponsorships and other contributions

Students involved with exhibiting at the gallery will gain experience in the following areas:

- Marketing themselves and their artwork to galleries
- Working with a gallery
- Valuing and pricing their works
- Establishing, retaining and growing a client base
- Networking with clientele
- Gaining realistic expectations of earnings in the industry

Notice that the art-related terms in the above bulleted lists could be replaced with terms from almost any other type of business. Every industry has its own traditional model and terminology; however, the same underlying principles for businesses exist across all fields and students will have the opportunity to gain an understanding of those principles through the gallery. This experiential approach will imbue involved students with intimate knowledge of the workings of the art world, of running their own business, whether it is art related or not, and will add invaluable skills to their skill set. After graduating, these students will have real-world experience that most other students will not have, which will set SLU students apart from the rest of crowd.

Another way that students will benefit from the gallery is that they will learn the importance of being resourceful, just as they would have to be if they owned their own business. The students will have limited resources to make the gallery sustainable, so they will have to find creative ways to do so. For example, this might entail initiating a quid pro quo relationship with the SLU AdClub. The club could create advertising copy for the gallery to use in its promotions. In turn, the gallery might host a special exhibition that showcases the club's premier works. Most art students are creative in respect to their own creations, but the gallery will provide the vehicle for them to become creative in business, which is a key element to success.

The gallery will encourage also cross-disciplinary involvement between students the in studio arts, art history, marketing, accounting, law and communications programs. Students running the gallery will most likely need to source advice or ideas from these students who may have a more developed background in their respective areas of study. As in the real world, outsourcing, partnering and collaborating will be a key to a healthy and successful gallery.

Saint Louis University Benefits

SLU will also benefit from the gallery by improving the art program's competitiveness with other schools, by raising awareness of the University's dedication to the arts to the public, and by increasing awareness of the University itself. The magnitude of these social benefits is difficult to measure but the benefits themselves are readily apparent.

The University has an established and well-respected arts program; however, it is the only local university or college without a student art gallery. Washington University, Webster University, St. Louis Community College, University of Missouri-St. Louis, Fontbonne University, Lindenwood University and Maryville University all have student galleries of some sort. Launching a student gallery just because a majority of schools in the area, and the nation for that matter, have one is not a justifiable reason in its own right. Nevertheless, student art galleries have become a requisite element of art programs around the country and SLU does not have one. The establishment of a permanent student art gallery on, or near, SLU's campus could provide the art program a more competitive footing in regards to attracting talented art students.

SLU could be known as one of the few schools in the country that has a commercial student art gallery completely run by students. This fact could prove to be an effective marketing tool to increase enrollment because prospective art students would view the department's program as a unique offering. The gallery could be the tipping point that brings a prospective student to SLU over Washington University or another school.

Additionally, the gallery's success will rely significantly on collaboration with Grand Center. The gallery's participation in Grand Center activities will increase cognizance and appreciation of SLU's effort with those who are active in the community. Many St. Louis business leaders are involved with Grand Center and are aware of the activities in the area. The establishment of the Pozzo Gallery will be noticed as it further showcases SLU's appreciation for the arts. This could develop into an opportunity to establish, or strengthen, relationships between community leaders and Saint Louis University, which may pay dividends in the future.

The University can use the gallery as a public relations tool by inviting local media outlets to appear at major gallery events. Positive publicity for the Pozzo Gallery is also positive publicity for the school.

The establishment of a gallery would also provide physical confirmation to the students in the fine arts department that the University is serious about supporting the program, its students and ensuring its long-term competitiveness. Students in the program will be incredibly appreciative of the University, which will translate into increased loyalty to SLU and possible future contributions.

The gallery will be another opportunity to reach out not only to alumni in general, but also to alumni from the fine arts' programs. It may engage Fine and Performing Arts alumni to get more involved with supporting the school, including financially. Some alumni may feel that by making a donation to the gallery, which is effectively a donation to the school, they are able to make a difference for those who are involved with something they deeply care about. These alumni can relate to what these students are experiencing. Increased alumni involvement is a constant objective for the University and the gallery could aid the school in meeting that objective.

Community Benefits

Saint Louis University has the responsibility to play an active role in the effort to continuously improve the health and growth of the community in which it belongs. The Pozzo Gallery will be another component in that endeavor, regardless of an on or off campus location. To do this, the gallery will become a member of the Grand Center arts district. Each additional art-related organization that becomes part of the district makes the district stronger as a whole, by reinforcing its purpose to make the area an arts and entertainment destination in St. Louis. The gallery's mere existence will further that purpose.

Part of the learning process for the students involved with the gallery will be to engage the neighborhood in which it resides. It is important for any business to build a support network with the surrounding businesses to increase its chance of survival. The gallery can strengthen the existing networks through community outreach and by working together with these businesses, thus, improving the gallery's and other businesses' likelihood for success.

Industry Description

The Pozzo Gallery will be a part of SLU, which is a not-for-profit organization, but will engage in activities that are typically commercial, i.e. selling drawings and paintings. For the purpose of industry analysis, the commercial art gallery industry was analyzed because the gallery's business model will more closely resemble the Pozzo Gallery than the noncommercial art gallery industry, which consists of nonprofit or public galleries and museums that do not sell art.

The commercial art gallery industry consists of businesses that showcase works of art for third parties, namely individual artists. Galleries effectively act as brokers for artists by procuring their art, providing a venue for viewing that art, providing a purchase mechanism for the art, and providing marketing and promotion for the artists and their works.

Most artists do not possess the means to create their art and then effectively market and distribute it. Artists' attempts to promote their own works might be limited by time constraints, by lack of business acumen, or by a multitude of other reasons. For most artists the gallery is the primary vehicle by which they can bring their art to the public and secure a livelihood.

Gallery responsibilities typically include the following operations:

- Working with artists to source works for the gallery
- Arranging the transportation of the pieces to the gallery
- Establishing the prices for which the works are offered and agreeing how the proceeds will be divided
- Scheduling exhibitions of the work
- Promoting the showings through various marketing efforts or by sending invitations to gallery clients and potential clients
- Arranging methods of payment

When many people think of art galleries, they envision large spaces with expensive art. The fact is that smaller galleries, which BizMiner classifies as independent companies with fewer than 25 employees, make up a respectable portion of the industry. These smaller galleries account for approximately 38.77% market share in the industry and generate average revenues of $240,403. Startup galleries, which primarily fall into the small business category, held .21% market share with average sales of $171,023, as of June 2010 (bizminer.com).

When industry sales are stratified by revenue classes, the class ranging from $1 to $500,000 annual sales contains 87% of the total industry's 17,000 plus firms. As of 2009, the average sales in this group were around $173,000. Nearly all small and startup galleries are included in this revenue group (bizminer.com).

Overall industry sales were $10 billion as of June 2010, which included an approximately $1 billion increase over the period from 2008 until June 2010. Likewise, the average annual sales by small businesses and startups have risen by 15.7% and 12.1%, respectively. Despite the sizable drop of nearly 2,000 firms from 2007 to 2008, the industry has shown evidence of a recovery as the number of firms in the industry has continued to rise year-to-year since 2008. While the trend is promising, the number of firms in the industry is lower today than in 2007 (bizminer.com).

Narrowing the scope of the analysis to the St. Louis Metropolitan area, one hundred and four firms made up the industry as of June 2010. Ninety-four of them were small businesses and two were considered startups. Compared to the national level, revenues have actually dropped from $72.2 million in June 2007 to $55.8 million in June 2010. Even though the trend line over this period is downward, it should be noted that firms generated an increase of revenues from June 2009 to June 2010 (bizminer.com).

The percentage of firms that have sales less than $500,000 in the St. Louis Metropolitan area closely mirrors that found on the national level, with 88%. Small business comprises a similar, but smaller, percentage of the market than at the national level (38.7%) with 33%. Startups in St. Louis actually command double the market share with .47%. One favorable statistic shows that failure rates for small and startup galleries are significantly lower than those in the total U.S. market. According to BizMiner, for the period between 2007 and 2009 small galleries had a failure rate of 26.5% and startups had a negative failure rate of 100%, meaning that startups actually increased in number; whereas, total U.S. market small and startup gallery failure rates were 34.9% and 51.64%, respectively. This may indicative of a community that is more supportive of the arts (bizminer.com).

MARKET ANALYSIS

Market and Target Customer

The Pozzo Gallery's typical customers are people who are looking for a relatively inexpensive piece of artwork to decorate their apartments, condos, homes or offices. Age, income and lifestyle of customers will vary considerably; however, a few common threads will exist for most customers, which include those who feel strongly about supporting one or more of the following: young artists and students, the surrounding business community, and Saint Louis University. Since the gallery will sell the works of non-established artists, prices will be reasonable and affordable for customers in nearly every income level.

The gallery's typical clientele will consist of the following:

- Family members of artists exhibiting in the gallery who wish show support for their relative

- SLU alumni visiting campus and looking for a way to support the University

- Upperclassmen at SLU who are moving into their first apartment and looking for something to hang on their walls; and their parents, who are helping them furnish their new apartment

- Neighborhood businesses who will want to show their support for a fellow business

- Guests at the Hotel Ignacio, who will most likely have some relationship with the University

- Attendees of the various events in the Grand Center and Mid Town Alley areas who park or visit the surrounding businesses

For the last three points above, location will determine the degree of involvement by those target audiences.

Competition and Competitive Advantage

Nearly every business has some sort of direct and indirect competition, and the Pozzo Gallery will be no different; however, the unique aspects of the business coupled with other factors may not result in the typical competition or level of intensity that a business normally faces for several reasons.

The primary reason is that the gallery exists to educate students about running an art-related business and to provide the experience of working with a gallery to sell their works. The focus of the gallery will not be to generate enough revenues to breakeven; doing so would be outstanding, albeit very unlikely. Therefore, the gallery will have to be subsidized to some extent by the University. Many of the galleries and museums in the area are nonprofit and have educational missions; however, they must at least breakeven to keep their doors open. Some of these organizations generate revenues through admission fees, membership dues, event hosting, and arts and craft sales, but mostly rely on donations and pledges to an endowment fund. As a result, these organizations must run similarly to typical for profit businesses in order to be sustainable. Ideally, the Pozzo Gallery would strive to stand on its own without subsidy from the University, but a more reasonable aim would be to lessen the level of that subsidy. This scenario provides protection from competition, in the sense that, it does not matter how well another nearby gallery is doing because even though it may have an effect on the Pozzo Gallery's bottom line, the bottom line has much less significance to the gallery. Of course, students should strive to improve the bottom line just as they would if it were their own business.

Another reason supporting a lower level of competition is that most of the organizations share a common goal in helping to rejuvenate the area known as the Grand Center district, which lies just north of the University. The district is championed by Grand Center, Inc. (GCI), a nonprofit corporation "established to create a vibrant, safe and secure urban neighborhood by facilitating the development of a regional district for arts, entertainment and education in the City of St. Louis" (grandcenter.org). Many nonprofit organizations now reside in the district as a result of this endeavor. While some of these galleries, museums and performing arts centers will attempt to garner as many visitors as possible, which implies some level of competition, the underlying goal is to bring visitors into the district to enjoy all that it has to offer. The health of an individual organization is dependent on the health of the district and by working together they are giving themselves the best chance of survival. As a result, the organizations have created a collaborative environment rather than a competitive one.

Several of SLU's galleries are part of Grand Center, including the Museum of Contemporary Religious Art (MOCRA), the Historic Samuel Couples House, and the Saint Louis University Museum of Art (SLUMA). Regardless of whether The Pozzo Gallery is located on or off campus, it would join their ranks and become part of Grand Center. The gallery would be welcomed to the area by the existing organizations because it reinforces what the district stands for, dedication to the fine arts, and not viewed as competition, an assertion supported by Kenton Christiansen, the VP for Communications and Marketing at Grand Center Inc.

While the prior points illustrate the altruistic environment of the area and the unique nature of competition, another aspect of competition that should be considered, assuming that the gallery is a nonprofit attempting to survive, is the similarity of the surrounding organizations' business focus and product offering to that of the gallery.

The Pozzo Gallery intends to offer reasonably priced paintings, drawings, ceramics and other handmade crafts. Ten Grand Center galleries' offerings and foci were compared against those of the Pozzo Gallery to determine what similarities exist (see table below).

Competitor	Business type*	Focus	Direct competitor
Bruno David Gallery	FP	High end contemporary art	No
Contemporary Art Museum St. Louis	NP	Contemporary all types of media	No
Craft Alliance in Grand Center	NP	Contemporary craft education and craft sales	Yes
Greenberg Van Doren Gallery	FP	High end contemporary art	No
Pace Framing/PSTL Window Gallery	FP	Framing/Photography	No
Portfolio Gallery & Education Center	NP	Education/African-American	No
Pulitzer Foundation for the Arts	NP	Visual, literary and performing arts	No
Schmidt Contemporary Art	FP	High end contemporary art	No
The Arthur and Helen Baer Visual Art Galleries	NP	Part of Centene Center for Arts and Education	No
The Sheldon Art Galleries	NP	Art appreciation and education, acts as a museum	No

*NP = Non profit; FP = For profit

Many of the galleries are educational and do not sell artwork, such as the Contemporary Art Museum, Sheldon Art Galleries, Arthur and Helen Baer Visual Art Galleries, Pulitzer Foundation for the Arts, rather they focus on art appreciation and awareness. The few for profit galleries that do sell artists' work, i.e. Schmidt Contemporary Art, Bruno David Gallery, and Greenberg Van Doren Gallery, are focused on the high end contemporary art pieces of established artists. This is not a product that the gallery will offer, thus diminishing the level of competition between them. The Craft Alliance does sell handmade jewelry and crafts made from fiber, glass, clay, wood and metal. The prices and offerings range tremendously depending on the work and the artist. The Pozzo Gallery will not offer nearly the breadth of products, but there may be a few products that the gallery will offer that the Craft Alliance also does. That may breed some competition; however, the gallery's target audience is SLU alumni, parents, students, and visitors to other businesses in the vicinity. Craft Alliances' products and services are geared toward people who are interested in learning how to create arts and crafts themselves. The Craft Alliance is known as an organization that provides workshops, classes and family programs.

As previously stated the business environment between the galleries, museums and performing arts centers in the area is less competitive than it is collaborative. This unique circumstance will provide a significant benefit to the gallery and will reinforce its competitive advantages.

Competitive advantages that the Pozzo Gallery possesses include the following:

- Close ties to Saint Louis University, in fact it is an extension of it, and can leverage these ties in promotional and marketing efforts. Channels will be available through the University that will enable the gallery to hone in on its target audience more effectively than the other institutions in the area.

- Involvement of passionate students who are investing themselves in this endeavor; therefore, they have the incentive to pursue its success, from a monetary perspective and from an invaluable, real-world educational experience perspective.

- A lock on the source of supply, meaning that the gallery has access to a continuous stream of product from students.

Another perspective on competition could include the competition with other area higher learning institutions that possess a student art gallery. This is not competition in the typical business sense, rather competition in a scholastic sense. The Pozzo Gallery will most likely not compete for sales with these schools' student galleries, even if they did sell regularly sell art; yet, competition exists with them because they offer an educational experience to their students that SLU does not. Students in these schools' art programs have the opportunity to experience the various facets of the art world outside of their classrooms, or studios, on a consistent basis. As a result, these students may be better prepared for art-related careers after they graduate. This could put SLU students at a competitive disadvantage as they try to establish themselves in their fields.

Competition related to institutional recruiting also exists. A hypothetical example of this could be that a local prospective student desires to stay in St. Louis for college and is planning on majoring in studio arts. This student is looking for a program that will best help her realize her dream to become a successful artist. Ignoring other potential factors that may influence her final choice, she will most likely select a program that offers an exciting experience that is not just confined to the studio. Knowing that she can gain exposure, experience and personal connections associated with involvement in a student gallery will probably sway her towards schools that offer this prospect. In this case, the student gallery is a marketing tool for the school. It also sends the message that the school is invested in the fine arts program. Therefore, the gallery factors into the level of institutional competitiveness.

St. Louis college and university student art galleries

Institution	Name	Type	Entity*	Focus**
Washington University	Weitman Gallery	Photography	NC	Students
	Des Lee Gallery	Studio Art	NC	Students
Webster University	Visual Arts Studios	Studio Art	NC	Students
St. Louis Community College	Meramec Contemporary Art Gallery	Studio Art	NC	Students
Fontbonne University	Fontbonne University Gallery of Art's	Studio Art	NC	Students
Lindenwood University	Studio East Gallery	Studio Art	NC	Students
	Studio West Gallery	Studio Art	NC	Students
Maryville University	Morton J. May Foundation Gallery	Studio Art	NC	Students
University of Missouri-St. Louis	Gallery Visio	Studio Art	NC	Students

NC = Non-commercial
**Galleries focus on students, but are also open to alumni, faculty, amateur and professional artists.

Marketing Strategy

The gallery's primary goal is to give students exposure to the business of art. One of the Pozzo Gallery Management Board's tasks is to create a marketing plan for the gallery. A marketing plan is an integral part of business operations, but many people have no experience developing one. As part of the educational experience, students will have the opportunity to create and implement one for the gallery. They will have to decide what may, or may not work, with the available resources. The process must be up to them, if it is going to be a truly educational experience. Students will have guidance from the faculty advisor, but the majority of the plan will be determined by them.

Listed below are some examples of promotional strategies and activities that the gallery may engage in, including:

1. Mini-galleries during events at Chaifetz Arena to create awareness and generate sales

2. Partnerships with restaurants and businesses near SLU and Grand Center that will allow them to display brochures, artwork or with whom the gallery can cosponsor an event. Potential partnerships could include the following businesses and institutions:

- Best Steak House
- Chuy Arzola's
- City Diner at the Fox
- College Church
- Hotel Ignacio
- Jupiter Studios
- KETC/Channel 9
- KOTA Wood Fire Grill
- Loyola Academy

- Nadoz Euro Bakery & Cafe
- Sunrise Chinese Restaurant
- The Bistro at Grand Center
- Continental Life Building
- The Coronado
- The Moto Museum
- Triumph Grill
- University Plaza
- Urban Chestnut Brewing
- Vito's Pizzeria & Ristorante
- Pasta House

3. Partnerships with student organizations for advertising and other promotional activities. Potential partnerships could include the following organizations:

- Student Activities Board
- CEO (Collegiate Entrepreneurs' Organization)
- Ad Club
- KSLU (Student radio station)
- SLU-TV (Student television station)
- Student Government Association
- The University News

4. A website where customers can view new works of art and learn about the artists and the gallery's mission

5. Participation in Midtown Alley events such as the Mid Town Alley Grand Prix and the Midtown Alley Street Fest

6. Participation in Grand Center events such as the Art Walk held annually in May

7. Invitational alumni and local artist exhibitions

8. Gallery membership with monthly e-newsletters and special events

9. Artist bio boards with pictures that are displayed next artist's works that provide insights about themselves and tell a story about how the work came to be

10. Co-hosted events at the gallery with businesses who deal in complimentary products, such as wine

11. "Plein-air" painting contests that are held outside and winners are awarded prizes

12. Campaigns to persuade St. Louis businesses to support local student artists by purchasing and displaying in their offices.

13. Themed-exhibitions featuring SLU or Saint Louis landmarks and venues

The mini-galleries mentioned above, may be a key aspect of the gallery's future operations. Students involved with the gallery would assemble temporary mobile galleries at certain SLU events where they could maximize their exposure and increase awareness of the gallery. At the event, the artists would display a limited number of works on portable folding display panels or individual easels. The motivation behind the mobile gallery is to increase the number of interactions artists have with potential clients. Most likely, sales will occur infrequently; however, the student is gaining exposure, getting practice in selling themselves as an artist, and building a foundation for future sales. These galleries would only be shown at events where they do not take away from the event itself. The mobile mini-gallery's basic schedule would revolve around major events that bring people to campus. Possible events or occasions could include: certain events at the Chaifetz Arena, Homecoming activities, Parents Weekends, and various alumni gatherings. This mobile gallery would be a market expansion because it brings the art to the customer instead of the customer coming to the art.

Business hours are typically a feature of a business' services, but hours are addressed in this section because they will play a role in the gallery's marketing strategy. The hours at the 3331 Locust St. location were based on the perceived prime foot traffic hours, as well as, on the other neighborhood galleries' hours in the area. As for any other location, the same kind of considerations would need to be made in order to determine a schedule for optimal business hours. By ascertaining peak traffic times, for the day and week, and for certain occasions and events, the gallery will be able to utilize its workforce more effectively. Moreover, the hours will be part of the promotional strategy geared towards these target audiences.

Business Hours Example: 3331 Locust St.

Another aspect of the marketing strategy will center on the gallery's business hours. The galleries in the area typically have daytime hours that end at 5:00 or 6:00 P.M, regardless of the day of the week. Tentative hours for the Pozzo Gallery are listed below:

*   Friday: 5:00-10:00 P.M.

*   Saturday: Noon-10:00 P.M

*   Sunday: 11:00 A.M.-4:00 P.M, and

*   Possible extensions on Thursdays for Fox shows and for other special events

The gallery's evening hours will coincide with many nighttime events in the area, especially those held at Fox Theater and Chaifetz Arena, and neighboring restaurant peak hours. Also, the Hotel Ignacio anticipates that the largest number of bookings will be for weekends. A frozen yogurt shop next door to the gallery is expected to open in May and the owners of the establishment anticipate that many of their evening customers will have just attended an event nearby or just dined at one of the nearby restaurants. Overall, this is an advantageous situation for the gallery and it will need to effectively promote to these evening and weekend visitors.

THE ORGANIZATION

Legal Structure

The Pozzo Gallery will fall under Saint Louis University's status as a 501(c)(3) non-profit organization.

Organizational Structure

The ideal structure for this endeavor will be through a course framework. The running and management of the Pozzo Gallery would be an actual course, or a series of courses, offered through the Fine and Performing Arts Department. Initially, the course could be advertised as an independent study taught by Assistant Professor of Studio Art Mark Hefner, M.F.A. The students involved in the course would run all aspects of the gallery. If demand for this course is high, which the survey in the appendix suggests that it is, then the next step would be to offer it as an actual course under the available experimental course number. Another option, if demand is sufficient, is to offer the experimental course first. Eventually, this course could become a prerequisite to another course. The first course may focus on certain aspects of the gallery, while the second focuses on leadership and overall management of the gallery. The course concept can be tailored in any way to meet the needs of the program; nonetheless, arranging the gallery's operations in a course context increases the feasibility of the idea.

The course framework is the best option to ensure student participation because it, at the very least, requires students to be actively involved in the gallery or risk receiving a failing grade. This is not a required class, so students who do register for it already have the desire to be part of the experience; for that reason, motivation and involvement is unlikely to be an issue. Ideally, the course would be open to all students. Any student with an entrepreneurial yearning may see the course as an opportunity to get a taste of running their own business. Eventually, the course could be an elective that counts towards an entrepreneurship major for business students.

While the course approach provides greater organizational stability than a volunteer system, it still faces its own set of hurdles. The main issue is that a fine arts faculty member has to teach the class. Mark Hefner has said he was more than willing to teach the course as an independent study, fully realizing that it would be in addition to his existing course load and that he would not be compensated for the additional work. He is willing to do this unpaid because he believes in the value it could have for students. If gallery is run through the experimental course, then the situation is more complicated. Mr. Hefner indicated that he would handle this course but he already has a full class schedule. He said that the department may need to bring in an adjunct professor to teach one of his classes, which would free him to teach the Pozzo class. The University will most likely have to pay an adjunct to teach the open class per semester.

The gallery will have a relatively unique organizational structure because it is both an educational and business organization. Inside the course framework, the Pozzo Gallery Management Board, consisting of the students who have registered for the class, will guide all aspects of the business. They will devise marketing and operational strategies for the gallery; keep records, run day-to-day operations and establish rules and policies for the staff and customers.

In addition to their strategic roles in the gallery, students will also act as staff, just as most small business owners do. Based on the business hours of the 3331 Locust St. location, only four five-hour shifts per week needed to be filled. Students in the fine arts program typically have two two-hour and forty-five minute classes a week. Besides the five and a half hours spent in the classroom, students have a homework load and are expected to spend time outside of class completing assignments. This class is fundamentally different, but will have similar hour requirements as the standard model, which should be sufficient for staffing the gallery. Since the business hours are somewhat dependent on location, a new venue may alter the business hours which may alter the staffing demand. Of course, more shifts may be required if the gallery begins opening for special events.

Advisory Team

The establishment of an advisory team is still in progress at this time; however, it will provide support and act as a sounding board for the PGMB.

Location

A space for the Pozzo Galley is currently not available. If a space were to open up the following list would serve as a guide to the essential and preferred attributes of a space when considering it for use as a student gallery.

Essential:

- Minimum of three walls where art can be hung

- Ample wall area to display twenty pieces without overcrowding

- Minimum of 460 ft2, which is the size of the 3331 Locust St. location, but preferably over 500 ft2

- High visibility. If located in an internal part of a campus building, the ability to place signage at the main entrance of the building. If off campus, in a higher traffic area with existing businesses, within two blocks of campus

- Access to a small storage area

Preferred:

- Street facing venue for maximum visibility

- A large open space with high ceilings where up to forty pieces could be hung at a time

- If off campus: Within one of campus; close to the Fox Theater

- If on campus: In a high traffic area easily accessible to non-student visitors, such as alumni; close proximity to a parking area

FINANCIALS

Once again, the original location of the gallery will be used as an example to demonstrate the potential revenues and expenses that an art gallery may incur. Depending on the location and other variables, the revenues and expenses may vary. These variations are addressed in the following section along with the example financial projections from the 3331 Locust St. location.

Startup Costs

Startup costs for a gallery depend on the location and whether or not the space needs to be modified to satisfy the gallery's needs. Unfortunately, without knowing the location it is difficult to estimate these costs. Most likely only minor construction, if any, would be needed to make the space gallery-ready. Another cost would be an initial outlay for a promotional budget. These funds would be used to publicize the gallery, send invitations for the grand opening, and purchase advertising, among other things. This is another phenomenal learning opportunity for students because, just as any business owner would, they will have to find the most effective use for their limited resources.

Other costs include mobile phone purchase and wireless service activation fee, which will be used for credit card transactions. Depending on the location, a security deposit may also be required. According to Pat McCarroll, Bush Student Center building manager, BSC requires a deposit equivalent to one month's rent. Monthly rent is dependent on the square footage of the place, so the deposit will vary by venue. Off campus sites may have similar requirements. In the example below, no security deposit was required for the Pozzo Gallery. Also, an off campus locale may require an alarm system for student safety and theft or vandalism prevention. The most likely startup costs that a gallery may incur are the following:

- Remodeling

- Promotional Budget

- Lease Deposit

- Alarm system

- Phone Service

Startup Cost Example: 3331 Locust St.

Startup costs for the gallery include reinforcing the walls that pieces will hang from; purchasing a mobile phone with a data plan in order to run credit cards for purchases; and funding for an initial promotional campaign.

The wall reinforcement will require plywood to be laid over existing drywall which will then be covered by another layer of drywall. This will allow for heavier pieces to be hung and repeated patching of the walls as pieces are switched out. The estimated cost for this is $2,000 and work will be performed by a SLU Facilities Management crew.

At first, only credit cards will be accepted for customer purchases. The simplest and most cost effective method to do this is to purchase a mobile phone with a data plan. The gallery will use the Square transaction application for an Android or iPhone and the free Square credit card reader. Purchasing a refurbished 3GS iPhone and activating the AT&T service will cost a combined one-time charge of $55; this does not include the monthly service fees.

The initial promotional campaign will require funds to print brochures, place ads, purchase an internet domain name, and support other publicity efforts. The amount needed has been estimated at $500.

Estimated startup costs

Construction	$2,000
Phone purchase and activation fee	$ 55
Promotional budget	$ 500
Total startup costs	**$2,555**

Revenues

Art gallery revenues are notoriously difficult to estimate because pieces of art can have a wide range of prices. Students who exhibit their work at the gallery will set their prices, but those prices depend on the size, medium, and perceived demand for each piece—it is not a standardized product. It is nearly impossible to forecast the creations of the artists; thus, it is difficult to set prices and determine revenues. The sales volume is also an uncertainty, as it is with any business, but especially in this situation because the effect of the recent openings of new businesses around the SLU neighborhood is unknown. These businesses will certainly bring visitors to the area, but no data exists yet as to the magnitude of the increase or as to how that might increase sales.

The revenues for the pro forma financial statements in this proposal were developed using sales from past student art shows at Boileau Hall. While not a perfect proxy, it is the best available option that can be used to estimate sales for the Pozzo Gallery. Students displaying in the previous show sold approximately ten pieces of art work over a two-week period. This show is promoted so there is increased awareness while it is occurring. Additionally, the show occurs over a short duration and has an established customer base. So, the approach, being conservative, is to use half of those sales for the Pozzo's monthly sales. Sales of five pieces per month, sixty pieces per year, seem to be a relatively safe number to realize. Naturally, if the gallery sells sixty pieces in a year, the monthly numbers will differ from the average which could affect cash flows.

Another method for estimating sales for the student gallery can be based on the proportion of for-sale works exhibited in the student show and the number of those works that actually sold. This year's Boileau show featured approximately forty-five two dimensional pieces for sale. Some artists opted to display, but not to sell their works in the exhibition. Sales data is not yet available for this show; however, assuming that the number of pieces sold this year is identical to the number sold last year, which was ten, then the ratio of works sold to works displayed is 1 to 4.5 over the duration of the show. Depending on the size of the work, the gallery on Locust could display eighteen to twenty-two pieces without appearing overly cramped. Applying the proportion from the Boileau show to the proposed gallery would result in an estimate of four to five pieces being sold. Instead of this occurring over a two-week period, the sales for the Pozzo Gallery would be stretched out over a month—a conservative, yet, realistic assumption. Consequently, this figure is similar to the figure derived before from the Boileau rate of sales over time.

The following analysis stems from the original gallery location and is useful to illustrate the effect costs and revenues have on the gallery's potential profitability.

Profitability Example: 3331 Locust St.

Although revenues calculations are challenging a breakeven analysis can be run because the fixed and variable costs are known. The analysis identified the amount of revenues needed to breakeven in the first year are $53,140. This figure includes the startup costs mentioned earlier and monthly sales of five works at $100 per piece of work. The breakeven point excluding the startup costs is $47,733. While some of the pricing assumptions may change in year two and three, it is expected that the gallery will need to generate about approximately $48,300 per year for each of those two years to break even. This analysis assumes that all expenses are hard dollar costs that are paid to parties outside of the University; however, in reality the gallery would be using SLU services, thus, SLU would effectively be paying itself. In this scenario certain operating expenses drop off, including lease, insurance and security, leaving only the expenses paid to third parties other than SLU. Using the same startup costs and revenue forecasts as before, but excluding expenses paid to SLU, the breakeven figures drop dramatically to $13,425. If startup costs are excluded in the calculation that number falls to $8,017. Assuming slight cost increases in years two and three, the breakeven point is around $8,500 for each year. (Financial statements are provided at the end of the financial section)

Breakeven analysis

ASSUMING ALL EXPENSES ARE HARD DOLLAR COSTS

		Breakeven revenues
Variable costs	52.75%	
Fixed costs including startup	$25,109	$53,140
Fixed costs excluding startup	$22,554	$47,733

ASSUMING EXPENSES PAID TO SLU ARE NOT HARD DOLLAR COSTS

		Breakeven revenues
Variable costs	52.75%	
Fixed costs including startup	$6,343	$13,425
Fixed costs excluding startup	$3,788	$ 8,017

Please Note: The financial statements and figures are illustrative of a specific location. Analysis of a different location requires new estimates for expenses.

Since the average monthly prices and sales are difficult to estimate, the charts on the following page provide a graphical illustration of the ranges of yearly profits that result from various average monthly prices and volumes.

Pozzo gallery profit matrix

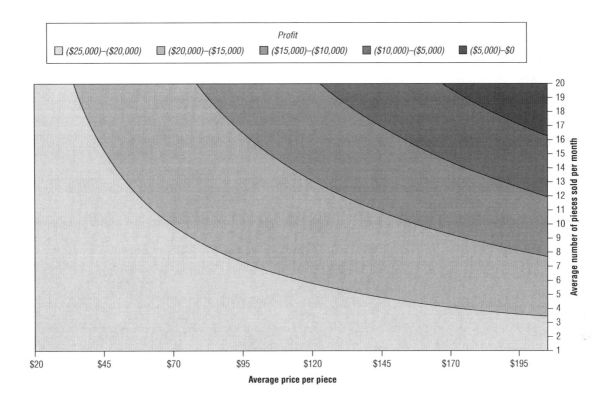

Pozzo gallery profit matrix (no payments to SLU)

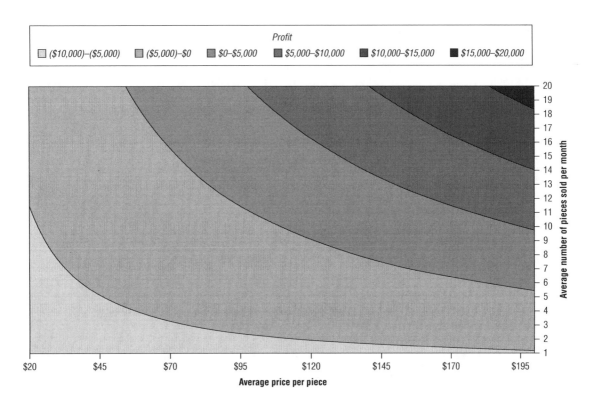

Variable Costs

Variable costs for the gallery include the artist's commission, which is 50% of the sale price, and the Square service transaction fee of 2.75% of the sale price. These costs are not dependent on location.

Fixed Costs

Lease

Lease year	$/ft²	Lease expense	
		Annual	Monthly
1	$10.00	$4,600	$383.33
2	$10.00	$4,600	$383.33
3	$10.75	$4,945	$412.08
4	$11.25	$5,175	$431.25
5	$11.25	$5,175	$431.25
6	$11.75	$5,405	$450.42

Total square footage: 460

- Lease rate for 3331 Locust St.

- In above table, rate increases are based on forecasted increase in lease rates and building costs.

- Rates for space in the BSC are $12.50 per square foot per year, this rate is comparable to most on campus venues.

- BSC requires a security deposit equivalent to one month's rent, which is dependent on square footage of the space.

Building Improvements

- For 3331 Locust St. are not anticipated for the first year because of the work that will be performed prior to the gallery opening.

- Depending on the location improvement may be required.

Utilities

- Previous data on utility usage for the space is unavailable, so the monthly expense is estimated at $100 per month. The gallery is illuminated by LED lights which require a relatively small amount of electricity. The majority utility usage, and expenses, will occur during business hours.

- Utilities are included in the BSC lease rate.

Hardware Supplies

- Light maintenance and cleaning supplies that the gallery will need to have on site, including: material and tools to patch walls; paint to touch up patched areas; hardware for picture hanging; tools to hang works; and cleaning supplies. The cost for these supplies is estimated at $25 per month.

Marketing

- A preliminary budget has been set at $100 per month for the first year; this budget is separate from the initial startup funds of $500.

Insurance

- For 3331 Locust St., liability insurance for the business is estimated to be $85 per month through a third party insurance provider, this includes a rider insuring the artwork.

- Depending on the location a plate glass rider may need to be attached to the policy. Annual premium rate is $1.80/sq. ft. for single pane; annual premium rate is $2.60/sq. ft. for double pane.

- The University does self-insure, so technically there would be no cost for insuring the gallery if he gallery is located on SLU property.

Mobile Phone Service

- AT&T mobile phone service with data plan and taxes will cost approximately $62 per month.

Security

- For 3331 Locust St., student safety is paramount, so during evening hours when the gallery is open DPSSS will post an officer at that location. The cost DPSSS security is $22 per hour; the gallery is anticipated to be open approximately 10 hours per week resulting in a monthly cost of $880. During daytime hours DPSSS has offered to increase patrols in the area.

- If the gallery is located off campus, but in a SLU building a similar security plan may be need.

- DPSSS services are only available on SLU-owned property and a gallery hosted on a non-SLU property would require an hiring an outside security service.

- A location on campus would not require hiring security for regular business hours.

- An alarm system may also be required depending on setting of an off campus location.

Unforeseen Expenses

- Many of gallery's costs have been identified and estimated conservatively; however, not every expense or situation can be anticipated so a contingency expense of 10% of operating expenses has been built in.

Capital Requirements

The capital requirements are based on the analysis for the 3331 Locust St. Location and funding needs may change based on a different location.

Capital Requirements Example: 3331 Locust St.

The gallery will require startup funds of approximately $2,500. In addition, cash flow at the end of year one is expected to be negative $22,274. Assuming the gallery is able to sell an average of five works per month at an average price of $100; the average monthly cash flow will be approximately negative $1,643. The figures listed above are based on averages, some months may be have higher sales than others; therefore, working capital requirements may also fluctuate. The difficulty in predicting price and volume also makes determining cash flow needs difficult. For the first year the gallery will require around $22,500 from the University. In years two and three, assuming that revenues and expenses stay roughly the same, the gallery would require a subsidy of $19,719 from the school. Ideally, these subsidies would be provided at the beginning of the gallery's fiscal year.

The above figures include all expenses as outlays; however, the services provided by SLU will not be hard dollar costs. In that case, the gallery would still need $2,500 in startup funds. Using the same revenue assumptions, cash flow at the end of year one would be negative $3,508. Cash flows for years two and three would be around negative $950, respectively.

Assuming all expenses are hard dollar costs

Cash flow statement	Includes startup costs			Excludes startup costs		
	Year			Year		
	1	2	3	1	2	3
Beginning cash	($ 2,555)	($22,274)	($41,993)	$ 0	($19,719)	($39,438)
Net income	($19,719)	($19,719)	($19,719)	($19,719)	($19,719)	($19,719)
Ending cash	($22,274)	($41,993)	($61,711)	($19,719)	($39,438)	($59,156)

Assuming expenses paid to SLU are not hard dollar costs

Cash flow statement	Includes startup costs			Excludes startup costs		
	Year			Year		
	1	2	3	1	2	3
Beginning cash	($2,555)	($3,508)	($4,462)	$ 0	($ 953)	($1,907)
Net income	($ 953)	($ 953)	($ 953)	($953)	($ 953)	($ 953)
Ending cash	($3,508)	($4,462)	($5,415)	($953)	($1,907)	($2,860)

Startup costs are estimated at $2,555.
Revenues are calculated assuming an average sales of five $100 pieces per month.

The potential to raise capital by other means also exists. One possibility is renting the space out for events or meetings for small groups. Another possibility is a donation campaign designed and run by the PGMB, which would target alumni and other art supporters. These activities would give students the experience of raising money for a commercial or nonprofit gallery and would lessen University's subsidy of the gallery.

While the gallery may not be attractive from a business perspective, the Pozzo Gallery does provide significant benefits to students, Saint Louis University and the community that offset the financial requirements. PGMB's ultimate goal is to develop and implement an overall strategy that will make it self-sustaining.

Pozzo gallery financial statements

Income statement	Month						
	1	2	3	4	5	6	7
Revenues*							
Number of works sold	5	5	5	5	5	5	5
Average price	$ 100	$ 100	$ 100	$ 100	$ 100	$ 100	$ 100
Sales revenue	$ 500	$ 500	$ 500	$ 500	$ 500	$ 500	$ 500
Artist commission (50%)	($ 250)	($ 250)	($ 250)	($ 250)	($ 250)	($ 250)	($ 250)
Square transaction fee (2.75%)	($ 14)	($ 14)	($ 14)	($ 14)	($ 14)	($ 14)	($ 14)
Gross margin	**$ 236**	**$ 236**	**$ 236**	**$ 236**	**$ 236**	**$ 236**	**$ 236**
Operating expenses							
Lease	$ 383	$ 383	$ 383	$ 383	$ 383	$ 383	$ 383
Building improvements	$ 0	$ 0	$ 0	$ 0	$ 0	$ 0	$ 0
Utilities	$ 100	$ 100	$ 100	$ 100	$ 100	$ 100	$ 100
Hardware supplies	$ 25	$ 25	$ 25	$ 25	$ 25	$ 25	$ 25
Marketing	$ 100	$ 100	$ 100	$ 100	$ 100	$ 100	$ 100
Insurance	$ 85	$ 85	$ 85	$ 85	$ 85	$ 85	$ 85
Mobile phone service	$ 62	$ 62	$ 62	$ 62	$ 62	$ 62	$ 62
Security**	$ 953	$ 953	$ 953	$ 953	$ 953	$ 953	$ 953
Unforeseen expense (10% of op exp)	$ 171	$ 171	$ 171	$ 171	$ 171	$ 171	$ 171
Total operating expenses	**$1,879**	**$1,879**	**$1,879**	**$1,879**	**$1,879**	**$1,879**	**$1,879**
Net income	**($1,643)**	**($1,643)**	**($1,643)**	**($1,643)**	**($1,643)**	**($1,643)**	**($1,643)**

Cash flow statement	Month						
	1	2	3	4	5	6	7
Beginning cash	($2,555)	($4,198)	($5,841)	($7,485)	($ 9,128)	($10,771)	($12,414)
Net income	($1,643)	($1,643)	($1,643)	($1,643)	($ 1,643)	($ 1,643)	($ 1,643)
Ending cash	($4,198)	($5,841)	($7,485)	($9,128)	($10,771)	($12,414)	($14,058)

Startup expenses prior to opening	
Building improvements	$2,000
Phone and activation	$ 55
Marketing	$ 500
Total	**$2,555**

		Breakeven revenues
Variable costs	52.75%	
Fixed costs including startup	$25,109	$53,140
Fixed costs excluding startup	$22,554	$47,733

Pozzo gallery financial statements (cont.)

Income statement	Month					Year one total
	8	9	10	11	12	
Revenues*						
Number of works sold	5	5	5	5	5	60
Average price	$ 100	$ 100	$ 100	$ 100	$ 100	—
Sales revenue	$ 500	$ 500	$ 500	$ 500	$ 500	$ 6,000
Artist commission (50%)	($ 250)	($ 250)	($ 250)	($ 250)	($ 250)	($ 3,000)
Square transaction fee (2.75%)	($ 14)	($ 14)	($ 14)	($ 14)	($ 14)	($ 165)
Gross margin	**$ 236**	**$ 236**	**$ 236**	**$ 236**	**$ 236**	**$ 2,835**
Operating expenses						
Lease	$ 383	$ 383	$ 383	$ 383	$ 383	$ 4,600
Building improvements	$ 0	$ 0	$ 0	$ 0	$ 0	$ 0
Utilities	$ 100	$ 100	$ 100	$ 100	$ 100	$ 1,200
Hardware supplies	$ 25	$ 25	$ 25	$ 25	$ 25	$ 300
Marketing	$ 100	$ 100	$ 100	$ 100	$ 100	$ 1,200
Insurance	$ 85	$ 85	$ 85	$ 85	$ 85	$ 1,020
Mobile phone service	$ 62	$ 62	$ 62	$ 62	$ 62	$ 744
Security**	$ 953	$ 953	$ 953	$ 953	$ 953	$11,440
Unforeseen expense (10% of op exp)	$ 171	$ 171	$ 171	$ 171	$ 171	$ 2,050
Total operating expenses	**$1,879**	**$1,879**	**$1,879**	**$1,879**	**$1,879**	**$22,554**
Net income	**($1,643)**	**($1,643)**	**($1,643)**	**($1,643)**	**($1,643)**	**($19,719)**

Cash flow statement	Month					Year one total
	8	9	10	11	12	
Beginning cash	($14,058)	($15,701)	($17,344)	($18,987)	($20,631)	($20,631)
Net income	($ 1,643)	($ 1,643)	($ 1,643)	($ 1,643)	($ 1,643)	($ 1,643)
Ending cash	($15,701)	($17,344)	($18,987)	($20,631)	($22,274)	($22,274)

*For illustrative purposes, gallery revenues are calculated assuming an average sales of five pieces per month at an average price of $100.

**Security provided by DPSSS at an average of 10 hours per week and rate of $22 per hour. Annual expense is estimated at $11,440, or $953 per month.

Pozzo gallery financial statements

Assumes services provided through SLU are not hard dollar outlays.

Income statement	Month 1	2	3	4	5	6	7
Revenues*							
Number of works sold	5	5	5	5	5	5	5
Average price	$100	$100	$100	$100	$100	$100	$100
Sales revenue	$500	$500	$500	$500	$500	$500	$500
Artist commission (50%)	($250)	($250)	($250)	($250)	($250)	($250)	($250)
Square transaction fee (2.75%)	($ 14)	($ 14)	($ 14)	($ 14)	($ 14)	($ 14)	($ 14)
Gross margin	**$236**	**$236**	**$236**	**$236**	**$236**	**$236**	**$236**
Operating expenses							
Lease	$ 0	$ 0	$ 0	$ 0	$ 0	$ 0	$ 0
Building improvements	$ 0	$ 0	$ 0	$ 0	$ 0	$ 0	$ 0
Utilities	$100	$100	$100	$100	$100	$100	$100
Hardware supplies	$ 25	$ 25	$ 25	$ 25	$ 25	$ 25	$ 25
Marketing	$100	$100	$100	$100	$100	$100	$100
Insurance	$ 0	$ 0	$ 0	$ 0	$ 0	$ 0	$ 0
Mobile phone service	$ 62	$ 62	$ 62	$ 62	$ 62	$ 62	$ 62
Security**	$ 0	$ 0	$ 0	$ 0	$ 0	$ 0	$ 0
Unforeseen expense (10% of op exp)	$ 29	$ 29	$ 29	$ 29	$ 29	$ 29	$ 29
Total operating expenses	**$316**	**$316**	**$316**	**$316**	**$316**	**$316**	**$316**
Net income	**($ 79)**	**($ 79)**	**($ 79)**	**($ 79)**	**($ 79)**	**($ 79)**	**($ 79)**

Cash flow statement	Month 1	2	3	4	5	6	7
Beginning cash	($2,555)	($2,634)	($2,714)	($2,793)	($2,873)	($2,952)	($3,032)
Net income	($ 79)	($ 79)	($ 79)	($ 79)	($ 79)	($ 79)	($ 79)
Ending cash	($2,634)	($2,714)	($2,793)	($2,873)	($2,952)	($3,032)	($3,111)

Startup expenses prior to opening	
Building improvements	$2,000
Phone and activation	$ 55
Marketing	$ 500
Total	**$2,555**

		Breakeven revenues
Variable costs	52.75%	
Fixed costs including startup	$6,343	$13,425
Fixed costs excluding startup	$3,788	$ 8,017

Pozzo gallery financial statements (cont.)

Assumes services provided through SLU are not hard dollar outlays.

	Month					Year one
Income statement	8	9	10	11	12	total
Revenues*						
Number of works sold	5	5	5	5	5	60
Average price	$100	$100	$100	$100	$100	—
Sales revenue	$500	$500	$500	$500	$500	$6,000
Artist commission (50%)	($250)	($250)	($250)	($250)	($250)	$3,000
Square transaction fee (2.75%)	($ 14)	($ 14)	($ 14)	($ 14)	($ 14)	($ 165)
Gross margin	**$236**	**$236**	**$236**	**$236**	**$236**	**$2,835**
Operating expenses						
Lease	$ 0	$ 0	$ 0	$ 0	$ 0	$ 0
Building improvements	$ 0	$ 0	$ 0	$ 0	$ 0	$ 0
Utilities	$100	$100	$100	$100	$100	$1,200
Hardware supplies	$ 25	$ 25	$ 25	$ 25	$ 25	$ 300
Marketing	$100	$100	$100	$100	$100	$1,200
Insurance	$ 0	$ 0	$ 0	$ 0	$ 0	$ 0
Mobile phone service	$ 62	$ 62	$ 62	$ 62	$ 62	$ 744
Security**	$ 0	$ 0	$ 0	$ 0	$ 0	$ 0
Unforeseen expense (10% of op exp)	$ 29	$ 29	$ 29	$ 29	$ 29	$ 344
Total operating expenses	**$316**	**$316**	**$316**	**$316**	**$316**	**$3,788**
Net income	**($ 79)**	**($ 79)**	**($ 79)**	**($ 79)**	**($ 79)**	**($ 953)**

	Month					Year one
Cash flow statement	8	9	10	11	12	total
Beginning cash	($3,111)	($3,191)	($3,270)	($3,349)	($3,429)	($3,429)
Net income	($ 79)	($ 79)	($ 79)	($ 79)	($ 79)	($ 79)
Ending cash	($3,191)	($3,270)	($3,349)	($3,429)	($3,508)	($3,508)

*For illustrative purposes, gallery revenues are calculated assuming an average sales of five pieces per month at an average price of $100.
**Security provided by DPSSS at an average of 10 hours per week and rate of $22 per hour. Annual expense is estimated at $11,440, or $953 per month.

Pozzo gallery financial statements (no revenues)

Income statement	Month						
	1	2	3	4	5	6	7
Revenues*							
Number of works sold	0	0	0	0	0	0	0
Average price	$ 100	$ 100	$ 100	$ 100	$ 100	$ 100	$ 100
Sales revenue	$ 0	$ 0	$ 0	$ 0	$ 0	$ 0	$ 0
Artist commission (50%)	$ 0	$ 0	$ 0	$ 0	$ 0	$ 0	$ 0
Square transaction fee (2.75%)	$ 0	$ 0	$ 0	$ 0	$ 0	$ 0	$ 0
Gross margin	**$ 0**	**$ 0**	**$ 0**	**$ 0**	**$ 0**	**$ 0**	**$ 0**
Operating expenses							
Lease	$ 383	$ 383	$ 383	$ 383	$ 383	$ 383	$ 383
Building improvements	$ 0	$ 0	$ 0	$ 0	$ 0	$ 0	$ 0
Utilities	$ 100	$ 100	$ 100	$ 100	$ 100	$ 100	$ 100
Hardware supplies	$ 25	$ 25	$ 25	$ 25	$ 25	$ 25	$ 25
Marketing	$ 100	$ 100	$ 100	$ 100	$ 100	$ 100	$ 100
Insurance	$ 85	$ 85	$ 85	$ 85	$ 85	$ 85	$ 85
Mobile phone service	$ 62	$ 62	$ 62	$ 62	$ 62	$ 62	$ 62
Security**	$ 953	$ 953	$ 953	$ 953	$ 953	$ 953	$ 953
Unforeseen expense (10% of op exp)	$ 171	$ 171	$ 171	$ 171	$ 171	$ 171	$ 171
Total operating expenses	**$1,879**	**$1,879**	**$1,879**	**$1,879**	**$1,879**	**$1,879**	**$1,879**
Net income	**($1,879)**	**($1,879)**	**($1,879)**	**($1,879)**	**($1,879)**	**($1,879)**	**($1,879)**

Cash flow statement	Month						
	1	2	3	4	5	6	7
Beginning cash	($2,555)	($4,434)	($6,314)	($ 8,193)	($10,073)	($11,952)	($13,832)
Net income	($1,879)	($1,879)	($1,879)	($ 1,879)	($ 1,879)	($ 1,879)	($ 1,879)
Ending cash	($4,434)	($6,314)	($8,193)	($10,073)	($11,952)	($13,832)	($15,711)

Startup expenses prior to opening	
Building improvements	$2,000
Phone and activation	$ 55
Marketing	$ 500
Total	**$2,555**

		Breakeven revenues
Variable costs	52.75%	
Fixed costs including startup	$25,109	$53,140
Fixed costs excluding startup	$22,554	$47,733

Pozzo gallery financial statements (no revenues cont.)

Income statement	Month					Year one total
	8	9	10	11	12	
Revenues*						
Number of works sold	0	0	0	0	0	0
Average price	$ 100	$ 100	$ 100	$ 100	$ 100	—
Sales revenue	$ 0	$ 0	$ 0	$ 0	$ 0	$ 0
Artist commission (50%)	$ 0	$ 0	$ 0	$ 0	$ 0	$ 0
Square transaction fee (2.75%)	$ 0	$ 0	$ 0	$ 0	$ 0	$ 0
Gross margin	**$ 0**	**$ 0**	**$ 0**	**$ 0**	**$ 0**	**$ 0**
Operating expenses						
Lease	$ 383	$ 383	$ 383	$ 383	$ 383	$ 4,600
Building improvements	$ 0	$ 0	$ 0	$ 0	$ 0	$ 0
Utilities	$ 100	$ 100	$ 100	$ 100	$ 100	$ 1,200
Hardware supplies	$ 25	$ 25	$ 25	$ 25	$ 25	$ 300
Marketing	$ 100	$ 100	$ 100	$ 100	$ 100	$ 1,200
Insurance	$ 85	$ 85	$ 85	$ 85	$ 85	$ 1,020
Mobile phone service	$ 62	$ 62	$ 62	$ 62	$ 62	$ 744
Security**	$ 953	$ 953	$ 953	$ 953	$ 953	$11,440
Unforeseen expense (10% of op exp)	$ 171	$ 171	$ 171	$ 171	$ 171	$ 2,050
Total operating expenses	**$1,879**	**$1,879**	**$1,879**	**$1,879**	**$1,879**	**$22,554**
Net income	**($1,879)**	**($1,879)**	**($1,879)**	**($1,879)**	**($1,879)**	**($22,554)**

Cash flow statement	Month					Year one total
	8	9	10	11	12	
Beginning cash	($15,711)	($17,591)	($19,470)	($21,350)	($23,229)	($23,229)
Net income	($ 1,879)	($ 1,879)	($ 1,879)	($ 1,879)	($ 1,879)	($ 1,879)
Ending cash	($17,591)	($19,470)	($21,350)	($23,229)	($25,109)	($25,109)

*For illustrative purposes, gallery revenues are calculated assuming an average sales of five pieces per month at an average price of $100.
**Security provided by DPSSS at an average of 10 hours per week and rate of $22 per hour. Annual expense is estimated at $11,440, or $953 per month.

Pozzo gallery financial statements (no revenues)

Assumes services provided through SLU are not hard dollar outlays.

				Month			
Income statement	1	2	3	4	5	6	7
Revenues*							
Number of works sold	0	0	0	0	0	0	0
Average price	$100	$100	$100	$100	$100	$100	$100
Sales revenue	$ 0	$ 0	$ 0	$ 0	$ 0	$ 0	$ 0
Artist commission (50%)	$ 0	$ 0	$ 0	$ 0	$ 0	$ 0	$ 0
Square transaction fee (2.75%)	$ 0	$ 0	$ 0	$ 0	$ 0	$ 0	$ 0
Gross margin	**$ 0**	**$ 0**	**$ 0**	**$ 0**	**$ 0**	**$ 0**	**$ 0**
Operating expenses							
Lease	$ 0	$ 0	$ 0	$ 0	$ 0	$ 0	$ 0
Building improvements	$ 0	$ 0	$ 0	$ 0	$ 0	$ 0	$ 0
Utilities	$100	$100	$100	$100	$100	$100	$100
Hardware supplies	$ 25	$ 25	$ 25	$ 25	$ 25	$ 25	$ 25
Marketing	$100	$100	$100	$100	$100	$100	$100
Insurance	$ 0	$ 0	$ 0	$ 0	$ 0	$ 0	$ 0
Mobile phone service	$ 62	$ 62	$ 62	$ 62	$ 62	$ 62	$ 62
Security**	$ 0	$ 0	$ 0	$ 0	$ 0	$ 0	$ 0
Unforeseen expense (10% of op exp)	$ 29	$ 29	$ 29	$ 29	$ 29	$ 29	$ 29
Total operating expenses	**$316**	**$316**	**$316**	**$316**	**$316**	**$316**	**$316**
Net income	**($316)**	**($316)**	**($316)**	**($316)**	**($316)**	**($316)**	**($316)**

				Month			
Cash flow statement	1	2	3	4	5	6	7
Beginning cash	($2,555)	($2,871)	($3,186)	($3,502)	($3,818)	($4,133)	($4,449)
Net income	($ 316)	($ 316)	($ 316)	($ 316)	($ 316)	($ 316)	($ 316)
Ending cash	($2,871)	($3,186)	($3,502)	($3,818)	($4,133)	($4,449)	($4,765)

Startup expenses prior to opening					Breakeven revenues
Building improvements	$2,000		Variable costs	52.75%	
Phone and activation	$ 55		Fixed costs including startup	$6,343	$13,425
Marketing	$ 500		Fixed costs excluding startup	$3,788	$ 8,017
Total	**$2,555**				

Pozzo gallery financial statements (no revenues cont.)

Assumes services provided through SLU are not hard dollar outlays.

			Month			Year one
Income statement	8	9	10	11	12	total
Revenues*						
Number of works sold	0	0	0	0	0	0
Average price	$100	$100	$100	$100	$100	—
Sales revenue	$ 0	$ 0	$ 0	$ 0	$ 0	$ 0
Artist commission (50%)	$ 0	$ 0	$ 0	$ 0	$ 0	$ 0
Square transaction fee (2.75%)	$ 0	$ 0	$ 0	$ 0	$ 0	$ 0
Gross margin	**$ 0**	**$ 0**	**$ 0**	**$ 0**	**$ 0**	**$ 0**
Operating expenses						
Lease	$ 0	$ 0	$ 0	$ 0	$ 0	$ 0
Building improvements	$ 0	$ 0	$ 0	$ 0	$ 0	$ 0
Utilities	$100	$100	$100	$100	$100	$1,200
Hardware supplies	$ 25	$ 25	$ 25	$ 25	$ 25	$ 300
Marketing	$100	$100	$100	$100	$100	$1,200
Insurance	$ 0	$ 0	$ 0	$ 0	$ 0	$ 0
Mobile phone service	$ 62	$ 62	$ 62	$ 62	$ 62	$ 744
Security**	$ 0	$ 0	$ 0	$ 0	$ 0	$ 0
Unforeseen expense (10% of op exp)	$ 29	$ 29	$ 29	$ 29	$ 29	$ 344
Total operating expenses	**$316**	**$316**	**$316**	**$316**	**$316**	**$3,788**
Net income	**($316)**	**($316)**	**($316)**	**($316)**	**($316)**	**($3,788)**

			Month			Year one
Cash flow statement	8	9	10	11	12	total
Beginning cash	($4,765)	($5,081)	($5,396)	($5,712)	($6,028)	($6,028)
Net income	($ 316)	($ 316)	($ 316)	($ 316)	($ 316)	($ 316)
Ending cash	($5,081)	($5,396)	($5,712)	($6,028)	($6,343)	($6,343)

*For illustrative purposes, gallery revenues are calculated assuming an average sales of five pieces per month at an average price of $100.
**Security provided by DPSSS at an average of 10 hours per week and rate of $22 per hour. Annual expense is estimated at $11,440, or $953 per month.

FUTURE DIRECTIONS AND GROWTH

Many factors will determine the possible paths the gallery will take and when these variables are known a more detailed roadmap can established. However, future directions and growth opportunities for a student gallery could include:

- Creating a mobile mini-gallery that could be set up around campus for specific events

- Exhibiting alumni and local artists' works to increase community involvement with the gallery

- Renting out the gallery for private events

- Establishing a satellite gallery at SLU's Madrid campus

Tattoo Studio/Art Gallery

LivingArts Inc.

2159 Summit Ave.
Spokane, WA 99201

Paul Greenland

LivingArts Inc. is a tattoo studio that differentiates itself from the competition by doubling as an art gallery.

EXECUTIVE SUMMARY

After graduating from Brighton Art Academy in Minneapolis, Brian Thompson pursued a career in the commercial sector. For 10 years he has made his mark in two ways: producing and selling original works of traditional art, and working as a graphic designer for a large advertising agency in St. Paul. When his agency was acquired by another firm one year ago, Thompson found himself out of work for the first time in a decade. However, as is often the case, a new opportunity emerged in the midst of these difficult circumstances.

During college, Thompson worked as an apprentice in a Minneapolis tattoo parlor, learning the trade from an artist who had studied in Japan and produced unique designs that were unlike any other in the city. After several conversations with his former mentor, Thompson has decided to establish his own tattoo studio in his hometown of Spokane, Washington, which also will double as an art gallery with other unique offerings. This will allow him to leverage his traditional art skills in a market with great economic potential.

Although he will perform some tattooing, Thompson's primary responsibility will be managing and growing the business, producing/selling works of original art, and developing tattoo designs for clients. He will be joined in the business by two independent tattoo artists (Tom "Lefty" Harris and Lindsay Greene), who will bring a unique blend of skill and experience to LivingArts.

MARKET ANALYSIS

Over the last decade, a number of revitalization efforts have taken place in downtown Spokane. By the mid-2000s many young people and well-funded baby boomers began relocating to former industrial spaces and historic buildings that had been converted to apartments, condominiums, and lofts. According to data from *DemographicsNow*, the larger Spokane area was home to 1.12 million people in 2010. By 2015 this figure was projected to reach 1.19 million.

The local market has shown an affinity for tattoo establishments in recent years. In June of 2006 the *Spokesman-Review* reported that the number of tattoo parlors increased 77 percent between 1995 and 2005 in Spokane. Likewise, retail sales from these establishments increased 550 percent during the same time period, climbing to $1.3 million. The local market continued to grow during the second half of the decade, and by mid-2011 there were more than 30 tattoo establishments in Spokane. These establishments catered to a wide spectrum of customers, hailing from a variety of age, ethnic, and demographic groups.

Competition

LivingArts Inc. will face competition from the following establishments:

- Screamin Ink Tattoos & Piercing

- Living Skin Tattoo

- Sweet Ink Tattoo

- Rage Studios

- 509 Tattoo Shop

- All American Tattoo

- Barking Dog Tattooz

- Bird's Eye Tattoo

- Boar Head Tattoo Parlor

- Body Grafix Tattoo Studio

- Body Language Tattoo

- Bulletproof Tattoo

- Dark Arts Tattoo Studio

- Ghost Writer Ink

- Jade Dragon Custom Tattoo

- Lady Bug Tattoo

- Lady Luck Tattoo

- Northstar Tattoos

- Rage Studios LLC

- R Tattoo

- Self Expression Body Art Studio

- Shamrock Tattoo

- Skin Candy Tattooing & Piercing

- Sweet Ink Tattoo

- Tattoo Room

- Tattoos by DJ

- Tattoos by Jim

- The Missing Piece LLC

- Tiger Tattoo North

- Wicked Needles Inc.

Differentials

Many tattoo parlors advertise their services with neon lights and sell typical stencil-based tattoos. However, LivingArts will differentiate itself from the competition by serving as a unique destination with broad appeal. Located in a renovated storefront in downtown Spokane, Thompson's establishment will host live acoustic entertainment, wine and beer tastings, and showings that will include his own drawings and paintings, as well as the works of other area artists.

INDUSTRY BACKGROUND

Some consider tattoos to be the world's oldest art form, with evidence of their use dating back to the Egyptians and the Nubians in 2000 BC. The explorer James Cook mentioned them in his notes regarding a South Pacific expedition in 1769. According to a September 6, 2010, article on Basilandspice.com, Samuel O'Reily is credited with pioneering the technique of producing tattoos with electricity, via the development of the electric tattoo machine. In the United States some sources indicate that, at first, tattoos were mainly limited to wealthy individuals. The arrival of Japanese tattoo artists helped increase the popularity of tattooing, and by the early 20th century they had become common among the mass population. According to an October 2010 *Dermatology Times* article, 6 percent of Americans had a tattoo in 1936, based on an estimate from *Life* magazine.

By the 1990s tattoos had become more mainstream. Shedding their "outlaw" image, it became increasingly common for professionals, housewives, and even grandparents to get tattoos. Estimates regarding the number of Americans with tattoos during the early 21st century have varied. For example, a June 14, 2006, article in the *Spokesman-Review* cited research from the *Journal of the American Academy of Dermatology* which found that, in the 18-50 age group, approximately 25 percent of individuals had a tattoo. Commentary regarding this study from industry players found that, in many markets, this figure is actually estimated to be much higher (in the neighborhood of 66%). A 2008 Harris poll estimated that only 15 percent of Americans had a tattoo.

Regardless of the data, one thing is clear: tattoos are more accepted and popular than ever before. Their popularity is evident by major related events, such as the Ninth Boston Tattoo Convention held in September 2010. In addition, reality television programs such as TLC's "LA Ink" and "Miami Ink" have been well received. The network planned to introduce a New York-based spinoff of the program in mid-2011.

PERSONNEL

Brian Thompson (owner/manager)

A native of Spokane, Washington, Brian Thompson has had an affinity for art since he was a child. During elementary school, his parents and teachers began recognizing that he had both unusual and exceptional artistic abilities. This eventually resulted in a full scholarship to the Brighton Art Academy in Minneapolis, followed by a successful 10-year career in the commercial arts sector.

Over the last decade, Thompson has made his mark in two ways: producing and selling original works of traditional art, and working as a graphic designer for Webster & Pratt, a large advertising agency in St. Paul. When his agency was acquired by another firm one year ago, Thompson found himself out of work for the first time. However, as is often the case, a new opportunity emerged in the midst of these difficult circumstances.

During college, Thompson worked as an apprentice in a Minneapolis tattoo parlor, learning the trade from an artist who had studied in Japan and produced unique designs that were unlike any other in the city. After several conversations with his former mentor, Thompson has decided to establish his own tattoo studio, which also will double as an art gallery with other unique offerings. This will allow him to leverage his traditional art skills in a market with great economic potential.

Thompson knows that it takes more than artistic ability to run a successful business. After working at Webster & Pratt for four years, he was promoted to the role of lead designer because of his leadership and teambuilding skills. Through exceptional teamwork, Thompson's design team developed a reputation for creative excellence and efficiency, doing whatever it took to turn around concepts for clients. During Thompson's fifth year with the agency, he was named manager of the art department. Webster & Pratt provided him with basic management training in areas such as budgeting and human resources management.

Brian Thompson has always had an entrepreneurial spirit. Although he once considered establishing his own advertising agency, and has diligently saved money in support of that plan (see Financial Analysis section), he is energized about the creative and economic potential of LivingArts, along with the ability to return to his hometown when he can be closer to family. Although he will perform some tattooing, Brian's primary responsibility will be managing and growing the business, producing/selling works of original art, and developing tattoo designs for clients.

Independent Contractors

In addition to Thompson, LivingArts' initial location will have space for two additional artists. After careful consideration, the following independent contractors have agreed to rent space within the business:

Tom "Lefty" Harris—Lefty has been tattooing for 25 years. He has worked at tattoo parlors in Chicago, Las Vegas, and Los Angeles. Lefty will be relocating to Spokane from California in one month. His artwork will further differentiate LivingArts from the competition, and he will serve as an excellent resource for Brian Thompson and Lindsay Greene.

Lindsay Greene—Lindsay learned about LivingArts from Stanley Hawk, Brian Thompson's former mentor in St. Paul. Already planning to relocate to the West, she will bring unique expertise to LivingArts with her ability to perform body piercings. She also has considerable experience creating tattoo designs especially for women, which will add yet another unique dimension to the business.

Professional & Advisory Support

LivingArts has established a business banking account with Spokane National Bank, as well as a merchant account for accepting credit card payments. Spokane Accounting Services, a local accounting firm, will provide the business with accounting and tax advisory services. Finally, an online legal document service has been utilized to cost-effectively prepare the paperwork necessary for incorporating the new business.

BUSINESS STRATEGY

LivingArts' strategy is to become Spokane's premier tattoo studio. Brian Thompson will utilize his advertising expertise to achieve a position of market leadership in the downtown area. This will be accomplished via the use of social media, word-of-mouth marketing, special events, and traditional advertising (see the Marketing & Sales section). While marketing always will be an important part of the studio's business strategy, a heavy emphasis will be placed upon marketing during the first 18 months of operation. Once the LivingArts brand has been established, the emphasis of marketing activities will shift toward maintaining the brand.

Visitors will quickly discover that the LivingArts studio is a unique destination, and that "our art sets us apart." In order to encourage new business and generate positive word-of-mouth, great care will be taken to ensure that individuals who stop by are comfortable. The gallery atmosphere will, in part, accomplish this. However, our artists also will put a premium on being courteous and approachable. In addition to perusing the gallery, we will encourage guests to enjoy a complimentary cup of coffee and watch our artists at work.

SERVICES

Tattoos

We will provide customers with custom tattoo designs that are truly unique in our local market. In addition, customers also may supply their own artwork.

Although they are unique, many of the tattoos that we offer fall into established categories, including:

- Angel
- Ankle
- Arm
- Aztec
- Back
- Behind the Ear
- Black & White
- Bird
- Butterfly
- Celebrity
- Celtic
- Chest
- Chinese
- Christian
- Cross
- Dolphin
- Dragon
- Eagle
- Fairy
- Fire
- Fish
- Flag
- Flower
- Foot
- Friends
- Hawaiian
- Heart
- Irish
- Japanese
- Lettering
- Lion

- Lower Back

- Moon

- Mouth

- Neck

- Religious

- Rose

- Shoulder

- Spanish

- Skull

- Sleeve

- Snake

- Tribal

- Urban

- Wings

- Wrist

- Zodiac

MARKETING & SALES

A marketing plan has been developed for LivingArts that includes the following primary tactics:

- Web Site: LivingArts will develop a Web site that lists basic information about the establishment, such as our location and hours. In addition, the site will include profiles of our artists, as well as a gallery of each artist's designs. A special section will highlight the artwork of Brian Thompson, and provide details about artwork that is for sale within the traditional gallery. Finally, a calendar section will list upcoming special events and performances by local artists.

- A YouTube channel will be developed so that prospective customers can view a series of video profiles about our artists, what it's like to get a tattoo, and how to care for a new tattoo as the skin heals. In addition, we will include clips from various special events.

- LivingArts will have a presence on social media sites, including Facebook and Twitter.

- Brian Thompson will maintain a blog, providing insight into his experiences as an artist and a tattoo studio operator.

- An estimate for the development of an eye-catching external sign has been received from Johnson's Sign Co. Unlike the typical neon signs characteristic of so many tattoo establishments, a crisp, professional design has been developed that incorporates elements of Brian Thompson's artwork.

- Window displays will showcase a regular rotation of Brian Thompson's artwork, catching the attention of passersby.

- Four benches, located in high-traffic areas throughout the city, have been identified for potential display advertising.

- A proposed advertising agreement has been drafted with local a radio station, providing the opportunity for on-air promotion, as well as periodic live broadcasts from Living Arts. Thompson has agreed to provide a select number of autographed prints, suitable for framing, for use as giveaways in on-air promotional contests.

- Live entertainment & events will be hosted at LivingArts on a regular basis. This will provide an opportunity to engage with individuals who might not otherwise visit a tattoo studio. Acoustic entertainment, wine tastings, and beer tastings are among the types of events we will host.

- LivingArts will run a quarter-page, color Yellow Page ad.

- A proposed advertising schedule (quarter-page advertisement, print and electronic) has been developed in partnership with *The Pacific Northwest Inlander,* a local, alternative newspaper.

Brian Thompson will evaluate Living Arts' marketing plan on a quarterly basis during the first three years of operations, and semi-annually thereafter.

OPERATIONS

Location

LivingArts will be located in a high traffic area in downtown Spokane. The business will be situated in a renovated storefront, the front portion of which will be used as gallery space. An area toward the back of the store will be utilized for intimate performances by local artists. Finally, there is space for three artists to perform tattooing and body piercing, along with a small office for the business.

Hours of Operation

- Monday-Thursday: Noon - 8:00 p.m.

- Friday & Saturday: Noon - 10:00 p.m.

- Closed on Sundays

Appointments & Consultations

Customers can either phone ahead to schedule a free consultation, or simply stop by. Prior to any tattooing or body piercing, our artists will have thorough discussions with customers, so that they have a complete understanding of costs and the process.

Health & Safety Precautions

LivingArts will adhere to the most stringent sterilization standards, including ultrasonic cleaning, autoclave sterilization, and the use of disposable products. Disposable needles will be opened in front of the customer, to provide them with the greatest assurance.

Business Management Software

Brian Thompson has found a tattoo studio management software application from MINDBODY, which is available on a hosted basis for a subscription of $70 per month (2-5 users). The software offers the following features:

- Appointment Management

- Point-of-sale & e-Commerce

- Inventory Management

- Business Analytics

- Staff & Client Management

Equipment

The following equipment will be needed prior to our first day of business. Note: The two independent contractors have agreed to provide their own tattoo machines:

- Tattoo Kit ($300) [includes machine, power supply, foot switch, clip cord, and a variety of inks/supplies]

- Stereo System ($300)

- Autoclave ($2,985)

- Speakers ($200)

- 42" Flat Panel Television ($400)

- Leather Chairs ($750)

- Leather Sofa ($1,350)

- Mirrors ($250)

- Computer ($400)

Total investment: $6,935

Inventory

LivingArts will require approximately $7,500 worth of supplies prior to startup (detailed inventory breakdown available upon request):

- Tattoo Refill Kits

- Tattoo Ink

- Tubes

- Needles

- Grips

- Sterilization Supplies

- Medical Supplies

- Tattoo Reference Books

- Piercing Supplies

- Flash

- Practice Skin

- Jewelry

- Power Supply Adapters

Insurance

LivingArts will secure appropriate business insurance and liability coverage from our agent, Spokane General Insurance Associates. In addition, we have secured a standard customer liability waiver form from a legal document service, which we will utilize for all jobs.

LEGAL & REGULATORY

In addition to carrying adequate liability coverage, LivingArts meets all requirements established by the Washington State Department of Licensing for tattoo artists and body piercing artists. Complete information is available here:

http://www.dol.wa.gov/business/tattoo

Copies of our practitioners' licenses are available upon request.

FINANCIAL ANALYSIS

Sales Forecast

In order to gauge the sales potential of LivingArts, Thompson has evaluated several established tattoo parlors in other Western urban markets that are currently for sale. This research revealed the following gross revenues for establishments of a similar size:

Portland: $248,000

Seattle: $175,000

Denver: $205,000

Based upon this information, and his knowledge of the local market, Thompson is confident that LivingArts can generate gross revenues of $125,000 during its first year of operation, $150,000 during year two, and $175,000 by year three. After factoring in lease payments, inventory purchases, and payments to artists (detailed projections and a three-year income statement are available upon request), Thompson is projecting a positive variance during the first three years of operations:

	2012	2013	2014
Gross revenue	$125,000	$150,000	$175,000
Expenses	$ 98,750	$112,500	$126,250
Net revenue	$ 26,250	$ 37,500	$ 48,750

Thompson estimates that 80 percent of revenues will be attributed to tattooing, body art services, and related merchandise sales. The remainder will be attributed to sales of traditional artwork and special events, which mainly will serve to attract new prospective customers to the establishment (especially those who may not otherwise visit a tattoo establishment).

Financing

Thompson will contribute $20,000 of his own money to the business, from personal savings and investment income, as well as a $10,000 loan from his father, Rex. He is seeking a small business loan of $15,000 to cover remaining start-up and operational costs.

Toy Rental Business
Granny's Attic

579 Main St.
Sarasota, Florida 34231

Heidi Denler

Granny's Attic will serve the Bradenton-Sarasota, Florida, area, offering rental of children's toys and games. It is a private, family-owned business, with four members of the Johnston family investing equally and being equally responsible for the business.

GRANNY'S ATTIC

After a few years of traveling with their young children and trying keep them happy with a small selection of toys that could be packed into corners of suitcases or under the seat of a car, Alex and Jenny Johnston came up with the idea of opening a toy rental store in the Sarasota-Bradenton area where Alex's parents, Jim and Kay Johnston, had retired. The Sarasota-Bradenton area consists of many retirement communities where grandparents welcome their grandchildren; however, many children are bored due to a lack of interesting toys when staying at Grandma's and Grandpa's.

EXECUTIVE SUMMARY

Granny's Attic will be established by the owners as an LLC (limited liability corporation) serving the Bradenton-Sarasota, Florida, area, offering rental of children's toys and games. It is a private, family-owned business, with four members of the Johnston family investing equally and being equally responsible for the business. Jim and Kay Johnston moved to the area following their retirement. Jim spent 40 years as a CPA and Kay was an elementary school teacher and principal for 35 years. Their son, Alex, is an attorney, and their daughter-in-law, Jenny, is a stay-at-home mom, taking care of 7-year-old daughter Mandy and 5-year-old son Josh. Alex and Jenny are moving from their home in Illinois to start Granny's Attic.

MISSION STATEMENT

The mission of Granny's Attic is to provide families visiting the Sarasota-Bradenton area the opportunity for their children to play with favorite games and toys without the inconvenience of trying to pack them for the vacation trip.

VISION STATEMENT

The Johnstons will build their customer base through customer service, customer loyalty club cards, and advertising by word of mouth, flyers, and newspaper advertising.

VALUES STATEMENT

Granny's Attic will offer high-quality, well-maintained, sanitized toys, games, and puzzles in four age categories in clean, welcoming surroundings with a warm and friendly atmosphere to encourage repeat business.

BUSINESS PHILOSOPHY

The Johnstons will provide excellent service in a warm, friendly setting where children and adults can try out the games before they rent them. Repeat business and customer goodwill, combined with customer service, and an Internet presence, as well as word of mouth, newspaper, and flyer advertising, will foster future growth.

THE MARKET

The Johnstons chose the Bradenton-Sarasota area for two reasons: (1) the proximity to the elder Johnstons, Kay and Jim, and (2) the high population of retirees whose families visit for a week or two a year. Kay and Jim Johnston have a made many social connections through their condominium complex, college alumni associations, and fraternity/sorority alumni chapters. Grandparents who have retired to the area are not likely to maintain a toy closet for the annual visits of their grandchildren, and traveling families do not have space in their luggage, even if they drive, to haul more than one or two favorite toys or games when they come to visit the grandparents.

Within the first six months of operation the Johnstons plan to have contracts with local family resorts to provide toys and games from Granny's Attic for their guests.

SERVICES

Granny's Attic has a variety of toys, games, and play equipment for ages 1 to 12. Those over 12 tend to prefer electronic games, a segment the Johnstons do not plan to enter for two to four years. Within each age group (toddler, pre-school, 5-8, and 9-12), playthings available for rental are separated into categories: puzzles, educational, board games, and physical/outdoor play. Rental times will be a minimum of three days and a maximum of ten days. The rental costs for more than 10 days would result in a cost to the client that would be equal to the purchase price of the toy or game in most situations.

COMPETITIVE EDGE

As a CPA, Jim Johnston brings his 30 years of experience to the business/accounting side of Granny's Attic. His son, Alex, can review legal documents for all aspects of the business. Kay's experiences with education and working with children provides insight into what children want and need. Jenny has the ability to connect easily with other moms and is up-to-date on trends in children's toys and games thanks to her own two offspring. All four have social connections in the area that will further assist in their marketing plans.

The four owners plan to forge relationships with the major toy manufacturers to purchase traditional, classic toys, as well as trendy ones, in order to offer high-quality toys and games in all categories. Maintenance of each toy, in addition to sanitizing, will be of key importance to the Johnstons for safety and health concerns. When a toy or game begins to show wear, it will be donated to a local shelter and replaced.

Customer service will be a key component of Granny's Attic from price point to toy selection. Rental prices in most cases can be much less than buying the toy or game. The major marketing point for renting toys is that there is no storage involved for toys that will be outgrown before the child's next visit to grandma's. Grandparents will have the peace of mind from knowing that they are offering their grandchildren the latest in toy trends along with the classics, all in "like new" condition. They will also be assured that their grandchildren will enjoy the toys they rent because toys can be exchanged for other toys of equal value in stock within 24 hours of the child's arrival in town.

KEYS TO SUCCESS

- Maintain a sufficient inventory of classic and trending games and toys, sanitized and in "like new" condition.
- Assist in selection of toys and games.

OBJECTIVES

- To provide quality classic and trendy games and toys for grandparents and traveling families to rent while on vacation to avoid having to pack and haul favorite games and toys when going on vacation.
- To create working relationships with major toy and game manufacturers to get optimal purchasing power when buying toys and games for inventory.
- To be profitable within a year.

START-UP SUMMARY

Start-up expenses will include inventory, rental of a storefront in a high-traffic strip mall, office supplies, and state and local fees for registering the name and other documents necessary to open the business. As an attorney, Alex will be able to handle corporate formation and as a retired CPA, Jim will be able to maintain the company's financial records during the start-up phase of Granny's Attic.

Start up equipment (partial list)
- Computers: 3 workstations, 2 in the office and one as a cash register; Microsoft software and licensing; 2 HP Laser printers, 1 in the office and one to print receipts at the register; DSL Internet wireless connection
- Shelving for toys and games
- Light fixtures

- Sanitizing area behind office in workroom area

- Packaging area behind office in workroom area

- 2 desks and chairs in office

- Hard surface large worktables in workroom area

- Toys, puzzles and games from such manufacturers as Fisher Price, LeapFrog, VTech, Lego, Chicco, and Brio

- Web site construction (six months after launch of storefront)

- Sanitizing station

FINANCIAL

Included in start-up costs will be standard security deposits, rental fees, and licensing fees assessed by the state and federal government entities. Expenses will be incurred in separating the rental property into the four separate areas for display, storage, office, and preparation, as well as furnishings.

The display area of the shop will be divided into four age categories through color, with the walls painted red, yellow, green, or blue, depending on the age group. The floor will be tiled with shades of those colors to denote each area, with the play area comprising a combination of those four colors.

Other start-up costs that will be incurred will include fees for registering the name "Granny's Attic" with all federal, state, and local governments. The Johnstons will also have rent, taxes, payroll and payroll taxes, key man insurance on the four Johnstons, property insurance, liability insurance, inventory, telephone and other utilities, an alarm system, and advertising.

SERVICES

Granny's Attic will offer the Bradenton-Sarasota area a wide range of classic and trendy games and toys in four age categories for a minimum of 3 days and maximum of 10 days. The storefront will be in a strip mall in a high traffic area, near condos and retirement villages populated by grandparents. The showroom will be bright and cheerful, with sample of each toy and game in the inventory on display on shelves. An area will be set aside for those families who bring their children with them, so the children can try the games before renting them. At least two people will be available to assist customers during business hours. A pick-up and delivery service will be available for a percentage of the rental for customers who pre-pay over the telephone or via the company Web site.

STORE DESIGN AND EQUIPMENT

When customers enter Granny's Attic they will get the feeling of walking into Santa's Workshop. Plastic-coated wire shelving units will line the walls, with the four age groups (toddler, pre-school, 5-8, and 9-12) clearly separated into color-coordinated sections in primary colors of red, yellow, blue, and green. In the center of the room there will be a play area where toys and games can be played by children, parents, and grandparents. A checkout counter will be near the front door.

Behind the display area will be a storage area where sanitized and shrink-wrapped toys, puzzles, and games will be stored, ready for rental.

The office area will be behind the display area, along with a small area for the Johnstons and employees to relax between clients or have lunch or a snack. This space will be equipped with three desks and chairs, three computers, a printer, a small kitchen table with four to six chairs, a small refrigerator, and a microwave.

The back of the store will have four tables where toys will be prepared for rental. This will include inspection, sanitizing, and shrink wrapping.

PERSONNEL PLAN

The four Johnstons will be the primary employees for Granny's Attic. At key vacation times (mid-winter school break, Easter/spring vacation, Thanksgiving, and the December Christmas/Hanakkuh school holidays), the Johnstons will hire local collegians to assist with rentals, cleaning and sanitizing, packaging, and delivery. Within a year, Kay and Jim would like to start backing out of a day-to-day role in the business, maintaining a silent partnership. All four will work with a local employment agency to find replacements for the older Johnstons in the actual storefront.

Kay and Jenny will handle research and purchasing, Alex will handle legal and in-store duties, and Jim will maintain the books. All four will handle counter and rental responsibilities and work to train temporary holiday employees and future employees.

MARKET ANALYSIS SUMMARY

Two customer segments will be served by Granny's Attic: (1) grandparents with permanent residences in the Sarasota-Bradenton area who want to provide entertainment for their visiting grandchildren, and (2) parents traveling on vacation to the area who want to entertain their children without dragging personal games and toys with them on the plane or in a car.

COMPETITION

A general rental company offers beach toys for rent, but does not include puzzles, games, and general toys. That store also offers cribs, playpens, strollers, and ride-on toys for rent.

The only other competition for toy rentals are online companies that charge shipping and handling fees on top of rental fees. Those rental fees are significantly higher than the proposed rental charges for Granny's Attic selections.

COMPETITIVE EDGE

Granny's Attic will create and maintain a competitive edge by being the first of its kind in the region. High-quality, well-maintained, sanitized products that are offered for variable time frames at reasonable rates will be combined with caring, helpful, and knowledgeable customer service personnel to create return business and encourage new business. Word of mouth advertising will be a key component in building clientele, along with advertising at local retirement communities and in *The Bradenton Herald* and the *Sarasota Herald Tribune*.

STRATEGY AND IMPLEMENTATION

The Johnstons will work quickly to garner market share among grandparents. Marketing will focus on bringing in customers with special introductory rates and converting them into return customers who will promote Granny's Attic.

Granny's Attic will focus on client needs, including:

- Matching children's ages and abilities, along with their interests, to toys and games

- Delivery when requested

- Sanitized toys and games

- Like new toys and games

- A wide selection of toys, games, and puzzles

- Reservations to avoid disappointing visiting grandchildren

MARKETING STRATEGY

Visibility within the strip mall on a busy thoroughfare will be combined with advertising in the two main local newspapers, as well as neighborhood publications. Flyers will be distributed at area senior communities that have high levels of grandparents and at resorts that cater to families.

Customer service will focus on providing what the clients want and request to encourage repeat business and word of mouth advertising. Clients who have referred new customers to Granny's Attic will receive a 10 percent discount on their next rental. A Granny's Attic Loyalty Club card will have a magnetic strip that will hold information to enable the tracking of rentals and every twentieth rental will be free of charge. The tracking will be saved on a computer program that will allow the staff of Granny's Attic to suggest options for future choices of toys and games based on prior rentals.

WEB SITE

The Johnstons plan to launch a Web site after the storefront has been open six months. They will hire a local company to build their Web site, where clients and potential clients can preview the toy selection "catalog." Children will be able to visit the site and create a wish list from which their grandparents can choose which toys, puzzles, and games to rent, possibly after discussions with mom and dad. Keywords will be carefully chosen to optimize positive results from search engines.

CONCLUSION

The Johnstons expect Granny's Attic to be profitable within the first year of operation. Their location in a high-traffic strip mall on a busy thoroughfare near family resorts and retirement communities will offer a ready customer base for a unique service.

Location, store design, staff, customer service, and advertising will work together to ensure success for Granny's Attic. As the first in the area offering this type of service, the Johnstons project steady business from the outset of the shop.

BUSINESS PLAN TEMPLATE

USING THIS TEMPLATE

A business plan carefully spells out a company's projected course of action over a period of time, usually the first two to three years after the start-up. In addition, banks, lenders, and other investors examine the information and financial documentation before deciding whether or not to finance a new business venture. Therefore, a business plan is an essential tool in obtaining financing and should describe the business itself in detail as well as all important factors influencing the company, including the market, industry, competition, operations and management policies, problem solving strategies, financial resources and needs, and other vital information. The plan enables the business owner to anticipate costs, plan for difficulties, and take advantage of opportunities, as well as design and implement strategies that keep the company running as smoothly as possible.

This template has been provided as a model to help you construct your own business plan. Please keep in mind that there is no single acceptable format for a business plan, and that this template is in no way comprehensive, but serves as an example.

The business plans provided in this section are fictional and have been used by small business agencies as models for clients to use in compiling their own business plans.

GENERIC BUSINESS PLAN

Main headings included below are topics that should be covered in a comprehensive business plan. They include:

Business Summary

Purpose
Provides a brief overview of your business, succinctly highlighting the main ideas of your plan.

Includes

- Name and Type of Business
- Description of Product/Service
- Business History and Development
- Location
- Market

- Competition
- Management
- Financial Information
- Business Strengths and Weaknesses
- Business Growth

Table of Contents

Purpose
Organized in an Outline Format, the Table of Contents illustrates the selection and arrangement of information contained in your plan.

Includes

- Topic Headings and Subheadings
- Page Number References

Business History and Industry Outlook

Purpose

Examines the conception and subsequent development of your business within an industry specific context.

Includes

- Start-up Information
- Owner/Key Personnel Experience
- Location
- Development Problems and Solutions
- Investment/Funding Information
- Future Plans and Goals
- Market Trends and Statistics
- Major Competitors
- Product/Service Advantages
- National, Regional, and Local Economic Impact

Product/Service

Purpose

Introduces, defines, and details the product and/or service that inspired the information of your business.

Includes

- Unique Features
- Niche Served
- Market Comparison
- Stage of Product/Service Development
- Production
- Facilities, Equipment, and Labor
- Financial Requirements
- Product/Service Life Cycle
- Future Growth

Market Examination

Purpose

Assessment of product/service applications in relation to consumer buying cycles.

Includes

- Target Market
- Consumer Buying Habits
- Product/Service Applications
- Consumer Reactions
- Market Factors and Trends
- Penetration of the Market
- Market Share
- Research and Studies
- Cost
- Sales Volume and Goals

Competition

Purpose

Analysis of Competitors in the Marketplace.

Includes

- Competitor Information
- Product/Service Comparison
- Market Niche
- Product/Service Strengths and Weaknesses
- Future Product/Service Development

Marketing

Purpose

Identifies promotion and sales strategies for your product/service.

Includes

- Product/Service Sales Appeal
- Special and Unique Features
- Identification of Customers
- Sales and Marketing Staff
- Sales Cycles
- Type of Advertising/ Promotion
- Pricing
- Competition
- Customer Services

Operations

Purpose

Traces product/service development from production/inception to the market environment.

Includes

- Cost Effective Production Methods
- Facility
- Location
- Equipment
- Labor
- Future Expansion

Administration and Management

Purpose

Offers a statement of your management philosophy with an in-depth focus on processes and procedures.

Includes

- Management Philosophy
- Structure of Organization
- Reporting System
- Methods of Communication
- Employee Skills and Training
- Employee Needs and Compensation
- Work Environment
- Management Policies and Procedures
- Roles and Responsibilities

Key Personnel

Purpose

Describes the unique backgrounds of principle employees involved in business.

Includes

- Owner(s)/Employee Education and Experience
- Positions and Roles
- Benefits and Salary
- Duties and Responsibilities
- Objectives and Goals

Potential Problems and Solutions

Purpose

Discussion of problem solving strategies that change issues into opportunities.

Includes

- Risks
- Litigation
- Future Competition
- Economic Impact
- Problem Solving Skills

Financial Information

Purpose

Secures needed funding and assistance through worksheets and projections detailing financial plans, methods of repayment, and future growth opportunities.

Includes

- Financial Statements
- Bank Loans
- Methods of Repayment
- Tax Returns

- Start-up Costs
- Projected Income (3 years)
- Projected Cash Flow (3 Years)
- Projected Balance Statements (3 years)

Appendices

Purpose

Supporting documents used to enhance your business proposal.

Includes

- Photographs of product, equipment, facilities, etc.
- Copyright/Trademark Documents
- Legal Agreements
- Marketing Materials
- Research and or Studies

- Operation Schedules
- Organizational Charts
- Job Descriptions
- Resumes
- Additional Financial Documentation

Fictional Food Distributor

Commercial Foods, Inc.

3003 Avondale Ave.
Knoxville, TN 37920

This plan demonstrates how a partnership can have a positive impact on a new business. It demonstrates how two individuals can carve a niche in the specialty foods market by offering gourmet foods to upscale restaurants and fine hotels. This plan is fictional and has not been used to gain funding from a bank or other lending institution.

STATEMENT OF PURPOSE

Commercial Foods, Inc. seeks a loan of $75,000 to establish a new business. This sum, together with $5,000 equity investment by the principals, will be used as follows:

- Merchandise inventory $25,000

- Office fixture/equipment $12,000

- Warehouse equipment $14,000

- One delivery truck $10,000

- Working capital $39,000

- Total $100,000

DESCRIPTION OF THE BUSINESS

Commercial Foods, Inc. will be a distributor of specialty food service products to hotels and upscale restaurants in the geographical area of a 50 mile radius of Knoxville. Richard Roberts will direct the sales effort and John Williams will manage the warehouse operation and the office. One delivery truck will be used initially with a second truck added in the third year. We expect to begin operation of the business within 30 days after securing the requested financing.

MANAGEMENT

A. Richard Roberts is a native of Memphis, Tennessee. He is a graduate of Memphis State University with a Bachelor's degree from the School of Business. After graduation, he worked for a major manufacturer of specialty food service products as a detail sales person for five years, and, for the past three years, he has served as a product sales manager for this firm.

B. John Williams is a native of Nashville, Tennessee. He holds a B.S. Degree in Food Technology from the University of Tennessee. His career includes five years as a product development chemist in gourmet food products and five years as operations manager for a food service distributor.

Both men are healthy and energetic. Their backgrounds complement each other, which will ensure the success of Commercial Foods, Inc. They will set policies together and personnel decisions will be made jointly. Initial salaries for the owners will be $1,000 per month for the first few years. The spouses of both principals are successful in the business world and earn enough to support the families.

They have engaged the services of Foster Jones, CPA, and William Hale, Attorney, to assist them in an advisory capacity.

PERSONNEL

The firm will employ one delivery truck driver at a wage of $8.00 per hour. One office worker will be employed at $7.50 per hour. One part-time employee will be used in the office at $5.00 per hour. The driver will load and unload his own trucks. Mr. Williams will assist in the warehouse operation as needed to assist one stock person at $7.00 per hour. An additional delivery truck and driver will be added the third year.

LOCATION

The firm will lease a 20,000 square foot building at 3003 Avondale Ave., in Knoxville, which contains warehouse and office areas equipped with two-door truck docks. The annual rental is $9,000. The building was previously used as a food service warehouse and very little modification to the building will be required.

PRODUCTS AND SERVICES

The firm will offer specialty food service products such as soup bases, dessert mixes, sauce bases, pastry mixes, spices, and flavors, normally used by upscale restaurants and nice hotels. We are going after a niche in the market with high quality gourmet products. There is much less competition in this market than in standard run of the mill food service products. Through their work experiences, the principals have contacts with supply sources and with local chefs.

THE MARKET

We know from our market survey that there are over 200 hotels and upscale restaurants in the area we plan to serve. Customers will be attracted by a direct sales approach. We will offer samples of our products and product application data on use of our products in the finished prepared foods. We will cultivate the chefs in these establishments. The technical background of John Williams will be especially useful here.

COMPETITION

We find that we will be only distributor in the area offering a full line of gourmet food service products. Other foodservice distributors offer only a few such items in conjunction with their standard product line. Our survey shows that many of the chefs are ordering products from Atlanta and Memphis because of a lack of adequate local supply.

SUMMARY

Commercial Foods, Inc. will be established as a foodservice distributor of specialty food in Knoxville. The principals, with excellent experience in the industry, are seeking a $75,000 loan to establish the business. The principals are investing $25,000 as equity capital.

The business will be set up as an S Corporation with each principal owning 50% of the common stock in the corporation.

FICTIONAL HARDWARE STORE

OSHKOSH HARDWARE, Inc.

123 Main St.
Oshkosh, WI 54901

The following plan outlines how a small hardware store can survive competition from large discount chains by offering products and providing expert advice in the use of any product it sells. This plan is fictional and has not been used to gain funding from a bank or other lending institution.

EXECUTIVE SUMMARY

Oshkosh Hardware, Inc. is a new corporation that is going to establish a retail hardware store in a strip mall in Oshkosh, Wisconsin. The store will sell hardware of all kinds, quality tools, paint, and housewares. The business will make revenue and a profit by servicing its customers not only with needed hardware but also with expert advice in the use of any product it sells.

Oshkosh Hardware, Inc. will be operated by its sole shareholder, James Smith. The company will have a total of four employees. It will sell its products in the local market. Customers will buy our products because we will provide free advice on the use of all of our products and will also furnish a full refund warranty.

Oshkosh Hardware, Inc. will sell its products in the Oshkosh store staffed by three sales representatives. No additional employees will be needed to achieve its short and long range goals. The primary short range goal is to open the store by October 1, 1994. In order to achieve this goal a lease must be signed by July 1, 1994 and the complete inventory ordered by August 1, 1994.

Mr. James Smith will invest $30,000 in the business. In addition, the company will have to borrow $150,000 during the first year to cover the investment in inventory, accounts receivable, and furniture and equipment. The company will be profitable after six months of operation and should be able to start repayment of the loan in the second year.

THE BUSINESS

The business will sell hardware of all kinds, quality tools, paint, and housewares. We will purchase our products from three large wholesale buying groups.

In general our customers are homeowners who do their own repair and maintenance, hobbyists, and housewives. Our business is unique in that we will have a complete line of all hardware items and will be able to get special orders by overnight delivery. The business makes revenue and profits by servicing our customers not only with needed hardware but also with expert advice in the use of any product we sell. Our major costs for bringing our products to market are cost of merchandise of 36%, salaries of $45,000, and occupancy costs of $60,000.

303

Oshkosh Hardware, Inc.'s retail outlet will be located at 1524 Frontage Road, which is in a newly developed retail center of Oshkosh. Our location helps facilitate accessibility from all parts of town and reduces our delivery costs. The store will occupy 7500 square feet of space. The major equipment involved in our business is counters and shelving, a computer, a paint mixing machine, and a truck.

THE MARKET

Oshkosh Hardware, Inc. will operate in the local market. There are 15,000 potential customers in this market area. We have three competitors who control approximately 98% of the market at present. We feel we can capture 25% of the market within the next four years. Our major reason for believing this is that our staff is technically competent to advise our customers in the correct use of all products we sell.

After a careful market analysis, we have determined that approximately 60% of our customers are men and 40% are women. The percentage of customers that fall into the following age categories are:

Under 16: 0%
17-21: 5%
22-30: 30%
31-40: 30%
41-50: 20%
51-60: 10%
61-70: 5%
Over 70: 0%

The reasons our customers prefer our products is our complete knowledge of their use and our full refund warranty.

We get our information about what products our customers want by talking to existing customers. There seems to be an increasing demand for our product. The demand for our product is increasing in size based on the change in population characteristics.

SALES

At Oshkosh Hardware, Inc. we will employ three sales people and will not need any additional personnel to achieve our sales goals. These salespeople will need several years experience in home repair and power tool usage. We expect to attract 30% of our customers from newspaper ads, 5% of our customers from local directories, 5% of our customers from the yellow pages, 10% of our customers from family and friends, and 50% of our customers from current customers. The most cost effect source will be current customers. In general our industry is growing.

MANAGEMENT

We would evaluate the quality of our management staff as being excellent. Our manager is experienced and very motivated to achieve the various sales and quality assurance objectives we have set. We will use a management information system that produces key inventory, quality assurance, and sales data on a weekly basis. All data is compared to previously established goals for that week, and deviations are the primary focus of the management staff.

GOALS IMPLEMENTATION

The short term goals of our business are:

1. Open the store by October 1, 1994
2. Reach our breakeven point in two months
3. Have sales of $100,000 in the first six months

In order to achieve our first short term goal we must:

1. Sign the lease by July 1, 1994
2. Order a complete inventory by August 1, 1994

In order to achieve our second short term goal we must:

1. Advertise extensively in Sept. and Oct.
2. Keep expenses to a minimum

In order to achieve our third short term goal we must:

1. Promote power tool sales for the Christmas season
2. Keep good customer traffic in Jan. and Feb.

The long term goals for our business are:

1. Obtain sales volume of $600,000 in three years
2. Become the largest hardware dealer in the city
3. Open a second store in Fond du Lac

The most important thing we must do in order to achieve the long term goals for our business is to develop a highly profitable business with excellent cash flow.

FINANCE

Oshkosh Hardware, Inc. Faces some potential threats or risks to our business. They are discount house competition. We believe we can avoid or compensate for this by providing quality products complimented by quality advice on the use of every product we sell. The financial projections we have prepared are located at the end of this document.

JOB DESCRIPTION-GENERAL MANAGER

The General Manager of the business of the corporation will be the president of the corporation. He will be responsible for the complete operation of the retail hardware store which is owned by the corporation. A detailed description of his duties and responsibilities is as follows.

Sales

Train and supervise the three sales people. Develop programs to motivate and compensate these employees. Coordinate advertising and sales promotion effects to achieve sales totals as outlined in budget. Oversee purchasing function and inventory control procedures to insure adequate merchandise at all times at a reasonable cost.

Finance

Prepare monthly and annual budgets. Secure adequate line of credit from local banks. Supervise office personnel to insure timely preparation of records, statements, all government reports, control of receivables and payables, and monthly financial statements.

Administration

Perform duties as required in the areas of personnel, building leasing and maintenance, licenses and permits, and public relations.

Organizations, Agencies, & Consultants

A listing of Associations and Consultants of interest to entrepreneurs, followed by the ten Small Business Administration Regional Offices, Small Business Development Centers, Service Corps of Retired Executives offices, and Venture Capital and Finance Companies.

Associations

This section contains a listing of associations and other agencies of interest to the small business owner. Entries are listed alphabetically by organization name.

American Business Women's Association
9100 Ward Pkwy.
PO Box 8728
Kansas City, MO 64114-0728
(800)228-0007
E-mail: abwa@abwa.org
Website: http://www.abwa.org
Jeanne Banks, National President

American Franchisee Association
53 W Jackson Blvd., Ste. 1157
Chicago, IL 60604
(312)431-0545
E-mail: info@franchisee.org
Website: http://www.franchisee.org
Susan P. Kezios, President

American Independent Business Alliance
222 S Black Ave.
Bozeman, MT 59715
(406)582-1255
E-mail: info@amiba.net
Website: http://www.amiba.net
Jennifer Rockne, Director

American Small Businesses Association
206 E College St., Ste. 201
Grapevine, TX 76051
800-942-2722
E-mail: info@asbaonline.org
Website: http://www.asbaonline.org/

American Women's Economic Development Corporation
216 East 45th St., 10th Floor
New York, NY 10017
(917)368-6100

Fax: (212)986-7114
E-mail: info@awed.org
Website: http://www.awed.org
Roseanne Antonucci, Exec. Dir.

Association for Enterprise Opportunity
1601 N Kent St., Ste. 1101
Arlington, VA 22209
(703)841-7760
Fax: (703)841-7748
E-mail: aeo@assoceo.org
Website: http://www.micro enterpriseworks.org
Bill Edwards, Exec.Dir.

Association of Small Business Development Centers
c/o Don Wilson
8990 Burke Lake Rd.
Burke, VA 22015
(703)764-9850
Fax: (703)764-1234
E-mail: info@asbdc-us.org
Website: http://www.asbdc-us.org
Don Wilson, Pres./CEO

BEST Employers Association
2505 McCabe Way
Irvine, CA 92614
(949)253-4080
800-433-0088
Fax: (714)553-0883
E-mail: info@bestlife.com
Website: http://www.bestlife.com
Donald R. Lawrenz, CEO

Center for Family Business
PO Box 24219
Cleveland, OH 44124
(440)460-5409
E-mail: grummi@aol.com
Dr. Leon A. Danco, Chm.

Coalition for Government Procurement
1990 M St. NW, Ste. 400
Washington, DC 20036
(202)331-0975
E-mail: info@thecgp.org
Website: http://www.coalgovpro.org
Paul Caggiano, Pres.

Employers of America
PO Box 1874
Mason City, IA 50402-1874
(641)424-3187
800-728-3187
Fax: (641)424-1673
E-mail: employer@employerhelp.org
Website: http://www.employerhelp.org
Jim Collison, Pres.

Family Firm Institute
200 Lincoln St., Ste. 201
Boston, MA 02111
(617)482-3045
Fax: (617)482-3049
E-mail: ffi@ffi.org
Website: http://www.ffi.org
Judy L. Green, Ph.D., Exec.Dir.

Independent Visually Impaired Enterprisers
500 S 3rd St., Apt. H
Burbank, CA 91502
(818)238-9321
E-mail: abazyn@bazyn communications.com
http://www.acb.org/affiliates
Adris Bazyn, Pres.

International Association for Business Organizations
3 Woodthorn Ct., Ste. 12
Owings Mills, MD 21117
(410)581-1373
E-mail: nahbb@msn.com
Rudolph Lewis, Exec. Officer

International Council for Small Business
The George Washington University
School of Business and Public
Management
2115 G St. NW, Ste. 403
Washington, DC 20052
(202)994-0704
Fax: (202)994-4930
E-mail: icsb@gwu.edu
Website: http://www.icsb.org
Susan G. Duffy. Admin.

International Small Business Consortium
3309 Windjammer St.
Norman, OK 73072
E-mail: sb@isbc.com
Website: http://www.isbc.com

Kauffman Center for Entrepreneurial Leadership
4801 Rockhill Rd.
Kansas City, MO 64110-2046
(816)932-1000
E-mail: info@kauffman.org
Website: http://www.entreworld.org

National Alliance for Fair Competition
3 Bethesda Metro Center, Ste. 1100
Bethesda, MD 20814
(410)235-7116
Fax: (410)235-7116
E-mail: ampesq@aol.com
Tony Ponticelli, Exec.Dir.

National Association for the Self-Employed
PO Box 612067
DFW Airport
Dallas, TX 75261-2067
(800)232-6273
E-mail: mpetron@nase.org
Website: http://www.nase.org
Robert Hughes, Pres.

National Association of Business Leaders
4132 Shoreline Dr., Ste. J & H
Earth City, MO 63045
Fax: (314)298-9110
E-mail: nabl@nabl.com
Website: http://www.nabl.com/
Gene Blumenthal, Contact

National Association of Private Enterprise
PO Box 15550
Long Beach, CA 90815
888-224-0953

Fax: (714)844-4942
Website: http://www.napeonline.net
Laura Squiers, Exec.Dir.

National Association of Small Business Investment Companies
666 11th St. NW, Ste. 750
Washington, DC 20001
(202)628-5055
Fax: (202)628-5080
E-mail: nasbic@nasbic.org
Website: http://www.nasbic.org
Lee W. Mercer, Pres.

National Business Association
PO Box 700728
5151 Beltline Rd., Ste. 1150
Dallas, TX 75370
(972)458-0900
800-456-0440
Fax: (972)960-9149
E-mail: info@nationalbusiness.org
Website: http://www.national
business.org
Raj Nisankarao, Pres.

National Business Owners Association
PO Box 111
Stuart, VA 24171
(276)251-7500
(866)251-7505
Fax: (276)251-2217
E-mail: membershipservices@nboa.org
Website: http://www.rvmdb.com.nboa
Paul LaBarr, Pres.

National Center for Fair Competition
PO Box 220
Annandale, VA 22003
(703)280-4622
Fax: (703)280-0942
E-mail: kentonp1@aol.com
Kenton Pattie, Pres.

National Family Business Council
1640 W. Kennedy Rd.
Lake Forest, IL 60045
(847)295-1040
Fax: (847)295-1898
E-mail: lmsnfbc@email.msn.com
Jogn E. Messervey, Pres.

National Federation of Independent Business
53 Century Blvd., Ste. 250
Nashville, TN 37214
(615)872-5800
800-NFIBNOW
Fax: (615)872-5353
Website: http://www.nfib.org
Jack Faris, Pres. and CEO

National Small Business Association
1156 15th St. NW, Ste. 1100
Washington, DC 20005
(202)293-8830
800-345-6728
Fax: (202)872-8543
E-mail: press@nsba.biz
Website: http://www.nsba.biz
Rob Yunich, Dir. of Communications

PUSH Commercial Division
930 E 50th St.
Chicago, IL 60615-2702
(773)373-3366
Fax: (773)373-3571
E-mail: info@rainbowpush.org
Website: http://www.rainbowpush.org
Rev. Willie T. Barrow, Co-Chm.

Research Institute for Small and Emerging Business
722 12th St. NW
Washington, DC 20005
(202)628-8382
Fax: (202)628-8392
E-mail: info@riseb.org
Website: http://www.riseb.org
Allan Neece, Jr., Chm.

Sales Professionals USA
PO Box 149
Arvada, CO 80001
(303)534-4937
888-736-7767
E-mail: salespro@salesprofessionals-usa.com
Website: http://www.salesprofessionals-usa.com
Sharon Herbert, Natl. Pres.

Score Association - Service Corps of Retired Executives
409 3rd St. SW, 6th Fl.
Washington, DC 20024
(202)205-6762
800-634-0245
Fax: (202)205-7636
E-mail: media@score.org
Website: http://www.score.org
W. Kenneth Yancey, Jr., CEO

Small Business and Entrepreneurship Council
1920 L St. NW, Ste. 200
Washington, DC 20036
(202)785-0238
Fax: (202)822-8118
E-mail: membership@sbec.org
Website: http://www.sbecouncil.org
Karen Kerrigan, Pres./CEO

Small Business in Telecommunications
1331 H St. NW, Ste. 500
Washington, DC 20005
(202)347-4511
Fax: (202)347-8607
E-mail: sbt@sbthome.org
Website: http://www.sbthome.org
Lonnie Danchik, Chm.

Small Business Legislative Council
1010 Massachusetts Ave. NW, Ste. 540
Washington, DC 20005
(202)639-8500
Fax: (202)296-5333
E-mail: email@sblc.org
Website: http://www.sblc.org
John Satagaj, Pres.

Small Business Service Bureau
554 Main St.
PO Box 15014
Worcester, MA 01615-0014
(508)756-3513
800-343-0939
Fax: (508)770-0528
E-mail: membership@sbsb.com
Website: http://www.sbsb.com
Francis R. Carroll, Pres.

**Small Publishers Association
of North America**
1618 W COlorado Ave.
Colorado Springs, CO 80904
(719)475-1726
Fax: (719)471-2182
E-mail: span@spannet.org
Website: http://www.spannet.org
Scott Flora, Exec. Dir.

SOHO America
PO Box 941
Hurst, TX 76053-0941
800-495-SOHO
E-mail: soho@1sas.com
Website: http://www.soho.org

**Structured Employment Economic
Development Corporation**
915 Broadway, 17th Fl.
New York, NY 10010
(212)473-0255
Fax: (212)473-0357
E-mail: info@seedco.org
Website: http://www.seedco.org
William Grinker, CEO

Support Services Alliance
107 Prospect St.
Schoharie, NY 12157
800-836-4772

E-mail: info@ssamembers.com
Website: http://www.ssainfo.com
Steve COle, Pres.

**United States Association for Small
Business and Entrepreneurship**
975 University Ave., No. 3260
Madison, WI 53706
(608)262-9982
Fax: (608)263-0818
E-mail: jgillman@wisc.edu
Website: http://www.ususbe.org
Joan Gillman, Exec. Dir.

Consultants

This section contains a listing of consultants specializing in small business development. It is arranged alphabetically by country, then by state or province, then by city, then by firm name.

Canada

Alberta

Common Sense Solutions
3405 16A Ave.
Edmonton, AB, Canada
(403)465-7330
Fax: (403)465-7380
E-mail: gcoulson@comsense
solutions.com
Website: http://www.comsense
solutions.com

Varsity Consulting Group
School of Business
University of Alberta
Edmonton, AB, Canada T6G 2R6
(780)492-2994
Fax: (780)492-5400
Website: http://www.bus.ualberta.ca/vcg

Viro Hospital Consulting
42 Commonwealth Bldg., 9912 - 106
St. NW
Edmonton, AB, Canada T5K 1C5
(403)425-3871
Fax: (403)425-3871
E-mail: rpb@freenet.edmonton.ab.ca

British Columbia

SRI Strategic Resources Inc.
4330 Kingsway, Ste. 1600
Burnaby, BC, Canada V5H 4G7
(604)435-0627
Fax: (604)435-2782

E-mail: inquiry@sri.bc.ca
Website: http://www.sri.com

Andrew R. De Boda Consulting
1523 Milford Ave.
Coquitlam, BC, Canada V3J 2V9
(604)936-4527
Fax: (604)936-4527
E-mail: deboda@intergate.bc.ca
Website: http://www.ourworld.
compuserve.com/homepages/deboda

The Sage Group Ltd.
980 - 355 Burrard St.
744 W Haistings, Ste. 410
Vancouver, BC, Canada V6C 1A5
(604)669-9269
Fax: (604)669-6622

Tikkanen-Bradley
1345 Nelson St., Ste. 202
Vancouver, BC, Canada V6E 1J8
(604)669-0583
E-mail: webmaster@tikkanen
bradley.com
Website: http://www.tikkanenbradley.com

Ontario

The Cynton Co.
17 Massey St.
Brampton, ON, Canada L6S 2V6
(905)792-7769
Fax: (905)792-8116
E-mail: cynton@home.com
Website: http://www.cynton.com

Begley & Associates
RR 6
Cambridge, ON, Canada N1R 5S7
(519)740-3629
Fax: (519)740-3629
E-mail: begley@in.on.ca
Website: http://www.in.on.ca/~begley/
index.htm

CRO Engineering Ltd.
1895 William Hodgins Ln.
Carp, ON, Canada K0A 1L0
(613)839-1108
Fax: (613)839-1406
E-mail: J.Grefford@ieee.ca
Website: http://www.geocities.com/
WallStreet/District/7401/

Task Enterprises
Box 69, RR 2 Hamilton
Flamborough, ON, Canada L8N 2Z7
(905)659-0153
Fax: (905)659-0861

HST Group Ltd.
430 Gilmour St.
Ottawa, ON, Canada K2P 0R8
(613)236-7303
Fax: (613)236-9893

Harrison Associates
BCE Pl.
181 Bay St., Ste. 3740
PO Box 798
Toronto, ON, Canada M5J 2T3
(416)364-5441
Fax: (416)364-2875

TCI Convergence Ltd. Management Consultants
99 Crown's Ln.
Toronto, ON, Canada M5R 3P4
(416)515-4146
Fax: (416)515-2097
E-mail: tci@inforamp.net
Website: http://tciconverge.com/
index.1.html

Ken Wyman & Associates Inc.
64B Shuter St., Ste. 200
Toronto, ON, Canada M5B 1B1
(416)362-2926
Fax: (416)362-3039
E-mail: kenwyman@compuserve.com

JPL Business Consultants
82705 Metter Rd.
Wellandport, ON, Canada L0R 2J0
(905)386-7450
Fax: (905)386-7450
E-mail: plamarch@freenet.npiec.on.ca

Quebec

The Zimmar Consulting Partnership Inc.
Westmount
PO Box 98
Montreal, QC, Canada H3Z 2T1
(514)484-1459
Fax: (514)484-3063

Saskatchewan

Trimension Group
No. 104-110 Research Dr.
Innovation Place, SK, Canada S7N 3R3
(306)668-2560
Fax: (306)975-1156
E-mail: trimension@trimension.ca
Website: http://www.trimension.ca

Corporate Management Consultants
40 Government Road - PO Box 185
Prud Homme, SK, Canada, SOK 3K0
(306)654-4569
Fax: (650)618-2742

E-mail: cmccorporatemanagement@
shaw.ca
Website: http://www.Corporate
managementconsultants.com
Gerald Rekve

United States

Alabama

Business Planning Inc.
300 Office Park Dr.
Birmingham, AL 35223-2474
(205)870-7090
Fax: (205)870-7103

Tradebank of Eastern Alabama
546 Broad St., Ste. 3
Gadsden, AL 35901
(205)547-8700
Fax: (205)547-8718
E-mail: mansion@webex.com
Website: http://www.webex.com/~tea

Alaska

AK Business Development Center
3335 Arctic Blvd., Ste. 203
Anchorage, AK 99503
(907)562-0335
Free: 800-478-3474
Fax: (907)562-6988
E-mail: abdc@gci.net
Website: http://www.abdc.org

Business Matters
PO Box 287
Fairbanks, AK 99707
(907)452-5650

Arizona

Carefree Direct Marketing Corp.
8001 E Serene St.
PO Box 3737
Carefree, AZ 85377-3737
(480)488-4227
Fax: (480)488-2841

Trans Energy Corp.
1739 W 7th Ave.
Mesa, AZ 85202
(480)827-7915
Fax: (480)967-6601
E-mail: aha@clean-air.org
Website: http://www.clean-air.org

CMAS
5125 N 16th St.
Phoenix, AZ 85016

(602)395-1001
Fax: (602)604-8180

Comgate Telemanagement Ltd.
706 E Bell Rd., Ste. 105
Phoenix, AZ 85022
(602)485-5708
Fax: (602)485-5709
E-mail: comgate@netzone.com
Website: http://www.comgate.com

Moneysoft Inc.
1 E Camelback Rd. #550
Phoenix, AZ 85012
Free: 800-966-7797
E-mail: mbray@moneysoft.com

Harvey C. Skoog
PO Box 26439
Prescott Valley, AZ 86312
(520)772-1714
Fax: (520)772-2814

LMC Services
8711 E Pinnacle Peak Rd., No. 340
Scottsdale, AZ 85255-3555
(602)585-7177
Fax: (602)585-5880
E-mail: louws@earthlink.com

Sauerbrun Technology Group Ltd.
7979 E Princess Dr., Ste. 5
Scottsdale, AZ 85255-5878
(602)502-4950
Fax: (602)502-4292
E-mail: info@sauerbrun.com
Website: http://www.sauerbrun.com

Gary L. McLeod
PO Box 230
Sonoita, AZ 85637
Fax: (602)455-5661

Van Cleve Associates
6932 E 2nd St.
Tucson, AZ 85710
(520)296-2587
Fax: (520)296-3358

California

Acumen Group Inc.
(650)949-9349
Fax: (650)949-4845
E-mail: acumen-g@ix.netcom.com
Website: http://pw2.netcom.com/~janed/
acumen.html

On-line Career and Management Consulting
420 Central Ave., No. 314
Alameda, CA 94501

(510)864-0336
Fax: (510)864-0336
E-mail: career@dnai.com
Website: http://www.dnai.com/~career

Career Paths-Thomas E. Church & Associates Inc.
PO Box 2439
Aptos, CA 95001
(408)662-7950
Fax: (408)662-7955
E-mail: church@ix.netcom.com
Website: http://www.careerpaths-tom.com

Keck & Co. Business Consultants
410 Walsh Rd.
Atherton, CA 94027
(650)854-9588
Fax: (650)854-7240
E-mail: info@keckco.com
Website: http://www.keckco.com

Ben W. Laverty III, PhD, REA, CEI
4909 Stockdale Hwy., Ste. 132
Bakersfield, CA 93309
(661)283-8300
Free: 800-833-0373
Fax: (661)283-8313
E-mail: cstc@cstcsafety.com
Website: http://www.cstcsafety.com/cstc

Lindquist Consultants-Venture Planning
225 Arlington Ave.
Berkeley, CA 94707
(510)524-6685
Fax: (510)527-6604

Larson Associates
PO Box 9005
Brea, CA 92822
(714)529-4121
Fax: (714)572-3606
E-mail: ray@consultlarson.com
Website: http://www.consultlarson.com

Kremer Management Consulting
PO Box 500
Carmel, CA 93921
(408)626-8311
Fax: (408)624-2663
E-mail: ddkremer@aol.com

W and J PARTNERSHIP
PO Box 2499
18876 Edwin Markham Dr.
Castro Valley, CA 94546
(510)583-7751
Fax: (510)583-7645
E-mail: wamorgan@wjpartnership.com
Website: http://www.wjpartnership.com

JB Associates
21118 Gardena Dr.
Cupertino, CA 95014
(408)257-0214
Fax: (408)257-0216
E-mail: semarang@sirius.com

House Agricultural Consultants
PO Box 1615
Davis, CA 95617-1615
(916)753-3361
Fax: (916)753-0464
E-mail: infoag@houseag.com
Website: http://www.houseag.com/

3C Systems Co.
16161 Ventura Blvd., Ste. 815
Encino, CA 91436
(818)907-1302
Fax: (818)907-1357
E-mail: mark@3CSysCo.com
Website: http://www.3CSysCo.com

Technical Management Consultants
3624 Westfall Dr.
Encino, CA 91436-4154
(818)784-0626
Fax: (818)501-5575
E-mail: tmcrs@aol.com

RAINWATER-GISH & Associates, Business Finance & Development
317 3rd St., Ste. 3
Eureka, CA 95501
(707)443-0030
Fax: (707)443-5683

Global Tradelinks
451 Pebble Beach Pl.
Fullerton, CA 92835
(714)441-2280
Fax: (714)441-2281
E-mail: info@globaltradelinks.com
Website: http://www.globaltradelinks.com

Strategic Business Group
800 Cienaga Dr.
Fullerton, CA 92835-1248
(714)449-1040
Fax: (714)525-1631

Burnes Consulting
20537 Wolf Creek Rd.
Grass Valley, CA 95949
(530)346-8188
Free: 800-949-9021
Fax: (530)346-7704
E-mail: kent@burnesconsulting.com
Website: http://www.burnesconsulting.com

Pioneer Business Consultants
9042 Garfield Ave., Ste. 312
Huntington Beach, CA 92646
(714)964-7600

Beblie, Brandt & Jacobs Inc.
16 Technology, Ste. 164
Irvine, CA 92618
(714)450-8790
Fax: (714)450-8799
E-mail: darcy@bbjinc.com
Website: http://198.147.90.26

Fluor Daniel Inc.
3353 Michelson Dr.
Irvine, CA 92612-0650
(949)975-2000
Fax: (949)975-5271
E-mail: sales.consulting@fluordaniel.com
Website: http://www.fluordaniel
consulting.com

MCS Associates
18300 Von Karman, Ste. 710
Irvine, CA 92612
(949)263-8700
Fax: (949)263-0770
E-mail: info@mcsassociates.com
Website: http://www.mcsassociates.com

Inspired Arts Inc.
4225 Executive Sq., Ste. 1160
La Jolla, CA 92037
(619)623-3525
Free: 800-851-4394
Fax: (619)623-3534
E-mail: info@inspiredarts.com
Website: http://www.inspiredarts.com

The Laresis Companies
PO Box 3284
La Jolla, CA 92038
(619)452-2720
Fax: (619)452-8744

RCL & Co.
PO Box 1143
737 Pearl St., Ste. 201
La Jolla, CA 92038
(619)454-8883
Fax: (619)454-8880

Comprehensive Business Services
3201 Lucas Cir.
Lafayette, CA 94549
(925)283-8272
Fax: (925)283-8272

The Ribble Group
27601 Forbes Rd., Ste. 52
Laguna Niguel, CA 92677

Organizations, Agencies, & Consultants

(714)582-1085
Fax: (714)582-6420
E-mail: ribble@deltanet.com

Norris Bernstein, CMC
9309 Marina Pacifica Dr. N
Long Beach, CA 90803
(562)493-5458
Fax: (562)493-5459
E-mail: norris@ctecomputer.com
Website: http://foodconsultants.com/
bernstein/

Horizon Consulting Services
1315 Garthwick Dr.
Los Altos, CA 94024
(415)967-0906
Fax: (415)967-0906

Brincko Associates Inc.
1801 Avenue of the Stars, Ste. 1054
Los Angeles, CA 90067
(310)553-4523
Fax: (310)553-6782

**Rubenstein/Justman Management
Consultants**
2049 Century Park E, 24th Fl.
Los Angeles, CA 90067
(310)282-0800
Fax: (310)282-0400
E-mail: info@rjmc.net
Website: http://www.rjmc.net

F.J. Schroeder & Associates
1926 Westholme Ave.
Los Angeles, CA 90025
(310)470-2655
Fax: (310)470-6378
E-mail: fjsacons@aol.com
Website: http://www.mcninet.com/
GlobalLook/Fjschroe.html

Western Management Associates
5959 W Century Blvd., Ste. 565
Los Angeles, CA 90045-6506
(310)645-1091
Free: (888)788-6534
Fax: (310)645-1092
E-mail: gene@cfoforrent.com
Website: http://www.cfoforrent.com

Darrell Sell and Associates
Los Gatos, CA 95030
(408)354-7794
E-mail: darrell@netcom.com

Leslie J. Zambo
3355 Michael Dr.
Marina, CA 93933
(408)384-7086

Fax: (408)647-4199
E-mail: 104776.1552@compuserve.com

Marketing Services Management
PO Box 1377
Martinez, CA 94553
(510)370-8527
Fax: (510)370-8527
E-mail: markserve@biotechnet.com

William M. Shine Consulting Service
PO Box 127
Moraga, CA 94556-0127
(510)376-6516

Palo Alto Management Group Inc.
2672 Bayshore Pky., Ste. 701
Mountain View, CA 94043
(415)968-4374
Fax: (415)968-4245
E-mail: mburwen@pamg.com

BizplanSource
1048 Irvine Ave., Ste. 621
Newport Beach, CA 92660
Free: 888-253-0974
Fax: 800-859-8254
E-mail: info@bizplansource.com
Website: http://www.bizplansource.com
Adam Greengrass, President

The Market Connection
4020 Birch St., Ste. 203
Newport Beach, CA 92660
(714)731-6273
Fax: (714)833-0253

Muller Associates
PO Box 7264
Newport Beach, CA 92658
(714)646-1169
Fax: (714)646-1169

International Health Resources
PO Box 329
North San Juan, CA 95960-0329
(530)292-1266
Fax: (530)292-1243
Website: http://www.futureof
healthcare.com

NEXUS - Consultants to Management
PO Box 1531
Novato, CA 94948
(415)897-4400
Fax: (415)898-2252
E-mail: jimnexus@aol.com

Aerospcace.Org
PO Box 28831
Oakland, CA 94604-8831

(510)530-9169
Fax: (510)530-3411
Website: http://www.aerospace.org

Intelequest Corp.
722 Gailen Ave.
Palo Alto, CA 94303
(415)968-3443
Fax: (415)493-6954
E-mail: frits@iqix.com

McLaughlin & Associates
66 San Marino Cir.
Rancho Mirage, CA 92270
(760)321-2932
Fax: (760)328-2474
E-mail: jackmcla@msn.com

**Carrera Consulting Group, a division
of Maximus**
2110 21st St., Ste. 400
Sacramento, CA 95818
(916)456-3300
Fax: (916)456-3306
E-mail: central@carreraconsulting.com
Website: http://www.carreraconsulting.com

**Bay Area Tax Consultants and Bayhill
Financial Consultants**
1150 Bayhill Dr., Ste. 1150
San Bruno, CA 94066-3004
(415)952-8786
Fax: (415)588-4524
E-mail: baytax@compuserve.com
Website: http://www.baytax.com/

AdCon Services, LLC
8871 Hillery Dr.
Dan Diego, CA 92126
(858)433-1411
E-mail: adam@adconservices.com
Website: http://www.adconservices.com
Adam Greengrass

California Business Incubation Network
101 W Broadway, No. 480
San Diego, CA 92101
(619)237-0559
Fax: (619)237-0521

G.R. Gordetsky Consultants Inc.
11414 Windy Summit Pl.
San Diego, CA 92127
(619)487-4939
Fax: (619)487-5587
E-mail: gordet@pacbell.net

Freeman, Sullivan & Co.
131 Steuart St., Ste. 500
San Francisco, CA 94105
(415)777-0707

Free: 800-777-0737
Fax: (415)777-2420
Website: http://www.fsc-research.com

Ideas Unlimited
2151 California St., Ste. 7
San Francisco, CA 94115
(415)931-0641
Fax: (415)931-0880

Russell Miller Inc.
300 Montgomery St., Ste. 900
San Francisco, CA 94104
(415)956-7474
Fax: (415)398-0620
E-mail: rmi@pacbell.net
Website: http://www.rmisf.com

PKF Consulting
425 California St., Ste. 1650
San Francisco, CA 94104
(415)421-5378
Fax: (415)956-7708
E-mail: callahan@pkfc.com
Website: http://www.pkfonline.com

Welling & Woodard Inc.
1067 Broadway
San Francisco, CA 94133
(415)776-4500
Fax: (415)776-5067

Highland Associates
16174 Highland Dr.
San Jose, CA 95127
(408)272-7008
Fax: (408)272-4040

ORDIS Inc.
6815 Trinidad Dr.
San Jose, CA 95120-2056
(408)268-3321
Free: 800-446-7347
Fax: (408)268-3582
E-mail: ordis@ordis.com
Website: http://www.ordis.com

Stanford Resources Inc.
20 Great Oaks Blvd., Ste. 200
San Jose, CA 95119
(408)360-8400
Fax: (408)360-8410
E-mail: sales@stanfordsources.com
Website: http://www.stanfordresources.com

Technology Properties Ltd. Inc.
PO Box 20250
San Jose, CA 95160
(408)243-9898
Fax: (408)296-6637
E-mail: sanjose@tplnet.com

Helfert Associates
1777 Borel Pl., Ste. 508
San Mateo, CA 94402-3514
(650)377-0540
Fax: (650)377-0472

Mykytyn Consulting Group Inc.
185 N Redwood Dr., Ste. 200
San Rafael, CA 94903
(415)491-1770
Fax: (415)491-1251
E-mail: info@mcgi.com
Website: http://www.mcgi.com

Omega Management Systems Inc.
3 Mount Darwin Ct.
San Rafael, CA 94903-1109
(415)499-1300
Fax: (415)492-9490
E-mail: omegamgt@ix.netcom.com

The Information Group Inc.
4675 Stevens Creek Blvd., Ste. 100
Santa Clara, CA 95051
(408)985-7877
Fax: (408)985-2945
E-mail: dvincent@tig-usa.com
Website: http://www.tig-usa.com

Cast Management Consultants
1620 26th St., Ste. 2040N
Santa Monica, CA 90404
(310)828-7511
Fax: (310)453-6831

Cuma Consulting Management
Box 724
Santa Rosa, CA 95402
(707)785-2477
Fax: (707)785-2478

The E-Myth Academy
131B Stony Cir., Ste. 2000
Santa Rosa, CA 95401
(707)569-5600
Free: 800-221-0266
Fax: (707)569-5700
E-mail: info@e-myth.com
Website: http://www.e-myth.com

Reilly, Connors & Ray
1743 Canyon Rd.
Spring Valley, CA 91977
(619)698-4808
Fax: (619)460-3892
E-mail: davidray@adnc.com

Management Consultants
Sunnyvale, CA 94087-4700
(408)773-0321

RJR Associates
1639 Lewiston Dr.
Sunnyvale, CA 94087
(408)737-7720
E-mail: bobroy@rjrassoc.com
Website: http://www.rjrassoc.com

Schwafel Associates
333 Cobalt Way, Ste. 21
Sunnyvale, CA 94085
(408)720-0649
Fax: (408)720-1796
E-mail: schwafel@ricochet.net
Website: http://www.patca.org

Staubs Business Services
23320 S Vermont Ave.
Torrance, CA 90502-2940
(310)830-9128
Fax: (310)830-9128
E-mail: Harry_L_Staubs@Lamg.com

Out of Your Mind...and Into the Marketplace
13381 White Sands Dr.
Tustin, CA 92780-4565
(714)544-0248
Free: 800-419-1513
Fax: (714)730-1414
E-mail: lpinson@aol.com
Website: http://www.business-plan.com

Independent Research Services
PO Box 2426
Van Nuys, CA 91404-2426
(818)993-3622

Ingman Company Inc.
7949 Woodley Ave., Ste. 120
Van Nuys, CA 91406-1232
(818)375-5027
Fax: (818)894-5001

Innovative Technology Associates
3639 E Harbor Blvd., Ste. 203E
Ventura, CA 93001
(805)650-9353

Grid Technology Associates
20404 Tufts Cir.
Walnut, CA 91789
(909)444-0922
Fax: (909)444-0922
E-mail: grid_technology@msn.com

Ridge Consultants Inc.
100 Pringle Ave., Ste. 580
Walnut Creek, CA 94596
(925)274-1990
Fax: (510)274-1956
E-mail: info@ridgecon.com
Website: http://www.ridgecon.com

Bell Springs Publishing
PO Box 1240
Willits, CA 95490
(707)459-6372
E-mail: bellsprings@sabernet
Website: http://www.bellsprings.com

Hutchinson Consulting and Appraisal
23245 Sylvan St., Ste. 103
Woodland Hills, CA 91367
(818)888-8175
Free: 800-977-7548
Fax: (818)888-8220
E-mail: r.f.hutchinson-cpa@worldnet.
att.net

Colorado

Sam Boyer & Associates
4255 S Buckley Rd., No. 136
Aurora, CO 80013
Free: 800-785-0485
Fax: (303)766-8740
E-mail: samboyer@samboyer.com
Website: http://www.samboyer.com/

Ameriwest Business Consultants Inc.
PO Box 26266
Colorado Springs, CO 80936
(719)380-7096
Fax: (719)380-7096
E-mail: email@abchelp.com
Website: http://www.abchelp.com

GVNW Consulting Inc.
2270 La Montana Way
Colorado Springs, CO 80936
(719)594-5800
Fax: (719)594-5803
Website: http://www.gvnw.com

M-Squared Inc.
755 San Gabriel Pl.
Colorado Springs, CO 80906
(719)576-2554
Fax: (719)576-2554

Thornton Financial FNIC
1024 Centre Ave., Bldg. E
Fort Collins, CO 80526-1849
(970)221-2089
Fax: (970)484-5206

TenEyck Associates
1760 Cherryville Rd.
Greenwood Village, CO 80121-1503
(303)758-6129
Fax: (303)761-8286

Associated Enterprises Ltd.
13050 W Ceder Dr., Unit 11
Lakewood, CO 80228

(303)988-6695
Fax: (303)988-6739
E-mail: ael1@classic.msn.com

The Vincent Company Inc.
200 Union Blvd., Ste. 210
Lakewood, CO 80228
(303)989-7271
Free: 800-274-0733
Fax: (303)989-7570
E-mail: vincent@vincentco.com
Website: http://www.vincentco.com

Johnson & West Management Consultants Inc.
7612 S Logan Dr.
Littleton, CO 80122
(303)730-2810
Fax: (303)730-3219

Western Capital Holdings Inc.
10050 E Applwood Dr.
Parker, CO 80138
(303)841-1022
Fax: (303)770-1945

Connecticut

Stratman Group Inc.
40 Tower Ln.
Avon, CT 06001-4222
(860)677-2898
Free: 800-551-0499
Fax: (860)677-8210

Cowherd Consulting Group Inc.
106 Stephen Mather Rd.
Darien, CT 06820
(203)655-2150
Fax: (203)655-6427

Greenwich Associates
8 Greenwich Office Park
Greenwich, CT 06831-5149
(203)629-1200
Fax: (203)629-1229
E-mail: lisa@greenwich.com
Website: http://www.greenwich.com

Follow-up News
185 Pine St., Ste. 818
Manchester, CT 06040
(860)647-7542
Free: 800-708-0696
Fax: (860)646-6544
E-mail: Followupnews@aol.com

Lovins & Associates Consulting
309 Edwards St.
New Haven, CT 06511
(203)787-3367

Fax: (203)624-7599
E-mail: Alovinsphd@aol.com
Website: http://www.lovinsgroup.com

JC Ventures Inc.
4 Arnold St.
Old Greenwich, CT 06870-1203
(203)698-1990
Free: 800-698-1997
Fax: (203)698-2638

Charles L. Hornung Associates
52 Ned's Mountain Rd.
Ridgefield, CT 06877
(203)431-0297

Manus
100 Prospect St., S Tower
Stamford, CT 06901
(203)326-3880
Free: 800-445-0942
Fax: (203)326-3890
E-mail: manus1@aol.com
Website: http://www.RightManus.com

RealBusinessPlans.com
156 Westport Rd.
Wilton, CT 06897
(914)837-2886
E-mail: ct@realbusinessplans.com
Website: http://www.RealBusinessPlans.com
Tony Tecce

Delaware

Focus Marketing
61-7 Habor Dr.
Claymont, DE 19703
(302)793-3064

Daedalus Ventures Ltd.
PO Box 1474
Hockessin, DE 19707
(302)239-6758
Fax: (302)239-9991
E-mail: daedalus@mail.del.net

The Formula Group
PO Box 866
Hockessin, DE 19707
(302)456-0952
Fax: (302)456-1354
E-mail: formula@netaxs.com

Selden Enterprises Inc.
2502 Silverside Rd., Ste. 1
Wilmington, DE 19810-3740
(302)529-7113
Fax: (302)529-7442
E-mail: selden2@bellatlantic.net
Website: http://www.seldenenterprises.com

District of Columbia

Bruce W. McGee and Associates
7826 Eastern Ave. NW, Ste. 30
Washington, DC 20012
(202)726-7272
Fax: (202)726-2946

McManis Associates Inc.
1900 K St. NW, Ste. 700
Washington, DC 20006
(202)466-7680
Fax: (202)872-1898
Website: http://www.mcmanis-mmi.com

Smith, Dawson & Andrews Inc.
1000 Connecticut Ave., Ste. 302
Washington, DC 20036
(202)835-0740
Fax: (202)775-8526
E-mail: webmaster@sda-inc.com
Website: http://www.sda-inc.com

Florida

BackBone, Inc.
20404 Hacienda Court
Boca Raton, FL 33498
(561)470-0965
Fax: 516-908-4038
E-mail: BPlans@backboneinc.com
Website: http://www.backboneinc.com
Charles Epstein, President

Whalen & Associates Inc.
4255 Northwest 26 Ct.
Boca Raton, FL 33434
(561)241-5950
Fax: (561)241-7414
E-mail: drwhalen@ix.netcom.com

E.N. Rysso & Associates
180 Bermuda Petrel Ct.
Daytona Beach, FL 32119
(386)760-3028
E-mail: erysso@aol.com

Virtual Technocrats LLC
560 Lavers Circle, #146
Delray Beach, FL 33444
(561)265-3509
E-mail: josh@virtualtechnocrats.com;
info@virtualtechnocrats.com
Website: http://www.virtualtechno
crats.com
Josh Eikov, Managing Director

Eric Sands Consulting Services
6193 Rock Island Rd., Ste. 412
Fort Lauderdale, FL 33319
(954)721-4767

Fax: (954)720-2815
E-mail: easands@aol.com
Website: http://www.ericsandsconsultig.com

Professional Planning Associates, Inc.
1975 E. Sunrise Blvd. Suite 607
Fort Lauderdale, FL 33304
(954)764-5204
Fax: 954-463-4172
E-mail: Mgoldstein@proplana.com
Website: http://proplana.com
Michael Goldstein, President

Host Media Corp.
3948 S 3rd St., Ste. 191
Jacksonville Beach, FL 32250
(904)285-3239
Fax: (904)285-5618
E-mail: msconsulting@compuserve.com
Website: http://www.media
servicesgroup.com

William V. Hall
1925 Brickell, Ste. D-701
Miami, FL 33129
(305)856-9622
Fax: (305)856-4113
E-mail: williamvhall@compuserve.com

F.A. McGee Inc.
800 Claughton Island Dr., Ste. 401
Miami, FL 33131
(305)377-9123

Taxplan Inc.
Mirasol International Ctr.
2699 Collins Ave.
Miami Beach, FL 33140
(305)538-3303

T.C. Brown & Associates
8415 Excalibur Cir., Apt. B1
Naples, FL 34108
(941)594-1949
Fax: (941)594-0611
E-mail: tcater@naples.net.com

RLA International Consulting
713 Lagoon Dr.
North Palm Beach, FL 33408
(407)626-4258
Fax: (407)626-5772

Comprehensive Franchising Inc.
2465 Ridgecrest Ave.
Orange Park, FL 32065
(904)272-6567
Free: 800-321-6567
Fax: (904)272-6750
E-mail: theimp@cris.com
Website: http://www.franchise411.com

Hunter G. Jackson Jr. - Consulting Environmental Physicist
PO Box 618272
Orlando, FL 32861-8272
(407)295-4188
E-mail: hunterjackson@juno.com

F. Newton Parks
210 El Brillo Way
Palm Beach, FL 33480
(561)833-1727
Fax: (561)833-4541

Avery Business Development Services
2506 St. Michel Ct.
Ponte Vedra Beach, FL 32082
(904)285-6033
Fax: (904)285-6033

Strategic Business Planning Co.
PO Box 821006
South Florida, FL 33082-1006
(954)704-9100
Fax: (954)438-7333
E-mail: info@bizplan.com
Website: http://www.bizplan.com

Dufresne Consulting Group Inc.
10014 N Dale Mabry, Ste. 101
Tampa, FL 33618-4426
(813)264-4775
Fax: (813)264-9300
Website: http://www.dcgconsult.com

Agrippa Enterprises Inc.
PO Box 175
Venice, FL 34284-0175
(941)355-7876
E-mail: webservices@agrippa.com
Website: http://www.agrippa.com

Center for Simplified Strategic Planning Inc.
PO Box 3324
Vero Beach, FL 32964-3324
(561)231-3636
Fax: (561)231-1099
Website: http://www.cssp.com

Georgia

Marketing Spectrum Inc.
115 Perimeter Pl., Ste. 440
Atlanta, GA 30346
(770)395-7244
Fax: (770)393-4071

Business Ventures Corp.
1650 Oakbrook Dr., Ste. 405
Norcross, GA 30093
(770)729-8000
Fax: (770)729-8028

Informed Decisions Inc.
100 Falling Cheek
Sautee Nacoochee, GA 30571
(706)878-1905
Fax: (706)878-1802
E-mail: skylake@compuserve.com

Tom C. Davis & Associates, P.C.
3189 Perimeter Rd.
Valdosta, GA 31602
(912)247-9801
Fax: (912)244-7704
E-mail: mail@tcdcpa.com
Website: http://www.tcdcpa.com/

Illinois

TWD and Associates
431 S Patton
Arlington Heights, IL 60005
(847)398-6410
Fax: (847)255-5095
E-mail: tdoo@aol.com

Management Planning Associates Inc.
2275 Half Day Rd., Ste. 350
Bannockburn, IL 60015-1277
(847)945-2421
Fax: (847)945-2425

Phil Faris Associates
86 Old Mill Ct.
Barrington, IL 60010
(847)382-4888
Fax: (847)382-4890
E-mail: pfaris@meginsnet.net

Seven Continents Technology
787 Stonebridge
Buffalo Grove, IL 60089
(708)577-9653
Fax: (708)870-1220

Grubb & Blue Inc.
2404 Windsor Pl.
Champaign, IL 61820
(217)366-0052
Fax: (217)356-0117

ACE Accounting Service Inc.
3128 N Bernard St.
Chicago, IL 60618
(773)463-7854
Fax: (773)463-7854

AON Consulting Worldwide
200 E Randolph St., 10th Fl.
Chicago, IL 60601
(312)381-4800
Free: 800-438-6487
Fax: (312)381-0240
Website: http://www.aon.com

FMS Consultants
5801 N Sheridan Rd., Ste. 3D
Chicago, IL 60660
(773)561-7362
Fax: (773)561-6274

Grant Thornton
800 1 Prudential Plz.
130 E Randolph St.
Chicago, IL 60601
(312)856-0001
Fax: (312)861-1340
E-mail: gtinfo@gt.com
Website: http://www.grantthornton.com

Kingsbury International Ltd.
5341 N Glenwood Ave.
Chicago, IL 60640
(773)271-3030
Fax: (773)728-7080
E-mail: jetlag@mcs.com
Website: http://www.kingbiz.com

MacDougall & Blake Inc.
1414 N Wells St., Ste. 311
Chicago, IL 60610-1306
(312)587-3330
Fax: (312)587-3699
E-mail: jblake@compuserve.com

James C. Osburn Ltd.
6445 N. Western Ave., Ste. 304
Chicago, IL 60645
(773)262-4428
Fax: (773)262-6755
E-mail: osburnltd@aol.com

Tarifero & Tazewell Inc.
211 S Clark
Chicago, IL 60690
(312)665-9714
Fax: (312)665-9716

Human Energy Design Systems
620 Roosevelt Dr.
Edwardsville, IL 62025
(618)692-0258
Fax: (618)692-0819

China Business Consultants Group
931 Dakota Cir.
Naperville, IL 60563
(630)778-7992
Fax: (630)778-7915
E-mail: cbcq@aol.com

Center for Workforce Effectiveness
500 Skokie Blvd., Ste. 222
Northbrook, IL 60062
(847)559-8777
Fax: (847)559-8778

E-mail: office@cwelink.com
Website: http://www.cwelink.com

Smith Associates
1320 White Mountain Dr.
Northbrook, IL 60062
(847)480-7200
Fax: (847)480-9828

Francorp Inc.
20200 Governors Dr.
Olympia Fields, IL 60461
(708)481-2900
Free: 800-372-6244
Fax: (708)481-5885
E-mail: francorp@aol.com
Website: http://www.francorpinc.com

Camber Business Strategy Consultants
1010 S Plum Tree Ct
Palatine, IL 60078-0986
(847)202-0101
Fax: (847)705-7510
E-mail: camber@ameritech.net

Partec Enterprise Group
5202 Keith Dr.
Richton Park, IL 60471
(708)503-4047
Fax: (708)503-9468

Rockford Consulting Group Ltd.
Century Plz., Ste. 206
7210 E State St.
Rockford, IL 61108
(815)229-2900
Free: 800-667-7495
Fax: (815)229-2612
E-mail: rligus@RockfordConsulting.com
Website: http://www.Rockford
Consulting.com

RSM McGladrey Inc.
1699 E Woodfield Rd., Ste. 300
Schaumburg, IL 60173-4969
(847)413-6900
Fax: (847)517-7067
Website: http://www.rsmmcgladrey.com

A.D. Star Consulting
320 Euclid
Winnetka, IL 60093
(847)446-7827
Fax: (847)446-7827
E-mail: startwo@worldnet.att.net

Indiana

Modular Consultants Inc.
3109 Crabtree Ln.
Elkhart, IN 46514

(219)264-5761
Fax: (219)264-5761
E-mail: sasabo5313@aol.com

Midwest Marketing Research
PO Box 1077
Goshen, IN 46527
(219)533-0548
Fax: (219)533-0540
E-mail: 103365.654@compuserve

Ketchum Consulting Group
8021 Knue Rd., Ste. 112
Indianapolis, IN 46250
(317)845-5411
Fax: (317)842-9941

**MDI Management
Consulting**
1519 Park Dr.
Munster, IN 46321
(219)838-7909
Fax: (219)838-7909

Iowa

McCord Consulting Group Inc.
4533 Pine View Dr. NE
PO Box 11024
Cedar Rapids, IA 52410
(319)378-0077
Fax: (319)378-1577
E-mail: smmccord@hom.com
Website: http://www.mccordgroup.com

Management Solutions L.C.
3815 Lincoln Pl. Dr.
Des Moines, IA 50312
(515)277-6408
Fax: (515)277-3506
E-mail: wasunimers@uswest.net

Grandview Marketing
15 Red Bridge Dr.
Sioux City, IA 51104
(712)239-3122
Fax: (712)258-7578
E-mail: eandrews@pionet.net

Kansas

Assessments in Action
513A N Mur-Len
Olathe, KS 66062
(913)764-6270
Free: (888)548-1504
Fax: (913)764-6495
E-mail: lowdene@qni.com
Website: http://www.assessments-
in-action.com

Maine

Edgemont Enterprises
PO Box 8354
Portland, ME 04104
(207)871-8964
Fax: (207)871-8964

Pan Atlantic Consultants
5 Milk St.
Portland, ME 04101
(207)871-8622
Fax: (207)772-4842
E-mail: pmurphy@maine.rr.com
Website: http://www.panatlantic.net

Maryland

Clemons & Associates Inc.
5024-R Campbell Blvd.
Baltimore, MD 21236
(410)931-8100
Fax: (410)931-8111
E-mail: info@clemonsmgmt.com
Website: http://www.clemonsmgmt.com

Imperial Group Ltd.
305 Washington Ave., Ste. 204
Baltimore, MD 21204-6009
(410)337-8500
Fax: (410)337-7641

Leadership Institute
3831 Yolando Rd.
Baltimore, MD 21218
(410)366-9111
Fax: (410)243-8478
E-mail: behconsult@aol.com

Burdeshaw Associates Ltd.
4701 Sangamore Rd.
Bethesda, MD 20816-2508
(301)229-5800
Fax: (301)229-5045
E-mail: jstacy@burdeshaw.com
Website: http://www.burdeshaw.com

Michael E. Cohen
5225 Pooks Hill Rd., Ste. 1119 S
Bethesda, MD 20814
(301)530-5738
Fax: (301)530-2988
E-mail: mecohen@crosslink.net

World Development Group Inc.
5272 River Rd., Ste. 650
Bethesda, MD 20816-1405
(301)652-1818
Fax: (301)652-1250
E-mail: wdg@has.com
Website: http://www.worlddg.com

Swartz Consulting
PO Box 4301
Crofton, MD 21114-4301
(301)262-6728

Software Solutions International Inc.
9633 Duffer Way
Gaithersburg, MD 20886
(301)330-4136
Fax: (301)330-4136

Strategies Inc.
8 Park Center Ct., Ste. 200
Owings Mills, MD 21117
(410)363-6669
Fax: (410)363-1231
E-mail: strategies@strat1.com
Website: http://www.strat1.com

Hammer Marketing Resources
179 Inverness Rd.
Severna Park, MD 21146
(410)544-9191
Fax: (305)675-3277
E-mail: info@gohammer.com
Website: http://www.gohammer.com

Andrew Sussman & Associates
13731 Kretsinger
Smithsburg, MD 21783
(301)824-2943
Fax: (301)824-2943

Massachusetts

Geibel Marketing and Public Relations
PO Box 611
Belmont, MA 02478-0005
(617)484-8285
Fax: (617)489-3567
E-mail: jgeibel@geibelpr.com
Website: http://www.geibelpr.com

Bain & Co.
2 Copley Pl.
Boston, MA 02116
(617)572-2000
Fax: (617)572-2427
E-mail: corporate.inquiries@bain.com
Website: http://www.bain.com

Mehr & Co.
62 Kinnaird St.
Cambridge, MA 02139
(617)876-3311
Fax: (617)876-3023
E-mail: mehrco@aol.com

Monitor Company Inc.
2 Canal Park
Cambridge, MA 02141

(617)252-2000
Fax: (617)252-2100
Website: http://www.monitor.com

Information & Research Associates
PO Box 3121
Framingham, MA 01701
(508)788-0784

Walden Consultants Ltd.
252 Pond St.
Hopkinton, MA 01748
(508)435-4882
Fax: (508)435-3971
Website: http://www.waldencon
sultants.com

Jeffrey D. Marshall
102 Mitchell Rd.
Ipswich, MA 01938-1219
(508)356-1113
Fax: (508)356-2989

Consulting Resources Corp.
6 Northbrook Park
Lexington, MA 02420
(781)863-1222
Fax: (781)863-1441
E-mail: res@consultingresources.net
Website: http://www.consulting
resources.net

Planning Technologies Group L.L.C.
92 Hayden Ave.
Lexington, MA 02421
(781)778-4678
Fax: (781)861-1099
E-mail: ptg@plantech.com
Website: http://www.plantech.com

Kalba International Inc.
23 Sandy Pond Rd.
Lincoln, MA 01773
(781)259-9589
Fax: (781)259-1460
E-mail: info@kalbainternational.com
Website: http://www.kalbainter
national.com

VMB Associates Inc.
115 Ashland St.
Melrose, MA 02176
(781)665-0623
Fax: (425)732-7142
E-mail: vmbinc@aol.com

The Company Doctor
14 Pudding Stone Ln.
Mendon, MA 01756
(508)478-1747
Fax: (508)478-0520

Data and Strategies Group Inc.
190 N Main St.
Natick, MA 01760
(508)653-9990
Fax: (508)653-7799
E-mail: dsginc@dsggroup.com
Website: http://www.dsggroup.com

The Enterprise Group
73 Parker Rd.
Needham, MA 02494
(617)444-6631
Fax: (617)433-9991
E-mail: lsacco@world.std.com
Website: http://www.enterprise-group.com

PSMJ Resources Inc.
10 Midland Ave.
Newton, MA 02458
(617)965-0055
Free: 800-537-7765
Fax: (617)965-5152
E-mail: psmj@tiac.net
Website: http://www.psmj.com

Scheur Management Group Inc.
255 Washington St., Ste. 100
Newton, MA 02458-1611
(617)969-7500
Fax: (617)969-7508
E-mail: smgnow@scheur.com
Website: http://www.scheur.com

I.E.E.E., Boston Section
240 Bear Hill Rd., 202B
Waltham, MA 02451-1017
(781)890-5294
Fax: (781)890-5290

Business Planning and Consulting Services
20 Beechwood Ter.
Wellesley, MA 02482
(617)237-9151
Fax: (617)237-9151

Michigan

Walter Frederick Consulting
1719 South Blvd.
Ann Arbor, MI 48104
(313)662-4336
Fax: (313)769-7505

Fox Enterprises
6220 W Freeland Rd.
Freeland, MI 48623
(517)695-9170
Fax: (517)695-9174
E-mail: foxjw@concentric.net
Website: http://www.cris.com/~foxjw

G.G.W. and Associates
1213 Hampton
Jackson, MI 49203
(517)782-2255
Fax: (517)782-2255

Altamar Group Ltd.
6810 S Cedar, Ste. 2-B
Lansing, MI 48911
(517)694-0910
Free: 800-443-2627
Fax: (517)694-1377

Sheffieck Consultants Inc.
23610 Greening Dr.
Novi, MI 48375-3130
(248)347-3545
Fax: (248)347-3530
E-mail: cfsheff@concentric.net

Rehmann, Robson PC
5800 Gratiot
Saginaw, MI 48605
(517)799-9580
Fax: (517)799-0227
Website: http://www.rrpc.com

Francis & Co.
17200 W 10 Mile Rd., Ste. 207
Southfield, MI 48075
(248)559-7600
Fax: (248)559-5249

Private Ventures Inc.
16000 W 9 Mile Rd., Ste. 504
Southfield, MI 48075
(248)569-1977
Free: 800-448-7614
Fax: (248)569-1838
E-mail: pventuresi@aol.com

JGK Associates
14464 Kerner Dr.
Sterling Heights, MI 48313
(810)247-9055
Fax: (248)822-4977
E-mail: kozlowski@home.com

Minnesota

Health Fitness Corp.
3500 W 80th St., Ste. 130
Bloomington, MN 55431
(612)831-6830
Fax: (612)831-7264

Consatech Inc.
PO Box 1047
Burnsville, MN 55337
(612)953-1088
Fax: (612)435-2966

Robert F. Knotek
14960 Ironwood Ct.
Eden Prairie, MN 55346
(612)949-2875

DRI Consulting
7715 Stonewood Ct.
Edina, MN 55439
(612)941-9656
Fax: (612)941-2693
E-mail: dric@dric.com
Website: http://www.dric.com

Markin Consulting
12072 87th Pl. N
Maple Grove, MN 55369
(612)493-3568
Fax: (612)493-5744
E-mail: markin@markinconsulting.com
Website: http://www.markin
consulting.com

Minnesota Cooperation Office for Small Business & Job Creation Inc.
5001 W 80th St., Ste. 825
Minneapolis, MN 55437
(612)830-1230
Fax: (612)830-1232
E-mail: mncoop@msn.com
Website: http://www.mnco.org

Enterprise Consulting Inc.
PO Box 1111
Minnetonka, MN 55345
(612)949-5909
Fax: (612)906-3965

Amdahl International
724 1st Ave. SW
Rochester, MN 55902
(507)252-0402
Fax: (507)252-0402
E-mail: amdahl@best-service.com
Website: http://www.wp.com/amdahl_int

Power Systems Research
1365 Corporate Center Curve, 2nd Fl.
St. Paul, MN 55121
(612)905-8400
Free: (888)625-8612
Fax: (612)454-0760
E-mail: Barb@Powersys.com
Website: http://www.powersys.com

Missouri

Business Planning and Development Corp.
4030 Charlotte St.
Kansas City, MO 64110
(816)753-0495

E-mail: humph@bpdev.demon.co.uk
Website: http://www.bpdev.demon.co.uk

CFO Service
10336 Donoho
St. Louis, MO 63131
(314)750-2940
E-mail: jskae@cfoservice.com
Website: http://www.cfoservice.com

Nebraska

International Management Consulting Group Inc.
1309 Harlan Dr., Ste. 205
Bellevue, NE 68005
(402)291-4545
Free: 800-665-IMCG
Fax: (402)291-4343
E-mail: imcg@neonramp.com
Website: http://www.mgtcon
sulting.com

Heartland Management Consulting Group
1904 Barrington Pky.
Papillion, NE 68046
(402)339-2387
Fax: (402)339-1319

Nevada

The DuBois Group
865 Tahoe Blvd., Ste. 108
Incline Village, NV 89451
(775)832-0550
Free: 800-375-2935
Fax: (775)832-0556
E-mail: DuBoisGrp@aol.com

New Hampshire

Wolff Consultants
10 Buck Rd.
Hanover, NH 03755
(603)643-6015

BPT Consulting Associates Ltd.
12 Parmenter Rd., Ste. B-6
Londonderry, NH 03053
(603)437-8484
Free: (888)278-0030
Fax: (603)434-5388
E-mail: bptcons@tiac.net
Website: http://www.bptconsulting.com

New Jersey

Bedminster Group Inc.
1170 Rte. 22 E
Bridgewater, NJ 08807

(908)500-4155
Fax: (908)766-0780
E-mail: info@bedminstergroup.com
Website: http://www.bedminster
group.com
Fax: (202)806-1777
Terry Strong, Acting Regional Dir.

Delta Planning Inc.
PO Box 425
Denville, NJ 07834
(913)625-1742
Free: 800-672-0762
Fax: (973)625-3531
E-mail: DeltaP@worldnet.att.net
Website: http://deltaplanning.com

Kumar Associates Inc.
1004 Cumbermeade Rd.
Fort Lee, NJ 07024
(201)224-9480
Fax: (201)585-2343
E-mail: mail@kumarassociates.com
Website: http://kumarassociates.com

John Hall & Company Inc.
PO Box 187
Glen Ridge, NJ 07028
(973)680-4449
Fax: (973)680-4581
E-mail: jhcompany@aol.com

Market Focus
PO Box 402
Maplewood, NJ 07040
(973)378-2470
Fax: (973)378-2470
E-mail: mcss66@marketfocus.com

Vanguard Communications Corp.
100 American Rd.
Morris Plains, NJ 07950
(973)605-8000
Fax: (973)605-8329
Website: http://www.vanguard.net/

ConMar International Ltd.
1901 US Hwy. 130
North Brunswick, NJ 08902
(732)940-8347
Fax: (732)274-1199

KLW New Products
156 Cedar Dr.
Old Tappan, NJ 07675
(201)358-1300
Fax: (201)664-2594
E-mail: lrlarsen@usa.net
Website: http://www.klwnew
products.com

PA Consulting Group
315A Enterprise Dr.
Plainsboro, NJ 08536
(609)936-8300
Fax: (609)936-8811
E-mail: info@paconsulting.com
Website: http://www.pa-consulting.com

Aurora Marketing Management Inc.
66 Witherspoon St., Ste. 600
Princeton, NJ 08542
(908)904-1125
Fax: (908)359-1108
E-mail: aurora2@voicenet.com
Website: http://www.auroramarketing.net

Smart Business Supersite
88 Orchard Rd., CN-5219
Princeton, NJ 08543
(908)321-1924
Fax: (908)321-5156
E-mail: irv@smartbiz.com
Website: http://www.smartbiz.com

Tracelin Associates
1171 Main St., Ste. 6K
Rahway, NJ 07065
(732)381-3288

Schkeeper Inc.
130-6 Bodman Pl.
Red Bank, NJ 07701
(732)219-1965
Fax: (732)530-3703

Henry Branch Associates
2502 Harmon Cove Twr.
Secaucus, NJ 07094
(201)866-2008
Fax: (201)601-0101
E-mail: hbranch161@home.com

Robert Gibbons & Company Inc.
46 Knoll Rd.
Tenafly, NJ 07670-1050
(201)871-3933
Fax: (201)871-2173
E-mail: crisisbob@aol.com

PMC Management Consultants Inc.
6 Thistle Ln.
Three Bridges, NJ 08887-0332
(908)788-1014
Free: 800-PMC-0250
Fax: (908)806-7287
E-mail: int@pmc-management.com
Website: http://www.pmc-management.com

R.W. Bankart & Associates
20 Valley Ave., Ste. D-2

Westwood, NJ 07675-3607
(201)664-7672

New Mexico

Vondle & Associates Inc.
4926 Calle de Tierra, NE
Albuquerque, NM 87111
(505)292-8961
Fax: (505)296-2790
E-mail: vondle@aol.com

InfoNewMexico
2207 Black Hills Rd., NE
Rio Rancho, NM 87124
(505)891-2462
Fax: (505)896-8971

New York

Powers Research and Training Institute
PO Box 78
Bayville, NY 11709
(516)628-2250
Fax: (516)628-2252
E-mail: powercocch@compuserve.com
Website: http://www.nancypowers.com

Consortium House
296 Wittenberg Rd.
Bearsville, NY 12409
(845)679-8867
Fax: (845)679-9248
E-mail: eugenegs@aol.com
Website: http://www.chpub.com

Progressive Finance Corp.
3549 Tiemann Ave.
Bronx, NY 10469
(718)405-9029
Free: 800-225-8381
Fax: (718)405-1170

Wave Hill Associates Inc.
2621 Palisade Ave., Ste. 15-C
Bronx, NY 10463
(718)549-7368
Fax: (718)601-9670
E-mail: pepper@compuserve.com

Management Insight
96 Arlington Rd.
Buffalo, NY 14221
(716)631-3319
Fax: (716)631-0203
E-mail: michalski@foodservice
insight.com
Website: http://www.foodservice
insight.com

Samani International Enterprises, Marions Panyaught Consultancy
2028 Parsons
Flushing, NY 11357-3436
(917)287-8087
Fax: 800-873-8939
E-mail: vjp2@biostrategist.com
Website: http://www.biostrategist.com

Marketing Resources Group
71-58 Austin St.
Forest Hills, NY 11375
(718)261-8882

Mangabay Business Plans & Development Subsidiary of Innis Asset Allocation
125-10 Queens Blvd., Ste. 2202
Kew Gardens, NY 11415
(905)527-1947
Fax: 509-472-1935
E-mail: mangabay@mangabay.com
Website: http://www.mangabay.com
Lee Toh, Managing Partner

ComputerEase Co.
1301 Monmouth Ave.
Lakewood, NY 08701
(212)406-9464
Fax: (914)277-5317
E-mail: crawfordc@juno.com

Boice Dunham Group
30 W 13th St.
New York, NY 10011
(212)924-2200
Fax: (212)924-1108

Elizabeth Capen
27 E 95th St.
New York, NY 10128
(212)427-7654
Fax: (212)876-3190

Haver Analytics
60 E 42nd St., Ste. 2424
New York, NY 10017
(212)986-9300
Fax: (212)986-5857
E-mail: data@haver.com
Website: http://www.haver.com

The Jordan, Edmiston Group Inc.
150 E 52nd Ave., 18th Fl.
New York, NY 10022
(212)754-0710
Fax: (212)754-0337

KPMG International
345 Park Ave.
New York, NY 10154-0102
(212)758-9700

Fax: (212)758-9819
Website: http://www.kpmg.com

Mahoney Cohen Consulting Corp.
111 W 40th St., 12th Fl.
New York, NY 10018
(212)490-8000
Fax: (212)790-5913

Management Practice Inc.
342 Madison Ave.
New York, NY 10173-1230
(212)867-7948
Fax: (212)972-5188
Website: http://www.mpiweb.com

Moseley Associates Inc.
342 Madison Ave., Ste. 1414
New York, NY 10016
(212)213-6673
Fax: (212)687-1520

Practice Development Counsel
60 Sutton Pl. S
New York, NY 10022
(212)593-1549
Fax: (212)980-7940
E-mail: pwhaserot@pdcounsel.com
Website: http://www.pdcounsel.com

Unique Value International Inc.
575 Madison Ave., 10th Fl.
New York, NY 10022-1304
(212)605-0590
Fax: (212)605-0589

The Van Tulleken Co.
126 E 56th St.
New York, NY 10022
(212)355-1390
Fax: (212)755-3061
E-mail: newyork@vantulleken.com

Vencon Management Inc.
301 W 53rd St.
New York, NY 10019
(212)581-8787
Fax: (212)397-4126
Website: http://www.venconinc.com

Werner International Inc.
55 E 52nd, 29th Fl.
New York, NY 10055
(212)909-1260
Fax: (212)909-1273
E-mail: richard.downing@rgh.com
Website: http://www.wernertex.com

Zimmerman Business Consulting Inc.
44 E 92nd St., Ste. 5-B
New York, NY 10128

(212)860-3107
Fax: (212)860-7730
E-mail: ljzzbci@aol.com
Website: http://www.zbcinc.com

Overton Financial
7 Allen Rd.
Peekskill, NY 10566
(914)737-4649
Fax: (914)737-4696

Stromberg Consulting
2500 Westchester Ave.
Purchase, NY 10577
(914)251-1515
Fax: (914)251-1562
E-mail: strategy@stromberg_consul
ting.com
Website: http://www.stromberg_
consulting.com

Innovation Management Consulting Inc.
209 Dewitt Rd.
Syracuse, NY 13214-2006
(315)425-5144
Fax: (315)445-8989
E-mail: missonneb@axess.net

M. Clifford Agress
891 Fulton St.
Valley Stream, NY 11580
(516)825-8955
Fax: (516)825-8955

Destiny Kinal Marketing Consultancy
105 Chemung St.
Waverly, NY 14892
(607)565-8317
Fax: (607)565-4083

Valutis Consulting Inc.
5350 Main St., Ste. 7
Williamsville, NY 14221-5338
(716)634-2553
Fax: (716)634-2554
E-mail: valutis@localnet.com
Website: http://www.valutisconsulting.com

North Carolina

Best Practices L.L.C.
6320 Quadrangle Dr., Ste. 200
Chapel Hill, NC 27514
(919)403-0251
Fax: (919)403-0144
E-mail: best@best:in/class
Website: http://www.best-in-class.com

Norelli & Co.
Bank of America Corporate Ctr.
100 N Tyron St., Ste. 5160

Charlotte, NC 28202-4000
(704)376-5484
Fax: (704)376-5485
E-mail: consult@norelli.com
Website: http://www.norelli.com

North Dakota

Center for Innovation
4300 Dartmouth Dr.
PO Box 8372
Grand Forks, ND 58202
(701)777-3132
Fax: (701)777-2339
E-mail: bruce@innovators.net
Website: http://www.innovators.net

Ohio

Transportation Technology Services
208 Harmon Rd.
Aurora, OH 44202
(330)562-3596

Empro Systems Inc.
4777 Red Bank Expy., Ste. 1
Cincinnati, OH 45227-1542
(513)271-2042
Fax: (513)271-2042

Alliance Management International Ltd.
1440 Windrow Ln.
Cleveland, OH 44147-3200
(440)838-1922
Fax: (440)838-0979
E-mail: bgruss@amiltd.com
Website: http://www.amiltd.com

Bozell Kamstra Public Relations
1301 E 9th St., Ste. 3400
Cleveland, OH 44114
(216)623-1511
Fax: (216)623-1501
E-mail: jfeniger@cleveland.bozellk
amstra.com
Website: http://www.bozellk
amstra.com

Cory Dillon Associates
111 Schreyer Pl. E
Columbus, OH 43214
(614)262-8211
Fax: (614)262-3806

Holcomb Gallagher Adams
300 Marconi, Ste. 303
Columbus, OH 43215
(614)221-3343
Fax: (614)221-3367
E-mail: riadams@acme.freenet.oh.us

Young & Associates
PO Box 711
Kent, OH 44240
(330)678-0524
Free: 800-525-9775
Fax: (330)678-6219
E-mail: online@younginc.com
Website: http://www.younginc.com

Robert A. Westman & Associates
8981 Inversary Dr. SE
Warren, OH 44484-2551
(330)856-4149
Fax: (330)856-2564

Oklahoma

Innovative Partners L.L.C.
4900 Richmond Sq., Ste. 100
Oklahoma City, OK 73118
(405)840-0033
Fax: (405)843-8359
E-mail: ipartners@juno.com

Oregon

INTERCON - The International Converting Institute
5200 Badger Rd.
Crooked River Ranch, OR 97760
(541)548-1447
Fax: (541)548-1618
E-mail: johnbowler@
crookedriverranch.com

Talbott ARM
HC 60, Box 5620
Lakeview, OR 97630
(541)635-8587
Fax: (503)947-3482

Management Technology Associates Ltd.
2768 SW Sherwood Dr, Ste. 105
Portland, OR 97201-2251
(503)224-5220
Fax: (503)224-5334
E-mail: lcuster@mta-ltd.com
Website: http://www.mgmt-tech.com

Pennsylvania

Healthscope Inc.
400 Lancaster Ave.
Devon, PA 19333
(610)687-6199
Fax: (610)687-6376
E-mail: health@voicenet.com
Website: http://www.healthscope.net/

Elayne Howard & Associates Inc.
3501 Masons Mill Rd., Ste. 501

Huntingdon Valley, PA 19006-3509
(215)657-9550

GRA Inc.
115 West Ave., Ste. 201
Jenkintown, PA 19046
(215)884-7500
Fax: (215)884-1385
E-mail: gramail@gra-inc.com
Website: http://www.gra-inc.com

Mifflin County Industrial Development Corp.
Mifflin County Industrial Plz.
6395 SR 103 N
Bldg. 50
Lewistown, PA 17044
(717)242-0393
Fax: (717)242-1842
E-mail: mcide@acsworld.net

Autech Products
1289 Revere Rd.
Morrisville, PA 19067
(215)493-3759
Fax: (215)493-9791
E-mail: autech4@yahoo.com

Advantage Associates
434 Avon Dr.
Pittsburgh, PA 15228
(412)343-1558
Fax: (412)362-1684
E-mail: ecocba1@aol.com

Regis J. Sheehan & Associates
Pittsburgh, PA 15220
(412)279-1207

James W. Davidson Company Inc.
23 Forest View Rd.
Wallingford, PA 19086
(610)566-1462

Puerto Rico

Diego Chevere & Co.
Metro Parque 7, Ste. 204
Metro Office
Caparra Heights, PR 00920
(787)774-9595
Fax: (787)774-9566
E-mail: dcco@coqui.net

Manuel L. Porrata and Associates
898 Munoz Rivera Ave., Ste. 201
San Juan, PR 00927
(787)765-2140
Fax: (787)754-3285
E-mail: m_porrata@manuelporrata.com
Website: http://manualporrata.com

South Carolina

Aquafood Business Associates
PO Box 13267
Charleston, SC 29422
(843)795-9506
Fax: (843)795-9477
E-mail: rraba@aol.com

Profit Associates Inc.
PO Box 38026
Charleston, SC 29414
(803)763-5718
Fax: (803)763-5719
E-mail: bobrog@awod.com
Website: http://www.awod.com/gallery/
business/proasc

Strategic Innovations International
12 Executive Ct.
Lake Wylie, SC 29710
(803)831-1225
Fax: (803)831-1177
E-mail: stratinnov@aol.com
Website: http://www.
strategicinnovations.com

Minus Stage
Box 4436
Rock Hill, SC 29731
(803)328-0705
Fax: (803)329-9948

Tennessee

Daniel Petchers & Associates
8820 Fernwood CV
Germantown, TN 38138
(901)755-9896

Business Choices
1114 Forest Harbor, Ste. 300
Hendersonville, TN 37075-9646
(615)822-8692
Free: 800-737-8382
Fax: (615)822-8692
E-mail: bz-ch@juno.com

RCFA Healthcare Management Services L.L.C.
9648 Kingston Pke., Ste. 8
Knoxville, TN 37922
(865)531-0176
Free: 800-635-4040
Fax: (865)531-0722
E-mail: info@rcfa.com
Website: http://www.rcfa.com

Growth Consultants of America
3917 Trimble Rd.
Nashville, TN 37215

(615)383-0550
Fax: (615)269-8940
E-mail: 70244.451@compuserve.com

Texas

Integrated Cost Management Systems Inc.
2261 Brookhollow Plz. Dr., Ste. 104
Arlington, TX 76006
(817)633-2873
Fax: (817)633-3781
E-mail: abm@icms.net
Website: http://www.icms.net

Lori Williams
1000 Leslie Ct.
Arlington, TX 76012
(817)459-3934
Fax: (817)459-3934

Business Resource Software Inc.
2013 Wells Branch Pky., Ste. 305
Austin, TX 78728
Free: 800-423-1228
Fax: (512)251-4401
E-mail: info@brs-inc.com
Website: http://www.brs-inc.com

Erisa Adminstrative Services Inc.
12325 Hymeadow Dr., Bldg. 4
Austin, TX 78750-1847
(512)250-9020
Fax: (512)250-9487
Website: http://www.cserisa.com

R. Miller Hicks & Co.
1011 W 11th St.
Austin, TX 78703
(512)477-7000
Fax: (512)477-9697
E-mail: millerhicks@rmhicks.com
Website: http://www.rmhicks.com

Pragmatic Tactics Inc.
3303 Westchester Ave.
College Station, TX 77845
(409)696-5294
Free: 800-570-5294
Fax: (409)696-4994
E-mail: ptactics@aol.com
Website: http://www.ptatics.com

Perot Systems
12404 Park Central Dr.
Dallas, TX 75251
(972)340-5000
Free: 800-688-4333
Fax: (972)455-4100
E-mail: corp.comm@ps.net
Website: http://www.perotsystems.com

ReGENERATION Partners
3838 Oak Lawn Ave.
Dallas, TX 75219
(214)559-3999
Free: 800-406-1112
E-mail: info@regeneration-partner.com
Website: http://www.regeneration-partners.com

High Technology Associates - Division of Global Technologies Inc.
1775 St. James Pl., Ste. 105
Houston, TX 77056
(713)963-9300
Fax: (713)963-8341
E-mail: hta@infohwy.com

MasterCOM
103 Thunder Rd.
Kerrville, TX 78028
(830)895-7990
Fax: (830)443-3428
E-mail: jmstubblefield@master training.com
Website: http://www.mastertraining.com

PROTEC
4607 Linden Pl.
Pearland, TX 77584
(281)997-9872
Fax: (281)997-9895
E-mail: p.oman@ix.netcom.com

Alpha Quadrant Inc.
10618 Auldine
San Antonio, TX 78230
(210)344-3330
Fax: (210)344-8151
E-mail: mbussone@sbcglobal.net
Website:http://www.a-quadrant.com
Michele Bussone

Bastian Public Relations
614 San Dizier
San Antonio, TX 78232
(210)404-1839
E-mail: lisa@bastianpr.com
Website: http://www.bastianpr.com
Lisa Bastian CBC

Business Strategy Development Consultants
PO Box 690365
San Antonio, TX 78269
(210)696-8000
Free: 800-927-BSDC
Fax: (210)696-8000

Tom Welch, CPC
6900 San Pedro Ave., Ste. 147
San Antonio, TX 78216-6207

(210)737-7022
Fax: (210)737-7022
E-mail: bplan@iamerica.net
Website: http://www.moneywords.com

Utah

Business Management Resource
PO Box 521125
Salt Lake City, UT 84152-1125
(801)272-4668
Fax: (801)277-3290
E-mail: pingfong@worldnet.att.net

Virginia

Tindell Associates
209 Oxford Ave.
Alexandria, VA 22301
(703)683-0109
Fax: 703-783-0219
E-mail: scott@tindell.net
Website: http://www.tindell.net
Scott Lockett, President

Elliott B. Jaffa
2530-B S Walter Reed Dr.
Arlington, VA 22206
(703)931-0040
E-mail: thetrainingdoctor@excite.com
Website: http://www.tregistry.com/jaffa.htm

Koach Enterprises - USA
5529 N 18th St.
Arlington, VA 22205
(703)241-8361
Fax: (703)241-8623

Federal Market Development
5650 Chapel Run Ct.
Centreville, VA 20120-3601
(703)502-8930
Free: 800-821-5003
Fax: (703)502-8929

Huff, Stuart & Carlton
2107 Graves Mills Rd., Ste. C
Forest, VA 24551
(804)316-9356
Free: (888)316-9356
Fax: (804)316-9357
Website: http://www.wealthmgt.net

AMX International Inc.
1420 Spring Hill Rd. , Ste. 600
McLean, VA 22102-3006
(703)690-4100
Fax: (703)643-1279
E-mail: amxmail@amxi.com
Website: http://www.amxi.com

Charles Scott Pugh (Investor)
4101 Pittaway Dr.
Richmond, VA 23235-1022
(804)560-0979
Fax: (804)560-4670

John C. Randall and Associates Inc.
PO Box 15127
Richmond, VA 23227
(804)746-4450
Fax: (804)730-8933
E-mail: randalljcx@aol.com
Website: http://www.johncrandall.com

McLeod & Co.
410 1st St.
Roanoke, VA 24011
(540)342-6911
Fax: (540)344-6367
Website: http://www.mcleodco.com/

Salzinger & Company Inc.
8000 Towers Crescent Dr., Ste. 1350
Vienna, VA 22182
(703)442-5200
Fax: (703)442-5205
E-mail: info@salzinger.com
Website: http://www.salzinger.com

The Small Business Counselor
12423 Hedges Run Dr., Ste. 153
Woodbridge, VA 22192
(703)490-6755
Fax: (703)490-1356

Washington

Burlington Consultants
10900 NE 8th St., Ste. 900
Bellevue, WA 98004
(425)688-3060
Fax: (425)454-4383
E-mail: partners@burlington
consultants.com
Website: http://www.burlington
consultants.com

Perry L. Smith Consulting
800 Bellevue Way NE, Ste. 400
Bellevue, WA 98004-4208
(425)462-2072
Fax: (425)462-5638

St. Charles Consulting Group
1420 NW Gilman Blvd.
Issaquah, WA 98027
(425)557-8708
Fax: (425)557-8731
E-mail: info@stcharlesconsulting.com
Website: http://www.stcharlescon
sulting.com

Independent Automotive Training Services
PO Box 334
Kirkland, WA 98083
(425)822-5715
E-mail: ltunney@autosvccon.com
Website: http://www.autosvccon.com

Kahle Associate Inc.
6203 204th Dr. NE
Redmond, WA 98053
(425)836-8763
Fax: (425)868-3770
E-mail: randykahle@kahleassociates.com
Website: http://www.kahleassociates.com

Dan Collin
3419 Wallingord Ave N, No. 2
Seattle, WA 98103
(206)634-9469
E-mail: dc@dancollin.com
Website: http://members.home.net/
dcollin/

ECG Management Consultants Inc.
1111 3rd Ave., Ste. 2700
Seattle, WA 98101-3201
(206)689-2200
Fax: (206)689-2209
E-mail: ecg@ecgmc.com
Website: http://www.ecgmc.com

Northwest Trade Adjustment Assistance Center
900 4th Ave., Ste. 2430
Seattle, WA 98164-1001
(206)622-2730
Free: 800-667-8087
Fax: (206)622-1105
E-mail: matchingfunds@nwtaac.org
Website: http://www.taacenters.org

Business Planning Consultants
S 3510 Ridgeview Dr.
Spokane, WA 99206
(509)928-0332
Fax: (509)921-0842
E-mail: bpci@nextdim.com

West Virginia

**Stanley & Associates Inc./
BusinessandMarketingPlans.com**
1687 Robert C. Byrd Dr.
Beckley, WV 25801
(304)252-0324
Free: 888-752-6720
Fax: (304)252-0470
E-mail: cclay@charterinternet.com

Website: http://www.Businessand
MarketingPlans.com
Christopher Clay

Wisconsin

White & Associates Inc.
5349 Somerset Ln. S
Greenfield, WI 53221
(414)281-7373
Fax: (414)281-7006
E-mail: wnaconsult@aol.com

Small business administration regional offices

This section contains a listing of Small Business Administration offices arranged numerically by region. Service areas are provided. Contact the appropriate office for a referral to the nearest field office, or visit the Small Business Administration online at www.sba.gov.

Region 1

U.S. Small Business Administration
Region I Office
10 Causeway St., Ste. 812
Boston, MA 02222-1093
Phone: (617)565-8415
Fax: (617)565-8420
Serves Connecticut, Maine, Massachusetts, New Hampshire, Rhode Island, and Vermont.

Region 2

U.S. Small Business Administration
Region II Office
26 Federal Plaza, Ste. 3108
New York, NY 10278
Phone: (212)264-1450
Fax: (212)264-0038
Serves New Jersey, New York, Puerto Rico, and the Virgin Islands.

Region 3

U.S. Small Business Administration
Region III Office
Robert N C Nix Sr. Federal Building
900 Market St., 5th Fl.
Philadelphia, PA 19107
(215)580-2807
Serves Delaware, the District of Columbia, Maryland, Pennsylvania, Virginia, and West Virginia.

Region 4

U.S. Small Business Administration
Region IV Office
233 Peachtree St. NE
Harris Tower 1800
Atlanta, GA 30303
Phone: (404)331-4999
Fax: (404)331-2354
Serves Alabama, Florida, Georgia, Kentucky, Mississippi, North Carolina, South Carolina, and Tennessee.

Region 5

U.S. Small Business Administration
Region V Office
500 W. Madison St.
Citicorp Center, Ste. 1240
Chicago, IL 60661-2511
Phone: (312)353-0357
Fax: (312)353-3426
Serves Illinois, Indiana, Michigan, Minnesota, Ohio, and Wisconsin.

Region 6

U.S. Small Business Administration
Region VI Office
4300 Amon Carter Blvd., Ste. 108
Fort Worth, TX 76155
Phone: (817)684-5581
Fax: (817)684-5588
Serves Arkansas, Louisiana, New Mexico, Oklahoma, and Texas.

Region 7

U.S. Small Business Administration
Region VII Office
323 W. 8th St., Ste. 307
Kansas City, MO 64105-1500
Phone: (816)374-6380
Fax: (816)374-6339
Serves Iowa, Kansas, Missouri, and Nebraska.

Region 8

U.S. Small Business Administration
Region VIII Office
721 19th St., Ste. 400
Denver, CO 80202
Phone: (303)844-0500
Fax: (303)844-0506
Serves Colorado, Montana, North Dakota, South Dakota, Utah, and Wyoming.

Region 9

U.S. Small Business Administration
Region IX Office
330 N Brand Blvd., Ste. 1270
Glendale, CA 91203-2304
Phone: (818)552-3434
Fax: (818)552-3440
Serves American Samoa, Arizona, California, Guam, Hawaii, Nevada, and the Trust Territory of the Pacific Islands.

Region 10

U.S. Small Business Administration
Region X Office
2401 Fourth Ave., Ste. 400
Seattle, WA 98121
Phone: (206)553-5676
Fax: (206)553-4155
Serves Alaska, Idaho, Oregon, and Washington.

Small business development centers

This section contains a listing of all Small Business Development Centers, organized alphabetically by state/U.S. territory, then by city, then by agency name.

Alabama

Alabama SBDC
UNIVERSITY OF ALABAMA
2800 Milan Court Suite 124
Birmingham, AL 35211-6908
Phone: 205-943-6750
Fax: 205-943-6752
E-Mail: wcampbell@provost.uab.edu
Website: http://www.asbdc.org
Mr. William Campbell Jr, State Director

Alaska

Alaska SBDC
UNIVERSITY OF ALASKA - ANCHORAGE
430 West Seventh Avenue, Suite 110
Anchorage, AK 99501
Phone: 907-274 -7232
Fax: 907-274-9524
E-Mail: anerw@uaa.alaska.edu
Website: http://www.aksbdc.org
Ms. Jean R. Wall, State Director

American Samoa

American Samoa SBDC
AMERICAN SAMOA COMMUNITY COLLEGE
P.O. Box 2609
Pago Pago, American Samoa 96799
Phone: 011-684-699-4830
Fax: 011-684-699-6132
E-Mail: htalex@att.net
Mr. Herbert Thweatt, Director

Arizona

Arizona SBDC
MARICOPA COUNTY COMMUNITY COLLEGE
2411 West 14th Street, Suite 132
Tempe, AZ 85281
Phone: 480-731-8720
Fax: 480-731-8729
E-Mail: mike.york@domail.maricopa.edu
Website: http://www.dist.maricopa.edu.sbdc
Mr. Michael York, State Director

Arkansas

Arkansas SBDC
UNIVERSITY OF ARKANSAS
2801 South University Avenue
Little Rock, AR 72204
Phone: 501-324-9043
Fax: 501-324-9049
E-Mail: jmroderick@ualr.edu
Website: http://asbdc.ualr.edu
Ms. Janet M. Roderick, State Director

California

California - San Francisco SBDC
Northern California SBDC Lead Center
HUMBOLDT STATE UNIVERSITY
Office of Economic Development
1 Harpst Street 2006A, Siemens Hall
Arcata, CA, 95521
Phone: 707-826-3922
Fax: 707-826-3206
E-Mail: gainer@humboldt.edu
Ms. Margaret A. Gainer, Regional Director

California - Sacramento SBDC
CALIFORNIA STATE UNIVERSITY - CHICO
Chico, CA 95929-0765
Phone: 530-898-4598
Fax: 530-898-4734

E-Mail: dripke@csuchico.edu
Website: http://gsbdc.csuchico.edu
Mr. Dan Ripke, Interim Regional Director

California - San Diego SBDC
SOUTHWESTERN COMMUNITY
COLLEGE DISTRICT
900 Otey Lakes Road
Chula Vista, CA 91910
Phone: 619-482-6388
Fax: 619-482-6402
E-Mail: dtrujillo@swc.cc.ca.us
Website: http://www.sbditc.org
Ms. Debbie P. Trujillo, Regional Director

California - Fresno SBDC
UC Merced Lead Center
UNIVERSITY OF CALIFORNIA -
MERCED
550 East Shaw, Suite 105A
Fresno, CA 93710
Phone: 559-241-6590
Fax: 559-241-7422
E-Mail: crosander@ucmerced.edu
Website: http://sbdc.ucmerced.edu
Mr. Chris Rosander, State Director

California - Santa Ana SBDC
Tri-County Lead SBDC
CALIFORNIA STATE UNIVERSITY -
FULLERTON
800 North State College Boulevard, LH640
Fullerton, CA 92834
Phone: 714-278-2719
Fax: 714-278-7858
E-Mail: vpham@fullerton.edu
Website: http://www.leadsbdc.org
Ms. Vi Pham, Lead Center Director

California - Los Angeles Region SBDC
LONG BEACH COMMUNITY
COLLEGE DISTRICT
3950 Paramount Boulevard, Ste 101
Lakewood, CA 90712
Phone: 562-938-5004
Fax: 562-938-5030
E-Mail: ssloan@lbcc.edu
Ms. Sheneui Sloan, Interim Lead Center
Director

Colorado

Colorado SBDC
OFFICE OF ECONOMIC
DEVELOPMENT
1625 Broadway, Suite 170
Denver, CO 80202
Phone: 303-892-3864
Fax: 303-892-3848
E-Mail: Kelly.Manning@state.co.us

Website: http://www.state.co.us/oed/sbdc
Ms. Kelly Manning, State Director

Connecticut

Connecticut SBDC
UNIVERSITY OF CONNECTICUT
1376 Storrs Road, Unit 4094
Storrs, CT 06269-1094
Phone: 860-870-6370
Fax: 860-870-6374
E-Mail: richard.cheney@uconn.edu
Website: http://www.sbdc.uconn.edu
Mr. Richard Cheney, Interim State Director

Delaware

Delaware SBDC
DELAWARE TECHNOLOGY PARK
1 Innovation Way, Suite 301
Newark, DE 19711
Phone: 302-831-2747
Fax: 302-831-1423
E-Mail: Clinton.tymes@mvs.udel.edu
Website: http://www.delawaresbdc.org
Mr. Clinton Tymes, State Director

District of Columbia

District of Columbia SBDC
HOWARD UNIVERSITY
2600 6th Street, NW Room 128
Washington, DC 20059
Phone: 202-806-1550
Fax: 202-806-1777
E-Mail: hturner@howard.edu
Website: http://www.dcsbdc.com/
Mr. Henry Turner, Executive Director

Florida

Florida SBDC
UNIVERSITY OF WEST FLORIDA
401 East Chase Street, Suite 100
Pensacola, FL 32502
Phone: 850-473-7800
Fax: 850-473-7813
E-Mail: jcartwri@uwf.edu
Website: http://www.floridasbdc.com
Mr. Jerry Cartwright, State Director

Georgia

Georgia SBDC
UNIVERSITY OF GEORGIA
1180 East Broad Street
Athens, GA 30602
Phone: 706-542-6762
Fax: 706-542-6776
E-mail: aadams@sbdc.uga.edu

Website: http://www.sbdc.uga.edu
Mr. Allan Adams, Interim State Director

Guam

Guam Small Business Development
Center
UNIVERSITY OF GUAM
Pacific Islands SBDC
P.O. Box 5014 - U.O.G. Station
Mangilao, GU 96923
Phone: 671-735-2590
Fax: 671-734-2002
E-mail: casey@pacificsbdc.com
Website: http://www.uog.edu/sbdc
Mr. Casey Jeszenka, Director

Hawaii

Hawaii SBDC
UNIVERSITY OF HAWAII - HILO
308 Kamehameha Avenue, Suite 201
Hilo, HI 96720
Phone: 808-974-7515
Fax: 808-974-7683
E-Mail: darrylm@interpac.net
Website: http://www.hawaii-sbdc.org
Mr. Darryl Mleynek, State Director

Idaho

Idaho SBDC
BOISE STATE UNIVERSITY
1910 University Drive
Boise, ID 83725
Phone: 208-426-3799
Fax: 208-426-3877
E-mail: jhogge@boisestate.edu
Website: http://www.idahosbdc.org
Mr. Jim Hogge, State Director

Illinois

Illinois SBDC
DEPARTMENT OF COMMERCE
AND ECONOMIC OPPORTUNITY
620 E. Adams, S-4
Springfield, IL 62701
Phone: 217-524-5700
Fax: 217-524-0171
E-mail: mpatrilli@ildceo.net
Website: http://www.ilsbdc.biz
Mr. Mark Petrilli, State Director

Indiana

Indiana SBDC
INDIANA ECONOMIC
DEVELOPMENT CORPORATION
One North Capitol, Suite 900
Indianapolis, IN 46204

Phone: 317-234-8872
Fax: 317-232-8874
E-mail: dtrocha@isbdc.org
Website: http://www.isbdc.org
Ms. Debbie Bishop Trocha, State
Director

Iowa

Iowa SBDC
IOWA STATE UNIVERSITY
340 Gerdin Business Bldg.
Ames, IA 50011-1350
Phone: 515-294-2037
Fax: 515-294-6522
E-mail: jonryan@iastate.edu
Website: http://www.iabusnet.org
Mr. Jon Ryan, State Director

Kansas

Kansas SBDC
FORT HAYS STATE UNIVERSITY
214 SW Sixth Street, Suite 301
Topeka, KS 66603
Phone: 785-296-6514
Fax: 785-291-3261
E-mail: ksbdc.wkearns@fhsu.edu
Website: http://www.fhsu.edu/ksbdc
Mr. Wally Kearns, State Director

Kentucky

Kentucky SBDC
UNIVERSITY OF KENTUCKY
225 Gatton College of Business
Economics Building
Lexington, KY 40506-0034
Phone: 859-257-7668
Fax: 859-323-1907
E-mail: lrnaug0@pop.uky.edu
Website: http://www.ksbdc.org
Ms. Becky Naugle, State Director

Louisiana

Louisiana SBDC
**UNIVERSITY OF LOUISIANA -
MONROE**
College of Business Administration
700 University Avenue
Monroe, LA 71209
Phone: 318-342-5506
Fax: 318-342-5510
E-mail: wilkerson@ulm.edu
Website: http://www.lsbdc.org
Ms. Mary Lynn Wilkerson, State
Director

Maine

Maine SBDC
**UNIVERSITY OF SOUTHERN
MAINE**
96 Falmouth Street P.O. Box 9300
Portland, ME 04103
Phone: 207-780-4420
Fax: 207-780-4810
E-mail: jrmassaua@maine.edu
Website: http://www.mainesbdc.org
Mr. John Massaua, State Director

Maryland

Maryland SBDC
UNIVERSITY OF MARYLAND
7100 Baltimore Avenue, Suite 401
College Park, MD 20742
Phone: 301-403-8300
Fax: 301-403-8303
E-mail: rsprow@mdsbdc.umd.edu
Website: http://www.mdsbdc.umd.edu
Ms. Renee Sprow, State Director

Massachusetts

Massachusetts SBDC
UNIVERSITY OF MASSACHUSETTS
School of Management, Room 205
Amherst, MA 01003-4935
Phone: 413-545-6301
Fax: 413-545-1273
E-mail: gep@msbdc.umass.edu
Website: http://msbdc.som.umass.edu
Ms. Georgianna Parkin, State Director

Michigan

Michigan SBTDC
**GRAND VALLEY STATE
UNIVERSITY**
510 West Fulton Avenue
Grand Rapids, MI 49504
Phone: 616-331-7485
Fax: 616-331-7389
E-mail: lopuckic@gvsu.edu
Website: http://www.misbtdc.org
Ms. Carol Lopucki, State Director

Minnesota

Minnesota SBDC
**MINNESOTA SMALL BUSINESS
DEVELOPMENT CENTER**
1st National Bank Building
332 Minnesota Street, Suite E200
St. Paul, MN 55101-1351
Phone: 651-297-5773
Fax: 651-296-5287

E-mail: michael.myhre@state.mn.us
Website: http://www.mnsbdc.com
Mr. Michael Myhre, State Director

Mississippi

Mississippi SBDC
UNIVERSITY OF MISSISSIPPI
B-19 Jeanette Phillips Drive
P.O. Box 1848
University, MS 38677
Phone: 662-915-5001
Fax: 662-915-5650
E-mail: wgurley@olemiss.edu
Website: http://www.olemiss.edu/depts/
mssbdc
Mr. Doug Gurley, Jr., State Director

Missouri

Missouri SBDC
UNIVERSITY OF MISSOURI
1205 University Avenue, Suite 300
Columbia, MO 65211
Phone: 573-882-1348
Fax: 573-884-4297
E-mail: summersm@missouri.edu
Website: http://www.mo-sbdc.org/
index.shtml
Mr. Max Summers, State Director

Montana

Montana SBDC
DEPARTMENT OF COMMERCE
301 South Park Avenue, Room 114 /
P.O. Box 200505
Helena, MT 59620
Phone: 406-841-2746
Fax: 406-444-1872
E-mail: adesch@state.mt.us
Website: http://commerce.state.mt.us/
brd/BRD_SBDC.html
Ms. Ann Desch, State Director

Nebraska

Nebraska SBDC
**UNIVERSITY OF NEBRASKA -
OMAHA**
60th & Dodge Street, CBA Room 407
Omaha, NE 68182
Phone: 402-554-2521
Fax: 402-554-3473
E-mail: rbernier@unomaha.edu
Website: http://nbdc.unomaha.edu
Mr. Robert Bernier, State Director

Nevada

Nevada SBDC
UNIVERSITY OF NEVADA - RENO
Reno College of Business
Administration, Room 411
Reno, NV 89557-0100
Phone: 775-784-1717
Fax: 775-784-4337
E-mail: males@unr.edu
Website: http://www.nsbdc.org
Mr. Sam Males, State Director

New Hampshire

New Hampshire SBDC
UNIVERSITY OF NEW HAMPSHIRE
108 McConnell Hall
Durham, NH 03824-3593
Phone: 603-862-4879
Fax: 603-862-4876
E-mail: Mary.Collins@unh.edu
Website: http://www.nhsbdc.org
Ms. Mary Collins, State Director

New Jersey

New Jersey SBDC
RUTGERS UNIVERSITY
49 Bleeker Street
Newark, NJ 07102-1993
Phone: 973-353-5950
Fax: 973-353-1110
E-mail: bhopper@njsbdc.com
Website: http://www.njsbdc.com/home
Ms. Brenda Hopper, State Director

New Mexico

New Mexico SBDC
SANTA FE COMMUNITY COLLEGE
6401 Richards Avenue
Santa Fe, NM 87505
Phone: 505-428-1362
Fax: 505-471-9469
E-mail: rmiller@santa-fe.cc.nm.us
Website: http://www.nmsbdc.org
Mr. Roy Miller, State Director

New York

New York SBDC
STATE UNIVERSITY OF NEW YORK
SUNY Plaza, S-523
Albany, NY 12246
Phone: 518-443-5398
Fax: 518-443-5275
E-mail: j.king@nyssbdc.org
Website: http://www.nyssbdc.org
Mr. Jim King, State Director

North Carolina

North Carolina SBDTC
UNIVERSITY OF NORTH CAROLINA
5 West Hargett Street, Suite 600
Raleigh, NC 27601
Phone: 919-715-7272
Fax: 919-715-7777
E-mail: sdaugherty@sbtdc.org
Website: http://www.sbtdc.org
Mr. Scott Daugherty, State Director

North Dakota

North Dakota SBDC
UNIVERSITY OF NORTH DAKOTA
1600 E. Century Avenue, Suite 2
Bismarck, ND 58503
Phone: 701-328-5375
Fax: 701-328-5320
E-mail: christine.martin@und.nodak.edu
Website: http://www.ndsbdc.org
Ms. Christine Martin-Goldman, State
Director

Ohio

Ohio SBDC
OHIO DEPARTMENT OF DEVELOPMENT
77 South High Street
Columbus, OH 43216
Phone: 614-466-5102
Fax: 614-466-0829
E-mail: mabraham@odod.state.oh.us
Website: http://www.ohiosbdc.org
Ms. Michele Abraham, State Director

Oklahoma

Oklahoma SBDC
SOUTHEAST OKLAHOMA STATE UNIVERSITY
517 University, Box 2584, Station A
Durant, OK 74701
Phone: 580-745-7577
Fax: 580-745-7471
E-mail: gpennington@sosu.edu
Website: http://www.osbdc.org
Mr. Grady Pennington, State Director

Oregon

Oregon SBDC
LANE COMMUNITY COLLEGE
99 West Tenth Avenue, Suite 390
Eugene, OR 97401-3021
Phone: 541-463-5250
Fax: 541-345-6006
E-mail: carterb@lanecc.edu

Website: http://www.bizcenter.org
Mr. William Carter, State Director

Pennsylvania

Pennsylvania SBDC
UNIVERSITY OF PENNSYLVANIA
The Wharton School
3733 Spruce Street
Philadelphia, PA 19104-6374
Phone: 215-898-1219
Fax: 215-573-2135
E-mail: ghiggins@wharton.upenn.edu
Website: http://pasbdc.org
Mr. Gregory Higgins, State Director

Puerto Rico

Puerto Rico SBDC
INTER-AMERICAN UNIVERSITY OF PUERTO RICO
416 Ponce de Leon Avenue, Union Plaza,
Seventh Floor
Hato Rey, PR 00918
Phone: 787-763-6811
Fax: 787-763-4629
E-mail: cmarti@prsbdc.org
Website: http://www.prsbdc.org
Ms. Carmen Marti, Executive Director

Rhode Island

Rhode Island SBDC
BRYANT UNIVERSITY
1150 Douglas Pike
Smithfield, RI 02917
Phone: 401-232-6923
Fax: 401-232-6933
E-mail: adawson@bryant.edu
Website: http://www.risbdc.org
Ms. Diane Fournaris, Interim State Director

South Carolina

South Carolina SBDC
UNIVERSITY OF SOUTH CAROLINA
College of Business Administration
1710 College Street
Columbia, SC 29208
Phone: 803-777-4907
Fax: 803-777-4403
E-mail: lenti@moore.sc.edu
Website: http://scsbdc.moore.sc.edu
Mr. John Lenti, State Director

South Dakota

South Dakota SBDC
UNIVERSITY OF SOUTH DAKOTA
414 East Clark Street, Patterson Hall
Vermillion, SD 57069

Phone: 605-677-6256
Fax: 605-677-5427
E-mail: jshemmin@usd.edu
Website: http://www.sdsbdc.org
Mr. John S. Hemmingstad, State Director

Tennessee

Tennessee SBDC
TENNESSEE BOARD OF REGENTS
1415 Murfressboro Road, Suite 540
Nashville, TN 37217-2833
Phone: 615-898-2745
Fax: 615-893-7089
E-mail: pgeho@mail.tsbdc.org
Website: http://www.tsbdc.org
Mr. Patrick Geho, State Director

Texas

Texas-North SBDC
DALLAS COUNTY COMMUNITY COLLEGE
1402 Corinth Street
Dallas, TX 75215
Phone: 214-860-5835
Fax: 214-860-5813
E-mail: emk9402@dcccd.edu
Website: http://www.ntsbdc.org
Ms. Liz Klimback, Region Director

Texas-Houston SBDC
UNIVERSITY OF HOUSTON
2302 Fannin, Suite 200
Houston, TX 77002
Phone: 713-752-8425
Fax: 713-756-1500
E-mail: fyoung@uh.edu
Website: http://sbdcnetwork.uh.edu
Mr. Mike Young, Executive Director

Texas-NW SBDC
TEXAS TECH UNIVERSITY
2579 South Loop 289, Suite 114
Lubbock, TX 79423
Phone: 806-745-3973
Fax: 806-745-6207
E-mail: c.bean@nwtsbdc.org
Website: http://www.nwtsbdc.org
Mr. Craig Bean, Executive Director

Texas-South-West Texas Border Region SBDC
UNIVERSITY OF TEXAS - SAN ANTONIO
501 West Durango Boulevard
San Antonio, TX 78207-4415
Phone: 210-458-2742
Fax: 210-458-2464

E-mail: albert.salgado@utsa.edu
Website: http://www.iedtexas.org
Mr. Alberto Salgado, Region Director

Utah

Utah SBDC
SALT LAKE COMMUNITY COLLEGE
9750 South 300 West
Sandy, UT 84070
Phone: 801-957-3493
Fax: 801-957-3488
E-mail: Greg.Panichello@slcc.edu
Website: http://www.slcc.edu/sbdc
Mr. Greg Panichello, State Director

Vermont

Vermont SBDC
VERMONT TECHNICAL COLLEGE
PO Box 188, 1 Main Street
Randolph Center, VT 05061-0188
Phone: 802-728-9101
Fax: 802-728-3026
E-mail: lquillen@vtc.edu
Website: http://www.vtsbdc.org
Ms. Lenae Quillen-Blume, State Director

Virgin Islands

Virgin Islands SBDC
UNIVERSITY OF THE VIRGIN ISLANDS
8000 Nisky Center, Suite 720
St. Thomas, VI 00802-5804
Phone: 340-776-3206
Fax: 340-775-3756
E-mail: wbush@webmail.uvi.edu
Website: http://rps.uvi.edu/SBDC
Mr. Warren Bush, State Director

Virginia

Virginia SBDC
GEORGE MASON UNIVERSITY
4031 University Drive, Suite 200
Fairfax, VA 22030-3409
Phone: 703-277-7727
Fax: 703-352-8515
E-mail: jkeenan@gmu.edu
Website: http://www.virginiasbdc.org
Ms. Jody Keenan, Director

Washington

Washington SBDC
WASHINGTON STATE UNIVERSITY
534 E. Trent Avenue
P.O. Box 1495
Spokane, WA 99210-1495

Phone: 509-358-7765
Fax: 509-358-7764
E-mail: barogers@wsu.edu
Website: http://www.wsbdc.org
Mr. Brett Rogers, State Director

West Virginia

West Virginia SBDC
WEST VIRGINIA DEVELOPMENT OFFICE
Capital Complex, Building 6, Room 652
Charleston, WV 25301
Phone: 304-558-2960
Fax: 304-558-0127
E-mail: csalyer@wvsbdc.org
Website: http://www.wvsbdc.org
Mr. Conley Salyor, State Director

Wisconsin

Wisconsin SBDC
UNIVERSITY OF WISCONSIN
432 North Lake Street, Room 423
Madison, WI 53706
Phone: 608-263-7794
Fax: 608-263-7830
E-mail: erica.kauten@uwex.edu
Website: http://www.wisconsinsbdc.org
Ms. Erica Kauten, State Director

Wyoming

Wyoming SBDC
UNIVERSITY OF WYOMING
P.O. Box 3922
Laramie, WY 82071-3922
Phone: 307-766-3505
Fax: 307-766-3406
E-mail: DDW@uwyo.edu
Website: http://www.uwyo.edu/sbdc
Ms. Debbie Popp, Acting State Director

Service corps of retired executives (score) offices

This section contains a listing of all SCORE offices organized alphabetically by state/U.S. territory, then by city, then by agency name.

Alabama

SCORE Office (Northeast Alabama)
1330 Quintard Ave.
Anniston, AL 36202
(256)237-3536

SCORE Office (North Alabama)
901 South 15th St, Rm. 201
Birmingham, AL 35294-2060
(205)934-6868
Fax: (205)934-0538

SCORE Office (Baldwin County)
29750 Larry Dee Cawyer Dr.
Daphne, AL 36526
(334)928-5838

SCORE Office (Shoals)
612 S. COurt
Florence, AL 35630
(256)764-4661
Fax: (256)766-9017
E-mail: shoals@shoalschamber.com

SCORE Office (Mobile)
600 S Court St.
Mobile, AL 36104
(334)240-6868
Fax: (334)240-6869

SCORE Office (Alabama Capitol City)
600 S. Court St.
Montgomery, AL 36104
(334)240-6868
Fax: (334)240-6869

SCORE Office (East Alabama)
601 Ave. A
Opelika, AL 36801
(334)745-4861
E-mail: score636@hotmail.com
Website: http://www.angelfire.com/sc/
score636/

SCORE Office (Tuscaloosa)
2200 University Blvd.
Tuscaloosa, AL 35402
(205)758-7588

Alaska

SCORE Office (Anchorage)
510 L St., Ste. 310
Anchorage, AK 99501
(907)271-4022
Fax: (907)271-4545

Arizona

SCORE Office (Lake Havasu)
10 S. Acoma Blvd.
Lake Havasu City, AZ 86403
(520)453-5951
E-mail: SCORE@ctaz.com
Website: http://www.scorearizona.org/
lake_havasu/

SCORE Office (East Valley)
Federal Bldg., Rm. 104
26 N. MacDonald St.
Mesa, AZ 85201
(602)379-3100
Fax: (602)379-3143
E-mail: 402@aol.com
Website: http://www.scorearizona.
org/mesa/

SCORE Office (Phoenix)
2828 N. Central Ave., Ste. 800
Central & One Thomas
Phoenix, AZ 85004
(602)640-2329
Fax: (602)640-2360
E-mail: e-mail@SCORE-phoenix.org
Website: http://www.score-phoenix.org/

SCORE Office (Prescott Arizona)
1228 Willow Creek Rd., Ste. 2
Prescott, AZ 86301
(520)778-7438
Fax: (520)778-0812
E-mail: score@northlink.com
Website: http://www.scorearizona.org/
prescott/

SCORE Office (Tucson)
110 E. Pennington St.
Tucson, AZ 85702
(520)670-5008
Fax: (520)670-5011
E-mail: score@azstarnet.com
Website: http://www.scorearizona.org/
tucson/

SCORE Office (Yuma)
281 W. 24th St., Ste. 116
Yuma, AZ 85364
(520)314-0480
E-mail: score@C2i2.com
Website: http://www.scorearizona.org/
yuma

Arkansas

SCORE Office (South Central)
201 N. Jackson Ave.
El Dorado, AR 71730-5803
(870)863-6113
Fax: (870)863-6115

SCORE Office (Ozark)
Fayetteville, AR 72701
(501)442-7619

SCORE Office (Northwest Arkansas)
Glenn Haven Dr., No. 4
Ft. Smith, AR 72901
(501)783-3556

SCORE Office (Garland County)
Grand & Ouachita
PO Box 6012
Hot Springs Village, AR 71902
(501)321-1700

SCORE Office (Little Rock)
2120 Riverfront Dr., Rm. 100
Little Rock, AR 72202-1747
(501)324-5893
Fax: (501)324-5199

SCORE Office (Southeast Arkansas)
121 W. 6th
Pine Bluff, AR 71601
(870)535-7189
Fax: (870)535-1643

California

SCORE Office (Golden Empire)
1706 Chester Ave., No. 200
Bakersfield, CA 93301
(805)322-5881
Fax: (805)322-5663

SCORE Office (Greater Chico Area)
1324 Mangrove St., Ste. 114
Chico, CA 95926
(916)342-8932
Fax: (916)342-8932

SCORE Office (Concord)
2151-A Salvio St., Ste. B
Concord, CA 94520
(510)685-1181
Fax: (510)685-5623

SCORE Office (Covina)
935 W. Badillo St.
Covina, CA 91723
(818)967-4191
Fax: (818)966-9660

SCORE Office (Rancho Cucamonga)
8280 Utica, Ste. 160
Cucamonga, CA 91730
(909)987-1012
Fax: (909)987-5917

SCORE Office (Culver City)
PO Box 707
Culver City, CA 90232-0707
(310)287-3850
Fax: (310)287-1350

SCORE Office (Danville)
380 Diablo Rd., Ste. 103
Danville, CA 94526
(510)837-4400

SCORE Office (Downey)
11131 Brookshire Ave.
Downey, CA 90241
(310)923-2191
Fax: (310)864-0461

SCORE Office (El Cajon)
109 Rea Ave.
El Cajon, CA 92020
(619)444-1327
Fax: (619)440-6164

SCORE Office (El Centro)
1100 Main St.
El Centro, CA 92243
(619)352-3681
Fax: (619)352-3246

SCORE Office (Escondido)
720 N. Broadway
Escondido, CA 92025
(619)745-2125
Fax: (619)745-1183

SCORE Office (Fairfield)
1111 Webster St.
Fairfield, CA 94533
(707)425-4625
Fax: (707)425-0826

SCORE Office (Fontana)
17009 Valley Blvd., Ste. B
Fontana, CA 92335
(909)822-4433
Fax: (909)822-6238

SCORE Office (Foster City)
1125 E. Hillsdale Blvd.
Foster City, CA 94404
(415)573-7600
Fax: (415)573-5201

SCORE Office (Fremont)
2201 Walnut Ave., Ste. 110
Fremont, CA 94538
(510)795-2244
Fax: (510)795-2240

SCORE Office (Central California)
2719 N. Air Fresno Dr., Ste. 200
Fresno, CA 93727-1547
(559)487-5605
Fax: (559)487-5636

SCORE Office (Gardena)
1204 W. Gardena Blvd.
Gardena, CA 90247
(310)532-9905
Fax: (310)515-4893

SCORE Office (Lompoc)
330 N. Brand Blvd., Ste. 190
Glendale, CA 91203-2304

(818)552-3206
Fax: (818)552-3323

SCORE Office (Los Angeles)
330 N. Brand Blvd., Ste. 190
Glendale, CA 91203-2304
(818)552-3206
Fax: (818)552-3323

SCORE Office (Glendora)
131 E. Foothill Blvd.
Glendora, CA 91740
(818)963-4128
Fax: (818)914-4822

SCORE Office (Grover Beach)
177 S. 8th St.
Grover Beach, CA 93433
(805)489-9091
Fax: (805)489-9091

SCORE Office (Hawthorne)
12477 Hawthorne Blvd.
Hawthorne, CA 90250
(310)676-1163
Fax: (310)676-7661

SCORE Office (Hayward)
22300 Foothill Blvd., Ste. 303
Hayward, CA 94541
(510)537-2424

SCORE Office (Hemet)
1700 E. Florida Ave.
Hemet, CA 92544-4679
(909)652-4390
Fax: (909)929-8543

SCORE Office (Hesperia)
16367 Main St.
PO Box 403656
Hesperia, CA 92340
(619)244-2135

SCORE Office (Holloster)
321 San Felipe Rd., No. 11
Hollister, CA 95023

SCORE Office (Hollywood)
7018 Hollywood Blvd.
Hollywood, CA 90028
(213)469-8311
Fax: (213)469-2805

SCORE Office (Indio)
82503 Hwy. 111
PO Drawer TTT
Indio, CA 92202
(619)347-0676

SCORE Office (Inglewood)
330 Queen St.

Inglewood, CA 90301
(818)552-3206

SCORE Office (La Puente)
218 N. Grendanda St. D.
La Puente, CA 91744
(818)330-3216
Fax: (818)330-9524

SCORE Office (La Verne)
2078 Bonita Ave.
La Verne, CA 91750
(909)593-5265
Fax: (714)929-8475

SCORE Office (Lake Elsinore)
132 W. Graham Ave.
Lake Elsinore, CA 92530
(909)674-2577

SCORE Office (Lakeport)
PO Box 295
Lakeport, CA 95453
(707)263-5092

SCORE Office (Lakewood)
5445 E. Del Amo Blvd., Ste. 2
Lakewood, CA 90714
(213)920-7737

SCORE Office (Long Beach)
1 World Trade Center
Long Beach, CA 90831

SCORE Office (Los Alamitos)
901 W. Civic Center Dr., Ste. 160
Los Alamitos, CA 90720

SCORE Office (Los Altos)
321 University Ave.
Los Altos, CA 94022
(415)948-1455

SCORE Office (Manhattan Beach)
PO Box 3007
Manhattan Beach, CA 90266
(310)545-5313
Fax: (310)545-7203

SCORE Office (Merced)
1632 N. St.
Merced, CA 95340
(209)725-3800
Fax: (209)383-4959

SCORE Office (Milpitas)
75 S. Milpitas Blvd., Ste. 205
Milpitas, CA 95035
(408)262-2613
Fax: (408)262-2823

SCORE Office (Yosemite)
1012 11th St., Ste. 300
Modesto, CA 95354
(209)521-9333

SCORE Office (Montclair)
5220 Benito Ave.
Montclair, CA 91763

SCORE Office (Monterey Bay)
380 Alvarado St.
PO Box 1770
Monterey, CA 93940-1770
(408)649-1770

SCORE Office (Moreno Valley)
25480 Alessandro
Moreno Valley, CA 92553

SCORE Office (Morgan Hill)
25 W. 1st St.
PO Box 786
Morgan Hill, CA 95038
(408)779-9444
Fax: (408)778-1786

SCORE Office (Morro Bay)
880 Main St.
Morro Bay, CA 93442
(805)772-4467

SCORE Office (Mountain View)
580 Castro St.
Mountain View, CA 94041
(415)968-8378
Fax: (415)968-5668

SCORE Office (Napa)
1556 1st St.
Napa, CA 94559
(707)226-7455
Fax: (707)226-1171

SCORE Office (North Hollywood)
5019 Lankershim Blvd.
North Hollywood, CA 91601
(818)552-3206

SCORE Office (Northridge)
8801 Reseda Blvd.
Northridge, CA 91324
(818)349-5676

SCORE Office (Novato)
807 De Long Ave.
Novato, CA 94945
(415)897-1164
Fax: (415)898-9097

SCORE Office (East Bay)
519 17th St.
Oakland, CA 94612

(510)273-6611
Fax: (510)273-6015
E-mail: webmaster@eastbayscore.org
Website: http://www.eastbayscore.org

SCORE Office (Oceanside)
928 N. Coast Hwy.
Oceanside, CA 92054
(619)722-1534

SCORE Office (Ontario)
121 West B. St.
Ontario, CA 91762
Fax: (714)984-6439

SCORE Office (Oxnard)
PO Box 867
Oxnard, CA 93032
(805)385-8860
Fax: (805)487-1763

SCORE Office (Pacifica)
450 Dundee Way, Ste. 2
Pacifica, CA 94044
(415)355-4122

SCORE Office (Palm Desert)
72990 Hwy. 111
Palm Desert, CA 92260
(619)346-6111
Fax: (619)346-3463

SCORE Office (Palm Springs)
650 E. Tahquitz Canyon Way Ste. D
Palm Springs, CA 92262-6706
(760)320-6682
Fax: (760)323-9426

SCORE Office (Lakeside)
2150 Low Tree
Palmdale, CA 93551
(805)948-4518
Fax: (805)949-1212

SCORE Office (Palo Alto)
325 Forest Ave.
Palo Alto, CA 94301
(415)324-3121
Fax: (415)324-1215

SCORE Office (Pasadena)
117 E. Colorado Blvd., Ste. 100
Pasadena, CA 91105
(818)795-3355
Fax: (818)795-5663

SCORE Office (Paso Robles)
1225 Park St.
Paso Robles, CA 93446-2234
(805)238-0506
Fax: (805)238-0527

SCORE Office (Petaluma)
799 Baywood Dr., Ste. 3
Petaluma, CA 94954
(707)762-2785
Fax: (707)762-4721

SCORE Office (Pico Rivera)
9122 E. Washington Blvd.
Pico Rivera, CA 90660

SCORE Office (Pittsburg)
2700 E. Leland Rd.
Pittsburg, CA 94565
(510)439-2181
Fax: (510)427-1599

SCORE Office (Pleasanton)
777 Peters Ave.
Pleasanton, CA 94566
(510)846-9697

SCORE Office (Monterey Park)
485 N. Garey
Pomona, CA 91769

SCORE Office (Pomona)
485 N. Garey Ave.
Pomona, CA 91766
(909)622-1256

SCORE Office (Antelope Valley)
4511 West Ave. M-4
Quartz Hill, CA 93536
(805)272-0087
E-mail: avscore@ptw.com
Website: http://www.score.av.org/

SCORE Office (Shasta)
737 Auditorium Dr.
Redding, CA 96099
(916)225-2770

SCORE Office (Redwood City)
1675 Broadway
Redwood City, CA 94063
(415)364-1722
Fax: (415)364-1729

SCORE Office (Richmond)
3925 MacDonald Ave.
Richmond, CA 94805

SCORE Office (Ridgecrest)
PO Box 771
Ridgecrest, CA 93555
(619)375-8331
Fax: (619)375-0365

SCORE Office (Riverside)
3685 Main St., Ste. 350
Riverside, CA 92501
(909)683-7100

SCORE Office (Sacramento)
9845 Horn Rd., 260-B
Sacramento, CA 95827
(916)361-2322
Fax: (916)361-2164
E-mail: sacchapter@directcon.net

SCORE Office (Salinas)
PO Box 1170
Salinas, CA 93902
(408)424-7611
Fax: (408)424-8639

SCORE Office (Inland Empire)
777 E. Rialto Ave.
Purchasing
San Bernardino, CA 92415-0760
(909)386-8278

SCORE Office (San Carlos)
San Carlos Chamber of Commerce
PO Box 1086
San Carlos, CA 94070
(415)593-1068
Fax: (415)593-9108

SCORE Office (Encinitas)
550 W. C St., Ste. 550
San Diego, CA 92101-3540
(619)557-7272
Fax: (619)557-5894

SCORE Office (San Diego)
550 West C. St., Ste. 550
San Diego, CA 92101-3540
(619)557-7272
Fax: (619)557-5894
Website: http://www.score-
sandiego.org

SCORE Office (Menlo Park)
1100 Merrill St.
San Francisco, CA 94105
(415)325-2818
Fax: (415)325-0920

SCORE Office (San Francisco)
455 Market St., 6th Fl.
San Francisco, CA 94105
(415)744-6827
Fax: (415)744-6750
E-mail: sfscore@sfscore.
Website: http://www.sfscore.com

SCORE Office (San Gabriel)
401 W. Las Tunas Dr.
San Gabriel, CA 91776
(818)576-2525
Fax: (818)289-2901

SCORE Office (San Jose)
Deanza College
208 S. 1st. St., Ste. 137
San Jose, CA 95113
(408)288-8479
Fax: (408)535-5541

SCORE Office (Silicon Valley)
84 W. Santa Clara St., Ste. 100
San Jose, CA 95113
(408)288-8479
Fax: (408)535-5541
E-mail: info@svscore.org
Website: http://www.svscore.org

SCORE Office (San Luis Obispo)
3566 S. Hiquera, No. 104
San Luis Obispo, CA 93401
(805)547-0779

SCORE Office (San Mateo)
1021 S. El Camino, 2nd Fl.
San Mateo, CA 94402
(415)341-5679

SCORE Office (San Pedro)
390 W. 7th St.
San Pedro, CA 90731
(310)832-7272

SCORE Office (Orange County)
200 W. Santa Anna Blvd., Ste. 700
Santa Ana, CA 92701
(714)550-7369
Fax: (714)550-0191
Website: http://www.score114.org

SCORE Office (Santa Barbara)
3227 State St.
Santa Barbara, CA 93130
(805)563-0084

SCORE Office (Central Coast)
509 W. Morrison Ave.
Santa Maria, CA 93454
(805)347-7755

SCORE Office (Santa Maria)
614 S. Broadway
Santa Maria, CA 93454-5111
(805)925-2403
Fax: (805)928-7559

SCORE Office (Santa Monica)
501 Colorado, Ste. 150
Santa Monica, CA 90401
(310)393-9825
Fax: (310)394-1868

SCORE Office (Santa Rosa)
777 Sonoma Ave., Rm. 115E
Santa Rosa, CA 95404

(707)571-8342
Fax: (707)541-0331
Website: http://www.pressdemo.com/
community/score/score.html

SCORE Office (Scotts Valley)
4 Camp Evers Ln.
Scotts Valley, CA 95066
(408)438-1010
Fax: (408)438-6544

SCORE Office (Simi Valley)
40 W. Cochran St., Ste. 100
Simi Valley, CA 93065
(805)526-3900
Fax: (805)526-6234

SCORE Office (Sonoma)
453 1st St. E
Sonoma, CA 95476
(707)996-1033

SCORE Office (Los Banos)
222 S. Shepard St.
Sonora, CA 95370
(209)532-4212

SCORE Office (Tuolumne County)
39 North Washington St.
Sonora, CA 95370
(209)588-0128
E-mail: score@mlode.com

SCORE Office (South San Francisco)
445 Market St., Ste. 6th Fl.
South San Francisco, CA 94105
(415)744-6827
Fax: (415)744-6812

SCORE Office (Stockton)
401 N. San Joaquin St., Rm. 215
Stockton, CA 95202
(209)946-6293

SCORE Office (Taft)
314 4th St.
Taft, CA 93268
(805)765-2165
Fax: (805)765-6639

SCORE Office (Conejo Valley)
625 W. Hillcrest Dr.
Thousand Oaks, CA 91360
(805)499-1993
Fax: (805)498-7264

SCORE Office (Torrance)
3400 Torrance Blvd., Ste. 100
Torrance, CA 90503
(310)540-5858
Fax: (310)540-7662

SCORE Office (Truckee)
PO Box 2757
Truckee, CA 96160
(916)587-2757
Fax: (916)587-2439

SCORE Office (Visalia)
113 S. M St,
Tulare, CA 93274
(209)627-0766
Fax: (209)627-8149

SCORE Office (Upland)
433 N. 2nd Ave.
Upland, CA 91786
(909)931-4108

SCORE Office (Vallejo)
2 Florida St.
Vallejo, CA 94590
(707)644-5551
Fax: (707)644-5590

SCORE Office (Van Nuys)
14540 Victory Blvd.
Van Nuys, CA 91411
(818)989-0300
Fax: (818)989-3836

SCORE Office (Ventura)
5700 Ralston St., Ste. 310
Ventura, CA 93001
(805)658-2688
Fax: (805)658-2252
E-mail: scoreven@jps.net
Website: http://www.jps.net/scoreven

SCORE Office (Vista)
201 E. Washington St.
Vista, CA 92084
(619)726-1122
Fax: (619)226-8654

SCORE Office (Watsonville)
PO Box 1748
Watsonville, CA 95077
(408)724-3849
Fax: (408)728-5300

SCORE Office (West Covina)
811 S. Sunset Ave.
West Covina, CA 91790
(818)338-8496
Fax: (818)960-0511

SCORE Office (Westlake)
30893 Thousand Oaks Blvd.
Westlake Village, CA 91362
(805)496-5630
Fax: (818)991-1754

Colorado

SCORE Office (Colorado Springs)
2 N. Cascade Ave., Ste. 110
Colorado Springs, CO 80903
(719)636-3074
Website: http://www.cscc.org/score02/index.html

SCORE Office (Denver)
US Custom's House, 4th Fl.
721 19th St.
Denver, CO 80201-0660
(303)844-3985
Fax: (303)844-6490
E-mail: score62@csn.net
Website: http://www.sni.net/score62

SCORE Office (Tri-River)
1102 Grand Ave.
Glenwood Springs, CO 81601
(970)945-6589

SCORE Office (Grand Junction)
2591 B & 3/4 Rd.
Grand Junction, CO 81503
(970)243-5242

SCORE Office (Gunnison)
608 N. 11th
Gunnison, CO 81230
(303)641-4422

SCORE Office (Montrose)
1214 Peppertree Dr.
Montrose, CO 81401
(970)249-6080

SCORE Office (Pagosa Springs)
PO Box 4381
Pagosa Springs, CO 81157
(970)731-4890

SCORE Office (Rifle)
0854 W. Battlement Pky., Apt. C106
Parachute, CO 81635
(970)285-9390

SCORE Office (Pueblo)
302 N. Santa Fe
Pueblo, CO 81003
(719)542-1704
Fax: (719)542-1624
E-mail: mackey@iex.net
Website: http://www.pueblo.org/score

SCORE Office (Ridgway)
143 Poplar Pl.
Ridgway, CO 81432

SCORE Office (Silverton)
PO Box 480

Silverton, CO 81433
(303)387-5430

SCORE Office (Minturn)
PO Box 2066
Vail, CO 81658
(970)476-1224

Connecticut

SCORE Office (Greater Bridgeport)
230 Park Ave.
Bridgeport, CT 06601-0999
(203)576-4369
Fax: (203)576-4388

SCORE Office (Bristol)
10 Main St. 1st. Fl.
Bristol, CT 06010
(203)584-4718
Fax: (203)584-4722

SCORE office (Greater Danbury)
246 Federal Rd.
Unit LL2, Ste. 7
Brookfield, CT 06804
(203)775-1151

SCORE Office (Greater Danbury)
246 Federal Rd., Unit LL2, Ste. 7
Brookfield, CT 06804
(203)775-1151

SCORE Office (Eastern Connecticut)
Administration Bldg., Rm. 313
PO 625
61 Main St. (Chapter 579)
Groton, CT 06475
(203)388-9508

SCORE Office (Greater Hartford County)
330 Main St.
Hartford, CT 06106
(860)548-1749
Fax: (860)240-4659
Website: http://www.score56.org

SCORE Office (Manchester)
20 Hartford Rd.
Manchester, CT 06040
(203)646-2223
Fax: (203)646-5871

SCORE Office (New Britain)
185 Main St., Ste. 431
New Britain, CT 06051
(203)827-4492
Fax: (203)827-4480

SCORE Office (New Haven)
25 Science Pk., Bldg. 25, Rm. 366

New Haven, CT 06511
(203)865-7645

SCORE Office (Fairfield County)
24 Beldon Ave., 5th Fl.
Norwalk, CT 06850
(203)847-7348
Fax: (203)849-9308

SCORE Office (Old Saybrook)
146 Main St.
Old Saybrook, CT 06475
(860)388-9508

SCORE Office (Simsbury)
Box 244
Simsbury, CT 06070
(203)651-7307
Fax: (203)651-1933

SCORE Office (Torrington)
23 North Rd.
Torrington, CT 06791
(203)482-6586

Delaware

SCORE Office (Dover)
Treadway Towers
PO Box 576
Dover, DE 19903
(302)678-0892
Fax: (302)678-0189

SCORE Office (Lewes)
PO Box 1
Lewes, DE 19958
(302)645-8073
Fax: (302)645-8412

SCORE Office (Milford)
204 NE Front St.
Milford, DE 19963
(302)422-3301

SCORE Office (Wilmington)
824 Market St., Ste. 610
Wilmington, DE 19801
(302)573-6652
Fax: (302)573-6092
Website: http://www.scoredelaware.com

District of Columbia

SCORE Office (George Mason University)
409 3rd St. SW, 4th Fl.
Washington, DC 20024
800-634-0245

SCORE Office (Washington DC)
1110 Vermont Ave. NW, 9th Fl.

Washington, DC 20043
(202)606-4000
Fax: (202)606-4225
E-mail: dcscore@hotmail.com
Website: http://www.scoredc.org/

Florida

SCORE Office (Desota County Chamber of Commerce)
16 South Velucia Ave.
Arcadia, FL 34266
(941)494-4033

SCORE Office (Suncoast/Pinellas)
Airport Business Ctr.
4707 - 140th Ave. N, No. 311
Clearwater, FL 33755
(813)532-6800
Fax: (813)532-6800

SCORE Office (DeLand)
336 N. Woodland Blvd.
DeLand, FL 32720
(904)734-4331
Fax: (904)734-4333

SCORE Office (South Palm Beach)
1050 S. Federal Hwy., Ste. 132
Delray Beach, FL 33483
(561)278-7752
Fax: (561)278-0288

SCORE Office (Ft. Lauderdale)
Federal Bldg., Ste. 123
299 E. Broward Blvd.
Ft. Lauderdale, FL 33301
(954)356-7263
Fax: (954)356-7145

SCORE Office (Southwest Florida)
The Renaissance
8695 College Pky., Ste. 345 & 346
Ft. Myers, FL 33919
(941)489-2935
Fax: (941)489-1170

SCORE Office (Treasure Coast)
Professional Center, Ste. 2
3220 S. US, No. 1
Ft. Pierce, FL 34982
(561)489-0548

SCORE Office (Gainesville)
101 SE 2nd Pl., Ste. 104
Gainesville, FL 32601
(904)375-8278

SCORE Office (Hialeah Dade Chamber)
59 W. 5th St.
Hialeah, FL 33010

(305)887-1515
Fax: (305)887-2453

SCORE Office (Daytona Beach)
921 Nova Rd., Ste. A
Holly Hills, FL 32117
(904)255-6889
Fax: (904)255-0229
E-mail: score87@dbeach.com

SCORE Office (South Broward)
3475 Sheridian St., Ste. 203
Hollywood, FL 33021
(305)966-8415

SCORE Office (Citrus County)
5 Poplar Ct.
Homosassa, FL 34446
(352)382-1037

SCORE Office (Jacksonville)
7825 Baymeadows Way, Ste. 100-B
Jacksonville, FL 32256
(904)443-1911
Fax: (904)443-1980
E-mail: scorejax@juno.com
Website: http://www.scorejax.org/

SCORE Office (Jacksonville Satellite)
3 Independent Dr.
Jacksonville, FL 32256
(904)366-6600
Fax: (904)632-0617

SCORE Office (Central Florida)
5410 S. Florida Ave., No. 3
Lakeland, FL 33801
(941)687-5783
Fax: (941)687-6225

SCORE Office (Lakeland)
100 Lake Morton Dr.
Lakeland, FL 33801
(941)686-2168

SCORE Office (St. Petersburg)
800 W. Bay Dr., Ste. 505
Largo, FL 33712
(813)585-4571

SCORE Office (Leesburg)
9501 US Hwy. 441
Leesburg, FL 34788-8751
(352)365-3556
Fax: (352)365-3501

SCORE Office (Cocoa)
1600 Farno Rd., Unit 205
Melbourne, FL 32935
(407)254-2288

SCORE Office (Melbourne)
Melbourne Professional Complex
1600 Sarno, Ste. 205
Melbourne, FL 32935
(407)254-2288
Fax: (407)245-2288

SCORE Office (Merritt Island)
1600 Sarno Rd., Ste. 205
Melbourne, FL 32935
(407)254-2288
Fax: (407)254-2288

SCORE Office (Space Coast)
Melbourn Professional Complex
1600 Sarno, Ste. 205
Melbourne, FL 32935
(407)254-2288
Fax: (407)254-2288

SCORE Office (Dade)
49 NW 5th St.
Miami, FL 33128
(305)371-6889
Fax: (305)374-1882
E-mail: score@netrox.net
Website: http://www.netrox.net/~score/

SCORE Office (Naples of Collier)
International College
2654 Tamiami Trl. E
Naples, FL 34112
(941)417-1280
Fax: (941)417-1281
E-mail: score@naples.net
Website: http://www.naples.net/clubs/
score/index.htm

SCORE Office (Pasco County)
6014 US Hwy. 19, Ste. 302
New Port Richey, FL 34652
(813)842-4638

SCORE Office (Southeast Volusia)
115 Canal St.
New Smyrna Beach, FL 32168
(904)428-2449
Fax: (904)423-3512

SCORE Office (Ocala)
110 E. Silver Springs Blvd.
Ocala, FL 34470
(352)629-5959

Clay County SCORE Office
Clay County Chamber of Commerce
1734 Kingsdey Ave.
PO Box 1441
Orange Park, FL 32073
(904)264-2651
Fax: (904)269-0363

SCORE Office (Orlando)
80 N. Hughey Ave.
Rm. 445 Federal Bldg.
Orlando, FL 32801
(407)648-6476
Fax: (407)648-6425

SCORE Office (Emerald Coast)
19 W. Garden St., No. 325
Pensacola, FL 32501
(904)444-2060
Fax: (904)444-2070

SCORE Office (Charlotte County)
201 W. Marion Ave., Ste. 211
Punta Gorda, FL 33950
(941)575-1818
E-mail: score@gls3c.com
Website: http://www.charlotte-
florida.com/business/scorepg01.htm

SCORE Office (St. Augustine)
1 Riberia St.
St. Augustine, FL 32084
(904)829-5681
Fax: (904)829-6477

SCORE Office (Bradenton)
2801 Fruitville, Ste. 280
Sarasota, FL 34237
(813)955-1029

SCORE Office (Manasota)
2801 Fruitville Rd., Ste. 280
Sarasota, FL 34237
(941)955-1029
Fax: (941)955-5581
E-mail: score116@gte.net
Website: http://www.score-suncoast.org/

SCORE Office (Tallahassee)
200 W. Park Ave.
Tallahassee, FL 32302
(850)487-2665

SCORE Office (Hillsborough)
4732 Dale Mabry Hwy. N, Ste. 400
Tampa, FL 33614-6509
(813)870-0125

SCORE Office (Lake Sumter)
122 E. Main St.
Tavares, FL 32778-3810
(352)365-3556

SCORE Office (Titusville)
2000 S. Washington Ave.
Titusville, FL 32780
(407)267-3036
Fax: (407)264-0127

SCORE Office (Venice)
257 N. Tamiami Trl.
Venice, FL 34285
(941)488-2236
Fax: (941)484-5903

SCORE Office (Palm Beach)
500 Australian Ave. S, Ste. 100
West Palm Beach, FL 33401
(561)833-1672
Fax: (561)833-1712

SCORE Office (Wildwood)
103 N. Webster St.
Wildwood, FL 34785

Georgia

SCORE Office (Atlanta)
Harris Tower, Suite 1900
233 Peachtree Rd., NE
Atlanta, GA 30309
(404)347-2442
Fax: (404)347-1227

SCORE Office (Augusta)
3126 Oxford Rd.
Augusta, GA 30909
(706)869-9100

SCORE Office (Columbus)
School Bldg.
PO Box 40
Columbus, GA 31901
(706)327-3654

SCORE Office (Dalton-Whitfield)
305 S. Thorton Ave.
Dalton, GA 30720
(706)279-3383

SCORE Office (Gainesville)
PO Box 374
Gainesville, GA 30503
(770)532-6206
Fax: (770)535-8419

SCORE Office (Macon)
711 Grand Bldg.
Macon, GA 31201
(912)751-6160

SCORE Office (Brunswick)
4 Glen Ave.
St. Simons Island, GA 31520
(912)265-0620
Fax: (912)265-0629

SCORE Office (Savannah)
111 E. Liberty St., Ste. 103
Savannah, GA 31401
(912)652-4335

Fax: (912)652-4184
E-mail: info@scoresav.org
Website: http://www.coastalempire.com/
score/index.htm

Guam

SCORE Office (Guam)
Pacific News Bldg., Rm. 103
238 Archbishop Flores St.
Agana, GU 96910-5100
(671)472-7308

Hawaii

SCORE Office (Hawaii, Inc.)
1111 Bishop St., Ste. 204
PO Box 50207
Honolulu, HI 96813
(808)522-8132
Fax: (808)522-8135
E-mail: hnlscore@juno.com

SCORE Office (Kahului)
250 Alamaha, Unit N16A
Kahului, HI 96732
(808)871-7711

SCORE Office (Maui, Inc.)
590 E. Lipoa Pkwy., Ste. 227
Kihei, HI 96753
(808)875-2380

Idaho

SCORE Office (Treasure Valley)
1020 Main St., No. 290
Boise, ID 83702
(208)334-1696
Fax: (208)334-9353

SCORE Office (Eastern Idaho)
2300 N. Yellowstone, Ste. 119
Idaho Falls, ID 83401
(208)523-1022
Fax: (208)528-7127

Illinois

SCORE Office (Fox Valley)
40 W. Downer Pl.
PO Box 277
Aurora, IL 60506
(630)897-9214
Fax: (630)897-7002

SCORE Office (Greater Belvidere)
419 S. State St.
Belvidere, IL 61008
(815)544-4357
Fax: (815)547-7654

SCORE Office (Bensenville)
1050 Busse Hwy. Suite 100
Bensenville, IL 60106
(708)350-2944
Fax: (708)350-2979

SCORE Office (Central Illinois)
402 N. Hershey Rd.
Bloomington, IL 61704
(309)644-0549
Fax: (309)663-8270
E-mail: webmaster@central-illinois-
score.org
Website: http://www.central-illinois-
score.org/

SCORE Office (Southern Illinois)
150 E. Pleasant Hill Rd.
Box 1
Carbondale, IL 62901
(618)453-6654
Fax: (618)453-5040

SCORE Office (Chicago)
Northwest Atrium Ctr.
500 W. Madison St., No. 1250
Chicago, IL 60661
(312)353-7724
Fax: (312)886-5688
Website: http://www.mcs.net/~bic/

SCORE Office (Chicago–Oliver Harvey College)
Pullman Bldg.
1000 E. 11th St., 7th Fl.
Chicago, IL 60628
Fax: (312)468-8086

SCORE Office (Danville)
28 W. N. Street
Danville, IL 61832
(217)442-7232
Fax: (217)442-6228

SCORE Office (Decatur)
Milliken University
1184 W. Main St.
Decatur, IL 62522
(217)424-6297
Fax: (217)424-3993
E-mail: charding@mail.millikin.edu
Website: http://www.millikin.edu/
academics/Tabor/score.html

SCORE Office (Downers Grove)
925 Curtis
Downers Grove, IL 60515
(708)968-4050
Fax: (708)968-8368

SCORE Office (Elgin)
24 E. Chicago, 3rd Fl.
PO Box 648
Elgin, IL 60120
(847)741-5660
Fax: (847)741-5677

SCORE Office (Freeport Area)
26 S. Galena Ave.
Freeport, IL 61032
(815)233-1350
Fax: (815)235-4038

SCORE Office (Galesburg)
292 E. Simmons St.
PO Box 749
Galesburg, IL 61401
(309)343-1194
Fax: (309)343-1195

SCORE Office (Glen Ellyn)
500 Pennsylvania
Glen Ellyn, IL 60137
(708)469-0907
Fax: (708)469-0426

SCORE Office (Greater Alton)
Alden Hall
5800 Godfrey Rd.
Godfrey, IL 62035-2466
(618)467-2280
Fax: (618)466-8289
Website: http://www.altonweb.com/
score/

SCORE Office (Grayslake)
19351 W. Washington St.
Grayslake, IL 60030
(708)223-3633
Fax: (708)223-9371

SCORE Office (Harrisburg)
303 S. Commercial
Harrisburg, IL 62946-1528
(618)252-8528
Fax: (618)252-0210

SCORE Office (Joliet)
100 N. Chicago
Joliet, IL 60432
(815)727-5371
Fax: (815)727-5374

SCORE Office (Kankakee)
101 S. Schuyler Ave.
Kankakee, IL 60901
(815)933-0376
Fax: (815)933-0380

SCORE Office (Macomb)
216 Seal Hall, Rm. 214

Macomb, IL 61455
(309)298-1128
Fax: (309)298-2520

SCORE Office (Matteson)
210 Lincoln Mall
Matteson, IL 60443
(708)709-3750
Fax: (708)503-9322

SCORE Office (Mattoon)
1701 Wabash Ave.
Mattoon, IL 61938
(217)235-5661
Fax: (217)234-6544

SCORE Office (Quad Cities)
622 19th St.
Moline, IL 61265
(309)797-0082
Fax: (309)757-5435
E-mail: score@qconline.com
Website: http://www.qconline.com/
business/score/

SCORE Office (Naperville)
131 W. Jefferson Ave.
Naperville, IL 60540
(708)355-4141
Fax: (708)355-8355

SCORE Office (Northbrook)
2002 Walters Ave.
Northbrook, IL 60062
(847)498-5555
Fax: (847)498-5510

SCORE Office (Palos Hills)
10900 S. 88th Ave.
Palos Hills, IL 60465
(847)974-5468
Fax: (847)974-0078

SCORE Office (Peoria)
124 SW Adams, Ste. 300
Peoria, IL 61602
(309)676-0755
Fax: (309)676-7534

SCORE Office (Prospect Heights)
1375 Wolf Rd.
Prospect Heights, IL 60070
(847)537-8660
Fax: (847)537-7138

SCORE Office (Quincy Tri-State)
300 Civic Center Plz., Ste. 245
Quincy, IL 62301
(217)222-8093
Fax: (217)222-3033

SCORE Office (River Grove)
2000 5th Ave.
River Grove, IL 60171
(708)456-0300
Fax: (708)583-3121

SCORE Office (Northern Illinois)
515 N. Court St.
Rockford, IL 61103
(815)962-0122
Fax: (815)962-0122

SCORE Office (St. Charles)
103 N. 1st Ave.
St. Charles, IL 60174-1982
(847)584-8384
Fax: (847)584-6065

SCORE Office (Springfield)
511 W. Capitol Ave., Ste. 302
Springfield, IL 62704
(217)492-4416
Fax: (217)492-4867

SCORE Office (Sycamore)
112 Somunak St.
Sycamore, IL 60178
(815)895-3456
Fax: (815)895-0125

SCORE Office (University)
Hwy. 50 & Stuenkel Rd. Ste. C3305
University Park, IL 60466
(708)534-5000
Fax: (708)534-8457

Indiana

SCORE Office (Anderson)
205 W. 11th St.
Anderson, IN 46015
(317)642-0264

SCORE Office (Bloomington)
Star Center
216 W. Allen
Bloomington, IN 47403
(812)335-7334
E-mail: wtfische@indiana.edu
Website: http://www.brainfreezemedia.
com/score527/

SCORE Office (South East Indiana)
500 Franklin St.
Box 29
Columbus, IN 47201
(812)379-4457

SCORE Office (Corydon)
310 N. Elm St.
Corydon, IN 47112

(812)738-2137
Fax: (812)738-6438

SCORE Office (Crown Point)
Old Courthouse Sq. Ste. 206
PO Box 43
Crown Point, IN 46307
(219)663-1800

SCORE Office (Elkhart)
418 S. Main St.
Elkhart, IN 46515
(219)293-1531
Fax: (219)294-1859

SCORE Office (Evansville)
1100 W. Lloyd Expy., Ste. 105
Evansville, IN 47708
(812)426-6144

SCORE Office (Fort Wayne)
1300 S. Harrison St.
Ft. Wayne, IN 46802
(219)422-2601
Fax: (219)422-2601

SCORE Office (Gary)
973 W. 6th Ave., Rm. 326
Gary, IN 46402
(219)882-3918

SCORE Office (Hammond)
7034 Indianapolis Blvd.
Hammond, IN 46324
(219)931-1000
Fax: (219)845-9548

SCORE Office (Indianapolis)
429 N. Pennsylvania St., Ste. 100
Indianapolis, IN 46204-1873
(317)226-7264
Fax: (317)226-7259
E-mail: inscore@indy.net
Website: http://www.score-
indianapolis.org/

SCORE Office (Jasper)
PO Box 307
Jasper, IN 47547-0307
(812)482-6866

**SCORE Office (Kokomo/Howard
Counties)**
106 N. Washington St.
Kokomo, IN 46901
(765)457-5301
Fax: (765)452-4564

SCORE Office (Logansport)
300 E. Broadway, Ste. 103
Logansport, IN 46947
(219)753-6388

SCORE Office (Madison)

301 E. Main St.

Madison, IN 47250

(812)265-3135

Fax: (812)265-2923

SCORE Office (Marengo)

Rt. 1 Box 224D

Marengo, IN 47140

Fax: (812)365-2793

SCORE Office (Marion/Grant Counties)

215 S. Adams

Marion, IN 46952

(765)664-5107

SCORE Office (Merrillville)

255 W. 80th Pl.

Merrillville, IN 46410

(219)769-8180

Fax: (219)736-6223

SCORE Office (Michigan City)

200 E. Michigan Blvd.

Michigan City, IN 46360

(219)874-6221

Fax: (219)873-1204

SCORE Office (South Central Indiana)

4100 Charleston Rd.

New Albany, IN 47150-9538

(812)945-0066

SCORE Office (Rensselaer)

104 W. Washington

Rensselaer, IN 47978

SCORE Office (Salem)

210 N. Main St.

Salem, IN 47167

(812)883-4303

Fax: (812)883-1467

SCORE Office (South Bend)

300 N. Michigan St.

South Bend, IN 46601

(219)282-4350

E-mail: chair@southbend-score.org

Website: http://www.southbend-score.org/

SCORE Office (Valparaiso)

150 Lincolnway

Valparaiso, IN 46383

(219)462-1105

Fax: (219)469-5710

SCORE Office (Vincennes)

27 N. 3rd

PO Box 553

Vincennes, IN 47591

(812)882-6440

Fax: (812)882-6441

SCORE Office (Wabash)

PO Box 371

Wabash, IN 46992

(219)563-1168

Fax: (219)563-6920

Iowa

SCORE Office (Burlington)

Federal Bldg.

300 N. Main St.

Burlington, IA 52601

(319)752-2967

SCORE Office (Cedar Rapids)

2750 1st Ave. NE, Ste 350

Cedar Rapids, IA 52401-1806

(319)362-6405

Fax: (319)362-7861

E:mail: score@scorecr.org

Website: http://www.scorecr.org

SCORE Office (Illowa)

333 4th Ave. S

Clinton, IA 52732

(319)242-5702

SCORE Office (Council Bluffs)

7 N. 6th St.

Council Bluffs, IA 51502

(712)325-1000

SCORE Office (Northeast Iowa)

3404 285th St.

Cresco, IA 52136

(319)547-3377

SCORE Office (Des Moines)

Federal Bldg., Rm. 749

210 Walnut St.

Des Moines, IA 50309-2186

(515)284-4760

SCORE Office (Ft. Dodge)

Federal Bldg., Rm. 436

205 S. 8th St.

Ft. Dodge, IA 50501

(515)955-2622

SCORE Office (Independence)

110 1st. St. east

Independence, IA 50644

(319)334-7178

Fax: (319)334-7179

SCORE Office (Iowa City)

210 Federal Bldg.

PO Box 1853

Iowa City, IA 52240-1853

(319)338-1662

SCORE Office (Keokuk)

401 Main St.

Pierce Bldg., No. 1

Keokuk, IA 52632

(319)524-5055

SCORE Office (Central Iowa)

Fisher Community College

709 S. Center

Marshalltown, IA 50158

(515)753-6645

SCORE Office (River City)

15 West State St.

Mason City, IA 50401

(515)423-5724

SCORE Office (South Central)

SBDC, Indian Hills Community College

525 Grandview Ave.

Ottumwa, IA 52501

(515)683-5127

Fax: (515)683-5263

SCORE Office (Dubuque)

10250 Sundown Rd.

Peosta, IA 52068

(319)556-5110

SCORE Office (Southwest Iowa)

614 W. Sheridan

Shenandoah, IA 51601

(712)246-3260

SCORE Office (Sioux City)

Federal Bldg.

320 6th St.

Sioux City, IA 51101

(712)277-2324

Fax: (712)277-2325

SCORE Office (Iowa Lakes)

122 W. 5th St.

Spencer, IA 51301

(712)262-3059

SCORE Office (Vista)

119 W. 6th St.

Storm Lake, IA 50588

(712)732-3780

SCORE Office (Waterloo)

215 E. 4th

Waterloo, IA 50703

(319)233-8431

Kansas

SCORE Office (Southwest Kansas)

501 W. Spruce

Dodge City, KS 67801

(316)227-3119

SCORE Office (Emporia)
811 Homewood
Emporia, KS 66801
(316)342-1600

SCORE Office (Golden Belt)
1307 Williams
Great Bend, KS 67530
(316)792-2401

SCORE Office (Hays)
PO Box 400
Hays, KS 67601
(913)625-6595

SCORE Office (Hutchinson)
1 E. 9th St.
Hutchinson, KS 67501
(316)665-8468
Fax: (316)665-7619

SCORE Office (Southeast Kansas)
404 Westminster Pl.
PO Box 886
Independence, KS 67301
(316)331-4741

SCORE Office (McPherson)
306 N. Main
PO Box 616
McPherson, KS 67460
(316)241-3303

SCORE Office (Salina)
120 Ash St.
Salina, KS 67401
(785)243-4290
Fax: (785)243-1833

SCORE Office (Topeka)
1700 College
Topeka, KS 66621
(785)231-1010

SCORE Office (Wichita)
100 E. English, Ste. 510
Wichita, KS 67202
(316)269-6273
Fax: (316)269-6499

SCORE Office (Ark Valley)
205 E. 9th St.
Winfield, KS 67156
(316)221-1617

Kentucky

SCORE Office (Ashland)
PO Box 830
Ashland, KY 41105
(606)329-8011
Fax: (606)325-4607

SCORE Office (Bowling Green)
812 State St.
PO Box 51
Bowling Green, KY 42101
(502)781-3200
Fax: (502)843-0458

SCORE Office (Tri-Lakes)
508 Barbee Way
Danville, KY 40422-1548
(606)231-9902

SCORE Office (Glasgow)
301 W. Main St.
Glasgow, KY 42141
(502)651-3161
Fax: (502)651-3122

SCORE Office (Hazard)
B & I Technical Center
100 Airport Gardens Rd.
Hazard, KY 41701
(606)439-5856
Fax: (606)439-1808

SCORE Office (Lexington)
410 W. Vine St., Ste. 290, Civic C
Lexington, KY 40507
(606)231-9902
Fax: (606)253-3190
E-mail: scorelex@uky.campus.mci.net

SCORE Office (Louisville)
188 Federal Office Bldg.
600 Dr. Martin L. King Jr. Pl.
Louisville, KY 40202
(502)582-5976

SCORE Office (Madisonville)
257 N. Main
Madisonville, KY 42431
(502)825-1399
Fax: (502)825-1396

SCORE Office (Paducah)
Federal Office Bldg.
501 Broadway, Rm. B-36
Paducah, KY 42001
(502)442-5685

Louisiana

SCORE Office (Central Louisiana)
802 3rd St.
Alexandria, LA 71309
(318)442-6671

SCORE Office (Baton Rouge)
564 Laurel St.
PO Box 3217
Baton Rouge, LA 70801

(504)381-7130
Fax: (504)336-4306

SCORE Office (North Shore)
2 W. Thomas
Hammond, LA 70401
(504)345-4457
Fax: (504)345-4749

SCORE Office (Lafayette)
804 St. Mary Blvd.
Lafayette, LA 70505-1307
(318)233-2705
Fax: (318)234-8671
E-mail: score302@aol.com

SCORE Office (Lake Charles)
120 W. Pujo St.
Lake Charles, LA 70601
(318)433-3632

SCORE Office (New Orleans)
365 Canal St., Ste. 3100
New Orleans, LA 70130
(504)589-2356
Fax: (504)589-2339

SCORE Office (Shreveport)
400 Edwards St.
Shreveport, LA 71101
(318)677-2536
Fax: (318)677-2541

Maine

SCORE Office (Augusta)
40 Western Ave.
Augusta, ME 04330
(207)622-8509

SCORE Office (Bangor)
Peabody Hall, Rm. 229
One College Cir.
Bangor, ME 04401
(207)941-9707

SCORE Office (Central & Northern Arroostock)
111 High St.
Caribou, ME 04736
(207)492-8010
Fax: (207)492-8010

SCORE Office (Penquis)
South St.
Dover Foxcroft, ME 04426
(207)564-7021

SCORE Office (Maine Coastal)
Mill Mall
Box 1105
Ellsworth, ME 04605-1105

(207)667-5800

E-mail: score@arcadia.net

SCORE Office (Lewiston-Auburn)

BIC of Maine-Bates Mill Complex

35 Canal St.

Lewiston, ME 04240-7764

(207)782-3708

Fax: (207)783-7745

SCORE Office (Portland)

66 Pearl St., Rm. 210

Portland, ME 04101

(207)772-1147

Fax: (207)772-5581

E-mail: Score53@score.maine.org

Website: http://www.score.maine.org/

chapter53/

SCORE Office (Western Mountains)

255 River St.

PO Box 252

Rumford, ME 04257-0252

(207)369-9976

SCORE Office (Oxford Hills)

166 Main St.

South Paris, ME 04281

(207)743-0499

Maryland

SCORE Office (Southern Maryland)

2525 Riva Rd., Ste. 110

Annapolis, MD 21401

(410)266-9553

Fax: (410)573-0981

E-mail: score390@aol.com

Website: http://members.aol.com/

score390/index.htm

SCORE Office (Baltimore)

The City Crescent Bldg., 6th Fl.

10 S. Howard St.

Baltimore, MD 21201

(410)962-2233

Fax: (410)962-1805

SCORE Office (Bel Air)

108 S. Bond St.

Bel Air, MD 21014

(410)838-2020

Fax: (410)893-4715

SCORE Office (Bethesda)

7910 Woodmont Ave., Ste. 1204

Bethesda, MD 20814

(301)652-4900

Fax: (301)657-1973

SCORE Office (Bowie)

6670 Race Track Rd.

Bowie, MD 20715

(301)262-0920

Fax: (301)262-0921

SCORE Office (Dorchester County)

203 Sunburst Hwy.

Cambridge, MD 21613

(410)228-3575

SCORE Office (Upper Shore)

210 Marlboro Ave.

Easton, MD 21601

(410)822-4606

Fax: (410)822-7922

SCORE Office (Frederick County)

43A S. Market St.

Frederick, MD 21701

(301)662-8723

Fax: (301)846-4427

SCORE Office (Gaithersburg)

9 Park Ave.

Gaithersburg, MD 20877

(301)840-1400

Fax: (301)963-3918

SCORE Office (Glen Burnie)

103 Crain Hwy. SE

Glen Burnie, MD 21061

(410)766-8282

Fax: (410)766-9722

SCORE Office (Hagerstown)

111 W. Washington St.

Hagerstown, MD 21740

(301)739-2015

Fax: (301)739-1278

SCORE Office (Laurel)

7901 Sandy Spring Rd. Ste. 501

Laurel, MD 20707

(301)725-4000

Fax: (301)725-0776

SCORE Office (Salisbury)

300 E. Main St.

Salisbury, MD 21801

(410)749-0185

Fax: (410)860-9925

Massachusetts

SCORE Office (NE Massachusetts)

100 Cummings Ctr., Ste. 101 K

Beverly, MA 01923

(978)922-9441

Website: http://www1.shore.net/~score/

SCORE Office (Boston)

10 Causeway St., Rm. 265

Boston, MA 02222-1093

(617)565-5591

Fax: (617)565-5598

E-mail: boston-score-20@worldnet.att.net

Website: http://www.scoreboston.org/

SCORE office (Bristol/Plymouth County)

53 N. 6th St., Federal Bldg.

Bristol, MA 02740

(508)994-5093

SCORE Office (SE Massachusetts)

60 School St.

Brockton, MA 02401

(508)587-2673

Fax: (508)587-1340

Website: http://www.metrosouth

chamber.com/score.html

SCORE Office (North Adams)

820 N. State Rd.

Cheshire, MA 01225

(413)743-5100

SCORE Office (Clinton Satellite)

1 Green St.

Clinton, MA 01510

Fax: (508)368-7689

SCORE Office (Greenfield)

PO Box 898

Greenfield, MA 01302

(413)773-5463

Fax: (413)773-7008

SCORE Office (Haverhill)

87 Winter St.

Haverhill, MA 01830

(508)373-5663

Fax: (508)373-8060

SCORE Office (Hudson Satellite)

PO Box 578

Hudson, MA 01749

(508)568-0360

Fax: (508)568-0360

SCORE Office (Cape Cod)

Independence Pk., Ste. 5B

270 Communications Way

Hyannis, MA 02601

(508)775-4884

Fax: (508)790-2540

SCORE Office (Lawrence)

264 Essex St.

Lawrence, MA 01840

(508)686-0900

Fax: (508)794-9953

SCORE Office (Leominster Satellite)
110 Erdman Way
Leominster, MA 01453
(508)840-4300
Fax: (508)840-4896

SCORE Office (Bristol/Plymouth Counties)
53 N. 6th St., Federal Bldg.
New Bedford, MA 02740
(508)994-5093

SCORE Office (Newburyport)
29 State St.
Newburyport, MA 01950
(617)462-6680

SCORE Office (Pittsfield)
66 West St.
Pittsfield, MA 01201
(413)499-2485

SCORE Office (Haverhill-Salem)
32 Derby Sq.
Salem, MA 01970
(508)745-0330
Fax: (508)745-3855

SCORE Office (Springfield)
1350 Main St.
Federal Bldg.
Springfield, MA 01103
(413)785-0314

SCORE Office (Carver)
12 Taunton Green, Ste. 201
Taunton, MA 02780
(508)824-4068
Fax: (508)824-4069

SCORE Office (Worcester)
33 Waldo St.
Worcester, MA 01608
(508)753-2929
Fax: (508)754-8560

Michigan

SCORE Office (Allegan)
PO Box 338
Allegan, MI 49010
(616)673-2479

SCORE Office (Ann Arbor)
425 S. Main St., Ste. 103
Ann Arbor, MI 48104
(313)665-4433

SCORE Office (Battle Creek)
34 W. Jackson Ste. 4A
Battle Creek, MI 49017-3505

(616)962-4076
Fax: (616)962-6309

SCORE Office (Cadillac)
222 Lake St.
Cadillac, MI 49601
(616)775-9776
Fax: (616)768-4255

SCORE Office (Detroit)
477 Michigan Ave., Rm. 515
Detroit, MI 48226
(313)226-7947
Fax: (313)226-3448

SCORE Office (Flint)
708 Root Rd., Rm. 308
Flint, MI 48503
(810)233-6846

SCORE Office (Grand Rapids)
111 Pearl St. NW
Grand Rapids, MI 49503-2831
(616)771-0305
Fax: (616)771-0328
E-mail: scoreone@iserv.net
Website: http://www.iserv.net/
~scoreone/

SCORE Office (Holland)
480 State St.
Holland, MI 49423
(616)396-9472

SCORE Office (Jackson)
209 East Washington
PO Box 80
Jackson, MI 49204
(517)782-8221
Fax: (517)782-0061

SCORE Office (Kalamazoo)
345 W. Michigan Ave.
Kalamazoo, MI 49007
(616)381-5382
Fax: (616)384-0096
E-mail: score@nucleus.net

SCORE Office (Lansing)
117 E. Allegan
PO Box 14030
Lansing, MI 48901
(517)487-6340
Fax: (517)484-6910

SCORE Office (Livonia)
15401 Farmington Rd.
Livonia, MI 48154
(313)427-2122
Fax: (313)427-6055

SCORE Office (Madison Heights)
26345 John R
Madison Heights, MI 48071
(810)542-5010
Fax: (810)542-6821

SCORE Office (Monroe)
111 E. 1st
Monroe, MI 48161
(313)242-3366
Fax: (313)242-7253

SCORE Office (Mt. Clemens)
58 S/B Gratiot
Mt. Clemens, MI 48043
(810)463-1528
Fax: (810)463-6541

SCORE Office (Muskegon)
PO Box 1087
230 Terrace Plz.
Muskegon, MI 49443
(616)722-3751
Fax: (616)728-7251

SCORE Office (Petoskey)
401 E. Mitchell St.
Petoskey, MI 49770
(616)347-4150

SCORE Office (Pontiac)
Executive Office Bldg.
1200 N. Telegraph Rd.
Pontiac, MI 48341
(810)975-9555

SCORE Office (Pontiac)
PO Box 430025
Pontiac, MI 48343
(810)335-9600

SCORE Office (Port Huron)
920 Pinegrove Ave.
Port Huron, MI 48060
(810)985-7101

SCORE Office (Rochester)
71 Walnut Ste. 110
Rochester, MI 48307
(810)651-6700
Fax: (810)651-5270

SCORE Office (Saginaw)
901 S. Washington Ave.
Saginaw, MI 48601
(517)752-7161
Fax: (517)752-9055

SCORE Office (Upper Peninsula)
2581 I-75 Business Spur
Sault Ste. Marie, MI 49783
(906)632-3301

SCORE Office (Southfield)
21000 W. 10 Mile Rd.
Southfield, MI 48075
(810)204-3050
Fax: (810)204-3099

SCORE Office (Traverse City)
202 E. Grandview Pkwy.
PO Box 387
Traverse City, MI 49685
(616)947-5075
Fax: (616)946-2565

SCORE Office (Warren)
30500 Van Dyke, Ste. 118
Warren, MI 48093
(810)751-3939

Minnesota

SCORE Office (Aitkin)
Aitkin, MN 56431
(218)741-3906

SCORE Office (Albert Lea)
202 N. Broadway Ave.
Albert Lea, MN 56007
(507)373-7487

SCORE Office (Austin)
PO Box 864
Austin, MN 55912
(507)437-4561
Fax: (507)437-4869

SCORE Office (South Metro)
Ames Business Ctr.
2500 W. County Rd., No. 42
Burnsville, MN 55337
(612)898-5645
Fax: (612)435-6972
E-mail: southmetro@scoreminn.org
Website: http://www.scoreminn.org/
southmetro/

SCORE Office (Duluth)
1717 Minnesota Ave.
Duluth, MN 55802
(218)727-8286
Fax: (218)727-3113
E-mail: duluth@scoreminn.org
Website: http://www.scoreminn.org

SCORE Office (Fairmont)
PO Box 826
Fairmont, MN 56031
(507)235-5547
Fax: (507)235-8411

SCORE Office (Southwest Minnesota)
112 Riverfront St.

Box 999
Mankato, MN 56001
(507)345-4519
Fax: (507)345-4451
Website: http://www.scoreminn.org/

SCORE Office (Minneapolis)
North Plaza Bldg., Ste. 51
5217 Wayzata Blvd.
Minneapolis, MN 55416
(612)591-0539
Fax: (612)544-0436
Website: http://www.scoreminn.org/

SCORE Office (Owatonna)
PO Box 331
Owatonna, MN 55060
(507)451-7970
Fax: (507)451-7972

SCORE Office (Red Wing)
2000 W. Main St., Ste. 324
Red Wing, MN 55066
(612)388-4079

SCORE Office (Southeastern Minnesota)
220 S. Broadway, Ste. 100
Rochester, MN 55901
(507)288-1122
Fax: (507)282-8960
Website: http://www.scoreminn.org/

SCORE Office (Brainerd)
St. Cloud, MN 56301

SCORE Office (Central Area)
1527 Northway Dr.
St. Cloud, MN 56301
(320)240-1332
Fax: (320)255-9050
Website: http://www.scoreminn.org/

SCORE Office (St. Paul)
350 St. Peter St., No. 295
Lowry Professional Bldg.
St. Paul, MN 55102
(651)223-5010
Fax: (651)223-5048
Website: http://www.scoreminn.org/

SCORE Office (Winona)
Box 870
Winona, MN 55987
(507)452-2272
Fax: (507)454-8814

SCORE Office (Worthington)
1121 3rd Ave.
Worthington, MN 56187
(507)372-2919
Fax: (507)372-2827

Mississippi

SCORE Office (Delta)
915 Washington Ave.
PO Box 933
Greenville, MS 38701
(601)378-3141

SCORE Office (Gulfcoast)
1 Government Plaza
2909 13th St., Ste. 203
Gulfport, MS 39501
(228)863-0054

SCORE Office (Jackson)
1st Jackson Center, Ste. 400
101 W. Capitol St.
Jackson, MS 39201
(601)965-5533

SCORE Office (Meridian)
5220 16th Ave.
Meridian, MS 39305
(601)482-4412

Missouri

SCORE Office (Lake of the Ozark)
University Extension
113 Kansas St.
PO Box 1405
Camdenton, MO 65020
(573)346-2644
Fax: (573)346-2694
E-mail: score@cdoc.net
Website: http://sites.cdoc.net/score/

Chamber of Commerce (Cape Girardeau)
PO Box 98
Cape Girardeau, MO 63702-0098
(314)335-3312

SCORE Office (Mid-Missouri)
1705 Halstead Ct.
Columbia, MO 65203
(573)874-1132

SCORE Office (Ozark-Gateway)
1486 Glassy Rd.
Cuba, MO 65453-1640
(573)885-4954

SCORE Office (Kansas City)
323 W. 8th St., Ste. 104
Kansas City, MO 64105
(816)374-6675
Fax: (816)374-6692
E-mail: SCOREBIC@AOL.COM
Website: http://www.crn.org/score/

SCORE Office (Sedalia)
Lucas Place
323 W. 8th St., Ste.104
Kansas City, MO 64105
(816)374-6675

SCORE office (Tri-Lakes)
PO Box 1148
Kimberling, MO 65686
(417)739-3041

SCORE Office (Tri-Lakes)
HCRI Box 85
Lampe, MO 65681
(417)858-6798

SCORE Office (Mexico)
111 N. Washington St.
Mexico, MO 65265
(314)581-2765

SCORE Office (Southeast Missouri)
Rte. 1, Box 280
Neelyville, MO 63954
(573)989-3577

SCORE office (Poplar Bluff Area)
806 Emma St.
Poplar Bluff, MO 63901
(573)686-8892

SCORE Office (St. Joseph)
3003 Frederick Ave.
St. Joseph, MO 64506
(816)232-4461

SCORE Office (St. Louis)
815 Olive St., Rm. 242
St. Louis, MO 63101-1569
(314)539-6970
Fax: (314)539-3785
E-mail: info@stlscore.org
Website: http://www.stlscore.org/

SCORE Office (Lewis & Clark)
425 Spencer Rd.
St. Peters, MO 63376
(314)928-2900
Fax: (314)928-2900
E-mail: score01@mail.win.org

SCORE Office (Springfield)
620 S. Glenstone, Ste. 110
Springfield, MO 65802-3200
(417)864-7670
Fax: (417)864-4108

SCORE office (Southeast Kansas)
1206 W. First St.
Webb City, MO 64870
(417)673-3984

Montana

SCORE Office (Billings)
815 S. 27th St.
Billings, MT 59101
(406)245-4111

SCORE Office (Bozeman)
1205 E. Main St.
Bozeman, MT 59715
(406)586-5421

SCORE Office (Butte)
1000 George St.
Butte, MT 59701
(406)723-3177

SCORE Office (Great Falls)
710 First Ave. N
Great Falls, MT 59401
(406)761-4434
E-mail: scoregtf@in.tch.com

SCORE Office (Havre, Montana)
518 First St.
Havre, MT 59501
(406)265-4383

SCORE Office (Helena)
Federal Bldg.
301 S. Park
Helena, MT 59626-0054
(406)441-1081

SCORE Office (Kalispell)
2 Main St.
Kalispell, MT 59901
(406)756-5271
Fax: (406)752-6665

SCORE Office (Missoula)
723 Ronan
Missoula, MT 59806
(406)327-8806
E-mail: score@safeshop.com
Website: http://missoula.bigsky.net/
score/

Nebraska

SCORE Office (Columbus)
Columbus, NE 68601
(402)564-2769

SCORE Office (Fremont)
92 W. 5th St.
Fremont, NE 68025
(402)721-2641

SCORE Office (Hastings)
Hastings, NE 68901
(402)463-3447

SCORE Office (Lincoln)
8800 O St.
Lincoln, NE 68520
(402)437-2409

SCORE Office (Panhandle)
150549 CR 30
Minatare, NE 69356
(308)632-2133
Website: http://www.tandt.com/
SCORE

SCORE Office (Norfolk)
3209 S. 48th Ave.
Norfolk, NE 68106
(402)564-2769

SCORE Office (North Platte)
3301 W. 2nd St.
North Platte, NE 69101
(308)532-4466

SCORE Office (Omaha)
11145 Mill Valley Rd.
Omaha, NE 68154
(402)221-3606
Fax: (402)221-3680
E-mail: infoctr@ne.uswest.net
Website: http://www.tandt.com/score/

Nevada

SCORE Office (Incline Village)
969 Tahoe Blvd.
Incline Village, NV 89451
(702)831-7327
Fax: (702)832-1605

SCORE Office (Carson City)
301 E. Stewart
PO Box 7527
Las Vegas, NV 89125
(702)388-6104

SCORE Office (Las Vegas)
300 Las Vegas Blvd. S, Ste. 1100
Las Vegas, NV 89101
(702)388-6104

SCORE Office (Northern Nevada)
SBDC, College of Business
Administration
Univ. of Nevada
Reno, NV 89557-0100
(702)784-4436
Fax: (702)784-4337

New Hampshire

SCORE Office (North Country)
PO Box 34

Berlin, NH 03570
(603)752-1090

SCORE Office (Concord)
143 N. Main St., Rm. 202A
PO Box 1258
Concord, NH 03301
(603)225-1400
Fax: (603)225-1409

SCORE Office (Dover)
299 Central Ave.
Dover, NH 03820
(603)742-2218
Fax: (603)749-6317

SCORE Office (Monadnock)
34 Mechanic St.
Keene, NH 03431-3421
(603)352-0320

SCORE Office (Lakes Region)
67 Water St., Ste. 105
Laconia, NH 03246
(603)524-9168

SCORE Office (Upper Valley)
Citizens Bank Bldg., Rm. 310
20 W. Park St.
Lebanon, NH 03766
(603)448-3491
Fax: (603)448-1908
E-mail: billt@valley.net
Website: http://www.valley.net/~score/

SCORE Office (Merrimack Valley)
275 Chestnut St., Rm. 618
Manchester, NH 03103
(603)666-7561
Fax: (603)666-7925

SCORE Office (Mt. Washington Valley)
PO Box 1066
North Conway, NH 03818
(603)383-0800

SCORE Office (Seacoast)
195 Commerce Way, Unit-A
Portsmouth, NH 03801-3251
(603)433-0575

New Jersey

SCORE Office (Somerset)
Paritan Valley Community College,
Rte. 28
Branchburg, NJ 08807
(908)218-8874
E-mail: nj-score@grizbiz.com.
Website: http://www.nj-score.org/

SCORE Office (Chester)
5 Old Mill Rd.
Chester, NJ 07930
(908)879-7080

**SCORE Office
(Greater Princeton)**
4 A George Washington Dr.
Cranbury, NJ 08512
(609)520-1776

SCORE Office (Freehold)
36 W. Main St.
Freehold, NJ 07728
(908)462-3030
Fax: (908)462-2123

SCORE Office (North West)
Picantinny Innovation Ctr.
3159 Schrader Rd.
Hamburg, NJ 07419
(973)209-8525
Fax: (973)209-7252
E-mail: nj-score@grizbiz.com
Website: http://www.nj-score.org/

SCORE Office (Monmouth)
765 Newman Springs Rd.
Lincroft, NJ 07738
(908)224-2573
E-mail: nj-score@grizbiz.com
Website: http://www.nj-score.org/

SCORE Office (Manalapan)
125 Symmes Dr.
Manalapan, NJ 07726
(908)431-7220

SCORE Office (Jersey City)
2 Gateway Ctr., 4th Fl.
Newark, NJ 07102
(973)645-3982
Fax: (973)645-2375

SCORE Office (Newark)
2 Gateway Center, 15th Fl.
Newark, NJ 07102-5553
(973)645-3982
Fax: (973)645-2375
E-mail: nj-score@grizbiz.com
Website: http://www.nj-score.org

SCORE Office (Bergen County)
327 E. Ridgewood Ave.
Paramus, NJ 07652
(201)599-6090
E-mail: nj-score@grizbiz.com
Website: http://www.nj-score.org/

SCORE Office (Pennsauken)
4900 Rte. 70

Pennsauken, NJ 08109
(609)486-3421

SCORE Office (Southern New Jersey)
4900 Rte. 70
Pennsauken, NJ 08109
(609)486-3421
E-mail: nj-score@grizbiz.com
Website: http://www.nj-score.org/

SCORE Office (Greater Princeton)
216 Rockingham Row
Princeton Forrestal Village
Princeton, NJ 08540
(609)520-1776
Fax: (609)520-9107
E-mail: nj-score@grizbiz.com
Website: http://www.nj-score.org/

SCORE Office (Shrewsbury)
Hwy. 35
Shrewsbury, NJ 07702
(908)842-5995
Fax: (908)219-6140

SCORE Office (Ocean County)
33 Washington St.
Toms River, NJ 08754
(732)505-6033
E-mail: nj-score@grizbiz.com
Website: http://www.nj-score.org/

SCORE Office (Wall)
2700 Allaire Rd.
Wall, NJ 07719
(908)449-8877

SCORE Office (Wayne)
2055 Hamburg Tpke.
Wayne, NJ 07470
(201)831-7788
Fax: (201)831-9112

New Mexico

SCORE Office (Albuquerque)
525 Buena Vista, SE
Albuquerque, NM 87106
(505)272-7999
Fax: (505)272-7963

SCORE Office (Las Cruces)
Loretto Towne Center
505 S. Main St., Ste. 125
Las Cruces, NM 88001
(505)523-5627
Fax: (505)524-2101
E-mail: score.397@zianet.com

SCORE Office (Roswell)
Federal Bldg., Rm. 237

Roswell, NM 88201
(505)625-2112
Fax: (505)623-2545

SCORE Office (Santa Fe)
Montoya Federal Bldg.
120 Federal Place, Rm. 307
Santa Fe, NM 87501
(505)988-6302
Fax: (505)988-6300

New York

SCORE Office (Northeast)
1 Computer Dr. S
Albany, NY 12205
(518)446-1118
Fax: (518)446-1228

SCORE Office (Auburn)
30 South St.
PO Box 675
Auburn, NY 13021
(315)252-7291

SCORE Office (South Tier Binghamton)
Metro Center, 2nd Fl.
49 Court St.
PO Box 995
Binghamton, NY 13902
(607)772-8860

SCORE Office (Queens County City)
12055 Queens Blvd., Rm. 333
Borough Hall, NY 11424
(718)263-8961

SCORE Office (Buffalo)
Federal Bldg., Rm. 1311
111 W. Huron St.
Buffalo, NY 14202
(716)551-4301
Website: http://www2.pcom.net/score/
buf45.html

SCORE Office (Canandaigua)
Chamber of Commerce Bldg.
113 S. Main St.
Canandaigua, NY 14424
(716)394-4400
Fax: (716)394-4546

SCORE Office (Chemung)
333 E. Water St., 4th Fl.
Elmira, NY 14901
(607)734-3358

SCORE Office (Geneva)
Chamber of Commerce Bldg.
PO Box 587

Geneva, NY 14456
(315)789-1776
Fax: (315)789-3993

SCORE Office (Glens Falls)
84 Broad St.
Glens Falls, NY 12801
(518)798-8463
Fax: (518)745-1433

SCORE Office (Orange County)
40 Matthews St.
Goshen, NY 10924
(914)294-8080
Fax: (914)294-6121

SCORE Office (Huntington Area)
151 W. Carver St.
Huntington, NY 11743
(516)423-6100

SCORE Office (Tompkins County)
904 E. Shore Dr.
Ithaca, NY 14850
(607)273-7080

SCORE Office (Long Island City)
120-55 Queens Blvd.
Jamaica, NY 11424
(718)263-8961
Fax: (718)263-9032

SCORE Office (Chatauqua)
101 W. 5th St.
Jamestown, NY 14701
(716)484-1103

SCORE Office (Westchester)
2 Caradon Ln.
Katonah, NY 10536
(914)948-3907
Fax: (914)948-4645
E-mail: score@w-w-w.com
Website: http://w-w-w.com/score/

SCORE Office (Queens County)
Queens Borough Hall
120-55 Queens Blvd. Rm. 333
Kew Gardens, NY 11424
(718)263-8961
Fax: (718)263-9032

SCORE Office (Brookhaven)
3233 Rte. 112
Medford, NY 11763
(516)451-6563
Fax: (516)451-6925

SCORE Office (Melville)
35 Pinelawn Rd., Rm. 207-W
Melville, NY 11747
(516)454-0771

SCORE Office (Nassau County)
400 County Seat Dr., No. 140
Mineola, NY 11501
(516)571-3303
E-mail: Counse1998@aol.com
Website: http://members.aol.com/
Counse1998/Default.htm

SCORE Office (Mt. Vernon)
4 N. 7th Ave.
Mt. Vernon, NY 10550
(914)667-7500

SCORE Office (New York)
26 Federal Plz., Rm. 3100
New York, NY 10278
(212)264-4507
Fax: (212)264-4963
E-mail: score1000@erols.com
Website: http://users.erols.com/
score-nyc/

SCORE Office (Newburgh)
47 Grand St.
Newburgh, NY 12550
(914)562-5100

SCORE Office (Owego)
188 Front St.
Owego, NY 13827
(607)687-2020

SCORE Office (Peekskill)
1 S. Division St.
Peekskill, NY 10566
(914)737-3600
Fax: (914)737-0541

SCORE Office (Penn Yan)
2375 Rte. 14A
Penn Yan, NY 14527
(315)536-3111

SCORE Office (Dutchess)
110 Main St.
Poughkeepsie, NY 12601
(914)454-1700

SCORE Office (Rochester)
601 Keating Federal Bldg., Rm. 410
100 State St.
Rochester, NY 14614
(716)263-6473
Fax: (716)263-3146
Website: http://www.ggw.org/score/

SCORE Office (Saranac Lake)
30 Main St.
Saranac Lake, NY 12983
(315)448-0415

SCORE Office (Suffolk)
286 Main St.
Setauket, NY 11733
(516)751-3886

SCORE Office (Staten Island)
130 Bay St.
Staten Island, NY 10301
(718)727-1221

SCORE Office (Ulster)
Clinton Bldg., Rm. 107
Stone Ridge, NY 12484
(914)687-5035
Fax: (914)687-5015
Website: http://www.scoreulster.org/

SCORE Office (Syracuse)
401 S. Salina, 5th Fl.
Syracuse, NY 13202
(315)471-9393

SCORE Office (Utica)
SUNY Institute of Technology, Route 12
Utica, NY 13504-3050
(315)792-7553

SCORE Office (Watertown)
518 Davidson St.
Watertown, NY 13601
(315)788-1200
Fax: (315)788-8251

North Carolina

SCORE office (Asheboro)
317 E. Dixie Dr.
Asheboro, NC 27203
(336)626-2626
Fax: (336)626-7077

SCORE Office (Asheville)
Federal Bldg., Rm. 259
151 Patton
Asheville, NC 28801-5770
(828)271-4786
Fax: (828)271-4009

SCORE Office (Chapel Hill)
104 S. Estes Dr.
PO Box 2897
Chapel Hill, NC 27514
(919)967-7075

SCORE Office (Coastal Plains)
PO Box 2897
Chapel Hill, NC 27515
(919)967-7075
Fax: (919)968-6874

SCORE Office (Charlotte)
200 N. College St., Ste. A-2015

Charlotte, NC 28202
(704)344-6576
Fax: (704)344-6769
E-mail: CharlotteSCORE47@AOL.com
Website: http://www.charweb.org/
business/score/

SCORE Office (Durham)
411 W. Chapel Hill St.
Durham, NC 27707
(919)541-2171

SCORE Office (Gastonia)
PO Box 2168
Gastonia, NC 28053
(704)864-2621
Fax: (704)854-8723

SCORE Office (Greensboro)
400 W. Market St., Ste. 103
Greensboro, NC 27401-2241
(910)333-5399

SCORE Office (Henderson)
PO Box 917
Henderson, NC 27536
(919)492-2061
Fax: (919)430-0460

SCORE Office (Hendersonville)
Federal Bldg., Rm. 108
W. 4th Ave. & Church St.
Hendersonville, NC 28792
(828)693-8702
E-mail: score@circle.net
Website: http://www.wncguide.com/
score/Welcome.html

SCORE Office (Unifour)
PO Box 1828
Hickory, NC 28603
(704)328-6111

SCORE Office (High Point)
1101 N. Main St.
High Point, NC 27262
(336)882-8625
Fax: (336)889-9499

SCORE Office (Outer Banks)
Collington Rd. and Mustain
Kill Devil Hills, NC 27948
(252)441-8144

SCORE Office (Down East)
312 S. Front St., Ste. 6
New Bern, NC 28560
(252)633-6688
Fax: (252)633-9608

SCORE Office (Kinston)
PO Box 95

New Bern, NC 28561
(919)633-6688

SCORE Office (Raleigh)
Century Post Office Bldg., Ste. 306
300 Federal St. Mall
Raleigh, NC 27601
(919)856-4739
E-mail: jendres@ibm.net
Website: http://www.intrex.net/score96/
score96.htm

SCORE Office (Sanford)
1801 Nash St.
Sanford, NC 27330
(919)774-6442
Fax: (919)776-8739

SCORE Office (Sandhills Area)
1480 Hwy. 15-501
PO Box 458
Southern Pines, NC 28387
(910)692-3926

SCORE Office (Wilmington)
Corps of Engineers Bldg.
96 Darlington Ave., Ste. 207
Wilmington, NC 28403
(910)815-4576
Fax: (910)815-4658

North Dakota

**SCORE Office
(Bismarck-Mandan)**
700 E. Main Ave., 2nd Fl.
PO Box 5509
Bismarck, ND 58506-5509
(701)250-4303

SCORE Office (Fargo)
657 2nd Ave., Rm. 225
Fargo, ND 58108-3083
(701)239-5677

SCORE Office (Upper Red River)
4275 Technology Dr., Rm. 156
Grand Forks, ND 58202-8372
(701)777-3051

SCORE Office (Minot)
100 1st St. SW
Minot, ND 58701-3846
(701)852-6883
Fax: (701)852-6905

Ohio

SCORE Office (Akron)
1 Cascade Plz., 7th Fl.
Akron, OH 44308

(330)379-3163
Fax: (330)379-3164

SCORE Office (Ashland)
Gill Center
47 W. Main St.
Ashland, OH 44805
(419)281-4584

SCORE Office (Canton)
116 Cleveland Ave. NW, Ste. 601
Canton, OH 44702-1720
(330)453-6047

SCORE Office (Chillicothe)
165 S. Paint St.
Chillicothe, OH 45601
(614)772-4530

SCORE Office (Cincinnati)
Ameritrust Bldg., Rm. 850
525 Vine St.
Cincinnati, OH 45202
(513)684-2812
Fax: (513)684-3251
Website: http://www.score.
chapter34.org/

SCORE Office (Cleveland)
Eaton Center, Ste. 620
1100 Superior Ave.
Cleveland, OH 44114-2507
(216)522-4194
Fax: (216)522-4844

SCORE Office (Columbus)
2 Nationwide Plz., Ste. 1400
Columbus, OH 43215-2542
(614)469-2357
Fax: (614)469-2391
E-mail: info@scorecolumbus.org
Website: http://www.scorecolumbus.org/

SCORE Office (Dayton)
Dayton Federal Bldg., Rm. 505
200 W. Second St.
Dayton, OH 45402-1430
(513)225-2887
Fax: (513)225-7667

SCORE Office (Defiance)
615 W. 3rd St.
PO Box 130
Defiance, OH 43512
(419)782-7946

SCORE Office (Findlay)
123 E. Main Cross St.
PO Box 923
Findlay, OH 45840
(419)422-3314

SCORE Office (Lima)
147 N. Main St.
Lima, OH 45801
(419)222-6045
Fax: (419)229-0266

SCORE Office (Mansfield)
55 N. Mulberry St.
Mansfield, OH 44902
(419)522-3211

SCORE Office (Marietta)
Thomas Hall
Marietta, OH 45750
(614)373-0268

SCORE Office (Medina)
County Administrative Bldg.
144 N. Broadway
Medina, OH 44256
(216)764-8650

SCORE Office (Licking County)
50 W. Locust St.
Newark, OH 43055
(614)345-7458

SCORE Office (Salem)
2491 State Rte. 45 S
Salem, OH 44460
(216)332-0361

SCORE Office (Tiffin)
62 S. Washington St.
Tiffin, OH 44883
(419)447-4141
Fax: (419)447-5141

SCORE Office (Toledo)
608 Madison Ave, Ste. 910
Toledo, OH 43624
(419)259-7598
Fax: (419)259-6460

SCORE Office (Heart of Ohio)
377 W. Liberty St.
Wooster, OH 44691
(330)262-5735
Fax: (330)262-5745

SCORE Office (Youngstown)
306 Williamson Hall
Youngstown, OH 44555
(330)746-2687

Oklahoma

SCORE Office (Anadarko)
PO Box 366
Anadarko, OK 73005
(405)247-6651

SCORE Office (Ardmore)
410 W. Main
Ardmore, OK 73401
(580)226-2620

SCORE Office (Northeast Oklahoma)
210 S. Main
Grove, OK 74344
(918)787-2796
Fax: (918)787-2796
E-mail: Score595@greencis.net

SCORE Office (Lawton)
4500 W. Lee Blvd., Bldg. 100, Ste. 107
Lawton, OK 73505
(580)353-8727
Fax: (580)250-5677

SCORE Office (Oklahoma City)
210 Park Ave., No. 1300
Oklahoma City, OK 73102
(405)231-5163
Fax: (405)231-4876
E-mail: score212@usa.net

SCORE Office (Stillwater)
439 S. Main
Stillwater, OK 74074
(405)372-5573
Fax: (405)372-4316

SCORE Office (Tulsa)
616 S. Boston, Ste. 406
Tulsa, OK 74119
(918)581-7462
Fax: (918)581-6908
Website: http://www.ionet.net/~tulscore/

Oregon

SCORE Office (Bend)
63085 N. Hwy. 97
Bend, OR 97701
(541)923-2849
Fax: (541)330-6900

SCORE Office (Willamette)
1401 Willamette St.
PO Box 1107
Eugene, OR 97401-4003
(541)465-6600
Fax: (541)484-4942

SCORE Office (Florence)
3149 Oak St.
Florence, OR 97439
(503)997-8444
Fax: (503)997-8448

SCORE Office (Southern Oregon)
33 N. Central Ave., Ste. 216

Medford, OR 97501
(541)776-4220
E-mail: pgr134f@prodigy.com

SCORE Office (Portland)
1515 SW 5th Ave., Ste. 1050
Portland, OR 97201
(503)326-3441
Fax: (503)326-2808
E-mail: gr134@prodigy.com

SCORE Office (Salem)
416 State St. (corner of Liberty)
Salem, OR 97301
(503)370-2896

Pennsylvania

SCORE Office (Altoona-Blair)
1212 12th Ave.
Altoona, PA 16601-3493
(814)943-8151

SCORE Office (Lehigh Valley)
Rauch Bldg. 37
Lehigh University
621 Taylor St.
Bethlehem, PA 18015
(610)758-4496
Fax: (610)758-5205

SCORE Office (Butler County)
100 N. Main St.
PO Box 1082
Butler, PA 16003
(412)283-2222
Fax: (412)283-0224

SCORE Office (Harrisburg)
4211 Trindle Rd.
Camp Hill, PA 17011
(717)761-4304
Fax: (717)761-4315

SCORE Office (Cumberland Valley)
75 S. 2nd St.
Chambersburg, PA 17201
(717)264-2935

SCORE Office (Monroe County-Stroudsburg)
556 Main St.
East Stroudsburg, PA 18301
(717)421-4433

SCORE Office (Erie)
120 W. 9th St.
Erie, PA 16501
(814)871-5650
Fax: (814)871-7530

SCORE Office (Bucks County)
409 Hood Blvd.
Fairless Hills, PA 19030
(215)943-8850
Fax: (215)943-7404

SCORE Office (Hanover)
146 Broadway
Hanover, PA 17331
(717)637-6130
Fax: (717)637-9127

SCORE Office (Harrisburg)
100 Chestnut, Ste. 309
Harrisburg, PA 17101
(717)782-3874

SCORE Office (East Montgomery County)
Baederwood Shopping Center
1653 The Fairways, Ste. 204
Jenkintown, PA 19046
(215)885-3027

SCORE Office (Kittanning)
2 Butler Rd.
Kittanning, PA 16201
(412)543-1305
Fax: (412)543-6206

SCORE Office (Lancaster)
118 W. Chestnut St.
Lancaster, PA 17603
(717)397-3092

SCORE Office (Westmoreland County)
300 Fraser Purchase Rd.
Latrobe, PA 15650-2690
(412)539-7505
Fax: (412)539-1850

SCORE Office (Lebanon)
252 N. 8th St.
PO Box 899
Lebanon, PA 17042-0899
(717)273-3727
Fax: (717)273-7940

SCORE Office (Lewistown)
3 W. Monument Sq., Ste. 204
Lewistown, PA 17044
(717)248-6713
Fax: (717)248-6714

SCORE Office (Delaware County)
602 E. Baltimore Pike
Media, PA 19063
(610)565-3677
Fax: (610)565-1606

SCORE Office (Milton Area)
112 S. Front St.
Milton, PA 17847

(717)742-7341
Fax: (717)792-2008

SCORE Office (Mon-Valley)
435 Donner Ave.
Monessen, PA 15062
(412)684-4277
Fax: (412)684-7688

SCORE Office (Monroeville)
William Penn Plaza
2790 Mosside Blvd., Ste. 295
Monroeville, PA 15146
(412)856-0622
Fax: (412)856-1030

SCORE Office (Airport Area)
986 Brodhead Rd.
Moon Township, PA 15108-2398
(412)264-6270
Fax: (412)264-1575

SCORE Office (Northeast)
8601 E. Roosevelt Blvd.
Philadelphia, PA 19152
(215)332-3400
Fax: (215)332-6050

SCORE Office (Philadelphia)
1315 Walnut St., Ste. 500
Philadelphia, PA 19107
(215)790-5050
Fax: (215)790-5057
E-mail: score46@bellatlantic.net
Website: http://www.pgweb.net/score46/

SCORE Office (Pittsburgh)
1000 Liberty Ave., Rm. 1122
Pittsburgh, PA 15222
(412)395-6560
Fax: (412)395-6562

SCORE Office (Tri-County)
801 N. Charlotte St.
Pottstown, PA 19464
(610)327-2673

SCORE Office (Reading)
601 Penn St.
Reading, PA 19601
(610)376-3497

SCORE Office (Scranton)
Oppenheim Bldg.
116 N. Washington Ave., Ste. 650
Scranton, PA 18503
(717)347-4611
Fax: (717)347-4611

SCORE Office (Central Pennsylvania)
200 Innovation Blvd., Ste. 242-B
State College, PA 16803

(814)234-9415
Fax: (814)238-9686
Website: http://countrystore.org/
business/score.htm

SCORE Office (Monroe-Stroudsburg)
556 Main St.
Stroudsburg, PA 18360
(717)421-4433

SCORE Office (Uniontown)
Federal Bldg.
Pittsburg St.
PO Box 2065 DTS
Uniontown, PA 15401
(412)437-4222
E-mail: uniontownscore@lcsys.net

SCORE Office (Warren County)
315 2nd Ave.
Warren, PA 16365
(814)723-9017

SCORE Office (Waynesboro)
323 E. Main St.
Waynesboro, PA 17268
(717)762-7123
Fax: (717)962-7124

SCORE Office (Chester County)
Government Service Center, Ste. 281
601 Westtown Rd.
West Chester, PA 19382-4538
(610)344-6910
Fax: (610)344-6919
E-mail: score@locke.ccil.org

SCORE Office (Wilkes-Barre)
7 N. Wilkes-Barre Blvd.
Wilkes Barre, PA 18702-5241
(717)826-6502
Fax: (717)826-6287

SCORE Office (North Central Pennsylvania)
240 W. 3rd St., Rm. 227
PO Box 725
Williamsport, PA 17703
(717)322-3720
Fax: (717)322-1607
E-mail: score234@mail.csrlink.net
Website: http://www.lycoming.org/
score/

SCORE Office (York)
Cyber Center
2101 Pennsylvania Ave.
York, PA 17404
(717)845-8830
Fax: (717)854-9333

Puerto Rico

SCORE Office (Puerto Rico & Virgin Islands)
PO Box 12383-96
San Juan, PR 00914-0383
(787)726-8040
Fax: (787)726-8135

Rhode Island

SCORE Office (Barrington)
281 County Rd.
Barrington, RI 02806
(401)247-1920
Fax: (401)247-3763

SCORE Office (Woonsocket)
640 Washington Hwy.
Lincoln, RI 02865
(401)334-1000
Fax: (401)334-1009

SCORE Office (Wickford)
8045 Post Rd.
North Kingstown, RI 02852
(401)295-5566
Fax: (401)295-8987

SCORE Office (J.G.E. Knight)
380 Westminster St.
Providence, RI 02903
(401)528-4571
Fax: (401)528-4539
Website: http://www.riscore.org

SCORE Office (Warwick)
3288 Post Rd.
Warwick, RI 02886
(401)732-1100
Fax: (401)732-1101

SCORE Office (Westerly)
74 Post Rd.
Westerly, RI 02891
(401)596-7761
800-732-7636
Fax: (401)596-2190

South Carolina

SCORE Office (Aiken)
PO Box 892
Aiken, SC 29802
(803)641-1111
800-542-4536
Fax: (803)641-4174

SCORE Office (Anderson)
Anderson Mall
3130 N. Main St.

Anderson, SC 29621
(864)224-0453

SCORE Office (Coastal)
284 King St.
Charleston, SC 29401
(803)727-4778
Fax: (803)853-2529

SCORE Office (Midlands)
Strom Thurmond Bldg., Rm. 358
1835 Assembly St., Rm 358
Columbia, SC 29201
(803)765-5131
Fax: (803)765-5962
Website: http://www.scoremid
lands.org/

SCORE Office (Piedmont)
Federal Bldg., Rm. B-02
300 E. Washington St.
Greenville, SC 29601
(864)271-3638

SCORE Office (Greenwood)
PO Drawer 1467
Greenwood, SC 29648
(864)223-8357

SCORE Office (Hilton Head Island)
52 Savannah Trail
Hilton Head, SC 29926
(803)785-7107
Fax: (803)785-7110

SCORE Office (Grand Strand)
937 Broadway
Myrtle Beach, SC 29577
(803)918-1079
Fax: (803)918-1083
E-mail: score381@aol.com

SCORE Office (Spartanburg)
PO Box 1636
Spartanburg, SC 29304
(864)594-5000
Fax: (864)594-5055

South Dakota

SCORE Office (West River)
Rushmore Plz. Civic Ctr.
444 Mount Rushmore Rd., No. 209
Rapid City, SD 57701
(605)394-5311
E-mail: score@gwtc.net

SCORE Office (Sioux Falls)
First Financial Center
110 S. Phillips Ave., Ste. 200
Sioux Falls, SD 57104-6727

(605)330-4231
Fax: (605)330-4231

Tennessee

SCORE Office (Chattanooga)
Federal Bldg., Rm. 26
900 Georgia Ave.
Chattanooga, TN 37402
(423)752-5190
Fax: (423)752-5335

SCORE Office (Cleveland)
PO Box 2275
Cleveland, TN 37320
(423)472-6587
Fax: (423)472-2019

SCORE Office (Upper Cumberland Center)
1225 S. Willow Ave.
Cookeville, TN 38501
(615)432-4111
Fax: (615)432-6010

SCORE Office (Unicoi County)
PO Box 713
Erwin, TN 37650
(423)743-3000
Fax: (423)743-0942

SCORE Office (Greeneville)
115 Academy St.
Greeneville, TN 37743
(423)638-4111
Fax: (423)638-5345

SCORE Office (Jackson)
194 Auditorium St.
Jackson, TN 38301
(901)423-2200

SCORE Office (Northeast Tennessee)
1st Tennessee Bank Bldg.
2710 S. Roan St., Ste. 584
Johnson City, TN 37601
(423)929-7686
Fax: (423)461-8052

SCORE Office (Kingsport)
151 E. Main St.
Kingsport, TN 37662
(423)392-8805

SCORE Office (Greater Knoxville)
Farragot Bldg., Ste. 224
530 S. Gay St.
Knoxville, TN 37902
(423)545-4203
E-mail: scoreknox@ntown.com
Website: http://www.scoreknox.org/

SCORE Office (Maryville)
201 S. Washington St.
Maryville, TN 37804-5728
(423)983-2241
800-525-6834
Fax: (423)984-1386

SCORE Office (Memphis)
Federal Bldg., Ste. 390
167 N. Main St.
Memphis, TN 38103
(901)544-3588

SCORE Office (Nashville)
50 Vantage Way, Ste. 201
Nashville, TN 37228-1500
(615)736-7621

Texas

SCORE Office (Abilene)
2106 Federal Post Office and Court Bldg.
Abilene, TX 79601
(915)677-1857

SCORE Office (Austin)
2501 S. Congress
Austin, TX 78701
(512)442-7235
Fax: (512)442-7528

SCORE Office (Golden Triangle)
450 Boyd St.
Beaumont, TX 77704
(409)838-6581
Fax: (409)833-6718

SCORE Office (Brownsville)
3505 Boca Chica Blvd., Ste. 305
Brownsville, TX 78521
(210)541-4508

SCORE Office (Brazos Valley)
3000 Briarcrest, Ste. 302
Bryan, TX 77802
(409)776-8876
E-mail: 102633.2612@compuserve.com

SCORE Office (Cleburne)
Watergarden Pl., 9th Fl., Ste. 400
Cleburne, TX 76031
(817)871-6002

SCORE Office (Corpus Christi)
651 Upper North Broadway, Ste. 654
Corpus Christi, TX 78477
(512)888-4322
Fax: (512)888-3418

SCORE Office (Dallas)
6260 E. Mockingbird
Dallas, TX 75214-2619

(214)828-2471
Fax: (214)821-8033

SCORE Office (El Paso)
10 Civic Center Plaza
El Paso, TX 79901
(915)534-0541
Fax: (915)534-0513

SCORE Office (Bedford)
100 E. 15th St., Ste. 400
Ft. Worth, TX 76102
(817)871-6002

SCORE Office (Ft. Worth)
100 E. 15th St., No. 24
Ft. Worth, TX 76102
(817)871-6002
Fax: (817)871-6031
E-mail: fwbac@onramp.net

SCORE Office (Garland)
2734 W. Kingsley Rd.
Garland, TX 75041
(214)271-9224

SCORE Office (Granbury Chamber of Commerce)
416 S. Morgan
Granbury, TX 76048
(817)573-1622
Fax: (817)573-0805

SCORE Office (Lower Rio Grande Valley)
222 E. Van Buren, Ste. 500
Harlingen, TX 78550
(956)427-8533
Fax: (956)427-8537

SCORE Office (Houston)
9301 Southwest Fwy., Ste. 550
Houston, TX 77074
(713)773-6565
Fax: (713)773-6550

SCORE Office (Irving)
3333 N. MacArthur Blvd., Ste. 100
Irving, TX 75062
(214)252-8484
Fax: (214)252-6710

SCORE Office (Lubbock)
1205 Texas Ave., Rm. 411D
Lubbock, TX 79401
(806)472-7462
Fax: (806)472-7487

SCORE Office (Midland)
Post Office Annex
200 E. Wall St., Rm. P121
Midland, TX 79701
(915)687-2649

SCORE Office (Orange)
1012 Green Ave.
Orange, TX 77630-5620
(409)883-3536
800-528-4906
Fax: (409)886-3247

SCORE Office (Plano)
1200 E. 15th St.
PO Drawer 940287
Plano, TX 75094-0287
(214)424-7547
Fax: (214)422-5182

SCORE Office (Port Arthur)
4749 Twin City Hwy., Ste. 300
Port Arthur, TX 77642
(409)963-1107
Fax: (409)963-3322

SCORE Office (Richardson)
411 Belle Grove
Richardson, TX 75080
(214)234-4141
800-777-8001
Fax: (214)680-9103

SCORE Office (San Antonio)
Federal Bldg., Rm. A527
727 E. Durango
San Antonio, TX 78206
(210)472-5931
Fax: (210)472-5935

SCORE Office (Texarkana State College)
819 State Line Ave.
Texarkana, TX 75501
(903)792-7191
Fax: (903)793-4304

SCORE Office (East Texas)
RTDC
1530 SSW Loop 323, Ste. 100
Tyler, TX 75701
(903)510-2975
Fax: (903)510-2978

SCORE Office (Waco)
401 Franklin Ave.
Waco, TX 76701
(817)754-8898
Fax: (817)756-0776
Website: http://www.brc-waco.com/

SCORE Office (Wichita Falls)
Hamilton Bldg.
900 8th St.
Wichita Falls, TX 76307
(940)723-2741
Fax: (940)723-8773

Utah

SCORE Office (Northern Utah)
160 N. Main
Logan, UT 84321
(435)746-2269

SCORE Office (Ogden)
1701 E. Windsor Dr.
Ogden, UT 84604
(801)629-8613
E-mail: score158@netscape.net

SCORE Office (Central Utah)
1071 E. Windsor Dr.
Provo, UT 84604
(801)373-8660

SCORE Office (Southern Utah)
225 South 700 East
St. George, UT 84770
(435)652-7751

SCORE Office (Salt Lake)
310 S Main St.
Salt Lake City, UT 84101
(801)746-2269
Fax: (801)746-2273

Vermont

SCORE Office (Champlain Valley)
Winston Prouty Federal Bldg.
11 Lincoln St., Rm. 106
Essex Junction, VT 05452
(802)951-6762

SCORE Office (Montpelier)
87 State St., Rm. 205
PO Box 605
Montpelier, VT 05601
(802)828-4422
Fax: (802)828-4485

SCORE Office (Marble Valley)
256 N. Main St.
Rutland, VT 05701-2413
(802)773-9147

SCORE Office (Northeast Kingdom)
20 Main St.
PO Box 904
St. Johnsbury, VT 05819
(802)748-5101

Virgin Islands

SCORE Office (St. Croix)
United Plaza Shopping Center
PO Box 4010, Christiansted
St. Croix, VI 00822
(809)778-5380

SCORE Office (St. Thomas-St. John)
Federal Bldg., Rm. 21
Veterans Dr.
St. Thomas, VI 00801
(809)774-8530

Virginia

SCORE Office (Arlington)
2009 N. 14th St., Ste. 111
Arlington, VA 22201
(703)525-2400

SCORE Office (Blacksburg)
141 Jackson St.
Blacksburg, VA 24060
(540)552-4061

SCORE Office (Bristol)
20 Volunteer Pkwy.
Bristol, VA 24203
(540)989-4850

SCORE Office (Central Virginia)
1001 E. Market St., Ste. 101
Charlottesville, VA 22902
(804)295-6712
Fax: (804)295-7066

SCORE Office (Alleghany Satellite)
241 W. Main St.
Covington, VA 24426
(540)962-2178
Fax: (540)962-2179

SCORE Office (Central Fairfax)
3975 University Dr., Ste. 350
Fairfax, VA 22030
(703)591-2450

SCORE Office (Falls Church)
PO Box 491
Falls Church, VA 22040
(703)532-1050
Fax: (703)237-7904

SCORE Office (Glenns)
Glenns Campus
Box 287
Glenns, VA 23149
(804)693-9650

SCORE Office (Peninsula)
6 Manhattan Sq.
PO Box 7269
Hampton, VA 23666
(757)766-2000
Fax: (757)865-0339
E-mail: score100@seva.net

SCORE Office (Tri-Cities)
108 N. Main St.

Hopewell, VA 23860
(804)458-5536

SCORE Office (Lynchburg)
Federal Bldg.
1100 Main St.
Lynchburg, VA 24504-1714
(804)846-3235

SCORE Office (Greater Prince William)
8963 Center St
Manassas, VA 20110
(703)368-4813
Fax: (703)368-4733

SCORE Office (Martinsvile)
115 Broad St.
Martinsville, VA 24112-0709
(540)632-6401
Fax: (540)632-5059

SCORE Office (Hampton Roads)
Federal Bldg., Rm. 737
200 Grandby St.
Norfolk, VA 23510
(757)441-3733
Fax: (757)441-3733
E-mail: scorehr60@juno.com

SCORE Office (Norfolk)
Federal Bldg., Rm. 737
200 Granby St.
Norfolk, VA 23510
(757)441-3733
Fax: (757)441-3733

SCORE Office (Virginia Beach)
Chamber of Commerce
200 Grandby St., Rm 737
Norfolk, VA 23510
(804)441-3733

SCORE Office (Radford)
1126 Norwood St.
Radford, VA 24141
(540)639-2202

SCORE Office (Richmond)
Federal Bldg.
400 N. 8th St., Ste. 1150
PO Box 10126
Richmond, VA 23240-0126
(804)771-2400
Fax: (804)771-8018
E-mail: scorechapter12@yahoo.com
Website: http://www.cvco.org/score/

SCORE Office (Roanoke)
Federal Bldg., Rm. 716
250 Franklin Rd.
Roanoke, VA 24011

(540)857-2834
Fax: (540)857-2043
E-mail: scorerva@juno.com
Website: http://hometown.aol.com/
scorerv/Index.html

SCORE Office (Fairfax)
8391 Old Courthouse Rd., Ste. 300
Vienna, VA 22182
(703)749-0400

SCORE Office (Greater Vienna)
513 Maple Ave. West
Vienna, VA 22180
(703)281-1333
Fax: (703)242-1482

SCORE Office (Shenandoah Valley)
301 W. Main St.
Waynesboro, VA 22980
(540)949-8203
Fax: (540)949-7740
E-mail: score427@intelos.net

SCORE Office (Williamsburg)
201 Penniman Rd.
Williamsburg, VA 23185
(757)229-6511
E-mail: wacc@williamsburgcc.com

SCORE Office (Northern Virginia)
1360 S. Pleasant Valley Rd.
Winchester, VA 22601
(540)662-4118

Washington

SCORE Office (Gray's Harbor)
506 Duffy St.
Aberdeen, WA 98520
(360)532-1924
Fax: (360)533-7945

SCORE Office (Bellingham)
101 E. Holly St.
Bellingham, WA 98225
(360)676-3307

SCORE Office (Everett)
2702 Hoyt Ave.
Everett, WA 98201-3556
(206)259-8000

SCORE Office (Gig Harbor)
3125 Judson St.
Gig Harbor, WA 98335
(206)851-6865

SCORE Office (Kennewick)
PO Box 6986
Kennewick, WA 99336
(509)736-0510

SCORE Office (Puyallup)
322 2nd St. SW
PO Box 1298
Puyallup, WA 98371
(206)845-6755
Fax: (206)848-6164

SCORE Office (Seattle)
1200 6th Ave., Ste. 1700
Seattle, WA 98101
(206)553-7320
Fax: (206)553-7044
E-mail: score55@aol.com
Website: http://www.scn.org/civic/score-
online/index55.html

SCORE Office (Spokane)
801 W. Riverside Ave., No. 240
Spokane, WA 99201
(509)353-2820
Fax: (509)353-2600
E-mail: score@dmi.net
Website: http://www.dmi.net/score/

SCORE Office (Clover Park)
PO Box 1933
Tacoma, WA 98401-1933
(206)627-2175

SCORE Office (Tacoma)
1101 Pacific Ave.
Tacoma, WA 98402
(253)274-1288
Fax: (253)274-1289

SCORE Office (Fort Vancouver)
1701 Broadway, S-1
Vancouver, WA 98663
(360)699-1079

SCORE Office (Walla Walla)
500 Tausick Way
Walla Walla, WA 99362
(509)527-4681

SCORE Office (Mid-Columbia)
1113 S. 14th Ave.
Yakima, WA 98907
(509)574-4944
Fax: (509)574-2943
Website: http://www.ellensburg.com/
~score/

West Virginia

SCORE Office (Charleston)
1116 Smith St.
Charleston, WV 25301
(304)347-5463
E-mail: score256@juno.com

SCORE Office (Virginia Street)
1116 Smith St., Ste. 302
Charleston, WV 25301
(304)347-5463

SCORE Office (Marion County)
PO Box 208
Fairmont, WV 26555-0208
(304)363-0486

SCORE Office (Upper Monongahela Valley)
1000 Technology Dr., Ste. 1111
Fairmont, WV 26555
(304)363-0486
E-mail: score537@hotmail.com

SCORE Office (Huntington)
1101 6th Ave., Ste. 220
Huntington, WV 25701-2309
(304)523-4092

SCORE Office (Wheeling)
1310 Market St.
Wheeling, WV 26003
(304)233-2575
Fax: (304)233-1320

Wisconsin

SCORE Office (Fox Cities)
227 S. Walnut St.
Appleton, WI 54913
(920)734-7101
Fax: (920)734-7161

SCORE Office (Beloit)
136 W. Grand Ave., Ste. 100
PO Box 717
Beloit, WI 53511
(608)365-8835
Fax: (608)365-9170

SCORE Office (Eau Claire)
Federal Bldg., Rm. B11
510 S. Barstow St.
Eau Claire, WI 54701
(715)834-1573
E-mail: score@ecol.net
Website: http://www.ecol.net/~score/

SCORE Office (Fond du Lac)
207 N. Main St.
Fond du Lac, WI 54935
(414)921-9500
Fax: (414)921-9559

SCORE Office (Green Bay)
835 Potts Ave.
Green Bay, WI 54304
(414)496-8930
Fax: (414)496-6009

SCORE Office (Janesville)
20 S. Main St., Ste. 11
PO Box 8008
Janesville, WI 53547
(608)757-3160
Fax: (608)757-3170

SCORE Office (La Crosse)
712 Main St.
La Crosse, WI 54602-0219
(608)784-4880

SCORE Office (Madison)
505 S. Rosa Rd.
Madison, WI 53719
(608)441-2820

SCORE Office (Manitowoc)
1515 Memorial Dr.
PO Box 903
Manitowoc, WI 54221-0903
(414)684-5575
Fax: (414)684-1915

SCORE Office (Milwaukee)
310 W. Wisconsin Ave., Ste. 425
Milwaukee, WI 53203
(414)297-3942
Fax: (414)297-1377

SCORE Office (Central Wisconsin)
1224 Lindbergh Ave.
Stevens Point, WI 54481
(715)344-7729

SCORE Office (Superior)
Superior Business Center Inc.
1423 N. 8th St.
Superior, WI 54880
(715)394-7388
Fax: (715)393-7414

SCORE Office (Waukesha)
223 Wisconsin Ave.
Waukesha, WI 53186-4926
(414)542-4249

SCORE Office (Wausau)
300 3rd St., Ste. 200
Wausau, WI 54402-6190
(715)845-6231

SCORE Office (Wisconsin Rapids)
2240 Kingston Rd.
Wisconsin Rapids, WI 54494
(715)423-1830

Wyoming

SCORE Office (Casper)
Federal Bldg., No. 2215
100 East B St.

Casper, WY 82602
(307)261-6529
Fax: (307)261-6530

Venture capital & financing companies

This section contains a listing of financing and loan companies in the United States and Canada. These listing are arranged alphabetically by country, then by state or province, then by city, then by organization name.

Canada

Alberta

Launchworks Inc.
1902J 11th St., S.E.
Calgary, AB, Canada T2G 3G2
(403)269-1119
Fax: (403)269-1141
Website: http://www.launchworks.com

Native Venture Capital Company, Inc.
21 Artist View Point, Box 7
Site 25, RR 12
Calgary, AB, Canada T3E 6W3
(903)208-5380

Miralta Capital Inc.
4445 Calgary Trail South
888 Terrace Plaza Alberta
Edmonton, AB, Canada T6H 5R7
(780)438-3535
Fax: (780)438-3129

Vencap Equities Alberta Ltd.
10180-101st St., Ste. 1980
Edmonton, AB, Canada T5J 3S4
(403)420-1171
Fax: (403)429-2541

British Columbia

Discovery Capital
5th Fl., 1199 West Hastings
Vancouver, BC, Canada V6E 3T5
(604)683-3000
Fax: (604)662-3457
E-mail: info@discoverycapital.com
Website: http://www.discoverycapital.com

Greenstone Venture Partners
1177 West Hastings St.
Ste. 400
Vancouver, BC, Canada V6E 2K3
(604)717-1977
Fax: (604)717-1976
Website: http://www.greenstonevc.com

Growthworks Capital
2600-1055 West Georgia St.
Box 11170 Royal Centre
Vancouver, BC, Canada V6E 3R5
(604)895-7259
Fax: (604)669-7605
Website: http://www.wofund.com

MDS Discovery Venture Management, Inc.
555 W. Eighth Ave., Ste. 305
Vancouver, BC, Canada V5Z 1C6
(604)872-8464
Fax: (604)872-2977
E-mail: info@mds-ventures.com

Ventures West Management Inc.
1285 W. Pender St., Ste. 280
Vancouver, BC, Canada V6E 4B1
(604)688-9495
Fax: (604)687-2145
Website: http://www.ventureswest.com

Nova Scotia

ACF Equity Atlantic Inc.
Purdy's Wharf Tower II
Ste. 2106
Halifax, NS, Canada B3J 3R7
(902)421-1965
Fax: (902)421-1808

Montgomerie, Huck & Co.
146 Bluenose Dr.
PO Box 538
Lunenburg, NS, Canada B0J 2C0
(902)634-7125
Fax: (902)634-7130

Ontario

IPS Industrial Promotion Services Ltd.
60 Columbia Way, Ste. 720
Markham, ON, Canada L3R 0C9
(905)475-9400
Fax: (905)475-5003

Betwin Investments Inc.
Box 23110
Sault Ste. Marie, ON, Canada P6A 6W6
(705)253-0744
Fax: (705)253-0744

Bailey & Company, Inc.
594 Spadina Ave.
Toronto, ON, Canada M5S 2H4
(416)921-6930
Fax: (416)925-4670

BCE Capital
200 Bay St.

South Tower, Ste. 3120
Toronto, ON, Canada M5J 2J2
(416)815-0078
Fax: (416)941-1073
Website: http://www.bcecapital.com

Castlehill Ventures
55 University Ave., Ste. 500
Toronto, ON, Canada M5J 2H7
(416)862-8574
Fax: (416)862-8875

CCFL Mezzanine Partners of Canada
70 University Ave.
Ste. 1450
Toronto, ON, Canada M5J 2M4
(416)977-1450
Fax: (416)977-6764
E-mail: info@ccfl.com
Website: http://www.ccfl.com

Celtic House International
100 Simcoe St., Ste. 100
Toronto, ON, Canada M5H 3G2
(416)542-2436
Fax: (416)542-2435
Website: http://www.celtic-house.com

Clairvest Group Inc.
22 St. Clair Ave. East
Ste. 1700
Toronto, ON, Canada M4T 2S3
(416)925-9270
Fax: (416)925-5753

Crosbie & Co., Inc.
One First Canadian Place
9th Fl.
PO Box 116
Toronto, ON, Canada M5X 1A4
(416)362-7726
Fax: (416)362-3447
E-mail: info@crosbieco.com
Website: http://www.crosbieco.com

Drug Royalty Corp.
Eight King St. East
Ste. 202
Toronto, ON, Canada M5C 1B5
(416)863-1865
Fax: (416)863-5161

Grieve, Horner, Brown & Asculai
8 King St. E, Ste. 1704
Toronto, ON, Canada M5C 1B5
(416)362-7668
Fax: (416)362-7660

Jefferson Partners
77 King St. West
Ste. 4010

PO Box 136
Toronto, ON, Canada M5K 1H1
(416)367-1533
Fax: (416)367-5827
Website: http://www.jefferson.com

J.L. Albright Venture Partners
Canada Trust Tower, 161 Bay St.
Ste. 4440
PO Box 215
Toronto, ON, Canada M5J 2S1
(416)367-2440
Fax: (416)367-4604
Website: http://www.jlaventures.com

McLean Watson Capital Inc.
One First Canadian Place
Ste. 1410
PO Box 129
Toronto, ON, Canada M5X 1A4
(416)363-2000
Fax: (416)363-2010
Website: http://www.mcleanwatson.com

Middlefield Capital Fund
One First Canadian Place
85th Fl.
PO Box 192
Toronto, ON, Canada M5X 1A6
(416)362-0714
Fax: (416)362-7925
Website: http://www.middlefield.com

Mosaic Venture Partners
24 Duncan St.
Ste. 300
Toronto, ON, Canada M5V 3M6
(416)597-8889
Fax: (416)597-2345

Onex Corp.
161 Bay St.
PO Box 700
Toronto, ON, Canada M5J 2S1
(416)362-7711
Fax: (416)362-5765

Penfund Partners Inc.
145 King St. West
Ste. 1920
Toronto, ON, Canada M5H 1J8
(416)865-0300
Fax: (416)364-6912
Website: http://www.penfund.com

Primaxis Technology Ventures Inc.
1 Richmond St. West, 8th Fl.
Toronto, ON, Canada M5H 3W4
(416)313-5210
Fax: (416)313-5218
Website: http://www.primaxis.com

Priveq Capital Funds
240 Duncan Mill Rd., Ste. 602
Toronto, ON, Canada M3B 3P1
(416)447-3330
Fax: (416)447-3331
E-mail: priveq@sympatico.ca

Roynat Ventures
40 King St. West, 26th Fl.
Toronto, ON, Canada M5H 1H1
(416)933-2667
Fax: (416)933-2783
Website: http://www.roynatcapital.com

Tera Capital Corp.
366 Adelaide St. East, Ste. 337
Toronto, ON, Canada M5A 3X9
(416)368-1024
Fax: (416)368-1427

Working Ventures Canadian Fund Inc.
250 Bloor St. East, Ste. 1600
Toronto, ON, Canada M4W 1E6
(416)934-7718
Fax: (416)929-0901
Website: http://www.workingventures.ca

Quebec

Altamira Capital Corp.
202 University
Niveau de Maisoneuve, Bur. 201
Montreal, QC, Canada H3A 2A5
(514)499-1656
Fax: (514)499-9570

Federal Business Development Bank
Venture Capital Division
Five Place Ville Marie, Ste. 600
Montreal, QC, Canada H3B 5E7
(514)283-1896
Fax: (514)283-5455

Hydro-Quebec Capitech Inc.
75 Boul, Rene Levesque Quest
Montreal, QC, Canada H2Z 1A4
(514)289-4783
Fax: (514)289-5420
Website: http://www.hqcapitech.com

Investissement Desjardins
2 complexe Desjardins
C.P. 760
Montreal, QC, Canada H5B 1B8
(514)281-7131
Fax: (514)281-7808
Website: http://www.desjardins.com/id

Marleau Lemire Inc.
One Place Ville-Marie, Ste. 3601
Montreal, QC, Canada H3B 3P2

(514)877-3800
Fax: (514)875-6415

Speirs Consultants Inc.
365 Stanstead
Montreal, QC, Canada H3R 1X5
(514)342-3858
Fax: (514)342-1977

Tecnocap Inc.
4028 Marlowe
Montreal, QC, Canada H4A 3M2
(514)483-6009
Fax: (514)483-6045
Website: http://www.technocap.com

Telsoft Ventures
1000, Rue de la Gauchetiere
Quest, 25eme Etage
Montreal, QC, Canada H3B 4W5
(514)397-8450
Fax: (514)397-8451

Saskatchewan

Saskatchewan Government Growth Fund
1801 Hamilton St., Ste. 1210
Canada Trust Tower
Regina, SK, Canada S4P 4B4
(306)787-2994
Fax: (306)787-2086

United states

Alabama

FHL Capital Corp.
600 20th Street North
Suite 350
Birmingham, AL 35203
(205)328-3098
Fax: (205)323-0001

Harbert Management Corp.
One Riverchase Pkwy. South
Birmingham, AL 35244
(205)987-5500
Fax: (205)987-5707
Website: http://www.harbert.net

Jefferson Capital Fund
PO Box 13129
Birmingham, AL 35213
(205)324-7709

Private Capital Corp.
100 Brookwood Pl., 4th Fl.
Birmingham, AL 35209
(205)879-2722
Fax: (205)879-5121

21st Century Health Ventures
One Health South Pkwy.
Birmingham, AL 35243
(256)268-6250
Fax: (256)970-8928

FJC Growth Capital Corp.
200 W. Side Sq., Ste. 340
Huntsville, AL 35801
(256)922-2918
Fax: (256)922-2909

Hickory Venture Capital Corp.
301 Washington St. NW
Suite 301
Huntsville, AL 35801
(256)539-1931
Fax: (256)539-5130
E-mail: hvcc@hvcc.com
Website: http://www.hvcc.com

Southeastern Technology Fund
7910 South Memorial Pkwy., Ste. F
Huntsville, AL 35802
(256)883-8711
Fax: (256)883-8558

Cordova Ventures
4121 Carmichael Rd., Ste. 301
Montgomery, AL 36106
(334)271-6011
Fax: (334)260-0120
Website: http://www.cordova
ventures.com

Small Business Clinic of Alabama/AG Bartholomew & Associates
PO Box 231074
Montgomery, AL 36123-1074
(334)284-3640

Arizona

Miller Capital Corp.
4909 E. McDowell Rd.
Phoenix, AZ 85008
(602)225-0504
Fax: (602)225-9024
Website: http://www.themiller
group.com

The Columbine Venture Funds
9449 North 90th St., Ste. 200
Scottsdale, AZ 85258
(602)661-9222
Fax: (602)661-6262

Koch Ventures
17767 N. Perimeter Dr., Ste. 101
Scottsdale, AZ 85255
(480)419-3600

Fax: (480)419-3606
Website: http://www.kochventures.com

McKee & Co.
7702 E. Doubletree Ranch Rd.
Suite 230
Scottsdale, AZ 85258
(480)368-0333
Fax: (480)607-7446

Merita Capital Ltd.
7350 E. Stetson Dr., Ste. 108-A
Scottsdale, AZ 85251
(480)947-8700
Fax: (480)947-8766

Valley Ventures / Arizona Growth Partners L.P.
6720 N. Scottsdale Rd., Ste. 208
Scottsdale, AZ 85253
(480)661-6600
Fax: (480)661-6262

Estreetcapital.com
660 South Mill Ave., Ste. 315
Tempe, AZ 85281
(480)968-8400
Fax: (480)968-8480
Website: http://www.estreetcapital.com

Coronado Venture Fund
PO Box 65420
Tucson, AZ 85728-5420
(520)577-3764
Fax: (520)299-8491

Arkansas

Arkansas Capital Corp.
225 South Pulaski St.
Little Rock, AR 72201
(501)374-9247
Fax: (501)374-9425
Website: http://www.arcapital.com

California

Sundance Venture Partners, L.P.
100 Clocktower Place, Ste. 130
Carmel, CA 93923
(831)625-6500
Fax: (831)625-6590

Westar Capital (Costa Mesa)
949 South Coast Dr., Ste. 650
Costa Mesa, CA 92626
(714)481-5160
Fax: (714)481-5166
E-mail: mailbox@westarcapital.com
Website: http://www.westarcapital.com

Alpine Technology Ventures
20300 Stevens Creek Boulevard, Ste. 495
Cupertino, CA 95014
(408)725-1810
Fax: (408)725-1207
Website: http://www.alpineventures.com

Bay Partners
10600 N. De Anza Blvd.
Cupertino, CA 95014-2031
(408)725-2444
Fax: (408)446-4502
Website: http://www.baypartners.com

Novus Ventures
20111 Stevens Creek Blvd., Ste. 130
Cupertino, CA 95014
(408)252-3900
Fax: (408)252-1713
Website: http://www.novusventures.com

Triune Capital
19925 Stevens Creek Blvd., Ste. 200
Cupertino, CA 95014
(310)284-6800
Fax: (310)284-3290

Acorn Ventures
268 Bush St., Ste. 2829
Daly City, CA 94014
(650)994-7801
Fax: (650)994-3305
Website: http://www.acornventures.com

Digital Media Campus
2221 Park Place
El Segundo, CA 90245
(310)426-8000
Fax: (310)426-8010
E-mail: info@thecampus.com
Website: http://www.digital
mediacampus.com

BankAmerica Ventures / BA Venture Partners
950 Tower Ln., Ste. 700
Foster City, CA 94404
(650)378-6000
Fax: (650)378-6040
Website: http://
www.baventurepartners.com

Starting Point Partners
666 Portofino Lane
Foster City, CA 94404
(650)722-1035
Website: http://www.startingpoint
partners.com

Opportunity Capital Partners
2201 Walnut Ave., Ste. 210

Fremont, CA 94538
(510)795-7000
Fax: (510)494-5439
Website: http://www.ocpcapital.com

Imperial Ventures Inc.
9920 S. La Cienega Boulevar, 14th Fl.
Inglewood, CA 90301
(310)417-5409
Fax: (310)338-6115

Ventana Global (Irvine)
18881 Von Karman Ave., Ste. 1150
Irvine, CA 92612
(949)476-2204
Fax: (949)752-0223
Website: http://www.ventanaglobal.com

Integrated Consortium Inc.
50 Ridgecrest Rd.
Kentfield, CA 94904
(415)925-0386
Fax: (415)461-2726

Enterprise Partners
979 Ivanhoe Ave., Ste. 550
La Jolla, CA 92037
(858)454-8833
Fax: (858)454-2489
Website: http://www.epvc.com

Domain Associates
28202 Cabot Rd., Ste. 200
Laguna Niguel, CA 92677
(949)347-2446
Fax: (949)347-9720
Website: http://www.domainvc.com

Cascade Communications Ventures
60 E. Sir Francis Drake Blvd., Ste. 300
Larkspur, CA 94939
(415)925-6500
Fax: (415)925-6501

Allegis Capital
One First St., Ste. Two
Los Altos, CA 94022
(650)917-5900
Fax: (650)917-5901
Website: http://www.allegiscapital.com

Aspen Ventures
1000 Fremont Ave., Ste. 200
Los Altos, CA 94024
(650)917-5670
Fax: (650)917-5677
Website: http://www.aspenventures.com

AVI Capital L.P.
1 First St., Ste. 2
Los Altos, CA 94022

Organizations, Agencies, & Consultants

(650)949-9862
Fax: (650)949-8510
Website: http://www.avicapital.com

Bastion Capital Corp.
1999 Avenue of the Stars, Ste. 2960
Los Angeles, CA 90067
(310)788-5700
Fax: (310)277-7582
E-mail: ga@bastioncapital.com
Website: http://www.bastioncapital.com

Davis Group
PO Box 69953
Los Angeles, CA 90069-0953
(310)659-6327
Fax: (310)659-6337

Developers Equity Corp.
1880 Century Park East, Ste. 211
Los Angeles, CA 90067
(213)277-0300

Far East Capital Corp.
350 S. Grand Ave., Ste. 4100
Los Angeles, CA 90071
(213)687-1361
Fax: (213)617-7939
E-mail: free@fareastnationalbank.com

Kline Hawkes & Co.
11726 San Vicente Blvd., Ste. 300
Los Angeles, CA 90049
(310)442-4700
Fax: (310)442-4707
Website: http://www.klinehawkes.com

Lawrence Financial Group
701 Teakwood
PO Box 491773
Los Angeles, CA 90049
(310)471-4060
Fax: (310)472-3155

Riordan Lewis & Haden
300 S. Grand Ave., 29th Fl.
Los Angeles, CA 90071
(213)229-8500
Fax: (213)229-8597

Union Venture Corp.
445 S. Figueroa St., 9th Fl.
Los Angeles, CA 90071
(213)236-4092
Fax: (213)236-6329

Wedbush Capital Partners
1000 Wilshire Blvd.
Los Angeles, CA 90017
(213)688-4545
Fax: (213)688-6642
Website: http://www.wedbush.com

Advent International Corp.
2180 Sand Hill Rd., Ste. 420
Menlo Park, CA 94025
(650)233-7500
Fax: (650)233-7515
Website: http://www.adventinter
national.com

Altos Ventures
2882 Sand Hill Rd., Ste. 100
Menlo Park, CA 94025
(650)234-9771
Fax: (650)233-9821
Website: http://www.altosvc.com

Applied Technology
1010 El Camino Real, Ste. 300
Menlo Park, CA 94025
(415)326-8622
Fax: (415)326-8163

APV Technology Partners
535 Middlefield, Ste. 150
Menlo Park, CA 94025
(650)327-7871
Fax: (650)327-7631
Website: http://www.apvtp.com

August Capital Management
2480 Sand Hill Rd., Ste. 101
Menlo Park, CA 94025
(650)234-9900
Fax: (650)234-9910
Website: http://www.augustcap.com

Baccharis Capital Inc.
2420 Sand Hill Rd., Ste. 100
Menlo Park, CA 94025
(650)324-6844
Fax: (650)854-3025

Benchmark Capital
2480 Sand Hill Rd., Ste. 200
Menlo Park, CA 94025
(650)854-8180
Fax: (650)854-8183
E-mail: info@benchmark.com
Website: http://www.benchmark.com

Bessemer Venture Partners (Menlo Park)
535 Middlefield Rd., Ste. 245
Menlo Park, CA 94025
(650)853-7000
Fax: (650)853-7001
Website: http://www.bvp.com

The Cambria Group
1600 El Camino Real Rd., Ste. 155
Menlo Park, CA 94025
(650)329-8600

Fax: (650)329-8601
Website: http://www.cambriagroup.com

Canaan Partners
2884 Sand Hill Rd., Ste. 115
Menlo Park, CA 94025
(650)854-8092
Fax: (650)854-8127
Website: http://www.canaan.com

Capstone Ventures
3000 Sand Hill Rd., Bldg. One, Ste. 290
Menlo Park, CA 94025
(650)854-2523
Fax: (650)854-9010
Website: http://www.capstonevc.com

Comdisco Venture Group (Silicon Valley)
3000 Sand Hill Rd., Bldg. 1, Ste. 155
Menlo Park, CA 94025
(650)854-9484
Fax: (650)854-4026

Commtech International
535 Middlefield Rd., Ste. 200
Menlo Park, CA 94025
(650)328-0190
Fax: (650)328-6442

Compass Technology Partners
1550 El Camino Real, Ste. 275
Menlo Park, CA 94025-4111
(650)322-7595
Fax: (650)322-0588
Website: http://www.compass
techpartners.com

Convergence Partners
3000 Sand Hill Rd., Ste. 235
Menlo Park, CA 94025
(650)854-3010
Fax: (650)854-3015
Website: http://www.conver
gencepartners.com

The Dakota Group
PO Box 1025
Menlo Park, CA 94025
(650)853-0600
Fax: (650)851-4899
E-mail: info@dakota.com

Delphi Ventures
3000 Sand Hill Rd.
Bldg. One, Ste. 135
Menlo Park, CA 94025
(650)854-9650
Fax: (650)854-2961
Website: http://www.delphiventures.com

El Dorado Ventures
2884 Sand Hill Rd., Ste. 121
Menlo Park, CA 94025
(650)854-1200
Fax: (650)854-1202
Website: http://www.eldorado
ventures.com

Glynn Ventures
3000 Sand Hill Rd., Bldg. 4, Ste. 235
Menlo Park, CA 94025
(650)854-2215

Indosuez Ventures
2180 Sand Hill Rd., Ste. 450
Menlo Park, CA 94025
(650)854-0587
Fax: (650)323-5561
Website: http://www.indosuez
ventures.com

Institutional Venture Partners
3000 Sand Hill Rd., Bldg. 2, Ste. 290
Menlo Park, CA 94025
(650)854-0132
Fax: (650)854-5762
Website: http://www.ivp.com

Interwest Partners (Menlo Park)
3000 Sand Hill Rd., Bldg. 3, Ste. 255
Menlo Park, CA 94025-7112
(650)854-8585
Fax: (650)854-4706
Website: http://www.interwest.com

Kleiner Perkins Caufield & Byers (Menlo Park)
2750 Sand Hill Rd.
Menlo Park, CA 94025
(650)233-2750
Fax: (650)233-0300
Website: http://www.kpcb.com

Magic Venture Capital LLC
1010 El Camino Real, Ste. 300
Menlo Park, CA 94025
(650)325-4149

Matrix Partners
2500 Sand Hill Rd., Ste. 113
Menlo Park, CA 94025
(650)854-3131
Fax: (650)854-3296
Website: http://www.matrixpartners.com

Mayfield Fund
2800 Sand Hill Rd.
Menlo Park, CA 94025
(650)854-5560
Fax: (650)854-5712
Website: http://www.mayfield.com

McCown De Leeuw and Co. (Menlo Park)
3000 Sand Hill Rd., Bldg. 3, Ste. 290
Menlo Park, CA 94025-7111
(650)854-6000
Fax: (650)854-0853
Website: http://www.mdcpartners.com

Menlo Ventures
3000 Sand Hill Rd., Bldg. 4, Ste. 100
Menlo Park, CA 94025
(650)854-8540
Fax: (650)854-7059
Website: http://www.menloventures.com

Merrill Pickard Anderson & Eyre
2480 Sand Hill Rd., Ste. 200
Menlo Park, CA 94025
(650)854-8600
Fax: (650)854-0345

New Enterprise Associates (Menlo Park)
2490 Sand Hill Rd.
Menlo Park, CA 94025
(650)854-9499
Fax: (650)854-9397
Website: http://www.nea.com

Onset Ventures
2400 Sand Hill Rd., Ste. 150
Menlo Park, CA 94025
(650)529-0700
Fax: (650)529-0777
Website: http://www.onset.com

Paragon Venture Partners
3000 Sand Hill Rd., Bldg. 1, Ste. 275
Menlo Park, CA 94025
(650)854-8000
Fax: (650)854-7260

Pathfinder Venture Capital Funds (Menlo Park)
3000 Sand Hill Rd., Bldg. 3, Ste. 255
Menlo Park, CA 94025
(650)854-0650
Fax: (650)854-4706

Rocket Ventures
3000 Sandhill Rd., Bldg. 1, Ste. 170
Menlo Park, CA 94025
(650)561-9100
Fax: (650)561-9183
Website: http://www.rocketventures.com

Sequoia Capital
3000 Sand Hill Rd., Bldg. 4, Ste. 280
Menlo Park, CA 94025
(650)854-3927
Fax: (650)854-2977

E-mail: sequoia@sequoiacap.com
Website: http://www.sequoiacap.com

Sierra Ventures
3000 Sand Hill Rd., Bldg. 4, Ste. 210
Menlo Park, CA 94025
(650)854-1000
Fax: (650)854-5593
Website: http://www.sierraventures.com

Sigma Partners
2884 Sand Hill Rd., Ste. 121
Menlo Park, CA 94025-7022
(650)853-1700
Fax: (650)853-1717
E-mail: info@sigmapartners.com
Website: http://www.sigmapartners.com

Sprout Group (Menlo Park)
3000 Sand Hill Rd.
Bldg. 3, Ste. 170
Menlo Park, CA 94025
(650)234-2700
Fax: (650)234-2779
Website: http://www.sproutgroup.com

TA Associates (Menlo Park)
70 Willow Rd., Ste. 100
Menlo Park, CA 94025
(650)328-1210
Fax: (650)326-4933
Website: http://www.ta.com

Thompson Clive & Partners Ltd.
3000 Sand Hill Rd., Bldg. 1, Ste. 185
Menlo Park, CA 94025-7102
(650)854-0314
Fax: (650)854-0670
E-mail: mail@tcvc.com
Website: http://www.tcvc.com

Trinity Ventures Ltd.
3000 Sand Hill Rd., Bldg. 1, Ste. 240
Menlo Park, CA 94025
(650)854-9500
Fax: (650)854-9501
Website: http://www.trinityventures.com

U.S. Venture Partners
2180 Sand Hill Rd., Ste. 300
Menlo Park, CA 94025
(650)854-9080
Fax: (650)854-3018
Website: http://www.usvp.com

USVP-Schlein Marketing Fund
2180 Sand Hill Rd., Ste. 300
Menlo Park, CA 94025
(415)854-9080
Fax: (415)854-3018
Website: http://www.usvp.com

Venrock Associates
2494 Sand Hill Rd., Ste. 200
Menlo Park, CA 94025
(650)561-9580
Fax: (650)561-9180
Website: http://www.venrock.com

Brad Peery Capital Inc.
145 Chapel Pkwy.
Mill Valley, CA 94941
(415)389-0625
Fax: (415)389-1336

Dot Edu Ventures
650 Castro St., Ste. 270
Mountain View, CA 94041
(650)575-5638
Fax: (650)325-5247
Website: http://www.dotedu
ventures.com

Forrest, Binkley & Brown
840 Newport Ctr. Dr., Ste. 480
Newport Beach, CA 92660
(949)729-3222
Fax: (949)729-3226
Website: http://www.fbbvc.com

Marwit Capital LLC
180 Newport Center Dr., Ste. 200
Newport Beach, CA 92660
(949)640-6234
Fax: (949)720-8077
Website: http://www.marwit.com

Kaiser Permanente / National Venture Development
1800 Harrison St., 22nd Fl.
Oakland, CA 94612
(510)267-4010
Fax: (510)267-4036
Website: http://www.kpventures.com

Nu Capital Access Group, Ltd.
7677 Oakport St., Ste. 105
Oakland, CA 94621
(510)635-7345
Fax: (510)635-7068

Inman and Bowman
4 Orinda Way, Bldg. D, Ste. 150
Orinda, CA 94563
(510)253-1611
Fax: (510)253-9037

Accel Partners (San Francisco)
428 University Ave.
Palo Alto, CA 94301
(650)614-4800
Fax: (650)614-4880
Website: http://www.accel.com

Advanced Technology Ventures
485 Ramona St., Ste. 200
Palo Alto, CA 94301
(650)321-8601
Fax: (650)321-0934
Website: http://www.atvcapital.com

Anila Fund
400 Channing Ave.
Palo Alto, CA 94301
(650)833-5790
Fax: (650)833-0590
Website: http://www.anila.com

Asset Management Company Venture Capital
2275 E. Bayshore, Ste. 150
Palo Alto, CA 94303
(650)494-7400
Fax: (650)856-1826
E-mail: postmaster@assetman.com
Website: http://www.assetman.com

BancBoston Capital / BancBoston Ventures
435 Tasso St., Ste. 250
Palo Alto, CA 94305
(650)470-4100
Fax: (650)853-1425
Website: http://www.bancboston
capital.com

Charter Ventures
525 University Ave., Ste. 1400
Palo Alto, CA 94301
(650)325-6953
Fax: (650)325-4762
Website: http://www.charterventures.com

Communications Ventures
505 Hamilton Avenue, Ste. 305
Palo Alto, CA 94301
(650)325-9600
Fax: (650)325-9608
Website: http://www.comven.com

HMS Group
2468 Embarcadero Way
Palo Alto, CA 94303-3313
(650)856-9862
Fax: (650)856-9864

Jafco America Ventures, Inc.
505 Hamilton Ste. 310
Palto Alto, CA 94301
(650)463-8800
Fax: (650)463-8801
Website: http://www.jafco.com

New Vista Capital
540 Cowper St., Ste. 200

Palo Alto, CA 94301
(650)329-9333
Fax: (650)328-9434
E-mail: fgreene@nvcap.com
Website: http://www.nvcap.com

Norwest Equity Partners (Palo Alto)
245 Lytton Ave., Ste. 250
Palo Alto, CA 94301-1426
(650)321-8000
Fax: (650)321-8010
Website: http://www.norwestvp.com

Oak Investment Partners
525 University Ave., Ste. 1300
Palo Alto, CA 94301
(650)614-3700
Fax: (650)328-6345
Website: http://www.oakinv.com

Patricof & Co. Ventures, Inc. (Palo Alto)
2100 Geng Rd., Ste. 150
Palo Alto, CA 94303
(650)494-9944
Fax: (650)494-6751
Website: http://www.patricof.com

RWI Group
835 Page Mill Rd.
Palo Alto, CA 94304
(650)251-1800
Fax: (650)213-8660
Website: http://www.rwigroup.com

Summit Partners (Palo Alto)
499 Hamilton Ave., Ste. 200
Palo Alto, CA 94301
(650)321-1166
Fax: (650)321-1188
Website: http://www.summit
partners.com

Sutter Hill Ventures
755 Page Mill Rd., Ste. A-200
Palo Alto, CA 94304
(650)493-5600
Fax: (650)858-1854
E-mail: shv@shv.com

Vanguard Venture Partners
525 University Ave., Ste. 600
Palo Alto, CA 94301
(650)321-2900
Fax: (650)321-2902
Website: http://www.vanguard
ventures.com

Venture Growth Associates
2479 East Bayshore St., Ste. 710
Palo Alto, CA 94303

(650)855-9100
Fax: (650)855-9104

Worldview Technology Partners
435 Tasso St., Ste. 120
Palo Alto, CA 94301
(650)322-3800
Fax: (650)322-3880
Website: http://www.worldview.com

Draper, Fisher, Jurvetson / Draper Associates
400 Seaport Ct., Ste.250
Redwood City, CA 94063
(415)599-9000
Fax: (415)599-9726
Website: http://www.dfj.com

Gabriel Venture Partners
350 Marine Pkwy., Ste. 200
Redwood Shores, CA 94065
(650)551-5000
Fax: (650)551-5001
Website: http://www.gabrielvp.com

Hallador Venture Partners, L.L.C.
740 University Ave., Ste. 110
Sacramento, CA 95825-6710
(916)920-0191
Fax: (916)920-5188
E-mail: chris@hallador.com

Emerald Venture Group
12396 World Trade Dr., Ste. 116
San Diego, CA 92128
(858)451-1001
Fax: (858)451-1003
Website: http://www.emerald
venture.com

Forward Ventures
9255 Towne Centre Dr.
San Diego, CA 92121
(858)677-6077
Fax: (858)452-8799
E-mail: info@forwardventure.com
Website: http://www.forward
venture.com

Idanta Partners Ltd.
4660 La Jolla Village Dr., Ste. 850
San Diego, CA 92122
(619)452-9690
Fax: (619)452-2013
Website: http://www.idanta.com

Kingsbury Associates
3655 Nobel Dr., Ste. 490
San Diego, CA 92122
(858)677-0600
Fax: (858)677-0800

Kyocera International Inc.
Corporate Development
8611 Balboa Ave.
San Diego, CA 92123
(858)576-2600
Fax: (858)492-1456

Sorrento Associates, Inc.
4370 LaJolla Village Dr., Ste. 1040
San Diego, CA 92122
(619)452-3100
Fax: (619)452-7607
Website: http://www.sorrento
ventures.com

Western States Investment Group
9191 Towne Ctr. Dr., Ste. 310
San Diego, CA 92122
(619)678-0800
Fax: (619)678-0900

Aberdare Ventures
One Embarcadero Center, Ste. 4000
San Francisco, CA 94111
(415)392-7442
Fax: (415)392-4264
Website: http://www.aberdare.com

Acacia Venture Partners
101 California St., Ste. 3160
San Francisco, CA 94111
(415)433-4200
Fax: (415)433-4250
Website: http://www.acaciavp.com

Access Venture Partners
319 Laidley St.
San Francisco, CA 94131
(415)586-0132
Fax: (415)392-6310
Website: http://www.access
venturepartners.com

Alta Partners
One Embarcadero Center, Ste. 4050
San Francisco, CA 94111
(415)362-4022
Fax: (415)362-6178
E-mail: alta@altapartners.com
Website: http://www.altapartners.com

Bangert Dawes Reade Davis & Thom
220 Montgomery St., Ste. 424
San Francisco, CA 94104
(415)954-9900
Fax: (415)954-9901
E-mail: bdrdt@pacbell.net

Berkeley International Capital Corp.
650 California St., Ste. 2800
San Francisco, CA 94108-2609

(415)249-0450
Fax: (415)392-3929
Website: http://www.berkeleyvc.com

Blueprint Ventures LLC
456 Montgomery St., 22nd Fl.
San Francisco, CA 94104
(415)901-4000
Fax: (415)901-4035
Website: http://www.blue
printventures.com

Blumberg Capital Ventures
580 Howard St., Ste. 401
San Francisco, CA 94105
(415)905-5007
Fax: (415)357-5027
Website: http://www.blumberg-
capital.com

Burr, Egan, Deleage, and Co. (San Francisco)
1 Embarcadero Center, Ste. 4050
San Francisco, CA 94111
(415)362-4022
Fax: (415)362-6178

Burrill & Company
120 Montgomery St., Ste. 1370
San Francisco, CA 94104
(415)743-3160
Fax: (415)743-3161
Website: http://www.burrillandco.com

CMEA Ventures
235 Montgomery St., Ste. 920
San Francisco, CA 94401
(415)352-1520
Fax: (415)352-1524
Website: http://www.cmeaventures.com

Crocker Capital
1 Post St., Ste. 2500
San Francisco, CA 94101
(415)956-5250
Fax: (415)959-5710

Dominion Ventures, Inc.
44 Montgomery St., Ste. 4200
San Francisco, CA 94104
(415)362-4890
Fax: (415)394-9245

Dorset Capital
Pier 1
Bay 2
San Francisco, CA 94111
(415)398-7101
Fax: (415)398-7141
Website: http://www.dorsetcapital.com

Gatx Capital
Four Embarcadero Center, Ste. 2200
San Francisco, CA 94904
(415)955-3200
Fax: (415)955-3449

IMinds
135 Main St., Ste. 1350
San Francisco, CA 94105
(415)547-0000
Fax: (415)227-0300
Website: http://www.iminds.com

LF International Inc.
360 Post St., Ste. 705
San Francisco, CA 94108
(415)399-0110
Fax: (415)399-9222
Website: http://www.lfvc.com

Newbury Ventures
535 Pacific Ave., 2nd Fl.
San Francisco, CA 94133
(415)296-7408
Fax: (415)296-7416
Website: http://www.newburyven.com

Quest Ventures (San Francisco)
333 Bush St., Ste. 1750
San Francisco, CA 94104
(415)782-1414
Fax: (415)782-1415

Robertson-Stephens Co.
555 California St., Ste. 2600
San Francisco, CA 94104
(415)781-9700
Fax: (415)781-2556
Website: http://www.omegaad
ventures.com

Rosewood Capital, L.P.
One Maritime Plaza, Ste. 1330
San Francisco, CA 94111-3503
(415)362-5526
Fax: (415)362-1192
Website: http://www.rosewoodvc.com

Ticonderoga Capital Inc.
555 California St., No. 4950
San Francisco, CA 94104
(415)296-7900
Fax: (415)296-8956

21st Century Internet Venture Partners
Two South Park
2nd Floor
San Francisco, CA 94107
(415)512-1221
Fax: (415)512-2650
Website: http://www.21vc.com

VK Ventures
600 California St., Ste.1700
San Francisco, CA 94111
(415)391-5600
Fax: (415)397-2744

Walden Group of Venture Capital Funds
750 Battery St., Seventh Floor
San Francisco, CA 94111
(415)391-7225
Fax: (415)391-7262

Acer Technology Ventures
2641 Orchard Pkwy.
San Jose, CA 95134
(408)433-4945
Fax: (408)433-5230

Authosis
226 Airport Pkwy., Ste. 405
San Jose, CA 95110
(650)814-3603
Website: http://www.authosis.com

Western Technology Investment
2010 N. First St., Ste. 310
San Jose, CA 95131
(408)436-8577
Fax: (408)436-8625
E-mail: mktg@westerntech.com

Drysdale Enterprises
177 Bovet Rd., Ste. 600
San Mateo, CA 94402
(650)341-6336
Fax: (650)341-1329
E-mail: drysdale@aol.com

Greylock
2929 Campus Dr., Ste. 400
San Mateo, CA 94401
(650)493-5525
Fax: (650)493-5575
Website: http://www.greylock.com

Technology Funding
2000 Alameda de las Pulgas, Ste. 250
San Mateo, CA 94403
(415)345-2200
Fax: (415)345-1797

2M Invest Inc.
1875 S. Grant St.
Suite 750
San Mateo, CA 94402
(650)655-3765
Fax: (650)372-9107
E-mail: 2minfo@2minvest.com
Website: http://www.2minvest.com

Phoenix Growth Capital Corp.
2401 Kerner Blvd.
San Rafael, CA 94901
(415)485-4569
Fax: (415)485-4663

NextGen Partners LLC
1705 East Valley Rd.
Santa Barbara, CA 93108
(805)969-8540
Fax: (805)969-8542
Website: http://www.nextgen
partners.com

Denali Venture Capital
1925 Woodland Ave.
Santa Clara, CA 95050
(408)690-4838
Fax: (408)247-6979
E-mail: wael@denaliventurecapital.com
Website: http://www.denali
venturecapital.com

Dotcom Ventures LP
3945 Freedom Circle, Ste. 740
Santa Clara, CA 95045
(408)919-9855
Fax: (408)919-9857
Website: http://www.dotcom
venturesatl.com

Silicon Valley Bank
3003 Tasman
Santa Clara, CA 95054
(408)654-7400
Fax: (408)727-8728

Al Shugart International
920 41st Ave.
Santa Cruz, CA 95062
(831)479-7852
Fax: (831)479-7852
Website: http://www.alshugart.com

Leonard Mautner Associates
1434 Sixth St.
Santa Monica, CA 90401
(213)393-9788
Fax: (310)459-9918

Palomar Ventures
100 Wilshire Blvd., Ste. 450
Santa Monica, CA 90401
(310)260-6050
Fax: (310)656-4150
Website: http://www.palomar
ventures.com

Medicus Venture Partners
12930 Saratoga Ave., Ste. D8
Saratoga, CA 95070

(408)447-8600
Fax: (408)447-8599
Website: http://www.medicusvc.com

Redleaf Venture Management
14395 Saratoga Ave., Ste. 130
Saratoga, CA 95070
(408)868-0800
Fax: (408)868-0810
E-mail: nancy@redleaf.com
Website: http://www.redleaf.com

Artemis Ventures
207 Second St., Ste. E
3rd Fl.
Sausalito, CA 94965
(415)289-2500
Fax: (415)289-1789
Website: http://www.artemisventures.com

Deucalion Venture Partners
19501 Brooklime
Sonoma, CA 95476
(707)938-4974
Fax: (707)938-8921

Windward Ventures
PO Box 7688
Thousand Oaks, CA 91359-7688
(805)497-3332
Fax: (805)497-9331

National Investment Management, Inc.
2601 Airport Dr., Ste.210
Torrance, CA 90505
(310)784-7600
Fax: (310)784-7605

Southern California Ventures
406 Amapola Ave. Ste. 125
Torrance, CA 90501
(310)787-4381
Fax: (310)787-4382

Sandton Financial Group
21550 Oxnard St., Ste. 300
Woodland Hills, CA 91367
(818)702-9283

Woodside Fund
850 Woodside Dr.
Woodside, CA 94062
(650)368-5545
Fax: (650)368-2416
Website: http://www.woodsidefund.com

Colorado

Colorado Venture Management
Ste. 300
Boulder, CO 80301

(303)440-4055
Fax: (303)440-4636

Dean & Associates
4362 Apple Way
Boulder, CO 80301
Fax: (303)473-9900

Roser Ventures LLC
1105 Spruce St.
Boulder, CO 80302
(303)443-6436
Fax: (303)443-1885
Website: http://www.roserventures.com

Sequel Venture Partners
4430 Arapahoe Ave., Ste. 220
Boulder, CO 80303
(303)546-0400
Fax: (303)546-9728
E-mail: tom@sequelvc.com
Website: http://www.sequelvc.com

New Venture Resources
445C E. Cheyenne Mtn. Blvd.
Colorado Springs, CO 80906-4570
(719)598-9272
Fax: (719)598-9272

The Centennial Funds
1428 15th St.
Denver, CO 80202-1318
(303)405-7500
Fax: (303)405-7575
Website: http://www.centennial.com

Rocky Mountain Capital Partners
1125 17th St., Ste. 2260
Denver, CO 80202
(303)291-5200
Fax: (303)291-5327

Sandlot Capital LLC
600 South Cherry St., Ste. 525
Denver, CO 80246
(303)893-3400
Fax: (303)893-3403
Website: http://www.sandlotcapital.com

Wolf Ventures
50 South Steele St., Ste. 777
Denver, CO 80209
(303)321-4800
Fax: (303)321-4848
E-mail: businessplan@wolf
ventures.com
Website: http://www.wolfventures.com

The Columbine Venture Funds
5460 S. Quebec St., Ste. 270
Englewood, CO 80111

(303)694-3222
Fax: (303)694-9007

Investment Securities of Colorado, Inc.
4605 Denice Dr.
Englewood, CO 80111
(303)796-9192

Kinship Partners
6300 S. Syracuse Way, Ste. 484
Englewood, CO 80111
(303)694-0268
Fax: (303)694-1707
E-mail: block@vailsys.com

Boranco Management, L.L.C.
1528 Hillside Dr.
Fort Collins, CO 80524-1969
(970)221-2297
Fax: (970)221-4787

Aweida Ventures
890 West Cherry St., Ste. 220
Louisville, CO 80027
(303)664-9520
Fax: (303)664-9530
Website: http://www.aweida.com

Access Venture Partners
8787 Turnpike Dr., Ste. 260
Westminster, CO 80030
(303)426-8899
Fax: (303)426-8828

Medmax Ventures LP
1 Northwestern Dr., Ste. 203
Bloomfield, CT 06002
(860)286-2960
Fax: (860)286-9960

James B. Kobak & Co.
Four Mansfield Place
Darien, CT 06820
(203)656-3471
Fax: (203)655-2905

Orien Ventures
1 Post Rd.
Fairfield, CT 06430
(203)259-9933
Fax: (203)259-5288

ABP Acquisition Corporation
115 Maple Ave.
Greenwich, CT 06830
(203)625-8287
Fax: (203)447-6187

Catterton Partners
9 Greenwich Office Park
Greenwich, CT 06830
(203)629-4901

Fax: (203)629-4903
Website: http://www.cpequity.com

Consumer Venture Partners
3 Pickwick Plz.
Greenwich, CT 06830
(203)629-8800
Fax: (203)629-2019

Insurance Venture Partners
31 Brookside Dr., Ste. 211
Greenwich, CT 06830
(203)861-0030
Fax: (203)861-2745

The NTC Group
Three Pickwick Plaza
Ste. 200
Greenwich, CT 06830
(203)862-2800
Fax: (203)622-6538

Regulus International Capital Co., Inc.
140 Greenwich Ave.
Greenwich, CT 06830
(203)625-9700
Fax: (203)625-9706

Axiom Venture Partners
City Place II
185 Asylum St., 17th Fl.
Hartford, CT 06103
(860)548-7799
Fax: (860)548-7797
Website: http://www.axiomventures.com

Conning Capital Partners
City Place II
185 Asylum St.
Hartford, CT 06103-4105
(860)520-1289
Fax: (860)520-1299
E-mail: pe@conning.com
Website: http://www.conning.com

First New England Capital L.P.
100 Pearl St.
Hartford, CT 06103
(860)293-3333
Fax: (860)293-3338
E-mail: info@firstnewenglandcapital.com
Website: http://www.firstnewengland
capital.com

Northeast Ventures
One State St., Ste. 1720
Hartford, CT 06103
(860)547-1414
Fax: (860)246-8755

Windward Holdings
38 Sylvan Rd.
Madison, CT 06443
(203)245-6870
Fax: (203)245-6865

Advanced Materials Partners, Inc.
45 Pine St.
PO Box 1022
New Canaan, CT 06840
(203)966-6415
Fax: (203)966-8448
E-mail: wkb@amplink.com

RFE Investment Partners
36 Grove St.
New Canaan, CT 06840
(203)966-2800
Fax: (203)966-3109
Website: http://www.rfeip.com

Connecticut Innovations, Inc.
999 West St.
Rocky Hill, CT 06067
(860)563-5851
Fax: (860)563-4877
E-mail: pamela.hartley@ctin
novations.com
Website: http://www.ctinnovations.com

Canaan Partners
105 Rowayton Ave.
Rowayton, CT 06853
(203)855-0400
Fax: (203)854-9117
Website: http://www.canaan.com

Landmark Partners, Inc.
10 Mill Pond Ln.
Simsbury, CT 06070
(860)651-9760
Fax: (860)651-8890
Website: http://
www.landmarkpartners.com

Sweeney & Company
PO Box 567
Southport, CT 06490
(203)255-0220
Fax: (203)255-0220
E-mail: sweeney@connix.com

Baxter Associates, Inc.
PO Box 1333
Stamford, CT 06904
(203)323-3143
Fax: (203)348-0622

Beacon Partners Inc.
6 Landmark Sq., 4th Fl.
Stamford, CT 06901-2792

(203)359-5776
Fax: (203)359-5876

Collinson, Howe, and Lennox, LLC
1055 Washington Blvd., 5th Fl.
Stamford, CT 06901
(203)324-7700
Fax: (203)324-3636
E-mail: info@chlmedical.com
Website: http://www.chlmedical.com

Prime Capital Management Co.
550 West Ave.
Stamford, CT 06902
(203)964-0642
Fax: (203)964-0862

Saugatuck Capital Co.
1 Canterbury Green
Stamford, CT 06901
(203)348-6669
Fax: (203)324-6995
Website: http://www.sauga
tuckcapital.com

Soundview Financial Group Inc.
22 Gatehouse Rd.
Stamford, CT 06902
(203)462-7200
Fax: (203)462-7350
Website: http://www.sndv.com

TSG Ventures, L.L.C.
177 Broad St., 12th Fl.
Stamford, CT 06901
(203)406-1500
Fax: (203)406-1590

Whitney & Company
177 Broad St.
Stamford, CT 06901
(203)973-1400
Fax: (203)973-1422
Website: http://www.jhwhitney.com

Cullinane & Donnelly Venture Partners L.P.
970 Farmington Ave.
West Hartford, CT 06107
(860)521-7811

The Crestview Investment and Financial Group
431 Post Rd. E, Ste. 1
Westport, CT 06880-4403
(203)222-0333
Fax: (203)222-0000

Marketcorp Venture Associates, L.P. (MCV)
274 Riverside Ave.
Westport, CT 06880

(203)222-3030
Fax: (203)222-3033

Oak Investment Partners (Westport)
1 Gorham Island
Westport, CT 06880
(203)226-8346
Fax: (203)227-0372
Website: http://www.oakinv.com

Oxford Bioscience Partners
315 Post Rd. W
Westport, CT 06880-5200
(203)341-3300
Fax: (203)341-3309
Website: http://www.oxbio.com

Prince Ventures (Westport)
25 Ford Rd.
Westport, CT 06880
(203)227-8332
Fax: (203)226-5302

LTI Venture Leasing Corp.
221 Danbury Rd.
Wilton, CT 06897
(203)563-1100
Fax: (203)563-1111
Website: http://www.ltileasing.com

Delaware

Blue Rock Capital
5803 Kennett Pike, Ste. A
Wilmington, DE 19807
(302)426-0981
Fax: (302)426-0982
Website: http://www.bluerockcapital.com

District of Columbia

Allied Capital Corp.
1919 Pennsylvania Ave. NW
Washington, DC 20006-3434
(202)331-2444
Fax: (202)659-2053
Website: http://www.alliedcapital.com

Atlantic Coastal Ventures, L.P.
3101 South St. NW
Washington, DC 20007
(202)293-1166
Fax: (202)293-1181
Website: http://www.atlanticcv.com

Columbia Capital Group, Inc.
1660 L St. NW, Ste. 308
Washington, DC 20036
(202)775-8815
Fax: (202)223-0544

Core Capital Partners
901 15th St., NW
9th Fl.
Washington, DC 20005
(202)589-0090
Fax: (202)589-0091
Website: http://www.core-capital.com

Next Point Partners
701 Pennsylvania Ave. NW, Ste. 900
Washington, DC 20004
(202)661-8703
Fax: (202)434-7400
E-mail: mf@nextpoint.vc
Website: http://www.nextpointvc.com

Telecommunications Development Fund
2020 K. St. NW
Ste. 375
Washington, DC 20006
(202)293-8840
Fax: (202)293-8850
Website: http://www.tdfund.com

Wachtel & Co., Inc.
1101 4th St. NW
Washington, DC 20005-5680
(202)898-1144

Winslow Partners LLC
1300 Connecticut Ave. NW
Washington, DC 20036-1703
(202)530-5000
Fax: (202)530-5010
E-mail: winslow@winslowpartners.com

Women's Growth Capital Fund
1054 31st St., NW
Ste. 110
Washington, DC 20007
(202)342-1431
Fax: (202)341-1203
Website: http://www.wgcf.com

Sigma Capital Corp.
22668 Caravelle Circle
Boca Raton, FL 33433
(561)368-9783

North American Business Development Co., L.L.C.
111 East Las Olas Blvd.
Ft. Lauderdale, FL 33301
(305)463-0681
Fax: (305)527-0904
Website: http://
www.northamericanfund.com

Chartwell Capital Management Co. Inc.
1 Independent Dr., Ste. 3120

Jacksonville, FL 32202
(904)355-3519
Fax: (904)353-5833
E-mail: info@chartwellcap.com

CEO Advisors
1061 Maitland Center Commons
Ste. 209
Maitland, FL 32751
(407)660-9327
Fax: (407)660-2109

Henry & Co.
8201 Peters Rd., Ste. 1000
Plantation, FL 33324
(954)797-7400

Avery Business Development Services
2506 St. Michel Ct.
Ponte Vedra, FL 32082
(904)285-6033

New South Ventures
5053 Ocean Blvd.
Sarasota, FL 34242
(941)358-6000
Fax: (941)358-6078
Website: http://www.newsouth
ventures.com

Venture Capital Management Corp.
PO Box 2626
Satellite Beach, FL 32937
(407)777-1969

Florida Capital Venture Ltd.
325 Florida Bank Plaza
100 W. Kennedy Blvd.
Tampa, FL 33602
(813)229-2294
Fax: (813)229-2028

Quantum Capital Partners
339 South Plant Ave.
Tampa, FL 33606
(813)250-1999
Fax: (813)250-1998
Website: http://www.quantum
capitalpartners.com

South Atlantic Venture Fund
614 W. Bay St.
Tampa, FL 33606-2704
(813)253-2500
Fax: (813)253-2360
E-mail: venture@southatlantic.com
Website: http://www.southatlantic.com

LM Capital Corp.
120 S. Olive, Ste. 400
West Palm Beach, FL 33401

(561)833-9700
Fax: (561)655-6587
Website: http://www.lmcapital
securities.com

Georgia

Venture First Associates
4811 Thornwood Dr.
Acworth, GA 30102
(770)928-3733
Fax: (770)928-6455

Alliance Technology Ventures
8995 Westside Pkwy., Ste. 200
Alpharetta, GA 30004
(678)336-2000
Fax: (678)336-2001
E-mail: info@atv.com
Website: http://www.atv.com

Cordova Ventures
2500 North Winds Pkwy., Ste. 475
Alpharetta, GA 30004
(678)942-0300
Fax: (678)942-0301
Website: http://www.cordovaventures.
com

Advanced Technology Development Fund
1000 Abernathy, Ste. 1420
Atlanta, GA 30328-5614
(404)668-2333
Fax: (404)668-2333

CGW Southeast Partners
12 Piedmont Center, Ste. 210
Atlanta, GA 30305
(404)816-3255
Fax: (404)816-3258
Website: http://www.cgwlp.com

Cyberstarts
1900 Emery St., NW
3rd Fl.
Atlanta, GA 30318
(404)267-5000
Fax: (404)267-5200
Website: http://www.cyberstarts.com

EGL Holdings, Inc.
10 Piedmont Center, Ste. 412
Atlanta, GA 30305
(404)949-8300
Fax: (404)949-8311

Equity South
1790 The Lenox Bldg.
3399 Peachtree Rd. NE
Atlanta, GA 30326

(404)237-6222
Fax: (404)261-1578

Five Paces
3400 Peachtree Rd., Ste. 200
Atlanta, GA 30326
(404)439-8300
Fax: (404)439-8301
Website: http://www.fivepaces.com

Frontline Capital, Inc.
3475 Lenox Rd., Ste. 400
Atlanta, GA 30326
(404)240-7280
Fax: (404)240-7281

Fuqua Ventures LLC
1201 W. Peachtree St. NW, Ste. 5000
Atlanta, GA 30309
(404)815-4500
Fax: (404)815-4528
Website: http://www.fuquaventures.com

Noro-Moseley Partners
4200 Northside Pkwy., Bldg. 9
Atlanta, GA 30327
(404)233-1966
Fax: (404)239-9280
Website: http://www.noro-moseley.com

Renaissance Capital Corp.
34 Peachtree St. NW, Ste. 2230
Atlanta, GA 30303
(404)658-9061
Fax: (404)658-9064

River Capital, Inc.
Two Midtown Plaza
1360 Peachtree St. NE, Ste. 1430
Atlanta, GA 30309
(404)873-2166
Fax: (404)873-2158

State Street Bank & Trust Co.
3414 Peachtree Rd. NE, Ste. 1010
Atlanta, GA 30326
(404)364-9500
Fax: (404)261-4469

UPS Strategic Enterprise Fund
55 Glenlake Pkwy. NE
Atlanta, GA 30328
(404)828-8814
Fax: (404)828-8088
E-mail: jcacyce@ups.com
Website: http://www.ups.com/sef/
sef_home

Wachovia
191 Peachtree St. NE, 26th Fl.
Atlanta, GA 30303

(404)332-1000
Fax: (404)332-1392
Website: http://www.wachovia.com/wca

Brainworks Ventures
4243 Dunwoody Club Dr.
Chamblee, GA 30341
(770)239-7447

First Growth Capital Inc.
Best Western Plaza, Ste. 105
PO Box 815
Forsyth, GA 31029
(912)781-7131

Financial Capital Resources, Inc.
21 Eastbrook Bend, Ste. 116
Peachtree City, GA 30269
(404)487-6650

Hawaii

HMS Hawaii Management Partners
Davies Pacific Center
841 Bishop St., Ste. 860
Honolulu, HI 96813
(808)545-3755
Fax: (808)531-2611

Idaho

Sun Valley Ventures
160 Second St.
Ketchum, ID 83340
(208)726-5005
Fax: (208)726-5094

Illinois

Open Prairie Ventures
115 N. Neil St., Ste. 209
Champaign, IL 61820
(217)351-7000
Fax: (217)351-7051
E-mail: inquire@openprairie.com
Website: http://www.openprairie.com

ABN AMRO Private Equity
208 S. La Salle St., 10th Fl.
Chicago, IL 60604
(312)855-7079
Fax: (312)553-6648
Website: http://www.abnequity.com

Alpha Capital Partners, Ltd.
122 S. Michigan Ave., Ste. 1700
Chicago, IL 60603
(312)322-9800
Fax: (312)322-9808
E-mail: acp@alphacapital.com

Ameritech Development Corp.
30 S. Wacker Dr., 37th Fl.
Chicago, IL 60606
(312)750-5083
Fax: (312)609-0244

Apex Investment Partners
225 W. Washington, Ste. 1450
Chicago, IL 60606
(312)857-2800
Fax: (312)857-1800
E-mail: apex@apexvc.com
Website: http://www.apexvc.com

Arch Venture Partners
8725 W. Higgins Rd., Ste. 290
Chicago, IL 60631
(773)380-6600
Fax: (773)380-6606
Website: http://www.archventure.com

The Bank Funds
208 South LaSalle St., Ste. 1680
Chicago, IL 60604
(312)855-6020
Fax: (312)855-8910

Batterson Venture Partners
303 W. Madison St., Ste. 1110
Chicago, IL 60606-3309
(312)269-0300
Fax: (312)269-0021
Website: http://www.battersonvp.com

William Blair Capital Partners, L.L.C.
222 W. Adams St., Ste. 1300
Chicago, IL 60606
(312)364-8250
Fax: (312)236-1042
E-mail: privateequity@wmblair.com
Website: http://www.wmblair.com

Bluestar Ventures
208 South LaSalle St., Ste. 1020
Chicago, IL 60604
(312)384-5000
Fax: (312)384-5005
Website: http://www.bluestarventures.com

The Capital Strategy Management Co.
233 S. Wacker Dr.
Box 06334
Chicago, IL 60606
(312)444-1170

DN Partners
77 West Wacker Dr., Ste. 4550
Chicago, IL 60601
(312)332-7960
Fax: (312)332-7979

Dresner Capital Inc.
29 South LaSalle St., Ste. 310
Chicago, IL 60603
(312)726-3600
Fax: (312)726-7448

Eblast Ventures LLC
11 South LaSalle St., 5th Fl.
Chicago, IL 60603
(312)372-2600
Fax: (312)372-5621
Website: http://www.eblastventures.com

Essex Woodlands Health Ventures, L.P.
190 S. LaSalle St., Ste. 2800
Chicago, IL 60603
(312)444-6040
Fax: (312)444-6034
Website: http://www.essexwood
lands.com

First Analysis Venture Capital
233 S. Wacker Dr., Ste. 9500
Chicago, IL 60606
(312)258-1400
Fax: (312)258-0334
Website: http://www.firstanalysis.com

Frontenac Co.
135 S. LaSalle St., Ste.3800
Chicago, IL 60603
(312)368-0044
Fax: (312)368-9520
Website: http://www.frontenac.com

GTCR Golder Rauner, LLC
6100 Sears Tower
Chicago, IL 60606
(312)382-2200
Fax: (312)382-2201
Website: http://www.gtcr.com

High Street Capital LLC
311 South Wacker Dr., Ste. 4550
Chicago, IL 60606
(312)697-4990
Fax: (312)697-4994
Website: http://www.highstr.com

IEG Venture Management, Inc.
70 West Madison
Chicago, IL 60602
(312)644-0890
Fax: (312)454-0369
Website: http://www.iegventure.com

JK&B Capital
180 North Stetson, Ste. 4500
Chicago, IL 60601
(312)946-1200
Fax: (312)946-1103

E-mail: gspencer@jkbcapital.com
Website: http://www.jkbcapital.com

Kettle Partners L.P.
350 W. Hubbard, Ste. 350
Chicago, IL 60610
(312)329-9300
Fax: (312)527-4519
Website: http://www.kettlevc.com

Lake Shore Capital Partners
20 N. Wacker Dr., Ste. 2807
Chicago, IL 60606
(312)803-3536
Fax: (312)803-3534

LaSalle Capital Group Inc.
70 W. Madison St., Ste. 5710
Chicago, IL 60602
(312)236-7041
Fax: (312)236-0720

Linc Capital, Inc.
303 E. Wacker Pkwy., Ste. 1000
Chicago, IL 60601
(312)946-2670
Fax: (312)938-4290
E-mail: bdemars@linccap.com

Madison Dearborn Partners, Inc.
3 First National Plz., Ste. 3800
Chicago, IL 60602
(312)895-1000
Fax: (312)895-1001
E-mail: invest@mdcp.com
Website: http://www.mdcp.com

Mesirow Private Equity Investments Inc.
350 N. Clark St.
Chicago, IL 60610
(312)595-6950
Fax: (312)595-6211
Website: http://www.meisrow
financial.com

Mosaix Ventures LLC
1822 North Mohawk
Chicago, IL 60614
(312)274-0988
Fax: (312)274-0989
Website: http://www.mosaix
ventures.com

Nesbitt Burns
111 West Monroe St.
Chicago, IL 60603
(312)416-3855
Fax: (312)765-8000
Website: http://www.harrisbank.com

Polestar Capital, Inc.
180 N. Michigan Ave., Ste. 1905
Chicago, IL 60601
(312)984-9090
Fax: (312)984-9877
E-mail: wl@polestarvc.com
Website: http://www.polestarvc.com

Prince Ventures (Chicago)
10 S. Wacker Dr., Ste. 2575
Chicago, IL 60606-7407
(312)454-1408
Fax: (312)454-9125

Prism Capital
444 N. Michigan Ave.
Chicago, IL 60611
(312)464-7900
Fax: (312)464-7915
Website: http://www.prismfund.com

Third Coast Capital
900 N. Franklin St., Ste. 700
Chicago, IL 60610
(312)337-3303
Fax: (312)337-2567
E-mail: manic@earthlink.com
Website: http://www.third
coastcapital.com

Thoma Cressey Equity Partners
4460 Sears Tower, 92nd Fl.
233 S. Wacker Dr.
Chicago, IL 60606
(312)777-4444
Fax: (312)777-4445
Website: http://www.thomacressey.com

Tribune Ventures
435 N. Michigan Ave., Ste. 600
Chicago, IL 60611
(312)527-8797
Fax: (312)222-5993
Website: http://www.tribuneventures.com

Wind Point Partners (Chicago)
676 N. Michigan Ave., Ste. 330
Chicago, IL 60611
(312)649-4000
Website: http://www.wppartners.com

Marquette Venture Partners
520 Lake Cook Rd., Ste. 450
Deerfield, IL 60015
(847)940-1700
Fax: (847)940-1724
Website: http://www.marquette
ventures.com

Duchossois Investments Limited, LLC
845 Larch Ave.
Elmhurst, IL 60126

(630)530-6105
Fax: (630)993-8644
Website: http://www.duchtec.com

Evanston Business Investment Corp.
1840 Oak Ave.
Evanston, IL 60201
(847)866-1840
Fax: (847)866-1808
E-mail: t-parkinson@nwu.com
Website: http://www.ebic.com

Inroads Capital Partners L.P.
1603 Orrington Ave., Ste. 2050
Evanston, IL 60201-3841
(847)864-2000
Fax: (847)864-9692

The Cerulean Fund/WGC Enterprises
1701 E. Lake Ave., Ste. 170
Glenview, IL 60025
(847)657-8002
Fax: (847)657-8168

Ventana Financial Resources, Inc.
249 Market Sq.
Lake Forest, IL 60045
(847)234-3434

Beecken, Petty & Co.
901 Warrenville Rd., Ste. 205
Lisle, IL 60532
(630)435-0300
Fax: (630)435-0370
E-mail: hep@bpcompany.com
Website: http://www.bpcompany.com

Allstate Private Equity
3075 Sanders Rd., Ste. G5D
Northbrook, IL 60062-7127
(847)402-8247
Fax: (847)402-0880

KB Partners
1101 Skokie Blvd., Ste. 260
Northbrook, IL 60062-2856
(847)714-0444
Fax: (847)714-0445
E-mail: keith@kbpartners.com
Website: http://www.kbpartners.com

Transcap Associates Inc.
900 Skokie Blvd., Ste. 210
Northbrook, IL 60062
(847)753-9600
Fax: (847)753-9090

**Graystone Venture Partners, L.L.C. /
Portage Venture Partners**
One Northfield Plaza, Ste. 530
Northfield, IL 60093

(847)446-9460
Fax: (847)446-9470
Website: http://www.portage
ventures.com

Motorola Inc.
1303 E. Algonquin Rd.
Schaumburg, IL 60196-1065
(847)576-4929
Fax: (847)538-2250
Website: http://www.mot.com/mne

Indiana

Irwin Ventures LLC
500 Washington St.
Columbus, IN 47202
(812)373-1434
Fax: (812)376-1709
Website: http://www.irwinventures.com

Cambridge Venture Partners
4181 East 96th St., Ste. 200
Indianapolis, IN 46240
(317)814-6192
Fax: (317)944-9815

CID Equity Partners
One American Square, Ste. 2850
Box 82074
Indianapolis, IN 46282
(317)269-2350
Fax: (317)269-2355
Website: http://www.cidequity.com

Gazelle Techventures
6325 Digital Way, Ste. 460
Indianapolis, IN 46278
(317)275-6800
Fax: (317)275-1101
Website: http://www.gazellevc.com

Monument Advisors Inc.
Bank One Center/Circle
111 Monument Circle, Ste. 600
Indianapolis, IN 46204-5172
(317)656-5065
Fax: (317)656-5060
Website: http://www.monumentadv.com

MWV Capital Partners
201 N. Illinois St., Ste. 300
Indianapolis, IN 46204
(317)237-2323
Fax: (317)237-2325
Website: http://www.mwvcapital.com

First Source Capital Corp.
100 North Michigan St.
PO Box 1602
South Bend, IN 46601

(219)235-2180
Fax: (219)235-2227

Iowa

Allsop Venture Partners
118 Third Ave. SE, Ste. 837
Cedar Rapids, IA 52401
(319)368-6675
Fax: (319)363-9515

InvestAmerica Investment Advisors, Inc.
101 2nd St. SE, Ste. 800
Cedar Rapids, IA 52401
(319)363-8249
Fax: (319)363-9683

Pappajohn Capital Resources
2116 Financial Center
Des Moines, IA 50309
(515)244-5746
Fax: (515)244-2346
Website: http://www.pappajohn.com

Berthel Fisher & Company Planning Inc.
701 Tama St.
PO Box 609
Marion, IA 52302
(319)497-5700
Fax: (319)497-4244

Kansas

Enterprise Merchant Bank
7400 West 110th St., Ste. 560
Overland Park, KS 66210
(913)327-8500
Fax: (913)327-8505

Kansas Venture Capital, Inc. (Overland Park)
6700 Antioch Plz., Ste. 460
Overland Park, KS 66204
(913)262-7117
Fax: (913)262-3509
E-mail: jdalton@kvci.com

Child Health Investment Corp.
6803 W. 64th St., Ste. 208
Shawnee Mission, KS 66202
(913)262-1436
Fax: (913)262-1575
Website: http://www.chca.com

Kansas Technology Enterprise Corp.
214 SW 6th, 1st Fl.
Topeka, KS 66603-3719
(785)296-5272
Fax: (785)296-1160

E-mail: ktec@ktec.com
Website: http://www.ktec.com

Kentucky

Kentucky Highlands Investment Corp.
362 Old Whitley Rd.
London, KY 40741
(606)864-5175
Fax: (606)864-5194
Website: http://www.khic.org

Chrysalis Ventures, L.L.C.
1850 National City Tower
Louisville, KY 40202
(502)583-7644
Fax: (502)583-7648
E-mail: bobsany@chrysalisventures.com
Website: http://www.chrysalis
ventures.com

Humana Venture Capital
500 West Main St.
Louisville, KY 40202
(502)580-3922
Fax: (502)580-2051
E-mail: gemont@humana.com
George Emont, Director

Summit Capital Group, Inc.
6510 Glenridge Park Pl., Ste. 8
Louisville, KY 40222
(502)332-2700

Louisiana

Bank One Equity Investors, Inc.
451 Florida St.
Baton Rouge, LA 70801
(504)332-4421
Fax: (504)332-7377

Advantage Capital Partners
LLE Tower
909 Poydras St., Ste. 2230
New Orleans, LA 70112
(504)522-4850
Fax: (504)522-4950
Website: http://www.advantagecap.com

Maine

CEI Ventures / Coastal Ventures LP
2 Portland Fish Pier, Ste. 201
Portland, ME 04101
(207)772-5356
Fax: (207)772-5503
Website: http://www.ceiventures.com

Commwealth Bioventures, Inc.
4 Milk St.
Portland, ME 04101

(207)780-0904
Fax: (207)780-0913

Maryland

Annapolis Ventures LLC
151 West St., Ste. 302
Annapolis, MD 21401
(443)482-9555
Fax: (443)482-9565
Website: http://www.annapolis
ventures.com

Delmag Ventures
220 Wardour Dr.
Annapolis, MD 21401
(410)267-8196
Fax: (410)267-8017
Website: http://www.delmag
ventures.com

Abell Venture Fund
111 S. Calvert St., Ste. 2300
Baltimore, MD 21202
(410)547-1300
Fax: (410)539-6579
Website: http://www.abell.org

ABS Ventures (Baltimore)
1 South St., Ste. 2150
Baltimore, MD 21202
(410)895-3895
Fax: (410)895-3899
Website: http://www.absventures.com

Anthem Capital, L.P.
16 S. Calvert St., Ste. 800
Baltimore, MD 21202-1305
(410)625-1510
Fax: (410)625-1735
Website: http://www.anthemcapital.com

Catalyst Ventures
1119 St. Paul St.
Baltimore, MD 21202
(410)244-0123
Fax: (410)752-7721

Maryland Venture Capital Trust
217 E. Redwood St., Ste. 2200
Baltimore, MD 21202
(410)767-6361
Fax: (410)333-6931

New Enterprise Associates (Baltimore)
1119 St. Paul St.
Baltimore, MD 21202
(410)244-0115
Fax: (410)752-7721
Website: http://www.nea.com

T. Rowe Price Threshold Partnerships
100 E. Pratt St., 8th Fl.
Baltimore, MD 21202
(410)345-2000
Fax: (410)345-2800

Spring Capital Partners
16 W. Madison St.
Baltimore, MD 21201
(410)685-8000
Fax: (410)727-1436
E-mail: mailbox@springcap.com

Arete Corporation
3 Bethesda Metro Ctr., Ste. 770
Bethesda, MD 20814
(301)657-6268
Fax: (301)657-6254
Website: http://www.arete-
microgen.com

Embryon Capital
7903 Sleaford Place
Bethesda, MD 20814
(301)656-6837
Fax: (301)656-8056

Potomac Ventures
7920 Norfolk Ave., Ste. 1100
Bethesda, MD 20814
(301)215-9240
Website: http://www.potomac
ventures.com

Toucan Capital Corp.
3 Bethesda Metro Center, Ste. 700
Bethesda, MD 20814
(301)961-1970
Fax: (301)961-1969
Website: http://www.toucancapital.com

Kinetic Ventures LLC
2 Wisconsin Cir., Ste. 620
Chevy Chase, MD 20815
(301)652-8066
Fax: (301)652-8310
Website: http://www.kineticventures.com

Boulder Ventures Ltd.
4750 Owings Mills Blvd.
Owings Mills, MD 21117
(410)998-3114
Fax: (410)356-5492
Website: http://www.boulderventures.com

Grotech Capital Group
9690 Deereco Rd., Ste. 800
Timonium, MD 21093
(410)560-2000
Fax: (410)560-1910
Website: http://www.grotech.com

Massachusetts

Adams, Harkness & Hill, Inc.
60 State St.
Boston, MA 02109
(617)371-3900

Advent International
75 State St., 29th Fl.
Boston, MA 02109
(617)951-9400
Fax: (617)951-0566
Website: http://www.adventiner
national.com

American Research and Development
30 Federal St.
Boston, MA 02110-2508
(617)423-7500
Fax: (617)423-9655

Ascent Venture Partners
255 State St., 5th Fl.
Boston, MA 02109
(617)270-9400
Fax: (617)270-9401
E-mail: info@ascentvp.com
Website: http://www.ascentvp.com

Atlas Venture
222 Berkeley St.
Boston, MA 02116
(617)488-2200
Fax: (617)859-9292
Website: http://www.atlasventure.com

Axxon Capital
28 State St., 37th Fl.
Boston, MA 02109
(617)722-0980
Fax: (617)557-6014
Website: http://www.axxoncapital.com

BancBoston Capital/BancBoston Ventures
175 Federal St., 10th Fl.
Boston, MA 02110
(617)434-2509
Fax: (617)434-6175
Website: http://
www.bancbostoncapital.com

Boston Capital Ventures
Old City Hall
45 School St.
Boston, MA 02108
(617)227-6550
Fax: (617)227-3847
E-mail: info@bcv.com
Website: http://www.bcv.com

Boston Financial & Equity Corp.
20 Overland St.
PO Box 15071
Boston, MA 02215
(617)267-2900
Fax: (617)437-7601
E-mail: debbie@bfec.com

Boston Millennia Partners
30 Rowes Wharf
Boston, MA 02110
(617)428-5150
Fax: (617)428-5160
Website: http://www.millennia
partners.com

Bristol Investment Trust
842A Beacon St.
Boston, MA 02215-3199
(617)566-5212
Fax: (617)267-0932

Brook Venture Management LLC
50 Federal St., 5th Fl.
Boston, MA 02110
(617)451-8989
Fax: (617)451-2369
Website: http://www.brookventure.com

Burr, Egan, Deleage, and Co. (Boston)
200 Clarendon St., Ste. 3800
Boston, MA 02116
(617)262-7770
Fax: (617)262-9779

Cambridge/Samsung Partners
One Exeter Plaza
Ninth Fl.
Boston, MA 02116
(617)262-4440
Fax: (617)262-5562

Chestnut Street Partners, Inc.
75 State St., Ste. 2500
Boston, MA 02109
(617)345-7220
Fax: (617)345-7201
E-mail: chestnut@chestnutp.com

Claflin Capital Management, Inc.
10 Liberty Sq., Ste. 300
Boston, MA 02109
(617)426-6505
Fax: (617)482-0016
Website: http://www.claflincapital.com

Copley Venture Partners
99 Summer St., Ste. 1720
Boston, MA 02110
(617)737-1253
Fax: (617)439-0699

Corning Capital / Corning Technology Ventures
121 High Street, Ste. 400
Boston, MA 02110
(617)338-2656
Fax: (617)261-3864
Website: http://www.corningventures.com

Downer & Co.
211 Congress St.
Boston, MA 02110
(617)482-6200
Fax: (617)482-6201
E-mail: cdowner@downer.com
Website: http://www.downer.com

Fidelity Ventures
82 Devonshire St.
Boston, MA 02109
(617)563-6370
Fax: (617)476-9023
Website: http://www.fidelityventures.com

Greylock Management Corp. (Boston)
1 Federal St.
Boston, MA 02110-2065
(617)423-5525
Fax: (617)482-0059

Gryphon Ventures
222 Berkeley St., Ste.1600
Boston, MA 02116
(617)267-9191
Fax: (617)267-4293
E-mail: all@gryphoninc.com

Halpern, Denny & Co.
500 Boylston St.
Boston, MA 02116
(617)536-6602
Fax: (617)536-8535

Harbourvest Partners, LLC
1 Financial Center, 44th Fl.
Boston, MA 02111
(617)348-3707
Fax: (617)350-0305
Website: http://www.hvpllc.com

Highland Capital Partners
2 International Pl.
Boston, MA 02110
(617)981-1500
Fax: (617)531-1550
E-mail: info@hcp.com
Website: http://www.hcp.com

Lee Munder Venture Partners
John Hancock Tower T-53
200 Clarendon St.
Boston, MA 02103

(617)380-5600
Fax: (617)380-5601
Website: http://www.leemunder.com

M/C Venture Partners
75 State St., Ste. 2500
Boston, MA 02109
(617)345-7200
Fax: (617)345-7201
Website: http://www.mcventure
partners.com

Massachusetts Capital Resources Co.
420 Boylston St.
Boston, MA 02116
(617)536-3900
Fax: (617)536-7930

Massachusetts Technology Development Corp. (MTDC)
148 State St.
Boston, MA 02109
(617)723-4920
Fax: (617)723-5983
E-mail: jhodgman@mtdc.com
Website: http://www.mtdc.com

New England Partners
One Boston Place, Ste. 2100
Boston, MA 02108
(617)624-8400
Fax: (617)624-8999
Website: http://www.nepartners.com

North Hill Ventures
Ten Post Office Square
11th Fl.
Boston, MA 02109
(617)788-2112
Fax: (617)788-2152
Website: http://www.northhill
ventures.com

OneLiberty Ventures
150 Cambridge Park Dr.
Boston, MA 02140
(617)492-7280
Fax: (617)492-7290
Website: http://www.oneliberty.com

Schroder Ventures
Life Sciences
60 State St., Ste. 3650
Boston, MA 02109
(617)367-8100
Fax: (617)367-1590
Website: http://www.shroderventures.com

Shawmut Capital Partners
75 Federal St., 18th Fl.
Boston, MA 02110

(617)368-4900
Fax: (617)368-4910
Website: http://www.shawmutcapital.com

Solstice Capital LLC
15 Broad St., 3rd Fl.
Boston, MA 02109
(617)523-7733
Fax: (617)523-5827
E-mail: solticecapital@solcap.com

Spectrum Equity Investors
One International Pl., 29th Fl.
Boston, MA 02110
(617)464-4600
Fax: (617)464-4601
Website: http://www.spectrumequity.com

Spray Venture Partners
One Walnut St.
Boston, MA 02108
(617)305-4140
Fax: (617)305-4144
Website: http://www.sprayventure.com

The Still River Fund
100 Federal St., 29th Fl.
Boston, MA 02110
(617)348-2327
Fax: (617)348-2371
Website: http://www.stillriverfund.com

Summit Partners
600 Atlantic Ave., Ste. 2800
Boston, MA 02210-2227
(617)824-1000
Fax: (617)824-1159
Website: http://www.summitpartners.com

TA Associates, Inc. (Boston)
High Street Tower
125 High St., Ste. 2500
Boston, MA 02110
(617)574-6700
Fax: (617)574-6728
Website: http://www.ta.com

TVM Techno Venture Management
101 Arch St., Ste. 1950
Boston, MA 02110
(617)345-9320
Fax: (617)345-9377
E-mail: info@tvmvc.com
Website: http://www.tvmvc.com

UNC Ventures
64 Burough St.
Boston, MA 02130-4017
(617)482-7070
Fax: (617)522-2176

Venture Investment Management Company (VIMAC)
177 Milk St.
Boston, MA 02190-3410
(617)292-3300
Fax: (617)292-7979
E-mail: bzeisig@vimac.com
Website: http://www.vimac.com

MDT Advisers, Inc.
125 Cambridge Park Dr.
Cambridge, MA 02140-2314
(617)234-2200
Fax: (617)234-2210
Website: http://www.mdtai.com

TTC Ventures
One Main St., 6th Fl.
Cambridge, MA 02142
(617)528-3137
Fax: (617)577-1715
E-mail: info@ttcventures.com

Zero Stage Capital Co. Inc.
101 Main St., 17th Fl.
Cambridge, MA 02142
(617)876-5355
Fax: (617)876-1248
Website: http://www.zerostage.com

Atlantic Capital
164 Cushing Hwy.
Cohasset, MA 02025
(617)383-9449
Fax: (617)383-6040
E-mail: info@atlanticcap.com
Website: http://www.atlanticcap.com

Seacoast Capital Partners
55 Ferncroft Rd.
Danvers, MA 01923
(978)750-1300
Fax: (978)750-1301
E-mail: gdeli@seacoastcapital.com
Website: http://www.seacoast
capital.com

Sage Management Group
44 South Street
PO Box 2026
East Dennis, MA 02641
(508)385-7172
Fax: (508)385-7272
E-mail: sagemgt@capecod.net

Applied Technology
1 Cranberry Hill
Lexington, MA 02421-7397
(617)862-8622
Fax: (617)862-8367

Royalty Capital Management
5 Downing Rd.
Lexington, MA 02421-6918
(781)861-8490

Argo Global Capital
210 Broadway, Ste. 101
Lynnfield, MA 01940
(781)592-5250
Fax: (781)592-5230
Website: http://www.gsmcapital.com

Industry Ventures
6 Bayne Lane
Newburyport, MA 01950
(978)499-7606
Fax: (978)499-0686
Website: http://
www.industryventures.com

Softbank Capital Partners
10 Langley Rd., Ste. 202
Newton Center, MA 02459
(617)928-9300
Fax: (617)928-9305
E-mail: clax@bvc.com

Advanced Technology Ventures (Boston)
281 Winter St., Ste. 350
Waltham, MA 02451
(781)290-0707
Fax: (781)684-0045
E-mail: info@atvcapital.com
Website: http://www.atvcapital.com

Castile Ventures
890 Winter St., Ste. 140
Waltham, MA 02451
(781)890-0060
Fax: (781)890-0065
Website: http://www.castileventures.com

Charles River Ventures
1000 Winter St., Ste. 3300
Waltham, MA 02451
(781)487-7060
Fax: (781)487-7065
Website: http://www.crv.com

Comdisco Venture Group (Waltham)
Totton Pond Office Center
400-1 Totten Pond Rd.
Waltham, MA 02451
(617)672-0250
Fax: (617)398-8099

Marconi Ventures
890 Winter St., Ste. 310
Waltham, MA 02451
(781)839-7177

Fax: (781)522-7477
Website: http://www.marconi.com

Matrix Partners
Bay Colony Corporate Center
1000 Winter St., Ste.4500
Waltham, MA 02451
(781)890-2244
Fax: (781)890-2288
Website: http://www.matrix
partners.com

North Bridge Venture Partners
950 Winter St. Ste. 4600
Waltham, MA 02451
(781)290-0004
Fax: (781)290-0999
E-mail: eta@nbvp.com

Polaris Venture Partners
Bay Colony Corporate Ctr.
1000 Winter St., Ste. 3500
Waltham, MA 02451
(781)290-0770
Fax: (781)290-0880
E-mail: partners@polarisventures.com
Website: http://www.polar
isventures.com

Seaflower Ventures
Bay Colony Corporate Ctr.
1000 Winter St. Ste. 1000
Waltham, MA 02451
(781)466-9552
Fax: (781)466-9553
E-mail: moot@seaflower.com
Website: http://www.seaflower.com

Ampersand Ventures
55 William St., Ste. 240
Wellesley, MA 02481
(617)239-0700
Fax: (617)239-0824
E-mail: info@ampersandventures.com
Website: http://www.ampersand
ventures.com

Battery Ventures (Boston)
20 William St., Ste. 200
Wellesley, MA 02481
(781)577-1000
Fax: (781)577-1001
Website: http://www.battery.com

Commonwealth Capital Ventures, L.P.
20 William St., Ste.225
Wellesley, MA 02481
(781)237-7373
Fax: (781)235-8627
Website: http://www.ccvlp.com

Fowler, Anthony & Company
20 Walnut St.
Wellesley, MA 02481
(781)237-4201
Fax: (781)237-7718

Gemini Investors
20 William St.
Wellesley, MA 02481
(781)237-7001
Fax: (781)237-7233

Grove Street Advisors Inc.
20 William St., Ste. 230
Wellesley, MA 02481
(781)263-6100
Fax: (781)263-6101
Website: http://www.groves
treetadvisors.com

Mees Pierson Investeringsmaat B.V.
20 William St., Ste. 210
Wellesley, MA 02482
(781)239-7600
Fax: (781)239-0377

Norwest Equity Partners
40 William St., Ste. 305
Wellesley, MA 02481-3902
(781)237-5870
Fax: (781)237-6270
Website: http://www.norwestvp.com

Bessemer Venture Partners (Wellesley Hills)
83 Walnut St.
Wellesley Hills, MA 02481
(781)237-6050
Fax: (781)235-7576
E-mail: travis@bvpny.com
Website: http://www.bvp.com

Venture Capital Fund of New England
20 Walnut St., Ste. 120
Wellesley Hills, MA 02481-2175
(781)239-8262
Fax: (781)239-8263

Prism Venture Partners
100 Lowder Brook Dr., Ste. 2500
Westwood, MA 02090
(781)302-4000
Fax: (781)302-4040
E-mail: dwbaum@prismventure.com

Palmer Partners LP
200 Unicorn Park Dr.
Woburn, MA 01801
(781)933-5445
Fax: (781)933-0698

Michigan

Arbor Partners, L.L.C.
130 South First St.
Ann Arbor, MI 48104
(734)668-9000
Fax: (734)669-4195
Website: http://www.arborpartners.com

EDF Ventures
425 N. Main St.
Ann Arbor, MI 48104
(734)663-3213
Fax: (734)663-7358
E-mail: edf@edfvc.com
Website: http://www.edfvc.com

White Pines Management, L.L.C.
2401 Plymouth Rd., Ste. B
Ann Arbor, MI 48105
(734)747-9401
Fax: (734)747-9704
E-mail: ibund@whitepines.com
Website: http://www.whitepines.com

Wellmax, Inc.
3541 Bendway Blvd., Ste. 100
Bloomfield Hills, MI 48301
(248)646-3554
Fax: (248)646-6220

Venture Funding, Ltd.
Fisher Bldg.
3011 West Grand Blvd., Ste. 321
Detroit, MI 48202
(313)871-3606
Fax: (313)873-4935

Investcare Partners L.P. / GMA Capital LLC
32330 W. Twelve Mile Rd.
Farmington Hills, MI 48334
(248)489-9000
Fax: (248)489-8819
E-mail: gma@gmacapital.com
Website: http://www.gmacapital.com

Liberty Bidco Investment Corp.
30833 Northwestern Highway, Ste. 211
Farmington Hills, MI 48334
(248)626-6070
Fax: (248)626-6072

Seaflower Ventures
5170 Nicholson Rd.
PO Box 474
Fowlerville, MI 48836
(517)223-3335
Fax: (517)223-3337
E-mail: gibbons@seaflower.com
Website: http://www.seaflower.com

Ralph Wilson Equity Fund LLC
15400 E. Jefferson Ave.
Gross Pointe Park, MI 48230
(313)821-9122
Fax: (313)821-9101
Website: http://www.Ralph
WilsonEquityFund.com
J. Skip Simms, President

Minnesota

Development Corp. of Austin
1900 Eighth Ave., NW
Austin, MN 55912
(507)433-0346
Fax: (507)433-0361
E-mail: dca@smig.net
Website: http://www.spamtownusa.com

Northeast Ventures Corp.
802 Alworth Bldg.
Duluth, MN 55802
(218)722-9915
Fax: (218)722-9871

Medical Innovation Partners, Inc.
6450 City West Pkwy.
Eden Prairie, MN 55344-3245
(612)828-9616
Fax: (612)828-9596

St. Paul Venture Capital, Inc.
10400 Vicking Dr., Ste. 550
Eden Prairie, MN 55344
(612)995-7474
Fax: (612)995-7475
Website: http://www.stpaulvc.com

Cherry Tree Investments, Inc.
7601 France Ave. S, Ste. 150
Edina, MN 55435
(612)893-9012
Fax: (612)893-9036
Website: http://www.cherrytree.com

Shared Ventures, Inc.
6550 York Ave. S
Edina, MN 55435
(612)925-3411

Sherpa Partners LLC
5050 Lincoln Dr., Ste. 490
Edina, MN 55436
(952)942-1070
Fax: (952)942-1071
Website: http://www.sherpapartners.com

Affinity Capital Management
901 Marquette Ave., Ste. 1810
Minneapolis, MN 55402
(612)252-9900

Fax: (612)252-9911
Website: http://www.affinitycapital.com

Artesian Capital
1700 Foshay Tower
821 Marquette Ave.
Minneapolis, MN 55402
(612)334-5600
Fax: (612)334-5601
E-mail: artesian@artesian.com

Coral Ventures
60 S. 6th St., Ste. 3510
Minneapolis, MN 55402
(612)335-8666
Fax: (612)335-8668
Website: http://www.coralventures.com

Crescendo Venture Management, L.L.C.
800 LaSalle Ave., Ste. 2250
Minneapolis, MN 55402
(612)607-2800
Fax: (612)607-2801
Website: http://www.crescendo
ventures.com

Gideon Hixon Venture
1900 Foshay Tower
821 Marquette Ave.
Minneapolis, MN 55402
(612)904-2314
Fax: (612)204-0913

Norwest Equity Partners
3600 IDS Center
80 S. 8th St.
Minneapolis, MN 55402
(612)215-1600
Fax: (612)215-1601
Website: http://www.norwestvp.com

Oak Investment Partners (Minneapolis)
4550 Norwest Center
90 S. 7th St.
Minneapolis, MN 55402
(612)339-9322
Fax: (612)337-8017
Website: http://www.oakinv.com

Pathfinder Venture Capital Funds (Minneapolis)
7300 Metro Blvd., Ste. 585
Minneapolis, MN 55439
(612)835-1121
Fax: (612)835-8389
E-mail: jahrens620@aol.com

U.S. Bancorp Piper Jaffray Ventures, Inc.
800 Nicollet Mall, Ste. 800
Minneapolis, MN 55402

(612)303-5686
Fax: (612)303-1350
Website: http://www.paperjaffrey
ventures.com

The Food Fund, Ltd. Partnership
5720 Smatana Dr., Ste. 300
Minnetonka, MN 55343
(612)939-3950
Fax: (612)939-8106

Mayo Medical Ventures
200 First St. SW
Rochester, MN 55905
(507)266-4586
Fax: (507)284-5410
Website: http://www.mayo.edu

Missouri

Bankers Capital Corp.
3100 Gillham Rd.
Kansas City, MO 64109
(816)531-1600
Fax: (816)531-1334

Capital for Business, Inc. (Kansas City)
1000 Walnut St., 18th Fl.
Kansas City, MO 64106
(816)234-2357
Fax: (816)234-2952
Website: http://
www.capitalforbusiness.com

De Vries & Co. Inc.
800 West 47th St.
Kansas City, MO 64112
(816)756-0055
Fax: (816)756-0061

InvestAmerica Venture Group Inc. (Kansas City)
Commerce Tower
911 Main St., Ste. 2424
Kansas City, MO 64105
(816)842-0114
Fax: (816)471-7339

Kansas City Equity Partners
233 W. 47th St.
Kansas City, MO 64112
(816)960-1771
Fax: (816)960-1777
Website: http://www.kcep.com

Bome Investors, Inc.
8000 Maryland Ave., Ste. 1190
St. Louis, MO 63105
(314)721-5707
Fax: (314)721-5135

Website: http://www.gateway
ventures.com

Capital for Business, Inc. (St. Louis)
11 S. Meramac St., Ste. 1430
St. Louis, MO 63105
(314)746-7427
Fax: (314)746-8739
Website: http://www.capitalfor
business.com

Crown Capital Corp.
540 Maryville Centre Dr., Ste. 120
Saint Louis, MO 63141
(314)576-1201
Fax: (314)576-1525
Website: http://www.crown-
cap.com

Gateway Associates L.P.
8000 Maryland Ave., Ste. 1190
St. Louis, MO 63105
(314)721-5707
Fax: (314)721-5135

Harbison Corp.
8112 Maryland Ave., Ste. 250
Saint Louis, MO 63105
(314)727-8200
Fax: (314)727-0249

Heartland Capital Fund, Ltd.
PO Box 642117
Omaha, NE 68154
(402)778-5124
Fax: (402)445-2370
Website: http://www.heartland
capitalfund.com

Odin Capital Group
1625 Farnam St., Ste. 700
Omaha, NE 68102
(402)346-6200
Fax: (402)342-9311
Website: http://www.odincapital.com

Nevada

Edge Capital Investment Co. LLC
1350 E. Flamingo Rd., Ste. 3000
Las Vegas, NV 89119
(702)438-3343
E-mail: info@edgecapital.net
Website: http://www.edgecapital.net

The Benefit Capital Companies Inc.
PO Box 542
Logandale, NV 89021
(702)398-3222
Fax: (702)398-3700

Millennium Three Venture Group LLC
6880 South McCarran Blvd., Ste. A-11
Reno, NV 89509
(775)954-2020
Fax: (775)954-2023
Website: http://www.m3vg.com

New Jersey

Alan I. Goldman & Associates
497 Ridgewood Ave.
Glen Ridge, NJ 07028
(973)857-5680
Fax: (973)509-8856

CS Capital Partners LLC
328 Second St., Ste. 200
Lakewood, NJ 08701
(732)901-1111
Fax: (212)202-5071
Website: http://www.cs-capital.com

Edison Venture Fund
1009 Lenox Dr., Ste. 4
Lawrenceville, NJ 08648
(609)896-1900
Fax: (609)896-0066
E-mail: info@edisonventure.com
Website: http://www.edisonventure.com

Tappan Zee Capital Corp. (New Jersey)
201 Lower Notch Rd.
PO Box 416
Little Falls, NJ 07424
(973)256-8280
Fax: (973)256-2841

The CIT Group/Venture Capital, Inc.
650 CIT Dr.
Livingston, NJ 07039
(973)740-5429
Fax: (973)740-5555
Website: http://www.cit.com

Capital Express, L.L.C.
1100 Valleybrook Ave.
Lyndhurst, NJ 07071
(201)438-8228
Fax: (201)438-5131
E-mail: niles@capitalexpress.com
Website: http://www.capitalexpress.com

Westford Technology Ventures, L.P.
17 Academy St.
Newark, NJ 07102
(973)624-2131
Fax: (973)624-2008

Accel Partners
1 Palmer Sq.
Princeton, NJ 08542

(609)683-4500
Fax: (609)683-4880
Website: http://www.accel.com

Cardinal Partners
221 Nassau St.
Princeton, NJ 08542
(609)924-6452
Fax: (609)683-0174
Website: http://www.cardinal
healthpartners.com

Domain Associates L.L.C.
One Palmer Sq., Ste. 515
Princeton, NJ 08542
(609)683-5656
Fax: (609)683-9789
Website: http://www.domainvc.com

Johnston Associates, Inc.
181 Cherry Valley Rd.
Princeton, NJ 08540
(609)924-3131
Fax: (609)683-7524
E-mail: jaincorp@aol.com

Kemper Ventures
Princeton Forrestal Village
155 Village Blvd.
Princeton, NJ 08540
(609)936-3035
Fax: (609)936-3051

Penny Lane Parnters
One Palmer Sq., Ste. 309
Princeton, NJ 08542
(609)497-4646
Fax: (609)497-0611

Early Stage Enterprises L.P.
995 Route 518
Skillman, NJ 08558
(609)921-8896
Fax: (609)921-8703
Website: http://www.esevc.com

MBW Management Inc.
1 Springfield Ave.
Summit, NJ 07901
(908)273-4060
Fax: (908)273-4430

BCI Advisors, Inc.
Glenpointe Center W.
Teaneck, NJ 07666
(201)836-3900
Fax: (201)836-6368
E-mail: info@bciadvisors.com
Website: http://www.bci
partners.com

Demuth, Folger & Wetherill / DFW Capital Partners
Glenpointe Center E., 5th Fl.
300 Frank W. Burr Blvd.
Teaneck, NJ 07666
(201)836-2233
Fax: (201)836-5666
Website: http://www.dfwcapital.com

First Princeton Capital Corp.
189 Berdan Ave., No. 131
Wayne, NJ 07470-3233
(973)278-3233
Fax: (973)278-4290
Website: http://www.lytellcatt.net

Edelson Technology Partners
300 Tice Blvd.
Woodcliff Lake, NJ 07675
(201)930-9898
Fax: (201)930-8899
Website: http://www.edelsontech.com

New Mexico

Bruce F. Glaspell & Associates
10400 Academy Rd. NE, Ste. 313
Albuquerque, NM 87111
(505)292-4505
Fax: (505)292-4258

High Desert Ventures, Inc.
6101 Imparata St. NE, Ste. 1721
Albuquerque, NM 87111
(505)797-3330
Fax: (505)338-5147

New Business Capital Fund, Ltd.
5805 Torreon NE
Albuquerque, NM 87109
(505)822-8445

SBC Ventures
10400 Academy Rd. NE, Ste. 313
Albuquerque, NM 87111
(505)292-4505
Fax: (505)292-4528

Technology Ventures Corp.
1155 University Blvd. SE
Albuquerque, NM 87106
(505)246-2882
Fax: (505)246-2891

New York

New York State Science & Technology Foundation
Small Business Technology Investment Fund
99 Washington Ave., Ste. 1731
Albany, NY 12210

(518)473-9741
Fax: (518)473-6876

Rand Capital Corp.
2200 Rand Bldg.
Buffalo, NY 14203
(716)853-0802
Fax: (716)854-8480
Website: http://www.randcapital.com

Seed Capital Partners
620 Main St.
Buffalo, NY 14202
(716)845-7520
Fax: (716)845-7539
Website: http://www.seedcp.com

Coleman Venture Group
5909 Northern Blvd.
PO Box 224
East Norwich, NY 11732
(516)626-3642
Fax: (516)626-9722

Vega Capital Corp.
45 Knollwood Rd.
Elmsford, NY 10523
(914)345-9500
Fax: (914)345-9505

Herbert Young Securities, Inc.
98 Cuttermill Rd.
Great Neck, NY 11021
(516)487-8300
Fax: (516)487-8319

Sterling/Carl Marks Capital, Inc.
175 Great Neck Rd., Ste. 408
Great Neck, NY 11021
(516)482-7374
Fax: (516)487-0781
E-mail: stercrlmar@aol.com
Website: http://www.serling
carlmarks.com

Impex Venture Management Co.
PO Box 1570
Green Island, NY 12183
(518)271-8008
Fax: (518)271-9101

Corporate Venture Partners L.P.
200 Sunset Park
Ithaca, NY 14850
(607)257-6323
Fax: (607)257-6128

Arthur P. Gould & Co.
One Wilshire Dr.
Lake Success, NY 11020
(516)773-3000
Fax: (516)773-3289

Dauphin Capital Partners
108 Forest Ave.
Locust Valley, NY 11560
(516)759-3339
Fax: (516)759-3322
Website: http://www.dauphincapital.com

550 Digital Media Ventures
555 Madison Ave., 10th Fl.
New York, NY 10022
Website: http://www.550dmv.com

Aberlyn Capital Management Co., Inc.
500 Fifth Ave.
New York, NY 10110
(212)391-7750
Fax: (212)391-7762

Adler & Company
342 Madison Ave., Ste. 807
New York, NY 10173
(212)599-2535
Fax: (212)599-2526

Alimansky Capital Group, Inc.
605 Madison Ave., Ste. 300
New York, NY 10022-1901
(212)832-7300
Fax: (212)832-7338

Allegra Partners
515 Madison Ave., 29th Fl.
New York, NY 10022
(212)826-9080
Fax: (212)759-2561

The Argentum Group
The Chyrsler Bldg.
405 Lexington Ave.
New York, NY 10174
(212)949-6262
Fax: (212)949-8294
Website: http://www.argentum
group.com

Axavision Inc.
14 Wall St., 26th Fl.
New York, NY 10005
(212)619-4000
Fax: (212)619-7202

Bedford Capital Corp.
18 East 48th St., Ste. 1800
New York, NY 10017
(212)688-5700
Fax: (212)754-4699
E-mail: info@bedfordnyc.com
Website: http://www.bedfordnyc.com

Bloom & Co.
950 Third Ave.

New York, NY 10022
(212)838-1858
Fax: (212)838-1843

Bristol Capital Management
300 Park Ave., 17th Fl.
New York, NY 10022
(212)572-6306
Fax: (212)705-4292

**Citicorp Venture Capital Ltd.
(New York City)**
399 Park Ave., 14th Fl.
Zone 4
New York, NY 10043
(212)559-1127
Fax: (212)888-2940

CM Equity Partners
135 E. 57th St.
New York, NY 10022
(212)909-8428
Fax: (212)980-2630

Cohen & Co., L.L.C.
800 Third Ave.
New York, NY 10022
(212)317-2250
Fax: (212)317-2255
E-mail: nlcohen@aol.com

Cornerstone Equity Investors, L.L.C.
717 5th Ave., Ste. 1100
New York, NY 10022
(212)753-0901
Fax: (212)826-6798
Website: http://www.cornerstone-
equity.com

CW Group, Inc.
1041 3rd Ave., 2nd fl.
New York, NY 10021
(212)308-5266
Fax: (212)644-0354
Website: http://www.cwventures.com

DH Blair Investment Banking Corp.
44 Wall St., 2nd Fl.
New York, NY 10005
(212)495-5000
Fax: (212)269-1438

Dresdner Kleinwort Capital
75 Wall St.
New York, NY 10005
(212)429-3131
Fax: (212)429-3139
Website: http://www.dresdnerkb.com

East River Ventures, L.P.
645 Madison Ave., 22nd Fl.

New York, NY 10022
(212)644-2322
Fax: (212)644-5498

Easton Hunt Capital Partners
641 Lexington Ave., 21st Fl.
New York, NY 10017
(212)702-0950
Fax: (212)702-0952
Website: http://www.eastoncapital.com

Elk Associates Funding Corp.
747 3rd Ave., Ste. 4C
New York, NY 10017
(212)355-2449
Fax: (212)759-3338

EOS Partners, L.P.
320 Park Ave., 22nd Fl.
New York, NY 10022
(212)832-5800
Fax: (212)832-5815
E-mail: mfirst@eospartners.com
Website: http://www.eospartners.com

Euclid Partners
45 Rockefeller Plaza, Ste. 3240
New York, NY 10111
(212)218-6880
Fax: (212)218-6877
E-mail: graham@euclidpartners.com
Website: http://www.euclidpartners.com

Evergreen Capital Partners, Inc.
150 East 58th St.
New York, NY 10155
(212)813-0758
Fax: (212)813-0754

Exeter Capital L.P.
10 E. 53rd St.
New York, NY 10022
(212)872-1172
Fax: (212)872-1198
E-mail: exeter@usa.net

Financial Technology Research Corp.
518 Broadway
Penthouse
New York, NY 10012
(212)625-9100
Fax: (212)431-0300
E-mail: fintek@financier.com

4C Ventures
237 Park Ave., Ste. 801
New York, NY 10017
(212)692-3680
Fax: (212)692-3685
Website: http://www.4cventures.com

Fusient Ventures
99 Park Ave., 20th Fl.
New York, NY 10016
(212)972-8999
Fax: (212)972-9876
E-mail: info@fusient.com
Website: http://www.fusient.com

Generation Capital Partners
551 Fifth Ave., Ste. 3100
New York, NY 10176
(212)450-8507
Fax: (212)450-8550
Website: http://www.genpartners.com

Golub Associates, Inc.
555 Madison Ave.
New York, NY 10022
(212)750-6060
Fax: (212)750-5505

Hambro America Biosciences Inc.
650 Madison Ave., 21st Floor
New York, NY 10022
(212)223-7400
Fax: (212)223-0305

Hanover Capital Corp.
505 Park Ave., 15th Fl.
New York, NY 10022
(212)755-1222
Fax: (212)935-1787

Harvest Partners, Inc.
280 Park Ave, 33rd Fl.
New York, NY 10017
(212)559-6300
Fax: (212)812-0100
Website: http://www.harvpart.com

Holding Capital Group, Inc.
10 E. 53rd St., 30th Fl.
New York, NY 10022
(212)486-6670
Fax: (212)486-0843

Hudson Venture Partners
660 Madison Ave., 14th Fl.
New York, NY 10021-8405
(212)644-9797
Fax: (212)644-7430
Website: http://www.hudsonptr.com

IBJS Capital Corp.
1 State St., 9th Fl.
New York, NY 10004
(212)858-2018
Fax: (212)858-2768

InterEquity Capital Partners, L.P.
220 5th Ave.
New York, NY 10001

(212)779-2022
Fax: (212)779-2103
Website: http://www.interequity-capital.com

The Jordan Edmiston Group Inc.
150 East 52nd St., 18th Fl.
New York, NY 10022
(212)754-0710
Fax: (212)754-0337

Josephberg, Grosz and Co., Inc.
633 3rd Ave., 13th Fl.
New York, NY 10017
(212)974-9926
Fax: (212)397-5832

J.P. Morgan Capital Corp.
60 Wall St.
New York, NY 10260-0060
(212)648-9000
Fax: (212)648-5002
Website: http://www.jpmorgan.com

The Lambda Funds
380 Lexington Ave., 54th Fl.
New York, NY 10168
(212)682-3454
Fax: (212)682-9231

Lepercq Capital Management Inc.
1675 Broadway
New York, NY 10019
(212)698-0795
Fax: (212)262-0155

Loeb Partners Corp.
61 Broadway, Ste. 2400
New York, NY 10006
(212)483-7000
Fax: (212)574-2001

Madison Investment Partners
660 Madison Ave.
New York, NY 10021
(212)223-2600
Fax: (212)223-8208

MC Capital Inc.
520 Madison Ave., 16th Fl.
New York, NY 10022
(212)644-0841
Fax: (212)644-2926

**McCown, De Leeuw and Co.
(New York)**
65 E. 55th St., 36th Fl.
New York, NY 10022
(212)355-5500
Fax: (212)355-6283
Website: http://www.mdcpartners.com

Morgan Stanley Venture Partners
1221 Avenue of the Americas, 33rd Fl.
New York, NY 10020
(212)762-7900
Fax: (212)762-8424
E-mail: msventures@ms.com
Website: http://www.msvp.com

Nazem and Co.
645 Madison Ave., 12th Fl.
New York, NY 10022
(212)371-7900
Fax: (212)371-2150

Needham Capital Management, L.L.C.
445 Park Ave.
New York, NY 10022
(212)371-8300
Fax: (212)705-0299
Website: http://www.needhamco.com

Norwood Venture Corp.
1430 Broadway, Ste. 1607
New York, NY 10018
(212)869-5075
Fax: (212)869-5331
E-mail: nvc@mail.idt.net
Website: http://www.norven.com

Noveltek Venture Corp.
521 Fifth Ave., Ste. 1700
New York, NY 10175
(212)286-1963

Paribas Principal, Inc.
787 7th Ave.
New York, NY 10019
(212)841-2005
Fax: (212)841-3558

Patricof & Co. Ventures, Inc.
(New York)
445 Park Ave.
New York, NY 10022
(212)753-6300
Fax: (212)319-6155
Website: http://www.patricof.com

The Platinum Group, Inc.
350 Fifth Ave, Ste. 7113
New York, NY 10118
(212)736-4300
Fax: (212)736-6086
Website: http://www.platinumgroup.com

Pomona Capital
780 Third Ave., 28th Fl.
New York, NY 10017
(212)593-3639
Fax: (212)593-3987
Website: http://www.pomonacapital.com

Prospect Street Ventures
10 East 40th St., 44th Fl.
New York, NY 10016
(212)448-0702
Fax: (212)448-9652
E-mail: wkohler@prospectstreet.com
Website: http://www.prospectstreet.com

Regent Capital Management
505 Park Ave., Ste. 1700
New York, NY 10022
(212)735-9900
Fax: (212)735-9908

Rothschild Ventures, Inc.
1251 Avenue of the Americas, 51st Fl.
New York, NY 10020
(212)403-3500
Fax: (212)403-3652
Website: http://www.nmrothschild.com

Sandler Capital Management
767 Fifth Ave., 45th Fl.
New York, NY 10153
(212)754-8100
Fax: (212)826-0280

Siguler Guff & Company
630 Fifth Ave., 16th Fl.
New York, NY 10111
(212)332-5100
Fax: (212)332-5120

Spencer Trask Ventures Inc.
535 Madison Ave.
New York, NY 10022
(212)355-5565
Fax: (212)751-3362
Website: http://www.spencertrask.com

Sprout Group (New York City)
277 Park Ave.
New York, NY 10172
(212)892-3600
Fax: (212)892-3444
E-mail: info@sproutgroup.com
Website: http://www.sproutgroup.com

US Trust Private Equity
114 W.47th St.
New York, NY 10036
(212)852-3949
Fax: (212)852-3759
Website: http://www.ustrust.com/
privateequity

Vencon Management Inc.
301 West 53rd St., Ste. 10F
New York, NY 10019
(212)581-8787
Fax: (212)397-4126
Website: http://www.venconinc.com

Venrock Associates
30 Rockefeller Plaza, Ste. 5508
New York, NY 10112
(212)649-5600
Fax: (212)649-5788
Website: http://www.venrock.com

Venture Capital Fund of America, Inc.
509 Madison Ave., Ste. 812
New York, NY 10022
(212)838-5577
Fax: (212)838-7614
E-mail: mail@vcfa.com
Website: http://www.vcfa.com

Venture Opportunities Corp.
150 E. 58th St.
New York, NY 10155
(212)832-3737
Fax: (212)980-6603

Warburg Pincus Ventures, Inc.
466 Lexington Ave., 11th Fl.
New York, NY 10017
(212)878-9309
Fax: (212)878-9200
Website: http://www.warburgpincus.com

Wasserstein, Perella & Co. Inc.
31 W. 52nd St., 27th Fl.
New York, NY 10019
(212)702-5691
Fax: (212)969-7879

Welsh, Carson, Anderson, & Stowe
320 Park Ave., Ste. 2500
New York, NY 10022-6815
(212)893-9500
Fax: (212)893-9575

Whitney and Co. (New York)
630 Fifth Ave. Ste. 3225
New York, NY 10111
(212)332-2400
Fax: (212)332-2422
Website: http://www.jhwitney.com

Winthrop Ventures
74 Trinity Place, Ste. 600
New York, NY 10006
(212)422-0100

The Pittsford Group
8 Lodge Pole Rd.
Pittsford, NY 14534
(716)223-3523

Genesee Funding
70 Linden Oaks, 3rd Fl.
Rochester, NY 14625
(716)383-5550
Fax: (716)383-5305

Gabelli Multimedia Partners
One Corporate Center
Rye, NY 10580
(914)921-5395
Fax: (914)921-5031

Stamford Financial
108 Main St.
Stamford, NY 12167
(607)652-3311
Fax: (607)652-6301
Website: http://www.stamford
financial.com

Northwood Ventures LLC
485 Underhill Blvd., Ste. 205
Syosset, NY 11791
(516)364-5544
Fax: (516)364-0879
E-mail: northwood@northwood.com
Website: http://www.north
woodventures.com

Exponential Business Development Co.
216 Walton St.
Syracuse, NY 13202-1227
(315)474-4500
Fax: (315)474-4682
E-mail: dirksonn@aol.com
Website: http://www.exponential-ny.com

Onondaga Venture Capital Fund Inc.
714 State Tower Bldg.
Syracuse, NY 13202
(315)478-0157
Fax: (315)478-0158

Bessemer Venture Partners (Westbury)
1400 Old Country Rd., Ste. 109
Westbury, NY 11590
(516)997-2300
Fax: (516)997-2371
E-mail: bob@bvpny.com
Website: http://www.bvp.com

Ovation Capital Partners
120 Bloomingdale Rd., 4th Fl.
White Plains, NY 10605
(914)258-0011
Fax: (914)684-0848
Website: http://www.ovation
capital.com

North Carolina

Carolinas Capital Investment Corp.
1408 Biltmore Dr.
Charlotte, NC 28207
(704)375-3888
Fax: (704)375-6226

First Union Capital Partners
1st Union Center, 12th Fl.
301 S. College St.
Charlotte, NC 28288-0732
(704)383-0000
Fax: (704)374-6711
Website: http://www.fucp.com

Frontier Capital LLC
525 North Tryon St., Ste. 1700
Charlotte, NC 28202
(704)414-2880
Fax: (704)414-2881
Website: http://www.frontierfunds.com

Kitty Hawk Capital
2700 Coltsgate Rd., Ste. 202
Charlotte, NC 28211
(704)362-3909
Fax: (704)362-2774
Website: http://www.kittyhawk
capital.com

Piedmont Venture Partners
One Morrocroft Centre
6805 Morisson Blvd., Ste. 380
Charlotte, NC 28211
(704)731-5200
Fax: (704)365-9733
Website: http://www.piedmontvp.com

Ruddick Investment Co.
1800 Two First Union Center
Charlotte, NC 28282
(704)372-5404
Fax: (704)372-6409

The Shelton Companies Inc.
3600 One First Union Center
301 S. College St.
Charlotte, NC 28202
(704)348-2200
Fax: (704)348-2260

Wakefield Group
1110 E. Morehead St.
PO Box 36329
Charlotte, NC 28236
(704)372-0355
Fax: (704)372-8216
Website: http://www.wakefiel
dgroup.com

Aurora Funds, Inc.
2525 Meridian Pkwy., Ste. 220
Durham, NC 27713
(919)484-0400
Fax: (919)484-0444
Website: http://www.aurora
funds.com

Intersouth Partners
3211 Shannon Rd., Ste. 610
Durham, NC 27707
(919)493-6640
Fax: (919)493-6649
E-mail: info@intersouth.com
Website: http://www.intersouth.com

Geneva Merchant Banking Partners
PO Box 21962
Greensboro, NC 27420
(336)275-7002
Fax: (336)275-9155
Website: http://www.geneva
merchantbank.com

The North Carolina Enterprise Fund, L.P.
3600 Glenwood Ave., Ste. 107
Raleigh, NC 27612
(919)781-2691
Fax: (919)783-9195
Website: http://www.ncef.com

Ohio

Senmend Medical Ventures
4445 Lake Forest Dr., Ste. 600
Cincinnati, OH 45242
(513)563-3264
Fax: (513)563-3261

The Walnut Group
312 Walnut St., Ste. 1151
Cincinnati, OH 45202
(513)651-3300
Fax: (513)929-4441
Website: http://www.thewal
nutgroup.com

Brantley Venture Partners
20600 Chagrin Blvd., Ste. 1150
Cleveland, OH 44122
(216)283-4800
Fax: (216)283-5324

Clarion Capital Corp.
1801 E. 9th St., Ste. 1120
Cleveland, OH 44114
(216)687-1096
Fax: (216)694-3545

Crystal Internet Venture Fund, L.P.
1120 Chester Ave., Ste. 418
Cleveland, OH 44114
(216)263-5515
Fax: (216)263-5518
E-mail: jf@crystalventure.com
Website: http://www.crystal
venture.com

Key Equity Capital Corp.
127 Public Sq., 28th Fl.
Cleveland, OH 44114
(216)689-3000
Fax: (216)689-3204
Website: http://www.keybank.com

Morgenthaler Ventures
Terminal Tower
50 Public Square, Ste. 2700
Cleveland, OH 44113
(216)416-7500
Fax: (216)416-7501
Website: http://www.morgenthaler.com

National City Equity Partners Inc.
1965 E. 6th St.
Cleveland, OH 44114
(216)575-2491
Fax: (216)575-9965
E-mail: nccap@aol.com
Website: http://www.nccapital.com

Primus Venture Partners, Inc.
5900 LanderBrook Dr., Ste. 2000
Cleveland, OH 44124-4020
(440)684-7300
Fax: (440)684-7342
E-mail: info@primusventure.com
Website: http://www.primusventure.com

Banc One Capital Partners (Columbus)
150 East Gay St., 24th Fl.
Columbus, OH 43215
(614)217-1100
Fax: (614)217-1217

Battelle Venture Partners
505 King Ave.
Columbus, OH 43201
(614)424-7005
Fax: (614)424-4874

Ohio Partners
62 E. Board St., 3rd Fl.
Columbus, OH 43215
(614)621-1210
Fax: (614)621-1240

Capital Technology Group, L.L.C.
400 Metro Place North, Ste. 300
Dublin, OH 43017
(614)792-6066
Fax: (614)792-6036
E-mail: info@capitaltech.com
Website: http://www.capitaltech.com

Northwest Ohio Venture Fund
4159 Holland-Sylvania R., Ste. 202
Toledo, OH 43623
(419)824-8144

Fax: (419)882-2035
E-mail: bwalsh@novf.com

Oklahoma

Moore & Associates
1000 W. Wilshire Blvd., Ste. 370
Oklahoma City, OK 73116
(405)842-3660
Fax: (405)842-3763

Chisholm Private Capital Partners
100 West 5th St., Ste. 805
Tulsa, OK 74103
(918)584-0440
Fax: (918)584-0441
Website: http://www.chisholmvc.com

Davis, Tuttle Venture Partners (Tulsa)
320 S. Boston, Ste. 1000
Tulsa, OK 74103-3703
(918)584-7272
Fax: (918)582-3404
Website: http://www.davistuttle.com

RBC Ventures
2627 E. 21st St.
Tulsa, OK 74114
(918)744-5607
Fax: (918)743-8630

Oregon

Utah Ventures II LP
10700 SW Beaverton-Hillsdale Hwy.,
Ste. 548
Beaverton, OR 97005
(503)574-4125
E-mail: adishlip@uven.com
Website: http://www.uven.com

Orien Ventures
14523 SW Westlake Dr.
Lake Oswego, OR 97035
(503)699-1680
Fax: (503)699-1681

OVP Venture Partners (Lake Oswego)
340 Oswego Pointe Dr., Ste. 200
Lake Oswego, OR 97034
(503)697-8766
Fax: (503)697-8863
E-mail: info@ovp.com
Website: http://www.ovp.com

Oregon Resource and Technology Development Fund
4370 NE Halsey St., Ste. 233
Portland, OR 97213-1566
(503)282-4462
Fax: (503)282-2976

Shaw Venture Partners
400 SW 6th Ave., Ste. 1100
Portland, OR 97204-1636
(503)228-4884
Fax: (503)227-2471
Website: http://www.shawventures.com

Pennsylvania

Mid-Atlantic Venture Funds
125 Goodman Dr.
Bethlehem, PA 18015
(610)865-6550
Fax: (610)865-6427
Website: http://www.mavf.com

Newspring Ventures
100 W. Elm St., Ste. 101
Conshohocken, PA 19428
(610)567-2380
Fax: (610)567-2388
Website: http://www.news
printventures.com

Patricof & Co. Ventures, Inc.
455 S. Gulph Rd., Ste. 410
King of Prussia, PA 19406
(610)265-0286
Fax: (610)265-4959
Website: http://www.patricof.com

Loyalhanna Venture Fund
527 Cedar Way, Ste. 104
Oakmont, PA 15139
(412)820-7035
Fax: (412)820-7036

Innovest Group Inc.
2000 Market St., Ste. 1400
Philadelphia, PA 19103
(215)564-3960
Fax: (215)569-3272

Keystone Venture Capital Management Co.
1601 Market St., Ste. 2500
Philadelphia, PA 19103
(215)241-1200
Fax: (215)241-1211
Website: http://www.keystonevc.com

Liberty Venture Partners
2005 Market St., Ste. 200
Philadelphia, PA 19103
(215)282-4484
Fax: (215)282-4485
E-mail: info@libertyvp.com
Website: http://www.libertyvp.com

Penn Janney Fund, Inc.
1801 Market St., 11th Fl.
Philadelphia, PA 19103

(215)665-4447
Fax: (215)557-0820

Philadelphia Ventures, Inc.
The Bellevue
200 S. Broad St.
Philadelphia, PA 19102
(215)732-4445
Fax: (215)732-4644

Birchmere Ventures Inc.
2000 Technology Dr.
Pittsburgh, PA 15219-3109
(412)803-8000
Fax: (412)687-8139
Website: http://www.birchmerevc.com

CEO Venture Fund
2000 Technology Dr., Ste. 160
Pittsburgh, PA 15219-3109
(412)687-3451
Fax: (412)687-8139
E-mail: ceofund@aol.com
Website: http://www.ceoventure
fund.com

Innovation Works Inc.
2000 Technology Dr., Ste. 250
Pittsburgh, PA 15219
(412)681-1520
Fax: (412)681-2625
Website: http://www.innovation
works.org

Keystone Minority Capital Fund L.P.
1801 Centre Ave., Ste. 201
Williams Sq.
Pittsburgh, PA 15219
(412)338-2230
Fax: (412)338-2224

Mellon Ventures, Inc.
One Mellon Bank Ctr., Rm. 3500
Pittsburgh, PA 15258
(412)236-3594
Fax: (412)236-3593
Website: http://www.mellon
ventures.com

Pennsylvania Growth Fund
5850 Ellsworth Ave., Ste. 303
Pittsburgh, PA 15232
(412)661-1000
Fax: (412)361-0676

Point Venture Partners
The Century Bldg.
130 Seventh St., 7th Fl.
Pittsburgh, PA 15222
(412)261-1966
Fax: (412)261-1718

Cross Atlantic Capital Partners
5 Radnor Corporate Center, Ste. 555
Radnor, PA 19087
(610)995-2650
Fax: (610)971-2062
Website: http://www.xacp.com

Meridian Venture Partners (Radnor)
The Radnor Court Bldg., Ste. 140
259 Radnor-Chester Rd.
Radnor, PA 19087
(610)254-2999
Fax: (610)254-2996
E-mail: mvpart@ix.netcom.com

TDH
919 Conestoga Rd., Bldg. 1, Ste. 301
Rosemont, PA 19010
(610)526-9970
Fax: (610)526-9971

Adams Capital Management
500 Blackburn Ave.
Sewickley, PA 15143
(412)749-9454
Fax: (412)749-9459
Website: http://www.acm.com

S.R. One, Ltd.
Four Tower Bridge
200 Barr Harbor Dr., Ste. 250
W. Conshohocken, PA 19428
(610)567-1000
Fax: (610)567-1039

Greater Philadelphia Venture Capital Corp.
351 East Conestoga Rd.
Wayne, PA 19087
(610)688-6829
Fax: (610)254-8958

PA Early Stage
435 Devon Park Dr., Bldg. 500, Ste. 510
Wayne, PA 19087
(610)293-4075
Fax: (610)254-4240
Website: http://www.paearlystage.com

The Sandhurst Venture Fund, L.P.
351 E. Constoga Rd.
Wayne, PA 19087
(610)254-8900
Fax: (610)254-8958

TL Ventures
700 Bldg.
435 Devon Park Dr.
Wayne, PA 19087-1990
(610)975-3765
Fax: (610)254-4210
Website: http://www.tlventures.com

Rockhill Ventures, Inc.
100 Front St., Ste. 1350
West Conshohocken, PA 19428
(610)940-0300
Fax: (610)940-0301

Puerto Rico

Advent-Morro Equity Partners
Banco Popular Bldg.
206 Tetuan St., Ste. 903
San Juan, PR 00902
(787)725-5285
Fax: (787)721-1735

North America Investment Corp.
Mercantil Plaza, Ste. 813
PO Box 191831
San Juan, PR 00919
(787)754-6178
Fax: (787)754-6181

Rhode Island

Manchester Humphreys, Inc.
40 Westminster St., Ste. 900
Providence, RI 02903
(401)454-0400
Fax: (401)454-0403

Navis Partners
50 Kennedy Plaza, 12th Fl.
Providence, RI 02903
(401)278-6770
Fax: (401)278-6387
Website: http://www.navis
partners.com

South Carolina

Capital Insights, L.L.C.
PO Box 27162
Greenville, SC 29616-2162
(864)242-6832
Fax: (864)242-6755
E-mail: jwarner@capitalinsights.com
Website: http://www.capitalin
sights.com

Transamerica Mezzanine Financing
7 N. Laurens St., Ste. 603
Greenville, SC 29601
(864)232-6198
Fax: (864)241-4444

Tennessee

Valley Capital Corp.
Krystal Bldg.
100 W. Martin Luther King Blvd.,
Ste. 212

Chattanooga, TN 37402
(423)265-1557
Fax: (423)265-1588

Coleman Swenson Booth Inc.
237 2nd Ave. S
Franklin, TN 37064-2649
(615)791-9462
Fax: (615)791-9636
Website: http://
www.colemanswenson.com

Capital Services & Resources, Inc.
5159 Wheelis Dr., Ste. 106
Memphis, TN 38117
(901)761-2156
Fax: (907)767-0060

Paradigm Capital Partners LLC
6410 Poplar Ave., Ste. 395
Memphis, TN 38119
(901)682-6060
Fax: (901)328-3061

SSM Ventures
845 Crossover Ln., Ste. 140
Memphis, TN 38117
(901)767-1131
Fax: (901)767-1135
Website: http://www.ssm
ventures.com

Capital Across America L.P.
501 Union St., Ste. 201
Nashville, TN 37219
(615)254-1414
Fax: (615)254-1856
Website: http://
www.capitalacrossamerica.com

Equitas L.P.
2000 Glen Echo Rd., Ste. 101
PO Box 158838
Nashville, TN 37215-8838
(615)383-8673
Fax: (615)383-8693

Massey Burch Capital Corp.
One Burton Hills Blvd., Ste. 350
Nashville, TN 37215
(615)665-3221
Fax: (615)665-3240
E-mail: tcalton@masseyburch.com
Website: http://www.masseyburch.com

Nelson Capital Corp.
3401 West End Ave., Ste. 300
Nashville, TN 37203
(615)292-8787
Fax: (615)385-3150

Texas

Phillips-Smith Specialty Retail Group
5080 Spectrum Dr., Ste. 805 W
Addison, TX 75001
(972)387-0725
Fax: (972)458-2560
E-mail: pssrg@aol.com
Website: http://www.phillips-smith.com

Austin Ventures, L.P.
701 Brazos St., Ste. 1400
Austin, TX 78701
(512)485-1900
Fax: (512)476-3952
E-mail: info@ausven.com
Website: http://www.austinventures.com

The Capital Network
3925 West Braker Lane, Ste. 406
Austin, TX 78759-5321
(512)305-0826
Fax: (512)305-0836

Techxas Ventures LLC
5000 Plaza on the Lake
Austin, TX 78746
(512)343-0118
Fax: (512)343-1879
E-mail: bruce@techxas.com
Website: http://www.techxas.com

Alliance Financial of Houston
218 Heather Ln.
Conroe, TX 77385-9013
(936)447-3300
Fax: (936)447-4222

Amerimark Capital Corp.
1111 W. Mockingbird, Ste. 1111
Dallas, TX 75247
(214)638-7878
Fax: (214)638-7612
E-mail: amerimark@amcapital.com
Website: http://www.amcapital.com

AMT Venture Partners / AMT Capital Ltd.
5220 Spring Valley Rd., Ste. 600
Dallas, TX 75240
(214)905-9757
Fax: (214)905-9761
Website: http://www.amtcapital.com

Arkoma Venture Partners
5950 Berkshire Lane, Ste. 1400
Dallas, TX 75225
(214)739-3515
Fax: (214)739-3572
E-mail: joelf@arkomavp.com

Capital Southwest Corp.
12900 Preston Rd., Ste. 700
Dallas, TX 75230
(972)233-8242
Fax: (972)233-7362
Website: http://
www.capitalsouthwest.com

Dali, Hook Partners
One Lincoln Center, Ste. 1550
5400 LBJ Freeway
Dallas, TX 75240
(972)991-5457
Fax: (972)991-5458
E-mail: dhook@hookpartners.com
Website: http://www.hookpartners.com

HO2 Partners
Two Galleria Tower
13455 Noel Rd., Ste. 1670
Dallas, TX 75240
(972)702-1144
Fax: (972)702-8234
Website: http://www.ho2.com

Interwest Partners (Dallas)
2 Galleria Tower
13455 Noel Rd., Ste. 1670
Dallas, TX 75240
(972)392-7279
Fax: (972)490-6348
Website: http://www.interwest.com

Kahala Investments, Inc.
8214 Westchester Dr., Ste. 715
Dallas, TX 75225
(214)987-0077
Fax: (214)987-2332

MESBIC Ventures Holding Co.
2435 North Central Expressway, Ste. 200
Dallas, TX 75080
(972)991-1597
Fax: (972)991-4770
Website: http://www.mvhc.com

North Texas MESBIC, Inc.
9500 Forest Lane, Ste. 430
Dallas, TX 75243
(214)221-3565
Fax: (214)221-3566

Richard Jaffe & Company, Inc,
7318 Royal Cir.
Dallas, TX 75230
(214)265-9397
Fax: (214)739-1845

Sevin Rosen Management Co.
13455 Noel Rd., Ste. 1670
Dallas, TX 75240

(972)702-1100
Fax: (972)702-1103
E-mail: info@srfunds.com
Website: http://www.srfunds.com

Stratford Capital Partners, L.P.
300 Crescent Ct., Ste. 500
Dallas, TX 75201
(214)740-7377
Fax: (214)720-7393
E-mail: stratcap@hmtf.com

Sunwestern Investment Group
12221 Merit Dr., Ste. 935
Dallas, TX 75251
(972)239-5650
Fax: (972)701-0024

Wingate Partners
750 N. St. Paul St., Ste. 1200
Dallas, TX 75201
(214)720-1313
Fax: (214)871-8799

Buena Venture Associates
201 Main St., 32nd Fl.
Fort Worth, TX 76102
(817)339-7400
Fax: (817)390-8408
Website: http://www.buenaventure.com

The Catalyst Group
3 Riverway, Ste. 770
Houston, TX 77056
(713)623-8133
Fax: (713)623-0473
E-mail: herman@thecatalystgroup.net
Website: http://www.thecatalyst
group.net

Cureton & Co., Inc.
1100 Louisiana, Ste. 3250
Houston, TX 77002
(713)658-9806
Fax: (713)658-0476

Davis, Tuttle Venture Partners (Dallas)
8 Greenway Plaza, Ste. 1020
Houston, TX 77046
(713)993-0440
Fax: (713)621-2297
Website: http://www.davistuttle.com

Houston Partners
401 Louisiana, 8th Fl.
Houston, TX 77002
(713)222-8600
Fax: (713)222-8932

Southwest Venture Group
10878 Westheimer, Ste. 178

Houston, TX 77042
(713)827-8947
(713)461-1470

AM Fund
4600 Post Oak Place, Ste. 100
Houston, TX 77027
(713)627-9111
Fax: (713)627-9119

Ventex Management, Inc.
3417 Milam St.
Houston, TX 77002-9531
(713)659-7870
Fax: (713)659-7855

MBA Venture Group
1004 Olde Town Rd., Ste. 102
Irving, TX 75061
(972)986-6703

First Capital Group Management Co.
750 East Mulberry St., Ste. 305
PO Box 15616
San Antonio, TX 78212
(210)736-4233
Fax: (210)736-5449

The Southwest Venture Partnerships
16414 San Pedro, Ste. 345
San Antonio, TX 78232
(210)402-1200
Fax: (210)402-1221
E-mail: swvp@aol.com

Medtech International Inc.
1742 Carriageway
Sugarland, TX 77478
(713)980-8474
Fax: (713)980-6343

Utah

First Security Business Investment Corp.
15 East 100 South, Ste. 100
Salt Lake City, UT 84111
(801)246-5737
Fax: (801)246-5740

Utah Ventures II, L.P.
423 Wakara Way, Ste. 206
Salt Lake City, UT 84108
(801)583-5922
Fax: (801)583-4105
Website: http://www.uven.com

Wasatch Venture Corp.
1 S. Main St., Ste. 1400
Salt Lake City, UT 84133
(801)524-8939

Fax: (801)524-8941
E-mail: mail@wasatchvc.com

Vermont

North Atlantic Capital Corp.
76 Saint Paul St., Ste. 600
Burlington, VT 05401
(802)658-7820
Fax: (802)658-5757
Website: http://www.north
atlanticcapital.com

Green Mountain Advisors Inc.
PO Box 1230
Quechee, VT 05059
(802)296-7800
Fax: (802)296-6012
Website: http://www.gmtcap.com

Virginia

Oxford Financial Services Corp.
Alexandria, VA 22314
(703)519-4900
Fax: (703)519-4910
E-mail: oxford133@aol.com

Continental SBIC
4141 N. Henderson Rd.
Arlington, VA 22203
(703)527-5200
Fax: (703)527-3700

Novak Biddle Venture Partners
1750 Tysons Blvd., Ste. 1190
McLean, VA 22102
(703)847-3770
Fax: (703)847-3771
E-mail: roger@novakbiddle.com
Website: http://www.novakbiddle.com

Spacevest
11911 Freedom Dr., Ste. 500
Reston, VA 20190
(703)904-9800
Fax: (703)904-0571
E-mail: spacevest@spacevest.com
Website: http://www.spacevest.com

Virginia Capital
1801 Libbie Ave., Ste. 201
Richmond, VA 23226
(804)648-4802
Fax: (804)648-4809
E-mail: webmaster@vacapital.com
Website: http://www.vacapital.com

Calvert Social Venture Partners
402 Maple Ave. W
Vienna, VA 22180

(703)255-4930
Fax: (703)255-4931
E-mail: calven2000@aol.com

Fairfax Partners
8000 Towers Crescent Dr., Ste. 940
Vienna, VA 22182
(703)847-9486
Fax: (703)847-0911

Global Internet Ventures
8150 Leesburg Pike, Ste. 1210
Vienna, VA 22182
(703)442-3300
Fax: (703)442-3388
Website: http://www.givinc.com

Walnut Capital Corp. (Vienna)
8000 Towers Crescent Dr., Ste. 1070
Vienna, VA 22182
(703)448-3771
Fax: (703)448-7751

Washington

Encompass Ventures
777 108th Ave. NE, Ste. 2300
Bellevue, WA 98004
(425)486-3900
Fax: (425)486-3901
E-mail: info@evpartners.com
Website: http://www.encom
passventures.com

Fluke Venture Partners
11400 SE Sixth St., Ste. 230
Bellevue, WA 98004
(425)453-4590
Fax: (425)453-4675
E-mail: gabelein@flukeventures.com
Website: http://www.flukeventures.com

Pacific Northwest Partners SBIC, L.P.
15352 SE 53rd St.
Bellevue, WA 98006
(425)455-9967
Fax: (425)455-9404

Materia Venture Associates, L.P.
3435 Carillon Pointe
Kirkland, WA 98033-7354
(425)822-4100
Fax: (425)827-4086

OVP Venture Partners (Kirkland)
2420 Carillon Pt.
Kirkland, WA 98033
(425)889-9192
Fax: (425)889-0152
E-mail: info@ovp.com
Website: http://www.ovp.com

Digital Partners
999 3rd Ave., Ste. 1610
Seattle, WA 98104
(206)405-3607
Fax: (206)405-3617
Website: http://www.digitalpartners.com

Frazier & Company
601 Union St., Ste. 3300
Seattle, WA 98101
(206)621-7200
Fax: (206)621-1848
E-mail: jon@frazierco.com

Kirlan Venture Capital, Inc.
221 First Ave. W, Ste. 108
Seattle, WA 98119-4223
(206)281-8610
Fax: (206)285-3451
Website: http://www.kirlanventure.com

Phoenix Partners
1000 2nd Ave., Ste. 3600
Seattle, WA 98104
(206)624-8968
Fax: (206)624-1907

Voyager Capital
800 5th St., Ste. 4100
Seattle, WA 98103
(206)470-1180
Fax: (206)470-1185
E-mail: info@voyagercap.com
Website: http://www.voyagercap.com

Northwest Venture Associates
221 N. Wall St., Ste. 628
Spokane, WA 99201
(509)747-0728
Fax: (509)747-0758
Website: http://www.nwva.com

Wisconsin

Venture Investors Management, L.L.C.
University Research Park
505 S. Rosa Rd.
Madison, WI 53719
(608)441-2700
Fax: (608)441-2727
E-mail: roger@ventureinvestors.com
Website: http://www.venture
investers.com

Capital Investments, Inc.
1009 West Glen Oaks Lane, Ste. 103
Mequon, WI 53092
(414)241-0303
Fax: (414)241-8451
Website: http://
www.capitalinvestmentsinc.com

Future Value Venture, Inc.
2745 N. Martin Luther King
Dr., Ste. 204
Milwaukee, WI 53212-2300
(414)264-2252
Fax: (414)264-2253
E-mail: fvvventures@aol.com
William Beckett, President

Lubar and Co., Inc.
700 N. Water St., Ste. 1200
Milwaukee, WI 53202
(414)291-9000
Fax: (414)291-9061

GCI
20875 Crossroads Cir., Ste. 100
Waukesha, WI 53186
(262)798-5080
Fax: (262)798-5087

Glossary of Small Business Terms

Absolute liability
Liability that is incurred due to product defects or negligent actions. Manufacturers or retail establishments are held responsible, even though the defect or action may not have been intentional or negligent.

ACE
See Active Corps of Executives

Accident and health benefits
Benefits offered to employees and their families in order to offset the costs associated with accidental death, accidental injury, or sickness.

Account statement
A record of transactions, including payments, new debt, and deposits, incurred during a defined period of time.

Accounting system
System capturing the costs of all employees and/or machinery included in business expenses.

Accounts payable
See Trade credit

Accounts receivable
Unpaid accounts which arise from unsettled claims and transactions from the sale of a company's products or services to its customers.

Active Corps of Executives (ACE)
A group of volunteers for a management assistance program of the U.S. Small Business Administration; volunteers provide one-on-one counseling and teach workshops and seminars for small firms.

ADA
See Americans with Disabilities Act

Adaptation
The process whereby an invention is modified to meet the needs of users.

Adaptive engineering
The process whereby an invention is modified to meet the manufacturing and commercial requirements of a targeted market.

Adverse selection
The tendency for higher-risk individuals to purchase health care and more comprehensive plans, resulting in increased costs.

Advertising
A marketing tool used to capture public attention and influence purchasing decisions for a product or service. Utilizes various forms of media to generate consumer response, such as flyers, magazines, newspapers, radio, and television.

Age discrimination
The denial of the rights and privileges of employment based solely on the age of an individual.

Agency costs
Costs incurred to insure that the lender or investor maintains control over assets while allowing the borrower or entrepreneur to use them. Monitoring and information costs are the two major types of agency costs.

Agribusiness
The production and sale of commodities and products from the commercial farming industry.

America Online
An online service which is accessible by computer modem. The service features Internet access, bulletin boards, online periodicals, electronic mail, and other services for subscribers.

Americans with Disabilities Act (ADA)
Law designed to ensure equal access and opportunity to handicapped persons.

Annual report
Yearly financial report prepared by a business that adheres to the requirements set forth by the Securities and Exchange Commission (SEC).

Antitrust immunity
Exemption from prosecution under antitrust laws. In the transportation industry, firms with antitrust immunity are permitted under certain conditions to set schedules and sometimes prices for the public benefit.

Applied research
Scientific study targeted for use in a product or process.

Asians
A minority category used by the U.S. Bureau of the Census to represent a diverse group that includes Aleuts, Eskimos, American Indians, Asian Indians, Chinese, Japanese, Koreans, Vietnamese, Filipinos, Hawaiians, and other Pacific Islanders.

Assets
Anything of value owned by a company.

Audit
The verification of accounting records and business procedures conducted by an outside accounting service.

Average cost
Total production costs divided by the quantity produced.

Balance Sheet
A financial statement listing the total assets and liabilities of a company at a given time.

Bankruptcy
The condition in which a business cannot meet its debt obligations and petitions a federal district court either for reorganization of its debts (Chapter 11) or for liquidation of its assets (Chapter 7).

Basic research
Theoretical scientific exploration not targeted to application.

Basket clause
A provision specifying the amount of public pension funds that may be placed in investments not included on a state's legal list (see separate citation).

BBS
See Bulletin Board Service

BDC
See Business development corporation

Benefit
Various services, such as health care, flextime, day care, insurance, and vacation, offered to employees as part of a hiring package. Typically subsidized in whole or in part by the business.

BIDCO
See Business and industrial development company

Billing cycle
A system designed to evenly distribute customer billing throughout the month, preventing clerical backlogs.

Birth
See Business birth

Blue chip security
A low-risk, low-yield security representing an interest in a very stable company.

Blue sky laws
A general term that denotes various states' laws regulating securities.

Bond
A written instrument executed by a bidder or contractor (the principal) and a second party (the surety or sureties) to assure fulfillment of the principal's obligations to a third party (the obligee or government) identified in the bond. If the principal's obligations are not met, the bond assures payment to the extent stipulated of any loss sustained by the obligee.

Bonding requirements
Terms contained in a bond (see separate citation).

Bonus
An amount of money paid to an employee as a reward for achieving certain business goals or objectives.

Brainstorming
A group session where employees contribute their ideas for solving a problem or meeting a company objective without fear of retribution or ridicule.

Brand name
The part of a brand, trademark, or service mark that can be spoken. It can be a word, letter, or group of words or letters.

Bridge financing
A short-term loan made in expectation of intermediateterm or long-term financing. Can be used when a company plans to go public in the near future.

Broker
One who matches resources available for innovation with those who need them.

Budget
An estimate of the spending necessary to complete a project or offer a service in comparison to cash-on-hand and expected earnings for the coming year, with an emphasis on cost control.

Bulletin Board Service (BBS)
An online service enabling users to communicate with each other about specific topics.

Business and industrial development company (BIDCO)
A private, for-profit financing corporation chartered by the state to provide both equity and long-term debt capital to small business owners (see separate citations for equity and debt capital).

Business birth
The formation of a new establishment or enterprise. The appearance of a new establishment or enterprise in the Small Business Data Base (see separate citation).

Business conditions
Outside factors that can affect the financial performance of a business.

Business contractions
The number of establishments that have decreased in employment during a specified time.

Business cycle
A period of economic recession and recovery. These cycles vary in duration.

Business death
The voluntary or involuntary closure of a firm or establishment. The disappearance of an establishment or enterprise from the Small Business Data Base (see separate citation).

Business development corporation (BDC)
A business financing agency, usually composed of the financial institutions in an area or state, organized to assist in financing businesses unable to obtain assistance through normal channels; the risk is spread among various members of the business development corporation, and interest rates may vary somewhat from those charged by member institutions. A venture capital firm in which shares of ownership are publicly held and to which the Investment Act of 1940 applies.

Business dissolution
For enumeration purposes, the absence of a business that was present in the prior time period from any current record.

Business entry
See Business birth

Business ethics
Moral values and principles espoused by members of the business community as a guide to fair and honest business practices.

Business exit
See Business death

Business expansions
The number of establishments that added employees during a specified time.

Business failure
Closure of a business causing a loss to at least one creditor.

Business format franchising
The purchase of the name, trademark, and an ongoing business plan of the parent corporation or franchisor by the franchisee.

Business license
A legal authorization issued by municipal and state governments and required for business operations.

Business name
Enterprises must register their business names with local governments usually on a "doing business as" (DBA) form. (This name is sometimes referred to as a "fictional name.") The procedure is part of the business licensing process and prevents any other business from using that same name for a similar business in the same locality.

Business norms
See Financial ratios

Business permit
See Business license

Business plan
A document that spells out a company's expected course of action for a specified period, usually including a detailed listing and analysis of risks and uncertainties. For the small business, it should examine the proposed products, the market, the industry, the management policies, the marketing policies, production needs, and financial needs. Frequently, it is used as a prospectus for potential investors and lenders.

Business proposal
See Business plan

Business service firm
An establishment primarily engaged in rendering services to other business organizations on a fee or contract basis.

Business start
For enumeration purposes, a business with a name or similar designation that did not exist in a prior time period.

Cafeteria plan
See Flexible benefit plan

Capacity
Level of a firm's, industry's, or nation's output corresponding to full practical utilization of available resources.

Capital
Assets less liabilities, representing the ownership interest in a business. A stock of accumulated goods, especially at a specified time and in contrast to income received during a specified time period. Accumulated goods devoted to production. Accumulated possessions calculated to bring income.

Capital expenditure
Expenses incurred by a business for improvements that will depreciate over time.

Capital gain
The monetary difference between the purchase price and the selling price of capital. Capital gains are taxed at a rate of 28% by the federal government.

Capital intensity
The relative importance of capital in the production process, usually expressed as the ratio of capital to labor but also sometimes as the ratio of capital to output.

Capital resource
The equipment, facilities and labor used to create products and services.

Caribbean Basin Initiative
An interdisciplinary program to support commerce among the businesses in the nations of the Caribbean Basin and the United States. Agencies involved include: the Agency for International Development, the U.S. Small Business Administration, the International Trade Administration of the U.S. Department of Commerce, and various private sector groups.

Catastrophic care
Medical and other services for acute and long-term illnesses that cost more than insurance coverage limits or that cost the amount most families may be expected to pay with their own resources.

CDC
See Certified development corporation

CD-ROM
Compact disc with read-only memory used to store large amounts of digitized data.

Certified development corporation (CDC)
A local area or statewide corporation or authority (for profit or nonprofit) that packages U.S. Small Business Administration (SBA), bank, state, and/or private money into financial assistance for existing business capital improvements. The SBA holds the second lien on its maximum share of 40 percent involvement. Each state has at least one certified development corporation. This program is called the SBA 504 Program.

Certified lenders
Banks that participate in the SBA guaranteed loan program (see separate citation). Such banks must have a good track record with the U.S. Small Business Administration (SBA) and must agree to certain conditions set forth by the agency. In return, the SBA agrees to process any guaranteed loan application within three business days.

Champion
An advocate for the development of an innovation.

Channel of distribution
The means used to transport merchandise from the manufacturer to the consumer.

Chapter 7 of the 1978 Bankruptcy Act
Provides for a court-appointed trustee who is responsible for liquidating a company's assets in order to settle outstanding debts.

Chapter 11 of the 1978 Bankruptcy Act
Allows the business owners to retain control of the company while working with their creditors to reorganize their finances and establish better business practices to prevent liquidation of assets.

Closely held corporation
A corporation in which the shares are held by a few persons, usually officers, employees, or others close to the management; these shares are rarely offered to the public.

Code of Federal Regulations
Codification of general and permanent rules of the federal government published in the Federal Register.

Code sharing
See Computer code sharing

Coinsurance
Upon meeting the deductible payment, health insurance participants may be required to make additional health care cost-sharing payments. Coinsurance is a payment of a fixed percentage of the cost of each service; copayment is usually a fixed amount to be paid with each service.

Collateral
Securities, evidence of deposit, or other property pledged by a borrower to secure repayment of a loan.

Collective ratemaking
The establishment of uniform charges for services by a group of businesses in the same industry.

Commercial insurance plan
See Underwriting

Commercial loans
Short-term renewable loans used to finance specific capital needs of a business.

Commercialization
The final stage of the innovation process, including production and distribution.

Common stock
The most frequently used instrument for purchasing ownership in private or public companies. Common stock generally carries the right to vote on certain corporate actions and may pay dividends, although it rarely does in venture investments. In liquidation, common stockholders are the last to share in the proceeds from the sale of a corporation's assets; bondholders and preferred shareholders have priority. Common stock is often used in firstround start-up financing.

Community development corporation
A corporation established to develop economic programs for a community and, in most cases, to provide financial support for such development.

Competitor
A business whose product or service is marketed for the same purpose/use and to the same consumer group as the product or service of another.

Computer code sharing
An arrangement whereby flights of a regional airline are identified by the two-letter code of a major carrier in the computer reservation system to help direct passengers to new regional carriers.

Consignment
A merchandising agreement, usually referring to secondhand shops, where the dealer pays the owner of an item a percentage of the profit when the item is sold.

Consortium
A coalition of organizations such as banks and corporations for ventures requiring large capital resources.

Consultant
An individual that is paid by a business to provide advice and expertise in a particular area.

Consumer price index
A measure of the fluctuation in prices between two points in time.

Consumer research
Research conducted by a business to obtain information about existing or potential consumer markets.

Continuation coverage
Health coverage offered for a specified period of time to employees who leave their jobs and to their widows, divorced spouses, or dependents.

Contractions
See Business contractions

Convertible preferred stock
A class of stock that pays a reasonable dividend and is convertible into common stock (see separate citation). Generally the convertible feature may only be exercised after being held for a stated period of time. This arrangement is usually considered second-round financing when a company needs equity to maintain its cash flow.

Convertible securities
A feature of certain bonds, debentures, or preferred stocks that allows them to be exchanged by the owner for another class of securities at a future date and in accordance with any other terms of the issue.

Copayment
See Coinsurance

Copyright
A legal form of protection available to creators and authors to safeguard their works from unlawful use or claim of ownership by others. Copyrights may be acquired for works of art, sculpture, music, and published or unpublished manuscripts. All copyrights should be registered at the Copyright Office of the Library of Congress.

Corporate financial ratios
The relationship between key figures found in a company's financial statement expressed as a numeric value. Used to evaluate risk and company performance. Also known as Financial averages, Operating ratios, and Business ratios.

Corporation
A legal entity, chartered by a state or the federal government, recognized as a separate entity having its own rights, privileges, and liabilities distinct from those of its members.

Cost containment
Actions taken by employers and insurers to curtail rising health care costs; for example, increasing

employee cost sharing (see separate citation), requiring second opinions, or preadmission screening.

Cost sharing
The requirement that health care consumers contribute to their own medical care costs through deductibles and coinsurance (see separate citations). Cost sharing does not include the amounts paid in premiums. It is used to control utilization of services; for example, requiring a fixed amount to be paid with each health care service.

Cottage industry
Businesses based in the home in which the family members are the labor force and family-owned equipment is used to process the goods.

Credit Rating
A letter or number calculated by an organization (such as Dun & Bradstreet) to represent the ability and disposition of a business to meet its financial obligations.

Customer service
Various techniques used to ensure the satisfaction of a customer.

Cyclical peak
The upper turning point in a business cycle.

Cyclical trough
The lower turning point in a business cycle.

DBA
See Business name

Death
See Business death

Debenture
A certificate given as acknowledgment of a debt (see separate citation) secured by the general credit of the issuing corporation. A bond, usually without security, issued by a corporation and sometimes convertible to common stock.

Debt
Something owed by one person to another. Financing in which a company receives capital that must be repaid; no ownership is transferred.

Debt capital
Business financing that normally requires periodic interest payments and repayment of the principal within a specified time.

Debt financing
See Debt capital

Debt securities
Loans such as bonds and notes that provide a specified rate of return for a specified period of time.

Deductible
A set amount that an individual must pay before any benefits are received.

Demand shock absorbers
A term used to describe the role that some small firms play by expanding their output levels to accommodate a transient surge in demand.

Demographics
Statistics on various markets, including age, income, and education, used to target specific products or services to appropriate consumer groups.

Demonstration
Showing that a product or process has been modified sufficiently to meet the needs of users.

Deregulation
The lifting of government restrictions; for example, the lifting of government restrictions on the entry of new businesses, the expansion of services, and the setting of prices in particular industries.

Desktop Publishing
Using personal computers and specialized software to produce camera-ready copy for publications.

Disaster loans
Various types of physical and economic assistance available to individuals and businesses through the U.S. Small Business Administration (SBA). This is the only SBA loan program available for residential purposes.

Discrimination
The denial of the rights and privileges of employment based on factors such as age, race, religion, or gender.

Diseconomies of scale
The condition in which the costs of production increase faster than the volume of production.

Dissolution
See Business dissolution

Distribution
Delivering a product or process to the user.

Distributor
One who delivers merchandise to the user.

Diversified company
A company whose products and services are used by several different markets.

Doing business as (DBA)
See Business name

Dow Jones
An information services company that publishes the Wall Street Journal and other sources of financial information.

Dow Jones Industrial Average
An indicator of stock market performance.

Earned income
A tax term that refers to wages and salaries earned by the recipient, as opposed to monies earned through interest and dividends.

Economic efficiency
The use of productive resources to the fullest practical extent in the provision of the set of goods and services that is most preferred by purchasers in the economy.

Economic indicators
Statistics used to express the state of the economy. These include the length of the average work week, the rate of unemployment, and stock prices.

Economically disadvantaged
See Socially and economically disadvantaged

Economies of scale
See Scale economies

EEOC
See Equal Employment Opportunity Commission

8(a) Program
A program authorized by the Small Business Act that directs federal contracts to small businesses owned and

operated by socially and economically disadvantaged individuals.

Electronic mail (e-mail)
The electronic transmission of mail via phone lines.

E-mail
See Electronic mail

Employee leasing
A contract by which employers arrange to have their workers hired by a leasing company and then leased back to them for a management fee. The leasing company typically assumes the administrative burden of payroll and provides a benefit package to the workers.

Employee tenure
The length of time an employee works for a particular employer.

Employer identification number
The business equivalent of a social security number. Assigned by the U.S. Internal Revenue Service.

Enterprise
An aggregation of all establishments owned by a parent company. An enterprise may consist of a single, independent establishment or include subsidiaries and other branches under the same ownership and control.

Enterprise zone
A designated area, usually found in inner cities and other areas with significant unemployment, where businesses receive tax credits and other incentives to entice them to establish operations there.

Entrepreneur
A person who takes the risk of organizing and operating a new business venture.

Entry
See Business entry

Equal Employment Opportunity Commission (EEOC)
A federal agency that ensures nondiscrimination in the hiring and firing practices of a business.

Equal opportunity employer
An employer who adheres to the standards set by the Equal Employment Opportunity Commission (see separate citation).

Equity
The ownership interest. Financing in which partial or total ownership of a company is surrendered in exchange for capital. An investor's financial return comes from dividend payments and from growth in the net worth of the business.

Equity capital
See Equity; Equity midrisk venture capital

Equity financing
See Equity; Equity midrisk venture capital

Equity midrisk venture capital
An unsecured investment in a company. Usually a purchase of ownership interest in a company that occurs in the later stages of a company's development.

Equity partnership
A limited partnership arrangement for providing start-up and seed capital to businesses.

Equity securities
See Equity

Equity-type
Debt financing subordinated to conventional debt.

Establishment
A single-location business unit that may be independent (a single-establishment enterprise) or owned by a parent enterprise.

Establishment and Enterprise Microdata File
See U.S. Establishment and Enterprise Microdata File

Establishment birth
See Business birth

Establishment Longitudinal Microdata File
See U.S. Establishment Longitudinal Microdata File

Ethics
See Business ethics

Evaluation
Determining the potential success of translating an invention into a product or process.

Exit
See Business exit

Experience rating
See Underwriting

Export
A product sold outside of the country.

Export license
A general or specific license granted by the U.S. Department of Commerce required of anyone wishing to export goods. Some restricted articles need approval from the U.S. Departments of State, Defense, or Energy.

Failure
See Business failure

Fair share agreement
An agreement reached between a franchisor and a minority business organization to extend business ownership to minorities by either reducing the amount of capital required or by setting aside certain marketing areas for minority business owners.

Feasibility study
A study to determine the likelihood that a proposed product or development will fulfill the objectives of a particular investor.

Federal Trade Commission (FTC)
Federal agency that promotes free enterprise and competition within the U.S.

Federal Trade Mark Act of 1946
See Lanham Act

Fictional name
See Business name

Fiduciary
An individual or group that hold assets in trust for a beneficiary.

Financial analysis
The techniques used to determine money needs in a business. Techniques include ratio analysis, calculation of return on investment, guides for measuring profitability, and break-even analysis to determine ultimate success.

Financial intermediary
A financial institution that acts as the intermediary between borrowers and lenders. Banks, savings and loan associations, finance companies, and venture capital companies are major financial intermediaries in the United States.

Financial ratios
See Corporate financial ratios; Industry financial ratios

Financial statement
A written record of business finances, including balance sheets and profit and loss statements.

Financing
See First-stage financing; Second-stage financing; Thirdstage financing

First-stage financing
Financing provided to companies that have expended their initial capital, and require funds to start full-scale manufacturing and sales. Also known as First-round financing.

Fiscal year
Any twelve-month period used by businesses for accounting purposes.

504 Program
See Certified development corporation

Flexible benefit plan
A plan that offers a choice among cash and/or qualified benefits such as group term life insurance, accident and health insurance, group legal services, dependent care assistance, and vacations.

FOB
See Free on board

Format franchising
See Business format franchising; Franchising

401(k) plan
A financial plan where employees contribute a percentage of their earnings to a fund that is invested in stocks, bonds, or money markets for the purpose of saving money for retirement.

Four Ps
Marketing terms referring to Product, Price, Place, and Promotion.

Franchising
A form of licensing by which the owner-the franchisor- distributes or markets a product, method, or service through affiliated dealers called franchisees. The product, method, or service being marketed is identified by a brand name, and the franchisor

Glossary

maintains control over the marketing methods employed. The franchisee is often given exclusive access to a defined geographic area.

Free on board (FOB)
A pricing term indicating that the quoted price includes the cost of loading goods into transport vessels at a specified place.

Frictional unemployment
See Unemployment

FTC
See Federal Trade Commission

Fulfillment
The systems necessary for accurate delivery of an ordered item, including subscriptions and direct marketing.

Full-time workers
Generally, those who work a regular schedule of more than 35 hours per week.

Garment registration number
A number that must appear on every garment sold in the U.S. to indicate the manufacturer of the garment, which may or may not be the same as the label under which the garment is sold. The U.S. Federal Trade Commission assigns and regulates garment registration numbers.

Gatekeeper
A key contact point for entry into a network.

GDP
See Gross domestic product

General obligation bond
A municipal bond secured by the taxing power of the municipality. The Tax Reform Act of 1986 limits the purposes for which such bonds may be issued and establishes volume limits on the extent of their issuance.

GNP
See Gross national product

Good Housekeeping Seal
Seal appearing on products that signifies the fulfillment of the standards set by the Good Housekeeping Institute to protect consumer interests.

Goods sector
All businesses producing tangible goods, including agriculture, mining, construction, and manufacturing businesses.

GPO
See Gross product originating

Gross domestic product (GDP)
The part of the nation's gross national product (see separate citation) generated by private business using resources from within the country.

Gross national product (GNP)
The most comprehensive single measure of aggregate economic output. Represents the market value of the total output of goods and services produced by a nation's economy.

Gross product originating (GPO)
A measure of business output estimated from the income or production side using employee compensation, profit income, net interest, capital consumption, and indirect business taxes.

HAL
See Handicapped assistance loan program

Handicapped assistance loan program (HAL)
Low-interest direct loan program through the U.S. Small Business Administration (SBA) for handicapped persons. The SBA requires that these persons demonstrate that their disability is such that it is impossible for them to secure employment, thus making it necessary to go into their own business to make a living.

Health maintenance organization (HMO)
Organization of physicians and other health care professionals that provides health services to subscribers and their dependents on a prepaid basis.

Health provider
An individual or institution that gives medical care. Under Medicare, an institutional provider is a hospital, skilled nursing facility, home health agency, or provider of certain physical therapy services.

Hispanic
A person of Cuban, Mexican, Puerto Rican, Latin American (Central or South American), European Spanish, or other Spanish-speaking origin or ancestry.

HMO
See Health maintenance organization

Home-based business
A business with an operating address that is also a residential address (usually the residential address of the proprietor).

Hub-and-spoke system
A system in which flights of an airline from many different cities (the spokes) converge at a single airport (the hub). After allowing passengers sufficient time to make connections, planes then depart for different cities.

Human Resources Management
A business program designed to oversee recruiting, pay, benefits, and other issues related to the company's work force, including planning to determine the optimal use of labor to increase production, thereby increasing profit.

Idea
An original concept for a new product or process.

Import
Products produced outside the country in which they are consumed.

Income
Money or its equivalent, earned or accrued, resulting from the sale of goods and services.

Income statement
A financial statement that lists the profits and losses of a company at a given time.

Incorporation
The filing of a certificate of incorporation with a state's secretary of state, thereby limiting the business owner's liability.

Incubator
A facility designed to encourage entrepreneurship and minimize obstacles to new business formation and growth, particularly for high-technology firms, by housing a number of fledgling enterprises that share an array of services, such as meeting areas, secretarial services, accounting, research library, on-site financial and management counseling, and word processing facilities.

Independent contractor
An individual considered self-employed (see separate citation) and responsible for paying Social Security taxes and income taxes on earnings.

Indirect health coverage
Health insurance obtained through another individual's health care plan; for example, a spouse's employersponsored plan.

Industrial development authority
The financial arm of a state or other political subdivision established for the purpose of financing economic development in an area, usually through loans to nonprofit organizations, which in turn provide facilities for manufacturing and other industrial operations.

Industry financial ratios
Corporate financial ratios averaged for a specified industry. These are used for comparison purposes and reveal industry trends and identify differences between the performance of a specific company and the performance of its industry. Also known as Industrial averages, Industry ratios, Financial averages, and Business or Industrial norms.

Inflation
Increases in volume of currency and credit, generally resulting in a sharp and continuing rise in price levels.

Informal capital
Financing from informal, unorganized sources; includes informal debt capital such as trade credit or loans from friends and relatives and equity capital from informal investors.

Initial public offering (IPO)
A corporation's first offering of stock to the public.

Innovation
The introduction of a new idea into the marketplace in the form of a new product or service or an improvement in organization or process.

Intellectual property
Any idea or work that can be considered proprietary in nature and is thus protected from infringement by others.

Internal capital
Debt or equity financing obtained from the owner or through retained business earnings.

Internet
A government-designed computer network that contains large amounts of information and is accessible through various vendors for a fee.

Intrapreneurship
The state of employing entrepreneurial principles to nonentrepreneurial situations.

Invention
The tangible form of a technological idea, which could include a laboratory prototype, drawings, formulas, etc.

IPO
See Initial public offering

Job description
The duties and responsibilities required in a particular position.

Job tenure
A period of time during which an individual is continuously employed in the same job.

Joint marketing agreements
Agreements between regional and major airlines, often involving the coordination of flight schedules, fares, and baggage transfer. These agreements help regional carriers operate at lower cost.

Joint venture
Venture in which two or more people combine efforts in a particular business enterprise, usually a single transaction or a limited activity, and agree to share the profits and losses jointly or in proportion to their contributions.

Keogh plan
Designed for self-employed persons and unincorporated businesses as a tax-deferred pension account.

Labor force
Civilians considered eligible for employment who are also willing and able to work.

Labor force participation rate
The civilian labor force as a percentage of the civilian population.

Labor intensity
The relative importance of labor in the production process, usually measured as the capital-labor ratio; i.e., the ratio of units of capital (typically, dollars of tangible assets) to the number of employees. The higher the capital-labor ratio exhibited by a firm or industry, the lower the capital intensity of that firm or industry is said to be.

Labor surplus area
An area in which there exists a high unemployment rate. In procurement (see separate citation), extra points are given to firms in counties that are designated a labor surplus area; this information is requested on procurement bid sheets.

Labor union
An organization of similarly-skilled workers who collectively bargain with management over the conditions of employment.

Laboratory prototype
See Prototype

LAN
See Local Area Network

Lanham Act
Refers to the Federal Trade Mark Act of 1946. Protects registered trademarks, trade names, and other service marks used in commerce.

Large business-dominated industry
Industry in which a minimum of 60 percent of employment or sales is in firms with more than 500 workers.

LBO
See Leveraged buy-out

Leader pricing
A reduction in the price of a good or service in order to generate more sales of that good or service.

Legal list
A list of securities selected by a state in which certain institutions and fiduciaries (such as pension funds, insurance companies, and banks) may invest. Securities not on the list are not eligible for investment. Legal lists typically restrict investments to high quality securities meeting certain specifications.

Generally, investment is limited to U.S. securities and investment-grade blue chip securities (see separate citation).

Leveraged buy-out (LBO)
The purchase of a business or a division of a corporation through a highly leveraged financing package.

Liability
An obligation or duty to perform a service or an act. Also defined as money owed.

License
A legal agreement granting to another the right to use a technological innovation.

Limited partnerships
See Venture capital limited partnerships

Liquidity
The ability to convert a security into cash promptly.

Loans
See Commercial loans; Disaster loans; SBA direct loans; SBA guaranteed loans; SBA special lending institution categories Local Area Network (LAN) Computer networks contained within a single building or small area; used to facilitate the sharing of information.

Local development corporation
An organization, usually made up of local citizens of a community, designed to improve the economy of the area by inducing business and industry to locate and expand there. A local development corporation establishes a capability to finance local growth.

Long-haul rates
Rates charged by a transporter in which the distance traveled is more than 800 miles.

Long-term debt
An obligation that matures in a period that exceeds five years.

Low-grade bond
A corporate bond that is rated below investment grade by the major rating agencies (Standard and Poor's, Moody's).

Macro-efficiency
Efficiency as it pertains to the operation of markets and market systems.

Managed care
A cost-effective health care program initiated by employers whereby low-cost health care is made available to the employees in return for exclusive patronage to program doctors.

Management Assistance Programs
See SBA Management Assistance Programs

Management and technical assistance
A term used by many programs to mean business (as opposed to technological) assistance.

Mandated benefits
Specific treatments, providers, or individuals required by law to be included in commercial health plans.

Market evaluation
The use of market information to determine the sales potential of a specific product or process.

Market failure
The situation in which the workings of a competitive market do not produce the best results from the point of view of the entire society.

Market information
Data of any type that can be used for market evaluation, which could include demographic data, technology forecasting, regulatory changes, etc.

Market research
A systematic collection, analysis, and reporting of data about the market and its preferences, opinions, trends, and plans; used for corporate decision-making.

Market share
In a particular market, the percentage of sales of a specific product.

Marketing
Promotion of goods or services through various media.

Master Establishment List (MEL)
A list of firms in the United States developed by the U.S. Small Business Administration; firms can be selected by industry, region, state, standard metropolitan statistical area (see separate citation), county, and zip code.

Maturity
The date upon which the principal or stated value of a bond or other indebtedness becomes due and payable.

Medicaid (Title XIX)
A federally aided, state-operated and administered program that provides medical benefits for certain low income persons in need of health and medical care who are eligible for one of the government's welfare cash payment programs, including the aged, the blind, the disabled, and members of families with dependent children where one parent is absent, incapacitated, or unemployed.

Medicare (Title XVIII)
A nationwide health insurance program for disabled and aged persons. Health insurance is available to insured persons without regard to income. Monies from payroll taxes cover hospital insurance and monies from general revenues and beneficiary premiums pay for supplementary medical insurance.

MEL
See Master Establishment List

MESBIC
See Minority enterprise small business investment corporation

MET
See Multiple employer trust

Metropolitan statistical area (MSA)
A means used by the government to define large population centers that may transverse different governmental jurisdictions. For example, the Washington, D.C. MSA includes the District of Columbia and contiguous parts of Maryland and Virginia because all of these geopolitical areas comprise one population and economic operating unit.

Mezzanine financing
See Third-stage financing

Micro-efficiency
Efficiency as it pertains to the operation of individual firms.

Microdata
Information on the characteristics of an individual business firm.

Mid-term debt
An obligation that matures within one to five years.

Midrisk venture capital
See Equity midrisk venture capital

Minimum premium plan
A combination approach to funding an insurance plan aimed primarily at premium tax savings. The employer self-funds a fixed percentage of estimated monthly claims and the insurance company insures the excess.

Minimum wage
The lowest hourly wage allowed by the federal government.

Minority Business Development Agency
Contracts with private firms throughout the nation to sponsor Minority Business Development Centers which provide minority firms with advice and technical assistance on a fee basis.

Minority Enterprise Small Business Investment Corporation (MESBIC)
A federally funded private venture capital firm licensed by the U.S. Small Business Administration to provide capital to minority-owned businesses (see separate citation).

Minority-owned business
Businesses owned by those who are socially or economically disadvantaged (see separate citation).

Mom and Pop business
A small store or enterprise having limited capital, principally employing family members.

Moonlighter
A wage-and-salary worker with a side business.

MSA
See Metropolitan statistical area

Multi-employer plan
A health plan to which more than one employer is required to contribute and that may be maintained through a collective bargaining agreement and required to meet standards prescribed by the U.S. Department of Labor.

Multi-level marketing
A system of selling in which you sign up other people to assist you and they, in turn, recruit others to help

them. Some entrepreneurs have built successful companies on this concept because the main focus of their activities is their product and product sales.

Multimedia
The use of several types of media to promote a product or service. Also, refers to the use of several different types of media (sight, sound, pictures, text) in a CD-ROM (see separate citation) product.

Multiple employer trust (MET)
A self-funded benefit plan generally geared toward small employers sharing a common interest.

NAFTA
See North American Free Trade Agreement

NASDAQ
See National Association of Securities Dealers Automated Quotations

National Association of Securities Dealers Automated Quotations
Provides price quotes on over-the-counter securities as well as securities listed on the New York Stock Exchange.

National income
Aggregate earnings of labor and property arising from the production of goods and services in a nation's economy.

Net assets
See Net worth

Net income
The amount remaining from earnings and profits after all expenses and costs have been met or deducted. Also known as Net earnings.

Net profit
Money earned after production and overhead expenses (see separate citations) have been deducted.

Net worth
The difference between a company's total assets and its total liabilities.

Network
A chain of interconnected individuals or organizations sharing information and/or services.

New York Stock Exchange (NYSE)
The oldest stock exchange in the U.S. Allows for trading in stocks, bonds, warrants, options, and rights that meet listing requirements.

Niche
A career or business for which a person is well-suited. Also, a product which fulfills one need of a particular market segment, often with little or no competition.

Nodes
One workstation in a network, either local area or wide area (see separate citations).

Nonbank bank
A bank that either accepts deposits or makes loans, but not both. Used to create many new branch banks.

Noncompetitive awards
A method of contracting whereby the federal government negotiates with only one contractor to supply a product or service.

Nonmember bank
A state-regulated bank that does not belong to the federal bank system.

Nonprofit
An organization that has no shareholders, does not distribute profits, and is without federal and state tax liabilities.

Norms
See Financial ratios

North American Free Trade Agreement (NAFTA)
Passed in 1993, NAFTA eliminates trade barriers among businesses in the U.S., Canada, and Mexico.

NYSE
See New York Stock Exchange

Occupational Safety & Health Administration (OSHA)
Federal agency that regulates health and safety standards within the workplace.

Optimal firm size
The business size at which the production cost per unit of output (average cost) is, in the long run, at its minimum.

Organizational chart
A hierarchical chart tracking the chain of command within an organization.

OSHA
See Occupational Safety & Health Administration

Overhead
Expenses, such as employee benefits and building utilities, incurred by a business that are unrelated to the actual product or service sold.

Owner's capital
Debt or equity funds provided by the owner(s) of a business; sources of owner's capital are personal savings, sales of assets, or loans from financial institutions.

P & L
See Profit and loss statement

Part-time workers
Normally, those who work less than 35 hours per week. The Tax Reform Act indicated that part-time workers who work less than 17.5 hours per week may be excluded from health plans for purposes of complying with federal nondiscrimination rules.

Part-year workers
Those who work less than 50 weeks per year.

Partnership
Two or more parties who enter into a legal relationship to conduct business for profit. Defined by the U.S. Internal Revenue Code as joint ventures, syndicates, groups, pools, and other associations of two or more persons organized for profit that are not specifically classified in the IRS code as corporations or proprietorships.

Patent
A grant made by the government assuring an inventor the sole right to make, use, and sell an invention for a period of 17 years.

PC
See Professional corporation

Peak
See Cyclical peak

Pension
A series of payments made monthly, semiannually, annually, or at other specified intervals during the lifetime of the pensioner for distribution upon retirement. The term is sometimes used to denote the portion of the retirement allowance financed by the employer's contributions.

Pension fund
A fund established to provide for the payment of pension benefits; the collective contributions made by all of the parties to the pension plan.

Performance appraisal
An established set of objective criteria, based on job description and requirements, that is used to evaluate the performance of an employee in a specific job.

Permit
See Business license

Plan
See Business plan

Pooling
An arrangement for employers to achieve efficiencies and lower health costs by joining together to purchase group health insurance or self-insurance.

PPO
See Preferred provider organization

Preferred lenders program
See SBA special lending institution categories

Preferred provider organization (PPO)
A contractual arrangement with a health care services organization that agrees to discount its health care rates in return for faster payment and/or a patient base.

Premiums
The amount of money paid to an insurer for health insurance under a policy. The premium is generally paid periodically (e.g., monthly), and often is split between the employer and the employee. Unlike deductibles and coinsurance or copayments, premiums are paid for coverage whether or not benefits are actually used.

Prime-age workers
Employees 25 to 54 years of age.

Prime contract
A contract awarded directly by the U.S. Federal Government.

Private company
See Closely held corporation

Private placement
A method of raising capital by offering for sale an investment or business to a small group of investors (generally avoiding registration with the Securities and Exchange Commission or state securities registration agencies). Also known as Private financing or Private offering.

Pro forma
The use of hypothetical figures in financial statements to represent future expenditures, debts, and other potential financial expenses.

Proactive
Taking the initiative to solve problems and anticipate future events before they happen, instead of reacting to an already existing problem or waiting for a difficult situation to occur.

Procurement
A contract from an agency of the federal government for goods or services from a small business.

Prodigy
An online service which is accessible by computer modem. The service features Internet access, bulletin boards, online periodicals, electronic mail, and other services for subscribers.

Product development
The stage of the innovation process where research is translated into a product or process through evaluation, adaptation, and demonstration.

Product franchising
An arrangement for a franchisee to use the name and to produce the product line of the franchisor or parent corporation.

Production
The manufacture of a product.

Production prototype
See Prototype

Productivity
A measurement of the number of goods produced during a specific amount of time.

Professional corporation (PC)
Organized by members of a profession such as medicine, dentistry, or law for the purpose of conducting their professional activities as a corporation. Liability of a member or shareholder is limited in the same manner as in a business corporation.

Profit and loss statement (P & L)
The summary of the incomes (total revenues) and costs of a company's operation during a specific period of time. Also known as Income and expense statement.

Proposal
See Business plan

Proprietorship
The most common legal form of business ownership; about 85 percent of all small businesses are proprietorships. The liability of the owner is unlimited in this form of ownership.

Prospective payment system
A cost-containment measure included in the Social Security Amendments of 1983 whereby Medicare payments to hospitals are based on established prices, rather than on cost reimbursement.

Prototype
A model that demonstrates the validity of the concept of an invention (laboratory prototype); a model that meets the needs of the manufacturing process and the user (production prototype).

Prudent investor rule or standard
A legal doctrine that requires fiduciaries to make investments using the prudence, diligence, and intelligence that would be used by a prudent person in making similar investments. Because fiduciaries make investments on behalf of third-party beneficiaries, the standard results in very conservative investments. Until recently, most state regulations required the fiduciary to apply this standard to each investment. Newer, more progressive regulations permit fiduciaries to apply this standard to the portfolio taken as a whole, thereby allowing a fiduciary to balance a portfolio with higher-yield, higher-risk investments. In

Glossary

states with more progressive regulations, practically every type of security is eligible for inclusion in the portfolio of investments made by a fiduciary, provided that the portfolio investments, in their totality, are those of a prudent person.

Public equity markets
Organized markets for trading in equity shares such as common stocks, preferred stocks, and warrants. Includes markets for both regularly traded and nonregularly traded securities.

Public offering
General solicitation for participation in an investment opportunity. Interstate public offerings are supervised by the U.S. Securities and Exchange Commission (see separate citation).

Quality control
The process by which a product is checked and tested to ensure consistent standards of high quality.

Rate of return
The yield obtained on a security or other investment based on its purchase price or its current market price. The total rate of return is current income plus or minus capital appreciation or depreciation.

Real property
Includes the land and all that is contained on it.

Realignment
See Resource realignment

Recession
Contraction of economic activity occurring between the peak and trough (see separate citations) of a business cycle.

Regulated market
A market in which the government controls the forces of supply and demand, such as who may enter and what price may be charged.

Regulation D
A vehicle by which small businesses make small offerings and private placements of securities with limited disclosure requirements. It was designed to ease the burdens imposed on small businesses utilizing this method of capital formation.

Regulatory Flexibility Act
An act requiring federal agencies to evaluate the impact of their regulations on small businesses before the regulations are issued and to consider less burdensome alternatives.

Research
The initial stage of the innovation process, which includes idea generation and invention.

Research and development financing
A tax-advantaged partnership set up to finance product development for start-ups as well as more mature companies.

Resource mobility
The ease with which labor and capital move from firm to firm or from industry to industry.

Resource realignment
The adjustment of productive resources to interindustry changes in demand.

Resources
The sources of support or help in the innovation process, including sources of financing, technical evaluation, market evaluation, management and business assistance, etc.

Retained business earnings
Business profits that are retained by the business rather than being distributed to the shareholders as dividends.

Revolving credit
An agreement with a lending institution for an amount of money, which cannot exceed a set maximum, over a specified period of time. Each time the borrower repays a portion of the loan, the amount of the repayment may be borrowed yet again.

Risk capital
See Venture capital

Risk management
The act of identifying potential sources of financial loss and taking action to minimize their negative impact.

Routing
The sequence of steps necessary to complete a product during production.

S corporations
See Sub chapter S corporations

SBA
See Small Business Administration

SBA direct loans
Loans made directly by the U.S. Small Business Administration (SBA); monies come from funds appropriated specifically for this purpose. In general, SBA direct loans carry interest rates slightly lower than those in the private financial markets and are available only to applicants unable to secure private financing or an SBA guaranteed loan.

SBA 504 Program
See Certified development corporation

SBA guaranteed loans
Loans made by lending institutions in which the U.S. Small Business Administration (SBA) will pay a prior agreed-upon percentage of the outstanding principal in the event the borrower of the loan defaults. The terms of the loan and the interest rate are negotiated between theborrower and the lending institution, within set parameters.

SBA loans
See Disaster loans; SBA direct loans; SBA guaranteed loans; SBA special lending institution categories

SBA Management Assistance Programs
Classes, workshops, counseling, and publications offered by the U.S. Small Business Administration.

SBA special lending institution categories
U.S. Small Business Administration (SBA) loan program in which the SBA promises certified banks a 72-hour turnaround period in giving its approval for a loan, and in which preferred lenders in a pilot program are allowed to write SBA loans without seeking prior SBA approval.

SBDB
See Small Business Data Base

SBDC
See Small business development centers

SBI
See Small business institutes program

SBIC
See Small business investment corporation

SBIR Program
See Small Business Innovation Development Act of 1982

Scale economies
The decline of the production cost per unit of output (average cost) as the volume of output increases.

Scale efficiency
The reduction in unit cost available to a firm when producing at a higher output volume.

SCORE
See Service Corps of Retired Executives

SEC
See Securities and Exchange Commission

SECA
See Self-Employment Contributions Act

Second-stage financing
Working capital for the initial expansion of a company that is producing, shipping, and has growing accounts receivable and inventories. Also known as Second-round financing.

Secondary market
A market established for the purchase and sale of outstanding securities following their initial distribution.

Secondary worker
Any worker in a family other than the person who is the primary source of income for the family.

Secondhand capital
Previously used and subsequently resold capital equipment (e.g., buildings and machinery).

Securities and Exchange Commission (SEC)
Federal agency charged with regulating the trade of securities to prevent unethical practices in the investor market.

Securitized debt
A marketing technique that converts long-term loans to marketable securities.

Seed capital
Venture financing provided in the early stages of the innovation process, usually during product development.

Self-employed person
One who works for a profit or fees in his or her own business, profession, or trade, or who operates a farm.

Self-Employment Contributions Act (SECA)
Federal law that governs the self-employment tax (see separate citation).

Self-employment income
Income covered by Social Security if a business earns a net income of at least $400.00 during the year. Taxes are paid on earnings that exceed $400.00.

Self-employment retirement plan
See Keogh plan

Self-employment tax
Required tax imposed on self-employed individuals for the provision of Social Security and Medicare. The tax must be paid quarterly with estimated income tax statements.

Self-funding
A health benefit plan in which a firm uses its own funds to pay claims, rather than transferring the financial risks of paying claims to an outside insurer in exchange for premium payments.

Service Corps of Retired Executives (SCORE)
Volunteers for the SBA Management Assistance Program who provide one-on-one counseling and teach workshops and seminars for small firms.

Service firm
See Business service firm

Service sector
Broadly defined, all U.S. industries that produce intangibles, including the five major industry divisions of transportation, communications, and utilities; wholesale trade; retail trade; finance, insurance, and real estate; and services.

Set asides
See Small business set asides

Short-haul service
A type of transportation service in which the transporter supplies service between cities where the maximum distance is no more than 200 miles.

Short-term debt
An obligation that matures in one year.

SIC codes
See Standard Industrial Classification codes

Single-establishment enterprise
See Establishment

Small business
An enterprise that is independently owned and operated, is not dominant in its field, and employs fewer than 500 people. For SBA purposes, the U.S. Small Business Administration (SBA) considers various other factors (such as gross annual sales) in determining size of a business.

Small Business Administration (SBA)
An independent federal agency that provides assistance with loans, management, and advocating interests before other federal agencies.

Small Business Data Base
A collection of microdata (see separate citation) files on individual firms developed and maintained by the U.S. Small Business Administration.

Small business development centers (SBDC)
Centers that provide support services to small businesses, such as individual counseling, SBA advice, seminars and conferences, and other learning center activities. Most services are free of charge, or available at minimal cost.

Small business development corporation
See Certified development corporation

Small business-dominated industry
Industry in which a minimum of 60 percent of employment or sales is in firms with fewer than 500 employees.

Small Business Innovation Development Act of 1982
Federal statute requiring federal agencies with large extramural research and development budgets to allocate a certain percentage of these funds to small research and development firms. The program, called the Small Business Innovation Research (SBIR) Program, is designed to stimulate technological innovation and make greater use of small businesses in meeting national innovation needs.

Small business institutes (SBI) program
Cooperative arrangements made by U.S. Small Business Administration district offices and local colleges and universities to provide small business firms with graduate students to counsel them without charge.

Small business investment corporation (SBIC)
A privately owned company licensed and funded through the U.S. Small Business Administration and private sector sources to provide equity or debt capital to small businesses.

Small business set asides
Procurement (see separate citation) opportunities required by law to be on all contracts under $10,000 or a certain percentage of an agency's total procurement expenditure.

Smaller firms
For U.S. Department of Commerce purposes, those firms not included in the Fortune 1000.

SMSA
See Metropolitan statistical area

Socially and economically disadvantaged
Individuals who have been subjected to racial or ethnic prejudice or cultural bias without regard to their qualities as individuals, and whose abilities to compete are impaired because of diminished opportunities to obtain capital and credit.

Sole proprietorship
An unincorporated, one-owner business, farm, or professional practice.

Special lending institution categories
See SBA special lending institution categories

Standard Industrial Classification (SIC) codes
Four-digit codes established by the U.S. Federal Government to categorize businesses by type of economic activity; the first two digits correspond to major groups such as construction and manufacturing, while the last two digits correspond to subgroups such as home construction or highway construction.

Standard metropolitan statistical area (SMSA)
See Metropolitan statistical area

Start-up
A new business, at the earliest stages of development and financing.

Start-up costs
Costs incurred before a business can commence operations.

Start-up financing
Financing provided to companies that have either completed product development and initial marketing or have been in business for less than one year but have not yet sold their product commercially.

Stock
A certificate of equity ownership in a business.

Stop-loss coverage
Insurance for a self-insured plan that reimburses the company for any losses it might incur in its health claims beyond a specified amount.

Strategic planning
Projected growth and development of a business to establish a guiding direction for the future. Also used to determine which market segments to explore for optimal sales of products or services.

Structural unemployment
See Unemployment

Sub chapter S corporations
Corporations that are considered noncorporate for tax purposes but legally remain corporations.

Subcontract
A contract between a prime contractor and a subcontractor, or between subcontractors, to furnish supplies or services for performance of a prime contract (see separate citation) or a subcontract.

Surety bonds
Bonds providing reimbursement to an individual, company, or the government if a firm fails to complete a contract. The U.S. Small Business Administration guarantees surety bonds in a program much like the SBA guaranteed loan program (see separate citation).

Swing loan
See Bridge financing

Target market
The clients or customers sought for a business' product or service.

Targeted Jobs Tax Credit
Federal legislation enacted in 1978 that provides a tax credit to an employer who hires structurally unemployed individuals.

Tax number
A number assigned to a business by a state revenue department that enables the business to buy goods without paying sales tax.

Taxable bonds
An interest-bearing certificate of public or private indebtedness. Bonds are issued by public agencies to finance economic development.

Technical assistance
See Management and technical assistance

Technical evaluation
Assessment of technological feasibility.

Technology
The method in which a firm combines and utilizes labor and capital resources to produce goods or services; the application of science for commercial or industrial purposes.

Technology transfer
The movement of information about a technology or intellectual property from one party to another for use.

Tenure
See Employee tenure

Term
The length of time for which a loan is made.

Terms of a note
The conditions or limits of a note; includes the interest rate per annum, the due date, and transferability and convertibility features, if any.

Third-party administrator
An outside company responsible for handling claims and performing administrative tasks associated with health insurance plan maintenance.

Third-stage financing
Financing provided for the major expansion of a company whose sales volume is increasing and that is breaking even or profitable. These funds are used for further plant expansion, marketing, working capital, or development of an improved product. Also known as Third-round or Mezzanine financing.

Time deposit
A bank deposit that cannot be withdrawn before a specified future time.

Time management
Skills and scheduling techniques used to maximize productivity.

Trade credit
Credit extended by suppliers of raw materials or finished products. In an accounting statement, trade credit is referred to as "accounts payable."

Trade name
The name under which a company conducts business, or by which its business, goods, or services are identified. It may or may not be registered as a trademark.

Trade periodical
A publication with a specific focus on one or more aspects of business and industry.

Trade secret
Competitive advantage gained by a business through the use of a unique manufacturing process or formula.

Trade show
An exhibition of goods or services used in a particular industry. Typically held in exhibition centers where exhibitors rent space to display their merchandise.

Trademark
A graphic symbol, device, or slogan that identifies a business. A business has property rights to its trademark from the inception of its use, but it is still prudent to register all trademarks with the Trademark Office of the U.S. Department of Commerce.

Translation
See Product development

Treasury bills
Investment tender issued by the Federal Reserve Bank in amounts of $10,000 that mature in 91 to 182 days.

Treasury bonds
Long-term notes with maturity dates of not less than seven and not more than twenty-five years.

Treasury notes
Short-term notes maturing in less than seven years.

Trend
A statistical measurement used to track changes that occur over time.

Trough
See Cyclical trough

UCC
See Uniform Commercial Code

UL
See Underwriters Laboratories

Underwriters Laboratories (UL)
One of several private firms that tests products and processes to determine their safety. Although various firms can provide this kind of testing service, many local and insurance codes specify UL certification.

Underwriting
A process by which an insurer determines whether or not and on what basis it will accept an application for insurance. In an experience-rated plan, premiums are based on a firm's or group's past claims; factors other than prior claims are used for community-rated or manually rated plans.

Unfair competition
Refers to business practices, usually unethical, such as using unlicensed products, pirating merchandise, or misleading the public through false advertising, which give the offending business an unequitable advantage over others.

Unfunded accrued liability
The excess of total liabilities, both present and prospective, over present and prospective assets.

Unemployment
The joblessness of individuals who are willing to work, who are legally and physically able to work, and who are seeking work. Unemployment may represent the temporary joblessness of a worker between jobs (frictional unemployment) or the joblessness of a worker whose skills are not suitable for jobs available in the labor market (structural unemployment).

Uniform Commercial Code (UCC)
A code of laws governing commercial transactions across the U.S., except Louisiana. Their purpose is to bring uniformity to financial transactions.

Uniform product code (UPC symbol)
A computer-readable label comprised of ten digits and stripes that encodes what a product is and how much it costs. The first five digits are assigned by the Uniform Product Code Council, and the last five digits by the individual manufacturer.

Unit cost
See Average cost

UPC symbol
See Uniform product code

U.S. Establishment and Enterprise Microdata (USEEM) File
A cross-sectional database containing information on employment, sales, and location for individual enterprises and establishments with employees that have a Dun & Bradstreet credit rating.

U.S. Establishment Longitudinal Microdata (USELM) File
A database containing longitudinally linked sample microdata on establishments drawn from the U.S. Establishment and Enterprise Microdata file (see separate citation).

U.S. Small Business Administration 504 Program
See Certified development corporation

USEEM
See U.S. Establishment and Enterprise Microdata File

USELM
See U.S. Establishment Longitudinal Microdata File

VCN
See Venture capital network

Venture capital
Money used to support new or unusual business ventures that exhibit above-average growth rates,

significant potential for market expansion, and are in need of additional financing to sustain growth or further research and development; equity or equity-type financing traditionally provided at the commercialization stage, increasingly available prior to commercialization.

Venture capital company

A company organized to provide seed capital to a business in its formation stage, or in its first or second stage of expansion. Funding is obtained through public or private pension funds, commercial banks and bank holding companies, small business investment corporations licensed by the U.S. Small Business Administration, private venture capital firms, insurance companies, investment management companies, bank trust departments, industrial companies seeking to diversify their investment, and investment bankers acting as intermediaries for other investors or directly investing on their own behalf.

Venture capital limited partnerships

Designed for business development, these partnerships are an institutional mechanism for providing capital for young, technology-oriented businesses. The investors' money is pooled and invested in money market assets until venture investments have been selected. The general partners are experienced investment managers who select and invest the equity and debt securities of firms with high growth potential and the ability to go public in the near future.

Venture capital network (VCN)

A computer database that matches investors with entrepreneurs.

WAN

See Wide Area Network

Wide Area Network (WAN)

Computer networks linking systems throughout a state or around the world in order to facilitate the sharing of information.

Withholding

Federal, state, social security, and unemployment taxes withheld by the employer from employees' wages; employers are liable for these taxes and the corporate umbrella and bankruptcy will not exonerate an employer from paying back payroll withholding. Employers should escrow these funds in a separate account and disperse them quarterly to withholding authorities.

Workers' compensation

A state-mandated form of insurance covering workers injured in job-related accidents. In some states, the state is the insurer; in other states, insurance must be acquired from commercial insurance firms. Insurance rates are based on a number of factors, including salaries, firm history, and risk of occupation.

Working capital

Refers to a firm's short-term investment of current assets, including cash, short-term securities, accounts receivable, and inventories.

Yield

The rate of income returned on an investment, expressed as a percentage. Income yield is obtained by dividing the current dollar income by the current market price of the security. Net yield or yield to maturity is the current income yield minus any premium above par or plus any discount from par in purchase price, with the adjustment spread over the period from the date of purchase to the date of maturity.

Index

Index

Index